D1131362

Time, Space, and Women's Lives in Early Modern Europe

Habent sua fata libelli

SIXTEENTH CENTURY ESSAYS & STUDIES SERIES

GENERAL EDITOR
RAYMOND A. MENTZER
University of Iowa

EDITORIAL BOARD OF SIXTEENTH CENTURY ESSAYS & STUDIES

ELAINE BEILIN
Framingham State College

ROGER MANNING
Cleveland State University, Emeritus

MIRIAM U. CHRISMAN
University of Massachusetts, Emerita

MARY B. MCKINLEY
University of Virginia

BARBARA B. DIEFENDORF
Boston University

HELEN NADER
University of Arizona

PAULA FINDLEN
Stanford University

CHARLES G. NAUERT
University of Missouri, Emeritus

SCOTT H. HENDRIX
Princeton Theological Seminary

THEODORE K. RABB
Princeton University

JANE CAMPBELL HUTCHISON
University of Wisconsin–Madison

MAX REINHART
University of Georgia

CHRISTIANE JOOST-GAUGIER
University of New Mexico, Emerita

JOHN D. ROTH
Goshen College

RALPH KEEN
University of Iowa

ROBERT V. SCHNUCKER
Truman State University, Emeritus

ROBERT M. KINGDON
University of Wisconsin, Emeritus

NICHOLAS TERPSTRA
University of Toronto

MERRY WIESNER-HANKS
University of Wisconsin–Milwaukee

TIME, SPACE, and WOMEN'S LIVES in EARLY MODERN EUROPE

Edited by
Anne Jacobson Schutte
Thomas Kuehn
Silvana Seidel Menchi

SIXTEENTH CENTURY ESSAYS & STUDIES
VOLUME LVII

Copyright © 2001 Truman State University Press
Kirksville, Missouri 63501 USA
All rights reserved
http://tsup.truman.edu
All rights reserved

Library of Congress Cataloging-in-Publication Data

Tempi e spazi di vita femminile tra medioevo ed età moderna. English
      Time, space, and women's lives in early modern Europe / edited
by Anne Jacobson Schutte, Thomas Kuehn, Silvana Seidel Menchi.
      p.   cm - (Sixteenth century essays & studies : 57)
      Includes bibliographical references and index.
      ISBN 0-943549-82-5 (alk paper) — ISBN 0-943549-90-6 pbk :
alk. paper)
      1. Women—History—Middle Ages, 500–1500—Congresses. 2.
Women—Europe—History—Congresses. 3. Women—Europe—
Social conditions—Congresses. I. Schutte, Anne Jacobson. II.
Kuehn, Thomas, 1950– III. Seidel Menchi, Silvana. IV. Title. V.
Series.
HQ1143.T4613 2001
305.4'09'02—dc21

                                                            2001043061

Text is set in Adobe Garamond 10/12. Display type is DTC Optimum.
Cover and title page by Teresa Wheeler, Truman State University designer.
Printed in U.S.A.

No part of this work may be reproduced or transmitted in any format by any means, elec-
tronic or mechanical, including photocopying and recording, or by any information storage
or retrieval system, without permission in writing from the publisher.

The paper in this publication meets or exceeds the minimum requirements of the American
National Standard for Permanence of Paper for Printed Library materials Z39.48 (1984).

Contents

Contents

Part 4

Part 5

Introduction

Thomas Kuehn and Anne Jacobson Schutte

This volume grows out of an international conference held in October 1997 in Trento and nearby Rovereto under the sponsorship of the Istituto Storico Italo–Germanico and the Dipartimento di Scienze Filologiche e Storiche of the Università degli Studi di Trento.[1] Some thirty scholars from Italy, Germany, France, Austria, and the United States, with the help of numerous auditors, attempted to address a set of problems associated with "Time and Space in Women's Lives in Early Modern Europe."

In planning the conference, the organizing committee (Silvana Seidel Menchi, Anne Jacobson Schutte, Thomas Kuehn, Gabriella Zarri, and Heide Wunder) sought to move beyond the question "Did women have a Renaissance?" posed twenty years earlier by Joan Kelly-Gadol,[2] which was soon criticized as being narrowly framed and based solely on literary evidence.[3] Instead, we conceived the agenda in terms of the female life cycle, from birth to old age and death.[4] And we thought in terms of the social and physical spaces within which women lived their

---

[1]The history departments of Clemson University and the University of Virginia provided moral endorsement.

[2]Joan Kelly-Gadol, "Did Women Have a Renaissance?" in *Becoming Visible: Women in European History*, ed. Renate Bridenthal and Claudia Koonz (Boston: Houghton Mifflin, 1977), 137–64; *Becoming Visible: Women in European History*, ed. Renate Bridenthal, Claudia Koonz, and Susan Stuard, 2nd ed. (Boston: Houghton Mifflin, 1987), 175–201; also in Joan Kelly, *Women, History, and Theory* (Chicago: University of Chicago Press, 1984), 19–50.

[3]Kelly's formulation of the question no longer seems useful; it was omitted from *Becoming Visible: Women in European History*, ed. Renate Bridenthal, Susan Mosher Stuard, and Merry E. Wiesner, 3rd ed. (Boston: Houghton Mifflin, 1998). For a selective list of responses to Kelly's question, see Carole Levin, "Women in the Renaissance," in *Becoming Visible*, 3rd. ed., 169–70 (n. 3).

[4]This inspiration came from an anthology used by one of the organizers with great success in the classroom: *Victorian Women: A Documentary Account of Women's Lives in Nineteenth-Century England, France, and the United States*, ed. Erna Olafson Hellerstein, Leslie Parker Hume, and Karen M. Offen (Stanford: Stanford University Press, 1981). See also Merry E. Wiesner, chap. 2, *Women and Gender in Early Modern Europe* (Cambridge: Cambridge University Press, 1993).

BRIDWELL LIBRARY
SOUTHERN METHODIST UNIVERSITY
DALLAS, TEXAS 75275

lives and influenced their societies, communities, and families.[5] We asked presenters to emphasize the options available to women in various regions, social classes, and statuses of life, while not neglecting the ways in which women's choices were conditioned and limited. In addition, we requested that they pay attention to major theoretical issues in the historical study of women: the older "oppression" model versus the newer "agency" model; the advantages and disadvantages of focusing exclusively on women as a distinct social group (history of women) or concentrating on relations between the sexes and the construction of "femaleness" and "maleness" (history of gender). Thus we aimed to foster a refinement of scholarly investigation that would reveal the existence of, or at least point the way toward, a new paradigm.

Predictably, this ambitious charge, formulated in distinctively North American terms, proved more congenial to some presenters than to others. Practical limitations, furthermore, precluded exhaustive coverage of early modern Europe: with a few exceptions, the essays gathered here focus upon two geographical areas, Italy and Germany, in the sixteenth and seventeenth centuries.[6] Nonetheless, we believe that the volume as a whole succeeds in offering fresh insights drawn from research in a variety of sources, many of them not fully explored (if at all) in earlier scholarship. Perhaps more important, it serves as a methodological benchmark. Focusing on stages of the life cycle, these essays demonstrate, opens a wider window on gender— mainly but not exclusively the female gender—than did some previous approaches. This focus reformulates the "woman question" in two ways: by moving out from the realm of elite men's prescriptive pronouncements about female nature (although that subject still merits attention and receives it in several essays included here) to women's lived experience; and by changing the singular, "woman," to the plural, "women."

Here readers will encounter women of different ages in a variety of socioeconomic and cultural situations—from the much studied but not fully understood noblewomen of fifteenth- and sixteenth-century Florence and Venice, to their counterparts in Rome and England, to the women who chose or were compelled to take

---

[5]Here we were guided by other anthologies: *Connecting Spheres: Women in the Western World, 1500 to the Present*, ed. Marilyn J. Boxer and Jean H. Quataert (New York: Oxford University Press, 1987); *Gendered Domains: Rethinking Public and Private in Women's History*, ed. Dorothy O. Helly and Susan M. Reverby (Ithaca: Cornell University Press, 1992).

[6]For various reasons, four papers presented at the conference did not find their way into this volume. Two of them are included in the Italian version, *Tempi e spazi di vita femminile tra medioevo ed età moderna*, ed. Silvana Seidel Menchi, Anne Jacobson Schutte, and Thomas Kuehn (Bologna: Il Mulino, 1999): Isabelle Chabot, "Seconde nozze e identità materna nella Firenze del medioevo"; and Luise Schorn-Schütte, "Il matrimonio come professione: La moglie del pastore evangelico." Two other contributions were not submitted for publication: Mary Garrard, "Artemisia Gentileschi: A New Painting and Another Identity"; and Beate Schuster, "Zeit und Raum für Prostitution vom 14. bis 16. Jahrhundert."

BRIDWELL LIBRARY
SOUTHERN METHODIST UNIVERSITY
DALLAS, TEXAS 75275

religious vows, to the bourgeois women of eighteenth-century Salzburg. Significantly, these women do not stand alone in a monolithic, unambiguously subordinate, and passive position. On the contrary, we see them interacting with their parents, husbands, and other male "superiors," as well as with their children, in an effort to shape their own lives.

One of the concomitants of new approaches to the study of women is a new form of periodization, addressed in part 1. Kelly-Gadol's question began from a conventional—some would say overly male—periodization in which the Renaissance figures as the beginning of the modern world. Although she saw herself challenging accepted schemes of periodization in her essay, Kelly-Gadol did not shift temporal markers so much as recast the quality of periods, mainly the Renaissance, in terms of their effects on women. In her wide-ranging essay, Merry Wiesner-Hanks works through themes of capitalism and patriarchy and asks whether one can find a structure or fashion a master narrative for women in early modern Europe. Prodded in part by consideration of the interplay between historical and literary studies, she offers searching criticism of the term "early modern." The other essays in this section pursue this theme of literature and history and the conjoined theme of periodization. Margarete Zimmermann examines the literary *querelle des femmes* as a vehicle by which women's voices came eventually to be heard, tracking its changing terms to twentieth-century feminism. Gabriele Beck-Busse compares two Arcadian dialogues intended to provide instruction in language in terms of their depictions of women. Finally, Silvana Seidel Menchi surveys multiple literary and artistic depictions of the stages of women's lives, ending with legally significant ages. Her essay thus addresses the stages of the life course as usually laid out by men and wrapped around changes in the female reproductive cycle.

Part 2 contains essays by the three male contributors to the conference and this volume, all from the United States. No papers were presented by males from other countries, notably not the host nation, Italy—which speaks about the academic status and acceptability of women's history in European countries. These three are grouped not in order to set them apart from those of the women contributors but because they are similar in several ways. All three are Italian in focus, and in chronological terms they are the earliest papers in the book, covering fourteenth- and fifteenth-century events and developments. But they are consistent in more than temporal and spatial terms, which may indicate something about the sorts of concerns that bring men to the study of women's history. The problem of female agency in the face of the ideology and laws of patriarchy is a common concern. In investigating that problem, all three also exploit legal and bureaucratic sources (in contrast to the literary sources at the heart of the essays in the first section): notarial texts, statutes, lawyers' *consilia*, civic and fiscal records. Study of female agency and of these sorts of sources is not a uniquely male endeavor. Christiane Klapisch-Zuber, who served as a commentator at the Trento conference, set the tone and direction of research in a series of forceful and elegant essays that first began to appear over twenty years ago.[7] Interestingly, to varying degrees all three male authors seek to modify Klapisch-Zuber's judgment that (largely Florentine) women were subordinated to family structures that "remained under the control of level-headed males" and that women "were not permanent elements in the lineage."[8] Dowry emerges as central in all these reassessments.

Stanley Chojnacki attempts to demonstrate that Venetian husbands, in contrast to their Florentine counterparts, even in the face of dowry inflation that he pegs at 350 percent over two centuries, pledged property and securities to back return of their wives' dowries following their (the husbands') deaths. These women were thus given incentive not to remarry but to remain in their husbands' homes and raise their children. Thomas Kuehn's essay examines how Florentine women, against the legal backdrop of the academic *ius commune* and civic statutes, grew into greater legal responsibility and activity over the life course. Not surprisingly, he finds that widows, directly possessed of property (including the now returned dowry) and facing family responsibilities without a husband, had the most potential and need to be active in the disposal and use of property and legal rights. Their relationships with marital and natal kin also shifted during their lives; attention to such relationships is crucial to understanding their activities. This is perhaps most clear in Julius Kirshner's analysis of the relatively anomalous case of the woman who married a man from a different city (more common in places like Modena and Milan than in Florence and Venice), thus calling into question her citizenship rights in both her city of birth and that of her husband. Here the law was ambiguous, the main position being a compromise worked out by the great fourteenth-century jurist Bartolus of Sassoferrato between the enlarged citizenship of late Roman law (enshrined in the *Corpus iuris civilis*) and the localism and nativism of the medieval communes. Within the contingencies of cases, as the examples from the jurist Baldus de Ubaldis demonstrate, rules designed to protect male interests (some of which persisted into the recent past) had effects not always deleterious to female interests and actions.

One of the implicit themes in these essays is the existence of laws and extralegal conventions restricting women's access to the halls of political power and other public domains. The essays in part 3 gravitate around the prominent presence in Italian cities of a very special zone of female activity: religious life within and outside convents. We begin with Anne Jacobson Schutte's presentation of sainthood and witchcraft as opposite ends of a continuum, both best seen in the employment of rather harsh inquisitory procedures of proof. While female saints tended to come from socially privileged groups and witches from poorer and marginalized social origins, both gave occasion for the expression of male distrust of female nature. The same

---

[7]These are gathered in an English translation: Christiane Klapisch-Zuber, *Women, Family, and Ritual in Renaissance Italy*, trans. Lydia G. Cochrane (Chicago: University of Chicago Press, 1985).
[8]Christiane Klapisch-Zuber, "The 'Cruel Mother': Maternity, Widowhood, and Dowry in Florence in the Fourteenth and Fifteenth Centuries," in idem, *Women, Family, and Ritual*, 117–31, at 118.

sort of distrust, running especially high in the menacing circumstances of the Counter-Reformation, produced severe rules for the enclosure of those women who chose or were forced to enter convents. Francesca Medioli's essay shows that male authorities were tolerant of breaches of the rules that resulted in no scandal but also that some of these women resisted constraints, even to the point of escaping from their convents. Here again we encounter the theme of agency, but this time in relation to women's identity and life choices rather than control over property and children. Gabriella Zarri examines the search in Counter-Reformation Italy for a "third status" (between marriage and strict enclosure in a convent) in which women could dedicate themselves to a celibate and religious existence. The educational and charitable work of the Dimesse and the Company of St. Ursula provides examples of what women who crafted a novel form of religious life could accomplish.

Marriage constitutes the theme of part 4. Just as some women disliked and rebelled against the life in the convent foisted upon them by their families (as seen in Medioli's essay), some women expressed their displeasure at the husbands selected for them. Daniela Hacke looks at Venetian annulment cases in which women claimed that they had not given their consent (required by canon law) to marriage.[9] In sketching out the role of neighbors as witnesses in these suits, moreover, she raises questions about the degree to which the familial sphere was truly private. Marina d'Amelia's analysis of the correspondence between Eugenia Spada and her mother is a revealing account of women's relationships within families, including Eugenia's dealings with her difficult mother-in-law. Much of this correspondence concerns the quintessentially female experiences of pregnancy, parturition, and motherhood. Fascinating details from morning sickness to weaning show how a woman's body was culturally constructed, observed, and commented upon, and what one woman, at any rate, went through. Eugenia was later widowed, remarried, took her daughter into the new home, and had a child by her second husband, but remained profoundly interested in and attached to the sons she had to leave behind. D'Amelia's sources and what they reveal about women's lives stand at the opposite end from the laws and prescriptions drafted by men that constitute so much of our source material about women in the past.

The two other essays in this group deal with northern European evidence. Using a wide variety of sources, including letters and diaries, Barbara Harris looks at English aristocratic wives. She notes that despite the English legal rule of coverture, by which a wife's personality was absorbed into that of her husband, aristocratic husbands came to rely on their wives as guardians, agents, and executors. These women were effective managers of their own dowers and the property that would go to their children. In a similar vein, examining judicial and notarial records from late-eighteenth-century

---

[9]This is one of several themes covered in Chiara Valsecchi, "'Causa matrimonialis est gravis et ardua': *Consiliatores* e matrimonio fino al Concilio di Trento," *Studi di storia del diritto* 2 (1999): 407–580.

Salzburg, Gunda Barth-Scalmani finds that spouses utilized legal devices to arrive at joint or partial community of property depending on their social and economic position. The weight and authority of women in these peasant, artisan, and bourgeois households (in contrast to Harris's aristocrats) were marked by their joint role in decision making. Only in the 1811 Austrian codification was the husband unequivocally elevated from partner with his wife to head of household.

In recent years, gender relations and cultural construction of gender have entered historical discourse—especially, though not without controversy, in the history of women.[10] Most of the essays in this volume skirt the issue when they confront matters of male patriarchy versus female agency. In part 5, Kristin Zapalac and Heide Wunder confront the issue of gender directly, both by looking at constructions not of female but of male identity. Zapalac's essay poses a contrast between Jewish and Hellenistic-Christian views of gender: the Jewish sense of miracle in the story of the man able to nurse versus the gender anxiety of the "pregnant" man in an English version of one of Boccaccio's tales. The metaphysical separation between body and soul that allowed for the fear that a bodily development called into question one's masculine identity (at least for comic effect) may also have been at work in the life of Hans von Schweinichen. Mining his *Memorial* up to the time of his marriage, the point at which he became a full-fledged adult, Wunder shows that under the influence of Lutheran piety, acquired largely from his mother's influence, this courtier came to reject some components of his peers' lifestyle. The masculinity he developed was different from that of the intellectualized courtier in Castiglione's famous sixteenth-century dialogue, but it would live on in later bourgeois models of adult masculinity.

Perhaps what all these essays best demonstrate is that, aside from medical and theological-moral treatises (and perhaps in the works of some historians), historical sources do not present men and women in the abstract. Even laws take on different dimensions when read in terms of the actions and experiences of those who faced, or framed, those laws. There are those today, including some of the authors of these essays, who are using literary materials in new, imaginative, sophisticated ways and avoid the old persistent pitfall of confusing prescription with reality.[11] There are others, again including authors whose essays appear below, who struggle to locate and use the sorts of sources, largely documentary, that reveal social practices. Neither sort of sources can be neglected. Dimensions of meaning of practices will remain uncaptured if we are not aware of prescriptive contexts; ranges of meaning in prescriptive

[10]Here an undoubtedly seminal and visible work is Joan Scott, "Gender: A Useful Category of Historical Analysis," *American Historical Review* 91 (1986): 1053–75; reprinted in Joan Scott, *Gender and the Politics of History* (New York: Columbia University Press, 1988), 28–50.

[11]Kelly-Gadol did not avoid this trap. Cf. Judith C. Brown, "A Woman's Place Was in the Home: Women's Work in Renaissance Tuscany," in *Rewriting the Renaissance: The Discourses of Sexual Difference in Early Modern Europe*, ed. Margaret W. Ferguson, Maureen Quilligan, and Nancy J. Vickers (Chicago: University of Chicago Press, 1986), 206–24.

forms (intended or not) will escape those who do not look to social practices. We certainly do not assert that historians who are more comfortable with or better equipped to handle one sort of source must also work with another. Rather, we suggest that they will profit from participating in a community of discourse that does not privilege one type of source over another. Even those precious sources that give direct expression to women's voices in the past, like the letters at the heart of d'Amelia's essay, take meaning against the largely male realm of prescriptive literature, and Heide Wunder has succeeded in exploiting a male voice for insight into both genders.

A related methodological insight arising from these essays is the utility of mingling approaches ranging from the broad and synthetic to the microhistorical—by which we mean something more than provision of specific examples to back up general points. Case studies, at once narrative and analytical, lay at the heart of the genre of *microstoria* spawned around Bologna and the journal *Quaderni storici* in the late 1970s and earlquerelle80s. Microhistory as a narrative genre has been subject to various postmodernist attacks, as any reader of the journal *History and Theory* can attest. Yet at their best, microhistorical studies are sensitive to the nuances of power, shifts of voice, and even silences in documents and texts. They can elucidate intention and causation on the level of persons and small groups, opening history to women and others more liable to be left out or on the margins of totalizing accounts.[12] None of the authors in this volume is a particular advocate of microhistory or any other distinctive methodology. They do not engage in methodological or theoretical speculation. But they represent a variety of approaches in terms of scale.

This variety has enormously enriched the themes of time and space, so much so that we hesitate to advance gross, premature generalizations. It is clear that women's lives, both prescriptively and in reality, changed over their life course. That course varied for women according to their marital or vocational choices, or those made for them, as Hacke and Medioli demonstrate. Death too—especially of spouses, but also of parents, siblings, children, and others—bent the trajectories of their lives in different directions. Social status and wealth played their part as well. Some contributors see women gaining more influence, control, and freedom in their lives over the life course, culminating in a widow's single-handed management of household and finances—more so the more wealthy and socially prominent they were. Kuehn and Kirshner show, however, that women often had to operate in the unfamiliar and very male domain of law to manage their property and retrieve their inheritances, including the dowries that continued to tie them, as in Chojnacki's Venice, to men in both natal and marital families and also, as Kirshner shows, to cities. Conversely, Schutte

[12]See *Microhistory and the Lost Peoples of Europe*, ed. Edward Muir and Guido Ruggiero (Baltimore: Johns Hopkins University Press, 1991); Gianna Pomata, "Close-Ups and Long Shots: Combining Particular and General in Writing the Histories of Women and Men," in *Geschlechtergeschichte und Allgemeine Geschichte: Herausforderungen und Perspektiven*, ed. Hans Medick and Anne-Charlott Trepp (Göttingen: Wallstein, 1998), 99–124, esp. 114–16.

and Zarri argue that women entering convents and thus subordinating themselves to that most patriarchal of institutions, the church, did not forfeit all sense of self; hence the desire of some to find a third status.

Another dimension of time, not to be forgotten on the verge of a millennium, is its passage over the centuries. On this score, although it is true that the essays in this volume range from the fourteenth to the eve of the nineteenth century, venturing generalizations still seems hazardous. It may be that developments such as the prolonged *querelle des femmes* and the efforts of Protestantism and Catholicism alike to channel women's religious activities led to a more continual and self-conscious gender sense in cultural terms, as Wunder and Zapalac suggest. Yet gender was a category of law all along, and neither for Venetian nor English noblewomen did that category and its concomitant rights shift. Kirshner's stunning conclusion tracing the persistence of a gendered sense of citizenship into the modern Italian civil code and right up to legislation of 1983 and 1992 provides eloquent testimony to that.

Kelly-Gadol intended to quarrel with the direction of change toward the modern world as one of liberation for both sexes. More than two decades after the publication of her essay, seeing a direction of change for women over the centuries covered in this anthology, let alone determining by what criteria to measure it, remains difficult. Were women freer in law? Freer in conscience? More literate? More self-aware? The postmodern abhorrence of metanarratives has had its effect on histories of women and gender too.[13]

The largest generalizations we are confident about advancing relate to the conference's spatial theme. In cultural forms and substance, in the realities of life, there were differences for women (and men) between Italy—at least in cities between Rome and Venice—and northern European lands, mainly Germany. That this should be so will not surprise even a student beginning to learn about the Renaissance and Reformation, national histories, and modern languages. The differences between regions that emerge in this volume, however, should put to rest once and for all any timeless, classless, essentializing notion of "woman" in the abstract. The continuing option for women (or for their families) of entering the convent, the continued presence of feudal relationships and impartible inheritance (notable for Harris's English women), and—perhaps more important than usually allowed—the use of academic legal traditions and written procedure in preference to customary law were just some of the factors that had different impacts across the regions of western and central Europe.

In our view, the essays in this volume render problematic the commonly assumed spatial and social distinction between public and private. This distinction was axiomatic for Kelly-Gadol, who measured the deleterious effects of the Renais-

---

[13]See Lynn Hunt, "The Challenge of Gender: Deconstruction of Categories and Reconsideration of Narratives in Gender History," in *Geschlechtergeschichte und Allgemeine Geschichte*, ed. Medick and Trepp, 57–97, esp. 74–97.

sance on women in terms of noble women's loss of public power and the disappearance of bourgeois women "into a private realm of family and domestic concerns."[14] Since 1977, it has received a great deal of criticism on methodological grounds.[15] This is not to say that the terms "public" and "private" were not known and used in Latin and Western European vernaculars. Even in a domain of their privileged use, the development of modern state forms, they have been questioned and subjected to more nuanced treatment.[16] In the domain of women's history the distinction has proven murky. While, for example, matters of pregnancy and parturition might seem quintessentially private and domestic, totally female, as in the letters between Eugenia Spada and her mother explored by d'Amelia, the same matters could become visibly public where sainthood or witchcraft was at issue. In the early modern era marriage and inheritance were enormously public issues. Hacke's essay shows how deeply private disputes emerged in public, even through intermediary testimony of neighbors and friends. The very existence of so many legal documents that can shed light on women's lives is due to the fact that the "private" had to become "public" at times.

These essays force us to reject a simple equation of public space gendered as male space and private space gendered as female. For one thing, since men came home, the "private" was also their space. For another, no matter how absolutely women were legally and constitutionally excluded from official forms of power, they had reason (including reasons of male interest) to become "public" agents on occasion, as one can see in Barth-Scalmani's essay. The public/private dichotomy, a product of the nineteenth century's social, political, and legal developments, ill serves historical analysis of earlier eras—or even of the nineteenth century, for that matter. This volume enables us to understand how public and private interpenetrated in shaping the lives of specific historical persons, who moved between house and street, church and market, office and field, thus shaping each of these spaces. Zarri offers perhaps the most eloquent evidence of this in her account of women trying to forge an existence as celibate and studious but nonconventual, neither public nor cloistered.

Public/private is but one set of oppositional categories that must yield before the sorts of evidence and analysis presented here. In organizing the Trento conference, we initially asked the participants to pay attention to two particular oppositions—that between an "older" model of women's oppression by men and a newer model of women's agency; and that between a history of women (as opposed to

[14]Kelly-Gadol, *Becoming Visible*, 2nd ed., 197.

[15]See Susan M. Reverby and Dorothy O. Helly, "Introduction: Converging on History," in *Gendered Domains*, 1–24, esp. 6–8.

[16]See Giorgio Chittolini, "Il 'privato,' il 'pubblico,' lo Stato," in *Origini dello Stato*, ed. Giorgio Chittolini, Anthony Molho, and Pierangelo Schiera (Bologna: Il Mulino, 1994), 553–89; English translation: *The Origins of the State in Italy, 1300–1600*, ed. Julius Kirshner (Chicago: University of Chicago Press, 1995), 34–61.

men) and a history of gender. In his or her own way, each author tends to emphasize one side or the other of each opposition, but all shy away from taking a firm position on one side or the other. The cumulative effect enables us to conclude that we have moved beyond such oppositions or at least can operate comfortably within them without feeling compelled to resolve them in a definitive but reductionistic manner.

The notion of agency arose to recover a sense of women's lives and a reason to study them in opposition to an older contention that women were merely oppressed victims of patriarchy, whose lives were marked by exclusion, vulnerability, and powerlessness. Seeking women's agency rendered them both historical subjects worthy of investigation and active protagonists of change. We can now understand that women were both oppressed objects of hegemony and, within limits, agents in shaping their lives. Especially on the microhistorical level, their agency—despite limitations placed on them in culture, law, and the economy—becomes visible. We can also gain a sense of how such agency could reshape, however indirectly, the larger engines of patriarchy.

Much the same can be said about gender. Like agency, gender as an analytical construct seems to offer a way out of the impasse of women's victimization, of their seemingly timeless quality of object in history. Pioneers in the study of gender have stressed the dichotomy, or at least the analytical distinction, between sex (as biology) and gender (as culture). Gender is something women can be perceived to construct themselves, or at least change. Their agency is both in gender and engendered; therefore it is historical. Gender had the added utility of bringing together study of male and female identities, of breaking down dichotomies.[17] Yet even those most eager to see gender replace women's history as a category of analysis have voiced misgivings about it. It may only displace a male-female opposition from the level of life and economy to that of meaning and metaphor; it may not get us past the distinction between prescriptive and descriptive sources.[18] Some feminists fear that women's oppression and exploitation are lost sight of in the new celebration of gender—or worse, women emerge as participants in their own victimization. Nancy Partner, furthermore, has warned that approaches from the perspective of gender run the risk of leaving out an essential element, the individual self:

> Sex and gender offer an inadequate conceptual framework. A middle or third term is always needed—"self" or "sexuality" will do quite well—to acknowledge the developmental associations of mind with world which produce men and women who tend to be recognizably like others of their same sex (and class, society, etc.) when regarded collectively, but yet are quite distinct and individual seen "close up." Gender, as a concept carrying

[17]See the introduction to *Gender and Society in Renaissance Italy*, ed. Judith C. Brown and Robert C. Davis (London: Longman, 1998), 1–15, at 4–5.
[18]Here note Joan Scott's concerns, "Gender," 1064–65. See also Hunt, "The Challenge of Gender," 60–74.

all the explanatory weight for human behavior, thins out and dehumanizes the individual while never accounting for the deviance, rebellion, and simple idiosyncrasy which happily fill the historical record.[19]

Certain contributors to this volume are clearly more at home in gender history, others in the history of women. None of them commits the error identified by Partner. Indeed, in offering examples of behavior that challenged gender stereotypes, their essays reveal both the operation of patriarchy, notably in limiting fields of action, and the agency of those subject to it. The peculiarities of times, spaces, or situations remain: particular findings are not parlayed into vast generalizations. Selves—or, to invoke a related term, persons[20]—figure here, if not exactly as a new paradigm, as a privileged focal point for analysis. Selfhood mediated the experiences of women in the past.

Where and how we approach these experiences depends upon our own experiences. Over ten years ago, Karen M. Offen framed a contrast between Anglo-American feminism, which operated with a vocabulary of (equal) rights that implicitly took "the standard of male adulthood as the norm," and a European focus on "elaborations of womanliness" celebrating "sexual difference rather than similarity within a framework of male/female complementarity."[21] Setting the essays by North Americans (Wiesner-Hanks, Chojnacki, Kuehn, Kirshner, Schutte, Harris, Zapalac) against those by Europeans, readers can ask themselves whether such a distinction is still the case, and if so to what extent. While this volume by itself cannot bring about a Copernican revolution in the study of women and gender in early modern Europe, it certainly suggests new ways of approaching this field in all its interdisciplinary dimensions. We confidently predict that it will help to clear the path leading toward the new paradigm we need.

[19]Nancy F. Partner, "No Sex, No Gender," in *History and Theory: Contemporary Readings*, ed. Brian Fay, Philip Pomper, and Richard T. Vann (Oxford: Blackwell, 1998), 268–96, at 288.

[20]See Thomas Kuehn, "Person and Gender in the Laws," in *Gender and Society in Renaissance Italy*, 87–106.

[21]Karen M. Offen, "Defining Feminism: A Comparative Historical Approach," *Signs* 14 (1988–89): 119–57, at 123–24.

PART 1

Women's History and Social History
Are Structures Necessary?

Merry Wiesner-Hanks

As so often happens when one is asked for a title far in advance of a conference, I originally proposed a very general title which I hoped would allow me to discuss some aspects of the relationship between women's history and social history—the topic I was asked to address—and also to speak more specifically to the subject of the conference. Since I will, of course, not be able to consider *all* structures which have some bearing on women's lives in the early modern period, I would like to focus on two particular questions, and two particular types of structures. The question I will be addressing in the first part of my paper involves economic and social structures and is often linked with the broader debate about the relations between social history and women's history in this period: Do women need capitalism? In the second part of my paper, I will turn to a question of chronological structure, one which underlies—though perhaps not stated explicitly—this entire conference: Do women need the Renaissance? I will approach these questions both analytically and historiographically, surveying the work of a number of historians and scholars of literature over the last twenty years. I apologize here at the outset for narrowing my original vast question to just these two, for my title implies that I might be doing an intertextual reworking of post-Certeauian explications of the interactivity between event and structure combined with a neo-Althusserian privileging of structure over agency set in the context of a Foucaultian paradigm of phallologocentric self-referential discourse pre/overdetermined by positionalities of subjectivity and authority. That will have to wait for another time (and another historian).

Do women need capitalism? Though phrased rather inelegantly, this captures what has been the key debate among historians of women's economic role in premodern Europe, the importance of general economic change (usually labeled something like "the rise of capitalism") in changing the work and thus the lives of women (and, in its most recent phases, the role of economic change in changing the lives of men *as men*). Here two general positions have emerged, one which views capitalism as significant for women and one which views it as less significant; what we might in shorthand term the battle between capitalism and patriarchy. (This is only rarely an actual battle; the debate between Bridget Hill and Judith Bennett in *Women's History Review* is unusual in this regard.[1]) Not surprisingly, those who see significant change tend to emphasize capitalism, and those who see more continuity emphasize patriarchy.

Those who regard capitalism as an important development in women's history in general regard capitalism as a bad thing. This, of course, is no new idea: it was put forth by Alice Clark in *Working Life of Women in the Seventeenth Century* almost eighty years ago.[2] Though some of these studies see capitalism as an unremitting evil, pulling women down from a "golden age" of precapitalist household production in which their labor and ideas were valued (here Caroline Barron and Susan Cahn are the clearest voices), most recent work has been more qualified.[3] It stresses that women's experience varied according to social class, economic status, and geographic region—factors that have traditionally been taken into account when examining men's experience of economic change—and that it also varied according to age, marital status, family size, and life span, factors that the recent decades of research in women's history have taught us to investigate.

Those who argue that capitalism brought significant changes do not completely neglect continuity. The majority of women and men in Europe during these four centuries continued to work in agriculture, for at least three-quarters—and in some areas more like 95 percent—of the population remained in the countryside. Historians such as Michael Roberts, Keith Snell, Ann Kussmaul, and Christina Vanja are investigating the rural scene more closely, tracing both structures and techniques that were slow to change and innovations which directly affected women's lives, such as the introduction of the scythe, stall feeding, and silk production.[4] Historians who continue to concentrate on cities—where the sources are more prevalent and concentrated—stress that much of the economy was still precapitalist, and many occupations, such as domestic service and selling at the public market, changed very little during the period.

[1]Bridget Hill and Judith Bennett, "Women's History: A Study in Change, Continuity or Standing Still?" *Women's History Review* 2 (1993): 5–22, 173–84.

[2]Alice Clark, *Working Life of Women in the Seventeenth Century* (London: Routledge, 1919; reprints, 1968, 1982, 1992).

[3]Susan Cahn, *Industry of Devotion: The Transformation of Women's Work in England, 1500–1660* (New York: Columbia University Press, 1987); Caroline Barron, "The 'Golden Age' of Women in Medieval London," in *Medieval Women of Southern England* (Reading: Graduate Centre for Medieval Studies, University of Reading, 1989), 35–58.

[4]Michael Roberts, "Sickles and Scythes: Women's Work and Men's Work at Harvest Time," *History Workshop Journal* 7 (1979): 3–29; Keith Snell, *Annals of the Labouring Poor* (Cambridge: Cambridge University Press, 1985); Ann Kussmaul, *Servants in Husbandry in Early Modern England* (Cambridge: Cambridge University Press, 1981); Christina Vanja, "Frauen im Dorf: Ihre Stellung unter besonderer Berücksichtigung landgräflich-hessischer Quellen im Mittelalter," *Zeitschrift für Agrargeschichte und Agrarsoziologie* 34 (1986): 147–59.

For many historians, however, wide variety and strong continuities do not negate the fact that this is an era of significant change in women's work. Occupations which required university education or formal training were closed to women, as they could not attend universities or humanist academies, or participate in most apprenticeship programs. Women rarely controlled enough financial resources to enter occupations which required large initial capital outlay, and social norms or outright prohibition kept them from occupations with political functions. Family responsibilities prevented them from entering occupations which required extensive traveling. Capitalism created opportunities for wage labor, but most of these jobs were poorly paid and offered little job security.

Some historians, such as Bridget Hill and Pamela Tharpe, have focused on the economic causes and effects of these changes, while others, such as Martha Howell, Michael Roberts, Jean Quataert, Maxine Berg, and I, have been more interested in changes in meaning. (*The Historical Meanings of Work* is, in fact, the title of a recent collection.[5]) We stress—though we do not agree on everything—that it is in the meaning of work as much as the actual tasks that women were doing that we can see the most change during this period. As Clark noted so long ago, women were excluded or stepped back from certain areas of production, but, more importantly, their productive tasks were increasingly defined as reproductive (as housekeeping) or as assisting (as helping out). Thus a woman who sewed clothes, took in boarders, did laundry, and gathered herbs—and who was paid for all of these activities—was increasingly thought of as a housewife, a title that became enshrined in statistical language in the nineteenth century, when her activities were not regarded as contributing to the gross national product or other sorts of economic measurements.[6]

[5]Bridget Hill, *Women, Work and Sexual Politics in Eighteenth-Century England* (Oxford: Basil Blackwell, 1989); Pamela Sharpe, *Adapting to Capitalism: Working Women in the English Economy 1700–1850* (New York: St. Martin's, 1996); Maxine Berg, "Women's Work, Mechanization, and the Early Phases of Industrialization," in *On Work: Historical and Theoretical Approaches*, ed. R. E. Pahl (Oxford: Basil Blackwell, 1988), 61–94; Martha Howell, *Women, Production, and Patriarchy in Late Medieval Cities* (Chicago: University of Chicago Press, 1986); idem, "Citizenship and Gender: Women's Political Status in Northern Medieval Cities," in *Women and Power in the Middle Ages*, ed. Mary Erler and Maryanne Kowaleski (Athens: University of Georgia Press, 1988); Michael Roberts, "'Words They Are Women, Deeds They Are Men': Images of Work and Gender in Early Modern England," in *Women and Work in Pre-Industrial England*, ed. Lindsey Charles and Lorna Duffin (London: Croom Helm, 1985), 122–81; Jean Quataert, "The Shaping of Women's Work in Manufacturing: Guilds, Households, and the State in Central Europe," *American Historical Review* 90 (1985): 1122–48; Merry E. Wiesner, *Working Women in Renaissance Germany* (New Brunswick: Rutgers University Press, 1986); idem, "Guilds, Male Bonding and Women's Work in Early Modern Germany," in *Gender and History* 1 (1989): 125–37; idem, "*Wandervögels* and Women: Journeymen's Concepts of Masculinity in Early Modern Germany," *Journal of Social History* 24/4 (summer 1991): 767–82; *The Historical Meanings of Work*, ed. Patrick Joyce (Cambridge: Cambridge University Press, 1987).

[6]Marilyn Waring, *If Women Counted: A New Feminist Economics* (San Francisco: Harper and Row, 1988).

This gender division between production and reproduction was reinforced in the early modern period by parish, city, and state governments, which often allowed women to support themselves and their families with various tasks because these were not really "work," but simply "support." This even included allowing women to sell items which they had made, so that authorities clearly knew that "production" as we would define it was involved. Women themselves sometimes adopted the same rhetoric, for they knew that arguing they had a right to work would be much less effective than describing the children they had to support, or how much public money might otherwise be spent on them if they did not work.

And work women did. One of the clearest results of the last twenty years of scholarship is that capitalism—or other changes—did not bring an end to women's participation in the labor market. Peter Earle's recent study of the London labor market has found that 72 percent of the women who served as witnesses in court in 1700 were doing paid work outside the home, most of it low status, but certainly not a retreat from economic activity.[7] A few voices, Heide Wunder's among them, note that the continuation or expansion of wage labor, despite its low-pay, low-status nature, may actually have benefited some women, as it allowed them to support themselves without marrying. She thus emphasizes the great concern with "masterless" women and the laws which attempted to force women into service or into male-headed households as a result of the expansion of wage labor; such laws had not been necessary earlier because the opportunities for women to live alone and support themselves by their labor were much fewer.[8]

Statistical data like Earle's, and also statistical data which confirm women's lower wages for all types of tasks across centuries and countries, are often used by those who reject the notion that this is a period of dramatic change in women's work or who at least do not see capitalism as the most important agent of what change there was. Here Olwen Hufton, Katrina Honeyman and Jordan Goodman, Chris Middleton, and Judith Bennett have all been strong voices in favor of continuity, viewing gender ideology—what Honeyman and Goodman term "gender conflict" and Bennett, more boldly, "patriarchy"—as the most significant shaper of women's work experience.[9] They note that even dramatic changes in the structure and organi-

[7]Peter Earle, "The Female Labour Market in London in the Late Seventeenth and Early Eighteenth Centuries," *Economic History Review* 42 (1989): 338.

[8]Heide Wunder, *"Er ist die Sonn', sie ist der Mond": Frauen in der frühen Neuzeit* (Munich: Beck, 1992), 188–90; now available in English, *He Is the Sun, She Is the Moon: Women in Early Modern Germany,* trans. Thomas Dunlap (Cambridge: Harvard University Press, 1998).

[9]Olwen Hufton, "Women, Work, and Family," in *A History of Women in the West,* ed. Natalie Zemon Davis and Arlette Farge, vol. 3, *Renaissance and Enlightenment Paradoxes* (Cambridge: Harvard University Press, 1993), 15–45; Judith Bennett, "History That Stands Still: Women's Work in the European Past: Review Essay," *Feminist Studies* 14 (1988): 269–83; idem, *Ale, Beer and Brewsters in England: Women's Work in a Changing World* (New York: Oxford University Press, 1996); Chris Middleton, "The Familiar Fate of the *Famulae:* Gender Divisions in the History of Wage Labour," in *On Work,* 21–46; Kat-

zation of institutions and industries may not have been evident to the women work-ing in them, who were often clustered in the lowest-skilled or poorest-paid jobs. Whether an industry was organized capitalistically or by guilds, or whether a hospi-tal was run by the church or the city, made little difference to the woman who spun wool or washed bedding. Women remained in these low-status positions because they often fit their work around the life cycle of their families, moving in and out of various jobs as children were born and grew up, or as their husbands died and they remarried. Work for many women during this period was a matter of makeshifts and expedients, a pattern which some historians see continuing with only minor alter-ations until the twentieth century, or even until today, considering the role of ill-paid women and children in developing countries in today's global economy.

This position stems to some degree from the feminist critique of Marxism, which in its more theoretical guises has usually not focused on the premodern period for evidence but on the Industrial Revolution, the contemporary global economy or, following Engels, very early human cultures. This theory began with dramatic denunciations of patriarchy, such as those of Kate Millett and Shulamith Firestone, then developed through sophisticated analyses of the workings of both capitalism and patriarchy such as those of Heidi Hartmann, Christine Delphy, and Sylvia Walby (usually termed "dual systems approaches"), and now seems to have settled (for a time at least, for theory never settles for very long) on asserting what Anne Phillips describes as the "intertwining" of capitalism and patriarchy.[10] Some of these theorists, most prominently Carol Pateman, see that intertwining as necessary and point to its roots not only in the realm of work but also in the realms of property and contract, while others, such as Carol Johnson and Mary Murray, emphasize the contradictions and tensions between capitalism and patriarchy.[11]

At the same time that political and economic theorists are meshing or splitting capitalism and patriarchy, and historians are exploring changes and continuities in work and property ownership, other theorists and historians are asserting that all of this is a delusion, that what matters most—or, in the opinions of some, *all* that mat-ters—is language. This "linguistic turn," associated with the ideas of French theorists

---

rina Honeyman and Jordan Goodman, "Women's Work, Gender Conflict and Labour Markets in Europe, 1500–1900," *The Economic History Review* 44 (1991): 608–28.

[10]Kate Millett, *Sexual Politics* (London: Sphere, 1971); Shulamith Firestone, *The Dialectic of Sex* (London: The Women's Press, 1979); Heidi Hartmann, *The Unhappy Marriage of Marxism and Feminism: A Debate of Class and Patriarchy* (London: Pluto Press, 1981); Christine Delphy, "The Main Enemy," in Christine Delphy, *Close to Home: A Materialist Analysis of Women's Oppression,* trans. and ed. Diana Leonard (London: Hutchinson, 1984), 57–77; Sylvia Walby, *Theorizing Patriarchy* (Oxford: Basil Black-well, 1990); Anne Phillips, *Divided Loyalties: Dilemmas of Sex and Class* (London: Virago, 1987).

[11]Carole Pateman, *The Sexual Contract* (Oxford: Basil Blackwell, 1988); Carol Johnson, "Does Capitalism Really Need Patriarchy? Some Old Issues Reconsidered," *Women's Studies International Forum* 19 (1996):193–202; Mary Murray, *The Law of the Father: Patriarchy in the Transition from Feudalism to Capitalism* (London: Routledge, 1995).

BRIDWELL LIBRARY
SOUTHERN METHODIST UNIVERSITY
DALLAS. TEXAS 75275

whose names are constantly cited, affects (some of my colleagues would say *infects*) all of history in the United States, but particularly women's and gender history. "Theory" for most younger historians of women is not the economic theory I have been discussing, but linguistic theory, and the questions they are interested in are ones of representation, subjectivity, and discourse. A decade ago some women's historians worried that the links between social and women's history were too strong, that women's history spent too much of its time addressing questions that came from social history, such as class formation or protoindustrialization. As Judith Bennett phrased this in a response to Louise Tilly at the 1988 meeting of the Social Science History Association, "Who asks the questions for women's history?"[12] That question can still be put, of course, but the answer would not be social history, but literature. This "linguistic turn," what is usually loosely called "deconstruction," has also suggested that the question is flawed at its core, for—to take the most extreme position—there are no "women" and there is no "history." "Women" is a social construct, and "history" is just a text.

This position provoked acrimonious debate and denunciations (the exchange between Joan Scott and Linda Gordon in *Signs* is one notorious example[13]), with opponents of deconstruction asserting that it denies women's agency in both past and present by positing unchangeable linguistic structures, and proponents asserting that to talk about women's agency or experience, or to think one can discover them in historical records, is both naive and imperialistic. The debate became a familiar one—and was ably reviewed, along with other key issues in women's history, by Sonja Rose and others in a recent issue of the *Journal of Women's History*.[14] Rather than dwell on the dispute any longer, I would like to explore what I see as a fruitful *collaboration* between literature and history, an issue on which they have worked together to develop some interesting rethinking. This is the issue addressed by my second question: Do women need the Renaissance? Answering this question leads us into the issue of chronological structures, and brings together two larger questions: How useful is the term "Renaissance" in general? How useful are chronological categories derived from male experience for telling women's story, whether that story is conceived in terms of representation or reality? My question also derives, of course, from Joan Kelly's pathbreaking essay "Did Women Have a Renaissance?" which

---

[12]Judith Bennett, comment on Louise Tilly, "Gender, Women's History and Social History," *Social Science History* 13 (1989): 471.

[13]The debate was framed in Scott's review of Gordon's book, *Heroes of Their Own Lives* and in Gordon's review of Scott's book, *Gender and the Politics of History*, in *Signs* 15 (1990): 848-60.

[14]Sonja Rose et al., "Gender History/Women's History: Is Feminist Scholarship Losing Its Critical Edge?" *Journal of Women's History* 5 (1993): 89–128. There is a similar review of issues in women's and gender history in Eve Rosenhaft, "Zwei Geschlechter—eine Geschichte? Frauengeschichte, Männergeschichte, Geschlechtergeschichte und ihre Folgen für unsere Geschichtswahrnehmung," in *Was sind Frauen? Was sind Männer? Geschlechterkonstruktionen im historischen Wandel*, ed. Christiane Eifert et al. (Frankfurt: Suhrkamp, 1996), 257–74.

BRIDWELL LIBRARY
SOUTHERN METHODIST UNIVERSITY
DALLAS, TEXAS 75275

inspired so many of us to begin to question periodization, to (though we didn't call it that) deconstruct chronological categories.[15]

At the time Kelly asked her now famous question, the term "Renaissance" was already being contested. In his 1978 presidential address to the American Historical Association, William Bouwsma surveyed historians' reservations about the term, seeing these as part of a larger "collapse of the traditional dramatic organization of Western history."[16] Bouwsma was writing only a year after Kelly's essay appeared, and the critique of the term coming from women's history was not part of his considerations. His justification for resurrecting the Renaissance, however, nicely captures what has inspired feminist historical and literary critiques of the label. Bouwsma advocates a return to the dramatic organization of history, with the Renaissance as a key pivotal event, important because it created an "anthropological vision...that culture is a product of the creative adjustment of the human race to its varying historical circumstances rather than a function of universal and changeless nature, and the perception that culture accordingly differs from time to time and group to group." That statement anticipates the spirit of what we now oddly call the "new cultural history," but in a later rewording of his idea, Bouwsma also inadvertently captures the feminist critique of the Renaissance. He notes, "as the creator of language, man also shapes through language the only world he can know directly, including even himself...the notion of man as the creator of himself and the world was heady stuff." Some of you may be thinking "but Bouwsma *meant* women, too," and others may be thinking that I am unfairly criticizing a marvelous historian for sensitivities about language that other marvelous historians have yet to adopt twenty years later. But I don't think Bouwsma was being insensitive here; he was simply being accurate. As countless discussions of "self-fashioning" since have pointed out, it was *man* who was to be the creator of *himself*, *man* who was the measure of all things.[17]

The highly gendered nature of the Renaissance's "anthropological vision" is a steady theme in the work of Margaret King on female humanists, Constance Jordan on Renaissance feminism, and the huge number of studies of—mostly English—women writers.[18] Although it appeared originally that most of this feminist analysis of the Renaissance would be a further move away from the "drama of history"

[15]Joan Kelly, "Did Women Have a Renaissance?" in *Becoming Visible: Women in European History*, ed. Renate Bridenthal, Claudia Koonz, and Susan Stuard, 2nd ed. (Boston: Houghton-Mifflin, 1987), 175–201.

[16]William J. Bouwsma, "The Renaissance and the Drama of Western History," *American Historical Review* 84 (1979): 1–15.

[17]Stephen J. Greenblatt, *Renaissance Self-Fashioning: From More to Shakespeare* (Chicago: University of Chicago Press, 1980).

[18]Margaret King, *Women of the Renaissance* (Chicago: University of Chicago Press, 1993); Constance Jordan, *Renaissance Feminism: Literary Texts and Political Models* (Ithaca: Cornell University Press, 1990); Margaret Hannay, *Silent but for the Word: Tudor Women as Patrons, Translators, and Writers of Religious Works* (Kent, Ohio: Kent State University Press, 1985); Elaine Beilin, *Redeeming Eve: Women Writers*

(Bouwsma's words), dethroning the Renaissance yet again, in many ways it is not. The drama is still there, but the outcome is tragedy rather than triumph. The Renaissance is still the beginning of a trajectory, but that trajectory leads to Rousseau, the banning of women's clubs in the French Revolution, the restrictions of the Napoleonic Code, and separate spheres. (Though women's history of the nineteenth century rarely searches for roots in the Renaissance, that of the eighteenth century, such as the work of Christine Fauré, Joan Landes, and Olwen Hufton, certainly does.[19])

Though some feminist scholarship thus intentionally continues to use the term "Renaissance," with the understanding that there are quotation marks around it the same way there are around the "Golden Age" of Athens or even the "Enlightenment," it continues to be a source of discomfort. One would have thought that in twenty years the issue of what to call "this period" would have disappeared, like most academic questions we were arguing about twenty years ago, but the debate has instead widened. This conference is focusing on time. An entire session at the Berkshire Women's History Conference in June 1996 dealt with just this issue: "Complicating Categories, Crossing Chronologies: Periodization in the History of Women from Medieval to Modern." A session at the interdisciplinary conference "Gender in Perspective in the Early Modern Period" (sponsored by the Zentrum zur Erforschung der Frühen Neuzeit at the University of Frankfurt in the fall of 1996) was intended to focus (though it did not) on just this issue: "Defining Moments: Feminist Stakes in the Late Medieval/Renaissance/Early Modern Conundrum."

The debate, which has now spread to literary studies as well as history, is highlighted in Leah Marcus's essay in *Redrawing the Boundaries: The Transformation of English and American Literary Studies.*[20] She notes there that literary scholars are more loath than historians to give up the Renaissance because it allows them to preserve literature as a separate discipline in these days of ever-increasing interdisciplinarity. I was intrigued by this comment, and it led me to investigate a quite prominent example of the rejection of the "Renaissance," the renaming and redefinition of the *Journal of Medieval and Renaissance Studies* as the *Journal of Medieval and Early Modern Studies.* The "Statement of Purpose" for the renamed journal provides good evidence for Marcus's point. In two paragraphs which use the words "history"

---

of the Renaissance (Princeton: Princeton University Press, 1987); Elaine Hobby, *Virtue of Necessity: English Women's Writing 1649–88* (Ann Arbor: University of Michigan Press, 1989).

[19]Christine Fauré, *Democracy without Women: Feminism and the Rise of Liberalism in France* (Bloomington: Indiana University Press, 1991); Joan Landes, *Women and the Public Sphere in the Age of the French Revolution* (Ithaca: Cornell University Press, 1988); Olwen Hufton, *Women and the Limits of Citizenship in the French Revolution* (Toronto: University of Toronto Press, 1992).

[20]Leah Marcus, "Renaissance/Early Modern Studies," in *Redrawing the Boundaries: The Transformation of English and American Literary Studies,* ed. Stephen Greenblatt and Giles Gunn (New York: Modern Language Association, 1992), 41–63.

and "theory" or variations of them many times, the words "literature" and "literary" never appear (though the word "texts" does appear, in a phrase downplaying their centrality). I was so struck by this I wrote to Michael Cornett, the new managing editor, who answered with his reflections about both the journal and periodization in general. He confirmed my initial impression, commenting that "there has been a conscious attempt to keep literary study from dominating the journal because of its great success in opening up all these questions of a conscious engagement with the past and the artifice of historical study."[21]

There are two ways to view this comment, of course. One is to see it as confirming the fears of Marcus's colleagues in literature that if you dump the Renaissance, you dump literary studies as a separate field. The other is the way some of my colleagues in history will no doubt see it, as representing not the abandonment of literature but its total triumph, a point of view which might find further support in Cornett's later comment that "if literary work seems to lead the way, that's because literary scholars have led the way in rethinking historical study and it will take time for other disciplines to catch up."[22] Harrumph, we historians might say, perhaps we don't *want* to catch up? If scholars of literature wanted to rethink historical study, why didn't they become historians in the first place? If they want to tell us that all history is text, wouldn't it be nice if they could read the texts in their original? (We social historians who work with handwritten sources can always feel superior with that question.) Besides, since historians were actually the first to use the term "early modern" anyway—largely to escape the label "Reformation," not "Renaissance"—in this, isn't literature simply following history without admitting it?

The debate about who is swallowing whom in the intersection between literature and history depends to a great degree upon one's own allegiances, and goes far beyond the issue of what one calls a journal, or one's own scholarly specialty, or a period. Like the debate over deconstruction in women's history, it remains acrimonious. I could trace it further, but because I am emphasizing collaboration rather than conflict here, I would like to return to the question of labels again, and consider the term "early modern." If "Renaissance" carries too much baggage to use other than ironically, does "early modern" solve the problem? This is also a question that is at least twenty years old, for Bouwsma and many other analysts have pointed to some general problems with the term: its assumption that there is something that can unambiguously be called "modernity," and its retaining of a notion of linear trajectory with a final act, whether that final act is termed the Second Coming, the dictatorship of the proletariat, or "the end of history."[23] Lee Patterson, in an article in

---

[21]Michael Cornett, personal communication. My thanks to Professor Cornett for his very long and thoughtful comments.

[22]Michael Cornett, personal communication.

[23]"The end of history" is the title of Francis Fukayama's philosophical reflections, *The End of History and the Last Man* (New York: Free Press, 1992).

Speculum, sharply critiques this "crude binarism that locates modernity ('us') on one side and premodernity ('them') on the other."[24]

In the last several years these discussions have also included historians of areas beyond Europe. Anthony Reid, Vicente Rafael, and Leonard and Barbara Andaya, for example, have debated its use for Southeast Asia, and Leonard Blussé and Harriet Zurndorfer for China.[25] They have noted that (in the words of the Andayas) "especially in light of subaltern writings that reject the notion of modernity as a universal... the very invocation of the word implicitly sets a 'modern Europe' against a 'yet-to-be modernized' non-Europe." Thus non-Europe joins the Middle Ages as a "them" as compared to "us," both of them orientalized. David Wallace judges this linkage extremely harshly in "Carving Up Time and the World," noting that "Renaissance critics today continue to imitate the temporal and territorial expansionism of their Renaissance forbears," whose "restless and destructive individualism" led to "the erasure of pre-Columbian America" and the "genocidal violence of European colonialism."[26]

Both Wallace and Marcus warn that "early modern" might be even more expansionary than "Renaissance," and Nancy Partner agrees, noting that "even the Renaissance is rapidly losing its metaphorical romantic substance and is being engulfed in the rapacious maw of the Early Modern academic machine."[27] This problem arises particularly from its indeterminate beginning. When does the "early modern" period start? Is it meant to be a substitute for the Renaissance or Reformation, or is it a subsequent period? Some German scholars use the term "early modern" easily for the whole fifteenth century, though most scholars in the English-speaking world have some difficulty with this. Even in Germany, seeing the great change as occurring some time other than roughly 1500 can bring harsh criticism. A review in the *Frankfurter Allgemeine* of the new *Handbook of European History 1400–1600* was headlined "The Beginning of Modern Times Did Not Take Place" ("Das Beginn der Neuzeit findet nicht statt").[28] It describes the book as one in which the forty-one

[24]Lee Patterson, "On the Margin: Postmodernism, Ironic History, and Medieval Studies," *Speculum* 65 (1990): 87–108.

[25]Anthony Reid, "Introduction: A Time and a Place," in Anthony Reid, *Southeast Asia in the Early Modern Era: Trade, Power and Belief* (Ithaca: Cornell University Press, 1993); Leonard Y. Andaya and Barbara Watson Andaya, "Southeast Asia in the Early Modern Period: Twenty-Five Years On," *Journal of Southeast Asian Studies* 26.1 (1995): 92–98; Leonard Blussé and Harriet T. Zurndorfer, eds., *Conflict and Accommodation in Early Modern Asia: Essays in Honour of Erik Zürcher* (Leiden: Brill, 1993).

[26]David Wallace, "Carving Up Time and the World: Medieval-Renaissance Turf Wars; Historiography and Personal History," University of Wisconsin–Milwaukee, Center for Twentieth Century Studies, Working Paper No. 11 (1990–91): 6–7.

[27]Nancy F. Partner, "Did Mystics Have Sex?" in *Desire and Discipline: Sex and Sexuality in the Premodern West*, ed. Jacqueline Murray and Konrad Eisenbichler (Toronto: University of Toronto Press, 1996), 297.

[28]*Handbook of European History 1400–1600: Late Middle Ages, Renaissance, and Reformation,* ed. Thomas Brady, Heiko Oberman, and James Tracy (Leiden: E. J. Brill, 1994–95). The reviewer was Wilhelm Ribhegge, *Frankfurter Allgemeine Zeitung*, 8.8, 1996.

authors set out "with the fresh energy of foresters who are fitted out with chain saws and fell lofty but rotten trees in the forest of historiography." Though I did not mind being labeled a "forester" (I was one of the forty-one), being outfitted with chain saws clearly made us unacceptable, which is the general opinion of the reviewer about the entire *Handbook* and its attempt to dethrone the year 1500 and to stress continuities.

If "early modern" creates some general problems, what about its particular problems for the history of women? The standard periodization comes primarily from the near-conjuncture of Columbus and Luther, but the relation of the voyages of exploration to the lives of European women has been almost entirely neglected, and not everyone agrees about the significance of the Protestant Reformation for women. Since Joan Kelly taught us that all periodization is suspect when considering women's lives, does "early modern" leave us in the same dilemma that Renaissance does? That is, does it leave us using a periodization for women's history drawn rather unreflectively from men's? (Earlier I decided that it did, and used the—at that point—more suspect term "Renaissance" in the title for my book on working women in Germany from 1400 to 1650, hoping that people would just take it as a chronological designation. They didn't.)

One of the most powerful voices arguing that "early modern" has just as many problems as "Renaissance" has been Judith Bennett's. In "Medieval Women, Modern Women: Across the Great Divide" and her new book on brewsters, she uses examples from women's work experiences and other areas of life to challenge what she terms the "assumption of a dramatic change in women's lives between 1300 and 1700." She notes that historians who focus on issues other than women are questioning the "master narrative of a great transformation" and asserts that "women's history should ally itself with those who are questioning the master narrative" because "the paradigm of a great divide in women's history is undermined by many factual anomalies."[29]

Bennett's call rings true for those of us who have heard and participated in many conference sessions which bring together quite comfortably papers ranging from the Black Death to the Thirty Years' War—or beyond. But those of us who organize such sessions remain stumped as to what to call them. "Late medieval and early modern" is so long, and it reinforces the division instead of bridging it. Historians of England can use the names of ruling houses and historians of Germany use

---

[29]Judith Bennett, "Medieval Women, Modern Women: Across the Great Divide," in *Culture and History 1350–1600: Essays on English Communities, Identities, and Writing*, ed. David Aers (London: Harvester Wheatsheaf, 1992), 147–75. An abridged version of this appears in *Feminists' Revision History*, ed. Ann-Louise Shapiro, (New Brunswick: Rutgers University Press, 1994), 47–72. See also Bennett's *Ale, Beer, and Brewsters* (see n. 9). Bennett broadens her focus and calls for an emphasis on continuities in women's history and on what she terms the "patriarchal equilibrium" across all periods, not simply across "the great divide" of 1500. See her "Confronting Continuities," *Journal of Women's History* 9 (1997): 73–94, with responses by Sandra E. Greene, Karen Offen, and Gerda Lerner, 95–118.

"the long sixteenth century," getting ever longer as it stretches from the invention of the printing press in about 1450 to the end of the Thirty Years' War in 1648. Neither of these works very well for all of Europe, and both have the additional problem of still implying a great change, for I have seen few analyses which cut across the divide, and talk about, for example, "Lancastrian/York/Tudor England," or "Germany in the short fifteenth and long sixteenth century." And neither of these has been developed out of considerations of the lives of women, except perhaps for childbirth, or lack of childbirth, in the lives of certain English queens.

We are thus not much further than we were with Kelly twenty years ago, critiquing traditional periodization without finding a substitute with which everyone can agree. Perhaps we should just give up periodization altogether? We could easily latch on to the *Annales* school historians, who have posited a *longue durée* stretching from the eleventh century to the nineteenth, a period Le Roy Ladurie termed "motionless."[30] In fact, as Susan Stuard has recently pointed out, women already appear in some *Annales* school works—a historical school Natalie Davis termed a "sodality of French brothers"—as the perfect example of motionless history, primarily part of a household, serving as a means of exchange between families.[31] This approach was adopted at least in part by Bonnie Anderson and Judith Zinsser in their survey of European women's history, for they discuss peasant women from the ninth century to the twentieth in a single section, going beyond the time frame of even Le Roy Ladurie.[32] Motionless indeed.

Such wholesale rejection of periodization makes me and a number of other women's historians uneasy. In reviewing Zinsser and Anderson's textbook, Gianna Pomata comments, "I perceive here the shade of essentialism, the idea of an unchanging female nature."[33] "Essentialist" is about the worst thing one can call someone in feminist scholarship. The equivalent in history would probably be "ahistorical" and in literature perhaps being an "untheorized reductivist" or reading literature mimetically. The always-gracious Pomata softens her review by seeing only the "shade" of essentialism, a softness not found in the critique of subaltern studies coming from Indian feminists, who point out that women sometimes emerge only as a

---

[30]Emmanuel Le Roy Ladurie, "Motionless History," *Social Science History* 1 (1977): 115–36.

[31]Susan Mosher Stuard, "Fashion's Captives: Medieval Women in French Historiography," in *Women in Medieval History and Historiography*, ed. Susan Mosher Stuard (Philadelphia: University of Pennsylvania Press, 1987), 59–80. Davis's comment is from her address as president of the American Historical Association; see Natalie Davis, "History's Two Bodies," *American Historical Review* 93 (1988): 23. She later explored the work of women in the *Annales* school, where they served as assistants and researchers, in Natalie Davis, "Women and the World of Annales," *History Workshop Journal* 33 (1992): 121–37.

[32]Judith Zinsser and Bonnie Anderson, *A History of Their Own*, 2 vols. (New York: Harper and Row, 1988).

[33]Gianna Pomata, "History, Particular and Universal: On Reading Some Recent Women's History Textbooks," *Feminist Studies* 19 (1993): 7–50.

type of "eternal feminine," victimized and abject.[34] In discussing women in *Annales* school works, Stuard notes: "By such formulations gender for women, if not for men, was assumed to be a historical constant, not a dynamic category that changed in Europe's formative centuries and changed again with the transition into modern times."[35] With this critique Stuard hints at both essentialism and ahistoricism, but here we are back to a medieval /modern transition again!

I could end here, recapping the fact that all structures—social, chronological, political, economic, intellectual—are problematic in women's history, a conclusion which sounds both depressing and self-evident. I would like to suggest that it is neither, but instead reflects how far we have come in the last twenty-five years. In just one generation—the blink of an eye in the history of history—we came to recognize both that the structures we traditionally impose on history are male derived (a conclusion many of our colleagues still refuse to accept) and that they often do not work for understanding the lives of women. We deconstructed structures and categories in ways that were unthinkable just a short time ago, exploring axes of difference which have gone far beyond Joan Kelly's call for a "double vision" (essentially gender plus class), and beyond the "Holy Trinity" of race, class, and gender, to include age, sexuality, place of residence, ethnicity, religion, physical ability, etc. (Those axes are now so numerous, in fact, that when we were writing the call for papers for the 1996 Berkshire Women's History Conference, we gave up trying to list them, and titled the conference "Complicating Categories: Women, Gender and Difference.") This deconstruction has led us to question master narratives, of which the rise of capitalism and the Renaissance are only two examples. As I hope my tracing of these two issues has made clear, this deconstruction has arisen both from the intellectual movement of "deconstruction" and from our work in archives, exploring the lives of those whom we—perhaps naively—still believe to be real people.

Along with this deconstruction, however, we are also engaged in construction, suggesting alternative or additional structures that do help us understand the lives of women—and men—of the past. Some of these structures have been their own master narratives, such as the dichotomies of public/private or nature/culture, which have been so forceful in women's history over the last two decades but which have also themselves been challenged and deconstructed. Some of these have been less dramatic cross-temporal, cross-cultural comparisons, such as the recognition that structures are not only problematic for women's *history*, but also for *women*, that

---

[34]This point was made explicitly by Tanika Sarkar, St. Stephen's College, Delhi, in her paper at the plenary session entitled "Gendering Historiography" at the 1996 Berkshire Conference on Women's History, and is made tangentially in her "Rhetoric against the Age of Consent: Resisting Colonial Reason and the Death of a Child-Wife," *Economic and Political Weekly* (4 September 1993): 1869–78. See also Kamala Visweswaran, "Small Speeches, Subaltern Gender: Nationalist Ideology and Its Historiography," in *Subaltern Studies IX: Writings on South Asian History and Society*, ed. Shahid Amin and Dipesh Chakrabarty (New Delhi: Oxford University Press, 1996), 83–125.

[35]Stuard, "Fashion's Captives," 71.

periods of structural breakdown—war, revolution, religious transformation—have been those in which women had a wider role and found a louder voice. Some of these have been very specific, such as the current discussion among medievalists such as Susan Stuard and JoAnn McNamara about the twelfth century as period of significant change in ideas about gender and gender relations.[36]

This creation of new structures is only beginning, as we still—to stay within an architectural metaphor—have only a small pile of bricks with which to work. But many of us are steadily making bricks, mixing together different materials to construct a small part of the past. Others have discovered, in demolishing other structures labeled "capitalism," "Renaissance," "Enlightenment," or "Reformation," useful bricks which we could carry back to our building site. Others decided that brick-making or brick-carrying was boring, and have designed structural plans, often with little concern for the capabilities of the bricks to support such structures. Others decided to carry their bricks to new building sites, labeled "the body," "sexuality," or "the history of masculinity." We need to continue to do all these things—but to spend more time building on the work of others, and less time accusing others of having chosen the wrong task or of doing something useless. We also need to worry less about whether our structure will ultimately be labeled "women" or "gender" or exactly what rooms it will contain. We understand now that the structure we have labeled "history" is, to use a famous architectural metaphor, a City of Men, or to be more precise, a city of some men. That structure now has a few holes in it, but it is millennia old and very sturdy; we must make sure that our new structure, though smaller, is just as sturdy, and that our City of Ladies welcomes all immigrants. We may build high towers, but we need open gates.

[36]JoAnn McNamara, "The *Herrenfrage:* The Restructuring of the Gender System, 1050–1150," in *Medieval Masculinities: Regarding Men in the Middle Ages*, ed. Clare Lees (Minneapolis: University of Minnesota Press, 1994), 3–30; Susan Stuard, "The Dominion of Gender: Women's Fortunes in the High Middle Ages," in *Becoming Visible: Women in European History*, ed. Renate Bridenthal et al., 3rd ed. (Boston: Houghton Mifflin, 1998), 129–50.

The *Querelle des Femmes* as a Cultural Studies Paradigm

Margarete Zimmermann

> *I hesitated a long time over writing a book on women. The topic is irritating, particularly for women; and it is not new. A lot of ink has been spent on the quarrel over feminism. At present it is nearly ended, so let us not speak anymore about it. But it is discussed nevertheless. And it does not seem as if the voluminous follies turned out during the last century have helped much to throw any light on the problem. Incidentally—is there a problem? And what does it consist of?*[1]

With these words Simone de Beauvoir opens her essay *The Second Sex* (1949), one of the most famous feminist manifestos of our century. She quotes the long tradition of that debate about texts, images, and gender identities which since the early twentieth century has been known as the *querelle des femmes*, or occasionally as the more encompassing *querelle des sexes*, and which sometimes appears as *polemiche sul sesso femminile* (polemics on the female sex)[2] in older Italian publications. With her "revolutionary essay"[3] and "foundational text of a materialist feminism for the twentieth century,"[4] de Beauvoir situates herself within that late-nineteenth-century phase of the *querelle*, which she calls "the quarrel over feminism." In *Le deuxième sexe* one can detect a clear echo of older, even classic motifs of the historical *querelle des femmes* when de Beauvoir deals with the alleged creative and artistic inferiority of women. Toril Moi summarizes the discussion as follows:

> As long as conditions for women are not equal to those of men, Beauvoir declares, the product of their creativity will evidently be inferior to that

---

[1]Simone de Beauvoir, *Le Deuxième Sexe*, 2 vols. (Paris: Gallimard, 1971), 1: 11. (Unless otherwise stated, all translations are by Gesa Stedman.)

[2]As in G. Battista Marchesi, "Le polemiche sul sesso femminile ne' secc. XVI e XVIII," *Giornale storica della letteratura italiana* 25 (1895): 362–69.

[3]Toril Moi, *Simone de Beauvoir: Conflits d'une intellectuelle* (Paris: Diderot, 1995), 288.

[4]Moi, *Simone de Beauvoir*, 340.

produced by men. This disparity is entirely due to the advantageous situation which men enjoy at the heart of patriarchy....⁵

In spite of such obvious parallels, and a decidedly historical perspective which prompts de Beauvoir to look back at the "old quarrel"—*la vieille querelle*—she refrains from defining the term *querelle des femmes* and from specifying the debate's historical periods. Thus, we are confronted with a curious indeterminacy when dealing with this terminological and imaginary complex that the *querelle des femmes* represents. A similar case can be made for the German equivalent, "the battle of the sexes," which "became between 1850 and 1930, but in particular between 1890 and the First World War, a determining topic in art."⁶ Again, one encounters an almost irritating casualness in the use of a term with rather fuzzy boundaries. These few examples first of all indicate the different ways in which the historical *querelle des femmes* is called to mind in cultural memory, as well as creating a connection with modern feminism, which—although in need of further definition—is almost always made when the *querelle des femmes* is discussed. Thus, in this term a historical dimension always overlaps with a contemporary dimension.

In view of the sometimes uncomfortably fuzzy use of this key term of European gender history, and in view of the creation in 1994 of an interdisciplinary yearbook for gender studies, christened *Querelles*,⁷ it seemed a tempting as well as a necessary undertaking to pursue the trail of the European *querelle des femmes* since the fifteenth century. The result has been available since 1997 in the essay collection *Die europäische Querelle des Femmes: Geschlechterdebatten seit dem 15. Jahrhundert*, which Gisela Bock and I edited.⁸ In what follows, I will take up some conclusions from the introductory essay in that volume, "Die *Querelle des Femmes* in Europa: Eine begriffs- und forschungsgeschichtliche Einführung," by beginning with a short survey of the term's history. Secondly, I will give an overview of the *querelle des femme's* reception history. Finally, I intend to show why the *querelle des femmes* is—like the term feminism—a key word within a modern concept of cultural studies in which

---

⁵Moi, *Simone de Beauvoir*, 312.
⁶Barbara Eschenburg, "Der Kampf der Geschlechter: Der neue Mythos in Literatur, Philosophie und Kunst," in *Der Kampf der Geschlechter: Der neue Mythos in der Kunst 1850-1930*, ed. Helmut Friedel (Munich: DuMont Buchverlag, 1995), 9–42, at 9 (my translation).
⁷The yearbook is published by J. B. Metzler, Stuttgart, and Weimar. It includes volumes 1 through 3: (1) *Gelehrsamkeit und kulturelle Emanzipation*, ed. Angelika Ebrecht, Irmela von der Lühe, Ute Pott, Cettina Rapisarda, and Anita Runge (1996); (2) *Die europäische Querelle des Femmes: Geschlechterdebatten seit dem 15. Jahrhundert*, ed. Gisela Bock and Margarete Zimmermann (1997); (3) *Freundschaft im Gespräch*, ed. Sabine Eickenrodt and Cettina Rapisarda (1998). Cf. Hania Siebenpfeiffer and Gesa Stedman, "*Querelles*: Ein neuer Ort der Streitkultur," in *Virginia*, no. 24 (March 1998): 10, on the yearbook's conceptual background.
⁸Bock and Zimmermann, eds., *Die europäische Querelle des Femmes*.

gender history is considered a natural as well as an indispensable element.[9]

* *

Let us therefore begin with a little *Begriffsgeschichte*, following the famous maxim by Marc Bloch: "The best way to avoid being fooled by a word is by looking at its history."[10] But the term *querelle des femmes* immediately causes some confusion since it is ambiguous from a linguistic point of view. It leaves unresolved the question whether the complement "des femmes" is a *genetivus objectivus* and therefore refers to a quarrel of which women are the object; or whether it is a *genetivus subjectivus*, and therefore refers to a quarrel of which women are the subject. In the latter case, we would be dealing with a quarrel in which women were advocating their own cause. I suspect—but this will need further research—that this Janus-faced terminology reflects the historical development itself. The ambiguity reflects the development from a defense of women by the *champions des dames* (defenders of women), which dominated into the sixteenth century, to an increasing participation in this gender debate by the women themselves.

But before we delve into the history of the word, let us look at a modern definition of the phenomenon:

> The Querelle des Femmes/des Sexes draws on the sources' terminology but, as a more encompassing concept and a kind of technical term, it is a twentieth-century formation and as such refers to a much more complex phenomenon: an all-encompassing gender quarrel in which not only women but—and that has been insufficiently realized—men are at issue as well. It is a quarrel in word and image but also about words and images.... The points of debate are the delimitation of an "imaginaire," an imaginary space of masculinity and femininity, of gender hierarchies, and the stands taken in the relevant areas of the discussion that were topical during each period.[11]

Those "allusions to topical discussions" in particular allow cross-references to social and cultural history: for example, the debate over women's access to reading, writing, and education in the sixteenth century;[12] the assessment of marriage; the controversies

---

[9]In this essay, I will not deal with the problem that periodizing the *querelle des femmes* poses. Cf. in detail Gisela Bock and Margarete Zimmermann, "Die *Querelle des Femmes* in Europa: Eine begriffs- und forschungsgeschichtliche Einführung," in *Die europäische Querelle des Femmes*, ed. Gisela Bock and Margarete Zimmermann (Stuttgart: J. B. Metzler, 1997), 9–38; in this context, esp. 16–18.

[10]Quoted from Ulrich Raulff, *Ein Historiker im 20. Jahrhundert: Marc Bloch* (Frankfurt a/M: S. Fischer, 1995), 118.

[11]Bock and Zimmermann, *Die europäische Querelle*, 16.

[12]I pursued these questions in "Querelle des Femmes, querelles du livre," in *Des Femmes & des livres*, ed. Dominique de Courcelles; Actes du Colloque du 30 avril 1998 à l'Ecole des Chartes (forthcoming).

over feminine *bellezza* (beauty) and *ornamenti* (frills) in early modern Italy;[13] or over the *femme savante*[14] (learned woman) and the *femme poète* (female poet) in the seventeenth century.[15]

Concerning the part played by Christine de Pizan, who is mentioned again and again in the context of the *querelle des femmes* and is often even considered its initiator, let me make only the following short remarks. The Pizan corpus of *querelle* texts comprises three works: the *Epistre au Dieu d'Amours* (*The Letter to Cupid*) completed in May 1399;[16] the letters against the *Romance of the Rose*, written between 1401 and 1402,[17] which the author handed over to the French queen Isabeau de Bavière with a request for assistance in 1402; and the important defense of women *Le livre de la cité des dames* (*The Book of the City of Ladies*) (1404–5),[18] whose title quotes Augustine's important apology for Christianity, *De civitate dei*. That it was Christine de Pizan who initiated the *querelle* is nowadays regarded as rather unlikely, since numerous clues have been found to indicate that *querelle* discourses existed prior to the debate over the *Romance of the Rose* which Christine sparked off.[19]

Christine's keen awareness of the importance of texts and writing for the process of defining gender identities over the centuries, as well as her knowledge of the importance of canonized authors and texts within these processes is, however, notable. Thus, Christine makes it her business in the letters against the *Romance of the Rose* and in the *City of Ladies* to decanonize such authors as Jean de Meun and Ovid, or at least to dethrone them from their previously almost unquestioned authorial positions. Furthermore, her texts are the first examples of the doubling of a feminine text-persona and an empirical female *auctor*-persona. And finally, all textual and argumentative strategies of the *querelle des femmes* are already unfolded in Christine's three central *querelle* texts. These strategies include composing defamatory pam-

---

[13]Esther Lauer, "'Bellezza' und 'ornamenti' im italienischen Geschlechterstreit um 1600," in *Die europäische Querelle,* ed. Bock and Zimmermann, 269–91.

[14]An impressive study on this topic is found in Linda Timmermanns' *L'accès des femmes à la culture (1598–1715): Un débat d'idées de Saint François de Sales à la Marquise de Lambert* (Paris: H. Champion, 1993).

[15]Cf. Renate Kroll, *Femme poète: Madeleine de Scudéry und die poésie précieuse* (Tübingen: Niemeyer, 1996).

[16]Edited in Christine de Pizan, *Œuvres poétiques*, ed. Maurice Roy (Paris, 1886–96), 2: 1–27. In 1402, this text was translated into English by Thomas Hoccleve as *The Letter of Cupide*.

[17]The definitive edition is *Le Débat sur le Roman de la Rose: Edition critique*, ed. Erick Hicks (Paris: H. Champion Editeur, 1977).

[18]The Middle French text and an Italian translation are available in the edition supervised by Patrizia Caraffi and Earl Jeffrey Richards, *La città delle dame* (Milano: Luni, 1997).

[19]Cf. Helen Solterer's stimulating study *The Master and Minerva: Disputing Women in French Medieval Culture* (Berkeley: University of California Press, 1995). Cf. also the anthology *Woman Defamed and Woman Defended: An Anthology of Medieval Texts*, ed. Alcuin Blamires (Oxford: Clarendon, 1992), as well as *Grundriß der Romanischen Literaturen des Mittelalters*, 8:1: *La littérature française aux XIVe et XVe siècle* (Heidelberg, 1988), 158–60: "Pour et contre les femmes."

phlets directed against men as counterparts to defamatory pamphlets directed against women; establishing catalogues of women centering on specific topics; resorting to gender-specific anthropologies; and invalidating and obliterating misogynist exempla and text traditions and replacing them with philogynous traditions.

*   *   *

Let us now take a more precise look at the history of the term.[20] *Querelle* goes back to the Latin etymon *querel(l)a*, which means "lament" and "expression of pain," displeasure and "complaint" in the sense of a charge or criticism, and a legal charge. The lexeme *querelle* has been found in Old French texts since the twelfth century, mainly in the sense of "objection," "legal charge," and "case." It is in this sense—in relation to women who have been deprived of their lawful claim to land, property, and honor, and whose "justified cases and quarrels" have not been taken up by anyone—that Jean de Boucicaut uses the term in his memoirs *Le Livre des fais du bon messire Jehan Maingre, dit Bouciquaut* (1409) (*Book of the Excellent Deeds of the Good Lord Jehan Maingre, called Bouciquaut*).[21] Surprisingly, although the phenomenon of the *querelle* as a gender debate can be observed at least since the early fifteenth century and since the time of Christine de Pizan, its terminological definition only occurs some decades later, namely in Martin Le Franc's *Le Champion des dames (The Defender of Ladies)*, written around 1440.

In this immense allegorical poem, in the tradition of the *Romance of the Rose* as well as the *City of Ladies*, the *querelle des dames* is mentioned for the first time. But here the *dames* ("ladies") are only the objects of male discourses, those of the defender of women Franc Vouloir on the one hand, and those of the misogynist Malebouche and his infamous followers on the other. In this text, *querelle des dames* therefore refers to the "women's complaint" and the "quarrel over women" in which the women themselves do not actively participate. Women had already gained the status of subjects defending their own sex, as we have seen, in the works of Christine de Pizan; in this respect Martin decidedly falls behind Christine's example. He does follow her in the tradition of setting up catalogues of exemplary women, which he calls *clergesses* or *grandes dames de France* ("intellectuals" or "great French ladies") and

---

[20]Some information on the history of the word can be found in D. Zévaco, "Querelle," *Revue de philologie française* 30 (1917–18): 36–40.

[21]Jean de Boucicaut, *Le Livre des fais du bon messire Jehan Le Maingre, dit Bouciquaut*, ed. Denis Lalande (Geneva: Droz, 1985), 160–61: "It so happened that some charges were brought before the King that several ladies and girls, widows and others, were oppressed and put upon by some powerful men who with their force and power wanted to disinherit them of their land, their property and their honour, and indeed disinherited some of them. In that manner the women suffered a great deal and no knight, no squire, no gentleman and no one else stood up to defend them nor took up their justified cases and quarrels." Boucicaut further speaks of the "champions and defenders of their quarrels" (162), which the women lacked.

whose embedding in cultural memory he assists by constructing numerous memorial portraits.

The term *querelle des dames/femmes*, however, did not really catch on during the early modern period. During the sixteenth and seventeenth centuries, when this gender debate in word and image reached its apogee all over Europe, the term's usage strangely tended to diminish. This holds true, for example, in the widely read misogynist tract of the sixteenth century, the *Controverses des sexes masculin et femenin* (*Controversies of the Male and Female Sexes*), written in 1536 by the lawyer Gratien Du Pont of Toulouse.[22] The text is remarkable in that it is an apology for the male sex. In that respect it clearly resembles Boccaccio's *Il Corbaccio* (*The Raven*) (1360), which focuses on a Dantesque dream-vision experienced by the male narrator. He is a scholar suffering from unrequited love for a widow whose deceased husband he meets in his dream. Between both men a kind of teacher-pupil dialogue develops. It focuses on the transmission of knowledge concerning feminine perfidy and slyness, and most of all a systematic deconstruction of feminine beauty. The female body as a projection space for male desire is replaced by a view of the female physique as a space for male disgust.

In Gratien's *Controverses*, the male first-person narrator also dreams of an encounter with a *beau vieillard*, a handsome old man, in this case a decidedly run-down specimen. He is an allegorical representation of the male sex, who complains that he is constantly mistreated by *le sexe femenin*, the female sex, and therefore urgently asks for succor. An illustration from this enormous compendium, the "chessboard in the shape of Eve" (*Eschequier en forme deve*), provides a graphic impression of this form of heavily formalized attacks on women: the white squares contain moral and physical vilifications ending on the feminine syllable -ante, whereas the black squares contain those ending in -esse. The enormous textual edifice of the *Controverses du sexe masculin et femenin* is erected on the fictional foundation of the above-mentioned male pact. Within the overall context of the *querelle*, this treatise occupies an exceptional position, for it is the only example of a male voice taking up the defense of the *sexe masculin* under threat.

On the one hand, contemporary tracts, also of male origin, taking up the opposite position, such as Symphorien Champier's *La Nef des dames vertueuses* (*The Ship of Virtuous Ladies*) (1515) and Jean Bouchet's *Jugement poëtic de l'honneur femenin* (*Poetic Judgment on Female Honor*) (1536), act against the misogynist polemical force of the *Controverses*. On the other hand, the frequency of female interventions into this debate increases in the sixteenth and early seventeenth centuries: in France with women writers such as Marie de Romieu, Madeleine and Catherine des Roches, Hélisenne de Crenne, and Marie de Gournay; in Italy with the *tre corone,* Moderata Fonte, Lucrezia Marinella, and Arcangela Tarabotti; and in numerous anonymous

---

[22]On Gratien Du Pont, cf. Charles Oulmont, "Gratien Du Pont Sieur de Drusac et les femmes," *Revue des études rabelaisiennes* 4 (1906): 1–28; 5 (1907): 135–53.

female *querelle* authors whom we can only hear today as textual voices, or whose identity remains hidden behind the protecting mask of a male pseudonym.

Even though Jean Bouchet in *Le Jugement poëtic de l'honneur femenin* (1536) still speaks of "the quarrel which the woman suffers at the hands of the man,"[23] one can observe that this lexeme is replaced more and more often by *apologie, défense,* or, in the famous text by Marie de Gournay, *le grief des dames* (in the sense of women's complaint).[24] After 1630, it seems that the *querelle* in its original form had passed its climax;[25] the lexeme *querelle* also took on a markedly pejorative connotation. New forms of the debate over male/female inferiority or superiority include the catalogues of women originating from the older *querelle des femmes,* to which contemporary examples or at least those dating from the immediate past were added more and more often. Such a development can be considered as an early form of anthologizing and cataloguing of women's literature. A further indication of the "continuation of the old *querelle* in new media" is the presence of *querelle* topics in literary texts such as Pierre Marivaux's one-act play *La Colonie* (1729–50) and Christoph Martin Wieland's *Bildungsroman: Geschichte des Agathon* (1794),[26] to mention just two random examples.

This "continuation of the *querelle* by other means" forms a relatively continuous and straight line, which in Italy runs from Ludovico Domenichi's *Rime diverse d'alcune nobilissime e virtuosissime donne* (*Diverse Rhymes by Noble and Virtuous Women*) (1559) to Luisa Bergalli's *Componimenti poetici delle più illustri rimatrici d'ogni secolo* (*Poetic Compositions by the Most Famous Poetesses of All Centuries*) (1726) to Yolanda De Blasis's *Le Scrittrici italiane, dalle origini al 1800* (*Italian Women Writers from the Beginnings up to 1800*) (1930). The first of these volumes are anthologies with a few added biographical commentaries (Domenichi and Bergalli), while their successor is a preliminary attempt at a gender-specific literary history (De Blasis), a rather unsatisfactory work owing to its lack of structuring categories. Nevertheless, all three examples are interesting for modern readers with regard to canonization processes. In France a similar but richer tradition developed during the same period. It begins with Jean de La Forge's *Le cercle des femmes sçavantes* (*The Circle of Learned Ladies*) (1665), which is no more than a list of names. But two eighteenth-century works are more important: Abbé de La Porte's *Histoire littéraire des femmes françoyses* (*Literary History of French Women*) (1769), and Louise-Félicité de Kéralio's *Collection*

---

[23]Jean Bouchet, *Le Jugement poëtic de l'honneur femenin* (Poitiers: I. G. E. de Marner, 1536): avverso.

[24]Parts of Gournay's "Grief des Dames" (1626) first appeared in the preface to her edition of the *Essais* by Michel de Montaigne (1595). Today the text is available in Marie de Gournay, *Fragments d'un discours féminin,* ed. Elyane Dezon-Jones (Paris: J. Corti, 1988), 129–33.

[25]On this topic, cf. Ian Maclean, *Woman Triumphant: Feminism in French Literature, 1610–52* (Oxford: Clarendon, 1977).

[26]Christoph Martin Wieland's *Bildungsroman: Geschichte des Agathon* (1794), esp. book 14, chapter 6, containing Aspasia's philippic against the male sex, carries clear traces of the *querelle des femmes.*

des meilleurs ouvrages françois, composés par des femmes (Collection of the Best French Works Written by Women) (1786–88). La Porte's learned reference work offers brief bio-bibliographical articles on a large number of women writers and shows how marked the interest in French *dames de lettres* still was shortly before the French Revolution. Kéralio's *Collection* is mainly an anthology; the editor introduces extracts of considerable length—in Christine de Pizan's case more than 500 pages—with her own period-specific comments and provides information concerning the authors. By contrast, Jean Larnac's *Histoire de la littérature féminine en France* (*History of French Literature Written by Women*) (1929), which has to be read against the backdrop of newly emerging images of women during the 1920s, is the first and so far the only history of French literature written by women. Larnac draws on the *querelle des femmes* as his structuring principle. Yet when he repeatedly explains women's writing as expressive of a lack—a lack of personal beauty or of emotional fulfillment—he does nothing more than furnish us with another proof of the gender bias dominating traditional literary history. These developments climaxed around 1900 and in the following decades,[27] during exactly that period in which we experience the surprising renaissance of the term *querelle des femmes.*

*   *

This renaissance occurred mainly thanks to the work done by the literary historians and *seiziémistes* Abel Lefranc and Emile Telle, who used the term *querelle* in their studies on Rabelais (*Le Tiers Livre de "Pantagruel" et la querelle des femmes,* 1904, reprinted in 1914, 1931) and on Marguerite de Navarre (*L'œuvre de Marguerite d'Angoulême, reine de Navarre et la querelle des femmes,* 1937). This return to a classic term of gender history was no accident but can be explained by a specific historical constellation: the encounter of early French feminism and historicism around 1900.[28] From both arose the tendency to historicize an important contemporary phenomenon, feminism, and to find its founders and precursors.[29]

A second phase of the *querelle des femmes* took place during the new women's movement of the sixties and seventies. The women's movement was not so much

---

[27]Cf. Gianna Pomata's argument in "Storia particolare e storia universale: In margine ad alcuni manuali di storia delle donne," *Quaderni storici* 74 (1990): 341–85. For a discussion of these developments, cf. Roswitha Böhm, "Unter Ausschluß der Wieblichkeit: Strategien französischer Literaturgeschichtsschreibung," in *Gender Studies in den romanischen Literaturen: Revisionen, Subversionen,* ed. Renate Kroll and Margarete Zimmermann, 2 vols. (Frankfurt a/M: Dipa, 1999), 1: 315–36; and Margarete Zimmermann, "Gender, Gedächtnis und literarische Kultur: Zum Projekt einer Autorinnen-Literaturgeschichte," in Kroll and Zimmermann, *Gender Studies,* 29–55.

[28]Concerning the current debates on historicism, cf. Otto Gerhard Oexle, *Geschichtswissenschaft im Zeichen des Historismus: Studien zu Problemgeschichten der Moderne* (Göttingen: Vandenhoeck and Ruprecht, 1996).

[29]Cf. Margarete Zimmermann, "Christine de Pizan et les féminismes 1900," in *Sur le Chemin de Longue Etude: Actes du IIᵉ Congrès International sur Christine de Pizan, Orléans 1995,* ed. Bernard Ribémont (Paris: H. Champion, 1998), 183–204.

interested in finding possible precursors; rather, it acknowledged the *querelle* as a phenomenon *sui generis*, important for the history of women, which became the center of attention. From this perspective, the works by Maïté Albistur and Daniel Armogathe,[30] Ian Maclean,[31] and Marc Angenot[32] appeared in 1977; and the influential and now classic essay by Joan Kelly, "Early Feminist Thought and the *Querelle des Femmes, 1400–1789*," was published in 1982.[33] In addition, several new editions of *querelle* texts were brought out during these years, finally reawakening them from their centuries-long sleep in the archives and providing them with a new lease on life.[34] Editors' activities of this kind had a snowball effect since they also encouraged new research.

Signs of a third boom within modern *querelle des femmes* research can be detected during the 1990s. Obvious indications are Linda Timmermans's groundbreaking study *L'accès des femmes à la culture (1598–1715)* (1993), with several references to seventeenth-century *querelle* texts; and Helen Solterer's book *The Master and Minerva: Disputing Women in French Medieval Culture* (1995). Solterer shows a new interest in the medieval forms of the gender quarrel, as well as a concern with the legal background and the development of a "disputational figure of a woman" and a "dialectic between masterful writing and women's response."[35] In this context, the term "woman" does not refer to biological sex or social gender but to a position within the debate which can be taken up by women as well as by men. And finally, one could also place the collection of essays on the European *querelle des femmes* edited by Gisela Bock and me, as well as Gisèle Mathieu-Castellani's study *La Quenouille et la lyre*,[36] within this new *querelle* boom of the nineties.

A final point: the fact that mainly specialists in French literature have used the term *querelle des femmes* has had a detrimental effect. France was foregrounded to

[30]Maïté Albistur and Daniel Armogathe,*Histoire du féminisme français*, 2 vols. (Paris: Des femmes, 1977).

[31]Maclean, *Woman Triumphant*.

[32]Marc Angenot, *Les Champions des femmes: Examen du discours sur la supériorité des femmes, 1400–1800* (Montréal: Presses de l'Université du Québec, 1977).

[33]Joan Kelly, "Early Feminist Thought and the *Querelle des Femmes, 1400–1789*," *Signs* 8 (1982): 4–28; reprinted in Joan Kelly, *Women, History, and Theory* (Chicago: University of Chicago Press, 1984) 65–109.

[34]Solterer, *Master and Minerva*, 18

[35]These include M. Screech's edition of François de Billon's *Le Fort inexpugnable de l'honneur féminin* (1970); the anthology *La femme dans la littérature française et les traductions en français du XVIᵉ siècle*, ed. Luce Guillerm-Curutchet, Jean-Pierre Guillerm, Laurence Hordoir-Louppe, and Marie-Françoise Piéjus (Lille: Université de Lille, 1971); Maureen Curnow, "The *Livre de la Cité des Dames* of Christine de Pizan: A Critical Edition" (Ph.D. diss., Vanderbilt University, 1975), which up to then was only available in manuscript; the new edition of texts by Marie de Gournay, beginning in the eighties; and *Archiv für philosophie- und theologiegeschichtliche Frauenforschung*, Elisabeth Gössmann (Munich: Iudicium, 1984).

[36]Gisele Mathieu-Castellani, *La Quenouille et la lyre* (Paris: José Corti, 1998).

such an extent that the *querelle* was at times even falsely seen to be a purely French affair. It was overlooked for a long time that the *querelle* is a historical phenomenon of European dimensions of which some offshoots can even be found in Latin American culture.[37] As a result, research into non-French aspects of the *querelle* began late.[38] In the essay collection *Die europäische Querelle des Femmes*, the French *querelle* was intentionally emphasized less than Italian, Spanish, and English *querelle* texts. Middle and Eastern European variants of this gender debate remain to be considered.

*   *

The title of this essay contains a proposition; namely, that the European *querelle des femmes* should be considered as a paradigm for historical cultural studies. If we agree with Roger Chartier that gender history is a part of historical cultural studies,[39] and see gender history as "inscribed in practices and facts, organizing reality and the everyday," as "always constructed by the discourse which founds and legitimizes it,"[40] and as grounded in social reality, then the *querelle des femmes* marks a point of intersection of cultural studies research interests. The *querelle* combines an intensive discourse of "man" and "woman" with reference to their respective social reality and its practices: exertion of political power, access to education, forms of control over the body, and marriage, to name only a very few relevant topics. The longer one studies the *querelle des femmes*, the more one gains the impression that we are confronted with a historical phenomenon of global importance which, in its numerous offshoots, reaches deep into the heart of the history of our disciplines. If new evidence from the most various disciplines of such an omnipresence of *querelle* structures in different fields were not constantly appearing, one could easily dismiss this as the misconceived idea of an academic in love with her own object. These research interests, however, have not been brought together and as yet await integration into a broader cultural studies context. I will content myself with just a few references.

Concerning Italian studies, Deanna Shemek[41] and Pamela Benson[42] prove that even classic texts such as Ariosto's *Orlando Furioso* or Castiglione's *Cortegiano* are

---

[37]Cf. Friederike Hassauer, *"Die Seele ist nicht Mann, nicht Weib:* Stationen der *Querelle des Femmes* in Spanien und Lateinamerika vom 16. bis zum 18. Jahrhundert," in *Die europäische Querelle,* ed. Bock and Zimmermann, 203–38.

[38]Friederike Hassauer draws attention to this phenomenon in Bock and Zimmermann, *Die europäische Querelle,* 207–8.

[39]Cf. Roger Chartier, "L'histoire culturelle entre 'Linguistic Turn' et retour au sujet," in *Wege zu einer neuen Kulturgeschichte,* ed. Hartmut Lehmann (Göttingen: Wallstein Verlag, 1995), 29–58.

[40]Chartier, "L'histoire culturelle," 53.

[41]Deanna Shemek, "Of Women, Knights, Arms, and Love: The *Querelle des Femmes* in Ariosto's Poem," *Modern Language Notes* 104, no. 1 (January 1989): 68–97.

[42]Pamela Benson, *The Invention of the Renaissance Woman: The Challenge of Female Independence in the Literature and Thought of Italy and England* (University Park: Pennsylvania State University Press, 1992). Franco-Italian literary relations within a *querelle* context are analyzed by Anna Slerca, "L'utilizzasione del De claris *mulieribus* in due testi della 'querelle des femmes': Il *Champion des Dames* di Martin Le Franc (1440) e il *Jugement poetic de l'honneur femenin* di Jean Bouchet (1538)," in *L'aube de la Renaissance:*

shot through with *querelle* references and therefore require rereading. The counterpart for German baroque literature has been presented by Cornelia Plume with her research on Daniel Casper von Lohenstein.[43] Concerning the history of art, I would like to refer only to Mary D. Garrard's work on Artemisia Gentileschi;[44] Sara Matthews Grieco's work on popular prints and emblems of the sixteenth century;[45] the exhibition *Die Galerie der starken Frauen/La Galerie des Femmes Fortes* (*The Gallery of Strong Women*), which was curated by Bettina Baumgärtel and Silvia Neysters in 1996 at the Kunstmuseum Düsseldorf;[46] and the illustrated book *La Guerre des Sexes* by Laure Beaumont-Maillet (1977), which includes important material on the early modern *querelle*.

Further examples from the fields of history,[47] philosophy, anthropology, theology, the history of fashion,[48] gender history, and literary history[49] round out the picture.[50] Since the "exceptional quality of feminist research... lies in its interdisciplinary approach"[51] and it must therefore be interested in working with precisely defined terms applicable across lines, the *querelle des femmes* offers itself as an exceptionally fertile key concept. It permits the focusing of similar research initiatives from the different disciplines involved in cultural studies but also allows us to uncover the considerable overlap in European *querelle* traditions. This will ultimately result in at least a partial rewriting of single-discipline histories such as literary history or art history. It may lead to the ultimate dissolution of monodisciplinary

---

Pour le dixième anniversaire de la disparition de Franco Simone, ed. Dario Cecchetti, Lionello Sozzi, and Louis Terreaux (Geneva: Editions Slatkine, 1991), 47–65.

[43]Cornelia Plume, *Heroinen in der Geschlechterordnung: Weiblichkeitsprojektionen bei Daniel Casper von Lohenstein und die "Querelle des Femmes"* (Stuttgart: Metzler, 1996).

[44]Mary P. Garrard, *Artemisia Gentileschi: The Image of the Female Hero in Italian Baroque Art* (Princeton: Princeton University Press, 1989), esp. chap. 2.

[45]Sara Matthews Grieco, *Ange ou Diablesse: La représentation de la femme au XVIe siècle* (Paris: Flammarion, 1991).

[46]See the catalogue *Kunstmuseum Dusseldorf*, ed. Bettina Baumgärtel and Silvia Neysters (Berlin: Klinkhardt & Biermann, 1995).

[47]Among many other studies, see Claudia Opitz, "Streit der Frauen? Die frühneuzeitliche *Querelle des femmes* aus sozial- und frauengeschichtlicher Sicht," *Historische Abhandlungen* 8, no. 1 (1995): 15–27.

[48]Cf. in this context Odile Blanc, *Parades et parures: L'invention du corps de mode à la fin du Moyen Age* (Paris: Gallimard, 1997).

[49]The attempt at structuring literary history with the help of the *querelle des femmes* can be observed already in Jean Larnac's *Histoire de la littérature féminine en France* (Paris: Editions Kra, 1929); and Germaine Brée, *Women Writers in France: Variations on a Theme* (New Brunswick, N.J.: Rutgers University Press, 1973), although this work covers a much more restricted time period.

[50]Among other studies, see Elisabeth Gössmann and Elisabeth Koch, *Maior dignitas est in sexu virili: Das weibliche Geschlecht im Normensystem des 16. Jahrhunderts* (Frankfurt a/M: V. Klostermann, 1991).

[51]Monika Kopyczinski, "Feministischer Diskurs und Wissenschaft," in *Feministische Literaturwissenschaft in der Romanistik*, ed. Renate Kroll and Margarete Zimmermann (Stuttgart: Metzler, 1995), 74–83; at 80.

histories in favor of a new cultural studies paradigm at whose center the *querelle des femmes* will find its place.[52]

---

[52]I am grateful to Gesa Stedman for translating this chapter into English.

Grammar in Arcadia

Gabriele Beck-Busse

This essay focuses on two works which, although published two hundred years apart, feature the arcadian setting evoked in the title as well as a number of other similarities. Both works, which present the French language and grammar, clearly have didactic aims. Peter Erondell's *French Garden*, published in 1605,[1] targets an English-speaking public that is learning French as a foreign language, whereas Alexandre (or Antoine) Tournon's *Promenades de Clarisse*, published between 1784 and 1787,[2] is aimed at a French public that wishes to be introduced to the principles of its own mother tongue or to the fundamentals of grammar in general. I intend to show some of the characteristics that help to determine the genre of "Grammars for Ladies" by means of these two textbooks, which can be considered a representative sample.[3]

The first work, Erondell's *French Garden*, can be characterized as a collection of dialogues that seek to convey not only practical language competence but also moral values as prescribed in innumerable earlier works. For example, the anonymous *Decor puellarum*,[4] Juan Luis Vives's *Institutio foeminae christianae*,[5] and Giovanni

---

[1]Peter Erondell, *The French Garden: for English Ladyes and Gentlewomen to walke in. Or, A Sommer dayes labour. Being an jnstruction for the attayning vnto the knowledge of the French Tongue: wherein for th[e] practise thereof, are framed thirteene Dialogues in French and English, concerning diuers matters from the rising in the morning till Bed-time. Also the Historie of the Centurion mencioned in the Gospell: in French Verses. Which is an easier and shortter Methode then hath beene yet set forth, to bring the louers of the French tongue to the perfection of the same* (London: printed for Ed[ward] White, 1605).

[2]Alexandre (or Antoine) Tournon, *Les Promenades de Clarisse et du Marquis de Valzé, ou Nouvelle méthode pour apprendre les principes de la langue et de l'ortographe françaises à l'usage des dames* (Paris: Cailleau, Jombert Jeune, Mérigot, Bailly et les Marchands de Nouveautés, 1784–87).

[3]See also Gabriele Beck-Busse, "Grammatik für Damen: Zur Geschichte der französischen und italienischen Grammatik in Deutschland, England, Frankreich und Italien (1605–1850)," (habilitationsschrift, Freie Universität Berlin, 1999).

[4]*Questa sie una opera quale si chiama Decor Puellarum: Zoe Honore de le donzelle: La quale da regola forma e modo al stato de le honeste donzelle* (Venice: Nicolaus Jenson, 1471) [Venice, Biblioteca Nazionale Marciana, Inc. V.609].

[5]For dating, see Manfred Lentzen, "Vives' Ideen über die Erziehung der Frau: Zu «De institutione

29

Michele Bruto's *Instituzione di una fanciulla nata nobilmente*[6] all present values that
are succinctly outlined by the term "Christian woman." But the protagonist of the
dialogues, simply called la Dame, not only strives to live up to Christian values and
morals; she also tries to live the life of a society lady. These contrasting goals make
her an interesting character.[7] One should not be surprised that her shopping list
contains things that a Christian author would warn against: jewelry and precious
stones are talked about without being condemned as "Devil's vanity"(*pompas de
Satanás* [Vives]), and la Dame savors her food instead of following the rules of a
moderate and ascetic life.[8]

It seems necessary to draw attention to a point that distinguishes Erondell's
French Garden from other language textbooks in dialogue form. Whereas normally
only standard utterances for some conversational situations (for example, "at the
dressmaker's") are offered, the choice and ordering of which are to a certain extent
arbitrary in other language textbooks, Erondell recounts a coherent story. As in a
play represented on stage, one accompanies la Dame during a day in her life. It is
thus no accident that Erondell subtitled his work *A summer day's labour.*[9]

As for the image of women evoked in the dialogues, the role of the mother and
that of the society lady are not incompatible.[10] But although Mother is "the sweetest

feminae christianae» (1523)," in *Juan Luis Vives: Sein Werk und seine Bedeutung für Spanien und Deutschland,* ed. Christoph Strosetzki, Akten der internationalen Tagung vom 14.–15. Dezember 1992 in Münster (Frankfurt a/M: Vervuert, 1995), 95; Juan Luis Vives, *Formación de la mujer cristiana (Institutio
Foeminae Christianae) (1523),* in *Obras completas,* ed. Lorenzo Riber (Madrid: M. Aguilar, 1947–48),
1:985–1175; Hendrik Brugmans, "Juan Luis Vives," in *Erasmus in Hispania, Vives in Belgio,* ed. Jozef
IJsewijn and Angel Losada, Acta Colloquii Brugensis, 23–26, IX 1985 (Louvain: Peeters, 1986), 5–15,
esp. 11; and Joachim Leeker, "Das Frauenbild in Vives' «De institutione feminae christianae» und Cas-
tigliones «Libro del cortegiano»," in *Juan Luis Vives,* ed. Strosetzki, 55–74.

[6]Giovanni Michele Bruto, *The Necessarie, Fit and Convenient Education of a yong Gentlewoman.
Written both in French and Italian, and translated into English by W. P. And now printed with the three Lan-
guages togither in one Volume, for the better instruction of such as are desirous to studie those Tongues* (London:
Adam Islip, 1598; reprint, Amsterdam: Theatrum Orbis Terrarum and Da Capo Press, 1969).

[7]Thanks to the abstract nature of her denomination, la Dame becomes the ideal of "the lady," the
example to be followed.

[8]See, for example, Erondell, *The French Garden,* K4v and particularly L7v, where la Dame mentions
to another lady in her company: "You drink your wine like a good Christian, you baptize well your wine;
how can you judge of the goodness of it?" For Vives' very different position, see Vives, *Formación,* 1013,
1019.

[9]Regarding the fragmentary nature of the usual textbook "dialogues," see Gabriele Beck-Busse,
review of Edgar Radtke, "Gesprochenes Französisch und Sprachgeschichte: Zur Rekonstruktion der
Gesprächskonstitution in Dialogen französischer Sprachlehrbücher des 17. Jahrhunderts unter besonderer Berücksichtigung der italienischen Adaptionen," *Zeitschrift für französische Sprache und Literatur* 107
(1997): 125–28.

[10]Elisabeth Badinter, *Emilie, Emilie: L'ambition féminine au XIIIe siècle* (Paris: Flammarion, 1983)
demonstrates that Madame du Châtelet, at the beginning of the eighteenth century, could still effortlessly
harmonize her role as a mother with her social obligations, whereas in the second half of the century,
Madame d'Epinay, in spite of comparable possibilities, felt obliged to choose between the two roles. Sim-

and most pleasant name," as la Dame informs us, we must not overlook the fact that her role as a mother is made rather easy because of the type of household she manages. The governess looks after the girls, the preceptor supervises the boys, and the wet nurse cares for the infant. The mother's duty is evidently limited to making certain that the children are adequately provided for, showing them once or twice a day her own care and affection, and above all, asking God to ensure their well-being.[11]

The girls' education, consisting of dancing, music, and French lessons, is quite conventional. In addition, the occupations with which girls counter idleness (needlework and edifying reading) are in keeping with the female norm.[12] The boys, on the other hand, counter idleness by gaining knowledge from books (see the sixth dialogue). For them, moral edification is not on the agenda.[13] In depicting girls and boys, Erondell makes it clear that knowledge and morals are sexually differentiated. This is particularly evident in the fourth dialogue, in which we follow the girls' French lesson. The presence of a male cousin, introduced as Monsieur du Petit-Sens and expressly known for his "little wit" and "small knowledge," is explicitly justified; he provides support, but also presumes to evaluate the girls' knowledge.[14] Although the language master has not left the scene, the cousin jumps at the chance to exercise his right by commenting on the girls' performance. He does not hesitate to test his youngest cousin, who has only just begun to learn French. The examination ends with the girl admitting her ignorance, whereupon the cousin condescendingly gives her a piece of "helpful" advice.[15]

---

ilarly, Erondell's *French Garden* illustrates that the role of the mother and that of the society lady in early-seventeenth-century England did not necessarily give rise to irreconcilable conflicts.

[11]Erondell, *French Garden*, E7v, E8v, G6v, H1v.

[12]It is significant that the *Quatrains* of Guy du Faur, seigneur de Pibracs, are mentioned here. By the second half of the seventeenth century at the latest, this work had become the epitome of a then obsolete moralizing education for girls. See Gustave Reynier, "La 'Science des Dames' au temps de Molière," *Revue des deux mondes* (15 May 1929): 436–64, esp. 458; Henri-Jean Martin, *Livre, pouvoirs et société à Paris au XVIIe siècle (1598–1701)*, 2 vols. (Geneva: Droz, 1969), 546. Regarding the importance of prayer book and spindle in girls' education in baroque Germany, see Barbara Becker-Cantarino, "Frauenzimmer Gesprächspiele: Geselligkeit, Frauen und Literatur im Barockzeitalter," in *Geselligkeit und Gesellschaft im Barockzeitalter*, ed. Wolfgang Adam et al., 2 vols. (Wiesbaden: Harrassowitz, 1997), 17–41, esp. 29.

[13]See Gérard Genette, *Seuils* (Paris: Editions du Seuil, 1987), for the "threshold-texts" of a book, such as preface, dedication, title page, etc. The paratexts (or threshold-texts) show a sharp differentiation between girls and boys. Whereas the former are described on the basis of their external aesthetic qualities (that is to say, beauty), the latter are characterized in terms of their intellectual capabilities: "Who with the busy Mother now and then/ May prattle of each point in phrases mild/ The witty Boys, of books, of sport and play,/ The pretty Lasses of their work all day." Erondell, *The French Garden*, A6r.

[14]Erondell, *The French Garden*, F5v, L6v.

[15]Since the corresponding linguistic devices and strategies (admission of one's own ignorance, request for an explanation) have already been conveyed (Erondell, *The French Garden*, F6v), there is no further practical reason for this scene. In quotations, spelling and to some extent punctuation have been modernized.

The girls, however, get the upper hand in a completely different domain. While their cousin judges the language teacher according to his exterior, namely his clothes, the girls appreciate his true, inner values: virtue, knowledge, reason, *esprit*. In other words, knowledge is assigned to the male, even to "Mister Little-Wit," while morals—the *bellezza dell'animo* ("the beauty of the mind"), as Bruto puts it[16]—are primarily the province of "the Sex," meaning the female sex.[17]

Perhaps the most significant dialogue in Erondell's *French Garden* is the twelfth, entitled "Of the walk." This dialogue illustrates the diversity of the Erondellian levels of discourse and the literary character of the work. Knowledge of language, such as grammatical structures and thematically ordered vocabulary, is associated with moral values and encyclopedic knowledge, including information about the target culture, France and the French people—all integrated into an elaborate form enhanced by literary allusions.

An impressive example of these literary allusions can be found at the beginning of the dialogue, in which the description of the landscape evokes several stereotypes of Arcadia:

Will you see a fair meadow? Is it not a great comfort to the eye to see so great variety of flowers? And then cast your eye upon that little hill, look how the little lambs do skip on the grass! See what a fair river with so many boats, which with their oars do slide and pass the course in swiftness.... See what infinite number of swans do deck the back of this river!... Let us enter into this grove to hear the nightingale. The sun did not shine here this day, for the grass is yet with dew. It is marvellous cool at the side of this brook; see how clear the water is. Master du Vault-l'Amour, I do not counsel you to see yourself in it for fear that it happen unto you, as to Echo's sweetheart, who bewails him yet every day in this wood. What sweet noise this water makes among the pible-stones [pebbles], it does enchant me almost to sleep.... Is not this a fair fountain compassed with small and great trees? Phoebus does not salute it but of the side [where] he rises, where he casts lively his beams to give strength to the herbs which do accompany it. (Erondell, *The French Garden,* M7v, M8v, N1v)

It is obvious that we have reached the place "where Diana was wont to bathe herself," as the little group is immediately moved to declare.[18]

[16]Bruto, *The Necessarie, Fit and Convenient Education,* G7v, G8r.

[17]Concerning the dichotomy between moral-female and intellectual-male reason in Torquato Tasso, as well as Lucrezia Marinella's reaction, see Becker-Cantarino, "Frauenzimmer Gesprächspiele," 31–33.

[18]Erondell, *The French Garden,* N1v. On Arcadia, see for example Ernst Robert Curtius, *Europäische Literatur und lateinisches Mittelalter* (1948), 5th ed. (Bern: Francke, 1965), chap. 10; Hellmuth Petriconi, "Das neue Arkadien," *Antike und Abendland* 3 (1948): 187–200; idem, "Die verlorenen Paradiese," *Romantistisches Jahrbuch* 10 (1959): 167–99; and Bruno Snell, "Arkadien / Die Entdeckung einer geistigen Landschaft," in his *Die Entdeckung des Geistes: Studien zur Entstehung des europäischen Denkens bei den Griechen,* 4th ed. (Göttingen: Vandenhoeck & Ruprecht, 1975), 257–74, 320–21.

The Arcadian landscape evoked here is by no means an isolated case: the well-known works of Bernard Le Bovier de Fontenelle[19] and Francesco Algarotti[20] also feature Arcadian settings. Less well known, perhaps, are language textbooks in which a central role is assigned to "the ladies," "the mother," or "the Demoiselles," and the action takes place at the family's manor, in the garden of the pupil's home, or in the vicinity of the *villeggiatura*. Among these are Joseph Baretti's *Easy Phraseology*,[21] Tournon's *Promenades*, B. Calbris's *The Rational Guide to the French Tongue*, and Sarina Corgialegno's *La grammatica della mamma*.[22]

Only Tournon's *Promenades de Clarisse* can be dealt with in detail here. Like Erondell's *French Garden*, the *Promenades de Clarisse* are surprising because of their literary features. Tournon develops a large-scale plot (the so-called *partie romanesque*, as a contemporary critic called it[23]), that is, a sort of novel that constitutes the background for the dialogues in which grammatical and orthographical issues are discussed. Since contemporary reviews explicitly criticized or praised just this aspect, we can infer that, for eighteenth-century readers as well as for us, the novelistic framework for a grammar book is not an obvious or usual choice, and therefore merits further reflection.[24]

Tournon's *Promenades de Clarisse* link various aspects which can be found in a series of other language textbooks addressed "to the Ladies": the setting in an idyllic landscape, the presentation in the form of a conversation,[25] the novelistic framework

---

[19]Bernard Le Bovier de Fontenelle, *Entretiens sur la pluralité des mondes (1686)*, ed. Alexandre Calame (Paris: Didier, 1966).

[20]Francesco Algarotti, *Il Newtonianismo per le dame ovvero dialoghi sopra la luce e i colori* (Naples: n.p., 1737).

[21]Joseph (Giuseppe) Baretti, *Easy Phraseology, For the Use of Young Ladies, Who intend to learn The Colloquial Part Of the Italian Language* (London: G. Robinson and T. Cadell, 1775).

[22]Sarina Corgialegno, *La Grammatica della Mamma ossia avviamento allo studio della grammatica* (Milan: Fratelli Treves, 1875).

[23]*Lettre critique sur les promenades de Clarisse, avec la réponse* (London: Cailleau, Jombert, Mérigot, and Bailly, 1785), 11.

[24]"[Q]u'importe donc que ce soit une Grammaire sous la forme d'un roman? Eh, tant mieux! les leçons en seront plus agréables," asserted the anonymous article of the *Lettre critique*, 14; see also 4–5, 11.

[25]The critic of the *Promenades*, for instance, compares Clarisse's garden to the "jardins de Calypso," *Année littéraire* 5 (1785): 205. For the utopian aspects of Arcadia, see Renate Baader, *Dames de Lettres: Autorinnen des preziösen, hocharistokratischen und "modernen" Salons (1649–1698): Mlle de Scudéry, Mlle de Montpensier, Mme d'Aulnoy* (Stuttgart: Metzler, 1986), 216, 223, 275. With respect to the idyllic landscape, Baader observes: "Den Konversationsraum bildet stereotyp eine Stätte idyllischer Freiheit: das Landhaus am Fluß, das Gartenkabinett, der Park." There are obvious affinities between the *genres saloniers* and some of the language textbooks "for Ladies." Conversation must not be confused with the form of question and answer, which is incompatible with the image of "the ladies" because it evokes *collèges* and *docteurs* and is understood not to correspond to *honnêteté*. See, for example, Monsieur N. C., *Les Femmes Sçavantes Ou Bibliotheque Des Dames Qui traite des Sciences qui conviennent aux Dames, de la conduite de leurs Etudes, des Livres qu'elles peuvent lire, Et L'Histoire de celles qui ont excellé dans les Sciences* (Amsterdam: Michel Charles Le Cene, 1718), 216–17, 267–69. Conversation, on the contrary, has the merit of naturalness. See Delphine Denis, *La muse galante: Poétique de la conversation dans l'oeuvre de Madeleine de Scudéry* (Paris: Champion, 1997), 125–28. On the imitation of the "méandres imprévus," which constitute

Gabriele Beck-Busse

that motivates the imparting of knowledge and incorporates grammatical issues in a literary scenario.[26] A further aspect is notable here. The *Promenades* were not published in the form of a book; rather, installments were delivered to subscribers by post month after month. Thus, just like the *Journal de la langue française*, which began publication at the very same time, Tournon's work promised topicality.[27]

Comparing Tournon's Clarisse and Francesco Algarotti's Marchesa in his *Newtonianismo per le Dame* brings to light some important differences. The Marchesa is explicitly conceived as Cartesian.[28] She wants to be convinced, she asks for explanations and examples, and she expresses her doubts. In short, she takes an active part in the conversation. The eighteen-year-old Clarisse, on the other hand, is pre-Romantic. She is a sensitive, attentive, interested, willing, and naive young lady full of questions but without any opinion of her own.[29] To show that she has understood her young teacher's explanations, she only slightly reformulates what he has already said.[30]

the "spirale de conversation," see Marc Fumaroli, "La conversation," in *Les lieux de mémoire,* ed. Pierre Nora, vol. 3.2 (Paris: Gallimard, 1992), 678–743, esp. 690–91; see also Peter Burke, *The Art of Conversation* (Cambridge: Polity Press, 1993), esp. 91, 100, 106, 108.

[26]Especially when writing for "le Monde," it is extremely important not to impart one's own knowledge without being asked for it, but rather to fit into the "compagnie," the group, as homogeneously and unobtrusively as possible, as observed by Claude Fleury, *Traité du choix et de la méthode des études* (Paris: Pierre Aubouin, Pierre Emery, and Charles Clousier, 1687), 135. See also Baader, *Dames de Lettres,* 216: "Diskret andeutend und undogmatisch gibt der Gebildete sein Wissen weiter, meidet den Monolog oder den Anschein lenkender Überlegenheit."

How to avoid pedantic undertones is shown in the anonymous *Les deux Perroquets,* the introduction of which recounts a rather fantastic story to explain the publication of the work. On the docks of Naples a traveler encounters a man holding on each fist a pretty gray parrot with a red collar. He takes no further notice of the two birds until, during a thunderstorm in the Tyrol, he meets the two birds again. These parrots are quite extraordinary, for they can recite dialogues of a bilingual French and English textbook. The man acquires the birds as well as the manuscript and continues traveling. After a rather long trip in the Orient, he arrives in England, where the manuscript is finally printed. See *Les deux Perroquets: Ouvrage français destiné à faciliter aux Anglais La Causerie Elégante, La Lettre et le Billet. A l'Usage des Dames, des Jeunes Filles et des Enfants. Par une dame* (London: David Nutt, 1850), vii–x [London, British Library, 12952.b.15].

[27]See Sylvain Auroux, Françoise Dougnac, and Tristan Hordé, "Les premiers périodiques linguistiques français (1784–1840)," *Histoire, Epistémologie, Langage* 4.1 (1982): 117–32. Regarding the positive features of topicality, see a reader's reaction in the *Journal de la langue française* (15 April 1785): 552–53; and also Winfried Busse and Françoise Dougnac, *François-Urbain Domergue: Le grammairien patriote (1745–1810)* (Tübingen: Narr, 1992), 54.

[28]Algarotti, *Il Newtonianismo,* H7.

[29]At the beginning of the work, Tournon raises the delicate question of whether, in view of their position in society, women need to learn the basics of French. In response to the question about what *she* thinks, Clarisse says nothing more substantial than "I do not set myself up as a judge in the discussions." Tournon, *Les Promenades,* 28–29.

[30]Tournon, *Les Promenades,* 44–45, 55, 57.

Another important difference is the way in which both characters deal with gallant allusions.[31] While these present no problem for the Marchesa (on the contrary, gallantry livens up conversation and lends it *esprit*), Clarisse feels compelled to react more or less brusquely, perhaps bearing in mind the words of Rousseau's *Julie:* "Indeed, using instruction as a way to corrupt a woman is the most condemnable of seductions."[32] These differences cannot be attributed exclusively to the difference in the protagonists' ages. More important are the influences of sensualism and the writings of an author whom Tournon does not fail to mention, the "author of *Emile.*"[33]

In spite of the considerable space of time that separates Erondell's *French Garden* and Tournon's *Promenades de Clarisse*, both works—and some other language textbooks intended "for the ladies" as well— share some of the following characteristics.[34] The grammatical issues are presented in an elaborate form. A background

[31]Concerning gallantry and its history, see Noémi Hepp, "La galanterie," in *Les lieux de mémoire,* ed. Nora, vol. 3.2: 744–83. The great significance which Madame de Scudéry's circle attached to gallantry as a constituent of conversation is demonstrated by Denis, *La muse galante,* 257–75, 330–33; see also Noémie Hepp, "Conversation et enjouement au XVIIe siècle: L'exemple de Madeleine de Scudéry," in *Du goût, de la conversation et des femmes,* ed. Alain Montandon (Clermont-Ferrand: Association des Publications de la Faculté des Lettres et Sciences Humaines de Clermont-Ferrand, 1994), 111–29, esp. 119–21. For gallantry in general, see also Christoph Strosetzki, *Konversation: Ein Kapitel gesellschaftlicher und literarischer Pragmatik im Frankreich des 17. Jahrhunderts* (Frankfurt a/M: Lang, 1978), 100–103.

[32]Jean-Jacques Rousseau, *Julie, ou, La Nouvelle Héloise,* ed. Réne Pomeau (Paris: Garnier, 1960), 1:13.

[33]See, for example, Tournon, *Les Promenades,* 23, 63. Sensualist points of view come to light in the discussion of whether women, because of their sensitivity and the "delicacy of their organs" (*la délicatesse de leurs organes*), are suited to studying. Even though Tournon initially assesses the vivacity of female sensory perception positively, he attaches a greater significance to the role of women in society, a role determined essentially by their physiological characteristics. "Besides, I do not believe that her existence in society and the end to which nature seems to have destined her require that she take up this career [studies]. But if the duty of a woman who has become a mother is to raise her child, will she not need to instruct him? Will moral education then be less precious than physical education? To practice learning, as I have already said, the first principles suffice: whoever possesses them can communicate them, and that is all a mother needs." Concerning the changing parameters in the *querelle des femmes,* see Lieselotte Steinbrügge, *Das moralische Geschlecht: Theorien und literarische Entwürfe über die Natur der Frau in der französischen Aufklärung* (Weinheim: Beltz, 1987), 48, 52. Rousseau's position is very similar: see, for example, Jean-Jacques Rousseau, *Emile, ou, de l'éducation,* ed. Michel Launay (Paris: Garnier-Flammarion, 1966), esp. 465, 475, 487, 508.

[34]For an inquiry into the so-called *Grammaire des Dames,* see *Histoire, Epistémologie, Langage* 16.2 (1994). On England and English grammar, see Carol Percy, "Paradigms for Their Sex? Women's Grammars in Late-Eighteenth-Century England," ibid, 121–41; and Vivian Salmon, "Women and the Study of Language in Sixteenth- and Seventeenth-Century England," ibid, 95–119. For Germany, see Edeltraud Dobnig-Jülch and Susanne Staudinger, "Frauen + (viel) Grammatik = (viel) Frauengrammatik? Zur Verbreitung und Typologie spezieller Grammatiken im 18. Jahrhundert," ibid, 143–68. On France, see Wendy Ayres-Bennett, "Le rôle des femmes dans l'élaboration des idées linguistiques au XVIIe siècle en France," ibid, 35–53; Madeleine Reuillon-Blanquet, "Les grammaires des dames en France et l'apprentissage des langues à la fin du XVIIIe siècle," ibid, 55–76; and idem, "Grammaires des Dames, ou comment rendre 'instructive et amusante' une étude généralement considérée comme rébarbative," *Langages de la Révolution (1770–1815),* éd. l'Equipe, "18ème et Révolution, Actes du 4ème colloque international de

story that has nothing to do with strictly grammatical questions serves to dispel the idea of pedantry: "gentle education"[35] tries to avoid the idea of selfish exhibition of one's own knowledge (that is, pedantry) by inventing a context in which a work's immanent public asks for explanations which the work's immanent grammarian often answers by stressing the fact that he does nothing but compile what others have said. The works use the style of convivial conversation to evoke informality, sociability, and gentle company, which even includes gallantry.[36]

The counterpart of this sociable setting can be characterized by the key words "church," "university," and "pedantry": the world of the so-called "serious studies" which are clearly associated with men, as Pietro Longhi's painting *Precettore dei Grimani* (fig. 1) illustrates.[37] Here we find nothing which livens up the studious atmosphere. On the contrary, the strict preceptor, dressed in black and probably a clergyman,[38] passes on his knowledge without digression, and not even the raised finger of instruction is lacking.

Longhi's *Lezione di Geografia* (fig. 2) conveys quite a different atmosphere. Here we encounter not instruction in a sober and specially equipped study, but the

---

lexicologie politique (Paris: INALF and Klincksieck, 1995). 163–75. An annotated bibliography of French textbooks for "young ladies" is to be found in Gabrielle Beck-Busse, "La grammaire française dédiée à mes jeunes amies: Bibliographie raisonnée de manuels de la langue française à l'usage de la jeunesse féminine (1564–1850)," *Histoire, Epistémologie, Langage* 16.2 (1994): 9–33. See also Günter Holtus, "'La gvirlande des ievnes filles' (1580) und 'La grammaire des dames' (1748): Überlegungen zu französischen Grammatiken und ihrem Zielpublikum," in *Sprache und Geschlecht in der Romania*, ed. Wolfgang Dahmen et al., Romanistisches Kolloquium 10 (Tübingen: Narr, 1997), 241–60; and Gabrielle Beck-Busse, "Les 'femmes' et les 'illitterati'; ou: La question du latin et de la langue vulgaire," *Histoire, Epistémologie, Langage* 16.2 (1994): 77–94.

[35] This expression is taken from a painting Jean Siméon Chardin was asked for; see Gabriel Naughton, *Chardin* (London: Phaidon Press, 1996), 18–19.

[36] This does not necessarily require two or more people conversing. As the anonymous *Eloquence* illustrates, colloquial language can also be imitated by a single speaker who anticipates a virtual interlocutor's objections and comments. *L'Eloquence Du Temps, Enseignée à une Dame de qualité, selon les regles d'une Rhetorique aisée & galante* (Brussels: n.p., 1699). Textbooks which copy the style of letters—for example, Karl Philipp Moritz, *Deutsche Sprachlehre in Briefen*, 2nd ed. (Berlin: Arnold Wever, 1791; reprint, Hildesheim: Georg Olms, 1990); and Salomon Reinach, *Sidonie, ou le français sans peine* (Paris: Hachette, 1913)—show considerable parallels, since a letter can be described as "une conversation écrite avec une personne absente." H. Ferté, *L'Art d'écrire une lettre* (Paris: Hachette, 1894), 1. Regarding the close relation between conversation and letter-writing style, see Strosetzki, *Juan Luis Vives*, 72–75.

[37] Unfortunately here the two paintings with the noteworthy titles *The Gentle Education* and *The Severe Education* that Chardin was asked for were not executed; see Naughton, *Chardin*. We therefore have to resign ourselves to two paintings which represent the eighteenth-century Venetian context of gentle (see also Algarotti's *Newtonianismo per le Dame*) and severe popularization.

[38] According to *Pietro Longhi dal disegno alla pittura*, ed. Teresio Pignatti (Venice: Alfieri, 1975), 29, we may suppose that the preceptor represented here is the Abate Melchiorre Cesarotti. In another *Lezione di Geografia* (Ca' d'Oro, Venice), formerly attributed to Longhi but also ascribed to Gramiccia, the boy's preceptor is represented in the usual clergyman's clothes. Terisio Pignatti, *Longhi*, 2nd ed. (Milan: Electa, 1972), 137, 446.

Fig. 1. Pietro Longhi, "The Teacher of the Grimani Family." Private collection of Alessandro Orsi, Milan. Photo courtesy of the Museo Correr, Venice. (Fototeca V.19209)

Fig. 2. Pietro Longhi, "The Geography Lesson." Pinacoteca Querini Stampalia, Venice. Photo courtesy of the Museo Correr, Venice. (Fototeca V.19213)

communication of knowledge in gentle company, in conviviality—that is, over a cup of tea or chocolate.[39] The loosely arranged books in the background on the left, the young man's curious glance (perhaps attracted more by the beauty of the young lady than by the globe), and the tray with the latest popular drink symbolize a way of imparting knowledge that employs new and unpedantic means. These means are stereotypically associated with the female sex—even if many of the works are expressly intended for a much wider public, including male members of the aristocracy—a fact that Longhi's *Lezione* illustrates as well.

Gilles Declercq characterizes the historical writings of the seventeenth-century Jesuit priest Louis Maimbourg by saying that this author aimed to be not only a historian but also a writer ("L'historien se veut écrivain").[40] The analogous statement about the grammarian who aims to be a writer characterizes some of those grammarians who address their works to "the ladies." "Ladies" here should be read as the "emblem of a worldly public, society, and a culture, emerging slowly under Louis XIV, that rejected the learned man and the pedant."[41] Both Erondell's *French Garden* and Tournon's *Promenades de Clarisse* clearly demonstrate that the grammarian, as a writer, does not hesitate to refer to stereotypes of pastoral poetry or, as Bruno Snell calls it, the "idea" or "scheme of the Arcadian landscape."[42] Thus we are justified in speaking not only of an "Arcadia of Philosophy," the term applied by Ettore

[39]Baader, *Dames de Lettres,* 217, for instance, speaks of the "Scheidung von Gelehrsamkeit und Konversation, (männlichem) Buchwissen und einer (frauenorientierten) gesellligen Mitteilsamkeit." Furthermore, I would like to draw attention to a passage of Bellegarde's *The Praise of Women.* While Urbanus, one of the protagonists, thinks "that the Time we bestow in the Company of Women is very idly thrown away," Philander, his counterpart, clearly emphasizes the positive aspects and does not forget to stress the importance of sociability for "a learned Man"—as long as he avoids pedantry. Bellegarde, just like Longhi in his *Lezione,* establishes a close relation between sociability and the tea (or coffee or chocolate) table:

A Man whose good Sense leads him to embellish his Mind with genteel Studies, will make a greater Proficiency therein by frequenting the Company of ingenious polite Women, than by poring over all the Books that were ever printed. He will acquire a fluent Diction, and a graceful Manner of Expression, without which Knowledge is despicable, or at least loses very much of its Worth and Beauty; for what does it avail to have the Memory loaded with an undigested Heap of Notions, if they are irre[gu]larly and in-elegantly displayed? The Discourse of a learned Man is insipid without these Talents, and he who totally sequesters himself from the Company of Women will never attain them. The Style, Gesture, Air, Delivery, and other Graces of Conversation are not to be acquired in a Library. To speak pertinently and politely... and to discern true Literature from Pedantry, I say, these Qualifications are better learned over a *Tea*-Table than at a University.

See Jean Baptiste Morvan de Bellegarde, *The Praise of Women: In Answer to this Question; Whether the Company of Women is useful, or hurtful, to young Gentlemen at their first Setting out in the World?*, trans. S. Macky (London: n.p., 1727), 29–30.

[40]Gilles Declercq, "Un adepte de l'histoire éloquente, le Père Maimbourg, S.J.," *XVIIe Siècle* 143 (1984): 119–32, esp. 126.

[41]Declerq, "Un adepte de l'histoire,"125.

[42]Snell, *Die Entdeckung des Geistes.*

Bonora to Algarotti's *Newtonianismo per le Dame*,[43] but also of an "Arcadia of Grammar." Just like its philosophical sister, this type of grammar is associated with the outstanding representatives of the non-academic world: the ladies.[44]

[43]Ettore Bonora, "Algarotti, Francesco," in *Dizionario Biografico degli Italiani* 2 (Rome: Istituto della Enciclopedia Italiana, 1960), 356–60, esp. 357.

[44]Thanks to Mary Copple for translation of this work into English, and to Gesa Stedman for revisions.

The Girl and the Hourglass
Periodization of Women's Lives
in Western Preindustrial Societies

Silvana Seidel Menchi

THE PROBLEM

The testimony of a contemporary German writer, Irmtraud Morgner, will serve to introduce this essay.[1] In *Amanda: Ein Hexenroman* (1983), the protagonist, Vilna, sketches the following plan of life:

> "Until age forty you defer yourself." I was twenty-four when I told myself this, with three healthy children, two abortions. But it wasn't a discussion: it was a decision, mine. I remember it as if it had happened today. It was in Leipzig, in a class on the history of philosophy. The professor was talking about Hegel, and I couldn't get the children's shoes and the plumber out of my head.... Thus, on Hegel, I decided: "At age forty I turn the page and close the book.... I close the book on my first life, of course, the one in which I've had to pay the debt that history and custom have laid on me. Specialization: the first life has made me specialize in the service of others and renunciation. The second belongs to me and to scholarship."[2]

A credible witness on East German society and a spokesperson for the "hard" feminism of the 1970s, Irmtraud Morgner tells us that in the German Democratic Republic, it was possible, or at least conceivable, to deploy a woman's life in two stages: that is, to actually divide one's biographical time into two lives to be lived in succession. The first would be rooted in the traditional humus of family and feeling, absorbed by the role of reproduction, which was taken for granted. The second would be dedicated to the construction of a personal identity, to the unfolding of the self in the sphere of culture, to the achievement of professional competence in

---

[1]I am grateful to Anne Jacobson Schutte for translating this chapter into English.

[2]Irmtraud Morgner, *Amanda: Ein Hexenroman* (Darmstadt: Luchterhard, 1983), 190 (my translation).

traditionally masculine fields. The age of forty signals the break between the two lives. Behind this fictional life project, we can glimpse the expectations nourished by the society of the German Democratic Republic in those years, and perhaps also the kind of experimentation it fostered in and among women. Contemporaneous western societies did not encourage similar plans: the rigorously monolithic calendars that underlay and still underlie professional careers, particularly academic ones, did not and do not allow for postponing specialization or planning two lives in succession. *Amanda* provides literary evidence in support of the fact that the conception of how life unfolds is a sociocultural variable that in different societies conditions the construction of personal itineraries in different ways.

In the social sciences, a well-established current of studies has arisen through and been nourished by attention to two themes: the unfolding and configuration of woman's life in various social contexts, and the way in which these diverse configurations affect individuals' life cycles. In its international ramifications and applications, the conceptual and linguistic tool kit utilized by sociologists of the life cycle beginning in the 1970s has proven to be highly productive.[3] Among the many assumptions put into circulation by this branch of sociology, one has become a given: the "natural" turning points of the life cycle (birth, sexual maturity, aging, and death), far from being facts of nature, are biological variables susceptible to quite divergent interpretations and sociocultural configurations.[4]

Historians' extension of the sociological discussion on the life cycle has been discontinuous.[5] Although the natural events which mark it—birth and death rates, life expectancy, age at marriage, average duration of marriage, age on first giving birth, reproductive rhythms, etc.—are among the richest themes in social history during the last half century, the issue of life stages is addressed only partially at its two extremes, childhood and old age.[6] Historians have not adequately answered crucial questions about the perceptions men and women had of age roles, the ways in which they represented them, and the projections of these roles into symbols organizing life in relationships. A persistent ahistorical vision of life stages, understood as

---

[3]Leopold Rosenmayr, ed., *Die menschlichen Lebensalter: Kontinuität und Krisen* (Munich: R. Pieper, 1978); Bernice L. Neugarten and Joan W. Moore, "The Changing Age-Status System," in *Middle Age and Aging: A Reader in Social Psychology,* ed. Bernice L. Neugarten (Chicago: University of Chicago Press, 1968), 2–21; *Età e corso della vita,* ed. Chiara Saraceno (Bologna: Il Mulino, 1986).

[4]Neugarten and Moore, "Changing Age-Status."

[5]The abundant historical literature, indicated in part in n. 11, examines theories on the life course and reviews the iconography connected with it; the extent to which these theories affected actual life experience is not among the problems the literature addresses.

[6]Klaus Arnold, *Kind und Gesellschaft in Mittelalter und Renaissance: Beiträge und Texte zur Geschichte der Kindheit* (Paderborn: Schöningh, and Munich: Martin Lutz, 1980); Georges Minois, *History of Old Age: From Antiquity to the Renaissance,* trans. Sarah Hanbury Tenison (Chicago: University of Chicago Press, 1989); Peter Borscheid, *Geschichte des Alters* (Munich: DTV, 1989); Ines Stahlmann, Klaus Arnold, and Beatrix Bastl, "Lebensalter," in *Europäische Mentalitätsgeschichte: Hauptthemen in Einzeldarstellungen,* ed. Peter Dinzelbacher (Stuttgart: A. Kröner, 1993), 208–30.

the expression of biologically determined potential,[7] is particularly noticeable in the history of women. Given how inexorably the factor of time conditioned, and still conditions, women's self-consciousness, their self-images, and their efforts to shape the future, the lack of specific historical discussion on age roles and the influence they exerted on the construction of female lives is very surprising. The close connection between age roles and sexual identity should serve as a stimulus to overcoming the deterministic rigidity of biological age, and to subjecting age roles to the same kind of analysis that sex roles have been receiving.[8]

To document the biologically determined vision of the female life curve, let us consider the sequence of ages sketched out by Giovanni Nevizano, a Piedmontese jurist of the early sixteenth century:

> Some enumerate female activities by dividing them into woman's ages, seven years each. In the first seven years she's a procuress, for her mother uses her, a child incapable of understanding evil, to go summon her lover. In the next seven years she's a virgin. Between fourteen and twenty-one she's the prey of love. In the following seven years, from twenty-one to twenty-eight, she's a whore. From twenty-eight to thirty-five she's a heifer or sow. In the next seven-year period she's a whore again. Between forty-two and forty-nine she's a junk dealer. From forty-nine to fifty-six she goes around begging wine with a jug. In the next seven years she becomes a witch. She ends up burned.[9]

This comes from the *Sylva nuptialis*, a compendium of marriage law assembled by Nevizano between 1520 and 1526. Placed in its context, his calendar divided into seven-year periods emanates from that age-old current of misogyny climaxing in the *querelle des femmes*, which the omnivorous, exceptionally curious, and entirely up-to-date Nevizano echoed without endorsing. When the sprouts of routine misogyny are pruned back, this sixteenth-century map of life turns out to be a variant of the reading of the female life cycle in terms of the process of aging, on which fixed biological rhythms confer a subhistorical character. Taken for granted like the passing of the seasons, the woman's life story coincides with the parabola of her body; woman's

---

[7]Chiara Saraceno, "Invecchiare: La sociologia dell'età e del corso della vita," *Memoria: Rivista di storia delle donne* 6 (1986): 5–20.

[8]See the chapters by Heide Wunder and Kristin Zapalac in this volume.

[9]Giovanni Nevizano, *Clarissimi iurisconsulti d. Joan. de Nevizanis civis Asten. Sylva nuptialis* (Lyon: Joannes Moylin alias de Cambrai, 1526), xx[x]viir–v: "Sunt enim qui enumerant septem mulierum proprietates: sanctas videlicet in ecclesia, angelos in accessu, demones in domo, bubones in fenestra, pichas in porta, capras in horto, fetorem in lecto. Alii enumerant per etates singulo septennio quod exerceat femina. Primo ergo septennio quod est lena, id est quia mater per eam, cum sit infantula, nec exinde concipere maliciam posset, mittit vocatum amasium. Secundo septennio est virgo. Tertio est philocapta. Quarto septennio est meretrix. Quinto est iuvenca seu porca. Sexto iterum lena. Septimo revenditrix. Octavo septennio mendicat cum dolio ad vinum. Nono septennio efficitur strigha, et tandem comburitur."

work is the management of her corporeality in its various phases. Virginity and falling in love are not stages of experience or psychosomatic conditions but "activities" or services, as immutable as the laws of nature, which the woman renders to the species. The active management of the female body peaks at age twenty-eight and finishes at age thirty-five. From then on, the activity or management of the body becomes passive. At that point, the arc begins its downward course, rapidly driving the woman, if she is not protected by privileged social standing, into professional marginalization (junk dealer), vice (drunkenness), antisocial criminality, witchcraft, ostracism, and ruin.

Comparison of Morgner's and Nevizano's testimonies is instructive because they converge. Four and a half centuries of history studded with social and political revolutions and dramatic transformations of habits, including the feminist revolution of the 1970s, have not brought changes in women's presumed specialties. Just like the woman of the early sixteenth century, the woman of the late twentieth century specializes in the management of her body and its sexual and reproductive functions. Not even the duration of this activity changed substantially: the end moved from age thirty-five to age forty, but forty figures in Morgner's view as the end of the line, after which the season of specialization in reproduction closes.

However, we also need to recognize the differences between Nevizano's and Morgner's schemes. Contrasted with the rigidly biological view of life stages, the testimony of Irmtraud Morgner opens the imagination to the horizon of the possible. Once female time is disconnected or removed from the reproductive function, it becomes a building ground for social creativity or clay to be molded in planning an individual life cycle.[10] Morgner's project of a double life and her adoption of turning forty as one's date of professional birth provides one of many models in which woman's time may be configured, just one of the outlines which a political orientation or a social agreement can fill in. When they recognize the horizon of the possible, women assume a pioneering role. Their self-consciousness guides them in reconfiguring the biographical calendar. On the basis of their lived experience, they sift through the variations of the possible and select feasible configurations of time, thus preserving social inventiveness from the danger of vaporizing into the ether of utopia. It is important to note that in the model proposed by Morgner, family life and professional life present themselves not as alternatives in competition but as successive lives—not either/or but before/after.

Between the determinism of biological periodization and the potentiality of future calendars, imagined or imaginable, lies a wide terrain to be explored: social calendars of woman's life elaborated by various cultures in response to different needs. Identifying some of these socially shaped calendars, noting their characteristics, and collecting some evidence on women's perceptions of the temporal phases that governed their lives form the objectives of a research project much more diffi-

[10]See introduction to Rosenmayr, *Menschliche Lebensalter,* 7–20, esp. 12, 18–19.

cult to carry out than I initially realized, of which this essay represents only a preliminary fragment.

LIFE MAPS

Historians who set out to study the female life cycle in societies of the Old Regime face the problem of finding sources. Some types of written sources—prescriptive statements, for instance—respond only in a fragmentary or laconic way to questions related to this theme. The figurative arts, as well as the literary works that inspire them, on the other hand, offer fuller and more diversified information. In the iconographic repertory of the medieval and early modern periods, the theme usually called "the ages of life" produced a rich range of interpretations and variations, which on account of their abundance poses major challenges of cataloguing, ordering, and comparing.[11]

Medieval and early modern literature and iconography attest to the existence of at least seven different life maps. The number of ages codified in these maps ranges from three to twelve, or if variants are taken into account, sixteen or more. Among them, the most durable and best documented divide life into three, four, six, seven, and ten ages. The theoretical foundations of the divisions are complex and many-sided. As a basis for understanding what follows, I shall outline briefly the most influential theories underlying the most persistent and widely diffused periodizations.

A.   The division into youth, maturity, and old age applies to human life the triadic arc of the sun: rising, zenith, setting. While the enigma of the sphinx contributed to the spread of this theory, Aristotle was its most influential *auctoritas* and most effective propagator. From Aristotle, the Christian Middle Ages derived the three-phase scheme *augmentum-status-decrementum* as the model of the curve traversed by every living being.[12]

B.   The division of life into four parts was inscribed in a system of interpretation based on the Pythagorean tetrad as the organizing principle of the universe: four

[11]See John Anthony Burrow, *The Ages of Man: A Study in Medieval Writing and Thought* (Oxford: Clarendon, and New York: Oxford University Press, 1986); Elizabeth Sears, *The Ages of Man: Medieval Interpretations of the Life Cycle* (Princeton: Princeton University Press, 1986); Michael E. Goodich, *From Birth to Old Age: The Human Life Cycle in Medieval Thought, 1250–1350* (Lanham, Md.: University Press of America, 1989); *Les âges de la vie au Moyen Âge*, Actes du colloque du Département d'Etudes Médiévales de l'Université de Paris-Sorbonne et de l'Université Friedrich-Wilhelm de Bonn, Provins, 16–17 mars 1990, ed. Henri Dubois and Michel Zink (Paris: Presses de l'Université de Paris–Sorbonne, 1992); Stahlmann, Arnold, and Bastl, *Europäische Mentalitätsgeschichte*, 208–30; Klaus T. Wirag, *Cursus Aetatis: Lebensalterdarstellungen vom 16. bis zum 18. Jahrhundert* (Ph.D. diss., Ludwig-Maximilian-Universität München, 1995), with an extensive up-to-date bibliography. I have not been able to see *The Seven Ages of Man*, ed. Robert R. Sears and S. Shirley Fellman (Los Altos, Calif.: W. Kaufmann, 1973).

[12]Franz Boll, "Die Lebensalter: Ein Beitrag zur antiken Ethologie und zur Geschichte der Zahlen," *Neue Jahrbücher für das klassische Altertum, Geschichte und deutsche Literatur und für Pedagogik* 31 (1913): 966–99; Sears, *The Ages of Man*, 91; Wirag, *Cursus Aetatis*, 11.

elements make up the cosmos; there are four primary qualities, four humors of the human body, four seasons of the year, four winds, four cardinal points. Similarly, man's life consists of four ages. The anthropological analogy of four humors of the human body to the four ages was Hippocratic and Galenic; the meteorological analogy of the four seasons and four winds to the four ages was of Ptolemaic origin. An important element in the success of this periodization of life was the harmony it established between macrocosm (the universe) and microcosm (man).[13]

C.   The division of life into six ages is based on Augustine's interpretation of the story of creation in the book of Genesis (1:1–2:3). Augustine established a relationship between the six days of creation, the six ages of universal history, and the six phases of human life. This interpretation of the life cycle is also based on a parallelism between microcosm and macrocosm. Among other texts, the *Bible moralisée* documents the broad diffusion of the Augustinian scheme. The division of human life into six ages survived until the eighteenth century, but it had already lost its connection with the ages of universal history in the sixteenth.[14]

D.   The division of life into seven ages is a projection of Pythagorean faith in the power of the number seven, the *numerus perfectus*, which gives shape to the world and its parts. The universe has seven spheres; seven celestial bodies control the cycle of seasons; the human body has seven parts; and according to Hippocrates, seven is the number that regulates the natural rhythm of growth and decay (every seven years an organism renews itself completely and begins a new cycle). The life cycle, therefore, is divided into seven equal phases, each lasting ten years; alternatively, it is divided into seven periods lasting seven years each. This division of life established a correspondence between the ages of man and the celestial bodies premised on the notion that the planets influence and control human life and determine the individual's character and physical constitution.[15]

E.   The abstract arithmetical speculation that divides life into ten periods of ten years each emanates from the decimal system. A variant of this theory, which had a classical precedent in Solon, divided human life into ten periods of seven years, but the decade system prevailed.[16] Diffused especially in central Europe, the nursery rhyme that articulated human life decade by decade is recorded in popular literature, above all in German, from the fourteenth to the eighteenth century. In the early sixteenth century this tradition found expression in a didactic play, Pamphilus Gengenbach's *Die X Alter dyser Welt* (*The Ten Ages of This World*), performed for the first time in Basel in 1515 and destined for considerable success on stage and in print.[17]

---

[13]Boll, "Die Lebensalter," 101–3.; Sears, *The Ages of Man*, 9–37; Wirag, *Cursus Aetatis*, 44–47. See also Rosenmayr, *Menschliche Lebensalter*.

[14]Boll, "Die Lebensalter," 107; Burrow, *The Ages of Man,* 80–82.; Sears, *The Ages of Man*, 54–79; Wirag, *Cursus Aetatis*, 153–54.

[15]Boll, "Die Lebensalter," 112–14.; Sears, *The Ages of Man*, 38–53; Wirag, *Cursus Aetatis*, 170–75.

[16]Boll, "Die Lebensalter," 110; Wirag, *Cursus Aetatis*, 199–201.

[17]Pamphilus Gengenbach, *Werke*, ed. Karl Goedeke, 2 vols. (Hannover: Carl Rümpel, 1855–56);

Through the fifteenth century, the periodization of life in ten ages remained linked to the metaphor of the wheel and was illustrated in the iconographic type known as the wheel of life. From the sixteenth century on, however, the decadic scheme generated a more durable and widely diffused iconographic representation, the so-called ladder of life.[18]

This brief review does not do justice to the refined interweaving of analogies and the imaginative counterpoint of symbols which combined and influenced one another in literary and iconographic sources. Still, it may serve to suggest the long-lasting fascination exercised by the theme of time, understood as life space, on western culture. For centuries, the aim of constructing a definitive or at least persuasive theory of the ages of life occupied philosophers' minds and artists' imaginations. From the systematic but admittedly not exhaustive research conducted by Elisabeth Sears on medieval interpretations and Klaus Wirag on early modern interpretations emerges a panorama of literary and iconographic testimonies running without a break from the twelfth to the eighteenth century. These testimonies are characterized by an impressive continuity in conceptual and symbolic referents. Vigorous roots in the culture and art of the ancient world,[19] illustrious sprigs in nineteenth- and twentieth-century art,[20] and a network of resonances and dependencies unlimited by linguistic and political frontiers confirm the inexhaustible vitality of a discourse which both lures historians by its currency and frustrates them by its evasiveness.[21] Even if the approximately 360 medieval and early modern iconographic interpretations of the *cursus aetatis* identified and analyzed by Sears and Wirag do not mirror real life, they nonetheless comprise an impressively large documentary mass. From it, one can draw information about the codified images of the various age brackets and about the socially defined behavior connected with them.[22] The quantitative abundance of iconographic documentation is reinforced by the literary evidence connected with it, although the considerations that followed are based above all on iconographic material.

Die Lebenstreppe: Bilder der menschlichen Lebensalter, catalogue of an exhibition of the Landschaftsverbandes Rheinland, Rheinisches Museumsamt, Brauweiler, in collaboration with the Städtische Museum Haus Koekkoek, Kleve (Cologne: Rheiland-Verlag, and Bonn: In Kommission bei R. Habelt, 1983), catalog no. 4, 104–5.

[18]Peter Joerißen, "Lebenstreppe und Lebensalterspiel im 16. Jahrhundert," in *Die Lebenstreppe*, 25–38.

[19]Boll, "Die Lebensalter."

[20]Suse Barth, *Lebensalter-Darstellungen im 19. und 20. Jahrhundert: Ikonographische Studien* (Ph.D. diss., Ludwig-Maximilian-Universität München, 1971.)

[21]Sears, *The Ages of Man*, xvii, 6.

[22]For examples of this type of reading of iconographical evidence, see Alain Charraud, "Analyse de la représentation des âges de la vie humaine dans les estampes populaires du XIXe siècle," *Ethnologie française* 1 (1971): 59–78; and Rudolph Schenda, "Die Alterstreppe: Geschichte einer Popularisierung," in *Die Lebenstreppe*, 11–24.

Long-standing interest in the theme of the ages of life promoted a multiform artistic output that involved even the great masters, necessitated large expenditures, employed artisans using a great variety of materials (including even majolica stoves), and invaded the print market, giving rise to a series of interpretations until the twentieth century and occupying a prominent position in popular art.[23] Feeding this inexhaustible interest was a basic need of self-consciousness; the sequence of the ages of life illuminated the human condition and led to the recognition of the limits to planning and predicting the future. Taken as a whole, this body of testimony expresses a high level of attention to humans' earthly reality, a lucid perception of time, and an inclination toward the active management of it. A culture that put so much effort into elaborating theories of life stages could neither consider time as destiny nor ignore the concept of long-term investments in resources for the individual's benefit.[24]

The coexistence of divergent or contradictory interpretations even within the work of a single artist makes it difficult to orient oneself in the general panorama of the theme's fortune. Some coordinates, however, emerge clearly from the mass of documentation. Elisabeth Sears has shown that in the fourteenth century the sequence of ages promoted interpretations of a predominantly cosmological character.[25] Representation of the life cycle thus followed an elementary cognitive map which included a set of information pertinent on the one hand to religious life (the Ten Commandments, the seven sacraments, the four evangelists, the twelve articles of the Creed, and so forth) and on the other to the organization of harmonious social life (the seven virtues and seven vices, the seven works of mercy, and the labors of the twelve months, for instance). In a culture dominated by the idea of correspondence between macrocosm and microcosm, the traits characterizing the different phases of life were considered and interpreted as projections of cosmic forces or astral cycles, particularly the four seasons, the six ages of the world, the seven planetary divinities. In the course of the fifteenth century, however, an anthropocentric interpretation emerged alongside the cosmological interpretation and finally displaced it. Sermons, hortatory orations, moralizing treatises, and the figurative expressions they inspired presented the ages of life as unpleasant aspects of a human condition mired in suffering, labor, and misery. Recognition of the stages of life thus served as a lesson in asceticism: training for flight from the world and meditation on death.[26] In the sixteenth century, interpretation of the theme in soteriological and eschatological terms intensified and remained prominent through the first half of the

[23]Jean Cuisenier, *L'art populaire en France: Rayonnement, modèles et sources* (Fribourg: Office du livre, and Paris: Société française du livre, 1975); *Die Lebenstreppe.*

[24]Louis Roussel and Alain Girard, "Régimes démographiques et âges de la vie," in *Les âges de la vie,* VIIe Colloque national de démographie, Strasbourg, 5, 6, 7 mai 1982, Travaux et documents, no. 46, vol. 1 (Paris: Presses Universitaires de France, 1982), 17–23.

[25]Sears, *The Ages of Man,* 97–120.

[26]Sears, *The Ages of Man,* 123–27, 133–34, 139–40.

seventeenth,[27] but it took on a different resonance, more intense and personal, designed to involve the observer emotionally. Iconographic references to the *memento mori* and the evocation of the Last Judgment which accompanied and framed representations of the earthly pilgrimage had specific goals. They aimed at promoting daily, unritualized exercises of meditation practiced by an individual or in the family (but in either case private), and at suggesting a vision of life in which the worldly and otherworldly dimensions were not opposed but complementary.[28]

The medium which then carried on this discourse—the woodcut, reproduced in quantity at a relatively low price—spread it into the homes of artisans, small businessmen, merchants (Thomas More's father, for example), and professionals.[29] That most of these prints came from the Rhine region, southern Germany, and the Netherlands, along with the provenance of some of the artists who designed them, allows us to link them with the spread of the Reformation. Reference to the Protestant ethic is particularly pertinent to a group of designs, often variations on the model of the ladder of life, the iconography of which crystallized in the second quarter of the sixteenth century and continued to be very popular until the middle of the seventeenth. Here the symbolism of *vanitas*, the reminder of the Last Judgment, and the christological references did not teach a lesson of asceticism and the devaluation of human time. On the contrary, they tended to exalt time as precious material for use in the construction of socially prized and praiseworthy values in the context of an earthly commitment intended to be in harmony with the divine design of creation.[30] During the seventeenth and eighteenth centuries, this iconographic variation on the theme of the ages of man underwent a further process of secularization. The eschatological component progressively weakened; the religious symbolism lost ground; the personification of individual ages signalled the complete social integration, the productivity, and the prestige of the figures in whom they were incarnated.[31] This tradition now codified models of worldly life. In the second half of the eighteenth and in the nineteenth century, the representation of life stages served the function of moral instruction in a protoindustrial and bourgeois mode: the behavioral models proposed taught lessons about the work ethic, professional success, and gain.[32] A rich series of popular prints prolonged the paradigmatic function of these images well into the twentieth century.[33]

---

[27]Wirag, *Cursus Aetatis,* 7, 101–6, 161, 208, 214–16.

[28]Schenda, "Die Alterstreppe," 21–22; Peter Joerißen, "Die Lebensalter des Menschen: Bildprogramm und Bildform im Jahrhundert der Reformation," in *Die Lebenstreppe,* 39–59; Wirag, *Cursus Aetatis,* 7.

[29]Boll, "Die Lebensalter," 98; *Die Lebenstreppe,*; Wirag, *Cursus Aetatis,* 3–4.

[30]Joerißen, "Die Lebensalter,"; Wirag, *Cursus Aetatis,* 7, 216, 233.

[31]Schenda, "Die Alterstreppe"; Wirag, *Cursus Aetatis,* 60.

[32]Cuisenier, *L'art populaire*; Schenda, "Die Alterstreppe," 22; Wirag, *Cursus Aetatis,* 8, 236–40.

[33]Charraud, "Analyse."

THE SEVEN AGES OF WOMAN

We have seen that although the conventionality and conservatism of iconographic language had a strong impact on the theme of the ages,[34] these characteristics did not impede its evolution and adaptation to new cultural and social needs. Now we are in a position to ask what this body of figurative documents can reveal about the periodization of woman's life. Synthesizing specialized studies of these sources, we can trace four phases of change.

A. In medieval and early modern iconography, as in the theories underlying it, the theme of the ages is almost always treated from an entirely male perspective.[35] In the late Middle Ages, the most notable exception to the rule is the fresco cycle by Guariento in the church of the Eremitani in Padua (c. 1360), illustrating "the influence exercised by the planets on human conduct."[36] Here, each of the seven planetary divinities sits on a throne between two smaller figures (a male on the right, a female on the left), who represent the characteristic activities or main interests of that particular phase of life for each sex.[37] Until the fifteenth century, apart from this Paduan example, the ages of life were personified almost exclusively by masculine figures. When a female figure appeared, she either fulfilled a formal need for symmetry or served as an attribute and/or symbol of a single period of life, youth.[38] The androcentric point of view is even more explicit in the labels on figures depicting the ages, which identify adolescence (*adolescentia*) as the period from age fourteen to age twenty-eight and youth (*iuventus*) as the phase from twenty-eight to forty-nine or fifty. For most medieval "sociologists" of the ages, fifty signalled the acme of life, the *aetas optima*.[39] Such judgments and comments clearly ignore the rhythms of woman's life. The presence—frequent in prints of the seventeenth century and universal in those of the nineteenth—of a female companion to the man in the various stages of life does not indicate any correction of the androcentric perspective. In nineteenth-century representations of the ladder of life, age fifty continued incongruously to signal the apex of an existence that, as far as the female figure is con-

---

[34]The doll, for instance, has represented female childhood for centuries. Sears, *The Ages of Man,* 110; Wirag, *Cursus Aetatis,* 208 and passim.

[35]Wirag, *Cursus Aetatis,* 6–8., 173, 201–2, and passim.

[36]Sears, *The Ages of Man,* 110–13, esp. 113.

[37]Francesca Flores D'Arcais, *Guariento* (Venice: Alfieri, 1965), 61–62.

[38]A representative document in a long iconographic tradition is the miniature attributed to the Maestro del Biadaiolo in a manuscript of Brunetto Latini's *Tesoro*: Florence, Biblioteca Laurenziana, cod. Plut. XLI, 19, 16r. See Stahlmann, Arnold, and Bastl, "Lebensalter," 216.

[39]Wilhelm Wackernagel, *Die Lebensalter: Ein Beitrag zur vergleichenden Sitten- und Rectsgeschichte* (Basel: Bahnmeier, 1862), 66; Heide Wunder, "*Er ist die Sonn', sie ist der Mond": Frauen in der frühen Neuzeit* (Munich: Beck, 1992), 51 (English edition: *He Is the Sun, She Is the Moon: Women in Early Modern Germany,* trans. Thomas Dunlap [Cambridge: Harvard University Press, 1998]); Wirag, *Cursus Aetatis,* 2, 7, 28, 50–55, 201–2, 223. The definition of "youth" as the period from twenty-eight to fifty (occasionally to sixty) goes back to Isidore of Seville.

cerned, was that of fiancée-wife-mother, which culminated fifteen or twenty years earlier.[40]

B. Toward the end of the fifteenth century, increasingly abundant documentation indicates a growth of interest in the exploration and use of times of life and a corresponding iconographic shift. Cosmological speculation, numerical symbolism, arithmetic abstractions, and connection with universal history became rarer.[41] The division of life into seven ages gained ground against other schemes of periodization but lost its attachment to astrology.[42] In Italian iconography, the ascetic-moralistic motifs (references to the transitoriness of life and the misery of the human condition) still predominant in central European interpretations appeared less frequently. Taking their place were attention to character and physiognomy and diagnoses of inclinations, passions, and states of mind.[43]

C. Along with iconographic change in the fifteenth century, we find diversification in the social profile of purchasers and in the locations in which they placed these images. Most medieval representations of the stages of life were destined for public spaces and a general, impersonal audience. From about 1470, these images tended to be commissioned by private individuals for use in the domestic sphere. The theme of life stages entered the repertory of interior decoration, appearing on such furnishing for the home as frescoes, tapestries, and chests.[44] The social range of purchasers widened with the advent of the printing press. From the early sixteenth century until the middle of the twentieth, prints representing the ages of life, available in vast quantities, reached people in the middle and lower orders. Those in the professions seem to have been the prime purchasers of these products.[45] We may conjecture that the change in the social profile of purchasers led artists to widen their perspective, thus favoring the entry of female figures into the visual lexicon.

D. In the first half of the sixteenth century, the woman came on stage as a principal player in the iconography of the ages.[46] Her entry coincides with the emergence of a fuller and more flexible conception of time. At the turn of the fifteenth century, in fact, we find a split between the two main conceptions of the life cycle: one division into long periods, three ages (of twenty-five years each) or four ages (of twenty years each); and another into brief periods of seven ages (of ten years each) or nine or ten (of seven or ten years each).[47] In Italian art, the three- or four-age division prevailed.[48] In central European art, while the four-age division never fell from

---

[40]Charraud, "Analyse," 70; Cuisenier, *L'art populaire*, 164 (pls. 291–92).

[41]Sears, *The Ages of Man*, 134–53.

[42]Wirag, *Cursus Aetatis*, 32, 174, 195.

[43]Wirag, *Cursus Aetatis*, 14–21.

[44]Sears, *The Ages of Man*, 134–38.

[45]Schenda, "Die Alterstreppe"; Wirag, *Cursus Aetatis*, 4, 209–40

[46]Wirag, *Cursus Aetatis*, 8, 206–8., 217, and passim.

[47]Wirag, *Cursus Aetatis*, 7–9.

[48]Wirag, *Cursus Aetatis*, 7, 14–21.

favor, seven-, nine-, and ten-phase schemes became more popular.[49] Beginning in the 1540s, these latter periodizations more and more often took the form of the ladder of life, which became the most widely diffused motif in iconographic representations of the ages (fig. 1).[50] Three- and four-part divisions were generally used for the male life cycle (as in fig. 2, Giorgione's "The Three Ages").[51] Six-, seven-, nine-, ten- and even twelve-part divisions seem to have been preferred to illustrate the female life cycle (figs. 3–4).[52] Beginning in the second half of the sixteenth century, the ladder of woman's life, whether she was shown by herself or with a male age-mate, typically had seven, nine, ten, or more rungs. Not surprisingly, it appears that in general,

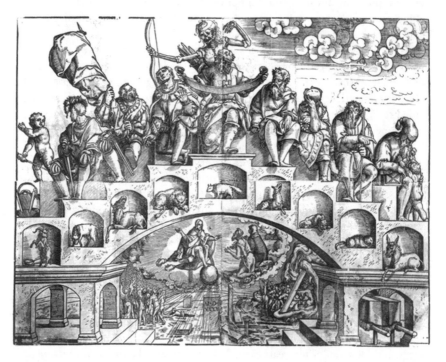

Fig. 1. Jörg Breu the Younger, "The Scale of Life" (1540). Courtesy of the Germanisches Nationalmuseum, Nürnberg.

[49]*Die Lebenstreppe*, 103–26, catalog nos. 1, 2, 4–6, 11–21; Wirag, *Cursus Aetatis,* 175–276.

[50]*Die Lebenstreppe*; Wirag, *Cursus Aetatis,* 209–39.

[51]Alessandro Ballarin, "Giorgio da Castelfranco, dit Giorgione, Les Trois Âges de l'homme," in *Le siècle de Titien: L'âge d'or de la peinture à Venise* (Paris: Réunion des Musées Nationaux, 1993), 309–13. Less persuasive is the interpretation offered by Mauro Lucco, "Le cosiddette 'Tre età dell'uomo' di Palazzo Pitti," in *'Le tre età dell'uomo' della Galleria Palatina* (Florence: Centro Di, 1989), 11–32.

[52]Wirag, *Cursus Aetatis,* passim.

Fig. 2. Giorgione, "The Three Ages of Man." Courtesy of the Galleria Palatinai, Florence.

central European artists depicting numerous brief life stages paid closer attention to the female life cycle than did their Italian counterparts, who tended to follow three- and four-part schemes.

Netherlandish, German, and Swiss draftsmen who systematically addressed the female experience in their treatment of the life cycle in seven or more stages did not hold revolutionary conceptions of woman's social position. All the attributes of the female figures on various steps of the life course refer to the domestic sphere. The bunch of keys carried by the fifty-year-old symbolizes her control of the house; the purse hanging from her belt refers to her management of family finances. A sixty- or seventy-year-old's spindle or distaff attests to work carried on until an advanced age. The book (possibly a Bible) with which one representation shows a fifty-year-old woman signals the fear of God or the prudence that governs her life; the rosary that representations from Catholic areas assign to seventy- and eighty-year-olds alludes to a life of prayer and meditation.[53]

As repetitive and conventional as this anchoring of women to the domestic sphere may seem, the figurative lexicon used by the draftsmen of the ladder of life

[53]*Die Lebenstreppe*, catalog; Wirag, *Cursus Aetatis*, 48–49, 208, 217, 231, and passim.

Fig. 3. Cristofano Bertelli, "The Ages of Woman's Life" (c. 1560). Courtesy of the Cabinet des Estampes, Bibliothèque Nationale, Paris.

opens up a new horizon of experience. With a clear but sympathetic eye, artists followed women's progress through the stages of life. That the power of seduction consciously exerted by the twenty-year-old—who in Cristofano Bertelli's interpretation boldly displays her tempting leg through the slit in her gown (fig. 3)—becomes a broken, useless weapon in the hands of the sixty-year-old (figs. 3, 4) did not escape them. Noble bearing and composed elegance of gesture, however, do not disappear, even in the very old woman depicted in melancholy meditation beside the coffin. Nor does the animal symbolism commenting on the steps in the female itinerary— for more than two centuries, birds—express negative judgments, despite the linkage of women with looseness which birds had originally suggested. Above all, this figurative lexicon, more innovative than the verbal lexicon accompanying it, characterized the declining years of woman's life as devoted to working hard, producing things of material and immaterial value, taking initiative, and fulfilling responsibilities.

In the work of these artists, the last stage of life is reevaluated: the grip of old age on woman is loosened. While the three-stage paradigm emphasizes the gap between youth and old age, the division into brief phases postpones old age and plays down its burdens. As opposed to the triadic division, in which turning forty signals becoming elderly, in some versions of the ladder of life the forty-year-old is represented by

Fig. 4. Anonymous Italian, "The Ages of Woman's Life" (mid-sixteenth century?). Courtesy of the Warburg Institute, London.

a pregnant woman.[54] Even in illustrating physical decay, the draftsmen and painters of the ladder of life neither resort to the rhetoric of *vanitas* nor brutally depict the ravages of time (fig. 5). They avoid allusions typical of the misogynist tradition to elderly female lust, in which the more beauty decays, the more obscene it becomes.[55] In the interpretations of the ladder of life included in the exhibition held in 1983, female old age appears domesticated. Dissociated from the idea of vice, it retains its decorum, even if tragic, all the way to the edge of the tomb.[56]

In support of the argument that the brief-period scheme of the life cycle mitigates the horror of old age, let me cite the testimony of Hans Baldung Grien (1484/5–1545). It is an obligatory citation, for the work of time on woman's body and soul has never had a more attentive observer and accurate chronicler than this disciple of Dürer, an inhabitant of reformed "sacramentarian" Strasbourg. The theme felicitously termed by Jean Wirth "the young girl and death" recurs with almost obsessive frequency in Baldung's work. In his many interpretations, this great variant on the topos *memento mori* attains allegorical polyvalence and sets off symbolic vibrations

[54]On the significance of turning forty in the three-phase calendar, see below, page 64. For the representation of the pregnant forty-year-old, see Wirag, *Cursus Aetatis,* 226, 229.

[55]Nevizano, *Sylva,* xxxvr; Minois, *History of Old Age,* 229–32.

[56]See *Die Lebenstreppe,* catalog.

Fig. 5. Bernardo Strozzi, "Old Woman at the Mirror." Courtesy of the Museum of Fine Arts, Moscow.

that are still provoking controversy.[57] These art-historical problems do not concern us here. Hans Baldung enters our field of observation as a meticulous recorder of the metamorphoses undergone by the female body during the life course. The literal meaning of his paintings and the scrupulous precision of his studies of the naked body make him a key witness.[58] Of particular relevance for our purposes is a comparison between his two interpretations of the ages of women, understood in the literal sense, which divide the female life cycle into three and ten ages respectively.

Baldung's painting in the Kunstmuseum of Vienna, dated between 1509 and 1511 and traditionally called "The Three Ages of Life and Death," reads the life course as a process of "natural degradation of the flesh" (Wirth). The contrast between the flowering fleshiness of the young woman in the middle and the desiccated old woman with sagging, wrinkled breasts, who stands to her left and holds the mirror for her, heightens the contrast between the young woman and the corpse in an advanced state of decomposition on her right, who holds over her head the real crown of beauty and sensuality: an hourglass through which half the sand has already run. The hourglass is the semantic fulcrum of the painting, the focal point at which the splendor and the ruin of the flesh, the force of seduction and the horror of degeneration, converge (fig. 6).[59]

Comparison with this early version highlights the extraordinary eloquence and density of meaning in the artist's late treatment of the same theme, a painting in the Staatsgalerie of Leipzig dated between 1544 and 1545 (fig. 7). In his tireless study of the female body and its metamorphoses, Baldung arrived, about thirty-five years after the Vienna picture, at a much more fully articulated and differentiated version of the life course. The arc of life in the later version, depicted in the two panels of a diptych, divides woman's time into ten ages. The ascending period of seven ages may be found in the Leipzig painting, "The Seven Ages of Woman"; the descending period, illustrating the last three ages, was covered in a painting now lost, of which a late-sixteenth-century copy, "The Three Ages of Woman and Death" or "The March toward Death," is held by the Musée des Beaux Arts of Rennes (fig. 8).[60] The

---

[57]Jean Wirth, *La jeune fille et la mort: Recherches sur les thèmes macabres dans l'art germanique de la Renaissance* (Geneva: Droz, 1979); Gert von der Osten, *Hans Baldung Grien: Gemälde und Dokumente* (Berlin: Deutscher Verlag für Kunstwissenschaft, 1983).

[58]In a history of adolescence Baldung ought to figure among the first artists who recognized the autonomy of this stage of life. I refer to the first standing figure in the painting "The Seven Ages of Woman"; Von der Osten, *Hans Baldung Grien*, no. 89. fig. 6.

[59]Von der Osten, *Hans Baldung Grien,* no. 10; Wirth, *La jeune fille,* 61–63.; Wirag, *Cursus Aetatis,* 21–22.

[60]Von der Osten, *Hans Baldung Grien,* 247–52, 253–54, fig. 89 and Kop. 90. More than forty years ago, Pariset connected the Rennes copy with the Leipzig painting and proposed to read the two in succession as part of a single discourse. F. G. Pariset, "Baldung et la 'Marche à la mort' du musée de Rennes," *La Revue des Arts* 7 (1957): 209–14. I follow Pariset's interpretation in spite of the objections raised by von der Osten, 254–55 to the two paintings as "fragments." Between the paintings in Vienna and Leipzig lie two paintings in the Prado (von der Osten, fig. 87), the interpretation of which is very controversial. Von der

ascending and descending structure of the composition suggests that Baldung had in mind the scheme of the ladder, which circulated from 1540 on in the high German and Rhenish area in the interpretation of Jörg Breu the Younger (fig. 1). On the other hand, the theoretical calendar underlying Baldung's ten-stage interpretation is probably the periodization of life into ten segments of seven years each, outlined by Giovanni Nevizano in the passage cited in the introduction to this essay.[61] But the figurative version diverges substantially from the literary one. With sober professionalism, the artist's eye registers the increasing heaviness of the body, the thickening of the stomach and hips, and the hardening of the features, which transform the slim adolescent, the tender and supple twenty-one-year-old, into the gruff forty-two-year-old (fig. 6) and the resolute forty-nine-year-old, who gathers her hair under her ruff and hides her body under her clothing. In contrast to the traditional view expressed by Nevizano, Baldung's thirty-five-year-old (fig. 7) is fresh and harmonious. Although the frown and heaviness of his forty-two-year-old make her unattractive, she shows no signs of physical decay. His forty-nine-year-old has firm features and an expression of efficiency and trustworthiness.

A woman who compared herself simultaneously with the three-stage calendar in the Vienna picture and the more diversified one in the Leipzig painting would have had before her two radically different prospects for life. For her, Baldung's move from the three-stage to the ten-stage calendar would have represented a conquest of living space and flexibility in planning. In the differentiated periodization of the Leipzig painting, the realm of old age is limited to the trio representing ages fifty-six, sixty-three, and seventy, pitilessly but not contemptuously depicted, whom Death guides and supports in their descent toward the grave (fig. 8). The flexible, diversified ten-age calendar of woman's life adds two constructive phases to the ascending curve, subtracts middle age from the shadow of decay, and gives the woman a maturity not inextricably linked to her reproductive function.

THE THREE AGES OF WOMAN

The iconographic model of the ladder and the periodization of the life course connected with it were promptly accepted in sixteenth-century Italy. Cristofano Bertelli's nine-rung ladder, designed between 1550 and 1560 to illustrate the female life cycle alongside the male life cycle, was a pioneering effort to integrate woman into the figurative lexicon of the ages (fig. 3).[62] Bertelli did not lack supporters and imitators (fig. 4). South of the Alps, however, the brief-stage scheme was less popular than the

---

Osten calls them "The Harmonic Elysium of the Youth" and "The Ages of Life and Death."

[61]See page 43 and n. 9 above.

[62]Joerißen, "Lebenstreppe," 30–32, figs. 4–5; Wirag, *Cursus Aetatis,* 217–18. Bertelli's print was preceded by two analogous interpretations of the theme, designed respectively by Jörg Breu the Younger (Augsburg, 1540) and Cornelis Anthonisz (Amsterdam, c. 1540–50), both including male figures. Joerißen, "Lebenstreppe und Lebensalterspiel," 25–30, figs. 1–2.

Fig. 6. Hans Baldung Grien, "The Three Ages of Life and Death" (1509–11). Courtesy of the Kunstmuseum, Vienna.

Fig. 7. Hans Baldung Grien, "The Seven Ages of Woman" (1544–45). Courtesy of the Staatsgalerie, Leipzig.

Fig. 8. Copy of Hans Baldung Grien, "The Three Ages of Woman and Death."
Courtesy of the Musée des Beaux Arts, Rennes.

long-stage one, which had deep roots in the collective mentality and enjoyed a strong cultural consensus. The Italian cultural horizon, I maintain, was dominated by the triadic pattern of ascent-apex-decline (*augmentum-status-decrementum*), to which Aristotle's authority had given immense longevity. In late medieval and Renaissance society, this scheme conditioned the construction of female biographies.

Except for representations of the Fates,[63] the three-phase calendar of woman's life was rarely cast in visual form. Nonetheless, its existence can be inferred from the statutes generated by Italian cities in the late Middle Ages and the early modern period, especially in sumptuary legislation. Although we have good reason to believe that social prescriptions of age-appropriate behavior coexisted with much more lenient practice,[64] the tripartite calendar formed part of individuals' cognitive maps and, at least as a model, influenced their choices. Through the reinforcement of canon law, which authorized marriage for women beginning at age twelve, the transition from childhood to adulthood for girls was fixed at that age. Sienese legislators, for example, allowed girls under twelve to wear certain garments popular since the 1330s which, on account of their being considered immodest, were prohibited to women in the rest of the population, except for prostitutes and servants, such as *cincte desuper* (dresses belted under their breasts). Childhood established a zone of freedom for the female population which terminated at age twelve.[65] In Genoa, too, childhood ended at the same time; legislation passed in 1449 required twelve-year-olds to put aside certain childish ornaments and subjected them to a different, pre-adult, sumptuary regimen characterized by specific impositions and restrictions.[66] In Venetian statues adulthood was fixed at age twelve for both males and females. A ruling of the Great Council, however, soon confirmed the adulthood of twelve-year-old girls, provided that they were married, but declared that males were not considered adults until they reached twenty-one.[67] In some Italian cities there was a tendency to end childhood before age twelve; in Lucca, a girl's ninth birthday brought certain freedoms in dress to an end.[68]

The generalized social expectation associating twelve-year-old-girls with marriage is reflected in the oldest series of matrimonial trials, those from the end of the

---

[63]Wirag, *Cursus Aetatis*, 22.

[64]Stanley Chojnacki, "Measuring Adulthood: Adolescence and Gender in Renaissance Venice," *Journal of Family History* 17 (1992): 371–95.

[65]Statuto del Donnaio (1343), in *Il mulino delle vanità: Lusso e cerimonie nella Siena medievale*, ed. Maria A. Ceppari Ridolfi and Patrizia Turrini (Siena: Il Lecchio, 1993), 141–209, esp. 172. Sienese women who declared at the beginning of their wills that they were over twelve intended to validate the testaments by declaring themselves adults: Samuel K. Cohn, Jr., *Death and Property in Siena, 1205–1800: Strategies for the Afterlife* (Baltimore: Johns Hopkins University Press, 1988), 131.

[66]Diane Owen Hughes, "Sumptuary Law and Social Relations in Renaissance Italy," in *Disputes and Settlements: Law and Human Relations*, ed. John Bossy (Cambridge: Cambridge University Press, 1983), 93–94.

[67]Chojnacki, "Measuring Adulthood," 373.

[68]Hughes, "Sumptuary Law," 93–94.

fourteenth century to the middle of the sixteenth. A considerable proportion of the requests for annulment presented to Italian episcopal tribunals in that period cited the minority of one of the partners—the bride in the great majority of cases—as the reason for the nullity of the conjugal bond.[69] This, of course, was a legal strategy recommended by the lawyers of parties wishing to dissolve marriages that in some cases had not been consummated, but the preadult age of the brides (nine, ten, and eleven) is frequently established by witnesses' statements and documents.[70] In cases in which the minority of the bride at the time of marriage could not be proven, lawyers' maneuvers suggest that she was not far beyond that age. The recognition that "girls became women much earlier than boys became men"[71] was widespread and scientifically based, for as Giovanni Nevizano, citing Egidius Romanus, states, "nature, little concerned with the female, carries her rapidly toward development."[72]

The effect of canon law extended beyond the Alps as well. In areas of Europe that mainly followed Germanic law, the passage of girls from childhood to the age at which they could be married occurred at age fourteen or fifteen. In some German legislation, however, the influence of Roman law pushed the legal age of marriage back to twelve. Historical or mythical examples of twelve-year-old brides corroborate the paradigmatic significance of this age even in the Germanic area.[73]

Another turning point that emerges from normative literature, this one within the phase of maturity, is the age of twenty-five. Its importance in Roman law, in which age twenty-five signalled the achievement of majority—and if the father had died or emancipated them, the removal of the son or daughter from the *patria potestas*—explains its presence in statutory literature. The Sienese statutes of 1337–39, for instance, put restrictions on an heiress's marriage until she reached twenty-five;[74] the Genoese statutes fixed twenty-five as the age after which a woman could marry

---

[69]Lucia Ferrante, "Il matrimonio disciplinato: Processi matrimoniali a Bologna nel Cinquecento," in *Disciplina dell'anima, disciplina del corpo e disciplina della società nel medioevo ed età moderna*, ed. Paolo Prodi (Bologna: Il Mulino, 1994), 914; Christine Meek, "La donna, la famiglia e la legge nell'epoca di Ilaria del Caretto," in *Ilaria del Caretto e il suo monumento: La donna nell'arte, la cultura e la società del '400*, ed. Stéphane Toussaint (Lucca: Istituto Storico Lucchese, 1995), 140–43. Cases of prepuberty marriages are particularly frequent in the series Matrimonialia of the Archivio Storico Diocesano of Naples; Pierroberto Scaramella, who catalogued the series, counts at least forty in the period 1499–1555.

[70]See, for example, Venice, Archivio Storico del Patriarcato di Venezia, Curia, Sezione antica, Causarum matrimoniorum, 1, fasc. 13, Maddalena di Sicilia and Giorgio Zaccaria (1455); 5, fasc. 14, Antonia filia q. Francisci and Iacopo de Papia (1490); 6, fasc. 2, Cassandra Badoer and Nicolò Venier (1491); 6, fasc. 10, Elisabetta Simoni and Natale da Cattaro (1496); 6, fasc. 15, Maddalena Fontana and Zuane Andrea Fragonà (1497–98).

[71]Chojnacki, "Measuring Adulthood," 373.

[72]Nevizano, *Sylva*, lxxxiiii: "Et cum citius pubescat femina quam masculus ponit.... Egidius De Regimine principum lib. I parte II, dicens quod est quare natura de ea modicum curans cito eam perducit ad augmentum."

[73]Wackernagel, *Die Lebensalter*, 49–50, 59–60, n. 275.

without her father's consent.[75] Jurists' writings provide a significant comment on this norm. Since the twenty-fifth year marks the acme of a woman's life (that is, the moment of maximum brilliance and simultaneously the beginning of decline), the father who "allows his daughter to pass twenty-five without having given her a husband" is derelict in his paternal duty; therefore the daughter, in addition to having the right to marry without his knowledge, can force him to assign her an appropriate dowry.[76] The Florentine jurist Francesco da Barberino assigns a symbolic as well as a juridical significance to the twenty-fifth birthday. In his *Documenti d'amore* (1315), this expert on women's problems assembles a parade of virtues, each allegorically represented by a female figure. "Glory" takes the form of a "most beautiful" woman with shining eyes, dressed in gold, who gathers flowers in a lush meadow; she enjoys the song of sweet little birds and the presence of meek animals who bring their young to her. To this vision, the highest form of earthly blessedness that the fourteenth-century imagination could conceive, Francesco da Barberino assigns "the perfect age of twenty-five." The God of Love, who guides the author's composition of the work and his design of the virtues' features, teaches him that "glory" must be twenty-five, for this age marks the summit of woman's life.[77]

Canon law, sumptuary legislation, and Germanic law agree in identifying the age of forty as the last decisive turning point in woman's life. Age forty was considered the tomb of female attractiveness and all its seductive powers. The *lex Visigothorum* reduced the *wergeld* for woman above forty.[78] A beguine who wished to take part in ecclesiastical organization and discipline had to be at least forty, and no nun could assume the role of abbess before she had reached the same age.[79] Underlying these regulations was the certainty that turning forty constituted an infallible antidote against the snares and disorders arising from a woman's presence. Bolognese sumptuary legislation incorporated into the statues of 1389 restricted the privilege of framing the face with a purely decorative cap, detached from the mantle (*ad gotas sine gabano*), to women forty and older and allowed the same age group to wear clothing lined with precious fur, otherwise reserved to the wives and daughters of

---

[74]Siena, Archivio di Stato, Statuto del comune di Siena (1341), 1, 121v. On the complex relationship between age, emancipation, and full legal capacity in fifteenth-century Florence, see Thomas Kuehn, *Emancipation in Late Medieval Florence* (New Brunswick, N.J.: Rutgers University Press, 1982).

[75]*Criminalium iurium civitatis Genuensis libri duo* (Genoa: Cristoforo Bellone, 1573), lib. II, 35–36, cited by Daniela Lombardi, "Fidanzamenti e matrimoni dal Concilio di Trento alle riforme settecentesche," in *Storia del matrimonio*, ed. Michela De Giorgio and Christiane Klapisch-Zuber (Rome: Laterza, 1996), 217, 236.

[76]Nevizano, *Sylva*, xxxix.

[77]Francesco da Barberino, *I documenti d'Amore*, ed. Francesco Egidi, 4 vols. (Rome: Presso la Società, 1905–27), 3: 253–58. In his note to the verse "Età di XXV anni aperfecta [ha perfecta]," Francesco remarks, "Ex hoc nota quod Amor, qui voluit hic pingi spetiosissimam mulierem, forte dixit in etate XXV annorum eligibiliorem esse."

[78]Barberino, *I documenti d'Amore*, 57, 65.

[79]Barberino, *I documenti d'Amore*, 65.

knights, physicians, and jurists.[80] These regulations may have stemmed from legislative cunning based on an assessment of collective psychology: the calculation that any woman would eschew clothing that, by marking her as having passed the fatal age of forty, excluded her from the sphere of social relations linked with her sexual identity. In Lombardy, an analogous calendar inspired the requirements that female domestic servants of parish priests and other ecclesiastics be over forty years of age.[81] Among the post-Tridentine rules enforcing strict cloistering of nuns, one prohibited nuns below age forty to linger near the door between the convent (a cloistered area) and the church (a public area); another required all nuns under forty to obtain a license from their superiors for going to the grate in the visiting room to talk with family members and others from the outside world.[82]

Bringing together sources far apart in time and space demonstrates the extraordinary tenacity of certain benchmarks of age and the durable tendency to assign a symbolic value to certain ages. Such long-lasting consensus on twelve and forty as watersheds and the resulting division into three ages suggest a codification of what experience showed: a curve based on reproductive function, with a phase of immaturity (childhood), maturity peaking at age twenty-five and ending at forty, and then extinction (old age). The way in which statutory and moralistic sources of the late Middle Ages altered the physiological calendar created a dramatic discrepancy between the rhythms of male and female life. Given a life expectancy of seventy, according to the most optimistic predictions, a woman in her last thirty-five years went into an inevitable and increasingly dramatic decline. A man with the same life expectancy reached his peak at fifty, thus enjoying more than twice as much time to achieve his goals and spending a considerably shorter period (twenty years) shuffling toward the grave.

We might assume that the three ages of woman defined in this way were a faithful reflection of the three faces of woman's sexual identity. Doing so would amount to jumping too hastily to an inaccurate conclusion. Closer examination reveals that the physiological calendar formed only a frame of reference for a sociocultural calendar that introduced substantial modifications of an anticipatory variety, especially as

---

[80]Maria Giuseppina Muzzarelli, "La disciplina delle apparenze: Vesti e ornamenti nella legislazione suntuaria bolognese fra XIII e XV secolo," in *Disciplina dell'anima*, ed. Prodi, 770.

[81]The Lombard provincial synods convoked by Carlo Borromeo to implement the Tridentine canons prohibited all clerics from keeping women, including mothers or sisters, in their homes without express and frequently monitored license from the archbishop. *Acta Ecclesiae Mediolanensis a Carlo Cardinali s. Praxedis Archiepiscopo condita* (Milan: Officina Typographica quon. Pacifici Pontij, 1599), 19, 413–14, 807. Subsequently, this norm shifted to the practice of reserving domestic service to the clergy to women over forty. Alessandro Manzoni, *I promessi sposi*, chap. 1, in *Opere*, ed. Riccardo Bacchelli (Milan: Ricciardi, 1953), 411.

[82]Gaetano Greco, "Monasteri femminili e patriziato a Pisa (1530–1630)," in *Città italiane del '500 tra Riforma e Controriforma*, Atti del Convegno Internazionale di Studi, Lucca, 13–15 ottobre 1983 (Lucca: Maria Pacini Fazzi, 1988), 321.

regards age twelve. The way in which statutory and moralistic sources of the late Middle Ages and early Renaissance altered the physiological calendar created a dramatic discrepancy between the rhythms of male and female life.

Putting girls on the marriage market at age twelve provides the clearest evidence of such anticipation. Although the age at which Florentine and Venetian girls in the fifteenth and early sixteenth century reached menarche can be verified only in a few cases, we can assume as a rough norm the median age of menarche in eighteenth-century France established by Edward Shorter: fifteen years, nine months in the period 1750–99.[83] Documents about adolescents in the Tucher family of Augsburg in the second half of the fifteenth century also suggest fifteen or sixteen as the age of menarche for girls in the patriciate, privileged in terms of diet and activities.[84] The sixteen-year-old Eleonora Gonzaga, eldest daughter of the marquis of Mantua, had not yet reached puberty when her parents arranged the consummation of her marriage, contracted more than four years earlier, with nineteen-year-old Francesco Maria della Rovere, duke of Urbino, on Christmas Day 1509.[85] Two Venetian women who in their wills of 1461 and 1474 identified age sixteen as the threshold of adulthood for their daughters—thus adopting the age at which Venetian statutes considered them emancipated—were perhaps indicating their expectation of when girls would reach menarche.[86] In late medieval and early Renaissance Italy, evidently, consummating marriage with a prepubescent bride was not unusual, and consummation with brides who had just reached menarche was common. To use Arnold van Gennep's terminology, in this period social puberty came considerably earlier than physiological puberty.[87]

Canon law had provided a corrective to this anticipatory tendency, suggesting that the consummation of marriage contracted before puberty should be postponed until the prepubescent spouse, almost always the bride, had reached menarche.[88] The canonical indication was exposed to the danger of being flouted by eager

[83]Jean-Noël Biraben, "L'évolution récente du temps biologique dans les sociétés industrielles," in *Âges de la vie,* VIIe Colloque National de Demographie, Travaux et Documents, Cahiers, no. 96 (Paris: Presses Universitaires de France, 1982), 3–10, esp. 8; but see also Merry E. Wiesner, *Women and Gender in Early Modern Europe* (Cambridge: Cambridge University Press, 1993), 44.

[84]Wunder, "*Er ist die Sonn',* 44.

[85]Alessandro Luzio and Rodolfo Renier, *Mantova e Urbino: Isabella d'Este ed Elisabetta Gonzaga nelle relazioni famigliari e nelle vicende politiche* (Turin: L. Roux, 1893; reprint, Bologna: Arnaldo Forni, 1976), 157, 186–87, 194–95. (The message awaited from Rome was evidently the papal dispensation that would authorize the consummation of the marriage of the prepubescent bride.)

[86]Chojnacki, "Measuring Adulthood," 371–72.

[87]Chojnacki, "Measuring Adulthood," 373. On the age at which Venetian girls were considered emancipated, see Anna Bellavitis, "La famiglia 'cittadina' veneziana nel XVI secolo: Dote e successione: Le leggi e le fonti," unpublished paper delivered at the Convegno Internazionale Mutamenti della famiglia nei paesi occidentali, Bologna, 6–8 October 1994.

grooms, confident about what they considered a sacrosanct right sealed by family rites and ecclesiastical ceremonies.[88] Great families found ways around this obstacle, one of those papal dispensations which the Apostolic Penitentiary rarely denied to those able to pay.[90] Hence the gap between social and physiological age exposed child brides to physical and psychological trials, about which not all their contemporaries were insensitive.[91]

Was the threshold of forty anticipated as well? We can hypothesize that here, too, there was a divergence between woman's social and psychological age. The gravity of sociocultural sanctions against violation of age norms and corresponding behavioral deviations by elderly women,[92] however, probably contributed to suppressing testimonies of that divergence.[93] Yet the contrast between social and psychological age emerges clearly in some documents.[94] When the marriage between a mature widow and a considerably younger man became troubled and came before the episcopal court, the conflict between spouses might well be framed as a dispute about age roles. The wife regulated her affective expectations and behavior in terms of a strong but socially transgressive perception of her psychological age; the husband, in contrast, expected his wife's conjugal behavior to conform to her social age, which put her in the category of the elderly.[95]

That age norms and corresponding behavioral parameters were social conventions relatively independent of the physiological—and in some cases, psychological—age of the women to whom they were applied was a fact of which contemporary observers were not unaware. The most systematic late medieval codifier of female

[88]Nevizano, *Sylva*, lxxxiiii. See in this regard Adhémar A. Esmein, *Le mariage en droit canonique* (Paris: Larose & Forcel, 1891), 1: 211–16.

[89]Ferrante, "Il matrimonio disciplinato," 914; Luzio and Renier, *Mantova e Urbino*, 194 (report by Alessandro Picenardi to Marchioness Isabella d'Este on the consummation of the marriage between her daughter Eleonora and Francesco Maria della Rovere).

[90]P. Ghinzoni, "Usi e costumi nuziali principeschi, Gerolamo Riario e Caterina Sforza (1473)," *Archivio storico lombardo* 15 (1888): 101–11; Luzio and Renier, 194.

[91]Luzio and Renier, *Mantova e Urbino*, 194–95 (reference to the consummation of Isabella d'Este's marriage to the marquis of Mantua). See also below.

[92]Minois, *History of Old Age:*, 273–75.

[93]To control the sexual behavior of mature women, some of whom enjoyed ample financial autonomy, Mediterranean culture had posed serious disincentives. The opinion that witches were lusty elderly women who, lacking spouses, had given themselves to the devil was widespread; thus the concept of age-inappropriate sexuality connected witchcraft with old age. Nevizano, *Sylva*, xxxvr. The sin of fornication was considered minor if committed *cum iuvene pulchra*; committed *cum vetula*, it was turpitude. Nevizano, *Sylva*, lxxiv.

[94]See Archivio Storico del Patriarcato di Venezia, Curia, Causarum Matrimoniorum, 1, fasc. 14, Clara Matafar and Michele Giustinian (1455).

[95]I refer to the case of Caterina Marescotti and Giovanni Sansedoni (Siena, 1629), which Oscar Di Simplicio edits and discusses: "'Un matrimonio reputato assai dispari e stralampato': Caterina Marescotti contro Giandomenico Sansedoni (Siena, 1629)," in *Coniugi nemici: La separazione in Italia dal XII al XVIII secolo*, ed. Silvana Seidel Menchi and Diego Quaglioni (Bologna,: Il Mulino, 2000), 453-88.

behavior, the jurist Francesco da Barberino, was very well aware of it. When he decided to write his book on female conduct, *Reggimento e costumi di donna* (1314), Francesco confronted the problem of structuring the treatise; would it be better to organize the discussion according to ages of life or social groups? Considering age too variable a factor, he discarded the first alternative, "for if one thinks about it carefully, some [girls become] women early and others late," and organized his work by class. The social pyramid offered him a secure frame of reference.[96] The life courses he designed for girls differ according to the social groups to which they belong. While Francesco gave no precise indications about years, believing that the criterion for age at marriage is "not the time but...the person,"[97] he sprinkled his discourse with revealing allusions to the social expectations he observed around him. In the higher social strata (kings, princes, feudal lords), with which he opened his discussion, entry into the marriageable age bracket occurs between the ages of nine and twelve. In this phase, elite girls must be removed from all contacts not directly under their mothers' control, shut in the house, and subjected to rigorous discipline of their behavior: going out rarely, looking neither left nor right while walking down the street, greeting no one, not standing at the window.[98] As one descends the social scale, the age of marriage rises and the rules of behavior become less strict. For the daughters of knights, judges, and physicians, marriageable age is between twelve and fifteen.[99] On the age of marriage appropriate for peasants' and artisans' daughters, Francesco refrained from making any quantitatively precise recommendation, but he suggested that they should not be put on the marriage market "as early" as their socially more fortunate contemporaries. As for behavior, the rigid author allowed them to dance, go walking around the city, and attend parties.[100] The social age of young girls, then, is a combination of two factors: social standing and biological age.

The periodization of woman's life according to the triadic calendar may be considered as both effect and cause of a social practice widely diffused in the Mediterranean area: early marriage for women. In the case of Florence, this practice has been thoroughly documented in the classic studies of David Herlihy and Christiane

[96]Francesco da Barberino, *Reggimento e costumi di donna,* ed. Giuseppe E. Sansone (Turin: Loescher, 1957), 8: "E questo libro già non partirò per numero d'etadi, ché, se dirittamente voglian considerar, è tal per tempo e tal tardi donna; e non sicondo etadi, ma sicondo suo grado conviene ognuna con senno passare."

[97]Barberino, *Reggimento e costumi,* 29.

[98]On the determination of the age of marriage, see Barberino, *Reggimento e costumi,* 20–22. (the story of Corrado di Savoia and Gioietta), 38, 60. On behavior, see Barberino, *Reggimento e costumi,* 24–29.

[99]Barberino, *Reggimento e costumi,* 16, 29–35. The indication of age comes from Barberino, *Reggimento e costumi,* 54–55 (the story of Oddo, a Norman knight, and his daughters Margarita and Joanna).

[100]On their behavior, see Barberino, *Reggimento e costumi,* 35: "Le voglio ricordare che lo suo tempo detto da marito ... non si conviene a lei così per tempo darlo a dimostrare." On behavior, see Barberino, *Reggimento e costumi,* 20, 35–36.

Klapisch-Zuber on Tuscan families,[101] Julius Kirshner and Anthony Molho on the Monte delle Doti, and Molho on marriage.[102] Venetian society presents a similar picture. Stanley Chojnacki has found thirty-four patrician wills in which parents specified the age they considered appropriate for their daughters' marriage. Exactly half of these (seventeen) preferred ages between fourteen and sixteen.[103] Early marriage—that is, the clearest expression of the determination by anticipation that marks woman's life course—appears in these studies to have been a structure fundamental to Italian society of the fifteenth and early sixteenth centuries. Since not only a high dowry[104] but also a young age[105] had a favorable influence on girls' marriage prospects, Venetian and Florentine fathers entered a frantic race with time to settle their daughters.[106] The tyranny of time was severe enough to induce Florentine fathers to consciously and systematically falsify public documents. By postdating their daughters' birth in communal registers, the fathers assured them at the time of marriage not only a dowry that had matured while on deposit in the Monte delle Doti but also a few more years of verdant youth.[107]

THE HOURGLASS

Of all the questions raised in this essay, woman's perception of the ages of life is certainly the most obscure. Was the cultural consensus on the three-stage map, which ensured its persistence, also and especially a female consensus? The rare testimonies I collected suggest that the female population internalized the three-stage calendar sketched in the preceding section and identified themselves with the age roles it prescribed, on the basis of which they constructed and evaluated their own lives.

Chief among the pieces of evidence supporting this hypothesis is the testimony of Alessandra Macinghi Strozzi, the best-known Florentine female writer of the fifteenth century. In a famous passage in her correspondence, Alessandra explained the urgency with which she was attempting to find her daughter Caterina a husband: "she is sixteen, and there must be no further delay in marrying her" (1447). Later, she chose as bride for her thirty-nine-year-old son Filippo a girl who had not yet turned

---

[101]David Herlihy and Christiane Klapisch-Zuber, *Les Toscans et leurs familles: Une étude du cataste florentin de 1427* (Paris: Presse de la Fondation nationale des sciences politiques, 1978).
[102]Julius Kirshner and Anthony Molho, "The Dowry Fund and the Marriage Market in Early Quattrocento Florence," *Journal of Modern History* 50 (1978): 403–38; idem, "Il Monte delle Doti a Firenze dalla sua fondazione nel 1425 alla metà del sedicesimo secolo: Abbozzo di una ricerca," *Ricerche storiche* 10 (1980): 21–47; Anthony Molho, *Marriage Alliance in Late Medieval Florence* (Cambridge: Harvard University Press, 1994).
[103]Chojnacki, "Measuring Adulthood," 373.
[104]Kirshner and Molho, "Il Monte delle doti," 38–40 and table 7.
[105]Anthony Molho, "Deception and Marriage Strategy in Renaissance Florence: The Case of Women's Ages," *Renaissance Quarterly* 41 (1988): 211.
[106]Chojnacki, "Measuring Adulthood," 373.
[107]Molho, "Deception and Marriage Strategy," 194.

fifteen, preferring her to sixteen- and eighteen-year old prospects (1466).[108] In 1448, when she was forty-two, she considered herself old and turned to meditation on her imminent death.[109] A few years later, in 1453, her contemporary Lena Tanagli, also a widow, requested repayment of a loan her late husband had made to the commune with the persuasive argument that the money constituted the dowry of her daughter, who at thirteen was "already close to marriageable age."[110] These Florentine voices are echoed by those of the Venetian patrician women whose wills Stanley Chojnacki has analyzed. Petronella Falier Morosini excluded her husband from the administration of her considerable property unless he found a husband for their daughter before her fifteenth birthday (1464), and Orsa Soranzo da Canal tied the payment of legacies to her daughters to their marrying before they reached seventeen.[111]

The hypothesis that women internalized the three-stage calendar, marked by watersheds at ages twelve and forty, is supported by literary sources. Although this type of source transmits women's voices only in indirect form, its use in this context is not improper. Both tellers of tales like Giovanni Boccaccio (1313–75) and Giovanni Sercambi (1348–1424) and authors of treatises like Francesco da Barberino wrote about women for women. Their narratives are nourished by experience of life, and members of their female public must have been able to recognize themselves in the evaluations, judgments, and choices which the writers attributed to their heroines. It is not irrelevant for our purposes, therefore, that the female protagonists of Boccaccio's *Decameron* are prepared to begin married life or sexual activity at fourteen or fifteen, some even at thirteen or twelve.[112] The adolescent girl whose father has not made arrangements to marry her becomes impatient, feels that her natural right has been withheld, and sets out by herself to find a male companion.[113] The age for extramarital affairs is between eighteen and twenty-eight; the oldest adulteresses in the *Decameron* whose ages are given are twenty-eight and thirty, but they are relatively rare birds in Boccaccio's gallery of women in love, and both are of the lower class.[114] Sercambi's *Novelle* presents a similar picture; his female protagonists marry or are sexually initiated between ages thirteen and fifteen, in one case at sixteen.[115] Just one tale presents a bride of twenty-five, who marries a *lavoratore* (peasant) described as

---

[108]Alessandra Macinghi Strozzi, *Lettere di una gentildonna fiorentina del secolo XV ai figliuoli esuli*, ed. Cesare Guasti (Florence: G. C. Sansoni, 1877); cited here in the reprint *Tempo di affetti, tempo di mercanti: Lettere ai figli esuli* (Milan: Garzanti, 1987), 62 (24 August 1447), 263 (2 November 1465), 267 (15 November 1465), 307 (7 February 1466); English edition, *Selected Letters of Alessandra Strozzi*, ed. and trans. Heather Gregory (Berkeley: University of California Press, 1997), 29–37, 169–82.

[109]Strozzi, *Tempo di affetti*, 66, 69.

[110]Molho, "Deception and Marriage Strategy," 205–6.

[111]Chojnacki, "Measuring Adulthood," 373.

[112]Giovanni Boccaccio, *Decameron*, II.6, III.10, IV.3, V.5, IX.6, X.8.

[113]Boccaccio, *Decameron*, IV.1.

[114]Boccaccio, *Decameron*, III.4.

[115]Giovanni Sercambi, *Novelle*, V, VI, LV, LX, LXII, LXXXVI, CII, CXL, CXLI.

"old."[116] Women who embark on extramarital adventures range between twenty-two and twenty-eight, with one exception at the advanced age of thirty-six.[117]

But the writers cast their eyes far beyond these data about age. They take their readers step by step to the threshold of a realm that often remains impenetrable to historians' gaze: the sphere of women's perception and evaluation of time. Through the occasional crannies in the wall of the sources opened by writers of stories and prescriptive works, we can glimpse a troubled dimension of lived experience. The social calendar based on anticipation which undergirded woman's life had the effect of increasing the distance between youth and old age by eliminating the periods of transition. Women were trained to situate themselves in a time which, in comparison to male time, was as closed and oppressive as a bad dream. "Men … are born able to do many things … and most of them are worth much more old than young; but women are born for nothing other than to make love and babies, and they are cherished only for this." The contrast between light and darkness to which the three-stage calendar reduced life allowed no room for chiaroscuro. For women, it was anguishingly necessary to "not wast[e] time … in her youth, because no sorrow is equal to that … of having lost time." This revelatory statement, which Boccaccio puts in the mouth of an old woman, equates woman's time with her youth; old age is non-time. "Women … have a much greater need to use time when they have it than men, because … when we get old, neither husband nor anyone else wants to see us; instead, they chase us into the kitchen to tell fairy tales to the cat and count the pots and pans." Given that "each one has as much of this world as he takes," recognition of the need to seize the day is tinged with anguish: "When I get old, I'll blame myself for having wasted my youth." The non-time of old age is seen not as an anticipation of death but as a fate worse than death: "And what the devil can we do, now that we're old, besides looking at the ashes in the fireplace?"[118] "God, don't let me survive into old age!" the prayer that Francesco da Barberino puts into the mouth of the girl Lisea of Genoa,[119] penetrates to the heart of the problem.

The crude contrast between youth and old age conferred a pressing urgency on the imperative of early marriage. Francesco da Barberino chronicled a domestic conflict on this issue which breaks out between an affectionate father and his firstborn daughter. When the father decides to leave it to chance, drawing lots, which of his two daughters, aged fifteen and thirteen, will marry first, the elder and more beautiful insists on her right of precedence.[120] The disastrous outcome of the marriage that the stubborn fifteen-year-old makes her father arrange for her is clearly intended to teach

---

[116]Sercambi, *Novelle*, CXI.

[117]Sercambi, *Novelle*, XXXII, XXXVI, LXXVI, LXXVII, XCIV, CLII (the thirty-six-year-old).

[118]All these quotations come from Boccaccio, *Decameron*, V.10. Similar ideas are expressed in Boccaccio, *Decameron*, III.5, and in Sercambi, *Novelle*, CXVIIII (the opening sonnet).

[119]Francesco da Barberino, *Reggimento*, 234.

[120]Barberino, *Reggimento*, 59.

adolescent female readers, and perhaps their mothers, not to push impatiently for marriage negotiations or plans, for which the males in the family are responsible. Francesco's celebration of "Madam Patience," patron and inspirer of the girl who has "passed the age of marriage" and arrived single at the frightening age of twenty, shows us that the female interference of which he was fearful was precisely the precipitation of very young girls into marriage.[121] The pressure that women themselves, whether as mothers or as candidates for marriage, exerted on the men of the family for the early opening and prompt conclusion of marriage negotiations should perhaps be added to those already adduced by historians to explain early marriage in late medieval and early Renaissance Italy.[122]

Despite the consensus on, and often the fervent endorsement of, the three-stage calendar I described, a few dissenting voices are worth listening to in conclusion. The Venetian Silvestro di Marco Morosini certainly did not favor early marriage; his will of 1432 stipulated that his daughters should not take husbands before they turned sixteen and guaranteed them an increment to their dowries of 250 ducats for every additional year they remained single.[123] Four decades later, in 1471, one Martino *veneziano* hesitated to accept the advantageous proposal of marriage to his daughter Angela, then fifteen, made by Enrico Bruno (Braun?) *teutonico*. Referring to the young woman as "a little girl and only daughter," he suggested that the wedding be put off for three years, thus indicating that he was swimming against the tide.[124]

The widowed noblewoman Gabriella Gonzaga Folgiani also opposed early marriage. In 1472, when the duke of Milan, Francesco Sforza, her brother-in-law, arranged the marriage of her daughter, Costanza, to Girolamo Riario, illegitimate son of the pope, she objected to the consummation of the marriage on the ground that the girl, "only 11, was not the proper age." She proposed to the mature spouse a pro forma substitute, putting the child in bed with him in her own presence without proceeding to actual consummation, which would have to be put off until the "proper age." Her resistance angered Duke Francesco, who found a way of taking revenge on a woman who in his opinion was somewhat "strange and savage." Anxious to secure his alliance with the pope, the duke immediately found Girolamo Riario another bride. The girl he wed and with whom, armed with a papal dispensation, he triumphantly consummated the marriage, was nine years old.[125]

---

[121]Barberino, *Reggimento*, 37–42. For the indication that twenty was an age of anguish for an unmarried girl, see Barberino, *Reggimento*, 40–42 (the story of Felice).

[122]Chojnacki, "Measuring Adulthood," 374 (referring to interpretations of the phenomenon by Herlihy and Klapisch-Zuber, and Kirshner and Molho).

[123]Stanley Chojnacki, "Dowries and Kinsmen in Early Renaissance Venice," *Journal of Interdisciplinary History* 5 (1975): 584–85, n. 30.

[124]Venice, Archivio Storico del Patriarcato di Venezia, Curia, Sezione antica, Causarum matrimoniorum, 3, fasc. 5, Angela Martini vs. Enrico Bruno *teutonico*.

[125]Ghinzoni, "Usi e costumi".

It seems likely that the "proper age" for the consummation of marriage, on which Gabriella Gonzaga insisted, was the age of puberty. The close connection established in the collective mentality between puberty and the consummation of marriage is attested by a Venetian document of the mid–fifteenth century. The young girl Giovanna di Giovanni, who came before the patriarch's vicar on 2 June 1452, believed that she was "close to puberty"; therefore she asked the vicar to record the fact that the promise of marriage she had made more than a year before to one Pietro Salmon had been extorted from her against her own will by her mother, and "in no way" did she want that man for her husband.[126] Understood in that way, the concept of "the proper age" explains why a variable period of time, sometimes more than a year, often passed between the signing of the marriage contract and consummation: the groom was waiting until his prepubescent bride reached menarche.[127] In a matrimonial trial from Vicenza of 1544, this necessity is explicitly stated. A Vicentine mother corroborated in the episcopal court the request for annulment of the marriage of her daughter, then thirteen, maintaining that "the girl was not of marriageable age because" when the wedding took place "she wasn't getting her period [*il suo male*], and it hasn't come yet."[128] This form of argument, however, seldom appears in matrimonial trials. The very young wives who asked the episcopal court to annul a marriage contracted before they had reached the canonical age put more emphasis on the force and violence by which their parents had extracted their consent than on their own physical and psychic immaturity at the time the contract was agreed to.[129] What appear to be courageous denunciations by adolescents who had been locked up and beaten were actually fabrications by the parents, who after having arranged a precocious marriage, changed their minds and went to court. Significantly, the father or mother who wanted to obtain the annulment of a child's marriage (or more accurately, the legal representative who suggested the legal strategy most likely to elicit the desired sentence) insisted in the case of a fourteen-year-old boy on the childish thoughtlessness, irresponsibility, and immaturity of the groom.[130] In the case of a twelve-year-old girl, it seemed more productive to employ the argument of force and violence. Thus, in a culture which deprived young girls of premarital adolescence, even childhood was eroded.

As I hope to have demonstrated, the expropriation of female time carried out by theorists of age schemes in late medieval and Renaissance Italy preempted and thereby annulled any possibility of young women's planning for the future: when

---

[126]Venice, Archivio Storico del Patriarcato, Sezione antica, *Actorum mandatorum praeceptorum*, 14, *ad datum*; see also Wunder, "*Er ist die Sonn'*, 44.

[127]Wunder, "*Er ist die Sonn'*, 44.

[128]Vicenza, Archivio della Curia Vescovile, b. 20/020, Caterina Dalla Gatta and Francesco Pavano (1544).

[129]Meek, "La donna," 140–43.

[130]Vicenza, Archivio della Curia Vescovile, b. 18/018 and b. 28/02, Iseppo Schebino and Caterina Piazoni di Castelgomberto (1556–57).

they were still children, their life course was already predetermined. Serving as a model even for those who did not fulfill it, the topos of the child bride was one of the social constants that contributed to the establishment and permanence of female passivity and dependence on males. My thesis remains to be tested in the following period of Italian history, the seventeenth through the nineteenth century.[131] The Italian, or Mediterranean, model outlined here must also be compared with those prevailing in other premodern societies, particularly those of central and northern Europe, in which patterns of women's lives were configured differently and the early arrival at each stage seems not to have been posited so rigidly.[132]

---

[131]One step in this direction is a recent study by Maria Fubini Leuzzi, *"Condurre a onore": Famiglia, matrimonio e assistenza dotale a Firenze in età moderna* (Florence: Leo S. Olschki, 1999).

[132]See Stahlman, Arnold, and Bastl, "Lebensalter," n. 5 above.

PART 2

Getting Back the Dowry
Venice, c. 1360–1530

Stanley Chojnacki

No subject has been as fruitful for studying the condition of elite women in late medieval and Renaissance Italy as the dowry.[1] Dowries have provided a gauge for assessing women's share of private wealth, their relations with their families of birth and marriage, the determination of their adult vocations, and their status vis-à-vis legal institutions, public authority, and prevailing cultural principles. Scholarship on Florence has been especially productive in exploring the dowry system's effects on the family orientation and economic resources of married women, though it has produced a mixed verdict. One influential tendency in that scholarship, led by Christiane Klapisch-Zuber and Isabelle Chabot, has been to view the dowry regime as inflicting economic and social distress upon women. In this body of writing, private and official spheres appear as collaborators in fashioning dowry practices that were detrimental to wives. Patrilineal imperatives led the families that sent their daughters into marriage to treat the dowry as a way of honoring the inheritance rights of daughters in appearance, but denying them in substance; family needs led men to make instrumental use of women to advance the interests of the patriline, and to deprive them of a secure membership in either natal or marital family. Simultaneously, Florence's government enacted statutes that severely limited women's rights to enjoy or dispose of their dowries.[2] Another body of scholarship, to which Giulia Calvi and Thomas Kuehn have contributed prominently, reaches a more nuanced conclusion, emphasizing adaptations in practice which attenuated or undermined

---

[1]See introduction to *Gender and Society in Renaissance Italy*, ed. Judith C. Brown and Robert C. Davis (London: Longman, 1998), 1–15.

[2]Christiane Klapisch-Zuber, "The 'Cruel Mother': Maternity, Widowhood, and Dowry in Florence in the Fourteenth and Fifteenth Centuries" and "The Griselda Complex: Dowry and Marriage Gifts in the Quattrocento," in Christiane Klapisch-Zuber, *Women, Family, and Ritual in Renaissance Italy*, trans. Lydia G. Cochrane (Chicago: University of Chicago Press, 1985), 117–31, 213–46; Isabelle Chabot, "'La sposa in nero': La ritualizzazione del lutto delle vedove fiorentine (secoli XIV–XV)," *Quaderni storici* 86 (1994): 421–62; idem, "Widowhood and Poverty in Late Medieval Florence," *Continuity and Change* 3

outright the patriarchal structure of the dowry regime. To proponents of this interpretation, women appear not merely as instruments of patriarchal policy, but also as
objects of concern on the part of their families, freely disposing of their property,
administering their deceased husbands' estates, exercising guardianship over their
children, and retaining enduring ties to their families of birth and marriage.[3]

In an effort to broaden the perspective on Italian women during this period,
and to provide a larger context for the Florentine case, I want to discuss the relationship of upper-class Venetian women to their dowries, especially the ways in which
dowries connected women with their families of birth and marriage, with the wealth
of those families, and with the institutional environment of gender relations in Venice. Exploring that relationship reveals a more unambiguously positive picture than
the Florentine one. From the beginning to the end of marriage and beyond, the
Venetian dowry regime gave women a broad and long-lived set of relationships and
economic influence within them. Isabelle Chabot has shown how the relationships
mobilized in a marriage lasted for its entire duration, and the final disposition of the
property whose transfer marked its beginning—the dowry and its satellite elements—mapped the kinship terrain around a marriage at its end.[4] The location of a
wife or widow on that terrain was tied to her continued stake in her dowry. In Venice

---

(1988): 291–311. See also Anthony Molho, *Marriage Alliance in Late Medieval Florence* (Cambridge,
Mass.: Harvard University Press, 1994); idem, "Deception and Marriage Strategy in Renaissance Flor-
ence: The Case of Women's Ages," *Renaissance Quarterly* 41 (1988): 193–217; Julius Kirshner, "Pursuing
Honor While Avoiding Sin: The Monte delle Doti of Florence," *Quaderni di Studi senesi* 41 (Milan: Giuffrè, 1978). On statutes restricting women's rights, see Julius Kirshner, "Materials for a Gilded Cage: Non-
Dotal Assets in Florence, 1300–1500," in *The Family in Italy from Antiquity to the Present*, ed. David I.
Kertzer and Richard P. Saller (New Haven: Yale University Press, 1991), 184–207; idem, "Maritus Lucretur Dotem Uxoris Sue Premortue in Late Medieval Florence," *Zeitschrift der Savigny-Stiftung für Rechtsgeschichte, Kanonistische Abteilung* 77 (1991): 111–55.

[3]Giulia Calvi, "Diritti e legami: Madri, figli, stato in Toscana (XVI–XVIII secolo)," *Quaderni storici*
86 (1994): 487–510; eadem, "Reconstructing the Family: Widowhood and Remarriage in Tuscany in the
Early Modern Period," in *Marriage in Italy, 1300–1650*, ed. Trevor Dean and K. J. P. Lowe (Cambridge:
Cambridge University Press, 1998), 275–96; Thomas Kuehn, "Some Ambiguities of Female Inheritance
Ideology in the Renaissance," in Thomas Kuehn, *Law, Family, and Women: Toward a Legal Anthropology of
Renaissance Italy* (Chicago: University of Chicago Press, 1991), 238–57; idem, "Understanding Gender
Inequality in Renaissance Florence: Personhood and Gifts of Maternal Inheritance by Women," *Journal of
Women's History* 8 (1996): 58–80. See also Anthony Molho et al., "Genealogia e parentado: Memorie del
potere nella Firenze tardo medievale: Il caso di Giovanni Rucellai," *Quaderni storici* 86 (1994): 365–403;
Susannah Foster Baxendale, "Exile in Practice: The Alberti Family in and out of Florence," *Renaissance
Quarterly* 44 (1991): 720–56, esp. 740–45; Elaine G. Rosenthal, "The Position of Women in Renaissance
Florence: Neither Autonomy nor Subjection," in *Florence and Italy: Renaissance Studies in Honour of Nico-
lai Rubinstein*, ed. Peter Denley and Caroline Elam (London: Westfield College, 1988), 369–81: Ann
Morton Crabb, "How Typical Was Alessandra Macinghi Strozzi of Fifteenth-Century Florentine Wid-
ows?" in *Upon My Husband's Death: Widows in the Literatures and Histories of Medieval Europe*, ed. Louis
Mirrer (Ann Arbor: University of Michigan Press, 1992), 47–68; Heather Gregory, "Daughters, Dowries,
and the Family in Fifteenth-Century Florence," *Rinascimento*, 2nd ser., 27 (1987): 215–37.

[4]Chabot, "Sposa in nero."

it was women, either acting personally as widows or designating agents to act for them, who managed the outcome of a marriage already ended or whose end was anticipated. In this they were supported by two powerful patriarchal structures, their families and government institutions.

Our route into the subject is through the end of marriage. Much of the writing on dowries has been concentrated on the efforts of families to provide dowries or of governments to regulate or facilitate the giving of dowries.[5] But the purposes of families in providing dowries and the attitudes of the young brides whom they accompanied had little bearing on the interests of widows or their heirs over the course of the ensuing years and decades. Marriage was a long and evolving experience, and the women who passed through the uxorial cycle from young bride to mature wife and mother to widow inevitably formed and reformed many times over the meaningful attachments and loyalties in their lives. Their relationship to their dowries underwent similar evolutions, especially as, with age, they contemplated the end of their marriage. To have a fuller sense of the social and economic meaning of wifehood, it is therefore useful to balance discussions of the beginnings of wifehood with consideration of how it ended, who got the dowries, how they got them, and who participated in getting them.

To begin with, let us review some information about dowry restitution in Venice. Incomplete records from the period 1366–90 provide information on 168 cases of dowry restitution to widows of nobles, whose counterparts in Florence have been the main objects of study there.[6] For the fifteenth century the court records are more complete. Here I use 139 cases regarding noble marriages from 1466 to 1477.[7] I was unable to complete a systematic study of dowry restitution in the early cinquecento, when the records are even more abundant, but I will make some anecdotal reference to them. These restitution acts, called in Venice *diiudicatus* or *de giudicato*, are useful in the first place for tracking the steady increase in marriage settlements from mid-trecento through early cinquecento. Between 1331 and 1360, wives conveyed to noble husbands dowries averaging 500 ducats; during the period 1361–90, the average grew to 873 ducats.[8] The upward pressure continued all

---

[5]See, in addition to the references above, Diane Owen Hughes, "From Brideprice to Dowry in Mediterranean Europe," *Journal of Family History* 3 (1978): 262–95. See also Stanley Chojnacki, "Daughters and Oligarchs: Gender in the Early Renaissance State," in *Gender and Society,* ed. Brown and Davis, 63–88; this and my other articles cited below may now be found in *Women and Men in Renaissance Venice: Twelve Essays on Patrician Society* (Baltimore: Johns Hopkins University Press, 2000).

[6]Archivio di Stato, Venice (henceforth ASV), Cancelleria Inferiore (henceforth CI), busta 114, Marino, S. Tomà, protocollo 1366–1391. (Unless otherwise indicated, all subsequent documentary citations are to the holdings of the ASV.)

[7]Giudici del Proprio, De Giudicato, regs. 1 and 2.

[8]The dates of dowry payments to husbands are given in only 142 of the 168 cases. The dates refer to the original conveyances of dowries repaid between 1366 and 1390 to widows or their designees. Amounts given in other moneys have been converted into ducats, using conversion tables in Frederic C. Lane and Reinhold C. Mueller, *Money and Banking in Medieval and Renaissance Venice*, vol. 1, *Coins and Moneys of Account* (Baltimore: Johns Hopkins University Press, 1985), 131, 291.

through the quattrocento. Among 122 noble dowries repaid from 1466 to 1477 in which the amounts are noted, the average was 1,230 ducats—nearly a 50 percent increase from 1361 to 1390.[9] And they still kept going up. In seventy-two noble marriage contracts from November 1505 to November 1507, the average dowry had risen to 1,732 ducats.[10] Altogether, average noble dowries grew by 350 percent over 180 years. It is important to note that these sums represent the amount technically designated as dowry, exclusive of the personal goods brought by the bride to her marriage and, more important, of the part of the settlement that remained as the property of the husband. By the early quattrocento this gift to the bridegroom, labeled the *corredo* (*corredum*), constituted one-third of the entire settlement. Thus, the amounts returned to widows were normally the remaining two-thirds.[11] Dowry inflation in Italy has been much discussed and well documented.[12] Equally important, the increase meant that the Venetian Giudici del Proprio, which had jurisdiction over dowry matters, was awarding to widows a steadily growing portion of private wealth in the dowry restitution procedure. That procedure and the roles of the government and private interests in it are the focus of this essay.

The government's regulations for dowry recovery were set in the statutes of 1242, and except for occasional refinements they remained constant through the period under discussion. Once a marriage ended, if the widow had not already recovered her dowry from her husband's estate, she, or the executors or heirs designated by deceased wives, reclaimed it in a two-stage process: the *vadimonium*, in which the widow or her heirs presented documentation of the dowry to the Giudici del Proprio, and the *diiudicatus*, in which the same judges authorized payment of it from her husband's estate and, when that was insufficient, from the property of the persons who had guaranteed the dowry.[13] A widow was required to notify the court of her intention to claim the dowry (*dare vadimonium comprobandi*) within a year and a day after the death of her husband (or her executors or heirs within a year and a day after her death); the claim then had to be documented within thirty days after

---

[9]Only 122 of the 139 quattrocento *diiudicatus* cases give precise dowry totals. Proprio, De Giudicato, regs. 1 and 2, passim.

[10]Avogaria di Comun, Contratti di nozze, reg. 140.1, fols. 1r–66v. The median dowry was 2,000 ducats; see Chojnacki, "Daughters and Oligarchs," 77. Note that this figure represents the two-thirds portion of the total marriage settlement which was designated as dowry strictly speaking, exclusive of gifts and *corredo* (on which see below).

[11]On the evolution of the *corredo* into a premium for the husband, see Stanley Chojnacki, "From Trousseau to Groomgift in Late Medieval Venice," in *Medieval and Renaissance Venice*, ed. Ellen E. Kittell and Thomas F. Madden (Urbana: University of Illinois Press, 1999), 141-65.

[12]For a brief review, see Chojnacki, "Daughters and Oligarchs," 77–80 and passim.

[13]The dowry-recovery procedures are in *Volumen statutorum, legum, ac iurium D. Venetorum* (Venice: Jacopo Novello, 1564), lib. 1, caps. 54–62, 24v–29v. A brief review of the relevant statutes is in Anna Bellavitis, "La famiglia 'cittadina' veneziana nel XVI secolo: Dote e successione: Le leggi e le fonti," *Studi veneziani*, n.s., 30 (1995): 55–68.

that.[14] Once this initial flurry was completed, the widow had thirty years to request actual restitution of the dowry by means of a *diiudicatus* decree from the Giudici del Proprio. All the while she could continue to live at the expense of her husband's estate. Although once she had received her *diiudicatus* she could no longer claim a living allowance, she could still remain in his house "until she has received full repayment of her dowry."[15] A statutory correction of 1343 added a further clarification to the effect that, unless a husband had specifically bequeathed his widow *statio*, she must vacate his house within two months if she received her dowry without having to go through the legal procedure.[16] This provision indicates that some husbands facilitated their widows' recovery of their dowries, enabling them to dispense with the courts.

Widows' entitlement to support from their husbands' property until they claimed their dowries gave them considerable latitude. This had widespread significance because the overwhelming majority of marriages ended with the death of the husband. Table 1 breaks down 454 fourteenth- and fifteenth-century *vadimonium* and *diiudicatus* cases involving nobles.[17]

Table 1: Spouse Survival
at *Vadimonium* or *Diiudicatus*

Wife survives	333 cases	73.3%
Husband survives	49 cases	10.8%
Both deceased	72 cases	15.9%
Total	454 cases	100.0%

The most striking information is that nearly three-quarters of the claims were filed by or on behalf of a living widow; the others were filed by her heirs or executors after her death. In reality, however, wives survived their husbands at an even higher rate than that. The table shows that in nearly three-fifths of the claims involving dead wives, the husbands also were deceased. In an indeterminate but undoubtedly large number of those cases, the widow had chosen not to claim her dowry but instead to live in her late husband's house, raising their children with her expenses paid by his estate.

[14]The documentation was to be presented to the court by the widow's *fideiussore*, or guarantor, whom she had convinced of the validity of her claim. The statutory correction of Doge Andrea Dandolo in 1343 required that the *fideiussore*'s brief (*breviarium*) could no longer merely be notarized but must be subscribed by the Giudici del Proprio. *Volumen statutorum*, lib. 6, cap. 7, 89v.

[15]*Volumen statutorum*, lib. 1, cap. 60, 27v.

[16]*Volumen statutorum*, lib. 6, cap. 17, 93v.

[17]Information from CI, busta 114, Marino, prot. 1366–1391; Proprio, De Giudicato, regs. 1, 2; Proprio, Vadimoni, regs. 1, 4, 5, 8, 9; Proprio, Testimoni, reg. 4; and Proprio, Parentelle, reg. 1. The 454 cases include only those *vadimonium* or *diiudicatus* procedures in which the vital status of both spouses is clearly indicated.

In doing so she acted in conformity with the wishes of many, if not most, husbands. Like their counterparts in Florence and elsewhere, Venetian men offered their wives economic inducements not to remarry.[18] In a will of 1420, Nicolò Mudazzo bequeathed to his wife, Elena, over and above her dowry of 1,100 ducats, the income from 1,000 ducats in shares in the state's funded debt (Monte), as well as food and clothing expenses for the rest of her life. Those bequests were unconditional. But if she was willing to remain with their children, "in the interest of greater love and peace," she would receive from his estate an additional fifty ducats a year, two beds, and all her clothing.[19] Mudazzo, like the countless men who imitated him, was supplementing his widow's statutory right to perpetual residence in the husband's house with additional material advantages, as long as she did not remarry. The reason was the conviction of such husbands that it was in the best interests of their children that their widows see to the children's upbringing. Equally important in the calculations of husbands was the desirability of inducing their widows to preserve their dowry wealth for the children rather than wrest it away and apply it to a remarriage, which in Florence occurred among one-third of women widowed in their twenties.[20]

It is critical to note, however, that the Venetian statutes also explicitly stated that in choosing to remain a widow a woman did not jeopardize her right to her dowry.[21] Many husbands acknowledged that their wives would eventually claim its restitution but asked them to defer it until the children were grown. Bartolomeo Grimani in 1469 acknowledged his wife's dowry of 1,066 ducats and 16 grossi but added, "I pray her that she be willing to delay requesting repayment of it (*indusiarse a pagar*)." Leonardo Priuli in 1477 was more precise, entreating his wife not to reclaim her dowry until five years after his death.[22] The text of his request conveys the concern of fathers and the strong position of mothers: "To my most beloved wife, Maria, I leave the entire dowry of 3,000 ducats which I had from her; however, I beseech (*oro*) her that it please her to leave the dowry in my estate for five years, or as long as she requires cash for the benefit of our children. In addition, I bequeath to her all the clothing and personal effects she received from her father, which she should freely

---

[18]On Florence, see Chabot, "Sposa in nero," 438–40.

[19]"Per plui amor et paxie." Archivio Notarile, Testamenti (henceforth abbreviated NT), busta 1255, Zane, protocollo, fols. 184v–86v. For other examples, see NT, busta 670, Marino, no. 116; NT, busta 1157, Croci, protocollo 2, fol. 14r; NT, busta 1233, Sorio, no. 257; NT, busta 558, Gambaro, no. 86; NT, busta 1149, Benedetto, no. 16; CI, Miscellanea Testamenti, busta 27, nos. 2578 and 2697.

[20]On the remarriage of widows in Florence, see Klapisch-Zuber, "Cruel Mother," 120, 125–27. In the seventeenth and eighteenth centuries, Florentine widows were chosen as guardians of their children in 75.4 percent of cases: see Calvi, "Diritti e legami," 490–91.

[21]"Nihil tamen noceat hoc in repromissa viduantis," *Volumen statutorum*, lib. 4, cap. 34, 76v.

[22]Proprio, Testimoni, reg. 4, 14r (Grimani); Proprio, Vadimoni, reg. 8, fol. 30r–v (Priuli). The reference to Leonardo Priuli's will is to the probated copy, dated 24 December 1478, but it was actually written in March 1477. See the following note.

possess together with all the items that I have had made for her, except for my jewels, which should be calculated as part of my residuary bequest. Item, I also leave her expenses for food and clothing for as long as she remains a widow, as my executors deem suitable for her status; but she should have more if she requires it and my estate can supply it. I commend to my most beloved wife our dear son, Zaccaria, and all other sons or daughters who might be born to us, that she be both mother and departed father to them and take the place of a father in seeing to their care."[23]

Despite all these inducements, Maria rejected Leonardo's request. She claimed her dowry one month after his will was probated and married the widower Piero Loredan within the year, undoubtedly making effective use of her handsome dowry and the trousseau to which both her father and her late husband had contributed. In that regard, she fits Klapisch-Zuber's typology of the "cruel mother," the young widow quickly remarried by her male kin—all the more so because she must have been quite young, having married Leonardo Priuli only two years before he wrote his will.[24] Yet her remarriage did not entail abandonment of Zaccaria, her son from the Priuli marriage; fifteen years after marrying her second husband, she launched Zaccaria on his political career by personally registering him for the Barbarella, the lottery for young patricians whose winners could enter the Great Council early, at age twenty.[25]

In reality, remarriage of widows like Maria Priuli was exceptional, accounting for fewer than 9 percent of women's marriages.[26] Most widows remained in their marital residence for many years, claiming their dowry decades after its conveyance to their husbands. In 138 fifteenth-century *vadimonium* claims which indicate the

---

[23]"Item Marie dilectissime uxori mee integre dimitto dotem suam quam habui, ducatorum triamillia, quamquam uxorem meam oro ut dictam dotem quandocumque non est ei numorum necessitas ad filiorum nostrorum utilitatem in mea commissarii per quinquennium si ei placuerit remanere permittat. Insuper ei dimitto vestimenta et res suas quas habuit a patre suo, et Item quas feci quae omnia eidem libere remanere volo et pro suis haberi. Exceptis omnibus meis iocalibus et zoiis quae in meo residuo remanere et computari volo. Item eidem dimitto viduando vitum et vestitum prout meis comissariis videbitur condicionibus suis convenire; plusque [?] ei dimittere si plus aut necessitas sua exigeret, aut facultati meae conveniret. Cui quidam dilectissime uxori meae commendo charissimum filium nostrum Zacariam omnesque alios filios et filias nostras nascituras ut patri amisso et matris et patris loco illorum curari suscipiret." I deciphered the text from Proprio, Testimoni, and a more elegantly legible copy, in Priuli's own hand, bearing the date "kalendis martii" 1477, in NT, busta 1239, Tomei, no. 413.

[24]Maria's marriage to the widower Piero Loredan and her 1475 marriage to Leonardo Priuli are in Marco Barbaro, "Libro di nozze patrizie," Biblioteca Marciana, Venice, codici italiani, classe 7, 156 (8492), fols. 246r, 368v.

[25]Avogadori di Comun, Balla d'Oro, reg. 164.3, fol. 140v. She was identified in the registration record as Maria Loredan, widow of Leonardo Priuli. I found no record of any children from her second marriage. On the participation of mothers in the Barbarella, or Balla d'Oro, see Stanley Chojnacki, "Kinship Ties and Young Patricians in Fifteenth-Century Venice," *Renaissance Quarterly* 38 (1985): 240–70.

[26]In a group of 859 marriages of patrician women in the quattrocento, only 74 (8.6 percent) were remarriages of widows. Barbaro, *Nozze,* passim. The 859 cases are marriages of women from, or into, sixteen selected noble clans; see Chojnacki, "Kinship Ties," 245, n. 12.

date of the marriage contract or dowry receipt (in effect, when the marriage began), the average length of time between that and the *vadimonium* filing was twenty-three and a half years, the median interval twenty-one years.[27] But that tells only part of the story. More widows or their heirs reclaimed the dowries at least three decades after their conveyance than did so after ten years or less of marriage. The information is displayed in table 2.

Table 2: Intervals from Dowry
to *Vadimonium*

>1–10 years	38 cases	27.5%
11–20 years	25 cases	18.1%
21–30 years	29 cases	21.0%
31–40 years	22 cases	15.9%
>40 years	24 cases	17.4%
Total	138 cases	99.9%

Brief marriages and young widows like Maria Priuli were thus the exception, accounting for just a bit over one-quarter of the *vadimonium* claims. Many and probably most widows, old and young, took advantage of statutory rights and husbands' inducements to refuse remarriage, staying in their marital residence and delaying claiming their dowry for years or even decades. *Vadimonium* filings frequently failed to meet the statutory deadline of a year and a day after the husband's death; in those cases, the women or their heirs made use of a loophole in the statutes extending the deadline to the full thirty years for those "ignorant of the law."[28] Those dilatory women enjoyed the best of both worlds, dwelling in the marital residence, raising their children at their late husband's expense, and then, when mothering—or life itself—was over, finally taking possession of their dowries or bestowing their dowry wealth on the heirs of their choice.

When they did eventually file, they did so in person. The statute outlining the *vadimonium* procedure required that "the woman ... must go before the doge and the *giudici* or send another person on her behalf."[29] Most took the first option: only 12.4 percent of the quattrocento *vadimonia* involving living widows were filed by

---

[27]Proprio, Vadimoni, regs. 1, 4, 5, 8, 9; Proprio, Parentelle, reg. 1; Proprio, Testimoni, reg. 4; CI, busta 126, Buosi, parchments. These 138 claims are part of the total sample of 163 fifteenth-century *vadimonia* studied; the other twenty-five are not clear about the beginning date of the marriage.

[28]*Volumen statutorum*, lib. 1, cap. 54, 25v. As one example, Alberto Badoer, filing his mother's *vadimonium* in 1477, documented her dowry with a dowry receipt of 1442; the scribe then noted: "Datum infra XXXta annos cum ipse dominus Albertus Badoer quondam domini Danielis uti scriptus in curia pro domina Helena eius matre juravit in anima sua nescivisse legem." Proprio, Vadimoni, reg. 8, fol. 13r.

[29]*Volumen statutorum*, lib. 1, cap. 54, 24v.

proctors; in the rest the women themselves appeared in court.[30] They made use of varied documentation to prove their claims. The preferred proof was the husband's notarized acknowledgment that he had received the full dowry (the *securitatis dotis carta* or the *instrumentum dotis*). Eighty-five (53.8 percent) of 158 *vadimonium* claims which identify the documentation presented were based on such receipts, a preference supported by the Maggior Consiglio, which in 1449 passed legislation requiring notaries to submit copies of all dowry receipts to the chancery office, in order that widows might claim their dowries without "great effort" (*labore magno*).[31] Another 22 percent were documented by means of marriage contracts; even though a contract is an undertaking to give a dowry rather than proof that it was actually given, the judges did make *diiudicatus* awards to widows on the basis of them.[32] Eleven percent offered entries in the husband's account book as proof of dowry payment, and 5 percent presented the husband's acknowledgment in his will, as in the case of Leonardo Priuli cited earlier. The remaining 8 percent used miscellaneous evidence, such as entries in the account books of the wife's or husband's father or brother, or the testimony of witnesses.

When women were deceased, their *vadimonium* claims and *diiudicatus* authorizations were managed by the executors or the beneficiaries they had designated in their wills.[33] The identities of these persons reveal much about the family orientation of married women and how much—or how little—it evolved during the course of the uxorial cycle. Broadly speaking, the wife's executors (*commissarii*) filed the *vadimonium* or claimed the *diiudicatus* when the marriage was briefer and the children were not old enough to make their own claims. The reverse was true in cases of long marriages or delayed claims; then, it was the heirs who managed the transaction. The difference is evident in the *vadimonium* filings, where the average interval from dowry receipt or marriage contract to *vadimonium* when executors filed was twenty-four years, but when heirs filed was 38.4 years.[34] As table 3 shows,

[30]Widows themselves lodged their claims in 106 (87.6 percent) of the 121 *vadimonia* involving living women. The other fifteen were filed by their proctors, usually family members. The survival of spouses at *vadimonia* filings: Wife survives, husband dead, 121 cases (74.2 percent); Wife dead, husband uncertain, 14 cases (8.6 percent); Both deceased, 22 cases (13.5 percent); Total, 163 cases (100 percent).

[31]Maggior Consiglio, reg. 22, Ursa, fol. 170r–v. Only 158 of the 163 fifteenth-century *vadimonium* claims studied indicate clearly the type of documentation presented.

[32]For example, Proprio, De Giudicato, reg. 1, fol. 12r; reg. 2, fols. 13r, 13v, 18r, etc. Among 105 *diiudicatus* awards for which the documentation was indicated, 10.1 percent used marriage contracts. (This *diiudicatus* figure should not be confused with the 22 percent of *vadimonium* claims that were based on contracts, as discussed here.)

[33]Eighty-five (28.1 percent) of 302 *vadimonia* and *diiudicatus* from the fifteenth century involved the dowries of deceased women and were therefore handled by the women's executors or beneficiaries. Note that this group does not include the fourteenth-century *diiudicatus* which are part of the total in table 1.

[34]Information from the 42 of the 163 quattrocento *vadimonia* that were filed for deceased women; see the table in n. 30 above.

the overwhelming majority of beneficiaries acting in these cases, just under 90 percent, were the woman's children.[35]

Table 3: Heirs Acting
in *Vadimonia* and *Diiudicatus*

Sons	22	45.8%
Daughters	8	16.7%
Sons and daughters	13	27.1%
Brothers and sisters	5	10.4%
Total	48	100.0%

Beneficence toward her children is what might be expected in a mother's will; the statutes themselves dictated that the property of intestate women was to be shared by all their children. This included their married daughters.[36] The statutes thus differentiated between mothers' property relations with their children, based on personal familial relations, and those of fathers, shaped by the imperatives of the male paternal line. The rules governing succession to intestate fathers excluded their married daughters, who had presumably received their share in the form of their dowries.[37]

When women nominated their executors, however, they looked to their natal as well as their marital families, as displayed in table 4. The complexity and variety of the family orientations of married women are revealed by the near parity between the natal and marital family members they chose to administer their estates: 44.2 percent were the women's husbands or children, 49.9 percent their parents or siblings. (Note that these figures apply only to the individual executor who filed the *vadimonium* claim; most testators entrusted their testaments to several executors, only one of whom acted in these proceedings.) Most revealing, and indeed startling, is that the largest category of the filing executors were the women's brothers, who made up 38 percent, compared with women's sons, who were 32 percent. It is really not surprising that a woman would enlist adult men from her family of birth to ensure that her property, including (but not limited to) her dowry, would be yielded

[35]The information in this and table 4 is derived from the eighty-five fifteenth-century *vadimonia* and *diiudicatus* in which women were deceased and the relationship between them and the filing beneficiaries or executors is certain. Proprio, Testimoni, reg. 4; Proprio, Vadimoni, regs. 1, 4, 5, 8, 9; Proprio, Parentelle, reg. 1; Proprio, De Giudicato, reg. 2.

[36]*Volumen statutorum*, lib. 4, cap. 28, 74v. For examples of married women filing their mother's *vadimonium*, see Proprio, Vadimoni, reg. 4, fols. 20r, 15r. In the latter instance, Agnesina, wife of Nicolò Loredan, filed for her one-sixth share of her mother's dowry seven months after her brother, Arsenio Vitturi, had filed for his one-sixth share; Proprio, Vadimoni, fol. 11r.

[37]Unmarried daughters were to succeed equally with unemancipated brothers to movables but not immovables, as long as their share was adequate to provide them with a suitable dowry. *Volumen statutorum*, lib. 4, cap. 25, 71v.

Table 4: Executors Acting
in *Vadimonia* and *Diiudicatus*

Sons	11	32.4%
Daughters	2	5.9%
Husbands	2	5.9%
Brothers	13	38.2%
Fathers	3	8.8%
Mothers	1	2.9%
Sons-in-law	1	2.9%
Daughters-in-law	1	2.9%
Total	34	99.9%

up by her husband after her death; nor is it surprising that those designated executors would comply, since in addition to sentiments of fraternal loyalty, they had expectations of their sister's grateful beneficence as an inducement.[38]

What is noteworthy is the enduring trust, sometimes spanning decades, between married women and their brothers. It is exemplified in the tie between Zanetta Trevisan and her brother, Nicolò, who in 1458 filed the *vadimonium* for the dowry that Zanetta had brought to Tolomeo Donà thirty-four years earlier, in 1424.[39] Equally revealing is the infrequency with which women named their husbands as executors; widowers made up less than 6 percent of executors filing *vadimonium* claims, the same percentage as the women's daughters and a smaller one than that of their fathers. No husbands appear as their wives' beneficiaries in the *vadimonium* and *diiudicatus* cases studied. This small representation of husbands, however, may result from the practice, discussed above, of widows' forgoing restitution of their dowries and living instead on their husbands' estates, then leaving their dowry wealth to their heirs; the husbands of such women would be unavailable as executors. But even when their husbands were alive, it made good sense for wives to designate executors other than their husbands to procure the restitution of their dowries from those same husbands or their estates.[40]

[38]On married women's testamentary bequests, see Stanley Chojnacki, "Patrician Women in Renaissance Venice," *Studies in the Renaissance* 21 (1974): 181–84.

[39]Zanetta had named Nicolò as an executor in her will of 1443, fifteen years before the *vadimonium* but nineteen years after she married; Proprio, Vadimoni, reg. 4, fol. 11v. In another example, Antonio Tron, as one of the *commissari* named in the will of his sister, the late Orsa Tron Foscarini, filed the *vadimonium* in 1460 for the dowry that had been conveyed to Orsa's late husband thirty-two years earlier, in 1428; Proprio, Testimoni, reg. 4, fol. 34v.

[40]For examples of both husbands and wives choosing their spouses as executors, see Stanley Chojnacki, "The Power of Love: Wives and Husbands in Late Medieval Venice," in *Women and Power in the Middle Ages*, ed. Mary Erler and Maryanne Kowaleski (Athens, Ga.: University of Georgia Press, 1988): 126–48. For Florentine husbands choosing their wives as executors, see Calvi, "Diritti e legami."

In filing their claims, widows or their executors were able to rely on government institutions mobilized to protect women's economic interests. According to the statutes, a widow's right to her dowry took precedence over all other claims on her husband's property, even those of his creditors, a principle reaffirmed by the Maggior Consiglio in 1403; and the estate of a man who died without a will had to repay his widow's dowry even before his children got their share.[41] The statutes also decreed that if a husband wished to sell property pledged for his wife's dowry, she could require him either to replace it with other real estate of equal value or to turn the sale price over to a government agency, which would invest it in the wife's name.[42] The *diiudicatus* judgments that formally awarded widows their dowries put these principles into practice. The procedure called for the widow to present proof of the amount of her dowry. The statutes imply that the process began with the filing of the *vadimonium*, but only one-third of the quattrocento *diiudicatus* judgments studied cite a previous *vadimonium* to document the dowry.[43] The others refer, to the evident satisfaction of the judges, to marriage contracts, husbands' wills and ledger entries, and above all notarized dowry receipts. Thus some women evidently bypassed the *vadimonium* step, proceeding directly to the *diiudicatus*. In any event, after the proof of the dowry was presented, the judges subtracted from that sum four types of deduction: the value of any property already deeded by the husband to his wife; any part of the dowry that she might have given him, for example in the form of a bequest; any partial repayment that his estate might have already made to her; and, I believe, any contributions that she might have made from her dowry toward those of her already married daughters.[44] The remainder was hers, and the judges authorized her to appropriate it—as well as twelve and a half lire *a grossi* (equal to just under five ducats) "for her widow's apparel [*pro sua veste viduali*]"—from her husband's entire estate, both movables and immovables.[45]

In many instances, however, the judges, doubtless at the urging of the widow or her executors, made provision for the possibility that her husband's estate would be

[41]*Volumen statutorum*, lib. 1, cap. 34, 17v.; lib. 4, cap. 24, 71v. The Maggior Consiglio act asserted that "maximus favor adhibetur super vindicationem dotium ipsarum [mulierum]." Maggior Consiglio, reg. 21, Leona, fol. 233v.

[42]*Volumen statutorum*, lib. 3, caps. 28 and 29, 49v[2] and 49v[3]. (The pagination names 49 twice.)

[43]Proprio, De Giudicato, regs. 1 and 2. The total number of *diiudicatus* judgments examined in these fifteenth-century registers is 139. This total includes the 122 mentioned earlier, as well as another seventeen in which the original amount of the dowry (though not the sum authorized in the judgment) is unclear or absent.

[44]The first three deductions are in *Volumen statutorum*, lib. 1, cap. 55, 25v. On the contributions of mothers to their daughters' dowries, see Donald E. Queller and Thomas F. Madden, "Father of the Bride: Fathers, Daughters, and Dowries in Late Medieval and Early Renaissance Venice," *Renaissance Quarterly* 46 (1993): 685–711; and Stanley Chojnacki, "'The Most Serious Duty': Motherhood, Gender, and Patrician Culture in Renaissance Venice," in *Refiguring Woman: Perspectives on Gender and the Italian Renaissance*, ed. Marilyn Migiel and Juliana Schiesari (Ithaca, N.Y.: Cornell University Press, 1991), 133–54.

[45]On the provision of widows' garb in Florence, see Chabot, "Sposa in nero," 433–36.

insufficient to repay the dowry, a prospect discussed by Julius Kirshner.[46] They therefore authorized her to sequester (*intromittere*) the remainder from the property of some other person who at the time of its conveyance had stood as surety for the dowry's restitution.[47] This brings us to the question of dowry security, to which I would like to devote the rest of the essay because, like the presence of brothers and fathers in *vadimonium* and *diiudicatus* proceedings, the practice of providing guarantees reveals how the dowry system made women participants in complex, evolving, but also durable social networks.

Venetians contrived a wide variety of dowry guarantees, but no contract was without some guarantee.[48] In most cases, the husband, if he was emancipated, pledged all his goods for the dowry's return. To cite one example, from 1424, among many: "ser Zorzi [Dolfin] promises to have a dowry receipt notarized (*carta de segurta de inpromessa*) for dona Barbarella [Contarini] ... obligating all his goods, movable and immovable, present and future."[49] A husband's sense of obligation led Nicolò Arimondo in 1422 to describe himself as "my wife's debtor."[50] That was in conformity with the statutory provision that all of a husband's property was obligated for the return of his wife's dowry from the moment of her *transductio* to his house; to clear up any uncertainty, the Great Council in 1413 reaffirmed that her precedence extended to both the movable and the immovable property.[51] Normally, the husband's promise in the contract to *meter in carta* his wife's dowry was fulfilled after its conveyance, when he acknowledged it in the notarized *securitatis dotis carta* or *instrumentum dotis*, pledging all his goods toward its restitution.[52]

Many families of prospective brides, however, were not satisfied with their future son-in-law's pledge; they insisted on more tangible assurance of his ability to repay the dowry. Husbands often complied by following the Florentine practice of assigning shares in the state's funded debt (Monte) or other government investment vehicles for the dowry's restitution.[53] Frequently, part of the dowry itself was invested in government funds, earmarked explicitly for its restitution. In such

---

[46]Julius Kirshner, "Wives' Claims against Insolvent Husbands in Late Medieval Italy," in *Women of the Medieval World: Essays in Honor of John H. Mundy*, ed. Julius Kirshner and Suzanne F. Wemple (Oxford: Basil Blackwell, 1985), 256–303.

[47]Twenty-nine of the 139 *diiudicatus* judgments included such assignments of secondary liability.

[48]This information is derived from an analysis of eighty-three marriage contracts or notarized dowry receipts from 1427 to 1541.

[49]Proprio, Testimoni, reg. 4, fol. 18r–v.

[50]"Son debitor a Prospera Arimondo mia consorte." Proprio, Vadimoni, reg. 4, fol. 45r.

[51]Maggior Consiglio, reg. 21, Leona, 233v. The statutory formula was "omnia bona viri obligata sint mulieri a tempore, quo est transducta." *Volumen statutorum*, lib. 4, cap. 34, 17v.

[52]One example of the formula: in 1407 Paolo Orio gave a notarized security to Elisabetta, "uxori sue dilecte, de tota illa repromissa que tempore sue desponsationis pro ea sibi dari promissa fuit, que repromissa fuit hucusque in toto libre ducentequinquaginta due denariorum venetorum grossorum [equal to 2,520 ducats]." Proprio, Vadimoni, reg. 1, fol. 2v.

[53]On the Florentine practice, see Molho, *Marriage Alliance*, 319–24.

arrangements, the husband usually, though not always, was to enjoy the income from the investment but had no control over the capital. Marcantonio Priuli agreed in his marriage contract of 1530 that "the capital of 2,000 ducats is always to remain as a dowry fund or security (*per fondo dotal o pro caucione*) for the dowry of madona Morosina," his wife.[54] Of the immense marriage portion of 7,600 ducats that Maria Morosini conveyed to her bridegroom in 1435, 6,000 were to be registered, in Maria's name, at the Monte office, the Camera degli Imprestiti.[55] Negotiating his daughter's marriage in 1453, Girolamo Dandolo prevailed on his new son-in-law to agree that she could require him, "at any time," to put 1,000 ducats in Monte shares in her name as dowry security.[56] To be on the safe side, fathers contracting their daughters' marriages took pains to ensure that changes in the market value of such shares would not erode dowry investments by spelling out precisely their equivalent in gold ducats, so that the dowry would be repaid "money for money, fund for fund (*danari per danari, monte per monte*)," as a contract of 1532 put it.[57] The government itself periodically enacted legislation affirming that when such investments were redeemed at the time of dowry restitution, they were to be calculated not according to the current market value of the shares but to their real value at the time of purchase.[58]

[54]Avogaria di Comun, Contratti di nozze, reg. 142.3, fol. 188r–v. If the fund in which the 2,000 ducats were invested should be liquidated, Marcantonio would be able to choose a substitute government fund or invest them in a bank; in any case, they were to remain Morosina's *fondo dotal.*

[55]Giudici del Esaminador, Vendizioni, reg. 7, fols. 15r–16r. The 6,000 ducats were designated not as dowry but as *dimissoria*, or inheritance, which, though under the husband's administration, was considered the wife's property outside the strict limits of the dowry. The part of the marriage portion designated as *dimissoria* was not subject to the dowry limit of 1,600 ducats set in 1420, and another act on the same day reaffirmed a wife's right to the income from her *dimissoria*. Senato, Misti, reg. 53, fol. 70r–v.

[56]"Si veramente che xe la dita dona Issabeta per nexun tempo vora chel dito ser tomado so mario faza scriver ala camera de imprestedi ducati mille de quella moneda, el dito ser tomado sia tenuto a farli scriver." Proprio, Testimoni, reg. 4, fol. 22r (1453). Of the 1,000 ducats in cash that Laura Montorio's mother contributed to her dowry, "500 ducats are to be invested in a [government] fund as the wife's dowry security." Contratti di nozze, reg. 142.3, fol. 173v (1530). Of the 1,600-ducat dowry that Girolamo Soranzo was to receive from his bride, Marina Tron, "400 are to be earmarked for the dowry's restitution." Contratti di nozze, reg. 140.1, fol. 9r (1506).

[57]Contratti di nozze, reg. 142.3, fol. 234r–v. Regina Barbaro's dowry in 1412 included 500 ducats' worth of *prestiti* shares, for which Regina's bridegroom was to "have a dowry receipt notarized indicating their current price." Proprio, Vadimoni, reg. 4, fol. 25v. Subsequently, the groom documented receipt of the 400 *prestiti* ducats, which equaled 232 gold ducats, "at the rate of 58 percent."

[58]The government periodically reaffirmed the principle. The Great Council passed a law to that effect in 1291, and a copy of it was inserted into the capitulary of the Giudici del Proprio, who had jurisdiction in dowry restitution. Proprio, Vadimoni, b. 2, fols. 34–35. The stricture was reiterated in a dowry-limiting act of 1505; Senato, Terra, reg. 15, fol. 93v.

Government investments were an attractive repository for dowry security, but in contrast with Florentine practice, Venetians were not hesitant to negotiate real estate as well, both as components of dowries and as security for their repayment.[59] The designation of immovables as dowry security was so normal that the statutes instructed that *diiudicatus* judgments must award widows contiguous properties, or at least "the ones most useful for the women (*utiliores pro mulieribus*)" in their husbands' estates.[60] The statutes also required husbands who sold real estate pledged toward repayment of dowries to file with the government, "in the wife's name," the title to any property purchased with the proceeds of such a sale; or if the proceeds were kept in cash, it was to be deposited with the Procuratori, also "in the name of the wives."[61] Those rules were enforced. In 1398 one of Gasparino Contarini's kinsmen sold real estate that had been partially obligated for the dowry of Gasparino's wife, Marina, whereupon the Giudici di Petizion ordered Gasparino either to secure the dowry on his own property or to deposit its cash value, 1,000 ducats, with the government's grain office, "as is customary," where it would earn interest. Gasparino was to carry out this order within one month "in order that the said domina Marina will have her dowry effectively secured and bonded."[62]

The judges' pressure on Gasparino reflected the determination of brides' families to ensure that their dowry investment would be protected. In a contract of 1531, Gian Francesco Bondumier prevailed on his sister's future husband to agree to turn over the 1,500-ducat cash portion of Ludovica's dowry to the Procuratori di San Marco, to be invested by them in "real estate…which investments are to be obligated for the dowry."[63] Other husbands pledged their own real estate. In 1365, Marco Ruzzini "gave and assigned" to his wife two apartments, appraised at exactly the amount of her dowry (30 lire *di grossi*, equal to 300 ducats), in the family palace (*domus maior*) of one of his kinsman; she would henceforth have "full power to delegate, have, hold, give, donate, sell, commit, and possess [the property] as your own, or to do anything else with it that might please you."[64] Giovanni Querini "gave, assigned, and transacted" to his wife the "the entire house he is currently dwelling

---

[59]On Florence, see Molho, *Marriage Alliance*, 324. On the practice in Venice, see Elisabeth Crouzet-Pavan, *"Sopra le acque salse": Espaces, pouvoir et société à Venise à la fin du Moyen Âge*, 2 vols. (Rome: École française de Rome, 1992), 1: 447–58.

[60]*Volumen statutorum*, lib. 1, cap. 61, 27v.

[61]*Volumen statutorum*, lib. 3, cap. 28, 49v[2].

[62]CI, busta 70, Darvasio, protocollo "1398," no foliation, 9 August 1398. The court action was initiated by Marina's father, Piero Zancani.

[63]Contratti di nozze, reg. 142.3, fol. 199v. The total dowry was 3,000 ducats.

[64]"A modo cum plenissima virtute et potestate intromittendi, habendi, tenendi, dandi, donandi, vendendi, committendi, et proprio possidendi, vel quicquid aliud inde tibi placuerit faciendi." The two apartments were contiguous (*insimul coniuncta*). CI, busta 15, Nicolò Benedetto, parchment, 14 November 1365.

in."[65] These were residential properties, but husbands also assigned their wives income-producing investments. Jacopo Morosini gave to his wife, Lucia, four rental properties at Rialto, valued at 500 ducats "as security for her dowry," and Luca Falier obligated to his wife, Maria, among other real estate, five rental properties in San Luca.[66] Paolo Contarini signed over to his wife eighty-eight campi in Camponogara which he had received as part of the dowry.[67]

Husbands earmarked real estate, Monte shares, or investments in the government's grain office as guarantees in order to satisfy their affines' demand for assurance of the dowry's restitution. But other husbands with insufficient property of their own had to call upon relatives or friends to back them up. In 1462, Francesco Morosini's three brothers had to pledge all their property to ensure repayment of his bride's dowry, unenthusiastically it seems: they stipulated that "if Francesco should purchase real estate or Monte shares (*prestiti*) for his wife's security, they wanted ipso facto to be freed from their pledge."[68] They had good reason to worry, because guarantors were called upon to honor their pledges. Because the estate of Francesco de Mezzo's late brother was insufficient, Francesco was forced to commit all his future *prestiti* income and all his profits from merchant ventures to repay his sister-in-law's dowry, of which he had been coguarantor.[69]

Not only brothers but other relatives stood surety for dowries, and their involvement maps the range of kin mobilized to protect women's economic interests. A sample of forty-six guarantors who joined with husbands to secure dowries from the 1420s to the 1530s, though small, can give an idea of the categories of pledges (table 5).[70] As with Francesco Morosini's contract, brothers took an active part in backing up a husband's capacity to repay the dowry. However, for most families of brides,

[65]"Tota domus a stacio in qua ad presens habitat ipse ser Joannes Querino." CI, busta 70, Darvasio, unfoliated fascicle beginning 17 June 1412; the act confirming his wife's ownership is dated 30 October 1413. On the meaning of *domus a statio* as noble residence, see Crouzet-Pavan, "Sopra le acque salse," 1: 471–526, passim.

[66]For Jacopo Morosini, see CI, busta 70, Darvasio, protocollo "1409," fol. 31r (1410). Lucia was confirmed in possession of it after being invested *ad proprium* by the judges. For Luca Falier, see Proprio, Vadimoni, reg. 4, fol. 11r (1457). Luca also assigned to Maria an inn (*hostellum*) and an adjacent house in Mirano. In both cases the term for rental property is *domus a sergentibus*, used in Venice to describe modest habitations, usually rented out by the owner. See Crouzet-Pavan, *"Sopra le acque salse,"* 1: 471–72, n. 13.

[67]Contratti di nozze, reg. 142.3, fols. 124v–25r (1529).

[68]"Et in caso chel dicto ser Francesco so fradello nel avegnir comprasse stabele over imprestedi per segurta dela dicta so moier, ipso facto i voleno esser liberi de tal prezaria over segurta." Proprio, Vadimoni, reg. 4, fol. 54v.

[69]CI, busta 96, Griffon, protocollo II, fol. 25r.

[70]Information from contracts and dowry receipts. These forty-six do not include the cases in which husbands pledged their own property without coguarantors. Sources: Proprio, Testimoni, reg. 4; Proprio, Parentelle, reg. 1; Proprio, Vadimoni, regs. 1, 4, 5, 8, 9; CI, busta 62, Buosi; Contratti di nozze, regs. 140.1 and 142.3.

Table 5: Coguarantees of Dowries
(By Relatives of Husbands).

Fathers	15 cases	32.6%
Brothers	12 cases	26.1%
Mothers or Grandmothers	18 cases	39.1%
Unknown relationship	1 case	2.2%
Total	46 cases	100.0%

one brother's pledge was not enough, and in nine of the twelve fraternal coguarantees, two, three, and even four brothers pledged their goods.[71]

It was more usual for fathers to counterpledge for their daughter-in-law's dowry or, in the case of unemancipated sons, to assume primary responsibility for its restitution. Fathers acted as guarantors one-third of the time; in fact, the practice and the principle were so well established that the priority of a woman's dowry among claims on their father-in-law's estate was written into the statutes, which mandated that if a man died intestate with his daughter-in-law's dowry in his possession, it was to be consigned to her husband before the estate was divided among the heirs.[72] Individual fathers made the same provision in their wills, allocating additional property to their unmarried sons in order to enable them to demonstrate to prospective in-laws the same dowry backing from their father's estate that their married brothers had received.[73] The economic resources of the bridegrooms' fathers loomed large in marriage bargaining, and not just as fallback dowry security. In 1412, Nicolò Coppo accepted his daughter-in-law and her dowry with the customary formula, "over all his goods (*in su i suo beni*)." He stated his willingness to emancipate his son, Agostino, but, like other fathers, also held out the reassuring alternative of housing and feeding the newly married couple and their children "as long as his son desires."[74] Although emancipation could be a way of disclaiming responsibility for repayment of a daughter-in-law's dowry, as Thomas Kuehn points out, convention weighed heavily on the side of the father-in-law's liability.[75] Even doges assumed their fatherly

[71]An example of four brothers pledging is in Proprio, Testimoni, reg. 4, fols. 26r. Examples of three are in Proprio, Testimoni, 32v; and Proprio, Vadimoni, reg. 4, fols. 19r–v, 25r–v, 54v, 64v.

[72]Only the movable portion of the father's estate was to be used for this purpose. *Volumen statutorum,* lib. 4, cap. 24, 71v; see also lib. 1, cap. 56, 26v.

[73]For example, the wills of Ermolao Pisani in 1469–70 and Prodocimo Arimondo in 1473–74: NT, busta 1238, Tomei, series 2, no. 15; NT, busta 1239, Tomei, no. 606.

[74]"Fin chel ditto so fio vora star cum lui in chaxa de so pare." Proprio, Vadimoni, reg. 4, fols. 25v–26v. For another example of fathers providing housing and living expenses to their sons and daughters-in-law, see Esaminador, Vendizioni, reg. 7, fols. 15r–16r.

[75]Thomas Kuehn, *Emancipation in Late Medieval Florence* (New Brunswick, N.J.: Rutgers University Press, 1982), 143–44.

responsibility. In 1393 Doge Antonio Venier secured his daughter-in-law's dowry upon all his property.[76]

It is only to be expected that in the patrilineal environment of the Venetian patriciate fathers and brothers would act as coguarantors, as they did in nearly three-fifths of the cases examined, twenty-seven of forty-six (58.7 percent). They stood to benefit most from the infusion into the family's collective resources of a daughter- or sister-in-law's dowry, so they had the best motive to encourage prospective in-laws by obligating their property as security for its restitution. For that reason it is remarkable that the mothers and grandmothers of husbands secured the dowry upon their property in nearly two-fifths of the cases. The frequency of their appearances in contracts provides powerful evidence both of women's loyalty to family and kin and of the substantial economic resources they were able to deploy in demonstrating it. Women's wealth was an element in guaranteeing dowries in indirect ways as well. In the case just mentioned of Nicolò Coppo pledging for the dowry of 1,500 ducats received by his son, Agostino, he carefully pointed out that Agostino also possessed, in his own name, 1,500 ducats in inheritance from his mother and grandmother.[77]

This was doubtless reassuring to Agostino's future parents-in-law, but living women also negotiated their wealth directly in dowry negotiations. To back up Domenico Barbaro's pledge of his own goods for his wife's dowry, his maternal grandmother promised that she would bequeath him "a large residential house (*chaxa granda da stacio*), a courtyard of houses, and other houses," and his mother promised that at her death he would get one-third of her property in San Paternian, "freely and without any contradiction." In addition, the two women signed over to Domenico, "free and clear (*senza alguna eception*)," 420 ducats which they had received in a civil judgment against one of their male relatives, as well as 200 ducats in *prestiti*.[78] Finally, they agreed jointly (*chadauna de lor insolidum*) to receive Domenico's bride's dowry, pledging all their property for its restitution. For the reasons already discussed, these women were far from unusual in possessing enough real estate to satisfy the families of prospective brides.[79] But other kinds of female wealth served just as effectively as dowry security. In a contract of 1428, the bridegroom's

---

[76]"Manifestum facimus nos Anthonius Venerio dei gratia dux veneciarum nostro nomine speciali cum nostris heredibus vobis nobili mulieri peramabili Petronille nurui nostre, quod recepimus vos cum parte suprascripte vestre repromisse ... super omnibus bonis nostris mobilibus et immobilibus et sic vos de ipsis assecuramus et securam reddimus." He made two such declarations, upon payment of the two installments of the dowry. CI, busta 17, Belancini, protocollo IV, no foliation, acts of 6 February 1392–93 and 22 December 1393.

[77]"Ha da sij de beni de so mare e de so madona ducati mille e zinquezento zoe mv^c." Proprio, Vadimoni, reg. 4, fols. 25v–26v.

[78]The sum was 42 lire *di grossi*, "o circha," equal to 420 ducats. The judgment was against Francesco Loredan; the maternal grandmother identified herself as Agnesina Loredan, widow of Bernabò Loredan. Proprio, Vadimoni, fols. 29v–30v.

[79]Other examples are in Proprio, Vadimoni, fols. 58v–59v.

mother and grandmother promised to bequeath him half of their *prestiti* holdings of 5,000 ducats.[80] Their commitment of their imposing wealth was a necessary (and, in the event, sufficient) condition of the dowry offer. How important it was and how scrupulously the families of brides sought assurance of the security of the dowries they were bestowing are both conveyed in a contract of 1462. Maria Davanzago pledged two-thirds of her wealth, "movable and immovable," to secure the dowry of her daughter-in-law. To reinforce the credibility of the pledge, her two sons-in-law, acting for themselves and on behalf of their wives and heirs, "renounce[d] any gifts [that Maria might have promised them]; in sum (*intuto*), the donation that the above-mentioned madona Maria is making to her son Marino Davanzago is understood to have the primary claim [on her goods]."[81]

The wealth of these women came from their own dowries, as some stated explicitly. Cristina Renier in 1479 pledged "all her goods, whether dotal or present and future," to secure the dowry of her daughter-in-law, and Gabriella Barbo in 1528 likewise obligated "all her dotal goods and all other goods of whatever sort she has or may have, present and future," for the same purpose.[82] Both of these women possessed nondotal property, but by far the largest portion of the wealth upon which they and the many other female pledges could credibly secure the dowries received by their sons and grandsons came from their own dowries.[83] The key to women's prominence among coguarantors of dowries is thus to be found in the very credibility of their guarantees, conclusive evidence that women got back those carefully secured dowries.

Female guarantors of dowries demonstrate the importance of women in nourishing the dowry system that enabled their own marriages and those of their sons and daughters. Their marriage portions gave them the economic substance necessary to reassure anxious parents of the next generation of brides that their investments in their daughters' marriages would be available in turn to those women when they were widowed. That actually represented an enlargement of mothers' role in their children's marriages. At the same time that they guaranteed the dowries

[80]Proprio, Vadimoni, reg. 5, fol. 10v (Piero Bragadin and Maria Contarini).

[81]"Miser Lodovico Contarini et miser Baldo Querini, çeneri de madona Maria relicta miser Lorenço Davançago se obliga si per lor come per so moier over in suo heriedi che [se] per la dicta madona Maria li fosse facto alguna promission over donacion in suo beni si stabeli come mobeli sora dicti miser Lodovico e miser Baldo die renunciar le dicte donacion, et che intuto la donation che madona Maria sora dicta fa a suo fio Marin Davançago se intenda esser la prima obligation in pena et soto pena de tuto quelo che mai per algun tempo per algun de i dicti ala dicta madona Maria li podesse esser dimandado." Proprio, Vadimoni, fols. 4v–5r.

[82]Proprio, Vadimoni, reg. 8, fols. 38v–40r (1479); Contratti di nozze, reg. 142.3, fol. 95v (1528).

[83]Additional examples of women securing the dowries of their sons and grandsons on their property: Proprio, Vadimoni, reg. 4, fols. 48v, 64v; reg. 5, fol. 10r; reg. 8, fols. 42r–43v; Proprio, Testimoni, reg. 4, fols. 17r, 23v–24r, 26r; Contratti di nozze, reg. 140.1, fol. 3v; reg. 142.3, fols. 46r–v, 161v–62r, 173v–74r, 205v–6r.

of their daughters-in-law, they also made important contributions to the dowries of their daughters.[84] Isabetta Corner's three sons-in-law acknowledged in notarized declarations in 1476 that each had received from her 500 ducats in partial payment of their wives' dowries. Of the 6,600-ducat marriage portion that Laura Bragadin brought to Nicolò Querini in 1533, 4,500 were contributions from her mother, including Monte shares, furnishings and clothing (*mobeli et vestimenti*) for the bride, and rental property.[85] Similar instances appear regularly in the records, and it is not rare to encounter a marriage contract with women making contributions to both sides. In the contract, noted earlier, of Agostino Coppo, whose mother and grandmother bequeathed him the 1,500 ducats needed to secure his bride's dowry, that dowry itself was enriched by 500 ducats in Monte shares contributed by the bride's grandmother and aunt. In 1477, part of the dowry that Giovanni Dolfin's mother guaranteed with her own property was money that the mother of Giovanni's bride had won in a judgment against the estate of her late husband.[86] That case is a demonstration of women's involvement in the complete dowry cycle: its assembling, its conveyance, and its repayment—here, as usual, assured by the authority of Venice's judicial system.

The dowry system was the means of its own continuity and expansion, owing in no small measure to the active participation of dowered women at all stages. It was in the interest of men to keep their connections with their married sisters, daughters, aunts, wives, and mothers strong, even over the course of decades, to keep up their membership in the evolving social networks of these women of substance. It was the stake of such men in the wealth and benevolence of their married womenfolk that demanded the guarantees that secured dowries and sustained the government institutions which ensured their restitution. Families may have dreaded the dowry inflation that forced them to invest ever larger amounts of family wealth in their daughters' dowries. But the support with which they, in collaboration with the institutional structure of Venice's government, enabled their women to get back their dowries nourished their own ability to find places in the marriage market for the next generation of daughters and sons.

[84]On women's contributions to their daughters' dowries, see Queller and Madden, "Father of the Bride," 695–69; and Stanley Chojnacki, "Dowries and Kinsmen in Early Renaissance Venice," *Journal of Interdisciplinary History* 5 (1975): 580–90.

[85]For Isabetta Corner, see CI, busta 162, Colonna, protocollo 1457, fols. 4v–5r. For Laura Bragadin, see Contratti di nozze, reg. 142.3, fols. 265v–265.2r.

[86]For Agostino Coppo, see Proprio, Vadimoni, reg. 4, fol. 25v. For Giovanni Dolfin, see Proprio, Vadimoni, reg. 8.1, fols. 42r–43v.

Daughters, Mothers, Wives, and Widows
Women as Legal Persons

Thomas Kuehn

There can be no question about seeing late medieval and early modern women as legal equals of men. Legal differences between the sexes were crafted by civic legislators and jurists, who incorporated the language of womanly weakness into their academic discourses.[1] Law and lawgivers in the past were not concerned with equality. It was not the flourishing of the individual as a whole and unique entity, but the reproduction of family and kinship units that animated laws governing parental powers, marriage, inheritance, property, and so much more.[2] The person, as the bearer of rights and obligations and the conscious agent of them, was conceived in that context.

Law in Italian cities was dynamic and complex, as there were multiple sources of it. Alongside the learned law propounded to professionals in universities (itself multiply composed), lay local customs. This relationship between the texts and rules of *ius commune* and the rules of each *ius proprium* was itself complex.[3] It is also crucial to recognize that the personhood of women was conceived of differently than that of men in these sources of law.

---

[1]Cf. Maria Teresa Guerra Medici, "Diritto statutario e condizione della donna nella città medievale dei sec. xii–xiv," *Rivista di storia del diritto italiano* 65 (1992): 319–36; Manlio Bellomo, *La condizione giuridica della donna in Italia: Vicende antiche e moderne* (Turin: Edizioni RAI, 1970); Thomas Kuehn, "Person and Gender in the Laws," in *Gender and Society in Renaissance Italy*, ed. Judith Brown and Robert C. Davis (London: Longman, 1998), 87–86.

[2]Nancy Partner similarly distinguishes between the modern individuated subject, a key to the Renaissance since Burckhardt, and a more diffuse sense of personhood in "Did Mystics Have Sex?" in *Desire and Discipline: Sex and Society in the Premodern West*, ed. Jacqueline Murray and Konrad Eisenbichler (Toronto: University of Toronto Press, 1996), 296–311. For an anthropological sense of this distinction, see Marilyn Strathern, *After Nature: English Kinship in the Late Twentieth Century* (Cambridge: Cambridge University Press, 1992).

[3]Cf. Thomas Kuehn, "A Medieval Conflict of Laws: Inheritance by Illegitimates in *Ius Commune* and *Ius Proprium*," *Law and History Review* 15 (1997): 243–73; Paolo Grossi, *L'ordine giuridico medievale* (Bari: Laterza, 1995).

My inquiry is limited to the particular social and legal context of Florentine families from the fourteenth century to the early sixteenth. While Florence's legal experiences and institutions were not fully unique in an Italian context, they did have peculiarities regarding women. What follows will concern women defined by domestic and marital circumstances. We will not confront them as nuns, as prostitutes, or as practitioners of trades. We will confront them by examining the typical stages of a life course—from (someone's) daughter to (someone's) wife, to mother and widow in turn—aware that life is not necessarily lived, or lived meaningfully, in the "typical" (if by that we seek some architectonic ideal or average), but in the variations worked on the potential available at each stage.[4]

As our first premise, we have to gauge the lives and actions of particular women as legal persons. This personhood went beyond assertions that "the woman, while capable of having rights, was legally incapable of acting on them" or that "the woman was, in the end, rather an object than a subject of the law."[5] Even broad dispositions regarding control of property or physical person had their exceptions and allowed for situational adjustment. Overrating a dichotomy between public (as male space and roles) and private (as female space and roles) can make a matter of separation seem more like seclusion. To see the public as higher, as the basis of all power, is to succumb to an ethnocentric and presentist sense of the state and law. The women with whom we will be concerned could and did craft strategies in pursuit of interests that were personal as well as familial, but they were not thereby seeking power.[6]

A second premise is that roles and expectations regarding women vary with age, as well as with social and economic status (including marital status). "Women begin as daughters, attain adulthood only as daughters-in-law, get no satisfaction until they are mothers of sons, and become powerful only when they are mothers-in-law. Thus their lives communicate the inevitability and personal necessity of social connection. The most important connection is to family."[7] This comment about twentieth-century Greek women can apply to those of Renaissance Florence as well. Where there was some "substance" to women's rights (and family was *substantia* by a juristic maxim), legal capacities and personhood acquired practical resonance.

---

[4]As explained in Stephen Jay Gould, *Full House: The Spread of Excellence from Plato to Darwin* (New York: Harmony Books, 1996).

[5]P. M. Arcari, "La donna," in *Idee sulle donne nel Medioevo: Fonti e aspetti giuridici, antropologici, religiosi, sociali e letterari della condizione femminile*, ed. Maria Consiglia de Matteis (Bologna: Pàtron, 1981), 67–93, at 72, in remarking on Isidore of Seville and early medieval Germanic laws.

[6]For a parallel situation, see introduction to *Gender and Power in Rural Greece*, ed. Jill Dubisch (Princeton: Princeton University Press, 1986), 3–41.

[7]Muriel Dimen, "Servants and Sentries: Women, Power, and Social Reproduction in Kriovrisi," in *Gender and Power in Rural Greece*, 53–67, at 64.

LEGAL BACKGROUND

According to Yan Thomas, "Under Roman law women did not form a distinct juridical species. The law…never proposed the slightest definition of women as such, even though for many jurists the common belief in women's weakness of mind (*imbecillitas mentis*), flightiness, and general infirmity (*infirmitas sexus*) served as a handy explanation for her statutory incapacities."[8] Division of the sexes was treated as a juridical rather than a natural fact. Thus while a language of innate inferiority flitted through the law of Rome, women were not incapacitated for their own protection but were incapacitated with regard to representing others, largely "in order to protect male prerogatives."[9] Women could not hold civic office, and they could not be *paterfamilias*, with everything that status implied regarding power over children and succession.[10] Women were the beginning and end of their family, according to a juristic commonplace. So it was that women as mothers were excluded from exercising guardianship (*tutela*) even over their own children, because the children were not their successors. It was "not that women were incapable," but because "their sphere of action was limited to their own person," that women were denied "the capacity to transcend the narrow sphere of private interest, a capacity that 'desubjectivized' action and gave it the abstract character of a function."[11] In their own regard, women were seen as clever, cunning, and greedy—quite capable of realizing and pursuing their own interests.

As the rationale for *tutela* over women disappeared in the late Roman empire, it came to be explained in classical jurisprudence as a matter of protection from weakness (like *tutela* over minors).[12] Presumed female weakness resulted in valuing men's testimony over women's, among other things.[13] The major transactional incapacity that remained for women in Roman law—inability to act as surety for others—in fact both prevented them from fulfilling a masculine function (being surety) and kept their property separate from their husbands'.[14] Husbands and wives could not give each other gifts (dowry excepted, and that was administered under rules) and, in contrast to English common law later, spouses were not automatically heir to

[8]Yan Thomas, "The Division of the Sexes in Roman Law," in *A History of Women in the West*, ed. Georges Duby and Michelle Perrot, 5 vols., vol. 1: *From Ancient Goddesses to Christian Saints*, ed. Pauline Schmitt Pantel (Cambridge, Mass.: Harvard University Press, 1992), 83–137, at 83.

[9]Suzanne Dixon, "Infirmitas Sexus: Womanly Weakness in Roman Law," *Tijdschrift voor Rechtsgeschiedenis* 52 (1984): 343–71, at 344.

[10]Thomas, "Division," 87–95; on the medieval law, see Manlio Bellomo, *Problemi di diritto familiare nell'età dei comuni: Beni paterni e "pars filii"* (Milan: Giuffrè, 1968), 2–7; Thomas Kuehn, *Emancipation in Late Medieval Florence* (New Brunswick, N.J.: Rutgers University Press, 1982), 10–34 and passim.

[11]Thomas, "Division," 129, 137; Dixon, "Infirmitas Sexus," 359–60.

[12]Cf. Dixon, "Infirmitas Sexus," 344, 350–53.

[13]A nice summary is Annalisa Belloni, "Die Rolle der Frau in der Jurisprudenz der Renaissance," in *Die Frau in der Renaissance*, ed. Paul Gerhard Schmidt (Wiesbaden: Harrassowitz, 1994), 55–80, esp. 68–78.

[14]Belloni, "Die Rolle der Frau," 362–67.

each other.[15] Women's exclusion from the public functions of the church mirrored their secular political exclusion, and canon law reiterated their exclusion from other roles (judge, arbitrator, surety, witness in criminal proceedings or to testaments).[16] Canon law, however, expanded protection of women, in light of their presumed weakness, as with regard to *alimenta*, and pushed successfully for giving mothers guardianship over their own children (relying on maternal affection as favorable to the children).[17]

Onto this uneven legacy the statutes of Florence worked certain protective extensions and incapacities. Florentine laws paralleled those of many other cities in restricting female inheritance, in the presence of direct male heirs, to dowry. Beyond this, Florence notably retained a form of protective guardianship of women, under the Lombard term *mundualdus*, for just about all civil acts, or by an attorney (*procuratore*) for civil litigation.[18]

Florentine statutes had several functions:

- they exempted wives wishing to seek their property pledged or sold by their husbands from the one-year filing period;
- they set procedures for women who wished to recover dowries from a predeceased husband's heirs, and allowed them to recover their dowries (*consignatio dotis*) in case of a husband's bankruptcy;
- they made all of a husband's property subject to a hypothec for return of the dowry;
- they forbade a wife from acting to defend her husband's property from his creditors;

[15]Dixon, "Infirmitas Sexus," 364; Barry Nicholas, *An Introduction to Roman Law* (Oxford: Oxford University Press, 1962), 249–50.

[16]In general, see René Metz, "Le statut de la femme en droit canonique médiéval," *Recueils de la Société Jean Bodin pour l'Histoire Comparative des Institutions*, vol. 12: *La Femme* (1962): 59–113.

[17]See Gian Savino Pene-Vidari, *Ricerche sul diritto agli alimenti*, vol. 1: *L'obbligo 'ex lege' dei familiari nel periodo della Glossa e del commento* (Turin: Giappichelli, 1970), 349–54; Gigliola Villata di Renzo, "Note per la storia della tutela nell'Italia del Rinascimento," in *La famiglia e la vita quotidiana in Europa dal '400 al '600: Fonti e problemi* (Rome: Ministero per i Beni Culturali e Ambientali, 1986), 59–95, and idem, *La tutela: Indagini sulla scuola dei glossatori* (Milan: Giuffrè, 1975), 137–59. Canon law also enshrined the notion of the marriage debt, the overt equality of which (each spouse having to acquiesce to reasonable sexual demands) was belied by prevailing views of women as irrationally lustful and by lack of any notion of spousal rape; see Dyan Elliott, "Bernardino of Siena versus the Marriage Debt," in *Desire and Discipline*, 168–200.

[18]On these statutes, see Thomas Kuehn, chaps. 9 and 10 in *Law, Family, and Women: Toward a Legal Anthropology of Renaissance Italy* (Chicago: University of Chicago Press, 1991); see also Franco Niccolai, *La formazione del diritto successorio negli statuti comunali del territorio lombardo-tosco* (Milan: Giuffrè, 1940). Samuel K. Cohn, Jr., *Women in the Streets: Essays on Sex and Power in Renaissance Italy* (Baltimore: Johns Hopkins University Press, 1996), 28, sees the *mundualdus* as a new element in the fifteenth century further constraining women and thus a factor in the "decline in Italian women's status" from the late fourteenth century, when in fact it was a Lombard survival (not revival) evident in Florence's earliest statutes from 1321.

- they gave to husbands all revenue on any property acquired by their wives during marriage, unless expressly forbidden it in the deed of gift or will;
- they made fathers liable for unemancipated sons but not for daughters;
- they rendered valid the contract of any wife made with spousal consent, while forbidding her any alienation of dotal property;
- they expressly absolved married daughters from paternal debts, unless they were heirs to their fathers;
- they declared that no married woman's consent to alienation of dotal property would be considered valid unless rendered before a judge and in the presence of the woman's father or a special guardian given her in the absence of a father;
- they affirmed the priority of mothers and paternal grandmothers to act as guardians to young children as long as they wished to serve and did not remarry;
- they placed wives in the order of intestate succession to their husbands only in preference to the fisc, but gave husbands predeceased wives' dowries if there were no children and rights to one-third of nondotal goods.[19]

Rights and (dis)abilities varied by age and marital status. Gendered categories served to restrict the amounts and types of property that women might own, but they were not precluded from ownership. Gender was distinct from ownership. Women's agency—the ability to use and dispose of what they owned—was restricted by gender, but also by other factors.

DAUGHTERS

Like legitimate sons, daughters were subject to their father's *potestas*. Anything acquired was gained passively, by gift or inheritance, and thus fell into one or another form of *peculium*, to be administered by fathers, to whom daughters and sons alike owed *reverentia* and *obedientia*. Manlio Bellomo reports that one sixteenth-century jurist was able to list thirty-four limitations falling on a daughter *in potestate*.[20] In consequence of this legal condition, young Florentine girls seldom emerged into legal view. One indicator of how little a daughter's property or legal capacity could come into play in Florentine life lies in the relative infrequency of emancipations of women, especially of those under eighteen (the Florentine age of majority), from *patria potestas*. In the first half of the fifteenth century, whereas 224 boys eighteen or younger were emancipated, only fifty-eight girls in the same age group were (about one-fourth as many). On the other hand, women were likely to

---

[19] *Statuta communis Florentiae anno salutis mccccxv*, 3 vols. (Freiburg [Florence], 1778–83), vol. 1, bk. 2, rubrics 57 (151–52), 61 (156–59), 63 (160), 64 (161), 65 (161–62), 110 (201–2), 111 (203–4), 113 (205), 115 (206–7), 122 (210–14), 126 (217–18), 129 (222–23).
[20] Bellomo, *Condizione giuridica*, 38–39.

be emancipated at an earlier age than men.[21] Emancipation of such young women had a variety of purposes in Florence, including facilitating the girls' alienation of inherited property to fathers or brothers.[22] In that unparalleled survey of household wealth, the Florentine *catasto*, such *peculia* of daughters surface sporadically. In 1458 Carlo di Palla della Foresa, for example, reported that a small farm given to his daughter Spinetta by her maternal grandfather had been sold four years earlier.[23]

Daughters' legal personae were complicated by their inheritance rights to their mothers and by the paternal obligation to dower them. To a small extent one can see the legal complications in a legal opinion (*consilium*) of Filippo Corsini (1334–1421). Corsini argued that the farm Bernardo d'Ugolino Bonsi had bought was still obligated for the dowry of Dada di Giovanni Petriboni, despite the Florentine statute forbidding children to seek their mother's dowry while their father was alive, unless they had been emancipated for two years. Dada was seeking to regain property her father had alienated from her mother's dowry. Since Bernardo had not been among those personally obligated for the dowry, it was argued that he was not protected by the statute. Corsini concluded that the Florentine statute worked a singular exception to *ius commune* that should not be extended.[24] What we cannot know was the father's sense of this reversal of his legal action by his daughter.

The main legal right of the unmarried daughter was the paternal obligation to dower her. This was a powerful obligation legitimizing patriarchy that, according to the authoritative jurist Baldo degli Ubaldi (1327–1400), was rooted "in a sort of communion between a father and daughter" that remained even if her marriage ended.[25] Amassing a dowry and putting together a *corredo* for marriage were dominant economic events in a girl's youth—enough so that Florence was able to take advantage of it in the city's fiscal schemes with the establishment in 1425 of the Monte delle Doti (dowry fund).[26]

---

[21]Kuehn, *Emancipation*, 86–87.

[22]Kuehn, *Emancipation*, 116–20; Thomas Kuehn, "Understanding Gender Inequality in Renaissance Florence: Personhood and Gifts of Maternal Inheritance by Women," *Journal of Women's History* 8 (1996): 58–80.

[23]Archivio di Stato, Firenze (hereafter ASF), catasto 790, fol. 254v.

[24]ASF, Notarile Antecosimiano (hereafter NA), 13502 (1458–82), fols. 326r–27r, a sealed original bearing the date 11 August 1412. It is interesting that Corsini closed by exonerating Bonsi of the costs of losing his suit "Propter dubietatem negocii et suttilitatem iurium et varietatem opyniorum...."

[25]Baldo to l. Si cum dotem (D. 24.3.22), *Opera omnia*, 10 vols. (Venice, 1577), vol. 3, fol. 10va: "Quod pactum valet quo ad extraneum, non quo ad patrem, quia natura dotis et onus patris in dotanda filia non possunt removeri nudo pacto natura dotis est in quadam communione inter patrem et filiam ut l. ii quod si in patris supra e. et onus patris prospicit filiae etiam dissoluto matrimonio ut C. de rei uxo. acti."

[26]On which see the early article of Julius Kirshner and Anthony Molho, "The Dowry Fund and the Marriage Market in Early Quattrocento Florence," *Journal of Modern History* 50 (1978): 403–38; and Anthony Molho, *Marriage Alliance in Late Medieval Florence* (Cambridge, Mass.: Harvard Unversity Press, 1994).

In Florence, most women who were going to be married were wives by age eighteen or nineteen.[27] Thus for them marriage interestingly coincided with the statutory age of adulthood. Marriage made them someone's wife; it did not change the fact that they were daughters. Moreover, neither in Florence nor elsewhere did marriage emancipate women (or men, for that matter), who continued under their fathers' *potestas* as long as the father lived.[28] Thus it was that married daughters could continue to have legal importance to their fathers.[29] In 1484, for example, Giovanni di Matteo Corsi emancipated his married daughter so he could give her his mother's estate, keeping usufruct for his life while passing to her a debt he owed someone else.[30] In this fashion he seems to have protected some property from his creditors by lodging ownership with a married daughter who was not otherwise obligated for his debts. Another indicator of continued legal and material ties between married women and their families of origin lies in the number of wills by which their fathers left them property. Bartolomeo di Filippo di Bertoldo had no sons, so he generously left *alimenta* to his servant, now living with his married daughter, bequeathed 100 florins to his married granddaughter (excluding her husband from usufruct), and left everything else to this daughter.[31]

WIVES

In *ius commune* a man became *paterfamilias* not on marriage, nor on the birth of legitimate children, but on his *pater*'s death or emancipation. A woman's legal persona, however, underwent changes at marriage. A married woman was a mother (a social fiction) even without children and became *materfamilias* on their birth. In essence, a woman became a *mater* not by giving birth but by marrying. Law attached her status to the legal marriage contract, not to the natural act of birth (which, however, fixed her relations to a child, even if born outside marriage).[32] This social function of providing men and their lineage with children was reinforced by a social and religious sexual ethic.[33] It fell to the wife to safeguard a lineage's integrity, perpetuate it, and preserve its honor by premarital virginity and marital chastity.

[27]Cf. David Herlihy and Christiane Klapisch-Zuber, *Les toscans et leurs familles* (Paris: Fondation Nationale des Sciences Politiques, 1978), 393–400.

[28]And a Florentine father was much more liable to be alive when his daughter married than when his sons did, for the boys' marriages were postponed to later ages and thus generally came after their sisters had been settled. See David B. Rheubottom, "'Sisters First': Betrothal Order and Age at Marriage in Fifteenth-Century Ragusa," *Journal of Family History* 13 (1988): 359–76.

[29]Kuehn, *Law, Family, and Women*, chap. 8.

[30]ASF, NA 14721, fol. 178r–v (23 January 1484).

[31]ASF, NA 14721, fols. 67v–68r (29 December 1482); also NA 7046, 14 April 1427.

[32]Thomas, "The Division of the Sexes," 87–88, 117–18, 122.

[33]This ethic is nicely examined by Maria Serena Mazzi, *Prostitute e lenoni nella Firenze del Quattrocento* (Milan: Il Saggiatore, 1991), 46–57, 85–87; and for modern Greece by Juliet du Boulay, "Women: Images of Their Nature and Destiny in Rural Greece," in *Gender and Power in Rural Greece*, 139–68.

The common pattern in Florence and elsewhere was virilocal/patrilocal marriage. Sons brought their brides home with them; the very process of conducting a new bride through the streets to a man's house had both legal and ritual significance in establishing the fact of marriage and related property transfers.[34] This pattern meant also that, although *patria potestas* endured and persisting ties were also celebrated in a ritual *ritornata* to the paternal home, the wife effectively left one family for another.[35] The law itself described the situation of the wife on analogy to a freed slave. She was in the "service" of her husband; she owed him *obsequium* (obedience and deference) while he held a power of correction over her.[36] However, while jurists, under the influence of canonical texts, could talk of husband and wife as "one flesh," there was no equivalent in *ius commune* to the English rule of coverture, by which husband and wife were one person, and that person was the husband.[37] Her interests and property remained legally distinct from his. Attachment to her kin was always important to her husband and his kin, including their children, for cognatic ties were socially and economically useful.[38] Perhaps this separateness of spouses is nowhere more clear than in the fact that an alimentary obligation between spouses was *not* axiomatic. The wife's dowry was supposed to sustain the matrimonial *onera*, including her alimentation, so in law the husband's obligation arose only if he was in possession of her dowry. Her right to retrieve the dowry in case of his mismanagement spoke to this fact.

To be sure, some jurists tried to argue for an obligation even in the absence of dowry, on the basis of the wife's working for her husband's benefit—a contractual basis, in other words. If the wife left the house, left the *obsequium* of her husband, then there was doubt on whether he owed her *alimenta*. If she had separated as a result of behavior that was his fault, then he owed her *alimenta*, especially if he still held her dowry.[39] In July 1415, seven jurists in Florence posed a hypothetical case of a wife who left a physically abusive husband, who kept her 1100-florin dowry while agreeing to pay her brothers forty-four florins annually (exactly 4 percent) for her *alimenta*. The woman fell ill and incurred considerable additional expenses. Could her brothers seek a supplementary payment from her husband? In this hypothetical

---

[34]Cf. Christiane Klapisch-Zuber, "Le complexe de Griselda: Dot et dons de mariage au Quattrocento," *Mélanges de l'École française de Rome* 94 (1982): 7–43; translated as "The Griselda Complex: Dowry and Marriage Gifts in the Quattrocentro," in Christiane Klapisch-Zuber, *Women, Family, and Ritual in Renaissance Italy,* trans. Lydia G. Cochrane (Chicago: University of Chicago Press, 1985), 213–46.

[35]Isabelle Chabot, "'La sposa in nero': La ritualizzazione del lutto delle vedove fiorentine (secoli xiv–xv)," *Quaderni storici* 86 (1994): 421–62, at 431–32.

[36]Bellomo, *Condizione giuridica*, 39–40; Kuehn, *Law, Family, and Women*, chap. 8.

[37]Nicholas, "An Introduction to Roman Law," 81.

[38]Cf. Anthony Molho, Roberto Barducci, Gabriella Battista, and Francesco Donneni, "Genealogia e parentado: Memorie del potere nella Firenze tardo-medievale, il caso di Giovanni Rucellai," *Quaderni storici* 86 (1994): 365–403; and Christiane Klapisch-Zuber, "Albero genealogico e costruzione della parentela nel Rinascimento," *Quaderni storici* 86 (1994): 405–20.

[39]Pene-Vidari, *Richerche sul diritto*, 349–96.

case the woman was clearly not *in obsequio viri*, but just as clearly the results were his fault. The husband was liable for both ordinary and extraordinary expenses of his wife (including those related to her illness) but the forty-four-florin annuity was intended only to cover ordinary expenses; and as medicines were not *alimenta* "because they do not feed (*alant*)," an extra sum was due. It was not licit for the husband to have the benefits of the dowry without facing the burdens of marriage.[40]

One can find a number of interesting actual cases of marital separations in Florence. For instance, the septuagenarian Monte di Giovanni del Benino, who "on account of his bad behavior" had provoked his wife's departure, did not furnish *alimenta*, although he kept her 400-florin dowry. An arbitrator ordered him to retain only 150 florins, paying the rest to his son, who would use it to see to his mother's support.[41] In another example, the agreement of 18 November 1460 struck between Apollonia di Domenico Lulli and her husband of five years, Bencivenni di Neri Bartoli, stipulated that she would return to their home and could bring her girl servant to live at his expense. For his part, he was to treat her as a good husband (*bonus vir*) should, not hit her (*verberare*), and restrain his son by a previous marriage and his wife from verbally abusing Apollonia (*non dare aliqua verba iniuriosa*).[42] The son and daughter-in-law were to leave and live on their own. And in 1458 ser Giovanni di ser Fruosino da Radda, then seventy-six, reported to city officials that his wife had not lived with him since 1434 and he was bound to pay her twenty-two florins annually as *alimenta*.[43]

In the statute that governed property acquired by a wife during marriage, which both gave usufruct to the husband (contrary to *ius commune*) and forbade the wife to alienate any of it without his consent (also contrary to *ius commune*), Florence came close to a form of coverture. Yet an indicator of the convergence and divergence of interests and personhood between spouses reaches us in a case that came before the Florentine jurist Antonio Strozzi (1455–1523). In this case, a wife alienated property obtained during marriage by giving it to grandchildren, to the disadvantage of sons by her second marriage. She was treated badly by her first husband and separated from him, living as a servant in Florence and later with her sons by her first marriage. The second husband's treatment of her negated his enjoyment of proceeds on her property and his legal ability to forbid her to alienate it. When a husband did not enjoy revenues from such property, then his wife was legally free to manage it,

---

[40]Biblioteca Nazionale, Firenze (hereafter BNF), Landau-Finaly 98, fols. 331r–32v, 335r–35^bisv, a sealed original by (in order) Paolo di Castro (c. 1360–1441), Giovanni Buongirolami (1381–1454), Floriano da San Pietro (fl. 1400), Giovanni da Imola (1367–1436), Pietro d'Ancarano (c. 1330–1416), Agribiro da Perugia (?), and Bartolomeo Vulpi (c. 1359–1435).

[41]ASF, NA 14715 (1469–71), fols. 63v–64r (12 October 1470).

[42]ASF, NA P 128 (old designation) (1452–62), fols. 416v–17v (18 November 1460). In her will of 26 July 1461 (fols. 489v–90r) she is termed "uxor olim Johannis Bartholomei de Singnia" and she leaves everything to the hospital of San Paolo, so one surmises that the reconciliation did not last.

[43]ASF, catasto 785, fols. 260r–62r.

because she was not prejudicing any rights of his. Otherwise, when alienation somehow did not prejudice spousal usufructuary rights, a wife was free to alienate for "the rationale of the statute prohibiting alienation ceases." However, she had deprived her sons of their expected portion, the *legitim*, and they could seek that "because a mother could not take away from other children the *legitim* owed to them by means of such a gift."[44] The husband's treatment released her from a substantial partnership in which he was legally dominant, but it did not absolve her from her maternal obligations.

When such tensions surfaced, they made it apparent that married women had a legal persona and some options for exercising it. Such cases caution us from making sharp distinctions between male interests as familial and women's interests as somehow competing with them. For a number of wives, it became necessary to take legal steps to retrieve their dowries from the management of husbands who were headed toward insolvency (*vergentes ad inopiam*). This was a practice designed in *ius commune* and sanctioned by Florentine statute. By this means it was possible for someone like Antonia di Checcho to regain her fifty-florin dowry from her husband of fourteen years, Bastiano di Paolo di Lorenzo, in 1427.[45] Most women who sought their dowries, however, were looking for considerably larger sums, and their protection of those funds from spousal creditors worked to the advantage of their husbands (and children) as well as themselves.[46]

These women were unusual. Mainly we find married women entering into legal transactions in cooperation with their husbands or their fathers and brothers. They wrote wills, received gifts, sold or gave property away, entered into arbitrations, consented to alienations of dotal property.[47] Encountered in the *catasto*, these married women can seem submerged in their husbands' worlds. They are listed among household members (as another deductible "mouth"), almost always without a patronymic reference, simply as "my woman" (*mia donna*) or "his wife" (*sua moglie*).[48] The dowry is not usually listed apart, unless it became necessary to record it as a debt owed.[49] Paraphernalia, or nondotal goods, were sometimes disclosed as such.[50] One

[44]ASF, Carte strozziane, 3rd ser., 41.9, fols. 156r–57r.

[45]ASF, NA 9040 (1422–29), fols. 278v–79r (21 March 1427).

[46]Julius Kirshner, "Wives' Claims against Insolvent Husbands in Late Medieval Italy," in *Women of the Medieval World*, ed. Julius Kirshner and Suzanne F. Wemple (Oxford: Basil Blackwell, 1985), 256–303.

[47]Kuehn, *Law, Family, and Women*, 205–10, 223–24.

[48]ASF, catasto 825, fol. 479r–80r, offers an exception where a widow gives the family of her daughter-in-law.

[49]See ASF, catasto 832, fols. 417r, where ser Jacopo di ser Guido del maestro Pagholo reports a debt owed by his brothers-in-law on their obligation "di conservarmi senza danno quando non potessi ritrarre la dota della mia donna e sua figliuola la qual a trassi dopo lungho tempo et affanno et stesa con assai mio danno."

[50]Julius Kirshner, "Materials for a Gilded Cage: Nondotal Assets in Florence (1300-1500)," in *The Family in Italy from Antiquity to the Present*, ed. David I. Kertzer and Richard P. Saller (New Haven: Yale Unversity Press, 1991), 184–207.

woman's brothers reported that their married sister had a piece of land that her husband treated as his own.[51] Another Florentine reported that his wife had at least 400 florins due her from her father's estate.[52]

That the wife's interests were substantial, or that her role in the household might be more active, shines through at rare moments. Tommaso di Goro di Stagio Dati, under the heading of "goods sold" (*beni venduti*), said that his wife had sold a piece of land in Gangalandi to a widow who lived there.[53] Although he probably served as her *mundualdus* and was present at the sale, he in no way ascribes it to himself or to an inclusive "we." His father had taken a similar stance with regard to a transaction of his (third) wife years before in his "secret" records. There he recalled how in January 1413, "with my consent," she had given her brother all the lands that their mother "had long before given her secretly."[54] In a more intriguing case, Masa, the thirty-year-old wife of Giovanni d'Arrigo di Giovanni, himself just two years older, posed as the active (first person) voice in the *catasto*, listed first among household members.[55]

MOTHERS

In the normal course of events, the wife was supposed to become the mother. There were certain ambiguities about motherhood in the law. These went back to senses of nature that were not totally consistent. Women's role in reproduction was downplayed, but their "natural" attachment to their children was recognized, even by jurists, who conceded that maternal love was greater even than paternal love, but that fathers gained *patria potestas* because they were more suited to doing things useful for their children.[56] The interests of the agnatic lineage worked a sort of naturalization of the female contribution, and patrilocality put the woman at parturition in the keeping of mother- and sister-in-law.[57] Once she had given her husband children, she could be seen as more integrated into the lineage's interests. Motherhood

---

[51]ASF, catasto 832, fol. 14r.

[52]ASF, catasto 826, fols. 230r–31r.

[53]ASF, catasto 790, fols. 143r–44v.

[54]*Il libro segreto di Gregorio Dati*, ed. Carlo Gargiolli (Bologna, 1869; reprint, Bologna: Romagnoli, 1968), 63.

[55]ASF, catasto 832, fol. 293r–v.

[56]Ascanio Clemente Amerini, *Tractatus de patria potestate*, in *Tractatus universi iuris*, 29 vols. (Venice, 1584), vol. 8, pt. 2, fols. 98ra–127rb, at 100ra: "Immo matris amor in filio sit maior amore patris…sit etiam filius matri summopere obligatus, cum matri sit ante patrum onerosus, dolorosus in partu, post partum laboriosus.… Qua de causa debuisset haec patria potestas ei tradi, tamen deficiebat secunda causa ob quam diximus fuisse eam potestatem repertam, cum ad multa mater pro filiorum utilitate ob muliebrem sexum non esset apta sicut patri et leges magis confidunt de patre in providendo filiis, quam de matre apparet.…"

[57]Bruno Martinelli, "Matrimoine et patrimoine: Sur les fonctions successorales des femmes dans quelques exemples provençaux," in *Femmes et patrimoine dans les sociétés rurales de l'Europe méditerranéenne*, ed. G. Ravis-Giordani (Paris: Centre National de la Recherche Scientifique, 1987), 75–87.

and age mitigated her relative strangeness and young sexuality.[58] Now her dowry had heirs in her children. Now in *ius commune* and in statutes she had others—her children—obligated for her *alimenta*. As a parent she also acquired certain obligations to and control over others. The law recognized a natural obligation of parental upbringing (*educatio*), including *alimenta*, falling on both parents. The mother's obligation was seen as primary, however, only in the first three years of life. Here, then, wealthy Florentines' pattern of putting their children to wet-nurse substituted paternal funds for maternal milk and inserted the primacy of the paternal obligation even earlier into life.[59]

Mothers had reason, even while their husbands were still alive, to enter into certain legal dealings for the benefit of their children. The wife of Francesco di Neri Dietisalvi, for example, wrote a will in favor of her married daughter.[60] But generosity could move the other way, too. When Matteo di Francesco Lapucci emancipated his two sons and gave them various household furnishings and implements (explaining that it had been their labor that had gained them), they turned around and gave usufruct on it all to their mother.[61] She thus continued to enjoy the things she was using anyway, but now on the sufferance of her sons rather than her husband. Legal and economic evocations of motherhood crop up periodically even in the *catasto*, where sons report testamentary obligations for masses of remembrance and so forth.[62]

WIDOWS

Scholars have viewed widowhood as an especially active period in women's lives. Free of husband, probably of father, possessed of dowry and perhaps other property, but also likely to have children to care for, widows can be seen as having stepped into roles of greater legal responsibility, even to have before them "independent life choices."[63] But widowhood has also been described as a time of diminishing resources and growing poverty.[64] Certainly widows had long been recognized in

---

[58]Cf. du Boulay, "Women: Images of Their Nature," 158–59.

[59]Cf. Christiane Klapisch-Zuber, "Genitori naturali e genitori di latte nella Firenze del Quattrocento," *Quaderni storici* 44 (1980): 543–63, translated as "Blood Parents and Milk Parents: Wet-Nursing in Florence, 1300–1530," in *Women, Family, and Ritual*, 132–64.

[60]ASF, NA 16841 (1454–1505), fols. 39r–41r (4 May 1477).

[61]ASF, NA 14722 (1484–86), fol. 151v (5 February 1488–89).

[62]ASF, catasto 825, fols. 43r–47r.

[63]Chabot, "La sposa in nero," 424.

[64]Cf. introduction to *Upon My Husband's Death: Widows in the Literature and Histories of Medieval Europe*, ed. Louise Mirrer (Ann Arbor: University of Michigan Press, 1992), 1–17; Ann Morton Crabb, "How Typical Was Alessandra Macinghi Strozzi of Fifteenth-Century Florentine Widows?" in *Upon My Husband's Death*, 47–68; Chabot, "La sposa in nero"; and idem, "Widowhood and Poverty in Late Medieval Florence," *Continuity and Change* 3 (1988): 291–311. As one example of a response to widowly poverty, messer Agnolo di Giovanni took in a boy whose mother was too poor to care for him (ASF, catasto 795, fols. 366r–68v). In another example, Jacopo di Giovanni Ferravecchio married a widow and, in a fairly rare gesture, took in her daughter because she was poor (ASF, catasto 814, fols. 710r–13r).

canon law as a category of *miserabilis persona* in need of special protection.[65] Some
of those who emerge in the *catasto* were undoubtedly poor. Attaviano di Nicholaio
d'Amadore listed a debt of twenty florins from a widow who, he said, "is very poor
and has never been able to have anything."[66] Women without husbands or other
adult males willing to help them had to face the tasks of managing alone, and that
management had to involve them in legal actions. The more wealth they possessed,
the more likely it was that some men, in their husband's kin or their natal family,
would stay involved in their activities.

According to Barbara Diefendorf, "The important administrative role assumed
by widows contrasts sharply with the legal incapacity of married women and bears
out the truth of the statement that married women were incapable because they were
married and not because they were women."[67] Certainly one thing the absence of a
husband provoked was the need to establish guardianship (*tutela*) over young children. This was an important matter in a society in which men delayed their marriages and thus stood a strong chance of dying before all their children reached
adulthood. In Florence an entire civic board, the Magistrato dei Pupilli, was devoted
to overseeing this legal institution.

The widowed mother did not become her minor children's guardian just by virtue of being their mother. As children "belonged" to their father, it was up to him to
name their mother or anyone else as guardian. If he died intestate, the widow could
approach the magistrato and seek *tutela*, or the task fell to his kin in preference to
her.[68] Nor could the widow serve as guardian alone; there had to be other, male
guardians as well. Not herself possessed of *patria potestas*, a widow could not name
guardians for her children following her death. But a widow become *tutrix* had an
official legal and social role that helped to "blur the formal structure of the patrilinear system decomposing its rigidness with more horizontal practices and behaviors."
She might stand in some conflict with brothers-in-law, with their patrimonial interests, while often relying on her own brothers, who like her did not have succession
interests in the estate. To remain guardian she had to stay widowed. Thus there was a
double exclusion: "Guardian by agreement not to remarry, she guaranteed the separation between sexuality and the maternal role; trustee of minors because she would
never inherit from them, she assured to her children an absolutely disinterested,
'pure' love."[69]

[65]James A. Brundage, "Widows as Disadvantaged Persons in Medieval Canon Law," in *Upon My
Husband's Death*, 193–206.

[66]ASF, catasto 790, fol. 603r.

[67]Barbara B. Diefendorf, "Women and Property in *ancien régime* France: Theory and Practice in
Dauphiné and Paris," in *Early Modern Conceptions of Property*, ed. John Brewer and Susan Staves (New
York: Routledge, 1996), 170–93, at 177.

[68]Cf. di Renzo, *La tutela*, 140–59.

[69]Giulia Calvi, "Diritti e legami: Madri, figli, stato in Toscana (xvi–xviii secolo)," *Quaderni storici*
86 (1994): 487–510, quotes at 489, 494.

Within those confines it is not rare to run across widows as heads of households in the *catasto*. Ordinarily they had several children to care for, but as years went by their wealth diminished and they resided alone or were part of a son's family. Domenica, widow of Donato Maringhi, had been head of her household in the 1427 *catasto*, but in 1458, at age eighty, she ceded pride of place to her fifty-year-old son Antonio, who was married with five children and had back in 1449 purchased the home in which this household of eight lived.[70] Another widow with a thirty-four-year-old son and a twenty-eight-year-old daughter gave a first-person report to *catasto* officials, in which she revealed that she rented their home from another widow.[71]

One of the chief matters with which widows had to contend was the return of their own dowries. For one widow, it was noted that her *sustanze* were her dowry "as it appears from a lawsuit taken to the podestà."[72] Even if widows stayed with their husbands' kin, as they usually did, retrieving the dowry (legally due to them on the dissolution of the marriage) was a perpetual legal headache. They reported these problems to *catasto* officials, and they pursued these matters by legal means, often enlisting the help of men against their brothers-in-law or even their sons.

Agnola, twenty-five-year-old widow of Nozo di Tuccio Manetti, who had three children under five, reported to *catasto* officials that she had begun the long process of retrieving her dowry. She did not seem sanguine:

> I should have from the unclaimed estate of the abovesaid Nozo, my former husband, my dowry, which is 500 florins…which has been sought in the court of the podestà of Florence, and the lawsuit has begun and goes on continually and still it is not decided, so that I cannot yet know how it will turn out for me.[73]

She further reported that none of her husband's kin was willing to help her young children, even though "they have no substance." In a questionable maternal move, she had sent the two older sons to their paternal kin, who did not even let them in but chased them away. "Wandering through the land, late that evening, they were brought back to me, and it falls to me to keep and feed them because they [the paternal kin] did not want to hear any more of them in any way."

Once they had their dowry back, widows could tend to economic needs with some facility, even if they had only part of it.[74] But they also could more easily remarry. Fruosino and Antonio di Giovanni di Fruosino, who owed their step-

---

[70]ASF, catasto 818, fol. 167r.

[71]ASF, catasto 825, fol. 165r–v.

[72]ASF, catasto 826, fol. 33r–v.

[73]ASF, catasto 790, fol. 364r.

[74]ASF, catasto 798, fol. 574r–v, where a woman claims that one holding was held by a brother-in-law "chontro a ogni debito di ragione, e detta possessione è mio fondo dotale perchè fu del mio padre."

mother her dowry, also observed that their widowed sister had received 240 florins of her dowry and bought a vineyard as *fondo dotale*. She had remarried but not yet been conducted to her husband's house for lack of the rest of her dowry.[75] Remarriage has been provocatively examined by Christiane Klapisch-Zuber, who labeled as "cruel mothers" those (generally younger) widows who found themselves caught between the demands of two families and made to remarry, taking their dowry with them, abandoning the children of their first marriage to the care of paternal kin.[76] Giulia Calvi, in a study of widows' petitions to the Florentine magistrato dei pupilli between roughly 1550 and 1750, argues that these "cruel mothers" were the product of a social-cultural priority on female role as wife, versus mother, that was reversed by the eighteenth century.[77] In their wills husbands commonly included clauses leaving their widows usufruct on the house, furnishings, and other properties, as long as they lived there with their children in chaste widowhood. This testamentary device encouraged widows to stay in their husbands' homes and, according to Isabelle Chabot, became more frequent with more mature and settled couples.[78] On the other hand, the statutes of Florence guaranteed widows the right to return to live with their fathers or brothers; and these men too gave substance to these rights in their wills or other actions.

In fact, by witness of the *catasto*, most widows remained with their children in their husbands' homes. They did so often with the sort of rights conceded by messer Luigi di Piero Guicciardini to his wife Nanna by his testament of 1482. He left her the dowry of 1,800 florins and added that as long as she remained a widow and did not seek her dowry, she had right to use his house in Florence, which right also was left to each of their married daughters. Nanna received her clothing and use of all *mobilia* and the furnishings of the house, although she had to share the place with her husband's bastard son.[79]

Still, some women returned to their natal families. In the *catasto* of 1458, Lucrezia, daughter of the physician Angniolo di Cristofano, said that she with her four children (ages eight to fourteen) "returned to the house of the estate of maestro Angiolo with my brothers because I did not have elsewhere to turn and anything to feed these my children." She declared no assets and, surprisingly, did not give the name of her deceased husband, which we learn only from her brothers' report. There

---

[75]ASF, catasto 826, fol. 501r.

[76]Christiane Klapisch-Zuber, "La 'mère cruelle': Maternité, veuvage et dot dans la Florence des xive–xve siècles," *Annales* 38 (1983): 1097–1109; English translation, "The 'Cruel Mother': Maternity, Widowhood, and Dowry in Florence in the Fourteenth and Fifteenth Centuries," in *Women, Family, and Ritual*, 117–31.

[77]Giulia Calvi, "Dal margine al centro: Soggettività femminile, famiglia, Stato moderno in Toscana (xvi–xviii secc.)," in *Discutendo di storia: Soggettività, ricerca, biografia*, ed. Società italiana delle Storiche (Turin: Roseberg and Sellier, 1990), 103–18.

[78]Chabot, "La sposa in nero," 438–40.

[79]ASF, NA 15790 (testamenti, 1480–1513), 14 January 1481–82.

it was also reported that from Lucrezia's dowry it would be necessary to form dowries for her two daughters.[80]

Even before widowhood, men of women's natal lineages sometimes looked to add to their sisters' *sustanze*. Francesco Guasconi left usufruct on all his property to his married sister. Following her death, it was to be divided between two lines of Guasconi and two ecclesiastical institutions.[81] Another brother simply made his married sister universal heir and asked that masses be arranged for his soul.[82] This evidence leads one to wonder if "cruel mothers" were not simply being good sisters.[83]

It is as widows that women appear most often as active legal agents in notarial records. They variously disposed of or acquired property rights, engaged in arbitrations, and wrote wills.[84] They had to manage their assets both for day-to-day purposes and for the long-term passage of property to kin. The range of their interests and the true gauge of their legal personhood is perhaps best seen in their wills, where, as others have observed, they were freer than men to direct property to a variety of kin.[85] One widow, born in the Alderotti lineage, left fifty-two florins as a dowry to her son's illegitimate daughter and widowhood rights of *tornata* to her married daughter, with her sons as her universal heirs.[86] But there is also the case of the widow who left 100 florins each to her deceased husband's two illegitimate brothers, at the same time naming as her heirs her husband's three uncles.[87]

Married daughters (limited by Florentine statute from seeking more than the dowry they already had) were a frequent target of maternal generosity. Dea di Giovanni di Bonifazio gave her married daughter by her first marriage a house in the Via del Giardino (thus obviating any "cruelty" in this remarried mother).[88] One widow made her married daughter her heir, substituting her brothers if the girl died without children.[89] What was left to married daughters could be termed an addition to the

[80]ASF, catasto 832, fols. 118r, 120r–22r.

[81]ASF, NA 6752 (testamenti, 1473–1507), fols. 16r–17v (22 March 1477–78).

[82]ASF, NA 16841 (testamenti, 1454–1505), inserto 4, fols. 74r–75r (28 August 1503).

[83]According to Chabot, "La sposa in nero," 451, widows who returned to the paternal home experienced "una vera e propria regressione, fisica e giuridica, che sancisce il ritorno della vedova ad uno *status di figlia*." However, it seems that for many it was the status of sister (still, to be sure, a status in the family of origin) that mattered. Chabot's point is that remarriage required denying status as mother in the first marriage and taking back the dowry into the patrimony; but not all such widows remarried and they still had dotal inheritance rights.

[84]Kuehn, *Law, Family, and Women*, 227.

[85]Cf. Stanley Chojnacki, "'The Most Serious Duty': Motherhood, Gender, and Patrician Culture in Renaissance Venice" in *Refiguring Woman: Perspectives on Gender and the Italian Renaissance*, ed. Marilyn Migiel and Juliana Schiesari (Ithaca: Cornell University Press, 1991), 133–54.

[86]ASF, NA 14179 (testamenti, 1454–1494), fols. 103r–4r (22 September 1474).

[87]ASF, NA 16841 (testamenti, 1454–1505), fols. 143r–44r (14 June 1481). The 100 florins each were against a farm and a shop that had been given to three sisters whose relationship to the testatrix is not clear.

[88]ASF, NA 14721 (1482–84), fol. 226r (3 September 1484).

[89]ASF, NA 7002 (testamenti, 1473–1490), fol. 133r–v (13 July 1482).

dowry. A widow named Pippa in 1488 gave one son-in-law two pieces of land said to be worth 100 florins for one daughter's dowry, and to the other she gave 100 florins but reserved usufruct to herself for life.[90] When there were no daughters, there were perhaps sisters or nieces.[91]

According to Manlio Bellomo, women found it "practically impossible" to retrieve their dowries. Women's ideologically inscribed greedy attachment to their property helped cast juristic limits on them.[92] Yet, as we have seen, widows undertook a range of activities, took advantage of their separateness in law to direct property to children and even bastards, and made use of legal distinctions such as those between ownership, possession, and usufruct. As an example to sum it all up, Tommasa, the widow of Geppo di Guido, by his will of 1419 had been left a legacy of all their household furnishings, and her husband did not want her to be forced to draw up an inventory of household goods "because he wanted her to be able for her needs and for giving alms and other things that he imposed on her to sell and alienate, and he gave her the faculty and license to sell and alienate those things and from those things just as it should please her ... and to reside in her free and unrestrained conscience and will." Although he named two hospitals as his heirs, he showed full faith in his wife to oversee active affairs of the estate, on which the good of his immortal soul also rested. And she did her part. Following his death in 1425, Tommasa undertook to support and dower a poor girl and saw to her marriage in November 1429 to a Tuscan peasant. Having been able to supply only nine florins toward the thirty-five promised as dowry, the following March she gave him the right to choose from among the possessions left to her by her husband whatever he wanted up to the sum of twenty-six florins.[93] Gender stereotypes did not stand in the way of this woman of modest means, who found herself possessed of property that gave expression to her legal persona in connection with that of her deceased husband.

CONCLUSIONS

In discussing the "everyday" legal problem of those who used property "by reason of friendship or kinship" (*ratione amicitiae vel familiaritatis*) with the owner, the renowned jurist Bartolo da Sassoferrato (d. 1357) drew his examples from relationships between men and women. His treatment is revealing of the true legal power of women with regard to property through family relationships. His first example is that of a son who entered a maternal property and proclaimed that he possessed it. Bartolo said that he did not. He then used the example of a brother and sister living together on the undivided patrimony, in which case he alone rented it and enjoyed its fruits while "commonly she seems to do this by reason of family relationship"

[90]ASF, NA 14723 (1487–89), fol. 111v (15 August 1488).
[91]See ASF, NA 3373 (1428–32), fols. 104v–5r (15 July 1430).
[92]Bellomo, *Condizione giuridica*, 44–46.
[93]ASF, NA 9040, fols. 462r–63r (21 March 1429–30).

only. Presumably he was the heir. Finally, what a wife was said to possess belonged to her, even if she never set foot on it and possessed it through her husband.[94] The mother's and wife's right of ownership were not lost, even to the powerful social presumptions vesting ownership and agency in men, whereas the sister could not claim ownership as sibling in the absence of rules of inheritance passing it to her.

Overlapping relationships and roles across a woman's life added dimensions to her personhood. We have examined broad changes across the life cycle, beginning with the practical legal invisibility of a young daughter. Motherhood added little to a woman's legal agency, for all that it generated complicated relationships. Mothers did not gain *patria potestas*; they could neither adopt, legitimate, nor name *tutores*. They had no automatic inheritance rights to their children, and they became their guardians only if named to it. Marriage gained them dowry rights and status in a second family. Socially, it marked a first emergence of adulthood, which also coincided to some degree with legal age of maturity (eighteen in Florence). And, realistically if paradoxically, it was the dissolution of marriage that propelled the greatest expansion of the practical range of legal agency of the woman now become a widow. Widowhood put women's property rights primarily in their hands and high in the interest of potentially numerous others.

These life stages did not work uniformly for all women, nor should we expect them to. Being simultaneously—in the juristic aphorism—the beginning and end of her family nicely expressed the ambiguity of women. They were capable of doing and managing, of seeing interests and legal means to pursue them, but they could not carry them over a long term to others. Their property and personhood would be dissolved into others—probably men. Nonetheless, it is a personhood that acted and left traces in the devolution of property and the passage of the generations. In law, lessened somewhat in civic statutes, women had "full legal capacity." It cannot be maintained that they were not "among the protagonists of medieval life" or that consideration of their persona was solely at the discretion of male heads of household.[95]

Evocative gender stereotypes were both belied by what women did or were asked to do legally, and reinforced by how infrequently they did these things in com-

---

[94]Bartolo to l. Qui iure familiaritatis (D. 41.2.41), *Opera omnia*, 10 vols. (Venice, 1615), vol. 5, fol. 88rb: "Qui ingreditur fundum ratione amicitiae vel familiaritatis dicitur non possidere. Concor. supra de fideicom. lib. l. generaliter et tota die occurit casus huius l. Nam mater et filius stant simul et filius vadit ad fundum matris postmodum cum divideretur, dicit filius, ego possedi tanto tempore talem fundum. Ego credo quid in dubio videtur ire causa familiaritatis et amicitiae non ut possideat. Idem dico in fratre et sorore simul habitantibus et habentibus patrimonium individuum, ut frater vadit solus ad possessiones locandas, et fructus solos recolligit. Certe communiter videtur facere ex causa familiaritatis, per hanc l. et l. generaliter supra e. Et facit optime infra e. l. proxi. expressius sup. quib. mo. usufr. ami. l. si mulieri, quid bene no. Si ergo ad uxorem pertinet res, ipsa dicitur possidere, licet nunquam vadat, et possideat per virum."

[95]Which is the conclusion of Manlio Bellomo, "Dote (diritto intermedio)," in *Enciclopedia del diritto* 13 (1965): 8–32, at 31.

---

parison to men. The contradictions faced by married and widowed women—born in one family and married into another—were replicated in their role as preservers of the boundaries between the two families. Return of the dowry, residence in widowhood, gifts and testaments, even *alimenta* were all moments when it fell to women to state where boundaries fell and, in consequence, how well men were doing in giving them an active identification with one side of the boundary or the other. Women were always "citizens" of two families—sometimes, as we see in Julius Kirshner's essay, of two cities. Men's allegiances were supposedly simpler and stronger, and so their agency was clearer, less equivocal, and more powerful. But men too at times had to use women, protect property in them, or just acknowledge ties that were real and active. The deceased husband especially had to depend on his wife to take an active role in seeing to his soul, his offspring, and his property. None of this is to deny the realities or the ideology of sexual subordination, but it is to point to larger structural and processual features that transcend gender roles.[96]

Finally, with regard to the multiple sources of law, it seems that notions of ownership enshrined in *ius commune* further served women's albeit limited agency. The main reason is that, in contrast to English law, for example, women's personhood was not subsumed in their husbands'.[97] The nature of the functions behind dowry, for example, was not so narrowly conceived that it could not be exchanged to other sorts of items—by men or women. And differences among ownership, possession, and other forms of use arising from relationships were maintained, rather than blurred. It was not the nature of the things but the relationships in which they took meaning that mattered. For women these were defined by being daughters, wives, mothers, widows, and (we should add to our title) sisters.

[96]Cf. Jill Dubisch, "Culture Enters through the Kitchen: Women, Food, and Social Boundaries in Rural Greece," in *Gender and Power in Rural Greece*, 195–214.

[97]Thus Belloni concludes: "Zusammenfassend kann man sagen, daß die Rechslage der Frauen nach römischem Recht weniger schlecht war, als viele dies vermuten, und daß das *Ius Commune* diese Rechtsstellung hier und da verbessert, aber nirgends verschlechtert hat." Belloni, "Die Rolle der Frau," 80.

Women Married Elsewhere
Gender and Citizenship in Italy

Julius Kirshner[1]

GROUNDS

"In parts of our law," the early-third-century Roman jurist Papinian declared, "the position of females is inferior to that of males."[2] It is unnecessary to rehearse the gender-specific rules that disabled Roman women, unmarried and married, in the spheres of private and public law; these have been amply documented and discussed. It is also well known that three centuries later the *Corpus iuris* of Emperor Justinian eliminated various disabilities limiting women's capacity to contract, to make a last will, and to inherit. As O. F. Robinson states, "Public law remained a closed field, and social and economic realities kept women practically subordinate in Justinian's law, but the theoretical equality of the sexes before the private law was largely achieved."[3]

---

[1]I am grateful to Mario Ascheri, Vincenzo Colli, Maria Grazia Nico, Claudia Storti Storchi, and Romano Ferrari Zubini for generously responding to my requests for information and sending copies of works not available in Chicago; to Sandro Bulgarelli for making available to me the magnificent collection of *statuti* housed in the Biblioteca del Senato della Repubblica; and to Piero Fusi of the Biblioteca and Archivio Storico Comunale of Castiglion Fiorentino for placing at my disposal the archival riches of his town. As usual, I owe a debt to Osvaldo Cavallar for his valuable suggestions. The following standard abbreviations have been used for the *Corpus iuris civilis*: Dig. (*Omnia digesta seu pandectarum*); Cod. (*Codex Iustinianus*); Nov. (*Novellae*); Inst. (*Justiniani Institutiones*); Auth. (*Authenticum novellarum constitutionum Iustiniani versio vulgata*); for the *Corpus iuris canonici*: X. (*Decretales Gregorii IX*); VI. (*Liber sextus decretalium Bonifacii VIII*).

[2]Dig. 1. 5. 9: "In multis iuris nostri articulis deterior est condicio feminarum quam masculorum."

[3]O. F. Robinson, "The Historical Background," in *The Legal Relevance of Gender: Some Aspects of Sex-Based Discrimination*, ed. Sheila McLean and Noreen Burrows (Atlantic Highlands, N. J.: Humanities, 1988), 40–60, at 56. On the proprietary and contractual capacities of Roman women, see idem, "The Status of Women in Roman Private Law," *Juridical Review* 22 (1987): 143–62; Jane F. Gardner, *Women in Roman Law and Society* (London: Croom Helm, 1986), 5–29; Maria Teresa Guerra Medici, *Diritti delle donne nella società altomedievale* (Naples: Edizioni Scientifiche Italiane, 1986), 51–64; Antti Arajava, *Women and Law in Late Antiquity* (Oxford: Clarendon, 1996), esp. 230 ff.

In the patrilineal setting of medieval Italian communities, the legal capacities of women were again circumscribed, even more so than in Papinian's day. The social reproduction of patrilineal regimes depended on sons' succeeding their fathers as heads of the household and as masters of the family's patrimony.[4] Under the *Corpus iuris*, daughters and sons at least theoretically inherited equally, but under medieval patrilineal regimes, daughters were ordinarily excluded from inheritance by law.[5] They were entitled to a dowry, of course, which had to be commensurate with the social standing of the bride's father. Yet, even though the amount of the dowry might be sizable, the bulk of the paternal estate was generally destined for brothers and other male agnates. Medieval women, like their Roman counterparts, were excluded from public office and honors and from performing the truth-telling function of the jurist. Maria Teresa Guerra Medici reminds us that medieval urban "women did not take oaths, did not participate in the assemblies, and did not take part in public life. They had no access to public places where decisions were made on the life of the community."[6]

Although barred from active citizenship, a free Roman woman born legitimately in the late Roman Empire was a citizen of Rome (*civitas romana*), the common fatherland (*communis patria*).[7] She also enjoyed citizenship (*ius civitatis*) in the city of her origin (*origo*). The *ius civitatis* derived from paternal descent rather than from one's actual place of birth or residence. Legitimate children automatically acquired their father's *origo*; illegitimate children, their mother's *origo*. Upon marriage a Roman woman automatically assumed the status of a resident alien (*incola*) in her husband's *origo*, where she was liable for public duties and personal charges. The married woman's assumption of her husband's domicile did not entail the loss of her own *origo*. The immutability of one's *origo* was a hallowed principle of Roman law enshrined in *lex Adsumptio* [*Digest* (50. 1. 6)]. Although she was discharged from undertaking public duties in her own *origo*, the Roman wife remained accountable for charges on patrimonial property located there.

---

[4]Andrea Romano, *Famiglia, successioni e patrimonio familiare nell'Italia medievale e moderna* (Turin: G. Giappichelli, 1994).

[5]Manlio Bellomo, *Ricerche sui rapporti patrimoniali tra coniugi: Contributo alla storia della famiglia medievale* (Milan: Giuffrè, 1961), 163–85; Laurent Mayali, *Droit savant et coutumes: L'exclusion des filles dotées XIIème–XVème siècles*, Ius commune, Studien zur europäischen Rechtsgeschichte, no. 33 (Frankfurt a/M: Klostermann, 1987); Maria Teresa Guerra Medici, "L'esclusione delle donne dalla successione legitima e la *Constitutio super statutariis successionibus* di Innocenzo XI," *Rivista di storia del diritto italiano* 56 (1983): 261–94.

[6]Maria Teresa Guerra Medici, *L'aria di città: Donne e diritti nel comune medievale* (Naples: Edizioni Scientifiche Italiane, 1996), 19.

[7]Yan Thomas, *"Origine" et "commune patrie": Étude de droit public romain (89 av. J.-C–212 ap. J. C.)*, Collection de l'Ecole française de Rome, no. 221 (Rome: Ecole française de Rome, 1996); Fausto Goria, "'Romani,' cittadinanza ed estensione della legislazione imperiale nella costituzione di Giustiniano," in *La nozione di "romano" tra cittadinanza e universalità* (Naples: Edizioni Scientifiche Italiane, 1984), 277–342.

The *Corpus iuris* was the product of an empire, in which the status of a Roman citizen signified attachment to a common fatherland, not to a particular territorial community. Since the married couple shared a common Roman citizenship, inter-city marriage did not alter the wife's status as a *civis romana*. Dual citizenship, strictly speaking, was not practiced, for Roman citizenship superseded local citizenship.[8] At the same time, in the name of the juridical unity of the family, as Roman jurists conceived it, the wife's domicile followed that of her husband. The rule *mulier sequitur forum viri* meant that during marriage a wife could not have or acquire a domicile separate from her husband—known in modern law as a "domicile of choice."

On the treatment of married women's citizenship, the contrast between the *Corpus iuris* and medieval law is striking.[9] The Roman model of a married woman's *origo* and domicile may well have prevailed after the revival of Roman legal science in the twelfth century, but it was definitely modified in the early thirteenth with the appearance of Accursius's *Glossa ordinaria*, the standard guide to Justinian's *Corpus iuris*. In a nutshell, the *Glossa* held that a woman married to a foreigner necessarily becomes a citizen of her husband's *origo*, while she simultaneously ceases to be a citizen of her own native city.[10] The *Glossa* treated *lex Adsumptio* as a special case that does not to apply to a woman married elsewhere (*mulier alibi nupta*).[11] Her citizenship must be sacrificed, it appears, because she is no longer subject to taxes and obligations in her own *origo*.

The *Glossa*'s innovation was grounded in the mutating reality of localism, of hundreds of politically independent and law-making communities, each with its own citizenry, its campanilistic ethos. Medieval citizenship, by definition, signified attachment to a particular community (*origo*) with jurisdiction over a particular territory.[12] The immigration policies of medieval cities also allowed for dual citizenship—for example, one could be concurrently a citizen of Florence by descent and Pisa by municipal enactment. It was fairly common in the population-depleted fourteenth and fifteenth centuries for cities to grant citizenship to foreign men who

---

[8]Dieter Nörr, "Origo," in *Realencyclopädie der classischen Alterumswissenschaft*, ed. Georg Wissowa, *Supplementband* 10 (Stuttgart: A. Druckenmüller, 1965), 431–73.

[9]For the historical and jurisprudential background, see Julius Kirshner, "Mulier Alibi Nupta," in *Consilia im späten Mittelalter: Zum historischen Aussagewert einer Quellengattung*, ed. Ingrid Baumgärtner, Schriftenreihe des deutschen Studienzentrums, no. 13 (Sigmaringen: Thorbecke, 1995), 147–76.

[10]*Glossa ordinaria* to Cod. 10. 40(39). 7, *Cives quidem*, sv. *adlectio* (Venice, 1569), 53b: "Et tamen ex alterius etiam facto pendet matrimonium sed improprie dicitur ibi (Dig. 50. 1. 38. 3) incola, nam civis fit."

[11]*Glossa ordinaria* to Cod. 10. 39(38). 4, *Origine*.

[12]See Julius Kirshner, "*Civitas sibi faciat civem*: Bartolus of Sassoferrato's Doctrine on the Making of a Citizen," *Speculum* 48 (1973): 694–713; Diego Quaglioni, "La radice della dottrina bartoliana della cittadinanza," in his *Civilis sapienta: Dottrine giuridiche e dottrine politiche fra medioevo ed età moderna* (Rimini: Maggioli, 1989), 127–44; Joseph Canning, *The Political Thought of Baldus de Ubaldis* (Cambridge: Cambridge University Press, 1987), 93–184; Giorgio Chittolini, "The Italian City-State and Its Territory," in *City-States in Classical Antiquity and Medieval Italy: Athens and Rome, Florence and Venice*, ed. Anthony Molho, Kurt Raaflaub, and Julia Emlein (Stuttgart: F. Steiner, 1991), 589–602.

married native women and established residency in the wife's *origo*. Under Roman law, also known as *ius commune*, and local statutes, husbands married elsewhere retained their original citizenship. Dual citizenship, however, was not extended by statutes to women married elsewhere.[13] Cities also entered into expeditious bilateral agreements, as did Florence and Perugia in 1376,[14] whereby one city extended circumscribed privileges of citizenship to citizens of another city.

The *Glossa*'s unprecedented departure from the *Corpus iuris* validated contemporary political and economic conventions. Fearing the loss of taxable property, nearly all communities in north and central Italy introduced statutes prohibiting foreigners from acquiring real property subject to the community's jurisdiction. Foreign husbands of native women, who acquired valuable properties through the wife's dowry, were the primary targets of these laws. In order to prevent these men from controlling such properties, laws were enacted imposing penalties on native women with substantial dowries and inheritances who married foreigners and resided in the husband's *origo*. Penalties included monetary fines, forfeiture of property, and the inability to inherit from family members remaining in the native community. These penalties were not imposed on foreign husbands who established domicile in the wife's *origo*.

The transfiguration of the woman married elsewhere into a citizen of her husband's *origo*, the jurists explained, was linked to the unipersonality of the married couple, a sanctified partnership in which the wife, joined to the husband's flesh, was the subordinate partner. The proof texts were Eph. 5: 23 and Mt. 19: 5–6: "The husband is the head of the wife with whom she has joined in one flesh (*una caro*)."[15] As the couple through the sacrament of marriage is joined in one flesh, so are they joined in one citizenship and in one domicile, where the wife willingly submits to her husband's authority and leadership. Divine, natural, and civil law were thus harmonized in one body and one citizenship. In theory, the primacy given to the juridical unity of the family enhanced the dominance of the husband and his heirs over the wife and her property. Presumably, as a citizen of her husband's *origo*, she would be prevented from claiming an exemption from the laws of her husband's *origo*. Any benefits the husband might accrue from this change were offset by his wife's corresponding loss of native citizenship, which disqualified her from acquiring the legal benefits and protections (*beneficia statutorum*) reserved for citizens of her *origo*.[16] In

---

[13]This paragraph is based on Kirshner, "Mulier Alibi Nupta," 154–60.

[14]*Le Relazioni tra la Repubblica di Firenze e l'Umbria nel secolo XIV,* ed. Giustiniano Degli Azzi, 2 vols. (Perugia: Unione Tipografia Cooperativa, 1904), 1: 138–39, doc. 486.

[15]Daniela Müller, "Vir caput mulieris: Zur Stellung der Frau im Kirchenrecht unter besonder Berücksichtigung des 12. und 13. Jahrhunderts," in *Vom mittelalterlichen Recht zur neuzeitlichen Rechtswissenschaft,* ed. Norbert Brieskorn et al. (Paderborn: F. Schöningh, 1994), 223–46.

[16]For the theoretical basis of the rule *forenses non gaudent beneficiis statutorum*, see Claudia Storti Storchi, *Ricerche sulla condizione giuridica dello straniero in Italia dal tardo diritto comune all'età preunitaria: Aspetti civilistici* (Milan: Giuffrè, 1989), 67–93.

her native city, therefore, the woman-married-elsewhere's capacity as a citizen to enter into contracts, to collect the dowry, to receive gifts and legacies of nondotal goods, and to seek relief in the courts would be abridged.

Enter Bartolo of Sassoferrato (d. 1357), the preeminent jurist of the first half of the fourteenth century, who was respectfully critical of the *Glossa's* doctrine. He was as committed as any jurist to the unipersonality of the married couple, to the husband's supremacy, to gender-based distinctions, and to updating the *Corpus iuris* to complement custom and usage. Yet he was an independent-minded jurist, who viewed the woman-married-elsewhere's compulsory loss of citizenship and legal benefits as inequitable and materially harmful. And he was remarkably adept at crafting remedies for the disabilities, intentional and unintentional, inflicted upon women by ill-advised statutes. His remedy for a woman married elsewhere was presented in his influential commentary on the paragraph §*Item rescripserunt mulierum* in the *Digest* (50. 1. 38. 3), where he asked whether a wife loses her original citizenship, notwithstanding the force of *lex Adsumptio*.[17] He had recently addressed this question, he reported, in a dispute concerning a statute of a city that prohibited foreigners from purchasing immovable property in its territory. The prohibition was premised on the rule that statutory benefits enjoyed by citizens are not applicable to foreigners. Does the statute in question, he asked, apply to a woman married elsewhere who wishes to buy immovable property in her native city? His answer:

> Briefly, we can say that she changes her place of origin in regard to everything by which the person of the wife can be drawn away and separated from the services of her husband, and therefore she may not be called and forced in that city to shoulder personal burdens, perform public services, or be summoned to court, and this is what the laws cited above say. In regard to other things, she does not change her place of origin, as we say in the case of a freedwoman (*liberta*), married with the consent of her patron, who remains a freedwoman, although not with respect to the duties a freeborn owes to the patron. And consequently she can buy immovable property, which, in my opinion, is equitable. And if someone should kill her, that person should be punished just as if a citizen had been killed. And I believe that she also enjoys other privileges granted to citizens.[18]

---

[17]My discussion of Bartolo's theory in this paper amplifies my analysis in "Mulier Alibi Nupta," 161–66, where I also provide a working edition of his commentary on Dig. 50. 1. 38. 3, *Imperatores §ltem rescripserunt mulierum*, 173–75.

[18]Dig. 50. 1. 38. 3, *Imperatores*, 174: "Statuto civitatis cavetur, quod forensis non possit emere in territorio, queritur utrum mulier de illa civitate oriunda, alibi nupta, possit ibi emere, quid dicemus? Brevitur possumus sic dicere, quod originem mutat quantum ad omnia per que persona mulieris possit trahi et separari a servitiis viri, et ideo non potest ibi vocari vel trahi ad honores vel munera vel ad iudicia, ut dictum est, et ita loquuntur supra allegata, quo ad alia non mutat originem, ar. dicta l. Adsumptio. Sicut

Bartolo's principle of a distinct dual citizenship represented an artful compromise aimed at reconciling the conflict between the *Corpus iuris* and the *Glossa*. First, invoking *lex Adsumptio* and the authoritative analogy of the freedwoman, he repatriated the woman married elsewhere, who once again has recourse to the *beneficia statutorum* of her native city, and he repaired the wife's legal ties to the family she left behind. Yet, a return to the status quo before the *Glossa* was unthinkable. Accordingly, Bartolo concurred that the wife acquires her foreign husband's citizenship, thus assuring her respectful compliance, though he acknowledged that this change was not authorized by Roman law. Bartolo did not explicitly elaborate on the temporality of the wife's new civic status—namely, when she actually becomes a citizen of her husband's *origo* and whether she remains a citizen upon termination of marriage. Discussing the rule *mulier sequitur forum viri* at the beginning of his commentary on § *Item rescripserunt mulierum*, Bartolo asserted that the change in the wife's domicile was predicated on a valid marriage contracted through words of present consent (*verba de presenti*). A betrothal contracted through vows of future consent (*verba de futuro*) does not alter a fiancée's civic status. The formulaic "one flesh" signified consummation of marriage, but a valid marriage with the ensuing change in the wife's civic status was not dependent on consummation or public installation of the bride in the husband's home. The wife, upon her husband's predecease, even before moving to his *origo*, is deemed a resident there, so long as she remains a widow. Bartolo's position on the wife's domicile, understood within the unfolding logic of his commentary, was surely meant to apply to the citizenship of a woman married elsewhere.

Along with the *Corpus iuris* and the *Glossa*, Bartolo's commentary on § *Item resripserunt mulierum* became a controlling text for jurists occupied with the issue of intercity marriages. His compromise was fair, for it maximized the wife's and husband's benefits, while it minimized their costs. It pleased the majority of his successors, who intuitively believed that original citizenship derived from nature and was therefore immutable. But his compromise was never treated as a universal panacea for the problems arising from the practice of intercity marriage. Intercity marriage and dual citizenship generated inevitable jurisdictional conflicts, as we can see in the following examination of three oft-cited *consilia* (legal opinions) written by Baldo degli Ubaldi of Perugia.

---

dicimus in simili in liberta nupta voluntate patroni, quia remanet liberta non tamen quo ad operas. Et sic ibi posset emere, quod est equitas. Et si quis eam occideret, puniretur tanquam occidens civem, et credo quod guadeat aliis privilegiis civium." Osvaldo Cavallar and I have translated Bartolo's commentary, which will appear in our forthcoming *Medieval Italian Jurisprudence: A Selection of Texts in Translation*. On conceiving the relationship between husband and wife as that between *patronus* and *liberta*, see Thomas Kuehn, "Women, Marriage, and *Patria Potestas* in Late Medieval Florence," in *Law, Family, and Women: Toward a Legal Anthropology of Renaissance Italy* (Chicago: University of Chicago Press, 1991), 202–3.

BALDO DEGLI UBALDI

As Bartolo's postmortem reputation swelled in the second half of the fourteenth century, so did, contemporaneously, the reputation of his most brilliant and productive disciple, Baldo degli Ubaldi (1327?–1400), who soon became the leading Italian jurist and consultor. [19] The range of Baldo's work is impressive: commentaries on the *Corpus iuris* and on the canon and feudal law, treatises, and roughly three thousand *consilia*, most of which were occasioned by actual cases. [20] Manuscript copies of his *consilia* are found throughout Europe and even across the Atlantic, at the University of Chicago. His *consilia* were printed and reprinted—for instance, at Brescia (1490–91), Milan (1491–93), Venice (1575), and Frankfurt (1589). Touching on virtually every area of private and public law, his opinions were instantly consequential and remained influential into the eighteenth century. They illustrate that local law was not self-evident, self-enforcing, or self-rectifying, but required the continual intervention of cosmopolitan jurists applying the *ius commune* and their interpretative skills to local cases. For the historian, they furnish invaluable detailed snapshots of critical moments in the lives of fourteenth-century Italian women, from the cradle to the grave. Hundreds of his *consilia* are dedicated to married women's property (*bona mulieris*), especially the constitution, disposition, and devolution of dowries. [21]

In working with Baldo's *consilia* and those of other jurists, one must be alert to several methodological challenges. First and foremost, the printed editions are marred by grammatical errors, falsifications, lacunae, and interpolations. It is absolutely necessary to return to manuscript copies (which also contain errors) for the

[19]In lieu of a comprehensive study of Baldo's life and works, there are sundry studies dealing with aspects of his career and thought. For pre-1986 studies, consult Canning's *The Political Thought of Baldus*. Ennio Cortese provides an updated biographical profile in *Il diritto nella storia medievale*, 2: *Il basso medioevo* (Rome: Il Cigno Galileo Galilei, 1995), 436–45. See also Kenneth Pennington, "Baldus de Ubaldis," *Rivista internazionale di diritto comune* 8 (1997): 35–62.

[20]For the figure three thousand, which includes unpublished as well as published *consilia*, I relied on the research of Vincenzo Colli of the Max-Planck-Institut für Europäische Rechtsgeschichte, who is currently preparing an indexed census of Baldo's *consilia*. Firstfruits of his project are found in his "Il Cod. 351 della Biblioteca Capitolare Feliniana di Lucca: Editori quattrocenteschi e *Libri consiliorum* di Baldo degli Ubaldi (1327–1400)," in *Scritti di storia del diritto offerti dagli allievi a Domenico Maffei* (Padova: Antenore, 1991), 255–82. For more research on *consilia*, including a bibliography, see Baumgärtner, *Consilia im späten Mittelalter* (above n. 8) and a companion volume, *Legal Consulting in the Civil Law Tradition*, ed. Mario Ascheri, Ingrid Baumgärtner, and Julius Kirshner, Studies in Comparative Legal History (Berkeley: Robbins Collection, 1999). The essays by Padoa-Schioppa, Storti Storchi, Massetto, Di Renzo Villata, and Zorzoli in *Ius Mediolani: Studi di storia del diritto milanese offerti dagli allievi a Giulio Vismara* (Milan: Giuffrè, 1996) contain valuable materials on *consilia* in Milan and Lombardy.

[21]See Julius Kirshner and Jacques Pluss, "Two Fourteenth-Century Opinions on Dowries, Paraphernalia, and Non-dotal Goods," in *Bulletin of Medieval Canon Law* 9 (1979): 65–77; Jacques Pluss, "Reading Case Law Historically: A Consilium of Baldus de Ubaldis on Widows and Dowries," *American Journal of Legal History* 30 (1986): 241–65; idem, "Baldus of Perugia on Female and Male: The Case of Allumella," *Thought* 64 (1989): 221–30; Gian Paolo Massetto, "Il lucro dotale nella dottrina e nella legislazione statutaria lombarde dei secoli xiv–xvi," in *Ius Mediolani*, 213–54.

purpose of establishing reliable and intelligible texts. Fortunately, the Barberini manuscripts in the Biblioteca Apostolica Vaticana contain an excellent collection of Baldo's *consilia*, autographs as well as copies, with additions and corrections made by Baldo himself or by his scribe.[22]

Second, *consilia* were integral to the formal process of dispute resolution, but it is exceptional that readers are afforded more than a glimpse of the concrete contingent facts of the dispute (*punctus*) moving public officials (*podestà, capitano del popolo, vicario*), judges, or litigants to request Baldo's opinion. In addition, the outcome of a case and the presiding judge's sentence are rarely reported. With luck and laborious sleuthing, one can occasionally find supplementary materials providing answers to extratextual questions conventionally posed by historians.

Third, the applicability of local statutes was almost always a central issue. Normally, consultors like Baldo included in their *consilia* an abstract or brief citation of the relevant statutes, copies of which were surely on their desks at the moment of composition. To grasp the legal issues at stake in a case, it is necessary to consult the redactions of the statutes cited by Baldo—but most of them, let it be stressed, are no longer extant or remain in manuscript awaiting modern editions.

Fourth, the identity of the party commissioning a *consilium*, crucial to interpreting the direction of the jurist's arguments, is often difficult to discern. This is especially true regarding Baldo's *consilia*, for which there are only scant references throwing light on the source of his commissions. Undoubtedly, some of his opinions were *consilia sapientis* produced at the request of officials, judges, and both parties (one party with the consent of the other, or the two parties together).[23] A *consilium sapientis* was designed to be impartial and by convention almost always determined the judge's sentence. However, the overwhelming majority of Baldo's *consilia* were probably *pro parte*, commissioned by individual litigants.[24] Presiding judges were not strictly bound to follow an opinion rendered on behalf of a client. But beyond an instant case, a *consilium pro parte*, particularly when rendered by a distinguished consultor like Baldo, carried the same doctrinal authority for the consultocrats as a *consilium sapientis*.

Domina Agnes

Lady Agnes was the protagonist of a case in the town of Castiglion Aretino, situated in the Valdichiana between Arezzo and Cortona. The case and Baldo's *consilium*

---

[22]Giancarlo Vallone, "La raccolta Barberini dei consilia originali di Baldo," *Rivista di storia del diritto italiano* 52 (1989): 3–63.

[23]For example, a *consilium* dealing with nondotal goods opens: "Puncta super quibus petitur consilium sapientis sunt infrascripta…" (MS 6, Regenstein Library, University of Chicago, fols. 29vb–30va). Note that this incipit is missing in the Venetian edition, vol. 3, fol. 118va, cons. 418.

[24]For payment to Baldo in 1372 for having written a *consilium* for a client, see *Documentazione di vita assisana, 1300–1530*, ed. Cesare Cenci (Grottaferrata: Editiones Collegii S. Bonaventura ad Claris Aquas, 1974), 1:165.

perhaps date between 1379, when he returned from Padua to teach at Perugia, and December 1384, when Castiglion Aretino, having submitted to Florence, became Castiglion Fiorentino forever.[25] The reference in the opening line of the *consilium* to "dicta domina Agnes" may allude to a preceding summary of the factual and legal issues the jurist was asked to address. This summary, unfortunately, was not included in the Barberini manuscript and printed editions. Internal evidence indicates that the case involved a homicide and that Agnes was alive at the time of the crime.[26] Since a defendant in a criminal case could not request a *consilium*, Baldo's opinion must have been *consilium sapientis*, probably commissioned by the podestà.

Originally from neighboring Montecchio Vesponi, Agnes married a citizen of Castiglion Aretino. Baldo first considered the question of whether Agnes, by virtue of her marriage, is a citizen of her husband's *origo*:

> Granted that the said lady Agnes was and is the wife of a true, natural, and original citizen of Castiglion, she also—seeing that insofar as she is joined to her husband's *origo* by virtue of marriage and insofar as she is made a part of her husband's body—is said to be and is of Castiglion Aretino for the duration of the marriage. For marriage is of such capacity and nature that it transfers the wife's *origo* to that of her husband. This is also established by virtue of the union in which that which is stronger draws to itself that which is less worthy. But there is no greater union than the conjugal union by which husband and wife are made one flesh, even, as it were, one substance in two persons. For that reason, the said lady Agnes should be reckoned a true and original citizen of the land of Castiglion. Since by divine law there is one flesh and divine law stands as truth and not fiction, it follows that the wife is properly made a fellow-citizen of her husband.[27]

[25]Santino Gallorini, *Castiglion Fiorentino: Dalle origini etrusco-romane al 1384* (Cortona: Calosci, 1992), 123 ff.

[26]My search for this specific case in the trecento records of the podestà, preserved in the Archivio Storico Comunale di Castiglion Fiorentino, proved fruitless.

[27]The text cited here is based on my collation of BAV (Biblioteca Apostolica Vaticana), Barb. lat 1401, fol. 71r–v, cons. 108, with the Venetian edition of 1575, vol. 5, fol. 26r, cons. 100: "In Christi nomine, amen. Considerato, quod dicta domina Agnes fuit et est uxor veri, naturalis et originarii Castellionensis, etiam ipsa tanquam eidem origini unita per virtutem matrimonii et tanquam pars corporis viri effecta dicitur esse et est de Castellione Aretino durante matrimonio. Nam matrimonium est istius virtutis ac nature, quod transfundit originem uxoris in originem viri, ut legitur et notatur in l. Origine, de mu. et origi., li. Xo (Cod. 10. 39 [38].4). Hoc etiam probatur ex virtute unionis, in qua id quod potentius est trahit ad se id quod est minus dignum, ut plene legitur et notatur extra, Ne sede vacante, ci (X. 3. 9. 1). Sed nulla est maior unio, quam unio coniugalis, per quam vir et uxor efficiuntur una caro; etiam est quasi una substantia in duabus personis, ut l. 1, ff. rerum admotarum (Dig. 25. 2. 1), et ff. ad Sillaniano, l. I, § si vir aut uxor (Dig. 29. 5. 1. 15), et extra, de bigamis, c. Debitum (X. 1. 21. 5). Et ideo dicta domina Agnes tanquam vera et originaria civis dicte terre Castellionis debet reputari, cum.iure divino sit una caro, et ius divinum consistat in veritate et non in fictione, sequitur quod proprie uxor est effecta concivis viri,

As one would expect from an opinion aimed at being forensically persuasive, rather than doctrinally novel, Baldo's assertions were formulaic, yet they harbor subtleties that merit highlighting. Note that Bartolo was cited as an authority on a par with the *Corpus iuris civilis*, the *Corpus iuris canonici*, and the *Glossa* (see n. 26 below). But unlike Bartolo, the civilian, Baldo was a doctor of canon law as well as civil law (*utriusque iuris*), who reflexively invoked canon law to reinforce his argument. Baldo, like Bartolo, embraced heterosexist clichés derived from the *Corpus iuris*, the Bible, and the Church Fathers to explain why the wife involuntarily assumes her husband's *origo* and domicile. In addition, Baldo's penchant for medieval Aristotelian doctrines is noticeable in the image of a submissive and less worthy wife pulled away from her *origo* by her noble and stronger husband.[28] Baldo also subscribed to the conventional Aristotelian view that the male sex is characterized by an active generative force, the female sex by a passive generative force. Thomas Aquinas and his adherents, following Aristotle, contrasted females, who passively assist in the economy of procreation, with men, "who are ordained to a more noble vital activity, namely intellectual knowledge."[29]

Note, too, that the transfer of the wife's *origo* to that of the husband's is said to be authorized by divine, civil, and canon law, the *Glossa*, and Bartolo. But no mention is made of an authorizing statute. Drafted by learned jurists under the guidance of a committee of notable citizens, the statutory compilations of Italian communities omitted express declarations that a foreign woman married to a native man would be treated as a citizen, or conversely that a native woman married to a foreign man could look forward to an alteration or even loss of her citizenship. Pragmatic citizen-lawmakers of the fourteenth century had no incentive—fiscal, legal, or political—to expressly renounce jurisdiction over a group of citizens and their property. The nativist conviction that the attribute of original citizenship was a permanent feature of one's legal persona, and therefore could not be eradicated, impeded the translation of the *Glossa*'s and Bartolo's doctrine into statutory law. Instead, citizens

---

et ita tenet glossa in l. Cives, Cod. de incolis (Cod. 10. 40 (39). 7), et Bartolus, ff. ad municipalem, l. fi., § Item rescripserunt." This *consilium* and others by Baldo on women married elsewhere are cited and briefly discussed by Canning, *The Political Thought*, 182–83; and Charlotte C. Wells, *Law and Citizenship in Early Modern France* (Baltimore: Johns Hopkins University Press, 1995), 8. Both authors ignore the juridical and factual questions specifically addressed by Baldo in his opinions, the methodological and textual challenges his opinions present to modern scholars, and the broader historical context attending the construction of women's juridical personality.

[28]Baldo's predilection for philosophizing is discussed by Norbert Horn, "Philosophie in der Jurisprudenz der Kommentatoren: Baldus philosophus," *Ius commune* 1 (1967): 104–49.

[29]Kari Elisabeth Børreson, *Subordination and Equivalence: The Nature and Role of Woman in Augustine and Thomas Aquinas* (Kampen: Kok Pharos), 158, citing S. Th. I, 92, 1, c; Vern L. Bullough, "Medieval Medical and Scientific Views of Women," *Viator* 4 (1973): 485–501; Joan Cadden, *Meanings of Sex Difference in the Middle Ages: Medicine, Science, and Culture* (Cambridge: Cambridge University Press, 1993), 24 ff., 169 ff.

in violation of a community's statutes would be punished with fines and banishment, including confiscation of property. In this politico-legal setting, monetary penalties, rather than loss of citizenship, would suffice to inhibit native women from marrying elsewhere. Overall, it was best to tread softly, leaving the precise determination of the civic status of a married woman, complicated by the theory that her status is effected by divine and civil law, to jurists who would be asked to deal with individual cases as they arose.

What Bartolo left implicit, Baldo made explicit. Agnes is not merely a citizen of her husband's *origo*, but is made a "true and original citizen." That Agnes "is of Castiglion Aretino" signifies, technically, that she is a true and legally valid citizen, whether or not she has domicile in Castiglion Aretino.[30] Significantly, she retains her new citizenship as long as she is married. Conversely, does Agnes cease being a citizen of Montecchio Vesponi during marriage? Baldo's language suggests that she loses her original citizenship, since her *origo* is transferred to her husband's. And a few lines later, he refers to Agnes's status in the past tense (*erat Monticchiensis*). Such language runs counter to his insistence that marriage does not obliterate the wife's natural and original filiation to her own fatherland (see below).

In light of his general views on legal fictions and citizenship,[31] Baldo's denial of the fictional element of Agnes's newly minted true and original citizenship seems inconsistent. "Legal fiction," for Baldo, "is a falsehood accepted as truth on behalf of a most special just cause expressed in law."[32] He endorsed a city's capacity to create new citizens with all the benefits and privileges enjoyed by original citizens, save the ability to hold public office. But he insisted that statutory grants of original citizenship to nonnatives, though valid, were unequivocally predicated on legal fiction. Furthermore, the joining of the husband and wife into one flesh exemplified what Baldo called *fictio unitiva*.[33] These views were delivered by Baldo in his capacity as a civilian. By contrast, in *Domina Agnes,* Baldo was also writing as a canonist, and his treatment of marriage as one flesh and as a sacrament grounded in divine law consequently precluded legal fiction. That is why Baldo did not raise the issue of legal fiction in this case, but simply opined that a woman married elsewhere automatically becomes a true original citizen of her husband's *origo*.

---

[30]On the theory behind this point, see Julius Kirshner, "A Consilium of Rosello dei Roselli on the Meaning of 'Florentinus,' 'de Florentia,' and 'de populo,'" *Bulletin of Medieval Canon Law* 6 (1976): 87–91.

[31]See Lodovico Barassi, "Le *fictiones juris* in Baldo," in *L'opera di Baldo, per cura dell'Università di Perugia nel V centenario della morte del grande giureconsulto* (Perugia: Unione Tipografia Cooperativa, 1901), 113–38; Julius Kirshner, "*Ars imitatur naturam*': A Consilium of Baldus on Naturalization," *Viator* 5 (1974): 309–15; and Canning, *The Political Thought*, 174 ff.

[32]Baldo to Cod. 9. 2. 7, *Ea quidem*. See also Franco Todescan, *Diritto e realtà: Storia e teoria del "fictio iuris"* (Padua: CEDAM, 1979), 105 ff.

[33]Baldo to Dig. 23. 2. 57, *Qui in provincia*, n. 7 (Venice, 1577), vol. 2, fol. 190ra; from Baldo's addition to his *lectura antiqua*.

Next, Baldo asked whether Agnes, granted that she was formerly of Montecchio, can be regarded under the statutes of Castiglion Aretino as a *Castiglionensis* in civil and criminal cases.[34] The answer is no, because of an anomaly that renders the statute inoperable. The statutes of Castiglion Aretino prescribe that while in its jurisdiction *Monticchienses* should be regarded as *Castiglionenses*, and the reverse, while in Montecchio *Castiglionenses* should be regarded as *Monticchienses*. This applies to any legal situation or case (*in quocunque casu*). The statute of Montecchio carried an equal-treatment provision but was limited to three cases: civil, criminal, and damage caused by negligence, accident, or design (*damnum datum*). Because true reciprocity is lacking between the two statutes, Baldo argued, neither one applies in this case.[35] Moreover, the statutes of Montecchio were no longer in force, most likely since 1375, when the town had lost its autonomy to the English mercenary John Hawkwood.[36]

From the above, it is certain that Castiglion Aretino was the place of prosecution. It remains uncertain whether Agnes was the victim or the offender, whether the homicide was committed in Castiglion Aretino or Montecchio. Plausibly, this was a case of conjucide. Agnes may have been killed by her husband in Castiglion Aretino, where he would have been subject to the penalty imposed for the crime of homicide. But suppose that he killed Agnes in Montecchio or another place outside the jurisdiction of Castiglion Aretino; that would prompt the question of whether she should be treated as a citizen or a foreigner. If she were treated as a foreigner, her husband would then be immune from prosecution in his own *origo*, because the crime was committed beyond its jurisdiction. Recall that Bartolo dealt with a similar

---

[34]The statutes of Castiglion Aretino and Montecchio Vesponi are no longer extant.

[35]"Secundo, est considerandum de dicto statuto in libro secundo, nunquid sit pena de eo tanquam de persona, que debeat haberi et tractari in civilibus et criminalibus causis in communi Castillionis tanquam Castillionensis, considerato quod erat Monticchiensis. Et dicendum est, quod non. Nam verba statuti sub rubrica 'quod Monticchienses tractentur ut Castillionenses,' habent istam modificationem et conditionem, videlicet dummodo versa vice Castillionenses et districtuales tractentur in castro Monticchi ut Monticchienses in quocunque casu. Et nota hoc verbum 'in quocunque casu.' Nam, aut nos consideramus modum tractandi ex dispositione legis, aut ex contingentia factorum. Siquidem ex legum dispositione, apparet quod statutum, quod Castellionenses tractantur ut Monticchienses in tribus causis, scilicet, civilibus, criminalibus et in dampnis datis. Et de aliis nichil est statutum, puta in datiis, collectis et similibus. Ergo illa verba 'in quocumque casu' non sunt verificata, quia sunt verba universalia, et sic conditio, que requirit dictum statutum sub rubrica 'quod Monticchienses, etc.' non est impleta. Ergo dispositio illius statuti est nulla, ut ff. de pigno. ac., l. Si necessarias, § Si annua (Dig. 13. 7. 8. 3). Item, quia apparet statutum Monticchiensium cassum, nec ad mulierem pertinet de iuris apicibus disputare." Such reciprocal pacts were standard, especially between neighboring communities. Such a pact was concluded in 1337 between Arezzo and Castiglion, which was edited by Giuseppe Ghizzi, *Storia della terra di Castiglione Fiorentino* (Arezzo, 1883–86; reprint, Bologna: Forni, 1972), pt. 3, 203: "Item quod cives et comitatini civitatis Arretii tractentur, et tractare debeant Castilionenses in civilibus, et criminalibus quaestionibus tamquam Castilionenses; et eodem modo tractentur, et tractare debeant Castilionenses et eorum districtuales, Arretii in omnibus questionibus tamquam cives."

[36]Santino Gallorini, *Montecchio Vesponi: Un territorio, un castello e una comunità* (Cortona: Calosci, 1993), 117 ff.

case involving the murder of a woman married elsewhere and famously insisted that her murderer should be prosecuted for having killed a citizen. His opinion was cited in another case in which a husband who had killed his "foreign-born" wife was judged to be prosecutable in his own *origo* for killing a fellow citizen.[37]

It is remotely conceivable that Agnes killed her husband or another citizen of Castiglion Aretino. In that event, it was in her interest to be considered a citizen, not a foreigner. Again, at stake was the severity of punishment, which typically doubled when a foreigner offended a citizen.[38] The inapplicability of the equal-treatment provisions would be welcome news to Agnes, if indeed she had committed the crime. At any rate, the *ius commune*, which Baldo determined to be the operative law in this case, dictated that Agnes should be regarded as an original (*originaria*) of Castiglion Aretino. Under the *ius commune*, the penalty for homicide was capital punishment. But Baldo recommended a penalty of 500 pounds, intimating that the statutory penalty for the crime in question was monetary rather than capital punishment.[39] Without the statutes of Castiglion Aretino and knowledge of what events actually took place, any attempt to reconstruct the basis for the outcome of *Domina Agnes* is obviously hazardous.

[37]BAV, Vat. lat, 8068, fols. 88v–89r, a *consilium* of the fourteenth-century jurist Iacopo da Fermo. The English translation of his *consilium* based on my edition will appear in *Medieval Italian Jurisprudence* (n. 17 above).

[38]For example, the *Statuto di Arezzo (1327)*, ed. Giulia Marri Camerani (Florence: Deputazione di storia patria per la Toscana, 1946), 209, rub. XXII (*De pena homicidii*); 213, rub. XXXII (*De pena forensis offendentis civem et e contra*): The fine for homicide imposed by the statutes of Arezzo was 2,000 pounds. Foreigners who committed crimes against citizens had to pay double the fine citizens would pay for the same crimes. Castiglion Fiorentino, Biblioteca Comunale, *Statuti* (1384), fol. 130r, lib. 3, cap. 8 (*De pena forensis offendentis Castilionensis*): "Si quis forensis quomodocumque offenderet Castilionensem vel eius districtualem, condemnetur et condemnari debeat in duplo illius pene qua condemnaretur Castilionensis, si offendisset talium Castilionsenem" (my transcription). A complete transcription of these statutes, prepared by Ornella Catani and Daniela Serafini, is preserved in the Biblioteca Comunale. The statutes of Montepulciano prescribed a maximum monetary fine of 1,200 pounds for citizens who killed foreigners, in contrast to the penalty of capital punishment awaiting foreigners who killed citizens: *Statuto del comune di Montepulciano (1337)*, ed. Ubaldo Morandi (Florence: L. S. Olschki, 1966), 171, rub. XII (*De pena homicidii*).

[39]"Satis est enim, quod originaria dici potuit, ut ff. de adulteriis, l. Si ex lege (Dig. 48. 5. 44). Si vero nos consideramus facti contingentiam, <et> tunc si actendamus probationem, videtur probatum de non tractatu. Si vero consideramus iuris dispositionem, debuit et debet probari de dicto tractatu, de quo disponit statutum. Nam cum facti sit, non praesumitur, et quod in facto consistat, est textus ff. de verb. obli., l. Quidam cum filium (Dig. 45. 1. 132). Et ideo pro dicto homicidio debet imponi pena pecuniaria v^c librarum denariorum et non pena capitis." Under the statutes of Castiglion Fiorentino, capital punishment was the penalty for the premeditated murder of a citizen, 500 pounds for the murder of a foreigner, and 200 pounds for inflicting accidental death: *Statuti* of 1384, fol. 128r, lib. 3, cap. 3 (*De pena occidentis et veneno tossicantis*). According to Baldo, when penalties (for example, monetary) are lighter than those imposed by the *ius commune* (for example, capital punishment), they are enforceable, save when the monetary fine was ridiculously low. See his *Tractatus duo de vi et potestate statutorum*, ed. E. M. Meijers (Haarlem: H. D. Tjeenk Willink & Zoon, 1939), 22.

La Perugina

No married woman of the city or contado of Assisi (*Nulla mulier civitatis Assisii vel comitatus*), irrespective of legal position or rank, may enter into contracts or make a last will without the presence of her husband. So declared the trecento statutes of Assisi. Now a certain woman, by virtue of her father's and her own *origo*, is truly of Perugia. She married a man of Assisi, where she lived for a long time and where she made a last will in the presence of her husband. For reasons that are not given, she returned to Perugia and, in her husband's absence and without his consent, she unilaterally revoked the last will. She proceeded to make a second will in Perugia, where, Baldo observed, the *ius commune* remains in force. The validity of the second will hinged on the resolution of two questions. First, does the woman of Perugia, through her marriage to an Assisian, automatically become a woman of Assisi? Second, can a woman married to an Assisian who later returns to her own natural fatherland make a testament in conformity with the laws of Perugia wherever they may be in force, or is she bound by the laws of her husband's hometown? [40]

Assisi's trecento statute (*Nulla mulier*) cited by Baldo is no longer extant, but probably survived with modifications in the redaction of 1469, published at Perugia between 1534 and 1543, which is cited here.[41] His *consilium*, though undated, may have been composed around 1374, when Baldo served as a legal adviser to the commune of Assisi. He also authored several other *consilia* involving cases in Assisi, including another dealing with *Nulla mulier*.[42] Lacking concrete evidence, it is impossible to determine conclusively whether Baldo's opinion was written as a *consilium sapientis* or *pro parte*. Perhaps it was a *consilium sapientis*, rendered in his capac-

---

[40]The text cited here is based on a collation of BAV, Vat. lat. 1401, fol. 103r–v with the Venetian edition of 1575, vol. 5, fols. 35r–36v, cons. 139: "Statuto communis Assisii cavetur, quod nulla mulier civitatis Assisii vel comitatus eiusdem cuiuscumque conditionis et status existat, possit contrahere vel testari sine presentia sui viri, si nupta fuit. Modo quedam mulier paterna et propria origine et vere Perusina nupta fuit Assisii et ibidem cum viro longo tempore moram traxit et tandem fecit testamentum cum presentia sui viri. Demum ista mulier Perusina est reversa, et absente dicto suo viro et non consentiente, dictum primum testamentum mutavit et revocavit; quod secundum testamentum factum fuit in civitate Perusii ubi viget ius commune. Queritur, nunquid dictum secundum testamentum valeat necne? Ex isto temate dua oriuntur dubia. Primo, an mulier Perusina nupta Assisinati dicatur esse mulier civitatis vel comitatus Assisii. Secundo, an dicta mulier reversa ad propriam patriam naturalem possit facere testamentum secundum leges proprie patrie quocumque loco valuerint, an non ligetur legibus fori mariti."

[41]*Statuta*, lib. 2, rub. 23 (*Quod mulier non possit testari, contrahere, alienare nisi prout infra capitulum*), fol. 8v. I cite the copy in the Biblioteca del Senato, Rome (Statuti 1209).

[42]On Baldo as an *advocatus* of the commune of Assisi in 1374, see Cenci, *Documentazione*, 167; for Baldo's other Assisian *consilia*, see Cenci, *Documentazione*, 165 (year: 1372); MS 6 (n. 24 above), fol. 15rb–vb (Venetian edition, vol. 3, fol. 117rb–va, cons. 412); MS 6, fol. 25rb–vb; MS 6, fol. 45ra–vb (Venetian edition, vol. 3, fol. 6rab. cons.14); MS 6, fol. 82rb–va (Venetian edition, vol. 3, fol. 113ra, cons. 399): "Statuto civitatis Assisi cavetur nulla mulier posset testari seu aliam ultimam voluntatem condere." For the full contents of MS 6, see Thomas Izbicki and Julius Kirshner, "Consilia of Baldus of Perugia in the Regenstein Library of the University of Chicago," *Bulletin of Medieval Canon Law* 15 (1985): 95–115.

ity as official advocate. The tenor of its conclusion suggests to me, however, that it was more likely to have been commissioned by the husband.

Nulla mulier's exordium announced the necessity of restricting the testamentary and patrimonial capacities of Assisian women to promote civic tranquillity and to safeguard the proprietary rights of Assisian men. [43] The restriction was consistent with the statute's ideological subtext that women, because of their inherent mental incompetence and physical weakness (*imbecillitas sexus*), require special supervision in the performance of legal acts.[44] The exordium offered what contemporary jurists considered a legally effective defense against charges that *Nulla mulier* violated the *ius commune* and canon law, which granted all citizens the capacity to make last wills without obstruction and, moreover, granted women *sui iuris* the capacity to dispose of their property as they wished.[45] As a matter of strict law, such charges were true, but jurists tended to reject them on the grounds that in protecting women and promoting the city's welfare the statute performed a greater good. That would be accomplished by securing the rights of a woman's agnates to her property and the rights of her husband and their mutual children to her dowry.

According to the 1469 redaction of *Nulla mulier,* in addition to last wills and codicils, all forms of alienation of property and obligations (contracts of sale, gifts, and exchanges) were prohibited unless they were concluded in the presence and with the consent of both her husband and her father (if he was alive).[46] Whether the father's consent had been similarly required in the trecento redaction is not known. In any event, under the civil law the father's consent was deemed necessary because

[43]*Statuta,* "Pro tranquillo et pacifico statu hominum civitatis Assisii et comitatus eiusdem et ad conservationem iurium ipsorum."

[44]So alleged Baldo's brother, Angelo degli Ubaldi (d. 1400), in a *consilium* involving the application of Todi's *Nulla mulier* statute. See his *Consilia* (Lyon, 1551), fol. 184vb, cons. 333: "Quia dictum statutum emanavit in favorem mulieris propter imbecillitatem sexus." On the Roman sources for this (in)famous construct, see Joëlle Beaucamp, "Le vocabulaire de la faiblesse féminine dans les textes juridiques romains du IIIe au VIe siècle," *Revue historique de droit français et étranger* 54 (1976): 485–508; Suzanne Dixon, *"Infirmitas sexus*: Womanly Weakness in Roman Law," *Tijdschrift voor Rechtsgeschiedenis* 52 (1984): 343–71.

[45]For a sixteenth-century overview of these statutes, see Domenico Toschi, *Practicae conclusiones* (Lyon, 1634–70), 7:456–57, concl. 677 (*Statutum circa successionem mulierum nuptarum extra territorium excludens eas, quando habeat locum vel secus, et an valeat, vel non*). A crisp discussion of the constraints on medieval Italian testators is found in Romano, *Famiglia,* 49 ff. For canon law, see Michael M. Sheehan, "The Influence of Canon Law on the Property Rights of Married Women in England," in *Marriage, Family, and Law in Medieval Europe,* ed. James K. Farge (Toronto: University of Toronto Press, 1996), 16–30.

[46]*Statuta,* "Statuerunt et ordinaverunt, quod nulla mulier civitatis Assisii vel comitatus eiusdem cuiuscumque conditionis et status existat possi, nec debeat modo aliquo testari, codicillari, donare seu aliquam ultimam voluntatem facere vel disponere, seu venditionem, permutationem, donationem, concessio[n]em, transactionem vel aliquam alienationem seu obligationem cuiuscumque generis et conditionis existat facere sine presentia et consensu sui viri et patris, si virum et patrem habeat. Et si patrem tantum haberet et non virum, sine presentia et consensu patris." For Baldo's analysis of "presentia et consensu sui viri et patris," see his commentary to Dig. 24. 3. 2. 3, *Soluto matrimonio* § *Voluntatem.*

his married daughter, even though she had left his *origo*, did not escape the reach of his *potestas*. Without paternal consent, she could not make a last will, alienate property, or choose a tomb.[47] Before a husband could exercise his own *potestas*, he had to have legitimately contracted and consummated the marriage, and as a matter of public knowledge cohabited with his wife in the same house for at least two months.[48] The husband's *potestas* extended to the earnings of a wife for work performed outside the domestic sphere—for example, as an artisan, innkeeper, merchant, or midwife. Admittedly, such earnings technically belonged to the wife, not to her husband, so long as her work was not connected to her domestic duties.[49] Nonetheless, under *Nulla mulier*, her capacity to freely dispose of her earnings was also limited.

In the absence of her husband and father, the presence and consent of her sons were required; in their absence, her grandsons. Next in line were her brothers born of the same parents (*fratres carnales*), and so forth.[50] Bowing to the force of social and spiritual realities, the drafters allowed women to expend up to 20 percent of their patrimony, including dotal goods and their own earnings, for making traditional charitable donations and for acquiring necessities for themselves.[51] Statutes like Assisi's *Nulla mulier*, popular across northern and central Italy,[52] were a mainstay of the political-legal structure restricting the capacity of all women to dispose of their properties freely.

[47]Kuehn, "Women, Marriage, and *Patria Potestas.*"

[48]*Statuta*, "Et vir intelligatur ille ad prestandum presentiam et consensum modo predicto, qui cum muliere contraxerit matrimonium et consumaverit, vel cum ea steterit publice tamquam viri in una et edem domo saltim per duos menses. Et ad probandum consumationem matrimonii sufficiat iuramentum viri et uxoris."

[49]For example, Baldo to Cod. 6. 46. 5, *Si uxoren tuam*: "Ceterum si uxor faceret aliquam artem, vel mercantiam, vel esset chyrugia vel obstetrix, que quidem non sunt opere domestice et familiares, id quod acquirit ex istis operis, non acquireret viro, quia nec ad preceptum viri tenetur negociari."

[50]*Statuta*.

[51]*Statuta*, "Liceat tamen dictis mulieribus sine presentia et consensu dictarum personarum testari, codicillari et ultimam voluntatem disponere et facere de bonis ipsorum et dotibus eorundem usque in quantitatem viginti librarum denariorum pro qualibet centenario dotis ipsius mulieris et bonorum omnium que habent; et etiam pro necessitatibus suis inter vivos alienare usque in dictam quantitatem supradictam prohibitione aliqua non obstante...."

[52]Francesco Schupfer, "L'autorizzazione maritale: Studi sugli statuti municipali italiani," in *Pel cinquantesimo anni d'insegnamento del professore Francesco Pepere* (Naples: Società Anonima Cooperativa, 1900), 5–11; Franco Niccolai, *La formazione del diritto successorio negli statuti comunali del territorio lombardo-tosco* (Milan: Giuffrè, 1940), 291–93; Carlo Vernelli, "Note sulla condizione femminile negli statuti comunali dell'Italia centrale," *Proposte e ricerche* 31 (1993): 187–202. Not surprisingly, like all things in decentralized Italy, *Nulla mulier* statutes were marked by local differences. For example, at Spoleto women were given the right to dispose of one-fourth of their goods, including their earnings, in contrast to one-fifth at Assisi. See *Statutorum Magnificae Civitatis Spoleti...* (Spoleto, 1542), fol. 53v, lib. 3, cap. 25. See also Giovanni Chiodi, "Scelte normative degli statuti di Spoleto del 1296," in *Gli statuti comunali umbri*, ed. Enrico Menestò (Spoleto: Centro di Studi sull'Alto Medioevo, 1997), 254–55.

The Assissian husband's vested right in his Perugian wife's dowry upon her natural predecease was the core issue of *La Perugina*.[53] A few jurists pronounced that a husband's claim falls under the statutes of the locale where the dowry contract was executed,[54] which in *La Perugina* was probably Perugia. Accordingly, the Assissian husband, upon his wife's predecease without children, would acquire one-third of the dowry under the statutes of Perugia. But Bartolo's teaching that the husband's claim to the dowry is a special case falling under the statute of his domicile carried the day. [55] By coincidence, a Perugian husband and his Assissian wife were the protagonists of the hypothetical case used by Bartolo to illustrate his doctrine.[56] In his hypothetical case, the husband would acquire one-half of his wife's dowry under the statutes of Assisi. In reality, however, the statutes of Assisi provided surviving husbands one-third of the dowry. [57] Consequently, Bartolo's doctrine would not have benefited the husband, since his vested right in the dowry was identical in Perugia and Assisi.

Bartolo's successors, including Baldo, objected to his doctrine that the husband is entitled to his statutory share of the dowry, regardless of whether he supported the burdens of matrimony, so long as he contracted marriage *de presenti*. They held that a husband was entitled to receive the statutory share as compensation for supporting his wife.[58] Their holding applies to the three cases examined here, in which the husband publicly introduces the wife into his home, not those in which he lives in his wife's *origo*, which would place him under the jurisdiction of her city.

Baldo, in his lengthy exegesis of *lex Cunctos populos* (Cod. 1. 1. 1), shared the position that the husband's domicile prevails in regard to his dotal claims.[59] But he focused on the conflict between local statutes and the *ius commune* rather than on the conflict between two local jurisdictions. In Baldo's hypothetical case, the statute

---

[53]A husband pronounced guilty of killing his wife thereby forfeited his claim to her dowry.

[54]Bartolo of Sassoferrato to Dig. 1. 3. 32, *De quibus* (Venice, 1526), fol. 21vb, n. 27; to Dig. 5. 1. 65, *Exigere*, fol. 165vb; for a sixteenth-century overview, see Rolando della Valle, *Questiones de lucro dotis*, in *Tractatus universi iuris* (Venice, 1584), vol. 9, fol. 356va, *Quaestio* XIII. For a solid analysis, though limited to printed sources, Egon Lorenz, *Das Dotalstatut in der italienischen Zivilrechtslehre des 13. bis 16. Jahrhunderts* (Cologne: Böhlau, 1965).

[55]Antonio Briganti, "La donna commerciante (secc. XIII–XIV)," *Annali della Facoltà di Giurisprudenza di Perugia* 26 (1991): 31; *Statuti di Perugia dell'anno MCCCXLII*, ed. Giustiniano Degli Azzi (Rome: Ermanno Loescher, 1913), 291, lib. 2. cap. 3 (*De gle stromente dotaglie e che agiano forza de confessione.*)

[56]Bartolo to Cod. 1. 1.1, *Cunctos populos* (Venice, 1570–71), fol. 4ra, n. 18–19: "Statutum est Assissii, ubi est celebratus contractus dotis et matrimonii, quod vir lucretur tertiam partem dotis, uxore moriente sine liberis. In hac vero civitate Perusii, unde est vir, statutum est quod vir lucretur dimidiam; quid spectatibur? Certe statutum terrae viri, ut d. l. Exigere."

[57]*Statuta*, fol. 12v, lib. 2, rub. 43 (*Quod in adventu dotis restituende tertia pars remaneat viro.*)

[58]Rolando della Valle, *Quaestiones de lucro dotis*, fols. 352–53, *Quaestio* IV. Despite inconsistencies, Baldo generally held that the husband's statutory share should be treated as compensation for having supported his wife.

[59]Meijers, *Tractatus duo de vi et potestate statutorum*, 33–34 and for the following.

of the husband's domicile grants him one-half of his wife's dowry upon her predecease without children. He takes as his wife a woman of Assisi, where he accepted the dowry and where the *ius commune* is in force. It was not necessary for Baldo to spell out to his audience that under the *ius commune* a man who marries at Assisi would be obligated to restore the *whole* dowry of his predeceased wife to her father or his heirs unless the parties had expressly made contrary arrangements. The *ius commune* here is synonymous with Justinian's *Corpus iuris* or Roman law,[60] not the revisionist opinions of medieval jurists who championed local customs and statutes awarding widowers up to the entire dowry.[61]

In Baldo's hypothetical case the husband's domicile prevails, but not for Bartolo's reason that this is a special case favoring the husband. For Baldo, this reason was not so much wrong as simplistic. Suppose the *ius commune* operates in the husband's domicile. Under Bartolo's doctrine, the husband must restore the whole dowry, an absurd and noxious result that Bartolo himself would have deplored. Baldo therefore took another approach. Whatever amount of dowry is due the husband on his wife's predecease is determined by the custom of the husband's region. Yet, alleging the *ius commune*, he reasoned that since payment of the dowry to the husband is assumed to have occurred in his domicile, the law there has precedence.[62] And if the law of his domicile is the *ius commune*, he must restore the whole dowry to her father or his heirs. This in fact was Baldo's approach in an actual case that occurred at Asti in the 1390s.[63]

Baldo's "conflict of laws" analysis is crucial to any conjectural reconstruction of the material stakes of the dispute to which he devoted the *consilium* analyzed here. The wife's first will, redacted at Assisi, served to guarantee her husband's claim to one-third of the dowry as prescribed by the city's statutes. In the second will, redacted at Perugia without the husband's consent, the wife, perhaps near death, possibly stipulated that the dowry must be restored to her father or his heirs as prescribed by the *ius commune*. In that event, the husband would be obligated to restore the whole dowry. Yet it was precisely this outcome that both the *Glossa* and Bartolo, despite their differences on the status of the woman married elsewhere, sought to prevent. Whatever circumstances caused the wife to make a second will that likely favored her kinsmen, her act threatened her husband's mastery and the legal and ideological foundations on which it rested.

---

[60]The *ius commune* as Roman law is not unique to this passage; it is generally assumed throughout Baldo's civil law commentaries and *consilia*.

[61]On the Roman husband's obligation, upon his wife's predecease, to return the dowry (*dos profectitia*) to his father-in-law, see Jane F. Gardner, "The Recovery of the Dowry in Roman Law," *Classical Quarterly* 35 (1985): 449–53. For the medieval revisions of Roman dowry law, see Bellomo, *Richerche*, 187–205.

[62]These general points are ably discussed by Lorenz, *Das Dotalstatut*.

[63]In the Venetian edition, vol. 3, cons. 31, fol. 9va. My dating of the *consilium* is based on the assumption that Baldo wrote it while a professor at Pavia (1390–1400).

Baldo's zigzagging opinion opened by acknowledging the doubts arising from an identification of the wife with *nulla mulier civitatis Assisii*: "A woman of Perugia married to an Assisian retains her own natural origin, which may not be eradicated, though by a certain legal fiction it can be concealed, which at times happens when marriage forcibly carries off the wife to the husband's city as if she were born there."[64] However, *Nulla mulier* does not apply to the wife for a number of reasons. Legal fiction does not operate in statutes, as here, contravening the *ius gentium* and *ius commune*. Since the case of the woman married elsewhere is not specifically mentioned in *Nulla mulier*, the wife does not fall within the statute's general scope. In addition, prohibitory statutes like *Nulla mulier*, which impose disadvantages, call for literal, not liberal, interpretation.[65]

Baldo then advanced the Aristotelian-biblical argument already encountered in *Domina Agnes* that a wife is drawn to her husband's *origo*, which replaces her own, a transformation effected by the power of the matrimonial union. "But certainly," he objected immediately, "this argument does not seem to be true." Natural law dictates that one's *origo* is quintessentially immutable, and this holds for one's name, which may not be extinguished. To be of Perugia means to be Perugian forever. That the wife in question is of Perugia stands as fact in harmony with "natural truth." "A married woman, therefore, loses neither her privileges nor the common laws of her natural fatherland, because natural laws may not be changed." Although a wife is transferred to her husband's domicile, she retains, as if she were a son, a natural and intimate filiation with her fatherland.[66] By way of analogy, Baldo cited *lex Cum in*

[64]"Iste passus est michi satis dubius propter verba statuti dicentis 'quod nulla mulier civitatis Assisii' etc. Nam Perusina nupta Assisinati propriam et naturalem originem retinet que non potest extingui, licet possit velari quadam iuris fictione, que est, quoniam matrimonium rapit nuptam ad civitatem viri ac si ibi nata esset." By choosing the verb "rapit," Baldo was perhaps suggesting that the force uprooting and seizing the wife and propelling her to the husband's city was so great that it is tantamount to abduction (*raptus*). On abduction marriages in Roman law, see Judith Evans Grubb's close-grained study, "Abduction Marriages in Antiquity: A Law of Constantine and Its Social Context," *Journal of Roman Studies* 79 (1989): 59–83.

[65]"Tamen ibi est fictio, que non videtur habere locum in statutis aliquid disponentibus contra ius gentium et contra ius commune, ut ff. so. ma., l. Si vero, § De viro (Dig. 24. 3. 64. 9). Unde statutum non videtur loqui in hac muliere, de qua queritur, ut ff. ad municip., l. 1 (Dig. 50. 1. 1). Ad hoc facit glo. vulgaris in l. iiia § Hec autem, ff. de neg. ge. (Dig. 3. 5. 3. 7), ubi glo. notat quod de casibus fictis necesse est specialem legem fieri. Alias non comprehendentur sub lege generaliter loquente etiam sub iure communi, nedum sub iure municipali quod est stricte interpretationis." On literal and liberal interpretation, see Mario Sbriccoli, *L'interpretazione dello statuto: Contributo allo studio della funzione dei giurisiti nell'età comunale* (Milan: Giuffrè, 1969), 214–30, 422–29; Norbert Horn, *Aequitas in den Lehren des Baldus* (Cologne: Böhlau, 1968), 30–32.

[66]"Nam matrimonium sua natura novat originem mulieris et ad originem viri transfundit propter potentiam eiusdem unionis. Nam cum vir et uxor efficiantur unum corpus et una caro, id, quod est potentius, rapit id, quod minus potest, et in se totaliter transfert, ut not. Cod. de mu. et ori., l. Origine. Ad hoc facit quod not. in c. i. Ne sede va. (X. 3. 9. 1). Sed certe ista ratio non videtur vera. Nam sicut substantia originis non potest mutari, ita nec nomen potest perimi et ideo etiam de origine nupte mulieris

adoptivis, in which the bonds between a natural father and his son are not dissolved by adoption. Though the son is legally a full member of his adoptive family, he does not cease being a kinsman of his natural family. For Baldo, adoption cannot sever a natural father from his son because their bond is divine (*nexum divinum*).[67]

Furthermore, the designation "de civitate vel de comitatu" corresponds to someone whose *origo* is truly from Assisi. "For one is said to be truly and properly from someplace who is from that place according to natural truth and not according to fiction." Baldo, a virtuoso of legal fiction, opposed only its improper use. When used properly, legal fiction was perfectly acceptable, as in the interpretation of the utterance "de provincia." If the preposition "de" precedes the word province but not city, then "whoever is from the province of Tuscia," although an indefinite expression, is understood to include inhabitants domiciled in the province.

Baldo interjected yet another consideration. The designation "de civitate" can refer to the domain of civil law and legal relations—that is, to those things of a city that are governed by civil law. *Ius civile* encompasses the laws made by cities (*ius civile civitatis*) as well as Justinian's *Corpus iuris*.[68] In the domain of civil law, a woman of Perugia married to an Assisian is a true and proper citizen of Assisi. Baldo's point reflected Bartolo's doctrine that civil law has generative power, via municipal legislation, to produce newly minted true citizens partaking of the same privileges and benefits of citizenship as those enjoyed by original citizens.[69] This happens because all citizenship, nonoriginal as well as original, stems from civil rather than natural law. In short, the designation "de civitate," if understood civilly, applies to the Perugian wife, who, as a true citizen of Assisi, is subject to the provisos of *Nulla mulier*. Alternatively, if "de civitate" is understood materially, it refers to a specific city enclosed by walls, within which citizenship and civic filiation derive from the fact of natural and legitimate descent. Within this circumscribed

---

iura tractant et disponunt de origine secundum originem suam, ut legitur et notatur in l. 1, Cod. de mulieribus et in quo loco, libro x°. Unde mulier nupta non perdit privilegia nec iura communia patrie sue naturalis, quia naturalia mutari non possunt, ut ff. de cap. min., <l.>. Tutelas (Dig. 4. 5. 7) et l. Legatum (Dig. 4. 5. 10), et ff. ad muni., l. Assumptio. Nam origo facti est, et in facto consistit et facta cause quoad naturalem veritatem pro infectis haberi non possunt.... Et licet uxor transeat ad domicilium viri, ut ff. de iure o. iu., l. Cum quedam puella (Dig. 2. 1. 19) et ff. de iudiciis, l. Exigere dotem (Dig. 5. 1. 65), et ff. ad municip., l. De iuri. (Dig. 50. 1. 37), et l. Lucius (Dig. 50. 1. 21), tamen patriam et cognationem naturalem retinet, que inseparabilis est, ut arg. Cod. de adoptio, l. Cum in adoptivis, in penultima columpna (Cod. 8. 47[48]. 10. 1f.)." For another *consilium* in which Baldo opined that civil law or a municipal statute "non potest tollere naturalem affectionem," see the Venetian edition, vol. 5, fol. 16v, cons. 54.

[67]Baldo to Cod. 8. 47[48]. 10. 1f.

[68]For Baldo, Justinian's *Corpus iuris* is synonymous with both the *ius civile* and *ius commune*. See Horn, *Aequitas*, 54.

[69]See Julius Kirshner, "*Civitas sibi faciat civem.*" On the requirements that a foreigner must meet to become a citizen of Assisi, see *Statuta*, lib. 1, rub. 21 (*De novis civibus recipiendis*), fol. 19r. This statute does not apply to foreign women married to Assisians, because the citizenship of these women is governed by the provisions of the *ius commune*.

domain, the foreign-born wife can acquire fictive, but not true, Assisian citizenship—a civic status that, in Baldo's analysis, exempts her from *Nulla mulier*, which extends to true citizens exclusively.[70]

The pretzeled syntax of citizenship, as manipulated by Baldo, failed to resolve the questions precipitating his *consilium*. But he did not leave *La Perugina's* challenge unanswered. Baldo upheld Roman and Lombard law's golden rule of conjugal relations: a wife is always subject to her husband's power (*potestas viri*). As he explained in his lecture on *lex Si uxorem* (Cod. 6. 46. 5), she is in the *potestas* of her husband in three main respects: "namely, in residence, which she must take up with him; in works, because she must work for her husband; and in jurisdiction, because she must obey the court and laws and statutes of the husband."[71] Consequently, even though the *ius commune* says the opposite, *La Perugina* must obey Assisi's *Nulla mulier*, particularly regarding the disposition of her dowry[72]—an abrupt ending making Baldo's treatment of citizenship appear, retrospectively, as consummate shadow-boxing prefatory to his foreordained defense of the prerogatives of husbandhood.

But let us forgo the self-righteous pleasure of impugning Baldo's motives, which is anachronistic and methodologically simplistic. His opinion reads as a *consilium pro parte* rendered on behalf of the Assisian husband, making his ultimate determination forensically inevitable. The question of the legal effects of intercity marriage

---

[70]"Et ista nomina 'de civitate vel communitate' significant originem, ut not. ff. de excu. tuto., l. Sed reprobari, in verbo 'Cumanenses' (Dig. 7. 22. 9). Nam de aliquo loco proprie et vere dicitur ille, qui est de illo loco secundum originem et naturalem veritatem et non secundum fictionem, arg. Cod. de hiis qui veniam et., l. fi (Cod. 2. 44. 4); secus, si ista dictio 'de' apponeretur provincie sed non civitati, ut si verba dicerent 'quicumque de provincie Tuscie' et cetera. Nam nomen 'provincie' generalissimum est et etiam incolas comprehendit propter suam latitudinem in modo significandi ei attributo a iure, ut legitur et not. ff. de verborum signi., l. Provinciales (Dig. 50. 16. 190). Solo hic considerandum est primo, numquid, quando fictio sive interpretatio iuris communis disponit super interpretatione alicuius vocabuli, talis interpretatio habeat locum in statutis utentibus illo vocabulo, et dico, quod sic, ut ff. ad l. Falc., l. 1, § 1 (Dig. 35. 2. 1. 1). Secundo est considerandum, quid est dictum 'de civitate,' utrum sit dictum, id est de hiis, qui reguntur iure civili illius civitatis, an sit dictum et de loco sic confinato <et> muris cincto. Nam si verba accipiuntur civiliter, id est primo modo, ista mulier nupta Assisi est vere et proprie de civitate Assisii et de civilitate, id est, sub iure civili illius civitatis. Est enim vere civis, quia vera civilitas potest induci per dispositionem legalem et non solum per ius commune, sed etiam per ius municipale, ut not. Bartolus, ff. de usucap. l. Si is qui pro emptore (Dig. 41. 3. 15). Sed si ista verba intelliguntur materialiter 'pro loco muris cincto,' tunc vera sine fictione dici non potest." The restriction of true citizenship to those originating and residing within the city walls was designed to prevent *contadini* and rustics from claiming citizenship status. See Bartolo, *Consilia* (Venice, 1585), fol. 46ra, cons. 196, n. 6.

[71]Kuehn's translation, "Woman, Marriage, and *Patria Potestas*," 203.

[72]"Finaliter videtur dicendum, quod ius commune trahatur ad municipale et e contrario, et quod ista mulier debeat sequi statuta originis viri, per que statuta est quodam modo quoad hec in potestate viri, sicut etiam de iure longobardo, et ideo maxime de dote sua obstante statuto disponere non possit, licet de iure communi esset contrarium." On the husband's *potestas* in Lombard law, see Ennio Cortese, "Per la storia del mundio in Italia," *Rivista italiana per le scienze giuridiche* 8 (1955–56): 324–474, esp. 378–79; Claudia Storti Storchi, "La tradizione longobarda nel diritto bergamesco: I rapporti patrimoniali tra coniugi (secoli XII–XIV)," in *Diritto comune e diritti locali nella storia dell'Europa* (Milan: Giuffrè, 1980), 79 ff.

was equally inevitable in this type of case, and Baldo's arguments and verbal constructions were taken very seriously by succeeding generations of jurists.[73] They were acutely aware, as Baldo was, that the husband's *potestas* was hardly invincible. Indeed, husbands were perceived as vulnerable souls deserving legal protection in their struggle with women like La Perugina, who would ruin their men if left free to do as they wished.[74] It should come as no surprise that the drafters of the next redaction of Assisi's statutes (1469) granted additional protection to surviving husbands. The statute awarding the surviving husband one-third of his wife's dowry now applied to all persons deemed "original citizens of the city of Assisi and to all other persons of Assisi's contado and district and *to foreign women whom the men of Assisi take or may have taken as wives*"[75] (my italics).

Domina Stefania

Lady Stefania, a native citizen of Viterbo, married Raniero di Bussi of Baschi sometime in the late trecento. We do not know if the couple resided in Viterbo or in the husband's hometown, an agricultural center on the road leading to Orvieto. She and Ranerio had at least two children: Francesco, who survived his mother, and Giovanna, who predeceased her. In her last will Stefania divided her estate between her son and three granddaughters. Francesco was instituted heir for one-third of her goods, while Giovanna's three daughters were instituted heirs for the remaining two-thirds.[76] After Stefania's death, her will was contested for violating Viterbo's (in)famous *Nulla mulier* statute, probably by her son, for he had the most to lose.[77]

---

[73]Domenico Toschi, *Practicae conclusiones*, 8: 735, concl. 387 (*Uxor sortitur domicilium et forum mariti*), nn. 14–16, where Baldo's opinion on Assisi is cited.

[74]On the topos of women who refuse to be submissive to men, thereby challenging sexual hierarchies, see Susan L. Smith, *The Power of Women: A Topos in Medieval Art and Literature* (Philadelphia: University of Pennsylvania Press, 1995).

[75]*Statuta*, fol. 12v, lib. 2, rub. 43: "Et hoc locum habeat et intelligatur in originalibus civibus Assisii et in omnibus aliis eiusdem comitatus et districtus et in mulieribus forensibus quas homines de Assisio habent et haberent pro uxore. Et intelligatur et locum habeat in preteritiis, pendentibus et futuris et in aliis quorum matrimonium non est solutum."

[76]The text cited here is based on my collation of BAV, Barb. lat 1401, fols. 45v–46r with the Venetian edition, vol. 5, fol. 58rab, cons. 226: "Premissis verbis statutis Viterbiensis disponentis sub hac forma: 'Nulla mulier habens filios vel filias ex filio possit testari, codicillari vel aliquem contractum facere extra personas filiorum, et si secus fecerit testamentum, codicillarii et contractus sint nulli ipso iure.' Accidit, quod domina Stefania origine Viterbiensis nupta Baschiensis, quia uxor Ranerii Busse, dicto Ranerio mortuo, condidit testamentum, in quo inter cetera Franciscum eius filium etiam dicti quondam domini Ranerii in tertia parte hereditatis et bonorum suorum sibi heredem instituit et tres eius neptes ex Johanna, quondam ipsius domine Stefanie filia, in reliquis duabus partibus heredes instituit atque fecit. Mortua est dicta domina Stefania." For another *consilium* of Baldo on a case in Viterbo, see MS 6, fol. 35vab, and the Venetian edition, vol. 3, fol. 2vab, cons. 3.

[77]None of these characters appears in the following sources: for Viterbo, Cesare Pinzi, *Storia della città di Viterbo illustrata con note e nuovi documenti in gran parte inediti*, 4 vols. (Rome: Tip. della Camera dei Deputati, and Viterbo: Tip. Sociale Agnesotti, 1887–1913); Gabriella Dilonardo Buccolini, "Note sul

I have no direct evidence indicating that Baldo's *consilium* was written on behalf of the granddaughters. Yet I am inclined to treat his *consilium* as *pro parte*, because of Baldo's capacious defense of Stefania's last will.

"No woman," Viterbo's statute declared, "having sons or daughters from a son may make a last will, codicil, or contract beyond the persons of her children, and if she otherwise made such a last will, codicil, or contract they are *ipso iure* invalid." This passage, which Baldo cited, derived from the 1356 redaction of Viterbo's statutes, only a fraction of which is extant.[78] The statute was likely revised in the redaction of 1469,[79] in response, I believe, to the criticisms leveled by Baldo and like-minded jurists. The statute was designed to protect daughters as well as sons from a mother's acts serving to prejudice the children's claims to her estate. It was also designed to reserve the bulk of the maternal estate for descendants reckoned as agnates of the husband-father. In our case, Francesco and his direct male descendants were so reckoned, as was Giovanna, but, it must be emphasized, not her daughters, who were agnates of their own father.

Unlike *Domina Agnes* and *La Perugina*, where the central issue was whether the laws of the husband's *origo* were binding on his foreign-born wife, *Domina Stefania* focused on the obverse: whether the laws of the *origo* of a woman married to a foreigner continue to be binding on her. At first Baldo contended that under the laws of her native city Stefania's last will is invalid for several by-now familiar reasons. First, her attachment to Viterbo is permanent; it may not be voluntarily relinquished nor taken away forcibly. Second, the reality of her binding attachment to Viterbo is

---

popolazionismo a Viterbo nel secolo XV: La concessione della cittadinanza," in *Studi in onore di Amintore Fanfani* 2 (Milan: Giuffrè, 1962): 477–90. For Baschi, see Armando Ricci, "Storia di un comune rurale dell'Umbria," *Annali della Scuola Normale Superiore di Pisa* 25 (1913): 2–184; G. Celata, "La condizione contadina in una Signoria e in un comune rurale autonomo tra il Duecento e Trecento," *Rivista di storia dell'agricoltura* 19 (1979): 65–103; Marilena Rossi Caponeri, "Note su alcuni testamenti della fine del secolo XIV relativi alla zona di Orvieto," in *Nolens intestatus decedere: Il testamento come fonte della storia religiosa e sociale* (Perugia: Regione dell'Umbria, 1985), 105–11.

[78]The rubric cited by Baldo is found neither in the redaction of 1251–52 nor in the extract of the 1356 redaction, which is limited to criminal law. It is likely, however, that the rubric was originally included in the 1356 redaction, in the section dealing with civil matters. See *Statuti della provincia romana*, ed. Pietro Egidi, Fonti per la storia d'Italia pubblicate dall'Istituto storico italiano (Rome: Forzani, 1930), 93–269 (1251–52); 271–82 (1356). Giuseppe Signorelli's *Leggi e costumi nel medioevo* (Viterbo: 1887), an old study on marriage and family in late medieval Viterbo, is inadequate and needs to be updated. On the legal position of women in Lazio, see Mariano D'Alatri's summary, "Donne di ieri a Roma e nel Lazio," *Lunario romano* 7 (1978): 182–95; and the informative analysis of Maria Luisa Lombardo and Mirella Morelli, "Donne e testamenti a Roma nel Quattrocento," in *Donne a Roma tra medioevo e Età moderna* (Rome: Centro di Ricerca, 1993), 23–130.

[79]I used the copy in the Biblioteca degli Ardenti in Viterbo: fols. 175v–178r, lib. 2, rub. 74 (*Quod mulier habens filios vel filias non possit testari, codicillari nec aliquem contractum facere extra personas filiorum*). I also consulted a seventeenth-century copy of the 1469 statutes in the Biblioteca del Senato: Statuti 765, fols. 101v–102r, lib. 2, rub. 74.

anchored in natural truth that is not obscured by the image of marriage. Third, just as a married woman is not released from her father's *potestas*, she similarly remains yoked to the *potestas* of her fatherland. Fourth, the statute extends to all her property located in Viterbo's territory. Fifth, no law exists by which a native woman is liberated, through marriage, from Viterbo's statute-making authority and jurisdiction.[80]

Reversing course, as the pro-et-contra format required, Baldo argued that the *origo* and legal venue of a woman married elsewhere is changed by virtue of marriage. As a widow, she continues to be subject to the jurisdiction and laws of her husband's *origo*, where she can be summoned to court. This applies so long as she continues to reside in her husband's *origo*, suggesting that Stefania may have relocated to Baschi. Nor is Stefania subject to Viterbo's statute, since it pertains to persons, rather than to the properties they possess that are located within its jurisdiction.[81]

Even if one grants that as a woman married elsewhere Stefania is personally exempt from Viterbo's statute, jurists determined that such an exemption does not apply to her property located in Viterbo's territory. Her last will, with respect to such properties, must be judged null and void. In order to defend Stefania's last will, and the claims of the granddaughters to Stefania's Viterbo property, Baldo had to show that the statute itself was invalid. He began with the observation that the statute was concurrently prohibitory and beneficial; it prohibited mothers from bequeathing property unless beneficial to their children. But to whom does "children" refer? It includes the granddaughters, for when property is bequeathed for the

[80]"Queritur, nunquid dictum valeat testamentum et videtur quod non, quia vidua lege sue originis potest prohiberi testari, quia veritas nature matrimonii imagine non obumbravit<ur>. Est enim inseparabile quicquid origini coheret, ut ff. ad municipales, l. Adsumptio, et ff. de captivis, l. In bello, § Facte (Dig. 49. 15. 12. 2). Adeo ut naturalis veritas nec auctoritate senatus mutari possit, ut l. i et secunda, ff. de usufructu earum rerum, que usu consumuntur (Dig. 7. 5. 1. et 2). Cum enim sit subiecta ratione originis, ergo statutum valet in ipsius persona. Preterea ipsa adhuc remanet subiecta quoad bona, que habet in originis territorio, ut l. i, Cod. de mulieribus et in quo loco, libro x°. Ergo respectu talium bonorum valet statutum. Nam si testamentum militis potest valere respectu certorum bonorum, ergo et legis dispositio, ut notant doctores in l. Cunctos populos (Cod. 1. 1. 1). Preterea ista mulier prius fuit subiecta statuto quam nupta, et ideo nuptie non liberant eam a vinculo statuti, arg. ff. ad municip., l. Incola et hiis (Dig. 50. 1. 29). Preterea nupta non liberatur a potestate patris, ergo nec a potestate patrie, ut not. Cod. de condi. insertis, l. Si uxor (Cod. 6. 46. 5). Licet enim nupserit, tamen iura sue patrie non remictit, sicut nec patronus, qui non consensit nuptiis liberte, ymo et si consensit, ut Cod. de operis libertorum, l. Quod ex liberta (Cod. 6. 3. 11). Preterea facere statuta non est iurisdictionis contentiose, sed est quedam iurisdictio per se, ut ff. de adil. ed., l. Sciendum (Dig. 21. 1. 63), et nulla lege cavetur, quod a tali iurisdictione per matrimonium sit exemptus: ergo remanet sub statuto."

[81]"In contrarium videtur. Nam per matrimonium ius originis mutatur, ut Cod. de municipibus et originariis, l. Origine. Et fit quedam novatio et transumptio, ut ff. de iuri. omnium iudicum, l. Cum quedam puella (Dig. 2. 1. 19). Preterea non tenetur parere foro originis, ut ff. ad municipales, l. De iure (Dig. 50. 1. 37). Preterea istud statutum disponit respectu persone, sed hoc respectu non subiacet sue origini, ut not. in dicta l. 1, de mulieribus et in quo loco, et idem in vidua, quod in nupta, ut ff. de senatoribus, l. Femine (Dig. 1. 9. 8 pr)."

benefit of children, it is ordinarily understood that grandchildren are contemplated. This understanding operates in the statute as well, so that words "extra personas filiorum" must include granddaughters. In order to deprive grandmothers from naming as heirs their granddaughters, the statute must expressly state "extra filios qui neptes." But a proviso excluding children from an inheritance due them under natural law is inconsistent with the beneficial purport of the statute and the *ius commune*. Just as a parent may not disinherit a child except for a compelling reason, so the city may not exclude granddaughters from the maternal inheritance to which they are entitled.[82] The proof text is *lex Cum ratio naturalis* (Cod. 48. 20. 7 pr), which declares that natural reason in the manner of an unspoken law awards children an inheritance from their parents, while it bars the removal of children from succession except for good reasons.

Nor is the statute's purposeful beneficence toward children determined by their sex. The words "habens filios et filias" show that the statute includes daughters. But these words form part of a longer verbal construction, "habens filios et filias ex filio," which indicates that the statute wants to exclude from inheritance the mother's daughters and their children. The addition of "ex filio" was testimony to, and symbolic of, the driving force behind the statute: the masculinist desire to privilege and sustain agnate families. Yet the exclusionary thrust of the addition was exceptional, and Baldo admitted that he did not know whether the omission of the feminine gender from the addition was a case of faulty legal drafting. If taken literally, the statute can be said to exclude the granddaughters, since it is weighted clearly in favor of males. In the same breath, Baldo rejoined, a literal interpretation of the statute results in its invalidity. To be sure, the statute has much in common with the masculinist bias that had resulted in the inferior legal position of women in pre-Justinianic jurisprudence. But the jurisprudence of Papinian's day was no longer in force, Baldo declared, having been superseded by Justinian's *Corpus iuris*, which, in matters of inheritance, placed daughters and sons and grandsons and granddaughters on an equal footing. The statute, therefore, stands in violation of the *ius commune*.[83]

---

[82]"Solutio, in hoc puncto dicendum est, quod statutum duo disponere videtur: unum prohibendo et aliud tacite conferendo bona filiis in quorum favore disponit, ut ff. ad Trebel., l. Qui filium, in principio (Dig. 36. 1. 1. 76). Unde hoc respectu valet statutum quoad bona, que sunt in suo territorio, ut Cod. non licere habitatoribus metrocomie, l. 1., libro xi° (Cod. 11. 56. 1). Sed esto quod ita sit, tamen in casu nostro statutum non prohibet testari in neptis, quia non dicitur extra filios qui neptes instituit, ut Cod. de condi. insertis, l. 1 (Cod. 6. 46. 1), et quod not. ff. solu. ma., l. Si dotali (Dig. 24. 3. 48). Cum enim debeatur ei hereditas iure nature, absonum esset dicere quod non posset eis relinqui, ut l. Cum ratio, de bonis dampnatorum (Dig. 48. 20. 7)."

[83]"Statutum enim non videtur ponderasse sexum secundum naturalem, erga liberos habendam caritatem, cum dicat 'habens filios vel filias.' Ecce femininum genus. Nescio tamen si scriptura statuti sit corrupta, quia si diceretur 'habens filios vel filias ex filio,' tunc statutum magis precise loqueretur ad excludendum, quia ponderaret sexum masculinum, sicut in multis ponderatur, ut ff. de statu hominum, l. In multis (Dig. 1. 5. 9). Et de media iurisprudentia olim hoc erat, ut patet in l. Maximum vitium (Cod. 6. 28. 4), et institi., de hereditatibus § Item vetustas (Inst. 3. 1. 15)."

Viterbo's *Nulla mulier* statute also violates natural law and papal temporal jurisdiction in the lands of the church, in which the city was prominently situated. As Baldo reasoned:

> It seems wicked to say that a mother may not institute as heirs her daughter or granddaughter, and if it happens that a statute expressly wishes this, it may not do so, because it violates natural law. Take the case of a mother who has a son and a daughter with a father who dies insolvent. The mother wants to make a last will because, as it happens, she wants to leave something for spiritual bequests and, as a matter of necessity, something for the safety of her own soul, and she wishes to leave something for her daughter, lest she go begging. If the statute is understood verbatim, it would force the girl to go begging. If we attend to the externals of the statute, the designation of the daughter as heir (*instituto*) is invalid. Wherefore I say that in the lands of the church, where such statutes are not valid, and inasmuch as they are altogether wicked and against all natural reason, and inasmuch as the pope would in no way ratify them, either such a statute is invalid, or it must be understood rightly and it must be supplemented by natural reason.[84]

In support of his position, Baldo turned to the venerable opinions of his predecessors Dino of Mugello (d. 1303?) and Cino of Pistoia (d. 1336). Baldo attributed to these jurists the opinion that statutes prohibiting a father or grandfather from leaving daughters or granddaughters their legitimate share of the paternal estate (*legitima*) are null and void.[85] By analogy, for Baldo, their opinions can apply to mothers and grandmothers, too. Furthermore, the deficiencies making municipal ordinances invalid can be amended with the aid of the *ius commune*. This key principle licensed Baldo to refashion Viterbo's statute for the purpose of making it con-

---

[84]"Sed iniquum videtur dicere quod mater non possit instituere filiam vel neptem, et forte si statutum hoc vellet expresse, non posset: quia esset quid contra ius naturale. Et pone: mater habet filium et filiam, et pater decessit inops. Mater vult facere testamentum, quia forte vult relinquere aliqua ad pias causas et pro necessitate salutis anime sue, et vult filie aliquid relinquere, ne mendicent. Si intelligatur statutum ut verbum sonat, cogetur filia femina ire mendicando. Nam non valet institutio, si actendamus corticem statuti. Quapropter dico, quod in terris ecclesie, in quibus terris non valent statuta, qua sunt omnino iniqua et contra omnem naturalem rationem, et qua papa nullo modo confirmaret, aut tale statutum non valet, aut est intelligendum sane et supplendum mediante naturali ratione."

[85]"Et dominus Dynus tenet c. Indultum (VI. 5. 13. 7), quod non valet statutum quod pater vel avus non possit relinquere legitimam filie vel nepote. Ymo plus, quod non valet si diceret, quod non teneatur relinquere, et idem tenet Cynus Cod. de nuptiis, l. Sancimus (Cod. 5. 4. 27)." Dino's opinion, in fact, referred to the obligation of a father toward his children. He also allowed fathers to disinherit their children for the reasons expressly stated in the *ius commune*; for instance, if the children maltreated the father. See his discussion of *Indultum* in *De regulis iuris pontificis commentaria* (Lyon, 1577), 115, n. 5. Cino's opinion is more nuanced than one is led to believe from Baldo's citation, and Cino also restricts his discussion to fathers and their children. See his commentary to Cod. 5. 4. 27 (Frankfurt, 1578), fol. 294va, n. 10.

form to the normal standards of the *ius commune* and natural law. Under the elementary rules of statutory interpretation, the masculine gender includes the feminine in statutes enacted with the intention of providing benefits. In such statutes the feminine "filiae" is normally understood to be included in the masculine "filii," which means children as well as sons. Since Viterbo's statute, enacted for the benefit of sons, makes no mention of daughters or granddaughters, the latter may not be excluded from inheritance. In the wake of Baldo's reasoning, either the statute is invalid or, through equitable interpretation, it must be comprehended that the words "extra filios" are supplemented with "vel filias" and other children—namely, Stefania's granddaughters. In both cases "the last will made by lady Stefania is equitable and in accord with the precept of natural reason and so must be observed."[86]

Whether Baldo's staunch defense of the granddaughters' claims determined the judge's sentence, or sparked an out-of-court settlement or even further litigation, is unknown. On the issue of papal ratification, Baldo may have misspoken. Without ratification by the pope, Viterbo's overlord, the city's statutes would lack validity; yet the redaction cited by Baldo must have received papal ratification.[87] Baldo's critique of Viterbo's statute was implicitly rejected in the 1469 redaction, which stated that the statute was enacted to benefit a mother's sons ("in favorem filiorum masculinorum mulieris"). To that end, inheritance of the maternal estate was restricted to daughters and sons and the children of the sons. Still excluded from the maternal grandmother's estate were the children of daughters. The revised statute, because it patently contradicted the *ius commune* and natural law, was an easy target for litigants and their legal advisers, who would not have missed an opportunity to invoke Baldo's authority.

[86]"Preterea masculinum concipit feminum in actu favorabili, unde statutum factum favore filiorum non facta mentione de filiabus vel neptibus, nec pro nec contra. In suo favore includit feminas, sed non in hodio, ut ff. de ventre in possessionem mictendo, l. 1, § Quare (Dig. 37. 9. 1. 3). Ex quibus concluditur, quod aut statutum non valet in casu isto, aut iusta interpretatione debet intelligi, quod sub illo nomine 'extra filios' intelligatur conceptive 'extra filios vel filias' et idem de ceteris liberis. Et hoc probatur ex coniunctione duarum legum, C. familie hercis., l. fi. (Cod. 3. 36. 26), et C. de testamentis, l. Hac consultissima, § Ex imperfecto (Cod. 6. 23. 21. 3). Nam natura favorabilis est ex lege nature communis est, ut in Auth. de testamentis imperfectis, circa principium (Auth. 8. 3 = N. 107). Ex quibus concludo testamentum iustum, et secundum dictamen naturalis rationis factum a dicta domina Stefania servandum."

[87]On the pope's temporal authority over Viterbo and the rest of the papal state, see Daniel Waley, "Viterbo nello Stato della Chiesa nel secolo XIII," *Atti del Convegno di Studio: VII centenario del 1° conclave (1268–71)* (Viterbo: Azienda Autonoma di Cura, Soggiorno e Turismo di Viterbo, 1975), 97–111; Paolo Prodi, *Il sovrano pontifice* (Bologna: Il Mulino, 1982), 15–40; Joseph Canning, "A State like Any Other? The Fourteenth-Century Papal Patrimony through the Eyes of Roman Law Jurists," in *The Church and Sovereignty, c. 590–1918: Essays in Honour of Michael Wilks* (Oxford: Basil Blackwell for the Ecclesiastical History Society, 1991), 245–60. For a different approach that stresses relative local autonomy instead of papal sovereignty, see Angela Lanconelli, "Autonomie comunali e potere centrale nel Lazio dei secoli XIII–XIV," in *La libertà di decidere: Realità e parvenze di autonomia nella normativa locale del medioevo*, ed. Rolando Dondarini (Ferrara: Deputazione Provinciale Ferrarese di Storia Patria, 1995), 83–102, 132–34.

Viterbo's city fathers enacted uncompromising statutes, but lacking true princely authority, they could not prevent citizens from mounting legal challenges to their laws, nor could they stop notaries from drawing last wills and contracts in violation of the city's statutes. Understandably, they enlisted the majesty of papal authority to affirm the statute's validity. An addendum to the statute, issued by Pope Innocent VIII (1484–92), would have disappointed Baldo. It first reprimanded the "many women" who conveyed their dowries and other goods to the detriment of their male descendants and kin, and second, the notaries who helped these women circumvent the statute. Innocent pronounced that the statute must be wholly observed for the sake of the republic and the preservation of its agnate families. In particular, notaries were prohibited from drafting last wills and instruments making such violations possible.[88] An analysis of the various clauses of the 1469 statute and the papal addendum is beyond the scope of this essay. It is noteworthy, however, that among the family members who appear in the statute, the woman married elsewhere is made conspicuous by her absence. For surely widows like Stefania, who possessed an alternative legal base in their husband's hometown, acted as legally independent persons rather than as *nullae mulieres* and contributed to the undermining of the statute's viability, which eventually necessitated papal intervention.

THE PRESENCE OF THE PAST

The woman-married-elsewhere's citizenship in late medieval Italy was an arena of conflict, contradiction, and ambiguity. Her native and adoptive cities, her father and husband, her children and kinsmen all vied for control over her body, property, and personhood—that is, her capacity to contract, obligate, or commit any legal act. Bartolo's theory of dual citizenship served to mediate these conflicts by aligning municipal statutes with the *ius commune* and by providing remedies for women reduced to the status of *nullae mulieres*. While Baldo did not openly endorse Bartolo's theory, he did concur that women engaged in intercity marriage acquire dual citizenship. Pitting natural law against the *Glossa*, he insisted that marriage to a foreigner does not extinguish the wife's legal standing as an original citizen of her native city. The *Glossa*'s model of women-married-elsewhere's citizenship, though defanged and largely superseded by the theories of Bartolo and Baldo, persisted as a potential source for legal pundits and especially lawmakers intent on expatriating the woman married elsewhere. To understate the problem, a woman engaged in the practice of intercity marriage was placed in a precarious position; she was neither here nor there, penalized in her hometown for marrying out, while never accepted as a full-fledged citizen in her husband's hometown.

[88]Biblioteca degli Ardenti, *Statuti* (1469), fols. 177r–178r, lib. 2, rub. 74; Biblioteca del Senato, *Statuti* 765, fols. 101v–102r, lib. 2, rub. 74. On Innocent VIII's relations with Viterbo, see Pinzi, vol. 4, 291–326; this subject demands further investigation.

This was still the situation after the First World War, according to the American reformer Emma Wold, legislative secretary of the National Woman's Party. In her foreword to a 1928 compilation of nationality laws as affected by marriage, prepared for the House of Representatives Committee on Immigration and Naturalization, she explained:

> In some countries the wife is now out, now in one hour a national, the next upon her marriage, an alien, and not inconceivably, in a third upon her husband's death, a national again. The possible variations of nationality situations that may be imagined are no more dizzying than the actual situations resulting from the wedding of nationality and marriage.[89]

For Wold, the rule that upon marriage to a foreigner the wife ceases to be a national of her country and becomes a national of her husband's did not antedate the French Revolution.[90] The rule was firmly established in the French Civil Code of 1804 (Code Napoléon) and was imported into the civil codes of countries in central and southern Europe, including Italy.[91] Wold's history is shaky, but she is on target with her observation that the French Civil Code was a formative source of law for married women's citizenship and nationality.

With the unification of Italy in 1861 came the unification of citizenship. Unification did not at all eradicate the centrifugal forces of regionalism and localism, but

[89]Statement of Emma Wold, "Effects of Marriage upon Nationality," *Hearings before the House Committee on Immigration and Naturalization*, 70th Cong., 1st sess. (1928), 3. See also Virginia Sapiro, "Women, Citizenship, and Nationality: Immigration and Naturalization Policies in the United States," *Politics and Society* 13 (1984): 1–23; Leila J. Rupp, *Worlds of Women: The Making of the International Women's Movement* (Princeton: Princeton University Press, 1997), 146–50. On the repercussions of the Expatriation Act of 1907, see Candice Lewis Bredbener, *A Nationality of Her Own: Women, Marriage, and the Law of Citizenship* (Berkeley: University of California Press, 1998); and Nancy F. Cott, "Marriage and Women's Citizenship in the United States, 1830–1934," *American Historical Review* 103 (1998): 1440–74.

[90]Note that the parlement of Paris in 1668 deprived of citizenship any French woman who remained abroad after the death of her foreign husband. Marguerite Vanel, *Histoire de la nationalité française d'origine: Evolution historique de la notion de française d'origine du XVIe siècle au Code Civil* (Paris: Ancne imprimerie de la cour d'appel, 1945), 79.

[91]Under the French Civil Code, a French woman married to a foreigner follows the condition of her husband and is deprived of her civil rights and the quality of a French woman. If she becomes a widow and resides in France, she can apply for repatriation (bk. 1, tit. 1, chap. 2, sect. 1, art. 19). On the influence exercised by the French Civil Code on the norms concerning citizenship in the codes of other countries, including the preunification codes of Italy, see Orazio Secchi, "Cittadinanza: Diritto italiano e legislazione comparata," *Il digesto italiano* (Turin: Unione Tipografica-Editrice Torinese, 1897–1902), 7, pt. 2, 224ff.; Guido Astuti, "Il Code Napoléon in Italia e la sua influenza sui codice degli stati italiani successori," in *Atti del Convegno Napoleone e l'Italia* (Roma: Accademia Nazionale dei Lincei, 1973), 192–216. According to Waldo Emerson Waltz, *The Nationality of Married Women*, Illinois Studies in the Social Sciences 22, no. 1 (Urbana: University of Illinois, 1937), 65, as of May 1936 there were about twenty-five states in the world where, upon marriage to a foreigner and the acquisition of her husband's nationality, the wife lost her own nationality.

medieval doctrines of citizenship as they specifically related to defunct city-states and regional states had become obsolete. Citizenship referred to *status civitatis* in the territory of the new Kingdom of Italy and the Liberal State. The acquisition and loss of state citizenship now monopolized the attention of the legal community. However, the guiding assumption of medieval women's citizenship—that an innately inferior wife must yield to her husband's *potestas* and follow him like a dumb animal for the sake of family solidarity—continued to animate the laws and treatises on married women's citizenship and the encyclical *Rerum novarum* (1891) of Pope Leo XIII.[92]

Meanwhile, the antiquated doctrine, originating not with Roman law (as most legal scholars believe) but with the *Glossa*, that a native woman married to a foreigner involuntarily loses her original citizenship while she simultaneously acquires her husband's citizenship found fertile soil in the new Italian State.[93] In addition to its appealing transparency, the doctrine was undeniably compatible with the notion in the French Civil Code of the juridical unipersonality of the married couple and with the subordinate position of the woman married elsewhere. It was no accident that the jurists responsible for Italian Civil Code of 1865, drawing on French and native sources, expatriated female citizens upon marriage to a foreigner on the condition that they become citizens under the laws of the husband's country.[94] Likewise, they expatriated female citizens married to Italian men who became foreigners, provided that they maintain a common residence with their husbands, as well as acquire their husband's foreign citizenship. The double standard was also alive and well. Marriage conferred the Italian husband's citizenship upon his foreign-born wife, without exception.[95] These regulations were carried forward in the new law on citizenship promulgated in June 1912.[96]

---

[92]Mario Manfredi and Ada Mangano, *Alle origini del diritto femminile: Cultura giuridica e ideologie* (Bari: Dedalo, 1983); Diana Vincenzi Amato, "La famiglia e il diritto," in *La famiglia italiana dall'Ottocento a oggi*, ed. Piero Melograni (Rome: Laterza, 1988), 629ff.; Chiara Saraceno, "Women, Family, and the Law, 1750–1942," *Journal of Family History* 15 (1990): 427–42.

[93]Storti Storchi, *Ricerche*, 201–4.

[94]*Codice Civile*, lib. 1, tit. 1, art. 14: "La donna cittadina che si marita a uno straniero, diviene straniera, semprechè col fatto del matrimonio acquisti la cittadinanza del marito." The distinguished jurist Pasquale Mancini was responsible for the insertion of the proviso that loss of citizenship is contingent upon the wife's acquisition of her foreign husband's citizenship. Without this proviso, Mancini and his allies rightly feared, a number of Italian women who married foreigners would become stateless. See Secchi, "Cittadinanza," 283.

[95]Pasquale Fiore, *Della cittadinanza e del matrimonio* (Naples: E. Marghieri, 1909), 58–59, 73–75, 99–106, 133–34.

[96]Rolando Quadri, "Cittadinanza," *Novissimo digesto italiano* (Turin: Unione Tipografica-Editrice Torinese, 1959), 3, 328–34. For two illuminating studies on court cases and doctrinal issues relating to the citizenship law of 1912, see Roberta Clerici, "Problemi in tema di cittadinanza nella giurisprudenza italiana," *Rivista di diritto internazionale privato e processuale* (*Riv. dir. int.*) 8 (1972): 22–75; "Nuove prospettive in tema di cittadinanza della donna maritata," *Rivista di diritto internazionale privato e processuale* (*Riv. dir. int.*) 11 (1975): 678–714, esp. 678–86.

After the First World War Italian women attained substantial rights, with the termination of the requirement that a wife's legal acts (for example, managing her personal property and opening a bank account) must have her husband's permission (*autorizzazione maritale*), and with the removal of the barriers that prevented women from entering the professions. Italian women marrying foreigners, however, did so with the apprehension that they would become strangers in their own country. After the Second World War, women won the franchise and exercised their right to vote for the first time in the elections of 1946 for the Constituent Assembly. A few years later, in 1948, the constitution of the postwar republic declared that all citizens, regardless of sex, were considered to have equal social dignity and husbands and wives were to be treated as equal partners. Yet, the constitutional proclamation of conjugal equality had no impact on the 1912 law regulating married women's citizenship.

A pathbreaking agreement on married women's citizenship, developed at the United Nations and embodied in the Convention of New York of 1957, was ignored in Italy. Adopted by forty-six nations, the Convention provided among other things that "each contracting state agrees that neither the celebration nor the dissolution of a marriage between one of its nationals and an alien, nor the change of nationality by the husband during marriage, shall automatically affect the nationality of the wife."[97] Only in the 1970s did the gap between constitution-based conjugal equality (modernity) and the inferior status of married women (antimodernity) become a ripe topic for legal scholars of international private law, who called for reform of Italy's laws on citizenship.[98]

When change came, it was sudden. On 16 April 1975 the Constitutional Court declared that the citizenship law of 1912, as it pertained to a married woman's involuntary loss of citizenship, was unconstitutional. The law of 1912, which treated women as juridically inferior to men, was said to be inconsistent with "the principles of the Constitution that attribute equal social dignity and equality before the law to all citizens without regard to sex and regulate marriage on the basis of the moral and juridical equality of husband and wife."[99] The Constitutional Court's decision became a "leading case" protecting once and for all the citizenship of Italian women

---

[97]For the text of the Convention of New York, see *Yearbook on Human Rights for 1957* (New York: Secretariat of the United Nations, 1957), 301–2.

[98]Andrea Giardina, "L'egualianza dei coniugi nel diritto internazionale privato," *Riv dir. int.* 10 (1974): 5–31. According to Roberta Clerici, *La cittadinanza nell'ordinamento giuridico italiano* (Padua: CEDAM, 1993), 110: "Dal canto suo, il regime italiano sulla cittadinanza si dimostra sino all metà degli anni settanta impermeabile a quei valori, malgrado essi siano nel frattempo penetrati nell'ordinamento in virtù della Costituzione repubblicana."

[99]For the text of the decision, see "Corte Costituzionale, sentenza 16 aprile 1975, n. 87," *Giurisprudenza italiana* 20 (1975): 515–21. The court also recognized that involuntary loss of citizenship harmed women by barring them from public-sector jobs reserved for Italian citizens.

with foreign husbands.[100] The decision was made in anticipation of impending legislative action on married women's citizenship.[101] On 22 April 1975, with thousands of women demonstrating in Rome for the modernization of Italy's antiquated family law and the legalization of abortion, parliament enacted a comprehensive family law reform that included partial repeal of the citizenship law of 1912. Henceforth, a native woman kept her Italian citizenship when she married a foreigner or when her husband acquired foreign citizenship, except where she expressly renounced it.[102]

With the emancipatory family law reform of 1975, the tenacious legacy of the *ius commune* was in great measure overcome. Italian women achieved what had been unimaginable, indeed appalling, to generations of jurists and legislators: the status of autonomous citizens with legal capabilities equal to those of male citizens. In addition to the capacity to marry foreigners without penalty, the reform allowed women to retain their maiden names and to choose jointly with their husbands a place of domicile. The vestigial institution of the dowry, an archsymbol of women's subjugation, was abolished.[103] The march toward gender equality, however, was incomplete. As Roberta Clerici remarks, the law automatically conferred Italian citizenship on foreign wives of Italian men, yet failed to extend Italian citizenship automatically to foreign husbands; thus the decision of the Corte Costituzionale as well as the family reform law had maintained a double standard and created a constitutional anomaly.[104]

This situation was eventually rectified in 1983, when parliament made it possible for a foreign husband of an Italian citizen to acquire his wife's citizenship if he wished to do so and if he satisfied a residency requirement. As a matter of parity, no longer did a foreign wife of an Italian citizen automatically acquire her husband's citizenship.[105] For the first time, she was given a choice about becoming an Italian citizen. Finally, in 1992, parliament made it easier for Italian women with

---

[100]Roberta Clerici, "La nuova legge organica sulla cittadinanza: Prime riflessioni," *Riv. dir. int.* 29 (1993): 747 ff.

[101]I am not suggesting that there was official contact between the independent judges of the Corte Costituzionale and the senators, only the intersection of parallel developments.

[102]Alfio Finocchiaro and Mario Finocchiaro, *Riforma del diritto di famiglia: Commento teorico pratico alla legge 19 maggio 1975, n° 151* (Milan: Giuffrè, 1975), vol. 1, 266–69. Art. 143-ter. 25 reads: "(Cittadinanza della moglie).—La moglie conserva la cittadinanza italiana, salvo sua espressa rinunzia, anche se per effetto del matrimonio o del mutamento di cittadinanza da parte del marito assume una cittadinanza straniera." An early draft of this text was introduced on 25 May 1972—that is, roughly three years before the decision of the Corte Costituzionale. A penultimate draft of this text was finalized by a commission of the Senate on 23 January 1975. The family reform law was signed into law on 19 May 1975 by the president of the Republic, and went into effect on 20 September.

[103]Roberta Clerici, "Gleichheit im Familienrecht: Einfluß der Verfassung und italienischer Verträge," in *Gleichheit im Familienrecht*, ed. Bea Verschraegen (Bielefeld: Gieseking, 1997), 103–24, esp. 108–11.

[104]Clerici, "Nuove prospettive."

[105]For the text of the law (21 April 1983), see *Riv. dir. int.* 19 (1983): 675–76.

foreign husbands to retain their original citizenship in cases where they were required to become citizens of their husband's country.[106] And a decision in the same year by the Tribunale di Venezia held unconstitutional the 1912 citizenship law that barred children of Italian women with foreign husbands from acquiring their mother's citizenship.[107]

Much too little, much too late, decry feminist critics and legal scholars, who point to the inadequacy of an essentially male (il)liberal ideology of equality to eliminate gender-based discrimination through male dominance of political power, economic resources, and the media.[108] Bartolo and Baldo naturally would have opposed feminism as a total assault on the patrilineal, patrimonial, and paternalistic society in which they comfortably lived and which their jurisprudence brilliantly reproduced. But they might well have been receptive to the feminist critique of formal legal equality, for, if anything, they were experts on the baleful consequences of well-intentioned laws launching the future perfect worlds that all citizens, then as today, are compelled to inhabit.

---

[106] *Riv. dir. int.* 28 (1992), 655 ff. For an analysis of the law, see Clerici, "La nuova legge organica," 741–76.

[107] On the basis of a decision of 7 August 1992; *Riv. dir. int.* 29 (1993): 148 ff.

[108] The literature is vast, but one may consult Odile Dhavernas, *Droits des femmes, pouvoir des hommes* (Paris: Seuil, 1978); Maria Giuseppina Manfredini, *La posizione giuridica della donna nell'ordinamento costituzionale* (Padua: CEDAM, 1979), 77 ff.; Martha Albertson Fineman, *The Illusion of Equality: The Rhetoric and Reality of Divorce Reform* (Chicago: University of Chicago Press, 1991); *Il dilemma della cittadinanza: Diritti e doveri delle donne*, ed. Gabriela Bonacchi and Angela Groppi (Bari: Laterza, 1993); *I diritti delle donne*, ed. Carlo Alberto Graziani and Ines Corti (Milan: Giuffrè, 1996); Judith A. Baer, *Our Lives before the Law: Constructing a Feminist Jurisprudence* (Princeton: Princeton University Press, 1999).

PART 3

"Saints" and "Witches" in Early Modern Italy
Stepsisters or Strangers?

Anne Jacobson Schutte

The possibility of a close family relationship between female saints and witches is hardly a novel idea. Following the lead of structural anthropologists, most scholars who propose such a resemblance proceed morphologically. Concentrating on similar behavior patterns, they observe that both saints and witches go into trances, exhibit somatic signs of their special status, and so forth.[1] To be sure, as Carlo Ginzburg showed in *Storia notturna*, morphology can suggest the possibility of historical connections. In the view of semineopositivists like me, however, it cannot satisfactorily establish them. (Please notice that I refrain deliberately from employing the verb "prove"!)[2] In this paper I intend to take a different approach. Drawing on my research into sainthood and witchcraft in the Venetian Republic from the late sixteenth to the early eighteenth century, I shall try to show that women apparently inspired by God and women allegedly in the service of the devil were operating on two ends of a concrete historical spectrum.

To set the stage, a general methodological principle well known to all may still be worth reiterating. From the point of view of scholars in the human sciences, sainthood and witchcraft are eminently social phenomena. Saints and witches are made, not born. In any time and place, they are products of a historically specific milieu in which certain models of behavior, out of a much larger repertoire theoretically available in

---

[1]See, for instance, *Sante e streghe: Biografie e documenti dal XIV al XVII secolo*, ed. Marcello Craveri (Milan: Giangiacomo Feltrinelli, 1980), 7–62; Richard Kieckhefer, "The Holy and the Unholy: Sainthood, Witchcraft, and Magic in Late Medieval Europe," *Journal of Medieval and Renaissance Studies* 24 (1994): 355–85.

[2]Like all sensible historians, I accept the legitimacy of suggesting a strong "possibility" when we cannot adduce a conclusive "proof." See Carlo Ginzburg, "Prove e possibilità," postface to Natalie Zemon Davis, *Il ritorno di Martin Guerre* (Turin: Einaudi, 1984), 131–54. On the possibilities and problems of morphology as a tool for historians, see Florike Egmond and Peter Mason, *The Mammoth and the Mouse: Microhistory and Morphology* (Baltimore: Johns Hopkins University Press, 1997), esp. 67–82.

their religious tradition, recommend themselves for imitation. As the sociologist Pierre Delooz put it, holy people become "saints for others"[3]—that is, they achieve positive recognition from their contemporaries—if they are perceived to embody the religious and social values considered most important at that moment and to meet urgent needs. Conversely, if they appear to pose some challenge or threat to these values and needs, they are accorded negative recognition, which is frequently expressed in exemplary punishment. Going one step further, the historian Peter Burke suggests who the "others" are:

> It is impossible to explain the achievement of sanctity entirely in terms of the qualities of the individual, or even by the qualities which witnesses saw in each individual. The imputation of sainthood, like its converse, the imputation of heresy or witchcraft, should be seen as a process of interaction or "negotiation" between centre and periphery, each with its own definition of the situation.[4]

*   *

Let us work backwards, starting with the final determination of whether a woman is a saint or a witch and then returning to the beginning. In early modern Italy, as Burke goes on to make clear, lay people, even elites, and most members of the secular and regular clergy below the rank of cardinal were on the periphery. At the center, of course, stood the papacy and two of its highest councils, commissions of cardinals established in the sixteenth century and presided over by the pope. In the late sixteenth century the Congregation of the Holy Office managed to assume control over all cases of witchcraft.[5] As a consequence of reforms implemented between 1625 and

---

[3]Pierre Delooz, "Per uno studio sociologico della santità," in *Agiografia altomedioevale*, ed. Sofia Boesch Gajano (Bologna: Il Mulino, 1976), 233–39. See also idem, *Sociologie et canonisations* (The Hague: Martinus Nijhoff, 1969).

[4]Peter Burke, "How to Be a Counter-Reformation Saint," in his *The Historical Anthropology of Early Modern Italy: Essays on Perception and Communication* (Cambridge: Cambridge University Press, 1987), 59.

[5]See Giovanni Romeo, *Inquisitori, esorcisti e streghe nell'Italia della Controriforma* (Florence: Sansoni, 1990); and idem, "I processi di stregoneria," in *Storia dell'Italia religiosa*, 2: *L'età moderna*, ed. Gabriele De Rosa and Tullio Gregory (Rome: Laterza, 1994), 189–209. On rare occasions, secular judges managed to act first on accusations of witchcraft before the Inquisition became involved. See Adriano Prosperi, "Inquisitori e streghe nel Seicento fiorentino," in *Gostanza, la strega di San Miniato: Processo a un guaritrice nella Toscana medicea*, ed. Franco Cardini (Rome: Laterza, 1989), 217–50. In parts of northeastern Italy under imperial control, where the Inquisition did not operate, witchcraft remained under the jurisdiction of secular courts. See, for instance, *Sante e streghe*, ed. Craveri, 258–81; *La confessione di una strega: Un frammento di storia della Controriforma*, ed. Luisa Sambenazzi (Rome: Bulzoni, 1989).

1634 by Pope Urban VIII, the Congregation of Rites consolidated the center's hegemony in negotiations with the periphery about the making of saints.[6]

The two Congregations operated in almost identical ways: they put accused witches (along with other heretics) and prospective saints on trial, and they often shared information. At first sight there appears to be a major difference between trials for witchcraft and trials for holiness, namely that the latter are always postmortem operations. Unlike defendants charged with witchcraft, those whose holiness is being investigated by the Congregation of Rites cannot be summoned for questioning in court. The absence from court of a person accused of witchcraft or another heresy because he or she has fled or died, however, was (and may still be) no bar to a full-scale inquisitorial prosecution by the Inquisition (now called the Congregation for the Doctrine of the Faith).[7] Having removed this apparent difference, we can easily see the similarities. Both bureaucratic operations rely heavily on the work of functionaries on the local level, whose work is closely monitored by their supervisors in Rome. Final deliberations by the two Congregations take place in the presence of the pope, whose approval is required to render their decisions official and binding.[8]

In the final stages of the promotion of saints and the condemnation of witches, then, action at the center decisively shapes and ultimately controls what occurs on the periphery. Indeed, far beyond the territory in central Italy where it was directly engaged in state building, in the much larger realm over which it claimed spiritual hegemony, the early modern papal monarchy yields two prime examples of social discipline (*Disziplinierung, disciplinamento*).[9] These are no mere morphological

---

[6]On saint-making directed from the center, see *Enciclopedia Cattolica*, s.v. "Beatificazione," by Giuseppe Löw, 2:1090–100; s.v. "Canonizzazione," by idem, 2:569–607; *Enciclopedia del diritto*, s.v. "Processo di beatificazione e canonizzazione," by Giuseppe Dalla Torre, 37:932–43; and idem, "Santità ed economia processuale: L'esperienza giuridica da Urbano VIII a Benedetto XIV," in *Finzione e santità tra medioevo ed età moderna*, ed. Gabriella Zarri (Turin: Rosenberg & Sellier, 1991), 231–63.

[7]A published example of postmortem Inquisition proceedings in the sixteenth century is found in *Nuovi documenti su Vittoria Colonna e Reginald Pole*, ed. Sergio Pagano and Concetta Ranieri (Vatican City: Biblioteca Apostolica Vaticana, 1989). In 1975, when Paul VI created the Congregation for the Doctrine of the Faith as the successor to the Congregation of the Holy Office, the procedural norms followed in the handling of dissidents became "internal," that is, secret. The current edition of the *Corpus Iuris Canonici*, published in 1983, sheds no light on the subject. Andrea Del Col, personal communication.

[8]On changes in operation of the Congregation for the Doctrine of the Faith, see Kenneth L. Woodward, *Making Saints: How the Catholic Church Determines Who Becomes a Saint, Who Doesn't, and Why* (New York: Simon & Schuster, 1990; reprint, 1996).

[9]On the papal monarchy of the early modern period, see Paolo Prodi, *The Papal Prince: One Body and Two Souls: The Papal Monarchy in Early Modern Europe* (1982), trans. Susan Haskins (Cambridge: Cambridge University Press, 1987). For a remarkably lucid, concrete, and prescient anticipation of the historiographical paradigm social discipline, see Peter Burke, "The Triumph of Lent," in his *Popular Culture in Early Modern Europe* (New York: Harper & Row, 1978), 207–44. The current state of research and theoretical reflections on it are well represented by three articles in *Disciplina dell'anima, disciplina del corpo e disciplina della società in medioevo ed età moderna*, ed. Paolo Prodi (Bologna: Il Mulino, 1994): Pierangelo Schiera, "Disciplina, Stato moderno, disciplinamento: Considerazioni a cavallo fra la sociolo

similarities. On the contrary, they are—if one can still use the term—historical "facts." Popes, cardinals, inquisitors, and the women and men they put on trial for holiness or heresy were flesh-and-blood human beings who interacted with one another, not only within but also between the discourses of witchcraft and holiness. The judicial systems and methods they employed (not just parallel or analogous in some abstract, formal sense but closely connected) have left abundant concrete traces (not just suggestive but ambiguous clues). From manuscript trial records and correspondence—supplemented by such printed materials as papal pronouncements, legal disquisitions, theological treatises, manuals of procedure, guides to devout life, and lives of holy people—we can reconstruct with considerable confidence what really happened in negotiations about holiness and witchcraft. Unlike those who are forced or elect to rely on morphology, we are not restricted to speculating about what might have occurred.

*   *

In the final analysis, as we have seen, authorities at the center made the decisions about sanctity and witchcraft. At the beginning and in medias res, on the other hand, we hear voices from the periphery—those of the protagonists in careers of what would eventually be judged holiness or its opposite, and of their relatives, friends, neighbors, and spiritual advisers. They began the process of negotiation and set it on its initial course. Turning now to close examination of concrete cases, we can see how this happened.

For the Venetian Republic, a manuscript guide to local holy people not restricted to worthies from a single order provides a large array of cases from which to choose. During the last two decades of the seventeenth century Andrea Vescovi, longtime chancellor of the Venetian Holy Office, worked on compiling his *Catalogo de' santi, beati, venerabili e servi di Iddio venetiani*, which he completed in 1698.[10]

---

gia del potere e la storia costituzionale," 21–46; Wolfgang Reinhard, "Disciplinamento sociale, confessionalizzazione, modernizzazione: Un discorso storiografico," 101–23; Heinz Schilling, "Chiese confessionali e disciplinamento sociale: Un bilancio provvisorio della ricerca storica," 125–60. On Italy in particular, see Adriano Prosperi, "Riforma cattolica, Controriforma, disciplinamento sociale," in *Storia dell'Italia religiosa* 2, ed. De Rosa and Gregory, 3–48; and idem, *Tribunali della coscienza: Inquisitori, confessori, missionari* (Turin: Giulio Einaudi, 1996). Gabriella Zarri shows the relevance of social discipline to the determination of "genuine" and "false" holiness: "'Vera' santità, 'simulata' santità: Ipotesi e riscontri," in *Finzione e santità*, ed. Zarri, 9–36, esp. 14–19.

[10]Andrea Vescovi, *Catalogo de' santi, beati, venerabili, e servi d'Iddio venetiani, come pure d'altri santi e beati forastieri morti in Venetia o stati per qualche tempo in detta città, quali dalla Santa Chiesa overo da degni autori sono con tali titoli registrati*, Venice, Biblioteca Nazionale Marciana [hereafter VeNM], MS Ital. Cl. VII, 331 (8661), 2r–v. This is the autograph manuscript, authenticated by Vescovi's collaborator Giovanni Battista Ferretti, notary and vice-chancellor of the patriarch of Venice. Other copies of this work are listed by Giovanni Musolino, Antonio Niero, and Silvio Tramontin, *Santi e beati veneziani: Quaranta profili* (Venice: Studium Cattolico Veneziano, 1963), 26–27.

The first section lists 150 holy people born in the Venetian Republic; the second is devoted to eighty saintly foreigners who spent some time in or passed through Venice. The majority of them left no traces in records maintained by the center; the Congregation of Rites neither accorded them interim sanction as *beati* who could be publicly venerated in Venice nor promoted them to the status of saint. Vescovi's compilation of spiritual heroes and heroines—those not officially recognized he is careful to call by the proper term, "servants of God"—is an unusually valuable source for informal saint-construction on the periphery. Furthermore, unlike the *Acta Sanctorum*, the list could be called relatively gender-balanced. According to Burke's calculations, twelve (22 percent) of the fifty-five people whom the Congregation of Rites promoted to full honors of sainthood between 1588 and 1767 are women.[11] Among the 230 people on Vescovi's list, which covers a much longer period of time, eighty-five (37 percent) are women, a considerable number of them from the late sixteenth and seventeenth centuries.

Selecting one representative instance of a woman heading in the direction of sainthood is neither difficult nor dangerous; while small details differ from one life story to another, their careers conform to a single pattern. To illustrate it, I have chosen the Capuchin nun Maria Felice Spinelli. As in many other cases, the brief account of her life provided by Vescovi can be supplemented by the printed sources he cites: a collection of Franciscan lives by Benedetto Mazzara and a vita by Tommaso Baldassini.[12]

Born in Venice on 30 March 1621 to Giuseppe and Barbara Spinelli and christened Bianca, she was one of seven children, only three of whom survived infancy. Bianca's childhood, like those of all holy women in this period, was marked by prodigies: a fall into the fireplace from which she emerged unharmed, miraculous recovery from an illness, and the expulsion of devils from a possessed servant. Although her prosperous merchant father hired a female teacher for his daughters, Bianca neglected her lessons in order to pray; Mazzara claims that she learned how to read, write, and sew without instruction (another common topos in the vitae of prospective female saints). Following the death of her parents, relatives who paid no heed to

[11]Burke, "How to Be," 54.

[12]Benedetto Mazzara, *Leggendario francescano*, ed. Pietr'Antonio da Venezia, 3rd ed., 12 vols. (Venice: Domenico Lovisa, 1721–22). On the theologian Mazzara (d. 1692), see Ignazio Di Pietro, *Memorie storiche degli uomini illustri della città di Solmona* (L'Aquila: Grossiana, 1806), 192–93; and Giovanni Giacinto Sbaraglia, *Supplementum et castigatio ad Scriptores trium ordinum S. Francisci a Waddingo aliisve descriptos*, 3 vols. (Rome: A. Nardecchia, 1908–36), 3:197. I have not seen the two earlier editions of the *Leggendario* (Venice: Bartolomeo Tramontin, 1667–80; Venice: Andrea Poletti, 1689). Although Pietr'Antonio da Venezia, who prepared the third edition of this collection, did not list Spinelli's vita as one of those he added to Mazzara's collection, he must have been responsible for references to the Oratorian Tommaso Baldassini da Jesi's *Vita della serva di Dio suora Maria Felice Spinelli* (Bologna: Heirs of Antonio Pisarri, 1692), issued in the year of Mazzara's death. For reasons of economy, I shall follow and cite Mazzara's account rather than Baldassini's.

her early vow of virginity arranged a suitable marriage for her. Too frightened to say no at the altar, she confessed to her husband on their wedding night that she was already committed to God. Since he too wanted to become a religious, they lived as brother and sister until he died from penances too severe for his weak constitution.[13] For having pushed this marriage, Bianca's older sister, Santina, was punished by death in childbed—just like the sister of Catherine of Siena, Mazzara rather inaccurately observes.[14]

From her Capuchin spiritual director Spinelli "learned the rules of the spirit" and obtained permission to set up a chapel in her home, but he and other confessors opposed her plans to become a nun. So did her relatives and several greedy suitors, one of whom tried to rape her in her bedroom but desisted when she began to blister her flesh with melted candle wax. Devoting herself to charitable work, she tended the most loathsome cases at the hospital of the Incurabili and spent so much money supporting repentant prostitutes and other unfortunates that her servants locked up her cash box. At length she obtained admission to Santa Maria del Redentore, the Capuchin house near San Girolamo. On account of her humility, she specified that she wanted the status of lay sister rather than that of choir nun, to which her social standing and financial resources entitled her. Before entering the convent, she travelled to Rome with her sister Caterina to take part in the Jubilee of 1650. En route, while praying in the church of Santa Maria degli Angeli in Assisi, she heard a voice instructing her to found a convent of the same name in Venice. On her return, however, she made her profession in Santa Maria del Redentore, taking the name Maria Felice.[15]

With a sister in religion whom she had met in Bologna on the journey to Rome, Giovanna (Maria Orsola) Ricoli, Spinelli began to consider how to carry out God's will and found a new convent. Her plan was vigorously opposed not only by the devil, who employed a stunning variety of tricks and temptations, but also by a series of confessors, who treated her with harshness bordering on sadism. They denounced her to the patriarch, Giovanni Francesco Morosini, on the grounds that she was possessed by the devil. After interviewing her, he rejected this diagnosis, calling her "a great servant of God, whom I would compare to the holy mother Teresa."[16] Hence Morosini and other enthusiastic friends supported her purchase from the Venetian government of Santa Maria delle Grazie, a monastery on the small island of the same

---

[13]This episode in Spinelli's life has a rather archaic flavor, resembling a pattern more common in the lives of medieval holy women than in those of their early modern counterparts, most of whom succeeded in avoiding marriage. See Dyan Elliott, *Spiritual Marriage: Sexual Abstinence in Medieval Wedlock* (Princeton: Princeton University Press, 1993).

[14]Mazzara, *Leggendario francescano*, 1:339–42.

[15]Mazzara, *Leggendario francescano*, 1:339–46, 360–61.

[16]Mazzara, *Leggendario francescano*, 1:352. In his conclusion (366), Mazzara mentions other clerics who called her a saint in her lifetime: the canon Giovanni Andreis, the Theatine Pietro Piccini, and the Somaschan Giovanni Francesco Priuli.

name south of the Giudecca, recently vacated by the suppressed order of San Girolamo di Fiesole.[17] On 19 March 1671, when renovation of the building and negotiations about enclosure were well advanced, Spinelli, Maria Orsola, and ten novices bade a tearful farewell to their sisters at Santa Maria del Redentore and set off in gondolas for their new abode.[18]

Like other female "servants of God," Spinelli in her last years was plagued with multiple ailments: severe headaches, high fevers, fainting spells, asthma, erysipelas, and dropsy. With "holy hatred toward herself," she bore her suffering humbly and patiently, commenting that "my sins merit much worse than this." Thanks to frequent visits from her "special angel," she was able to cope effectively with the practical demands of convent life and carry on her devotional regimen. She performed numerous thaumaturgic miracles, predicted deaths and recoveries from mortal illnesses, and foresaw the destinations of recently deceased souls. Following a stroke, she died on 24 January 1683. In the coffin, all signs of her travail having disappeared, her body recovered its youthful beauty.[19]

Like all seventeenth-century hagiographers, Mazzara followed models, the vitae of certified saints. He made no effort to conceal his modus operandi; indeed, he drew attention to it. Given his objectives, to edify readers and promote his subjects to the honors of the altar, he could hardly have done otherwise. He knew that his two intended audiences, devout people on the periphery and the Congregation of Rites at the center, expected a particular form of presentation. That particular presentation was precisely what he provided: accounts of a prodigious childhood and a course from adolescence through maturity strewn with obstacles heroically overcome, followed by a topically arranged demonstration of virtues, a moving evocation of a pious death, and a presentation of selected miracles.[20] On more than one occasion, Mazzara, a gifted narrator, evinced discomfort with the constrictions imposed by the genre. In the "virtues" section of Spinelli's vita, for example, he apologized for having to reiterate incidents already recounted.[21] Striking out on a new creative path and telling stories of the "servants of God" in his own way was a risk he could not afford to take.

---

[17]The monastery and the island (formerly called Cavanella) took their name from a miraculous image of the Virgin, on which see Flaminio Cornaro, *Venezia favorita da Maria: Relazione delle imagini miracolose di Maria conservate in Venezia* (Padua: Stamperia del Seminario appresso Giovanni Manfrè, 1758), 67–74. The island is now the site of a hospital for infectious diseases.

[18]Mazzara, *Leggendario francescano*, 1:346–56.

[19]Mazzara, *Leggendario francescano*, 1:356–65.

[20]On this model, which emerged in the fourteenth century and was modified only slightly in the seventeenth to accommodate the new emphasis on heroic virtue, see André Vauchez, *La sainteté en Occident aux derniers siècles du Moyen Age d'après le procès de canonisation et les documents hagiographiques* (Rome: École française de Rome, 1981), 583–622. (English edition: *Sainthood in the Later Middle Ages*, trans. Jean Birrell [New York: Cambridge University Press, 1996].)

[21]Mazzara, *Leggendario francescano*, 1:362.

In all but one detail, her inability to avoid marriage (an obstacle soon and happily removed), Maria Felice Spinelli's life story is thoroughly typical of prospective female saints in this era. Burke has identified five main "saintly roles, or routes to sanctity" available to Catholics of the Counter-Reformation: founder of a religious order, missionary, charitable activist, pastor, and mystic/ecstatic.[22] Clearly Spinelli, like many of her female peers, comes closest to fitting into the first category; the status of nun was a rarely stated but essential requirement for being taken seriously as a holy woman, and that of foundress was an added advantage. Her activities extended into two other areas: she was a charitable activist and enjoyed access to extramundane sources of information and power, even if she cannot properly be termed a mystic/ecstatic. Neither she nor many of her female peers served in the mission field, and of course none was a pastor; these roles were reserved primarily in the first instance and exclusively in the second for men. She fits the socioeconomic profile of saintly women as well. Among the canonized saints studied by Burke and the unofficial holy people in Vescovi's *Catalogo*, most of the men and an even higher proportion of the women (ten of twelve, or 83 percent, on Burke's list) came from the nobility or the prosperous middling ranks.[23]

*   *

Finding a typical witch is not so easy. For one thing, the term has misleading connotations. In Italy from the end of the sixteenth century on, very few women prosecuted for witchcraft fit the classic profile: selling their bodies and souls to the devil, flying to the Sabbath to engage in feasting, sex, and worship of the Evil One.[24] The overwhelming majority were garden-variety sorceresses who cast spells, often enhanced by the employment of holy words and consecrated materials, which were designed to heal or cause illness, find lost objects, and win or regain sexual partners.[25] Relatively few of them fit the stereotypical northern European age profile of

[22]Burke, "How to Be," 55–56.

[23]Among the men, Burke counts twenty-six nobles, three "middle-class" (the quotation marks are his), eight agricultural workers (the majority of whom lived before the sixteenth century), and eighteen whose social origins are unclear; Burke, "How to Be," 54. Of the women (my calculation), ten of twelve (83 percent) were of royal, noble, or prosperous middling origin; only Margherita di Cortona and Rosa di Lima came from humble circumstances.

[24]For some exceptions, see *Gostanza*, ed. Cardini; and Anne Jacobson Schutte, "My Satanic Spouse: Nuns and Sexual Possession in Early Modern Italy," *Civis* 21 (1997): 163–75.

[25]On the Roman Inquisition's abandoning support for the diabolical witchcraft hypothesis, see Romeo, *Inquisitori*, 3–108, 247–74. On the prevalence of sorceresses in the Venetian Inquisition's caseload, see Anne Jacobson Schutte, "I processi dell'Inquisizione veneziana nel Seicento: La femminilizzazione dell'eresia," in *L'inquisizione romana in Italia nell'età moderna: Archivi, problemi di metodo e nuove ricerche*, ed. Andrea Del Col and Giovanna Paolin (Rome: Ministero per i beni culturali e ambientali, Ufficio centrale per i beni archivistici, 1991), 159–73; and eadem, "Donne, Inquisizione e pietà," in *La Chiesa di Venezia nel Seicento*, ed. Bruno Bertoli (Venice: Studium Cattolico Veneziano, 1992), 235–51. My discussion of Caterina Erba below is adapted from the latter essay.

the witch: a withered, postmenopausal, eccentric crone. On the contrary, most were young; many engaged for fun or profit in extramarital sex.[26]

As an exemplary though not thoroughly typical case, let us consider Caterina Erba, processed by the Venetian Inquisition in the late summer of 1669. Born in Milan twenty-five years before her trial, she had run away from home with a Piedmontese ensign, whom she married on the Lido before he shipped out for Crete to fight the Turks. She followed him as far as Split; then, pregnant, she returned to Venice with the wife of a French colonel. After being delivered of a stillborn baby girl, she found employment as a wet nurse in the house of a noble family. Soon she became the mistress of the master's son, Andrea Renier.[27]

It was her lover who denounced her to the Inquisition. Informed by Erba's servant that in her house he could find knotted cords, wax figurines stuck with pins, and other objects employed in occult practices against him, Renier left Erba in his country house and went into town with his gondolier to search the place. Once he had found the articles, he talked with his confessor, who advised him to go to the Holy Office "to unburden my conscience and liberate myself from sorcery." This was probably not friendly spiritual counsel but an order.[28] When asked "about the status and reputation of the said Caterina," Renier offered the information he thought the inquisitor wanted: "She's been my woman, but I believe that while I was involved with her, she had other friendships." To ensure that the Holy Office took the matter seriously and understood that he was not a perpetrator but a victim, he added: "It's true that, from what I've seen, she isn't very devout. I repeatedly reprimanded her for not wearing holy medals but sticking them under the tablecloth."[29]

After interrogating Erba's servant and Renier's gondolier, the Inquisition ordered a search of Erba's house. The compromising materials were found and she

---

[26]On sorcery and male-female relationships, see Ruth Martin, *Witchcraft in Venice, 1550–1650* (Oxford: Basil Blackwell, 1989), "love magic," *ad indicem*; Marisa Milani, "Il caso di Emilia Catena,. 'meretrice, striga et herbera,'" *Museum Patavinum* 3 (1985): 75–97; eadem, "L'incanto' di Veronica Franco," *Giornale storico della letteratura italiana* 162 (1985): 250–63; eadem, *Piccole storie di stregoneria nella Venezia dell'500* (Verona: Essedue, 1989); *La verità ovvero il processo contro Isabella Bellocchio (Venezia, 12 gennaio–14 ottobre 1589)*, ed. Marisa Milani (Padua: Centro Stampa Maldura, 1985); and Mary R. O'Neil, "Magical Healing and Love Magic in the Roman Inquisition," in *Inquisition and Society in Early Modern Europe*, ed. Stephen Haliczer (London: Croom Helm, and New York: Barnes & Noble, 1987), 88–114.

[27]Venice, Archivio di Stato [hereafter VeAS], SU, b. 115, dossier Caterina Erba, first interrogation of Erba, 22 August 1669.

[28]From the late sixteenth century on, a considerable part of the Inquisition's caseload was generated by confessors' denying absolution to their penitents unless they made "spontaneous appearances," either to confess their involvement in unorthodox activities and to name their accomplices or, as in this instance, to denounce those who they had reason to believe had committed some offense against the faith. Romeo, *Inquisitori*, 191–98; Prosperi, *Tribunali della coscienza*, 213–548.

[29]Dossier Caterina Erba, denunciation, 12 August 1669. For contrasting evaluations of the importance to the Holy Office of sorceresses' "reputations," see Martin, *Witchcraft in Venice*, 234–38; Romeo, *Inquisitori*, 266.

was arrested.[30] When she was brought before the tribunal, she did not wait for the inquisitor to ask questions but spoke right up:

> I'll tell you the honest truth. This gentleman who kept me, Andrea Renier, who lives in Calle de Meio at San Stae, after he'd kept me a year and got me pregnant, left me with not a thing except a little money for the delivery. I gave birth in the house of the midwife Andriana, where that gentleman had put me until I delivered.

At this point, poor Caterina, "complaining and crying because he'd abandoned me," found support in a female network. The midwife's daughter, Betta, a prostitute, told her not to worry because a solution to her problem could be found. Betta invited to the house one Marina, wife of a boatman, who "promised to bring it about that the noblewoman wouldn't abandon me but would come back, and not send me out to [domestic] service."[31]

Caterina and Betta paid close attention to Marina, knowing that with her assistance their neighbor Anzoletta, a singer, had managed to inveigle a rich merchant into maintaining her. For two weeks Marina gave them lessons in such techniques of sorcery as "throwing the cord"[32] and sticking pins into wax figurines. According to Erba, she also taught them how to recite certain spells. As a precaution against committing a prosecutable offense, diluting the potency of the spells, or both, Marina cautioned her pupils not to mix them with authorized forms of devout behavior. Before reciting spells, Erba explained, "I had to take off the medals I was wearing."

Trembling, Caterina recited spells and employed most of the other techniques Marina had taught her, refraining only from administering to Andrea a magical powder that she feared would poison him. It appears that they worked, but not perfectly. Renier accepted his responsibility for Caterina only intermittently and rendered her unable to support herself:

> He made me stay first in one house, then in another, and I had four children with him. After the first birth, he sent me into service, but when people found out about our relationship, they fired me. I went to the gentleman and begged him to take care of me. He kept me there for two nights, and I got pregnant. After more of the same, he's kept me until now, and I think I'm pregnant again.[33]

Erba's ability to articulate her plight and conform to a stereotype of subordination served her well. Taking into account her prompt admission of guilt, her promise never again to engage in sorcery, her renunciation of the right to mount a defense,

---

[30]Dossier Caterina Erba, 13 and 21 August 1669.
[31]Dossier Caterina Erba, first interrogation of Erba, 22 August 1669.
[32]See Martin, *Witchcraft in Venice*, 123.
[33]Dossier Caterina Erba, first interrogation of Erba, 22 August 1669.

and her poverty, the Holy Office assigned a lenient penalty. She was merely prohibited from leaving the city and instructed to perform salutary penances and report once a month to the tribunal with a certificate of good conduct from her parish priest.[34] Three days later, in response to her petition, the judges decided that if on account of common knowledge about her liaison with Renier she was unable to find work as a servant in Venice, she could move to Padua.[35]

*   *

One formal difference between Erba's case and Spinelli's immediately strikes the ear. Rather than having her words mediated first by a confessor in one of the "commanded autobiographies" so many holy women (though apparently not Spinelli) were compelled to write[36] and then after her death by a hagiographer, a live defendant summoned before the Inquisition had an opportunity to speak for herself. Another is social class. As I indicated, virtually all prospective saints were born to privilege, which permitted them to become nuns and automatically gave them a certain amount of credibility or at least the benefit of the doubt. Most witches lived on the socioeconomic margins; through sorcery, they tried to scrape together the means of survival. Considered to be "little women," who bore the full brunt of pervasive misogyny, they were distrusted as weak and potentially culpable in all circumstances, even if they were never denounced and put on trial.[37] The saints sublimated their sexuality, mortified their bodies, and sought rewards in the hereafter. The witches, who worked in and through the sexual body, struggled to live from day to day, thinking only intermittently about their eternal destinations. Rarely if ever did these two types of women meet.[38] In many senses, therefore, saints and witches were strangers.

---

[34]Dossier Caterina Erba, sentence, 7 September 1669.

[35]Dossier Caterina Erba, 10 September 1669.

[36]On "commanded autobiographies," see Romeo De Maio, *Donna e Rinascimento* (Milan: Il Saggiatore, 1987), 167–72; Alison Weber, *Teresa of Avila and the Rhetoric of Femininity* (Princeton: Princeton University Press, 1990); Jacques Le Brun, "Les biographies spirituelles françaises du XVIIème siècle: Écriture féminine? Écriture mystique?" in *Esperienza religiosa e scritture femminili tra Medioevo ed età moderna*, ed. Marilena Modica Vasta (Palermo: Bonnano, 1992), 135–51; and Isabelle Poutrin, *Le voile et la plume: Autobiographie et sainteté dans l'Espagne moderne* (Madrid: Casa de Velásquez, 1995).

[37]See Anne Jacobson Schutte, "Piccole donne, grandi eroine: Santità femminile, 'simulata' e 'vera,' nell'Italia della prima età moderna," in *Donne e fede: Santità e vita religiosa*, ed. Lucetta Scaraffia and Gabriella Zarri (Rome: Laterza, 1994), 277–301 (in English as "Little Women, Great Heroines: Female Sanctity, 'Simulated' and 'Genuine,' in Early Modern Italy," in *Women and Faith*, ed. Lucetta Scaraffia and Gabriella Zarri [Cambridge, Mass. and London: Harvard University Press, 1999], 144-59); and eadem, "Tra Scilla e Cariddi: Giorgio Polacco, donne e disciplina nella Venezia del Seicento," in *Donna, disciplina, creanza cristiana dal XV al XVII secolo: Studi e testi a stampa*, ed. Gabriella Zarri (Rome: Edizioni di Storia e Letteratura, 1996), 215–36.

[38]On an encounter between the prospective saint Angela Maria Pasqualigo and the "little woman" Cecilia Ferrazzi, who, although she did not engage in sorcery, was suspected of diabolic possession and later tried by the Inquisition for pretense of sanctity, see Schutte, "Piccole donne," 297–98.

But from another point of view, one that takes full account of their gendered situation, saints and witches bear a much closer family resemblance. The lives of both were conditioned by pervasive male distrust of female nature as something "other," inferior, and potentially dangerous unless tightly controlled. Spinelli's relatives, as we have seen, disregarded her vow of virginity and married her off; her confessors opposed her projects of becoming a nun and founding a convent, and at one point accused her of being possessed by the devil. Erba's patrician lover neglected fully to accept the consequences of impregnating her, questioned her fidelity, and suspected her (rightly, as it turned out) of using sorcery to turn proper relations between the sexes upside down; he objected to her trying to condition his will and actions, when by all that was right and natural he should control hers.

To view these women as passive, helpless objects manipulated and victimized by men, however, would be a mistake. Some men—Spinelli's husband, her first spiritual director, Patriarch Morosini, and (though her hagiographer neglects to mention them) the Provveditori sopra Monasteri and other Venetian officials who allowed her establishment of Santa Maria degli Angeli to go forward—accepted the genuineness of her inspirations and assisted her in actualizing them. In assigning Erba a light punishment and then mitigating it, members of the Inquisition tribunal categorized her as an unfortunate victim of social circumstances beyond her control, instead of stigmatizing her as a willing servant of the devil. Their reaction exemplifies standard procedure in the trial and sentencing of those sorceresses who understood current assumptions about gender well enough to manipulate them by articulating the difficulties of their situations and comporting themselves in an appropriately penitent and deferential manner.[39]

In the lives of early modern Italian saints and witches we can recognize some female agency. Those in both groups who found and penetrated the cracks in a gender system that was not, in fact, rock-solid were able to determine their destiny to a limited, nonetheless significant, degree. While in the most literal sense they were strangers, in more important ways they appear to be kin; not blood sisters but stepsisters—or better still, *sorelle di latte* (girls unrelated by blood but nourished by the same wet nurse).

---

[39]During and after their trials, recalcitrant female defendants received somewhat harsher treatment. See Schutte, "Donne, Inquisizione e pietà," 240–41.

The Dimensions of the Cloister
Enclosure, Constraint, and Protection
in Seventeenth-Century Italy

Francesca Medioli

The space of the cloister is the area enclosed within the walls of a convent. From an architectural point of view, it is a structure that remained unchanged for centuries.[1] Nonetheless, at a certain point in time it did change in character. While earlier it was circumscribed and hidden away, the privileged destination for the *fuga mundi*, it later developed into a closed space. Its closure occurred in both directions: it was a space from which it was not possible to go out, but also a space that could not be entered. It was therefore a space which communicated with the outside world only in specific cases, according to well-defined rules, first and foremost among which was that of gender. The key to understanding the transformation of this space is the implementation of strict legal enclosure.

From 1563, when it was introduced at the Council of Trent, until the French Revolution and beyond, strict enclosure not only determined the external and physical dimension of the cloister but also redefined its symbolic, religious significance. Enclosure was bound intrinsically to the place, not just specifically to nuns; it permeated and defined the life of anyone who passed the threshold of the cloister. Even though not all the women in the convent were necessarily religious, it was still the case that all who entered its gate were subjected to the rule of enclosure, whether they were professed nuns, lay sisters, novices, retired widows, wives experiencing difficulties with their husbands, or young girls. To some extent, enclosure placed them all on the same level.[2]

---

[1]See Fabrizia Macalli, "Abbazia, architettura della," in *Dizionario degli Istituti di Perfezione* (henceforth *DIP*) (Rome: Edizioni Paoline, 1974), 1: 28–48, esp. 33; Angiola Maria Romanini, "Architettura monastica occidentale," *DIP*, 1: 790–827.

[2]As Cardinal De Luca said concerning enclosure: "Respicit non solum materialem, sed etiam mores tam monialium, quam in coeterorum in monasteriis conservantium." Giovan Battista De Luca, *Repertorium seu Index generalis rerum notabilium quae continentur in Theatro veritatis et iustitiae cardinalis de Luca* (Venice: Paolo Bellonio, 1698), 140.

After the Council of Trent, nuns were expected to consider enclosure as something more than a form of levelling discipline, possibly as a state of mind and at any rate as a prerogative to be preserved above everything else. We are on the whole well informed on the practical aspects involved in enforcing the rule of enclosure, and above all on the fact that the rule did not allow exceptions. On the extremely rare occasions when a nun could leave the convent, a number of precautions were taken to ensure that enclosure would follow her every movement.[3]

But did the nuns actually perceive strict enclosure as a prerogative of the nun's condition? And if not, how was it seen from within? These questions, as well as the raison d'être of strict enclosure as an institution, are the fundamental issues underlying the present essay. In order to tackle these issues, I would like to examine how enclosure was viewed and put into practice a century after Trent, in a totally different historical context; that is, in Rome by the highest echelons of the Church. Furthermore, I would like to explore how enclosure was perceived and experienced by those who were subjected to it. This can best be achieved by focusing on a sample of cases that go against the rule, for they are the only ones that can highlight the contrast between the normative theory and the actual experience of enclosure. I will base my survey on a personal examination of the archive of the Roman Congregation of Bishops and Regulars. Because the Congregation was the centralized organ in charge of the ordinary administration of the female convents throughout Catholic Christendom, its records provide a fitting framework within which to consider the specific theme of enclosure as constriction and protection. This archival material, furthermore, enables us to determine the amount of room for maneuver available between the formulators of the rule (that is, those who had laid it down and ensured its enforcement), and the (female) subjects of the rule, whether oppressed or supported by it. The monastic institution of enclosure at one and the same time constrained and protected. It did not exclusively constrict nuns and protect the oppressed, but both things at once or in succession for the same person. Paradoxically, it also protected the constrained nuns and constricted those who were meant to be protected by enclosure.

At Trent the institution of enclosure had been introduced in order to discipline the convents. Even though this aim was not stated in the decree, one may infer as much from the preliminary discussion preceding its promulgation, in which the connection between abuses, immature age, and enforced taking of the veil was indeed mentioned explicitly. As a proof of such a gendered voice, there is the fact that the council did not mandate enclosure for male religious persons.[4] For some

---

[3]See, for example, Archivio Segreto Vaticano, Sacra Congregatio Episcoporum et Regularium, Monialium (henceforth A.S.V., S.C.E.R.), Registro (henceforth Reg.) 1 (1646), 35v–36r.

[4]On the relevant discussions held at the Council of Trent, see Francesca Medioli, "An Unequal Law: Nuns' Enforcement before and after the Council of Trent," in *On a Footing of Perfect Equality: Women in Renaissance and Early Modern Europe*, ed. Christine Meek (Dublin: Four Courts Press, forthcoming).

time after 1563, memories of the status quo ante persisted. Nuns in Naples, for instance, "were accustomed in spring and autumn to go to the geysers of Pozzuoli, where, according to their pleasure and free will, they would spend fifteen or twenty days, whichever was the more convenient for them."[5] In 1601 the nuns of Udine could still remember a time when "there was so much freedom that we could go out when we wanted and remain outside fifteen days, a month, at the time of the grape-harvest, even outside Udine."[6]

A century after the introduction of enclosure, however, one cannot find among the nuns even the vaguest recollection of a different lifestyle. By the mid–seventeenth century, enclosure constituted a well-established tradition, both for the cardinals responsible for its administration and for the women subjected to it. At the same time, however, it is quite clear that the cardinals were perfectly aware of how unpopular the rule was among those directly affected. Thus a bishop wrote in a letter to the Congregation in 1661: "I know well that the nuns are women, and for that matter women who unwillingly see themselves constrained."[7] On the other hand, some of the measures that were customarily taken, such as the custom of bolting the gate at night from outside as well as inside, appear, to our eyes at any rate, better fit for a prison than for a convent.[8] We ought to consider the fact that one locks up not only in order to protect but also to guard. This consideration, as well as the question of who should hold the keys to the convent after dusk, caused violent disputes between the bishop and the nuns in Cosenza between 1663 and 1664, in San Severo in 1665, and later also in Ancona.[9]

But how was enclosure considered from a theoretical point of view at this time in Rome? Giovan Battista De Luca, cardinal and member of the Holy Congregation of Bishops and Regulars, started with the premise that since the first vow taken by a person of the Church of either sex was that of chastity, "any act of fornication will be said to be sacrilegious." Accordingly,

For the better observance of this vow and in order to avoid occasions when

[5]Giuliana Boccadamo, "Una riforma impossibile? I papi e i primi tentativi di riforma dei monasteri femminili di Napoli nel'500," *Campania Sacra* 21 (1990): 96–122, esp. 121.

[6]Giovanna Paolin, "Monache e donne nel Friuli del Cinquecento," in *Società e cultura del Cinquecento nel Friuli occidentale: Studi*, ed. Andrea Del Col (Udine: Edizioni della Provincia di Pordenone, 1984), 219.

[7]A.S.V., S.C.E.R., Positiones (henceforth Posit.), 1661, May–July, 3 June 1661, Masseo Vitali, bishop of Mantua, to the Congregation.

[8]See for example, the indirect testimony found in A.S.V., S.C.E.R., Posit., 1661, September–November: "And since among other offices, she has held that of porter and of keeping the keys of the gate of the convent; as the gate was locked only from the inside, according to the custom of that convent and all the others in the state of Avignon, the above-mentioned sister Francesca had the freedom to leave the the convent by night as by day."

[9]See A.S.V., S.C.E.R., Reg. 12 (1663), 166v, 184r, 192r, 194v, 202v; Reg. 13 (1664), 47r; Reg. 14 (1665), 173r.

one might be in danger of violating it, the custom of enclosure has been very commendably introduced.... And everything... is structured to further the observance and preservation of this vow of chastity, and in order to preclude the opportunity and the danger of its violation.[10]

It is noteworthy that Monsignor De Luca expressed his views not in Latin but in Italian, the vernacular understood by all, including the nuns. Much more concerned with practice than with theory, he was quite explicit about the true nature of enclosure:

Among the pastoral cares of the greatest importance... is that concerning the governance of convents, because on the one hand one needs a certain degree of rigor and austerity in order to safeguard a section of the flock so delicate and prone to danger; on the other hand, one needs a considerable degree of leniency, since we must feel pity for these women imprisoned for life and deprived of all the satisfactions which lay women of comparable rank enjoy.[11]

In the case of nuns, the customary methods of coercion are ineffective, for "They are women imprisoned for life, and therefore one cannot count upon that fear that can be instilled in laypeople with the threat of prison and other personal punishments, such as in matters concerning personal property or titles."[12]

De Luca's maxim, which on the whole represents the position held by the Congregation (even if his views and assumptions about women in the cloister are by no means atypical), was "rigor outside with laypeople and flexibility inside with the nuns."[13] His statement reflects how well the cardinals understood the actual condition of the women subjected to enclosure. One should add that this understanding must to some extent have been enhanced by the fact that a considerable proportion of the nuns and the cardinals shared the same social background: among the nuns were the prelates' mothers, aunts, sisters, and cousins.[14]

---

[10] Giovan Battista De Luca, *Il religioso pratico dell'uno e dell'altro sesso nell'ozio tuscolano della primavera del 1676: Con la cronologia delle religioni* (Rome: Reverenda Camera Apostolica, 1679), 143, 145.

[11] Giovan Battista De Luca, *Il vescovo pratico, sopra le cose spettanti al buon governo delle chiese et all'offiti de' vescovi e degli altri prelati ecclesiastici* (Rome: Corbelletti, 1675), 302.

[12] De Luca, *Il vescovo pratico*, 304.

[13] De Luca, *Il vescovo pratico*, 316.

[14] For instance, Alderano Cybo (cardinal from 1645 and member of the Holy Congregation from 1667), travelling to his diocese of Iesi in the autumn of 1659, stopped in Florence at the convent of the Murate, where he had some female relatives. Two of the three sisters of Girolamo Colonna, cardinal from 1627 and member of the Congregation from 1636 to 1666, became Carmelite nuns, while five of the six sisters of Emilio Altieri, a member of the Congregation from 1669 and pope in 1670, took the veil. Vincenzo Maria Orsini, a member of the Congregation from 1673 and pope in 1724, had a niece who in that year held the office of abbess at the convent of Santa Patrizia in Naples, as well as a sister and another

Undoubtedly this awareness of the actual conditions of women subjected to enclosure underlay the relative degree of tolerance displayed by the Congregation toward breaches of it, as long as they did not cause trouble. There is no doubt that breaches did take place regularly, and that they came in all shapes and degrees. Some were of little account, such as the practice of vocal and instrumental music, a very substantial element in the life of nunneries at the time, and the comedies performed in the presence of laypeople during Carnival.[15] Other violations, while formally serious, could nonetheless be treated mildly, as for instance at Civita Castellana when enclosure was breached by a "boy of four years less two months," who, as the nuns speedily made clear, "was not allowed to set foot on the ground nor to be taken into the monastery";[16] at Cosenza, when laywomen would enter "with the excuse of having to do the laundry"; at Città di Penne, to "clean the hen-houses"; or at Telese, "in large numbers" [six women] to bring in the harvest."[17]

As Cardinal De Luca stressed, with the nuns it had to be remembered that one was dealing with "poor women who have been imprisoned ... since it is often the case that young women are induced to take this course (to wit, taking the vow of enclosure) by force." The examination of their willingness to do so, he observed, "is generally limited to a mere formality and worthless ceremony," since "young ladies generally are ashamed of saying explicitly ... that they desire to be married," and furthermore, "they are ... human beings who voluntarily endure that penance of everlasting imprisonment, which is perhaps the second greatest after capital punishment." Accordingly,

> We ought to tolerate some degree of flexibility in their observance, especially with regard to their communal life, their correspondence, and their

---

niece in the convent of the Sapienza. His mother, Giovanna Frangipani, had earlier founded the convent of the Dominican nuns of Gravina. See respectively: Florence, Archivio di Stato, MS 137: *Diario fiorentino*, compiled by Francesco Settimani, vol. 10 (1645–59), 635v: "Cardinal Cibo arrived at an early hour in Florence and went to visit some relatives of his who were nuns in the convent of the Murate, and later departed for Iesi, his bishopric"; Gino Benzoni, "Colonna, Federico," in *Dizionario Biografico degli Italiani* (Rome: Istituto dell'Enciclopedia Italiana, 1982), 27: 296. Federico Colonna was the elder brother of the cardinal Girolamo: see Franca Petrucci, "Colonna, Girolamo," in ibid., 346–47; Luciano Osbat, "Clemente X," in ibid., 26: 293.

[15]As, for instance, in Florence in 1664, Como in 1675, Naples in 1678, and Perugia in 1684: see respectively, A.S.V., S.C.E.R., Reg. 10 (1661), 135v; Reg. 31 (1684), 67v; Posit., January 1671, Genoa, and Reg. 13 (1664), 201r, 210r; Reg. 22 (1675), 10r; Reg. 25 (1678), 26r; Reg. 31 (1684), 320r; Reg., 43 (1698), 165v.

[16]A.S.V., S.C.E.R., Reg. 8 (1656), 211v–12r; see Reg. 9 (1660), 86r–v, the Congregation to the archbishop of Bari: the boy "had followed into the enclosure of the monastery of Santa Scolastica a young girl of nine years"; Reg. 11 (1662), 162v–63r: the Congregation to Michele Misserotti, bishop of Bitetto, concerning the introduction of "boys younger than six years" into the convent of San Paolo.

[17]A.S.V., S.C.E.R., Reg. 11 (1662), 162v–63r; Reg. 9 (1660), 155v; Reg. 24 (1677), 279r; see also Reg. 7 (1655), 147–48.

acquaintances with laypeople, as long as one makes sure that no suspicion about the crucial point of their honesty arises. For it is not easy—in fact, it is quite impossible, especially in the case of women—to erase completely the former habits in which they have been brought up. They are different from plants which have grown obliquely.[18]

Conversations at the grilles like those which took place in Macerata in 1660 in the most run-down convent, that of the Convertite, between some of the inmates and a certain Giuseppe Mattei, called il Rusticone, were one thing.[19] An altogether different matter were the conversations taking place in the respectable convent of Santa Maria Nuova in Ancona, where the parlors in 1661 were "frequented by all sorts of people, amidst generalized public scandal."[20] In cases such as the latter, the intervention of the authorities was inevitable, swift, and uniform. Exactly the same measures were taken in 1646 to deal with the convent of San Silvestro in Ferrara and the convent of the Virgins in Malta.[21] The slightest relaxation of rules could degenerate and give rise to serious scandals, which was exactly what had to be avoided. The nuns were by this time, as De Luca put it, meant to be "the guiding lights of the people... or truly as the candles lit on the chandeliers to give light to others."[22] This was seen increasingly as the social function of the enclosed nuns, and the Congregation could resort to the utmost severity to assure that the principle was respected. If a breach of the rule had no far-reaching consequences, the culprits might expect relatively lenient treatment, but public scandal deriving from exactly the same breach was bound to be viewed as a serious aggravating circumstance and handled accordingly.

When Paolo Corsi, an Augustinian friar in Pavia, entered the convent of Matiola to visit Sister Maria Clara, the Congregation decreed his expulsion from the city and the province, and a salutary penalty according to the bishop's best judgment. As far as she was concerned, since the occurrence had not become known to the public, the whole matter should be dealt with without too much fuss so as not "to cause damage to the convent."[23] When the same course of events led to public scandal in the Vallombrosan convent of Santa Verdiana in Florence in 1661, the punishment imposed was ruthless; the Vallombrosan monk Zenobio Piazza stood trial and was condemned to the galleys for life while the two nuns, Sister Margherita Angela Portinai and the lay sister Elisabetta, were condemned to life imprisonment.[24] At Lodi in 1662 Sister Antonia Margherita Limera stood trial for having

---

[18]De Luca, *Vescovo*, 312, 316; idem, *Religioso*, 242.

[19]A.S.V., S.C.E.R., Reg. 9 (1660), 136v, the Congregation to the local authorities.

[20]A.S.V., S.C.E.R., Reg. 9 (1660), 136v; for another example, see Reg. 1 (1646), 120v–21r, Ferrara, the Congregation to Cardinal Bishop Carlo Pio di Savoia.

[21]A.S.V., S.C.E.R., Reg. 14 (1665), 13r; Reg. 1 (1646), 120v–21r; Reg. 16 (1667), 112v.

[22]De Luca, *Religioso,* 11.

[23]A.S.V., S.C.E.R., Reg. 11 (1662), 81v.

[24]A.S.V., S.C.E.R., Reg. 10 (1661), 180r.

introduced a man into her cell and entertained him there for a few days; she was sentenced to being walled in alive on a diet of bread and water.[25] In the same year, the trial for breach of enclosure and sexual intercourse against the cleric Domenico Cagianella and Sister Vincenza Intanti of the convent of San Salvatore in Ariano had an identical outcome.[26]

We cannot look at sexual misdemeanors as unambiguously symptomatic of a condition of life endured against one's will. Nonetheless, enclosure was clearly an objective deterrent meant to safeguard convents as much as possible from scandals; and it represented an extremely effective element in the governance of those women on whom life in the convent had been imposed in the first place. Nor did the Tridentine decrees solve the problem posed by the phenomenon of enforced taking of the veil. Even today, this issue is on the whole avoided if possible by a certain type of Catholic historiography, but archival material repeatedly attests to the phenomenon and, as we saw earlier in the words of Cardinal De Luca, it was very much on the minds of those in charge of governing the nuns.

As a general principle, both enclosure and enforced monachization were perceived as gender-specific problems. Accordingly they raised some juridical difficulties. Paradoxically, at Trent enclosure was justified in order to restrain these "unstable, fragile, and weak women," but at the same time the establishment of proceedings for seeking annulment of monastic vows implied recognition of personal will.[27] From a practical point of view, the general principle safeguarding free will and thus personal freedom was complicated by several factors, but the evidence testifies both to vigorous enforcement of enclosure and to the fact that the possibility of seeking annulment was not merely theoretical. Out of roughly thirty cases in my sample from the records of the Congregation of Bishops and Regulars, about half the petitions for annulment were successful.[28]

When petitions for annulment of vows were not granted, it is interesting to consider the reasons. The women directly involved took their steps according to a strictly personal logic. Resorting to considerations such as the common good and public scandal, the Congregation acted according to criteria at a level more general

---

[25]A.S.V., S.C.E.R., Reg. 11 (1662), 139r.

[26]A.S.V., S.C.E.R., Reg. 38 (1662), 305r.

[27]Dionysius Cartusianus (1402–71), *De reformatione monialium*. I quote from idem, *Opera omnia* (Tornaci: Typis Cartusiae S. Maria de Pratis, 1911), 249. The complete passage reads: "Quia videlicet foeminae sunt specialiter ac naturaliter multum instabiles, fragiles, molles ac debiles ratione; ideo periculosissimum est monialibus inter saeculares personas, praecipue inter viros, apparere et conversari, ipsoque inspicere, alloqui et audire." This passage proved to be extremely influential at least until the end of the eighteenth century; see, for instance, Antonio Bonelli, *Processo teologico sopra la clausura dei monasteri delle monache contro Pio Cortesi autore del libro intitolato "La monaca ammaestrata nel diritto che ha il principe sopra la clausura"* (Assisi: Ottavio Sgariglia, 1784), 26.

[28]On this specific theme, see Francesca Medioli, "Monacazioni forzate: Donne ribelli al proprio destino," *Clio* 30 (1994): 431–51.

than the specific context of enclosure. Constriction, members of the Congregation believed, should be used to maintain the social order; anyone who opposed it they perceived as subversive and dangerous.

In 1683 a great scandal enveloped the Dominican monastery of Santa Caterina in Brescia, where, as was reported by some of the nuns and soon became generally known, some of the inmates were pregnant, dubious liaisons went on between the nuns and the regulars in charge of them, and a secret passage linked the convent to a neighboring house.[29] When, after twenty years of misdemeanors, the scandal finally exploded and repressive measures were taken, two of the nuns involved, Cecilia Rovetti and Bartolomea Cattani, decided to flee. On orders from the local Dominican prior, "they were chased by armed citizens of Brescia" as far as Governolo, where they were caught and handed over to "a notary so that he might convince them to let themselves be chained and transported in a screened carriage to Cremona." Here they were taken to the bishop's palace, where "they were kept under lock and key." Cecilia—twenty-two years old, of "fair appearance," and of "good character, and modest"—soon came to see reason and said that she was prepared to return to a convent, as long as it was not in Brescia. The other, Bartolomea—forty-three years old, ugly and without "outside supporters"—declared that she "no longer wished to be a nun and that she would rather commit suicide" than return to the convent.[30]

Bartolomea raised a legal question of some importance: she claimed that she had earlier obtained a papal brief granting her permission to institute proceedings for annulment, but that the Venetian authorities had blocked the action and the collection of evidence.[31] In cases like this, the interests of the Congregation were clearly opposed to those of the Serenissima. Bartolomea may have received a *restitutio adversus lapsus quinquenni*, a preliminary step necessary to institute proceedings for annul-

---

[29]On the case, see the reconstruction by A. Cassa, *Monasteri di Brescia e monache di Santa Caterina: Pagine di storia patria* (Brescia: F. Apollonio, 1900), esp. 18 ff.; on the two fugitives, see *Monasteri di Brescia*, 36–41, which contains passages drawn from the letters left in the convent at the time of the attempted escape that illustrate the motivations behind it. The letter of Sister Bartolomea (38) reads: "I decided to go to the feet of the Vicar of Christ so that he may do with me whatever he wishes," a topos frequently encountered among nuns who claimed that they had been forced into the convent. Cecilia, on the contrary, wrote: "It is true that I made a mistake, but I think also that I have done my penance, for I have been retired for a long period and living with my enemies. I wander in the world, seeking good fortune, and I beg all my sisters to pray God for me." See A.S.V., S.C.E.R., Posit., 1682, September, Bartolomeo Gradenigo, bishop of Brescia, to the Congregation about the necessity of transferring jurisdiction over the nunnery of Santa Caterina from the Dominican friars to himself; see A.S.V., S.C.E.R., Posit., 7 October, about the bishop's takeover. The matter was not entirely resolved, though; see A.S.V., S.C.E.R., Reg. 29 (1683), 192v, the Congregation to the bishop of Brescia, in which the bishop's jurisdiction, as well as the annulment of any previous bull about it, is reiterated.

[30]A.S.V., S.C.E.R., Posit., 1682, 19 August, letter of Ludovico Seitala, bishop of Cremona, to the Congregation about the two nuns in jail.

[31]A.S.V., S.C.E.R., Posit., 1682, 20 August, letter of the vicar of the chapter of Brescia, Antonio M. Ferrario, to the Congregation; A.S.V., S.C.E.R., Posit., 1682, 20 August, letter of the superior of the Dominicans of Brescia to the Congregation about the two nuns' having been seen around Governolo.

ment when more than five years had elapsed since the taking of vows, like the one granted in 1670 to Carlina Tonelli, another nun in Brescia.[32] In Bartolomea's case, the problem was solved when she died of tertian fever on 11 September 1682, not long after being apprehended. In order to dispel suspicions of poisoning, Bishop Ludovico Seitala ordered an autopsy to be performed by two doctors and a surgeon, with negative results. The bishop reported to the Congregation that

> While she lay sick, poor Bartolomea was reported to have had extravagant dreams of being led to the public gallows in Brescia, that the executioner was placing the noose around her neck, and that he was on the point of hanging her, and that her body was going to be cut in several parts to be placed on public show.[33]

His opinion that her dream represented "the righteous judgments of God" is representative of the mentality of the time. It may have no longer matched the perception of the cardinals in Rome, who by now saw enclosure as a useful instrument of government with few theological implications.

The fact remains, however, that like the first bull on enclosure issued by Boniface VIII in 1298, and in identical words, the fifth chapter of the twenty-fifth session of the Council of Trent prescribed that ecclesiastical superiors should enforce strict enclosure "under the divine judgment and eternal malediction."[34] It should be noted that this is the only explicit curse included in the whole body of regulations issued by the Council of Trent, and that it matches closely the anathema *Auctoritate omnipotentis Dei* recorded in the Roman Pontifical of 1520 against anyone who violated a consecrated virgin.[35] The anguish of the nun's dreams or, at least, the way they were reported, can indicate how also for some nuns enclosure had not only a strictly repressive force but also an almost magical significance. Bartolomea believed that its violation would lead to severe earthly punishments envisaged in neither canon law nor tradition.

[32]A.S.V., S.C.E.R., Reg. 19 (1670), 229r.

[33]A.S.V., S.C.E.R., Posit., 1682, 16 September, letter of Ludovico Seitala, bishop of Cremona, to Cardinal Cesare Facchinetti.

[34]For Boniface VIII, I quote from *Bullarum diplomatum et privilegiorum sanctorum romanorum pontificum* (Turin: Dalmazzo, 1862), 7: 808–10; and for the Council of Trent, *Concilii Tridentinii actorum: Pars sexta complectens acta post sessionem sextam (XXII) usque ad finem concilii (17 sept.1562–4 dec. 1563)*, ed. Stephan Ehses, in *Concilium Tridentinum: Diariorum, actorum, epistularum tractatuum: Actorum* (henceforth *CT,* 9) (Freiburg in Breisgau: Herder, 1924), 9:10, 1040.

[35]See I. M. Calabuig and R. Barbieri, "Consacrazione delle vergini," in *Nuovo dizionario di liturgia,* ed. Domenico Sartore and Achille M. Triacca (Rome: Edizioni Paoline, 1988), 299–300: "Quis praesentes virgines seu sanctimoniales a divino servitio, cui sub vexillo castitatis subjectae sunt, abducat ... maledictus ... in domo et extra domum, maledictus in civitate et in agro, maledictus vigilando et dormiendo, maledictus ambulando et sedendo, maledictus sint caro eius et ossa, a planta pedis usque ad verticem non habeat sanitatem."

Francesca Medioli

A woman who for whatever reason did not wish to remain in a convent had no reason to perceive strict enclosure as anything other than a form of imprisonment. Vittoria Possevino, grandniece of the Jesuit Antonio, escaped four times from three convents located in three different states. Although she started proceedings for annulment, she was never to be released from her vows, mainly because there was no place for her in the lay world. During her time in Venice, Vittoria was placed "in deposit" in the convent of the Convertite on the Giudecca. After a failed first attempt to flee, she managed to escape in April 1661 with no help from "outside supporters." Having sought refuge in the house of a woman "fifty years old, honest and charitable," she was picked up by the captain of the Provveditori sopra Monasteri (the lay magistracy in charge of convents) and taken to his house, where she was imprisoned. She let it be known that she would prefer, "should she again be forced [to return to the same convent], to take her own life," and that if she were to be taken back to the Convertite of the Giudecca, "she would set the convent on fire." It was not reclusion in itself that frightened Vittoria, but the cloister: "she refused to go back, declaring openly that she would rather take her own life, but at the same time stating she was prepared to go to prison as long as the proceedings of her action were dealt with speedily." The papal nuncio insisted that "this very bad example for the other nuns had to stop." Vittoria Possevino remained outside the convent until November, when the Senate decided to hand her back to the nuncio. As a consequence of this scandal, the nuncio reported, "every [Venetian] convent refuses to take on ever again a deposit such as this of a nun from another land who had run away from the same convent twice."[36] In the end, she was taken to the Convertite in Ferrara and subsequently to the Convertite of Mantua, her native city, from which she managed to escape, only to be caught again.[37]

That the convent was perceived as a prison is shown by the cases of those who fled simply because they wanted to escape, those who were playing their last card, and those who fled because they had been forced to enter the convent in the first place. The Convertite experienced perhaps the highest rate of both successful and failed escapes. This was so because, as the fifth chapter of the twenty-fifth session of the Council of Trent stated, women entering a convent of Convertite were not even required to give their formal approval. Among them one finds a large number of former prostitutes who had been made to enter the convent by little short of brute force.[38] According to the Congregation, escapes and "similar accidents cannot happen without the participation and assistance of people both outside and inside the convent."[39] In Rossano in 1652, orders were given to chase a fugitive and in the

[36]A.S.V., S.C.E.R., Posit., February–March 1660, April–May 1660, September–December 1660, miscellaneous papers.
[37] For an accurate account of her story, see Medioli, "Donne ribelli," 438–41.
[38]A.S.V., S.C.E.R., Reg. 5 (1652), 214r.
[39]See *CT,* 9, 1044.

174   *Ed. Kuehn, Schutte, & Seidel Menchi*

meantime "diligently to institute proceedings to identify the accomplices."[40] For anyone attempting to escape in this manner, the chances of success were practically nil unless she could rely on practical and very reliable support from protectors who would supply the most basic necessities, such as lay clothing.

This is what happened to two nuns who fled in 1685 from the convent of the Convertite in Venice. Apprehended in Mantua and placed in the prison of the Convertite house there, they were subjected to "salutary penitences" (for example, fasts) while awaiting judgment on whether they would be taken back to Venice.[41] Imprisonment, one ought to remember, was not mere custody but a form of punishment.[42] But theirs was, according to canon law, a "simple flight" and not an aggravated one, as would have been the case if they had abandoned the veil, caused damage to the convent, or fled in the company of a man. They were, however, automatically excommunicated, for since the time of Boniface VIII this penalty was incurred by anyone who left the cloister without formal permission.[43]

A professed nun could decide to try to escape because she had nothing to lose. Francesca Maria, a professed nun in the convent of Santa Chiara in Vercelli, for instance, escaped in 1693 with Antonio Rolando, also known as Bizzarro, when their relationship was discovered. Since she would be imprisoned in any event, it would make little difference if in addition to breaching her vow of chastity, she were also charged with apostasy. Once caught, Rolando and Francesca Maria were condemned respectively to the perpetual service on the galleys and life imprisonment.[44]

Alternatively, a nun could escape in order to raise the issue of the nullity of her solemn profession, as did the Veronese nun Andreana Vittoria, known in the lay world as Elisabetta Balestreri Valeggi. She escaped without external help on 18 August 1682 from the convent of Santa Elisabetta in Mantua in the company of the lay sister Laura Maria Nizzoli, who had also been forced to enter the convent. They climbed over the wall of the kitchen garden with the help of a ladder, "putting their lives in grave danger." Having sought refuge in an inn, they met the servant of a knight, an acquaintance of the lay sister, who refused to help them. Perhaps in order to get rid of them, the innkeeper provided them some men's clothes, shoes, and hats and placed them on a carriage travelling towards Guastalla. The Franciscan friars under whose jurisdiction the convent fell ordered the other nuns to keep quiet about it.[45] The fact that the bishop was informed of what had happened only eight days later, on 26 August, gave the two fugitives some advantage. The two, however, were betrayed and apprehended on 7 September in Parma and four days later were sent

[40]A.S.V., S.C.E.R., Reg. 5 (1652), 214r.

[41]A.S.V., S.C.E.R., Reg. 32 (1685), 54r.

[42]See E. Pacho, "Carcere," in *DIP* 2: 261–76.

[43]See J. Fernándes, "Fuga," in *DIP* 4: 988–95; A. Gauthier, "Apostasia," in *DIP* 1: 717–19

[44]A.S.V., S.C.E.R., Reg. 39 (1693), 6r; see Reg. 38 (1692), 305r, for an identical punishment.

[45]A.S.V., S.C.E.R., Posit. 1682, 11 and 18 September, Giovanni Lucido Cattaneo, bishop of Mantua, to the Congregation.

back for trial to Mantua, where they were first placed in the bishop's prison and later transferred to a different jail, the convent of Santa Teresa.[46] On 2 October they petitioned the Congregation for absolution at least *in forum conscientiae* and asked to be placed in the same cell.[47]

Before being caught, and therefore not yet under any pressure to fabricate some excuse, Andreana Vittoria had explained the reasons for her escape in a letter addressed to the Holy Congregation: she wished to reach Rome in order to throw herself "at the feet of Our Lord whom Jesus Christ has granted as father to all Christians, but especially to poor abandoned religious women like me." Her purpose was to plead for the annulment of her vows. As she explained, she had entered the convent out of desperation, and for the same reason she had tried to escape:

> At the age of three, I lost my father; my mother married again but died after only two years. I was left with my stepfather, who treated me worse than any tyrant, beating me and insulting me both with words and with ill treatment in the way I was fed and dressed. But what he also did to me is that when I reached the age of fourteen, fifteen, he tried more than once to rob me of my honor; and as I through divine help survived this, I said I wanted to accuse him. He persecuted me ... until I said that I would become a nun, not because I wanted to but in order to free myself from his bad treatment and the danger of being disgraced in my honor. I told him, however, that I would first try it out for six months as an *educanda*. He said that he wanted me to go without any trial period because I had said I would go, and thus he forced me. In the meantime, he was consuming my property with concubines while I was in misery in the convent, increasingly unhappy. When my sadness at having been forced was compounded by vexations at the hands of the abbess and the other nuns, who treated me badly as a foreigner, my desperate melancholy drove me to such a resolution [to flee].[48]

Upholders of the usefulness of convents argued that one of their functions was to protect young women from the possible abuses that might take place within the home.[49] In the case of Andreana Vittoria, the space of the cloister had at first appeared attractive as the only available shelter from the abuses of her stepfather, but had then revealed itself as so oppressive a place that she decided to flee.

[46]A.S.V., S.C.E.R., 18 September, Tommaso Saldini, bishop of Parma, to the Congregation.
[47]A.S.V., S.C.E.R., 2 October, Suor Andreana Vittoria Balestrieri Valeggi and Suor Laura Maria Nizzoli to the Congregation.
[48]A.S.V., S.C.E.R., 25 August, Elisabetta Balestrieri Valeggi to the Congregation.
[49]See, for instance, Bologna, Biblioteca Comunale dell'Archiginnasio, MS B 778, Giovanni Boccadiferro, *Discorso sopra il governo delle monache*, 165–199. I quote from 171–72: "So that young ladies should not remain in their paternal homes, at risk of losing their honor not only with strangers but also

By February 1683, Andreana Vittoria and Laura Maria had been brought back to the convent where they had professed and were imprisoned there.[50] In May directions arrived from Rome that they should be "treated well and charitably."[51] In July Andreana Vittoria, showing the first signs of repentance for the "error she had committed," begged to be freed and reintegrated in her former grade and level in the order on the ground that her escape had "no other purpose than to expose before Our Lord the reasons of the nullity of her profession."[52] The Congregation refused her request but conceded that she should receive the sacraments and confession—a first sign of softening on their part. In February 1684 Laura Maria Nizzoli gave way and sent the Congregation her supplication.[53] It is not possible to say whether, after the period spent in prison, the convent had in the end regained some of its appeal, or whether, once all alternative options proved unreasonable, the two women resigned themselves to remaining there. Resignation at any rate is a topos often mentioned by authors of edifying treatises of the time.[54]

A similar case from Mantua also reflects, albeit with a more positive outcome, the ambiguous nature of the space of the cloister. In 1662 Flavia Peverari admitted to being guilty of adultery and after negotiations with her husband, Pietro Catanio di Cossi, resolved to take religious vows at the Convertite. Her husband asked the Congregation to speed up the procedures for her profession because Flavia was trying to avoid the convent in order to avoid taking the vow of chastity, even though in the circumstances her bargaining power with her husband and with Rome was nonexistent. In 1678, however, she instituted proceedings for the annulment of her profession on the grounds that it had been forced by her husband, and fifteen years

---

with servants and (which is much worse) with their brothers and perhaps even with their fathers, which has occurred more than once (I tremble to say) in our times and of which old records are full." See also Rome, Archivio Segreto Vaticano, Miscellanea Armadi, II, 86, 29v, letter of Cosimo I de' Medici to Pope Pius V: "Apart from the great harm that [unchaste behavior] causes to convents, it brings so great a threat to the honor of the whole city that one can no longer describe it, for every single day, because of their lack of mothers and fathers and because of other circumstances, it is not possible to safeguard the honor and good fame of countless girls except by putting them in convents as boarders in the first place." See also A.S.V., S.C.E.R., Reg. 9 (1660), 100r–v, Rimini, the Congregation to Marco Gallio, bishop of Rimini, concerning Giacinta and Virginia Pisoni, who entered the convent of San Sebastiano because of "the domestic abuses they suffered in their paternal home and for the other reasons you gave."

[50] A.S.V., S.C.E.R., Posit. 1682, 13 November, Elisabetta Balestrieri Valeggi and Francesca Nizzoli to the Congregation; A.S.V., S.C.E.R., Reg. 30 (1683), 22r, the Congregation to Giovanni Lucido Cataneo, bishop of Mantua.

[51] A.S.V., S.C.E.R., Reg. 30 (1683), 74v.

[52] A.S.V., S.C.E.R., Reg. 30 (1683), 167r.

[53] A.S.V., S.C.E.R., Reg. 30 (1683), 64r.

[54] See, for instance, the manual for discontented novices by Giuseppe Agnelli, *Il verisimile finto nel vero: Pensieri suggeriti dal direttore ad una religiosa novizia scontenta, per disporla alla solenne professione: Raccolti per uso opportuno di meditazioni nel triduo o altro maggior tempo precedente alla Sagra operazione* (Rome: Placho, 1703).

later, in 1693, she was finally released from her vows.[55] Apparently she had in the meantime managed to build a personal network of people who could receive her once she left the convent.

The status of lay women consigned to convents was of crucial importance. In 1661 in Marsi, in an entirely different geographical, juridical, and legal context, a novice escaped at night from her convent by climbing over the wall. She claimed that she had been constrained by force to enter it. According to canon law, she could have returned to the world freely without any proceedings for annulment, for she had not yet made her solemn profession. The bishop, however, had her imprisoned in the convent and wrote to the Congregation in the following terms; "[Concerning] the safety of the novice, the reputation of her family and of the convent itself, I do not think one can find any better expedient than leaving her where she is, with the addition of those penances that will appear to your most prudent judgment as most suitable to her fault." There would of course be inevitable problems with her future sisters, who for their part must have been primarily preoccupied with safeguarding their few privileges and would not have appreciated the increased restrictions imposed on them because of her. Had she been allowed to leave, however, matters would have been even worse. As the bishop pointed out, she would have represented a problem with very wide repercussions, including "great uproar and disarray throughout the city. Furthermore, her brothers, who are people of quality, instead of doing something like that [take her back], would disappear to the countryside in despair, and as the young girl is an orphan, I would not know to whom she could be safely handed over."[56] It was better, therefore, to keep her in prison for a while and then convince her gently to remain in the convent.

At this point we should examine briefly the other side of the coin, for the opposite could indeed occasionally happen: the enclosure could protect a whole convent. In 1661, for instance, a group of nuns in Montefiascone reported to the Congregation that "last March, at night, a sacrilegious group of people attempted to breach the enclosure of our convent by breaking a gate and a wall." The rough fellows were immediately captured by the troops of the bishop, but the nuns wrote a letter furnished with twenty-five signatures *manu propria* and two *signa crucis* asking the bishop to put the invaders on trial immediately in order to reestablish the honor of their convent.[57]

Enclosure served to protect an individual in other less exceptional circumstances, as for instance when a girl educated in a convent decided against the will of her family to take vows. And the custom of withdrawing temporarily, even for long periods, to a convent was widespread among women of all social classes. This most often happened when a woman was widowed in old age, alone, orphaned as a child,

---

[55]A.S.V., S.C.E.R., Reg. 11 (1662), 288v; Reg. 39 (1693), 86r.
[56]A.S.V., S.C.E.R., Posit., 1661, April, Ascanio de Gaspari, bishop of Marsi, to the Congregation.
[57]A.S.V., S.C.E.R., Posit., 1661, the nuns to the Congregation.

found family life troublesome, or wished to avoid a forced marriage or domestic abuse.[58] Inevitably protection was always accompanied by constriction as, for instance, in the case of Caterina Orsini, princess of Trecase. "Having had serious differences with the prince her husband," the princess asked to be allowed to spend an initial six-month period at the convent of San Giovanni Evangelista in Lecce; she subsequently obtained permission to prolong her stay for a further six months. In 1660, wishing to leave halfway through her second term, she had to ask permission from Rome.[59] Once inside, even a laywoman found it difficult to come out. The convent, not unlike Jonah's whale, returned women to the world only grudgingly.[60]

Let me conclude by quoting Eileen Power's words concerning medieval English nunneries, which I believe apply equally well to the later period that I have been considering: "A career, a vocation, a prison, a refuge: to its different inmates the monastery was all these things."[61] What had actually changed after the introduction of strict enclosure? The Council of Trent marks the point when newly reiterated and strengthened rules regarding nuns began for the first time to be enforced consistently and rigorously. The world within the walls of the convent, however, had not changed, nor had the social customs outside which constituted its raison d'être.

Enclosure is thus like the Great Wall of Catholicism. Standing firmly by its principles, the Church staked out its distinctive identity with respect to the Protestant Reformation. Enclosure was one of the most characteristic products of the regulating spirit of Trent. It is quite evident that the state of enclosure cannot be traced back to any natural human condition; it was a conscious choice made by the Council fathers and their successors, and only as such can it be appraised and defended.

In the cases examined here, the breach of enclosure was severely punished by the restriction of the escapees' freedom—a restriction inflicted, albeit to a lesser extent, upon any nun of the period. There is no correspondence between the guilt incurred in breaching enclosure and the punishment meted out in order to preserve the existing order of things. The repressive element of cloistered life was increasingly emphasized, but the convent continued to perform the same social and economic functions as before Trent. A generic perception of the dangers threatening virgins, the abstract desire for protection, and the presumed need to withdraw from the world through

---

[58]For some examples, see Francesca Medioli, "L'amministrazione della clausura da parte della Congregazione romana sopra i Regolari," in *Il monachesimo femminile in Italia dall'Alto Medioevo al secolo XVII a confronto con l'oggi*, ed. Gabriella Zarri (Verona: Il Segno dei Gabrielli, 1997), 239–82.

[59]A.S.V., S.C.E.R., Reg. 9 (1660), 16r; for a similar case, see A.S.V., S.C.E.R., Reg. 9 (1660), 7r–8r, Ancona, the Congregation to the vicar of the chapter, in which, in order to solve the problems between Giuseppe Colombella and his wife, Ludovica Truglioni, it is decided that she must enter one of the convents in Osimo, Cingoli, or Recanati.

[60]This metaphor comes from Suor Arcangela Tarabotti (1604–1652): see Francesca Medioli, *L'"Inferno monacale" di Arcangela Tarabotti* (Turin: Rosenberg & Sellier, 1990), 35.

[61]Eileen Power, *Medieval English Nunneries c.1275 to 1535* (Cambridge: Cambridge University Press, 1922), 25.

enclosure may be justifications valid at a personal level, but cannot be deemed sufficient to determine a norm. That convents were useful in order to avoid the disper-
sion of family patrimony and the almost universal perception of women's inferiority
can only partly explain why enclosure was established.

Apart from the defensive and protective element and the repressive and disciplining one, convents undoubtedly aimed to constitute the ideal space for spiritual
life. The well-known motif of the *hortus conclusus* was not only a literary topos conceived a posteriori for apologetic purposes. It also represents an effort to provide
forms and structures for a deep religious inspiration. Such a worthwhile aim, however, could have been pursued without strict enclosure, as numerous earlier and later
manifestations of the female monastic tradition clearly demonstrate. We still need,
therefore, to seek a further explanation for the Council of Trent's radical curtailing of
personal freedom. The adoption of a legal institution does not by itself necessarily
ensure the modification of a deeply rooted preexisting state of affairs: a norm can
provide the structure for order, but does not automatically guarantee order.[62]

[62]I am grateful to Paolo Vaciago for translating this work into English.

The Third Status

Gabriella Zarri

I would have preferred to retain the original title of this paper, "the third way" (*la terza via*), an expression better suited than "the third status" (*il terzo stato*) for conveying the dynamic element that characterizes not only the theoretical formulation of voluntary female celibacy, first articulated during a period of intense cultural and social transformations—the age of the Reformation and Counter-Reformation—but also the different forms it assumed. The recently published ninth volume of the *Dizionario degli Istituti di perfezione*, however, has assigned to "the third way" a restricted technical meaning: a conception of the vow of chastity and sacerdotal celibacy developed especially in Dutch and American Catholicism beginning in the 1970s that holds the complete fulfillment of this commitment not to be obligatory in certain circumstances.[1] Fortunately, there is an alternative. In some sixteenth-century sources, the term "third status" connotes a female condition presented as a third possibility for women's lives in addition to the traditional alternatives of marriage or the convent—that is, voluntary celibacy. In this essay I shall explore several institutions developed in the late sixteenth and seventeenth centuries that allowed women who did not wish to or could not marry or enter a convent to live unmarried in their families or in a community.

At first sight, such a possibility does not appear to be an early modern innovation. In the late medieval Low Countries, France, and northern Germany, communities for women linked to the movement of the Beguines and the Devotio moderna had emerged.[2] From the fourteenth century on in central Italy, *bizzoche* or

---

[1] *Dizionario degli Istituti di perfezione* (hereafter *DIP*), ed. Guerrino Pelliccia and Giancarlo Rocca, 9 (Rome: Edizioni Paoline, 1997): cols. 1030–36.

[2] Florence W. J. Koorn, "Women without Vows: The Case of the Beguines and the Sisters of the Common Life in the Northern Netherlands," in *Women and Men in Spiritual Culture, XIV–XVII Centuries: A Meeting of North and South*, ed. Elisja Schulte van Kessel (The Hague: Netherlands Government Publishing Office, 1986), 135–47; Gerhard Rehm, *Die Schwestern von gemeinsamenen Leben im nordwestlichen Deutschland: Untersuchungen zur Geschichte der Devotio moderna und des weiblichen Religiosentums* (Berlin: Duncker & Humblot, 1985); idem, "Aspekte der Wirtschaftstatigkeit der Schwestern von gemeinsamenen Leben im 15. Jahrhundert," in *Erwerbspolitik und Wirtschaftsweise mittelalterlicher Orden und Kloster*, ed. Kaspar Elm (Berlin: Duncker & Humblot, 1992), 249–66.

pinzochere had proliferated. In the early fifteenth century, the Roman widow Francesca Bussi de' Ponziani had founded an institute of noncloistered women religious, the Oblates of Tor de' Specchi.[3] During the course of that century, furthermore, the expanding movement of tertiaries living in their own homes or in small groups had evolved toward forms of communal life.[4] In general terms, it is legitimate to say that already before the sixteenth century we encounter a kind of laicization and secularization of religious life that on the female side assumed the symbolic form of the conflict between action and contemplation represented by the opposing models of Martha and Mary. But only in the sixteenth century, when the fracture of western Christianity generated diversified and opposed confessions and models of life, did these alternative forms of female religious life acquire distinct configurations responding to the new circumstances. At the same time, the evolution of political and social structures laid the groundwork for a wider diffusion of female solitude, documented especially in the eighteenth century.[5]

It is in the sixteenth century, I maintain, that the nubile life presented and affirmed itself as a voluntary choice for women, and that through ecclesiastical approval of this new condition it gained social legitimacy.[6] Obviously, in this regard there was a distinction between Protestant and Catholic lands. In the former the monastic model disappeared, while it remained in the Catholic; but the prior experiences of semireligious female communities, like the *beguinages*, continued to provide a possible example for unmarried women in lands touched by Reform.[7] In Catholic lands, and above all in Italy, the country in which the "third status" developed in the

---

[3]Penelope Galloway, "'Discreet and Devout Maidens': Women's Involvement in Beguine Communities in Northern France, 1200–1500," in *Medieval Women in Their Communities*, ed. Diane Watt (Cardiff: University of Wales Press, 1997), 92–125; Katherine Gill, "Open Monasteries for Women in Late Medieval and Early Modern Italy: Two Roman Examples," in *The Crannied Wall: Women, Religion, and the Arts in Early Modern Europe*, ed. Craig A. Monson (Ann Arbor: University of Michigan Press, 1992), 15–47.

[4]On the evolution of regular and secular third orders, see the extensive bibliographical survey by several authors in *DIP*, 9: cols. 1042–1128.

[5]See Maura Palazzi, "Solitudini femminili e patrilignaggio: Nubili e vedove fra Sette e Ottocento," in *Storia della famiglia italiana, 1750–1950*, ed. Marzio Barbagli and David I. Kertzer (Bologna: Il Mulino, 1992), 129–58; idem, *Donne sole: Storia dell'altra faccia dell'Italia tra antico regime e società contemporanea* (Milan: Mondadori, 1997).

[6]The important role of the new religious orders of the Counter-Reformation and their active apostolate in the evolution of women's condition in the Catholic world is hardly a new idea. See, for example, Ruth P. Liebowitz, "Virgins in the Service of Christ: The Dispute over an Active Apostolate for Women during the Counter-Reformation," in *Women of Spirit: Female Leadership in the Jewish and Christian Traditions*, ed. Rosemary Ruether and Eleanor McLaughlin (New York: Simon & Schuster, 1979), 131–52. This and other studies emphasize virginity and celibacy as conditions necessary for the "promotion of women" in the Church. Here I am especially interested in documenting the social aspects of the acceptance and diffusion of the new female life status.

[7]See the rich recent synthesis of O. Hufton, *The Prospect before Her: A History of Women in Western Europe, 1500–1800* (New York: Knopf, 1996).

form described here, the unmarried woman did not acquire her own social identity but was assimilated to the nun. Both, as brides of Christ, were absorbed into the gender identity of wife. In developing my argument, I shall concentrate on a few exemplary episodes with abundant documentation.[8]

In 1554 the daughter of Margherita dal Giglio Fantuzzi, an important benefactor of the Society of Jesus, which had recently been established in Bologna under the guidance of Francesco Palmio, had "not yet been able to make up her mind whether to become a nun or marry."[9] Elena wished to continue living at home with her widowed mother, who favored her daughter's desire. Their relatives considered this status undesirable and dangerous. Ignatius Loyola himself intervened, managing to convince one of Elena's uncles, Monsignor Tommaso del Giglio, that this status was legitimate, indeed good. On 28 July 1554 the general of the Company of Jesus wrote to the noble Margherita to report that her brother Tommaso "is content and quite satisfied with your ladyship's daughter Elena's remaining in the status in which she now is as long as your ladyship lives."[10] But another powerful member of the Fantuzzi family, Maestro Ottaviano, would not give up. In 1555 he addressed himself directly to Ignatius, presenting the case of young Elena as a scandal for the city. As the Jesuits of Bologna learned from the General Curia of the Order,

> Fantuzzi was very insistent and demanded that our Father should write to Palmio, telling him to make every effort to make Elena either marry or enter a cloister. Otherwise (he said) it was a cause of scandal, and the occasion of gossip against Father Palmio too; it was a danger to Elena's soul, and a Dominican had said that to live in such a state was a mortal sin, for which the Jesuits would have to do penance.[11]

Elena's premature death in 1559, while her mother was still alive, resolved the Jesuits' dilemma; in this instance, they did not have to take a stand. Still, the episode reveals that from the beginning, the fathers of the Society of Jesus held advanced ideas about women's condition. In midcentury, notwithstanding the innovative religious experiences of the Ursulines and the Angeliche, conceptions of women's status were still limited to the three traditional states: virgin, married woman, and widow.

---

[8]For some recent reflections on female religious life during the Counter-Reformation, see Craig Harline, "Actives and Contemplatives: The Female Religious of the Low Countries before and after Trent," *Catholic Historical Review* 81 (1995): 541–67; Gabriella Zarri, "Gender, Religious Institutions, and Social Discipline: The Reform of the Regulars," in *Gender and Society in Renaissance Italy*, ed. Judith C. Brown and Robert C. Davis (London: Longman, 1998), 193–212.

[9]*Saint Ignatius Loyola: Letters to Women*, ed. Hugo Rahner (New York: Herder & Herder, 1960), 215. On the origin of the Society of Jesus in Bologna, see Gabriella Zarri, "La Compagnia di Gesù a Bologna: Dall'origine alla stabilizzazione (1546–1568)," in *I gesuiti a Bologna*, ed. Gian Paolo Brizzi and Anna Maria Matteucci (Bologna: Nuova Alfa Editoriale, 1988), 119–23.

[10]Zarri, *St. Ignatius Loyola*, 215.

[11]Zarri, *St. Ignatius Loyola*, 216.

Thanks to numerous recent studies on the two institutions that best represent the new spiritual currents of the early modern era, Angela Merici's Ursulines and Mary Ward's English Ladies, the meaning of "the third status" is now well known.[12] What needs clarification, I think, is the generic term "semireligious," used in historical writing to designate women belonging to the new post-Tridentine institutions.[13] It is necessary to recognize the diversity of institutional forms taken by this imprecisely defined apostolic activity of the new religious women. The Italian situation needs to be studied more thoroughly in order to proceed to a Europewide comparison. Above all, the religious need that inspired the historical phenomenon of the birth and diffusion of these institutions must be tied more closely to the political and social motivations which supported them. In this regard, studies like those of Renée Baernstein, who presents life in the convent of the Angeliche of San Paolo in Milan as a solution alternative to the family for noble widows, offer one way of understanding the mix of religious motives and social needs.[14]

Until such work of investigation and excavation is further along, it seems premature to rush to conclusions like that of Anne Conrad, which lend themselves to univocal, oversimplified explanations.[15] The German scholar tends to consider the diverse post-Tridentine female institutes as the expression of women's aspirations for the apostolic life, conceived as innovative in respect to the conservative position of the Church, exemplified by insistence on enclosed convents. In reality, for many of these institutes, opposition to enclosure signified not opportunity to lead the apostolic life but rather independence from ecclesiastical jurisdiction and conservation of individual property rights, albeit in a form of life similar in all respects to that within the cloister. Many women, in other words, did not reject the monastic model but desired to remain in a secular status. With this in mind, in order to confront a large subject that is still only partially explored, I propose to reflect on various aspects of the diverse forms of noncloistered religious life in the early modern period and on the typology of the institutes connected with them, attempting to situate them in Italian reality.

[12]For a review of the literature on the Ursulines and the Angeliche, see *Religious Orders of the Catholic Reformation: In Honor of John C. Olin on His Seventy-Fifth Birthday,* ed. Richard L. DeMolen (New York: Fordham University Press, 1994), 59–96 and 99–136. On Mary Ward, see Anne Conrad, *Zwischen Kloster und Welt: Ursulinen und Jesuitinnen in der Katolischen Reformbewegung des 16./17. Jahrhunderts* (Mainz: Zabern, 1991).

[13]See Elisja Schulte van Kessel, "Virgins and Mothers between Heaven and Earth," in *A History of Women in the West,* vol. 3, Renaissance and Enlightenment Paradoxes, ed. Natalie Zemon Davis and Arlette Farge (Cambridge, Mass.: Belknap Press of Harvard University Press, 1993), 132–66.

[14]Renée Baernstein, "In Widow's Habit: Women between Convent and Family in Sixteenth-Century Milan," *Sixteenth Century Journal* 25 (1994): 787–808.

[15]Anne Conrad, "Il Concilio di Trento e la (mancata) modernizzazione dei ruoli femminili ecclesiastici," in *Il Concilio di Trento e il moderno,* ed. Paolo Prodi and Wolfgang Reinhard (Bologna: Il Mulino, 1996), 415–36.

Aspiring to a "mixed" religious life, a combination of contemplation and action, is not, as I have already indicated, an innovative expression of sixteenth-century reality. In theoretical discussions the problem was already on the table in the era of humanism. In practice it had been realized earlier in the institutes of the third orders and in the form of life as a *bizzocca*. What appears new in the Companies of St. Ursula or in the first Angeliche of San Paolo is the refusal to take monastic vows, the appeal to apostolic life, and the first Christian community as the theological premise for a form of religious life lived in the world, accompanied by detachment from structures linked with monastic orders.[16] This is an aspiration analogous to the one that had led the Venetian diplomat Gasparo Contarini to part company with his friends who in the second decade of the sixteenth century had abandoned politics in order to become Camaldolese hermits. We can also see in it a product of the discussions which, from Lorenzo Valla to Erasmus to Luther, had led to reflection on the ultimate significance of the life of perfection. As Paolo Prodi has written, the central problem at issue was

> whether or not the vow reinforces virtue. If the obligation per se does not confer an advantage, promising chastity, obedience, and poverty is useless. In fact, the great drama among the religious at the beginning of the modern era is the calling into question of the assumption that on the road toward evangelical perfection, the religious vow represents something more than undertaking an obligation in the world.[17]

The practice of taking the monastic vow, furthermore, was of relatively recent historical origin. In the twelfth century the vow, substituted for the ancient *professio* or *promissio* made to the abbot and the community, became an obligation assumed directly to God, like a form of oath in which the proposal to conserve chastity, poverty, and obedience was made explicitly.[18] Although the vow concerned the relationship between an individual and God, it was translated in public form into a juridical recognition and a special relationship of obedience and submission to ecclesiastical jurisdiction.

In the Company of St. Ursula, the rejection of public vows and the configuration of the institute as a confraternity of women who continued to live in their own houses rather than as a religious order seems to have arisen from a cultural context in which these problems had been pondered and discussed. Rejection of vows also appears to reflect the desire to guarantee a lay character to the new congregation.

---

[16]On this and several of the following considerations, see Paolo Prodi, "Nel mondo o fuori del mondo: La vocazione alla perfezione all'inizio dell'età moderna," in *Angela Merici*, ed. Cataldo Naro (Caltanisetta: Salvatore Sciascia, 1980), 13–33.

[17]Prodi, "Nel mondo o fuori," 25.

[18]Paolo Prodi, *Il sacramento del potere: Il giuramento politico nella storia costituzionale dell'Occidente* (Bologna: Il Mulino, 1992), 134–36.

The apparently contradictory request to receive papal confirmation for the recently founded institute indicates awareness of having taken an innovative route, beyond traditional ideas about women's condition, which required recognition from the highest religious authority in order to obtain legitimacy on the social plane. That at the founder's death, the Company of St. Ursula was strongly criticized for offering an insecure means of conserving virginal purity and lacking ecclesiastical privileges and protection is no accident.[19] The fact remains that the institution was founded on a decidedly ambiguous plane. Renouncing the taking of vows did not indicate the absence of a clear choice in favor of the religious life. The choice of virginity, which excluded marriage, expressed itself in a "firm proposal" made publicly in a ceremony which closely resembled monastic profession. The Capuchin Mattia Bellentani da Salo, Angela Merici's first biographer, termed the novel Merician institution "the new way of marrying Christ."[20] On the organizational and jurisdictional level, however, the Company remained a lay female confraternity, run at first exclusively by women, with the aim of pursuing the road toward perfection and offering this possibility to young women who could not or did not wish to enter a convent.

Novel on the religious plane in that it proposed a form of consecration to God subject neither to monastic enclosure nor to the jurisdiction of a religious order (to which the tertiaries, in contrast, were subject) and new also on the social plane, the Company of St. Ursula constituted a model that, with adaptations and changes, spread during the post-Tridentine era. Following the Company's early diffusion in Brescian territory, its ability to respond to emerging needs of women was recognized in Bologna. In this city, through the inspiration of the same Jesuit, Francesco Palmio, who along with Ignatius Loyola had supported Elena dal Giglio's choice of uncloistered virginity, appeared a document composed around 1565 entitled "Regolamento di vita spirituale per un vescovo." Sent by Cardinal Gabriele Paleotti to Carlo Borromeo, it declared:

> Because there are many virgins who wish to serve God in this status but cannot shut themselves up in convents, and many others who even though they [would like to] embrace the religion of Christ, cannot on account of poverty fulfill their desire, it appears that to aid these [women] to serve God, a Congregation of Little Virgins might be established and given a few

---

[19]Prodi, "Nel mondo o fuori del mondo," 32–33.

[20]Mattia Bellentani da Salò, *Vita della Beata Angela da Desenzano*, manuscript of 21 leaves in the Biblioteca Queriniana di Brescia, B.VI.30, Proemio, f. 3. A partial version of this text may be found in Matthias a Salò, *Historia Capuccina*, ed. Melchiore da Pobladura, in *Monumenta Historica Ordinis Minorum Capuccinorum*, 6 (Rome: Institutum Historicum Ordinis Minorum Capuccinorum, 1946): 77–113. On the symbolic significance of the Company and on the argument that I restate and amplify here, see Gabriella Zarri, "Ursula and Catherine: The Marriage of Virgins in the Sixteenth Century," in *Creative Women in Medieval and Early Modern Italy: A Religious and Artistic Renaissance*, ed. E. Ann Matter and John Coakley (Philadelphia: University of Pennsylvania Press, 1994), 237–78.

little rules, with which, staying in their parents' homes, they could serve God in the virginal status. And from this there could accrue many advantages, such as having people to serve in various pious institutions such as the Baraccano, the Putte di Santa Marta, and others, for there is a great shortage of suitable people. In time, once they were spread in various parts of the city, these Little Virgins could also teach girls Christian Doctrine, and in this group one could find many people able to aid various noble families, and this work would be of great utility to the city, without financial burdens, for each one would support herself by her own labors.[21]

Contained in this document are the principal elements that were taken over by Borromeo in Milan and by the other bishops who encouraged a company of women analogous to that of Brescia in their own dioceses. It provides proof that those who rejected the obligatory life conditions for women were young and that beyond marriage or convent there were women who could not enter the monastic profession for economic reasons. This choice of an unmarried life in a family proved functional for the needs of the Counter-Reformation Church, of noble families, and of cities, without burdening religious or civil institutions insofar as the young unmarried women could maintain themselves by their own labor.

Despite this early proposal, the Company of St. Ursula was not established in Bologna until 1603.[22] The Milanese Company was founded much earlier; its rules were published in 1569. As early as 1566, Borromeo informed himself about the *forma vitae* of the Brescian confraternity and examined its statutes, perhaps because he planned to impose a tested model of life on the spontaneously established female congregations that had already sprung up in the city of Milan.[23] Borromeo's approval of and support for the new form of life proposed by Merici, which he adopted with some important modifications of the Company's governance and aims, served to stimulate the diffusion of the institute in Lombardy and Emilia, and also an opportunity to cast it in a different form: a life in community. At some unknown point before 1576, several Ursulines were able to assemble and live together in a house[24] without renouncing the prerogatives of their institute, formally approved by Pope Gregory XIII in 1572.

---

[21]Quoted by Carlo Marcora, "Nicolò Ormaneto, vicario di san Carlo," *Memorie storiche della Diocesi di Milano* 8 (1961): 384. The original document, which Marcora does not identify precisely, is held in Milan. Its Bolognese provenance can be deduced from the names of the two orphanages mentioned: the Baraccano and Santa Marta.

[22]See Mario Fanti, "Le Orsoline secolari a Bologna: Una vicenda di quattro secoli (1603–1988)," *Strenna storica bolognese* 39 (1989): 161–78.

[23]See Gualberto Vigotti, *San Carlo Borromeo e la Compagnia di S. Orsola nel centenario della ricostruzione in Milano della Compagnia di S. Orsola Figlie di S. Angela Merici (1872–1972)* (Milan: Polo, 1972), 10-11.

[24]Vigotti, *San Carlo Borromeo*, 29–34.

As mentioned earlier, the welcoming of the Brescian Company into the diocese of Milan and the beginning of an experience of communal life set in motion a process of expansion which soon reached the cities of Verona, Cremona,[25] Venice, Ferrara, Novara, Bologna, and Modena. It also represented the legitimation of a new life status, the "third status," as it was called by the author of the "notice to the reader" prefacing the Rule of the Company of St. Ursula of Ferrara.[26] In the statement "to the Christian reader" introducing the Ferrarese Rules of 1587, approved by Bishop Paolo Leoni and dedicated by him to the Lady Governesses of the recently founded local Company, the institute was defended against those who considered it impossible for virgins to protect themselves in the world and unsuitable for them to live in their fathers' houses. Affirming that this institution renewed a very ancient spirit in the Church, the anonymous author lauded the fact that there was a praiseworthy "third status," in which young women could maintain their virginity and serve God in their own homes:

> Because there are many who, not understanding the status of virginity, not only do not praise it, as they certainly ought to do, but charge it with all kinds of wrongs and discourage it (above all for those who do not wish or feel inclined to enter a convent), holding it impossible [for virgins] to conserve themselves in the world and unsuitable for them to live in their fathers' homes, I have resolved to put here at the beginning of these Rules of the Company of St. Ursula a brief summary of the institution and of the status of these virgins, which will serve to set straight those who are deceived and teach those who do not know, and to confirm and encourage those who have entered it.[27]

Although this warning should not be attributed to the bishop of Ferrara but to the editor of the Rule, who praises the "most zealous" Paolo Leoni, the opinions expressed and positions taken were clearly endorsed by the bishop himself, since they constitute an integral part of the Rules, preceded by the dedication to the Governesses signed by Leoni. On the religious and ecclesial role of the Company, the editor states:

> And certainly it can be said that this status is necessary in God's Church, for as His Divine Majesty has gently shown, in all ages and places one finds

---

[25]See Paolo Guerrini, "La Compagnia di S. Orsola dalle origini alla soppressione napoleonica (1535–1810)," *Memorie storiche della diocesi di Brescia*, 7th ser. (1936): 167.

[26]*Regole della Compagnia delle Vergini di Santa Orsola: Stampate per ordine del molto Ill. e R.mo Mons Paolo Leone Vescovo di Ferrara* (Ferrara: Vittorio Baldini, 1587).

[27]*Regole della Compagnia delle Vergini*, 8–9.

those who serve as burning lamps in this shadowy world and bring advantage and fruit to His Holy Church.[28]

The writer then raises considerations of a social nature:

And to tell the truth, should not every father of a family nobly born, with few resources or many daughters (being unable to marry them all or even make them nuns), welcome the fact that there is a praiseworthy third status, in which those who feel themselves disposed to it can quietly stay in their own homes serving God in virginity and at the same time helping their mother or sisters-in-law to raise the children in the fear of God and manage the house well?[29]

Agostino Valier, bishop of Verona, the first to compose a treatise on the mode of living of Ursulines and other young women who lived in a similar manner, also approved of this status, which he classified as a fourth status, assigning it a grade of perfection just below that of nuns:

I want you to consider that of the four laudable female states, yours is the second perfect grade, for in God's church some women are married, others widows, and others virgins; and among the virgins some have taken a vow and are enclosed in convents, others [live] outside convents in their own houses.[30]

In Lombardy and Emilia, the organization and management of a varied assortment of young women and widows who could not or did not wish to marry or enter the convent proceeded according to the Brescian rule. An inspiration fairly similar to that of Angela Merici but a quite different form of organization and internal discipline marked the Dimesse, established in the Veneto in 1579 by the Observant Franciscan Antonio Pagani.[31] The main principle of the Dimesse's organization was women's leaving their family homes to settle in small groups of six or eight. Virginity was not privileged: unmarried young women and widows entered with equal rights

---

[28] *Regole della Compagnia delle Vergini*, 8r.

[29] *Regole della Compagnia delle Vergini*, 8r–v.

[30] Agostino Valiero, *Modo di vivere proposto alle Vergini che si chiamano Dimesse: Overo che vivono nelle lor case con voto o proposito di perpetua castità* (1575), 2nd ed. (Padua: Giuseppe Comino, 1744), 5. I previously explored these concepts and employed these citations in "Ursula and Catherine" and in "Dalla profezia alla disciplina (1450–1650)," in *Donne e fede: Santità e vita religiosa in Italia*, ed. Lucetta Scaraffia and Gabriella Zarri (Rome: Laterza, 1994) [English edition: Oxford: Harvard University Press, 1999].

[31] We lack a thorough study of this interesting figure, first a Barnabite and then an Observant Franciscan. See Rosalba Ferraresso, "Il venerabile Antonio Pagani," *Le Venezie francescane*, n.s., 5 (1988): 17–28; Giovanni Mantese, "Il ven. Antonio Pagani nella storia religiosa del Cinquecento vicentino e veneto," *Le Venezie francescane*, n.s., 5 (1988): 29–55; and Massimo Firpo, "Paola Antonia Negri da 'Divina Madre Maestra' a 'spirito diabolico,'" *Barnabiti studi* 7 (1990): 7–61.

and obligations. Subject to a rule crafted by Pagani, they dedicated themselves to teaching Christian Doctrine or assisting the poor.[32]

For understanding the linkage between social motivations and the choice of the "third status" as a style of life that impelled the protagonists of this new foundation, as well as their aspiration toward complete independence from a religious order and ecclesiastical jurisdiction, the formation of the Company of the Dimesse in Vicenza is particularly important. Maddalena Pigafetta, a noblewoman related on her mother's side to St. Gaetano Thiene and governess of an orphanage in Vicenza, made two wills in which she aimed to establish a Company of St. Ursula. The first (1571) spoke of widows "who, possessing revenues sufficient to live on and having no duties, desire to flee the tumults and disturbances of their homes and relatives and live quietly and peacefully, devoting their souls and bodies to the service and pleasure of Jesus Christ." They would assume responsibility for governing poor young women who enrolled in the Company: "and each of these widows could take one of these virgins into her service for household work or company, having other servants, and she could keep others whose confessors and protectors deemed it suitable."[33] In her second will (1577), Pigafetta made more explicit the character of the new Company, which she now envisioned as including women of the same social stratum. The inhabitants were to be poor widows, and the virgins were no longer assigned to the role of servant:

> And the house should be disposed in such a way that it is always available as a habitation for poor young Dimesse, well born and of good reputation…along with some poor widows of the same condition who, if they have male children, may not keep them in the house, but if they have female children, they may keep them in order to raise them in good and holy exercises.[34]

This second will went on to specify the numbers of virgins and widows and to make clear that Dimesse must be women capable of earning their own living, not beggars.

Another aspect of the planned institution's profile requires emphasis. Pigafetta insisted on the secular character of the new Company and on the freedom of jurisdiction which the women should enjoy:

> And I wish that they can and should be governed in part or entirely, depending on the governesses' opinion, according to the rule of St. Ursula

---

[32]Preliminary bibliographical information in addition to that cited below may be found in the brief anonymous article "Devota Compagnia delle Dimesse," in *Congregazioni laicali femminili e promozione della donna in Italia nei secoli XVI e XVII*, single number of *Quaderni Franzoniani: Semestrale di bibliografia e cultura ligure* 8, no. 2 (1995): 89–94.

[33]See Mantese, "Il ven. Antonio," 45. This document, the location of which Mantese does not give, may be found in Vicenza, Archivio di Stato: Notarile, Matteo Cereto (1571–75), act of 17 October 1571.

[34]Mantese, "Il ven. Antonio," 51.

observed in Venice, Milan, and Brescia, and I do not intend or wish that they have superiors other than themselves, and that they be completely free from any other subjection. And that, not subjected to any ecclesiastical jurisdiction, but as lay persons in a free status and place, they serve the Lord God by working in the pious institutions of this city according to need and where and when it appears to them that they can do some good—with, however, the advice, consent, and permission of the governesses.[35]

Pigafetta's will clearly indicates the necessity of paying particular attention to the situation of widows, a large category of women who from the fifteenth century on were considered socially perilous.[36] Here, in contrast, widows, who were usually directed by the Church to fulfill St. Paul's ideal image of "true" widows, eschewing remarriage and supporting charitable institutions in the capacity of patrons, are depicted as being themselves in need of assistance. The problem of maintaining and educating their children comes to the fore; living together with other women could provide a way for poorer widows to take care of their daughters, often less protected than sons, who were recognized as legitimate descendants in the paternal line.[37]

Pigafetta's intention of welcoming into the proposed institution both virgins and widows also indicates that in the second half of the sixteenth century, the rigid classification of women in the anthropological-religious categories of life status was no longer considered in complete isolation from social practice. In the fourteenth and fifteenth century, in fact, all treatises on female comportment prescribed that the young women lead a very withdrawn life, avoiding conversation with married women and widows and, within the house, even with servants. For example, one of the most detailed treatises printed at the beginning of the cinquecento, the *Lima spirituale* of Francesco Rappi da Santerenzio, contains a "Useful and Necessary Rule of Good Living for Married Women and Widows." "And teach your sons and daughters fear of God and good customs. And see that they have shame, reverence for superiors, that they frequent holy things. They should learn good letters, flee bad companions, talk of women, chatter of servants...."[38]

In the second half of the Cinquecento, however, as the testament cited above indicates, virgins and widows could live together without such cohabitation being

[35]Mantese,"Il ven. Antonio," 52. Similar testamentary wishes are expressed in Pigafetta's final will, written and witnessed on 9 September 1581 by her noble friend Elisabetta Godi. Vicenza, Archivio di Stato, Notarile, Marco Dalla Valle (1575–77), 166–68.

[36]Christiane Klapisch-Zuber, "The 'Cruel Mother': Maternity, Widowhood, and Dowry in Florence in the Fourteenth and Fifteenth Centuries," in her *Women, Family, and Ritual in Renaissance Italy*, trans. Lydia G. Cochrane (Chicago: University of Chicago Press, 1985), 117–31.

[37]Giulia Calvi, *Il contratto morale: Madri e figli nella Toscana moderna* (Rome: Laterza, 1994).

[38]Francesco (Rappi) da Santerentio, *Lima spirituale* (Bologna: Hieronimus Benedetti, 1515), fol. 32. On behavioral and didactic literature of the fifteenth to the eighteenth centuries, see Gabriella Zarri, ed., *Donna, disciplina, creanza cristiana: Studi e testi a stampa* (Rome: Edizioni di Storia e Letteratura, 1996).

considered dangerous to the virgins' honor. Here we witness the beginning of a shift in the conception of women's honor and condition.

The foundation of the Company of St. Ursula in Vicenza of which Pigafetta had dreamed never took place. At the very time that her second will was being drafted, the young widow Deianira Valmarana, under the guidance of Pagani, established a company named after the Madonna which fulfilled practically all of Pigafetta's criteria. Here again, noble women initiated the formation of a new type of communal living for women: "Here in Vicenza, a number of widowed gentlewomen, Dimesse, live in their own homes with a few others.... And there are four houses of them; and there are not and should not be more than four or six per house, besides two housekeepers and a cook."[39] One of these widows, Elisabetta Chiericati-Franceschini, was accompanied by her daughter Dorotea. Although recognition of the foundation was delayed on account of Deianira's and other companions' belonging to the Third Franciscan Order, the group firmly insisted upon its lay character and independence from ecclesiastical jurisdiction. The women adopted the poverty of dress and lifestyle which qualified them as Dimesse, and as such they won protection and approval from the bishop, Matteo Priuli.

The Dimesse's insistence on their lay status was motivated not only by the desire to manage freely their own assets, which they intended to use according to their needs and aims. Above all, given that their founder was a Franciscan tertiary who had made her formal profession, they wanted to guarantee that they would not be forced to comply with the norm of enclosure recently enunciated by the Council of Trent.[40] The words with which Deianira claimed for her institution the freedom of association and cohabitation are significant:

> Now we are here in our houses, bought and built in cooperation with these Lady Dimesse [the governesses], and we remain and live under their orders.... Neither they nor we, speaking with all reverence of God and our superiors, intend to make our open houses enclosed convents, but free [houses] under a free rule; and bound not by violent bonds but by loving ones, we intend to go forward as best we can to honor our most sweet Lord Jesus Christ Crucified....[41]

Religious action also featured among the institution's objectives. The rules of the Company called for conducting a sort of "apostolic mission" in the Vicentine hinterland and other cities. Carrying out such a mission would have necessitated a

---

[39]Vicenza, Biblioteca Bertoliana, Libreria Gonzati, 26.4.3, 17 (report in Pagani's hand); cited also by Donatella Anolfi, "La fondazione delle Dimesse," *Le Venezie francescane*, n.s., 5 (1988): 109.

[40]On the Tridentine and post-Tridentine legislation obligating tertiaries to make solemn professions and submit to enclosure or else cease accepting new novices, see Raimondo Creytens, "La riforma dei monasteri femminili dopo i decreti tridentini," in *Il Concilio di Trento e la riforma tridentina* (Rome: Herder, 1965), 1: 45–79.

[41]Anolfi, "La fondazione delle Dimesse," 109.

liberty of movement unthinkable for one lone woman. Therefore the rules provided that groups of two or three sisters go into castle towns and villages outside the city to help the needy with work and alms, teach Christian Doctrine, furnish printed catechisms, and work to prevent or resolve public scandals.[42] Chapter 51 of the Rule of the Dimesse, "Of those women who are suited for and sent out to [employ themselves in] pious works," describes these activities in detail:

> Furthermore, this Company may on occasion assign some of its members (no fewer than two, suited to the job)...to some particular, important pious work necessary in the city, or also outside the city to some castle town or village, or even in another city, according to the opportunity that arises, to fulfill it with work and effort or with spiritual or corporeal alms, and to teach Christian Doctrine, or to make arrangements for instructing ignorant women in the things necessary to their salvation, giving them little books that teach Christian Doctrine, and to do what they can to impede and destroy the work of Satan and scandals and vices and public or private sins, and to use every means in favor of virtuous and Christian work.... And on those assignments they may stay and work as long as necessary.... And during that time they will live either in the private homes of spiritual women or in some women's hospital or in some other house assigned to such pious work, or in any other place where it is necessary to work in order to gain and benefit any soul, as long as there are women and they are all respectable and of good reputation.[43]

In addition, the Dimesse were authorized to provide assistance to sick women in hospitals or their own homes.[44]

As far as devotional practices, fasting, and partaking of the sacraments were concerned, however, the lives of these women living by themselves were regulated by norms similar to monastic ones. Dimesse did not take vows; unlike Ursulines, they were not bound by promises to remain virgins and stay forever in the houses. Whoever felt herself called to a fuller life of perfection, Pagani's *Ordini* stated, could enter a convent.[45] The founder insisted, however, on the inalterability of the constitutions he had drafted.[46] As for contacts between the Dimesse and the outside world, it should be noted that the norms promulgated in the statutes were explicit and rigorous. Colloquies with men, permitted for "treating temporal business," must take

---

[42]Antonio Pagani, *Gli Ordini della divota Compagnia delle Dimesse che vivono sotto il nome e la protettione della purissima Madre di Dio Maria Vergine* (Venice: Domenico Nicolini, 1587), 85.

[43]Pagani, *Gli Ordini della divota*, 84–85.

[44]Pagani, *Gli Ordini della divota*, chap. 3, 3; chap. 58, 98–99.

[45]Pagani, *Gli Ordini della divota*, chap. 1, 2.

[46]Pagani, *Gli Ordini della divota*, chap. 62, 106–9.

place in a designated part of the house analogous to a convent *parlatorio*.[47] Encounters with women or relatives were permitted only once a month.[48]

While the Companies of St. Ursula and the Dimesse had a common concern, meeting the needs of women who did not intend to marry or become nuns, they differed in several ways. The Ursulines addressed themselves exclusively to young women, providing for them a way to consecrate themselves to God while continuing to live with their families. The Dimesse addressed themselves to women of all ages outside the marriage market, offering them a living situation alternative to the family. Although both institutions enunciated religious aims and issued rules governing comportment, they maintained their secular character and did not prescribe public profession of vows. The institute of the Dimesse established in Vicenza spread especially in the Veneto. In the late sixteenth and seventeenth centuries, houses which adopted the rule opened in such major cities as Venice, Verona, Padua, Bergamo, and Udine and in minor centers including Thiene, Schio, and Feltre. As Antonio Pagani had intended, the rules of the Dimesse remained unaltered, and uniformity and contact between the various houses was maintained.[49]

During the sixteenth century, the celibate life for women, whether pursued in family homes or in houses following a *forma vitae* similar to that of convents, spread and gained social legitimacy. Determining the respective roles of individual choices and social motives in this process is probably impossible. We must not forget that in the latter half of the century, a growing emphasis on primogeniture in inheritance practices[50] coincided with the Tridentine legislation limiting access to convents and enforcing strict enclosure. The number of young women who could neither marry nor become nuns, as well as those in need of assistance, grew. Family structure itself was in the process of transformation: from the age of the Renaissance on, the nuclear family proliferated. In opposition to and competition with Protestantism, furthermore, the Tridentine Church rediscovered the value of marriage as a status of perfection not inferior to monasticism and assigned great responsibility to the family in the moral and religious education of children.[51]

---

[47]Pagani, *Gli Ordini della divota*, chap. 6, 4.

[48]Pagani, *Gli Ordini della divota*, chap. 11, 10–11.

[49]The various houses of the Dimesse have not been studied thoroughly. On the last of the seventeenth-century foundations, see Piero Bertolla, *Le Dimesse di Udine Figlie dell'Immacolata Concezione: Tre secoli di vita (1656–1956)* (Udine: Arti grafiche friulane, 1963). See also Gabriella Zarri, "Disciplina regolare e pratica di coscienza: Le virtù e i comportamenti sociali in comunità femminili (secc. XVI–XVIII)," in *Disciplina dell'anima, disciplina del corpo e disciplina della società tra medioevo ed età moderna*, ed. Paolo Prodi (Bologna: Il Mulino, 1994), 257–78.

[50]Gerard Delille, "Strategie di alleanza e demografia del matrimonio," in *Storia del matrimonio*, ed. Michela De Giorgio and Christiane Klapisch-Zuber (Rome: Laterza, 1996), 295.

[51]See Vittorio Frajese, *Il popolo fanciullo: Silvio Antoniano e il sistema disciplinare della Controriforma* (Milan: Franco Angeli, 1987).

At the same time, the need for acculturation—no longer limited to the elite but extending to a larger proportion of the population, including women—was increasingly recognized.[52] Female celibacy, freely chosen or imposed by the family or by conditions independent of free will, gained much of its legitimacy from the new demand for social services for women.[53] Unmarried women ran secular institutions aiming at assistance and exertion of social control: orphanages, refuges for girls "at risk" (*zitelle*), houses for repentant prostitutes (*convertite*) and for married women in difficulty (*malmaritate*). These were sometimes linked with institutes such as the Ursulines, which offered an opportunity for a consecrated life in the services of the house, sometimes as a simple oblate, free from juridical ties to the institutional church.[54]

The same is the case with those who dedicated themselves to teaching. Aside from the cases of private women teachers and instructors of Christian Doctrine, traditionally recruited among married and widowed women, boarding colleges for girls, which began to proliferate in the second half of the sixteenth century alongside analogous institutions for boys, drew their teaching corps from unmarried women dedicated to God but not subject to ecclesiastical jurisdiction. Since we still lack a census of the various colleges for young women which were founded especially in central and northern Italy between the sixteenth and the seventeenth century, it is difficult to outline a typology, for each was run according to its own rules and constitutions.[55] Clearly, however, such colleges were intended for girls from noble families and inspired by the Jesuit model. In most cases, a college was founded by a benefactress, but promoted and regulated by a Jesuit who assisted her and assumed the role of spiritual guide to the community.

Although such colleges were secular in character and sometimes subject directly to the authority of the state, they were run by unmarried women who adopted a

---

[52]On the role played by the Ursulines of Milan in the primary education of girls, see Angelo Turchini, *Sotto l'occhio del padre: Società confessionale e istruzione primaria nello stato di Milano* (Bologna: Il Mulino, 1996).

[53]For the application of this argument to the French world, see Elizabeth Rapley, *The Dévotes: Women and Church in Seventeenth-Century France* (Kingston, Ont.: McGill-Queen's University Press, 1990).

[54]There is a vast bibliography on these types of institutions. As an example, see Marina Romanello, *Le spose del principe: Una storia di donne: La Casa secolare delle Zitelle in Udine, 1595–1995* (Milan: Franco Angeli, 1995).

[55]Early studies include Massimo Marcocchi, *Le origini del Collegio della Beata Vergine di Cremona, istituzione della Riforma Cattolica (1610)* (Cremona: Annali della Biblioteca statale e libreria civica di Cremona, 1974); and Gabriella Zarri, "Le istituzioni dell'educazione femminile," in *Le sedi della cultura nell'Emilia Romagna: I secoli moderni, Le istituzioni e il pensiero*, ed. Adriano Prosperi (Cinisello Balsamo: A Pizzi, 1987), 84–109. See the first census of female colleges and secular congregations in *Congregazioni laicali femminili* (n. 31 above); and Manlio Paganella, *Cinzia, Olimpia e Gridonia Gonzaga: Profilo storico del Collegio delle Vergini di Gesù di Castiglione delle Stiviere* (Basilica Santuario di S. Luigi Gonzaga di Castiglione delle Stiviere: Cassa rurale ed artigiana di Castel Goffredo, 1994).

form of life similar to that in a convent—and sometimes, as in Piacenza, took vows of perpetual virginity. The women in the Florentine college of the Montalve, founded in the mid–seventeenth century by the noblewoman Eleonora Ramirez di Montalvo, also chose a semimonastic or even eremitical life. The population of these colleges was divided into two distinct but closely connected groups: the girls being educated, theoretically destined to leave the institution but often disposed to spend their entire lives there as teachers; and the affiliates, who lived in celibacy sometimes made manifest by a public affirmation and the donning of a habit, but not necessarily sealed by a formal vow.[56]

In Italy during the seventeenth and eighteenth centuries, other institutions with educational purposes emerged, different from the colleges for noble girls and not linked to the Jesuit Order but promoted and run by women who lived in communities guided by religiously inspired regulations. Some of these, like the Maestre Pie of Lazio, received ecclesiastical recognition from local bishops, but since they did not solemnly profess vows obligating enclosure, they did not acquire the status of religious institute.[57]

The institutions described thus far fulfilled a double function: they provided one way of satisfying the demand for a form of female religious life inspired by the ideal of the active life; and they offered a socially legitimate alternative for the increasing numbers of women consigned to celibacy by their families. We must not forget, however, that such institutions arose and developed mainly in northern and central Italy. In the vast south, only a few cities present the variety of lay female religious lifestyles described here. In the Kingdom of Naples, the figure of the *monaca di casa* emerged and became popular. Following the tradition of the tertiaries, young women who could not marry put on a penitent's habit, often without any formal tie to a religious order or the ecclesiastical structure, and continued to live with their families, evading repeated attempts by diocesan authorities to control and discipline them.[58]

The "third status" of virgins who wished to serve God outside convents, legitimated by the ecclesiastical hierarchy in the mid–sixteenth century with the approval of the Ursuline and Dimesse lifestyles, contributed to providing a social identity and protective structures for female celibates, whose numbers were on the rise in early modern Italy. Their insistence on jurisdictional independence from the religious orders and the religious hierarchy, however, did not provide them with a lay definition for the condition of an unmarried woman. Even though they were free from the

---

[56]"Eleonora Ramirez Montalvo," in *Congregazioni laicali femminili*, 145–49.

[57]On the historical context in which these institutions developed, see Marina Caffiero, "Dall'esplosione mistica tardo-barocco all'apostolato sociale (1650–1850)," in *Donne e fede,* ed. Scaraffia and Zarri, 327–73 (English edition, Oxford: Harvard University Press, 1999).

[58]See Giuliana Boccadamo, "Le bizzoche a Napoli tra '600 e '700," *Campania sacra* 22 (1991): 351–94.

requirements of religious profession, their social identity remained linked with that of nuns: virgins were still identified as brides of Christ.

Nonetheless, it is worth recalling that at the end of the sixteenth century, the status of Ursulines and Dimesse, although ambiguously situated between secular and religious life, was considered by one of the first Italian theoreticians of feminism to be the best life status. In the first *giornata* of her dialogue *Il merito delle donne*, published in 1600, the Venetian writer Modesta Pozzo de' Zorzi, who adopted the nom de plume Moderata Fonte, introduces seven women representing different conditions of life.[59] Among them is the Dimessa Corinna, to whom her companion Lucrezia, an unhappily married woman, attributes the greatest happiness. Lucrezia praises Corinna for having "already embarked on a celestial life while still surrounded by the trials and dangers of this world. Though such trials barely touch you, for, by rejecting all contact with those falsest of creatures, men, you have escaped the tribulations of this world and are free to devote yourself to those glorious pursuits that will win you immortality."

Because Corinna does not have to put up with the troubles of the widow, the married woman, or the young girl destined for marriage, Lucrezia suggests, she should put her "sublime intelligence" to work and write a book on the subject of her life-choice "as an affectionate warning to all those poor simple girls who don't know the difference between good and evil, to show them where their true interests lie."[60] In addition, Fonte has Corinna express in a sonnet the conviction that she has chosen the best status of life:

> Libero cor nel mio petto soggiorna,
> Non servo alcun, né d'altri son che mia,
> Pascomi di modestia e cortesia,
> Virtù m'essalta, e castità m'adorna…
> Così negli anni verdi, e nei maturi,
> Poiché fallacia d'uom non m'interrompe,
> Fama e gloria n'attendo in vita, e in morte.[61]

[The heart that dwells within my breast is free: I serve no one, and belong to no one but myself. Modesty and courtesy are my daily bread; virtue exalts me and chastity adorns me…. And thus in my green years, as in the

---

[59]I am grateful to Adriana Chemello for calling my attention to this text. See Moderata Fonte, *Il merito delle donne*, ed. Adriana Chemello (Mirano-Venezia: Eidow, 1988); Adriana Chemello, "Moderata Fonte," in *Le stanze ritrovate: Antologia di scrittrici venete dal Quattrocento al Novecento*, ed. Antonio Arslan, Adriana Chemello, and Gilberto Pizzamiglio (Mirano-Venezia: Eidos, 1991).

[60]Moderata Fonte, *The Worth of Women: Wherein Is Clearly Revealed Their Nobility and Their Superiority to Men*, ed. and trans. Virginia Cox (Chicago: University Press, 1997), 48–49.

[61]Fonte, *Il merito*, 18–19.

riper ones that await me, since men's deceptions cannot obstruct my path, I may expect fame and glory, in life as in death.][62]

Moderata Fonte's treatise attributes to the "third status" the character of a choice freely made by some women and associates with the lifestyle of the Dimesse: the possibility of dedicating oneself to study and teaching. This was a conviction already present in the "erudite" women of the Renaissance, those living miracles, as "literate" women were then considered, whose prototype can be considered to be Isotta Nogarola. From Verona, author of a Latin text that confronted the problem of sexual difference beginning from an exegesis of the creation verses in Genesis, known to the world of learned men and courts, she was declared a model of virtue who had chosen the virginal life in order to more thoroughly pursue letters and studies.[63] But even later, in the second half of the Seicento, a poetess well known to the Spanish world, Juana Inés de la Cruz, born and living in Mexico, educated at home and then at the viceregal court, had left her family and friends to withdraw into a convent. According to an autobiographical letter she wrote, the woman had wanted "to live alone, not wanting to have obligatory occupations that might block my freedom for studies nor the noise of a community that might disturb the tranquil silence of my books," but celibacy not being compatible with the customs of Mexican society in the seventeenth century, Juana Inés de la Cruz decided to make a monastic profession:

> I decided to become a religious although I knew that many things pertaining to that state are repugnant to my character (I speak of those things that are accessory, not those that are substantial) because for me who absolutely rejected marriage such a choice was the least inapt and most convenient that I could adopt considering my desire to pursue salvation.[64]

Aside from this precocious recognition by Nogarola and Moderata Fonte in Italy, and the increasingly well known writings of the Venetian nun Arcangela Tarabotti against paternal authority and forced monachizzation,[65] no literary tradition of feminist reflection on women's right to liberty in the choice of life status developed. Despite Italy's having taken the lead in the sixteenth century in developing and finding social and theoretical justification for the new mode of life of the

---

[62]Fonte, *The Worth*, 49–50.

[63]Margaret King, *Women of the Renaissance* (Chicago: University of Chicago Press, 1991), 194–98.

[64] Both citations are drawn and translated from Juana Inés de la Cruz, *Respueta a sor Filotea*, in her *Obras completas*, Alberto G. Salceda, vol. 4 (Mexico: Fondo de Cultura Economica, 1976), cited by Francesca Cantù, "Juana Inés de la Cruz: Identità femminile e modelli di vita religiosa nel Messico del secolo xvii," in *Trimestre: Storia, politica, società* 30 (1997): 493.

[65]On Tarabotti's life, see Emilio Zanette's *Suor Arcangela, monaca del Seicento veneziano* (Rome: Istituto per la Collaborazione Culturale, 1960); see also Francesca Medioli, *L'"Inferno monacale" di Archangela Tarabotti* (Turin: Rosenberg & Sellier, 1990). For a modern edition of another of her works in favor of women and recent bibliography, see Francesco Buoninsegni and Suor Arcangela Tarabotti, *Satira e Antisatira*, ed. Elissa Weaver (Rome: Salerno, 1998).

Ursulines and the Dimesse, it lost ground to the richer cultural and religious tradition of France. The next treatise devoted to this subject by a woman appeared at the end of the seventeenth century. Inspired by debates in salons over the *querelle des femmes*, the writer Gabrielle Suchon composed *Du celibat volontaire, ou la vie sans engagement*, published in 1700. She casts in theoretical terms her own successful quest, pursued amid innumerable difficulties, to obtain the annulment of monastic vows she had been forced to make as a young woman. Voluntary celibacy, according to Suchon, means a retired existence dedicated to study, in which the intellectual life comes to the fore. The "neutralists," those who freely adopt this third style of life, can govern themselves according to reason.[66] This "third way," Suchon insists, is the only style of life that gives women authentic liberty.

---

[66]On the author and her works, see Cecilia Nubola, "Libertà, cultura, potere per le donne: Il 'Traité de la morale e de la politique' di Gabrielle Suchon," in *Donna, disciplina, creanza cristiana*, 333–46; idem, "Libertà di rimanere nubili: Gabrielle Suchon tra scrittura e scelte di vita," in *Der ledige Un-wille: Zur Geschichte lediger Frauen in der Neuzeit* (Vienna: Folio Verlag, 1998), 287–308.

PART 4

"Non lo volevo per marito in modo alcuno"

Forced Marriages, Generational Conflicts, and the Limits of Patriarchal Power in Early Modern Venice, c. 1580–1680

Daniela Hacke

In July of 1628 Vittoria Cesana brought a charge against her husband, the patrician Giovanni Battista Barbaro, in the court of the Patriarch of Venice. In the accusation she listed three reasons for initiating the suit.[1] First, she informed the ecclesiastical judges that she had expressed quite clearly her indignation about her father's marital plans for her by stating that she would rather kill herself than marry the proposed Barbaro. Then, in order to break her resistance, her father had taken her by the hand, led her into a room and, with a knife in his hand, threatened that he would murder her if she did not obey him. Finally, after her marriage, she had continued not only to express her unwillingness but also to lament the means of violence and force by which she had been married, as a result of which her husband had left her after only three days.[2]

At first glance, a case of this kind seems to confirm the notion that early modern parent-child relations were emotionally detached and cruel. The family conflict made public by Vittoria Cesana appears to enrich studies of the history of the family by giving yet another example of the dominant parental influence over the choice of

[1]My thanks to the participants in the Historischer Arbeitskreis Dienste, Ehe Sexualität (HADES, Stuttgart, 1996), namely to Stefan Breit, Martin Dinges, Renate Därr, Heinrich Richard Schmidt, and Heike Talkenberger for their comments on an earlier version of this essay, and to all those who contributed suggestions at the conference "Time and Space in Women's Lives in Early Modern Europe" (1997), especially Julius Kirshner, Luise Schorn-Schütte, and Heide Wunder. I would also like to thank Jens Hammer and Ulrike Strasser for the careful reading and the suggestions they provided and Vicky Avery, who was invaluable in proofreading this essay.

[2]Archivio Storico del Patriarcato di Venezia (hereafter ASPV), *Causarum Matrimoniorum* (hereafter C.M.), Reg. 90: 1 July 1628, Victorie Cesana cum Joe Baptista Barbaro, fols. 1r–3r. All cases discussed in this article are to be found in the *Sezione Antica*. I modernized the Italian names.

spouse. Since marriages were subject to family interests such as property transactions and social status, the emotional disposition of children, one might conclude, was only rarely considered during early modern marriage formation.[3] On closer examination, however, this case shows that parents might encounter noticeable resistance if they enforced their marital plans against the will of their children. That this resistant attitude continued even after a forced marriage had taken place is clearly revealed by annulment suits. Matrimony as a union formed by means of violence and force was certainly an unacceptable option for those children who sued in court. By turning our attention from the more frequently stressed dictatorial parental influence to the only rarely explored conflicts within the family,[4] we obtain revealing insights about the challenge and the implementation of authority. Rather than focus primarily on the powerlessness of children, I intend to reconstruct both the domestic conflicts and the process of enforcement of parental will, and to explore the differing social practices of resolving family conflicts. Physical violence was by no means the first nor the only method for settling domestic disputes in early modern societies.

In order to highlight the domestic disputes rather than the powerlessness of children, I shall focus on the resistance of children to their authoritarian parents, the parents' methods of imposing their marital plans on disobedient children, and the gender-specific use of the patriarchal court (suing women clearly outnumbered suing

---

[3]Our notion of emotionally detached and rather affectionless parent-child relations in "premodern" societies has been shaped in particular by Edward Shorter, *The Making of the Modern Family* (New York: Basic Books, 1975); and Lawrence Stone, *Family, Sex, and Marriage in England, 1500–1800* (London: Weidenfeld and Nicolson, 1977). This argument has been twisted to just the opposite by Steven Ozment, *When Fathers Ruled: Family Life in Reformation Europe* (Cambridge, Mass.: Harvard University Press, 1983). For an early critique of Stone, see Alan Macfarlane, "Review Essay," *History and Theory* 18 (1979): 103–26. Hans Medick and David Sabean have criticized the ideological approach of these two historians (especially Shorter), according to whom a progressive sentimentalization took place in the middle-class family in Europe during the eighteenth and nineteenth centuries, while peasant family life was still shaped by material needs. See Hans Medick and David W. Sabean, "Interest and Emotion in Family and Kinship Studies: A Critique of Social History and Anthropology," in *Interest and Emotion: Essays on the Study of Family and Kinship,* ed. Hans Medick and David W. Sabean (Cambridge: Cambridge University Press, 1984), 9–27. Other classics in this field are Jean-Louis Flandrin, *Families in Former Times: Kinship, Household, and Sexuality* (Cambridge: Cambridge University Press, 1979); and Peter Laslett, *The World We Have Lost: England before the Industrial Age* (New York: Scribner, 1966). An extensive discussion of works concentrating on parent-child relations in earlier times, and of Philippe Ariès's work in particular, is provided by Linda A. Pollock, *Forgotten Children: Parent-Child Relations from 1500 to 1900* (Cambridge: Cambridge University Press, 1983).

[4]Important exceptions are Rainer Beck, "Frauen in Krise: Eheleben und Ehescheidung in der ländlichen Gesellschaft Bayerns während des Ancien Régime," in *Dynamik der Tradition: Studien zur historischen Kulturforschung,* ed. Richard van Dülmen (Frankfurt a/M: Fischer, 1992), 137–212; Lyndal Roper, *The Holy Household: Women and Morals in Reformation Augsburg* (Oxford: Clarendon Press, 1989); Lucia Ferrante, "Marriage and Women's Subjectivity in a Patrilineal System: The Case of Early Modern Bologna," in *Gender, Kinship, Power: A Comparative and Interdisciplinary History,* ed. Mary J. Maynes, Ann Waltner, Brigitte Soland, and Ulrike Strasser (New York: Routledge, 1996), 115–29; and Ulinka Rublack, *The Crimes of Women in Early Modern Germany* (Oxford: Clarendon Press, 1999), 197–230.

---

men).[5] By exploring such family conflicts, I shall illuminate some aspects of female agency and the daughters' role in domestic disputes.[6] Archival evidence reveals the extent to which these conflicts occurred between family members, the temporary limits of patriarchal power, and the challenge to parental authority before it was reinforced and implemented. Annulment suits reveal not only children's resistance but also the limits of paternal authority, for the patriarchal court could undermine the will and authority of parents by passing a verdict in favor of the daughter. The principle of consensual marriage established by the Catholic Church could run counter to the parents' notion of their authority, since it clearly limited parental power in favor of children's wishes.

In order to contextualize Vittoria Cesana's and other cases, I shall first discuss the legal context of family disputes. A detailed analysis of several accusations presented in court will clarify the argumentative framework of annulment suits. I shall conclude by investigating the limits of patriarchal power as it becomes perceptible in neighbors' assessments of parental violence.

THE LEGAL FRAMEWORK: THE THEORY OF CONSENT VERSUS CIVIL LAW

The case narrated above raises questions concerning the influence of parents over the choice of marital partner and thus relates directly to the implementation of the decrees passed by the Council of Trent (1545–1563). In various sessions of the Council of Trent, the influence of parents was the subject of heated debate. While advocates of consensual marriage insisted on the free will of the couple, opponents defended the interests of parents in marriage formation and demanded that clandestine marriages be declared invalid. The discussions were further complicated by the double meaning of the term "clandestine marriage," since it referred both to marriages contracted without the knowledge of parents and to those contracted informally, that is, without witnesses and the blessing of a priest. The decree *Tametsi* passed by the Council of Trent signified a compromise. It reaffirmed, on the one hand, the sacramental character of Catholic marriage and thus the consent of the couple as fundamental for the validity of the union. On the other hand, clandestine marriages, that is, unions not publicly solemnized, were declared invalid since they were not contracted in accordance with the Tridentine decrees, which stressed the

---

[5]In the *Causarum Matrimoniorum*, there are thirty-three cases between 1579 and 1681 in which annulment of a marriage because of fear and force was sought. Of these, only two cases were initiated by men. Since I have not systematically investigated the series *Filicae causarum*, these figures must be understood as a first result.

[6]Although Christiane Klapisch-Zuber does not discuss the participation of women in family conflicts in her fundamental book *Women, Family, and Ritual in Renaissance Italy* (Chicago: University of Chicago Press, 1987), she "remains sensitive to the potential for conflict between or even within lineages." Thomas Kuehn, *Law, Family, and Women: Toward a Legal Anthropology of Renaissance Italy* (Chicago: University of Chicago Press, 1991), 5. For marital litigation, see Joanne Ferraro, "The Power to Decide: Battered Wives in Early Modern Venice," *Renaissance Quarterly* 3 (1995): 492–512.

public nature of the union as a condition for its validity. Thus, only when a marriage was blessed by a priest *in facie ecclesiae* and in front of two or three witnesses were the new formal Tridentine criteria fulfilled. Tridentine marital law therefore held a potential for conflict, since it clearly placed the consent of children above the marital plans of the parents.[7] Even though children had to ask their parents respectfully for their agreement when marrying, parental consent was not essential to the validity of the marriage.[8]

In opposition to this legal paradigm stood the secular model of parent-child relations. Every family member had a natural, God-ordained place within the hierarchical structure of early modern households: the husband ruled over his wife, the parents over their children, and master and mistress over the domestic servants. Relations between members of the household, furthermore, embodied a symbolic capital, since the family was a microcosm of the city and a metaphor for the state. Just as magistrates ruled over citizens, so the father ruled over his household members.[9] In this social and legal union, the *paterfamilias* had the responsibility and duty of governing and educating the other household members, who in turn had to respect and obey him. Male and female children stood under his *patria potestas*, a limited power to educate and to correct his offspring, as the legal historian Nino Tamassia put it.[10] Legally, the *patria potestas* was not limited to the children alone, but also included their goods, since the father was the usufructuary of the presents and bequests his unemancipated sons and unmarried daughters received.[11] Only with the death of the head of the household did the *patria potestas* end,[12] unless a

---

[7]The Tridentine decrees were not accepted by the French crown, which insisted on parental consent as a condition for the validity of the marriage. See Patricia Seed, *To Love, Honor, and Obey in Colonial Mexico: Conflicts over Marriage Choice, 1574–1821* (Stanford: Stanford University Press, 1988), 34–35.

[8]Here I give only the fundamental works. See Hubert Jedin, *Geschichte des Konzils von Trient*, 4 vols. (Freiburg: Herder, 1975–82); an excellent summary is provided by Seed, *To Love, Honor, and Obey*, 32–36. On clandestine marriages, see Gaetano Cozzi, "Padri, figli e matrimoni clandestini (metà sec. XVI–metà sec. XVIII)," *La Cultura* 14 (1976): 169–213; and Beatrice Gottlieb, "The Meaning of Clandestine Marriage," in *Family and Sexuality in French History*, ed. Robert Wheaton and Tamara K. Hareven (Philadelphia: University of Pennsylvania, 1980), 49–83.

[9]Margaret L. King, "Caldiera and the Barbaros on Marriage and the Family: Humanistic Reflections of Venetian Realities," *Journal of Medieval and Renaissance Studies* 6 (1976): 19–50; and idem, "Personal, Domestic, and Republican Values in the Moral Philosophy of Giovanni Caldiera," *Renaissance Quarterly* 28 (1975): 535–74.

[10]Nino Tamassia, *La famiglia italiana nei secoli decimoquinto e decimosesto* (reprint, Rome: Multigrafica Editrice, 1971), 248.

[11]I wish to thank Linda Guzzetti for providing me with this information. Linda Guzzetti, *Venezianische Frauen im 14. Jahrhundert* (Ph.D. diss., Technical University of Berlin, 1997).

[12]Thomas Kuehn, *Emancipation in Late Medieval Florence* (New Brunswick, N.J.: Rutgers University Press, 1982), 10. According to medieval and Roman law, the *patria potestas* covered all legitimate descendants of the male line. "Thus, a grandfather (*avus*) who remained *paterfamilias* to his sons was also *paterfamilias* to his grandsons, the children of his sons; and the *paterfamilias* retained his *patria potestas* over them, no matter what their age." Kuehn, *Emancipation*, 11.

---

public emancipation of the sons, through which they acquired their full judicial capacity, had been made beforehand.[13] Daughters were not inevitably emancipated by marrying, since the passive power of the father coexisted with the more active power of the husband.[14] Even though the *patria potestas* limited the autonomy of children, it nevertheless entailed paternal responsibilities and duties. As the head of the household, the father had to take care of the material and spiritual well-being of his children, which demanded different methods of education according to their age, sex, and social class.[15] According to the eighteenth-century legal historian Marco Ferro, the *patria potestas* was intended both to protect children during their childhood and to guide them during their adolescence; it was to be based on mutual respect and affection after their marriage.[16] Educational methods also endorsed "moderate corrections" of disobedient children, since the social order had to be restored when authority was challenged.[17] Although legally and socially subordinated to their spouses, wives participated in governing the household and were thus entitled to the "power of correcting their children, even forcefully."[18]

Fathers, furthermore, had the duty to dower their daughters. Daughters had a claim to an appropriate dowry (*dote congrua*), their share of the patrimony, which claim expired after it was paid.[19] After the father's death, the duty of dowering his daughters passed to his brothers; only when no male descendants were living did the widow assume this function.[20] According to Venetian law, daughters ran the risk of

---

[13]Tamassia, *La famiglia italiana*, 203. According to Marco Ferro, *Dizionario del diritto comune e veneto*, 2 vols. (1778–81; Venice: Andrea Santini & Figlio, 1845), 1: 672, emancipation in Venice was not a public act. For the actual practice of emancipation in Venice during the late seventeenth and eighteenth centuries, see Volker Hunecke, *Der venezianische Adel am Ende der Republik 1646–1797: Demographie, Familie, Haushalt* (Tübingen: Niemeyer, 1995), 271ff.

[14]Thomas Kuehn, "Women, Marriage, and *Patria Potestas* in Late Medieval Florence," in *Law, Family, and Women*, 197–211.

[15]For a detailed description of the education of a patrician son, see Daniela Frigo, *Il padre di famiglia: Governo della casa e governo civile nella tradizione dell' "Economica" tra Cinque e Seicento* (Rome: Bulzoni, 1985), 116–22.

[16]Unfortunately, Ferro gives no concrete age when referring to the different stages of life. Ferro, *Dizionario*, 2: 453–56.

[17]See Tamassia, *La famiglia italiana*, 258, on the advice to punish with moderation.

[18]Tamassia, *La famiglia italiana*, 255.

[19]The term *dote congrua* does not refer to a specific amount. Cf. Ferro, *Dizionario*, 1: 642. According to Stanley Chojnacki, in late-fifteenth-century Venice the dowry of patrician daughters could even exceed the inheritance of patrician sons. Stanley Chojnacki, "The Power of Love: Wives and Husbands in Late Medieval Venice," in *Women and Power in the Middle Ages*, ed. Mary Erler and Maryanne Kowaleski (Athens, Ga.: University of Georgia Press, 1988), 126–48; and idem, "Dowries and Kinsmen in Early Renaissance Venice," *Women in Medieval Society*, ed. Susan Mosher Stuard (Philadelphia: University of Pennsylvania Press, 1976), 173–98.

[20]Ferro, *Dizionario*, 1: 643, though only in the case that "the mothers were rich and the father[s] poor."

losing their claim to a dowry and being disinherited if they engaged in sexual alliances without their fathers' consent.[21] The same destiny awaited sons and daughters who married in accordance with the theory of consent, but against the expressed will of their parents.[22] This right of parents to disinherit disobedient children constituted a considerable challenge to canon law. According to Volker Hunecke, it made the Tridentine principle of free choice concerning one's marital partner almost worthless.[23]

Venetian patrician marriages were subject to further secular restrictions. Following the decree passed by the Council of Ten on 26 April 1526, only those patrician sons whose parents had registered their marriage at the Avogaria di Comun in the *Libro d'oro* had a claim to membership on the Great Council. Even marriages considered incontestable according to canon law were regarded as illegitimate according to Venetian civil law if they were not registered with this office.[24] In practice, among the marriages not reported to this office were also those contracted with a secret ritual.[25] Secret marriages, in contrast to clandestine marriages, were canonically valid unions which had been solemnized without the publication of the banns. Since the banns were not necessary for the validity of a marriage, they could be overcome by a bishop's dispensation. These marriages were recorded in special registers of the patriarchal court (and not, as usual, in the books of the parish) and were not made public unless the couple later wished to do so. Secret marriages were allowed only

> *ex gravissima et urgentissima causa*, for example, with the aim of regularizing the situation of a couple living in concubinage who were taken for spouses in the community and therefore could not marry without compromising their honor; or in the case of a couple of markedly diverse social extractions or ages...who feared that the publication of banns or marrying in church would expose them to serious difficulties or grave harm.[26]

---

[21]Ferro, *Dizionario*, 1: 643. This, however, was only the case when daughters were younger than twenty-five.

[22]Ferro, *Dizionario*, 2: 252.

[23]Hunecke, *Der venezianische Adel*, 141.

[24]Stanley Chojnacki, "Marriage Legislation and Patrician Society in Fifteenth-Century Venice," in *Law, Custom, and the Social Fabric in Medieval Europe: Essays in Honor of Bryce Lyon,* ed. Bernard S. Bachrach and David Nicholas (Kalamazoo: Western Michigan University Press, 1990), 163–84; and Hunecke, *Der venezianische Adel*, 16.

[25]Other marriages not notified at the Avogaria included both canonically invalid clandestine marriages and those which had been validly contracted according to the Tridentine decrees. See Hunecke, *Der venezianische Adel*, 114.

[26]Joseph Wenner, "Gewissensehe," in *Lexikon für Theologie und Kirche,* 10 vols. (Freiburg: Herder, 1957–65), 4: 868f., quoted in Hunecke, *Der venezianische Adel*, 110.

Secret marriages thus defended the principle of consent and free will of couples and represented one way to avoid kin influence and parental opposition.[27] From the mid–seventeenth century onward, one out of eight patrician marriages was solemnized by the secret ritual,[28] but wealthy nonpatrician males also quite frequently contracted secret marriages with women of a lower social rank.[29]

These remarks gain greater significance in the context of the gender-specific and class-specific use of the court. While wealthy *popolane* women in the late sixteenth and seventeenth centuries often sued their husbands at the Venetian patriarchal court for an annulment of the marriage, patrician sons only very rarely relied on the court for the settlement of family conflicts,[30] a tendency noticeable also in the eighteenth century.[31] Instead, male patricians either resolved their family problems privately, avoided direct opposition with kin and family by contracting a secret marriage, or tried not to establish a collateral line with a claim to inheritance by simply not letting their marriages be registered by the Avogaria di Comun.[32] The records of the patriarchal court do not, therefore, allow us to draw any conclusions about the frequency of domestic disputes in the different social strata. Moreover, the low percentage of nonpatrician males who attempted to get their marriage annulled in court does not reflect concrete social realities. Informal ways of settling conflicts were undertaken especially by men, since male honor often ran counter to a public suit in court. Men without too many property ties simply deserted their wives[33]

[27]For this argument, see Seed, *To Love, Honor, and Obey*, 75–80. At the same time, Hunecke, *Der venezianische Adel*, 111–12, stresses that secret marriages could also be solemnized in accordance with the family interest of rich patricians. This was particularly the case when one of the sons of a patrician *casa* had already married validly. Since secret marriages were considered invalid according to civil law, contracting a secret marriage avoided creating a collateral line with a claim to inheritance. For strategies to preserve the property as a whole, see also James C. Davis, *A Venetian Family and Its Fortune, 1500–1900: The Donà and the Conservation of Their Wealth* (Philadelphia: University of Pennsylvania Press,1975).

[28]Hunecke, *Der venezianische Adel*, 15.

[29]From 1633 to 1699, approximately 330 secret marriages by both patrician and nonpatrician men were solemnized. See Gabriele Martini, "La donna veneziana del '600 tra sessualità legittima ed illegittima: Alcune riflessioni sul concubinato," *Atti dell'Istituto Veneto di Scienze, Lettere ed Arti* 145 (1986–87): 301–39. For some eighteenth-century figures, refer to Gaetano Cozzi, "Padri," 204–5.

[30]For the period 1579–1681, only one case of a male patrician plaintiff who sued his patrician wife in the patriarchal court is preserved in the *Causarum Matrimoniorum*; ASPV, C.M., Reg. 94: 14 September 1680, Hieronimi Cornelio cum Delphina Theupolo.

[31]During the eighteenth century, female patricians used the court quite frequently in order to annul their marriages or to separate. Cf. Luca De Biase, "Problemi ed osservazioni sul 'divorzio' nel patriziato veneziano del XVIII: Un tentativo di analisi storica seriale," *Atti dell'Istituto Veneto di Scienze, Lettere ed Arti* 140 (1981–82): 143–62, esp. 156–57; and Gaetano Cozzi, "Note e documenti sulla questione del 'divorzio' a Venezia (1782–1788)," *Annali dell'Istituto Italo-Germanico in Trento* 7 (1981): 275–360, esp. 326ff.

[32]Hunecke, *Der venezianische Adel*, 111, 241; see also Cozzi, "Padri," 184ff. and 204ff.

[33]James Casey, "Household Disputes and the Law in Early Modern Andalusia," in *Disputes and Settlements: Law and Human Relations in the West*, ed. John Bossy (Cambridge: Cambridge University Press, 1983), 189–217.

Daniela Hacke

without approaching the court and publicly discussing the force inflicted on them by their parents.

THE SPEECH IN COURT: THE ARGUMENTATIVE FRAMEWORK

Recent research has paid attention to the courtroom as a very particular locus of oral speech and has explored ways in which this institutional framework shaped the way in which gender conflicts were represented. Female plaintiffs, as has been argued, used the judicial public forum by relying on stereotypes of womanhood: conflicts with the other sex were thus addressed in terms of female weakness and male aggression. In this sense, the courtroom was a place where women could try to achieve their aims.[34] Such strategic negotiating only worked within the realm of a system of moral values and norms that were shared by the judicial authority and thus shaped the way conflicts were represented in court. Talking about sexual violence against women, for example, was only possible by stressing the male will as responsible for the "realized sexual act" and by underlining the honorable behavior of the woman at the same time. Thus, the conventions of the court not only shaped the way in which conflicts were addressed but also influenced the details which had to be suppressed, in this case the "lust" of women.[35] The dialectics of power led women and men in court to reconstruct their experiences differently.[36]

Realization of the importance of language has provided an important stimulus for further research. Through the linguistic analysis of various texts (statements of the cases, witnesses' testimonies, and interrogations), scholars have drawn attention to their nature as records produced by the judicial authorities. They have investigated these texts with an eye to their inherent categories of standardization, which made the construction of gender explicit.[37] Such a "deconstructive" approach pays less attention to the experiences of women and men than to the context of the production, the structure of the sources, and the significance of the words.[38] A very positive by-product of these linguistic analyses of court records is the increasing number

[34]Rebekka Habermas, "Frauen und Männer im Kampf um Leib, Ökonomie und Recht: Zur Beziehung der Geschlechter im Frankfurt der Frühen Neuzeit," in *Dynamik der Tradition*, ed. van Dülmen, 109–36, esp. 110–11.

[35]On argumentative strategies, see Susanna Burghartz, "Tales of Seduction, Tales of Violence: Argumentative Strategies before the Bosel Marriage Court," *German History* 17 (1999): 41–56.

[36]Lyndal Roper, "Will and Honor: Sex, Words, and Power in Augsburg Criminal Trials," in her *Oedipus and the Devil: Witchcraft, Sexuality, and Religion in Early Modern Europe* (New York: Routledge, 1994), 53–78.

[37]Ulrike Gleixner, *"Das Mensch" und "der Kerl": Die Konstruktion von Geschlecht in Unzuchtsverfahren der Frühen Neuzeit, 1700–1760* (Frankfurt a/M: Campus, 1994); and Monika Mommertz, "'Ich, Lisa Thielen': Text als Handlung und als sprachliche Struktur—ein methodischer Vorschlag," *Historische Anthropologie* 4 (1996): 303–29. For the discourse of accusation ("Klagediskurs"), see Martin Dinges, *Der Maurermeister und der Finanzrichter: Ehre, Geld und soziale Kontrolle im Paris des 18. Jahrhunderts* (Göttingen: Vandenhoeck & Ruprecht, 1994), 63–96.

[38]Gleixner, *"Das Mensch" und "der Kerl,"* 19 ff.

of detailed descriptions of various court records from different regions, which enhances our sensitivity to the peculiarities of our own sources. Scholars now realize that the production of court records followed different conventions in various regions, as for example with respect to the process of transforming oral speech into written words, and that the degree of transformation varied greatly in different sorts of court records.

Testimonies offered by witnesses, part of a predominantly oral culture, were shaped by previous experience in storytelling and memorizing. They were never neutral, even when male and female witnesses endeavored to remember the precise circumstances of the events. When neighbors advised a father to use his power with moderation, or if they witnessed extreme violence against a disobedient daughter, they remembered and memorized such details according to the expectations of contemporary culture; retold in court, the recollections were reshaped yet again.[39] Contrary to the assumption that male and female witnesses heavily relied on lawyers who suggested the right words to them, I agree with Miranda Chaytor that narratives in court carried emotional weight for the witnesses who provided them,[40] especially when they were directly involved in the domestic disputes.

The written statements produced by plaintiffs and defendants, although based initially on oral speech, form part of a predominantly written culture. In building up the written argumentation of the case, the litigant parties could rely on the ecclesiastical lawyers of the patriarchal court, who were trained in canon law. When clients described to their lawyers the events which had occurred before and after the formation of the marriage, it was certainly not the first time that they had spoken about their domestic difficulties. Before a suit was initiated in court, domestic disputes had been discussed between family members and described to and commented on by friends and neighbors. No doubt this telling and retelling of family conflicts strategically sharpened the way in which conflicts were represented in court ("interessensgeleitete Darstellung").[41] Additional relevant details and facts may have been elicited by the lawyers in order to strengthen the suit. Since it had to fulfill the formal requirements of canon law and those regarding content, the final product, the written statement of the case, while quite often dramatically and rhetorically well composed, was also very standardized. Oral speech was thus subject to a process of transformation which nevertheless allows us to draw conclusions regarding the initial descriptions of family conflicts. Direct speech is strategically and appropriately incorporated into the statements of the case in order to strengthen the argumentation. By remembering the precise words with which they

---

[39]Laura Gowing, *Domestic Dangers: Women, Words, and Sex in Early Modern London* (Oxford: Clarendon Press, 1996), 54–55. On this aspect, see also Miranda Chaytor, "Husband(ry): Narratives of Rape in the Seventeenth Century," *Gender and History* 7 (1995): 378–407, esp. 378–79.

[40]Chaytor, "Husband(ry)," 380.

[41]Martin Dinges has coined the term "interessensgeleitete Darstellung"; see his *Der Maurermeister*, 65.

expressed their unwillingness about their parents' marital plans, or with which parents tried to break their children's resistance, plaintiffs and defendants produced an impression of detailed authenticity.

The transformation of oral speech into written words involved a process of selection in which the lawyer suppressed all irrelevant details of the domestic dispute. In the written presentation of the case, explicit motives for the resistance of the children and for the force used are rarely given, placing the action, the violence, and the resistance at the center of attention. Thus the scope of action for children in court was limited. This also becomes evident in the (almost) identical argumentation of male and female plaintiffs and the lack of contextualization of family conflicts in a particular social stratum. In annulment suits, because of the emphasis on fear and force, cultural notions of womanhood and manhood were surprisingly not of prime importance.[42] Rather, generational conflict and resistance to the marital partner were emphasized in order to highlight the abusive use of patriarchal power.

The structure I have outlined is evident in the case of Vittoria Cesana related at the beginning. Her continuous resistance, her father's threats, and finally the threat of physical violence he employed were listed point by point in her accusation. Reference to the lack of consent was juridically crucial. According to canon law, marriages could be annulled if the suing party could offer sufficient proof that the marriage was contracted despite the existence of an impediment such as fear and force. By emphasizing her lack of consent, Vittoria Cesana and her lawyer were arguing in precisely the way the court expected. They stressed Vittoria's resistance even after the marriage was contracted, which suggested, as other cases make explicit, why the marriage was not consummated and why the partners separated before the conflict was made public in court.[43]

Often, however, the presentation of the case was not so brief and unemotional. The submission of a certain Maddalena, for example, claimed that she started crying immediately after her father had proposed that she marry the Venetian merchant Alvise Bonamico.[44] The purpose of stressing this unambiguous and spontaneous emotional outburst was to underline Maddalena's immediate emotional aversion, the basis for her future resistance. Directly expressed displeasure about marriage plans devised by the parents, the first visible sign of the disobedience to come, initiated the domestic dispute. As the suit of one Morosina claimed, when told by her father at dinner that she was to marry the journeyman Gianmaria, she expressed in no uncertain terms her unwillingness to comply. Then she left the table and locked herself in

---

[42]ASPV, C.M., Reg. 93: 12 November 1654, Jacobi Maccarini cum Lucretia Bianchi. This is, of course, only a first result and needs further verification by investigating the series *Filciae Causarum*.

[43]An exception is the case in ASPV, C.M., Reg. 82: 21 April 1593, Hersilie Pegorini cum Bernardio Struppiolo. This couple had lived together for sixteen years when the wife sued for an annulment of the marriage. In order to highlight the generational conflicts, I have not discussed resistance against the marital partner which resulted from the forced marriage.

[44]ASPV, C.M., Reg. 88: 20 September 1625, Magdalene de Franciscis cum Aloysio Bonamico, fol. 9v.

a room, refusing to eat and drink.[45] Calling this self-destructive gesture[46] to the court's attention made clear that she placed her will to resist her father's marriage plans above her physical well-being.

Highlighting a sacrifice was a strategy also used in other trials. In their written submissions, daughters sometimes claimed that they would rather become nuns than agree to the marriage plans of others.[47] In this way they played the card of the obvious alternative open to women in Catholic regions.[48] Life in the cloister was presented in terms of a sacrifice of the worldly life, since only in such a perspective did the allegation that a woman would rather become a nun than a particular man's wife make sense in court. Sacrifice could be accompanied by self-abasement, as made explicit in the trial initiated by a certain Orsetta. She told her mother in a gesture of subjugation that she would work as her servant day and night, eating only bread and water, if her mother gave up the intention of marrying her to Francesco the hunch-back.[49] This gesture of subjugation was intended to emphasize Orsetta's deep des-peration. By stressing the offer of working as a servant in her mother's household, furthermore, Orsetta made her obedience explicit. Working as a domestic servant, no realistic alternative to marriage, was brought forward to demonstrate her general acceptance of the power relationships between parents and children. By this means, Orsetta may have tried to gain control and power in this domestic dispute before the case reached court. Much more drastic tactics can be found in cases in which a daughter claimed that she would rather kill herself than marry the proposed man.[50] Daughters used self-destructive threats in response to marriage plans both before the conflict reached the court and in their representations to the court.

These family disputes demonstrate that young women could exert counterpres-sure on their parents and that they could, at least for a time, turn the social order in early modern households upside down. By refusing to consent to marriages arranged for them, they clearly challenged their parents' authority, or in the case of orphaned children, that of their legal guardians. The expressed *will* of women, not audible in other trials,[51] emerges in annulment suits in order to motivate their resistance to

[45]ASPV, C.M., Reg. 74: 10 January 1579, Morosine filie Leonardi Pectinary cum Joanne Maria Pectinario, fol. 8v.

[46]Burghartz, "Tales of Seduction."

[47]See, for example, ASPV, *Filcia Causarum*, Reg. 9 (1563–1565): 14 May 1565, Franceschina fia Mag.ci Aloysy Duodo cum Battista, fol. 12r.

[48]On this alternative, see Volker Hunecke, "Kindsbett oder Kloster: Lebenswege venezianischer Patrizierinnen im 17. und 18. Jahrhundert," *Geschichte und Gesellschaft* 18 (1992): 446–76.

[49]ASPV, C.M., Reg. 74: 4 November 1579, Francisci de Vulgaris cum Orsetta de Coltis, not foli-ated, 27 November 1579.

[50]ASPV, C.M., Reg. 74: 4 November 1579, Francisci de Vulgaris cum Orsetta de Coltis, not foli-ated, 27 November 1579; ASPV, C.M., Reg. 74: 10 January 1579, Morosine filie Leonardi Pectinary cum Joanne Maria Pectinario, fol. 24v; and ASPV, C.M., Reg. 90: 1 July 1628, Victorie Cesana cum Joe Bap-tista Barbaro, fol. 11v.

[51]Cf. Roper, "Will and Honour"; and Burghartz, "Tales of Seduction."

superiors. One can only estimate the potential for tension in these family disagreements and how much they disrupted the communal life of the household. Each member was obliged to adopt a position in regard to the contest of wills. A mother, especially, was forced by the domestic dispute to behave unambiguously, since she had to decide whether to support her husband or her daughter. If she refused to side with her husband and thus remain loyal to him, the generation conflict would turn into a battle of the sexes in which the male head of the household struggled against the female members.[52]

Thus, household order and discipline was not always immediate; it had to be regained and implemented. The restoration of social order in the conflicts discussed so far meant the realization of the proposed marriage and the breaking of the daughter's resistance, thus turning disobedience into obedience and respect. In court, the amount of the violence inflicted was decisive, since the female plaintiffs had to explain convincingly why they finally consented to a marriage which they would later claim in court had been contracted without the necessary consent. Therefore plaintiffs had to reveal the means of fear and force that had been used against them by providing concrete examples. Since the litigants in an annulment suit were the wife and the husband, not the parents or the legal guardian, this presentation of the family conflict comes almost exclusively from the version of the offspring. Only in rare cases did Venetian parents reveal to the court their understanding of power relations and social order in early modern households. Hence we usually lack a counter-version which would elucidate the superiors' point of view.

According to the accusations, violence was not invariably the first measure taken by parents against their daughters' disobedience. Talk, persuasion, and insistent pleas mentioned in various trials show the different methods adopted in early modern society for the settling of family conflicts.[53] Since no explicit pressure was exercised during these attempts at persuasion,[54] such ways of exerting influence were not in direct conflict with the theory of consent, although the Spanish canonist Tomás Sánchez rejected excessive pleas and psychological pressure as morally wrong.[55] Only when these nonviolent means of achieving an agreement within the family were, according to the statements of the offspring, succeeded by violent expressions of power did they run counter to the theory of consent. Verbal insistence was followed by threats to break the resistance with blows. In some cases the threat of violence was sufficient to break the resistance, as in the previously mentioned case

---

[52]See, for example, ASPV, C.M., Reg. 88: 20 September 1625, Magdalene de Franciscis cum Aloysio Bonamico.

[53]See, for example, ASPV, C.M., Reg. 93: 30 March 1661, Benedicta Gregory Marinary cum Jacobi Muschietti, fol. 2r.

[54]Sixteenth-century Spanish Catholic parents could "persuade, counsel, or show by precept that they wanted a child to marry a particular person, or that they wished to dissuade a child from a choice independently made." Seed, *To Love, Honor, and Obey,* 41.

[55]Seed, *To Love, Honor, and Obey,* 41.

of Maddalena, whose suit stated that she was so frightened after her father had threatened to beat her that she immediately agreed to marry Alvise Bonamico.[56] But in the majority of cases, offspring claimed to have suffered extreme violence and abuse from fathers, mothers, occasionally brothers and uncles, and in one exceptional case a grandmother and aunt. The repertory of corporal punishment listed in the statements of the cases went from slaps and blows (with hands and sticks) to life-threatening assaults such as attempts at strangulation and other murderous attacks.

Additional material and psychological means of exerting pressure are described. The orphaned Elisabetta, under the guardianship of her uncle, accused him of having threatened her in one breath that he would neither pay her the dowry nor care for her anymore if she did not consent to marry the musician Iseppo Sanson.[57] Similar examples of exerting pressure can be found in other cases with slight variations, such as, for example, the threat of expulsion from the parental household, or, according to the patrician Marietta Raimondo, that of her uncle to withdraw from his caring role and the supervision of her estates since they were now enemies.[58] In this way, the suing parties argued in court, parents and legal guardians exploited the dependence of their children. These accusations functioned both to reveal the force exerted on the children and to demonstrate the breach of canon law, since daughters had a claim to a dowry even if they married against the will of their parents.[59]

By focusing on the repertory of physical punishment and psychological pressure, offspring provided conclusive evidence about why their resistance had finally been broken. Thus, descriptions of physical violence had a specific juridical function: to prove an impediment to a valid marriage. At the same time, the behavior of parents and their use of authority was placed at the center of attention in court. Exclamations like "voglio che tu il togli" (I want to you to marry him), [60] "voglio che tu fai quello che io ti comando" (I want you to do what I command),[61] and "mi son Padrone" (I'm the boss)[62] vividly expressed the will of implementing power. The obedience demanded by parents was an expression of their authority; its biggest obstacle was the free will the Church accorded to the couple entering into the marriage. Nonetheless, in marriage formation parents did not inevitably modify or reflect on their use of authority, as becomes evident in one rare example. One mother who testified in court stated that her daughter Paulina was living under her

---

[56]ASPV, C.M., Reg. 88: 20 Sept. 1625, Magdalene de Franciscis cum Aloysio Bonamico, fol. 10r–v.

[57]ASPV, C.M., Reg. 90: 21 February 1629, Helisabeth Damiani cum Josepho Sanson, fol. 32r.

[58]ASPV, C.M., Reg. 87: 18 December 1622, Mariete Rimundo cum Marco Maripetro, not foliated, *scriptura petitionis.*

[59]Ferro, *Dizionario,* 1: 479–80.

[60]ASPV, C.M., Reg. 74: 4 November 1579, Francisci de Vulgaris cum Ursetta de Coltis, not foliated, 27 November 1579.

[61]ASPV, Reg. 90: 1 July 1628, Victorie Cesana cum Joe Baptista Barbaro, fol. 21v. I changed the quotation slightly.

[62]ASPV, C.M., Reg. 88: 20 September 1625, Magdalene de Franciscis cum Aloysio Bonamico, fol. 4v.

and her husband's strict rule and that she was very much afraid of both her parents, for she had been reared severely and cruelly.[63] Because corporal punishment was an expression of parental authority, parents did not deny it in court,[64] even though it could be interpreted in the context of annulment suits as a means of fear and force. Nor was physical violence always an expression of superior authority. Isabella Vancastra, for example, admitted in court in 1619 that she was so furious about her illegitimate daughter's resistance to marrying Anzolo Faniente that she first threatened and then almost murdered her.[65] Strangely enough, extreme violence can be understood as an expression of powerlessness, which conveys the experience of parents' and legal guardians' reaching their limits before they could implement their will. In this sense annulment suits elucidate the (temporary) limits of patriarchy and the fragility of authority connected with the fear of losing control.

Thus, suing women (with the help of their lawyers) composed dramatic and well-constructed accusations in which the undesired marriage was presented as the result of fear and force. Although offspring expressly referred to their own will, their accusations nevertheless evoke the image of their powerlessness in the face of parents' tyranny: successful resistance was virtually impossible. This impression is reinforced by the descriptions of the characters of the litigating generations. Parents and legal guardians were described as cruel, vindictive, and frightening,[66] and as ruling over shy, intimidated, and frightened offspring.[67] The accusations, then, were not built up only by addressing juridical arguments but also by evoking the image of tyrannical rule, a type of governance which ran counter to the myth of Venice as a free and righteous republic. The city's distinctive tradition was decisive for the emergence of the myth of Venice, handed down almost unchanged in chronicles until it found its fullest expression at the beginning of the sixteenth century.[68] Gasparo Contarini, whose *De magistratibus et Republica Venetorum* spread the fame of Venice in Europe, propagated the constitutional aspect of the Venetian myth.[69] According to Con-

---

[63]ASPV, C.M., Reg. 90: 20 April 1629, Pauline filie Joannis Sutoris cum Laurentio Comelli, fols. 19v–20r.

[64]ASPV, C.M., Reg. 90: 20 April 1629, Pauline filie Joannis Sutoris cum Laurentio Comelli, fols. 21v–22r.

[65]ASPV, C.M., Reg. 86: 13 August 1618, Magdalene Filosi cum Angelo Faniente, fol. 62r–v.

[66]See, for example, ASPV, C.M., Reg. 93: 30 March 1661, Benedicta Gregory Marinary cum Jacobi Muschietti, fol. 3v.

[67]See, for example, ASPV, C.M., Reg 92: 12 May 1648, Angelice Pellizzoli cum Scipione Albano, fol. 13r–v: the daughter is described as "timida, quieta, modesta e obediente"; ASPV, C.M., Reg. 83: 8 August 1597, Cornelie q.m Jacobi Calzago cum Joanne Francisco Fisaro, fol. 11v: the mother is characterized as "terribile, di sua voglia, vendicosa, et che difficilmente s'acquieta."

[68]James Grubb, "When Myths Lose Power: Four Decades of Venetian Historiography," *Journal of Modern History* 58 (1986): 43–94, esp. 44; and Edward Muir, *Civic Ritual in Renaissance Venice* (Princeton and New York: Princeton University Press, 1981), 23–34.

[69]Robert Finley, *La vita politica nella Venezia del Rinascimento*, trans. Adria Pedrazzi Marconi (Milan: Jaca Book, 1982), 53.

tarini, the mixed Venetian constitution promoted the stability, order, and freedom of the Republic. Integrating the monarchical (the doge), the aristocratic (the senate), and the democratic element (the Great Council), Venice possessed a unique and harmonious constitution.[70] Monarchical rule was limited by the control of the magistracies and by the laws which secured public welfare, so that "all dangerous inconveniences, whereby the commonwealth might sustain harm, are thereby removed."[71] Summarizing, Contarini stated that in this way an abuse of authority by the doge and tyrannical rule in general were prevented.[72] Tyrannical rule as an abuse of power was thus the antithesis of republican ideals, which placed the public welfare, the stability, and the freedom of the Republic in the center of political behavior.[73]

The significance of the family as a metaphor for the state, mentioned earlier, gained a specific relevance in this context. According to Paolo Paruta, named *storiografo pubblico* in February 1580, the head of the household was, like the ruler of a city, limited in his monarchical power. In his treatise *Della perfezione della vita politica,* written around 1570, the royal government (*regia amministrazione*) of the *paterfamilias* was ideally limited by transferring the principle of the *governo misto* (mixed government) to the household. With the cooperation of the wife in ruling the household, autocratic rule was modified into a government of the few, while the services of the *fratelli* (brothers), oriented toward the public welfare of the household members, symbolized the democratic element.[74] The much-praised republican ideal of the Venetian mixed constitution thus paralleled the ideal government of the household.

[70]Apart from this model, fifteenth- and sixteenth-century humanists also referred to Venice as a combination of democracy and oligarchy, or as a classical aristocracy. See Finley, *La vita politica*, 53.

[71]Gasparo Contarini, *The Commonwealth and Government of Venice* (London, 1599; Amsterdam: Da Capo Press, 1969), 40. On *Venezia stato misto*, see Franco Gaeta, "Alcune considerazioni sul mito di Venezia," *Bibliothèque d'humanisme et Renaissance* 23 (1961): 58–75; and Myron Gilmore, "Myth and Reality in Venetian Political Theory," in *Renaissance Venice,* ed. John R. Hale (London: Faber and Faber, 1973), 431–44.

[72]Gasparo Contarini, *The Commonwealth*, 42: "Whereby I think any man may easily understand, that the Duke of Venice is deprived of all meanes, whereby he might abuse his authoritie, or become a tyrant."

[73]Dietmar Herz and Diego Neumann, "Das Hohelied der venezianischen Verfassung: Gasparo Contarini und sein 'De Magistratibus et Republica Venetorum,'" *Juristische Schulung* 12 (1997): 1146–49.

[74]Paolo Paruta, *Della perfezione della vita politica* (Venice, 1579), in *Storici e politici veneti del Cinquecento e del Seicento*, ed. Gino Benzoni and Tiziano Zanato (Milan: Ricciardi, 1982), 491–642, esp. 632: "L'istesso nella casa avenir si vede, ove l'imperio del padre sopra i figliuoli, e per l'auttorità che tiene sopra di loro e per la pietà con la quale gli governa, è certa somiglianza d'una regia amministrazione; onde si può dire che il padre di famiglia sia quasi un picciol re nella sua casa, sì come il re è quasi un gran padre di famiglia nella città. In quanto poi l'uomo, non solo, ma col consiglio della donna, dispone di ciascuna cosa famigliare, l'uno e l'altra per sé particolare carico o dentro o fuori prendendosi per beneficio della loro famiglia, si vede ben espressa una maniera di governo di pochi buoni ottimamente ordinato; ma li fratelli, uguali in ogni parte, che nella casa né servi sono né signori, ma cambievolmente s'adoprano nelle cure domestiche, sono figura di uno stato più popolare."

Paternal tyranny, Paruta seems to suggest, was prevented by the mechanism of control. The moderate use of power is also discussed in treatises on household organization and management, which focused on the household ruler and therefore on his duties and responsibilities. According to Giovanni Caldiera, since the family is an instrument for the socialization of future citizens, the *paterfamilias'* ability to govern his family in a well-balanced way, promoting desired virtues in his children, is crucial.[75] "Above all, the paterfamilias has to be wise and prudent."[76] The main characteristics of a *buon economo* (good household manager) are virtue, moderation, and soundness of decisions; he has to govern strictly but righteously, caring for the physical and spiritual well-being of his household members.[77]

Since they offered much useful information and advice on its organization, these treatises on household management enjoyed widespread popularity. Although most of these works were composed for male patricians and described patrician households, their messages could make their way to "women, children, and servants via sermons, plays and verbal orders."[78] Thanks to the diary of Marin Sanudo, we know that some aspects of the Venetian myth reached the lower strata of the population via sermons.[79] In the process of appropriation of cultural ideals, offspring had at their disposal lawyers who were almost certainly acquainted with the constitutional aspect of the Venetian myth and probably also with those works dealing with the *governo della famiglia*.[80] These cultural images of a rule oriented toward balanced, righteous, and prudent use of authority were utilized to support the accusation by evoking its opposite: the frightful image of despotic and tyrannical rule. Hence the harsh behavior of parents and legal guardians was stressed because it could be represented as an abuse of authority.[81]

As we are about to see, the ideal of moderate and well-balanced rule was also decisive in the perception of domestic disputes by neighbors. It is not my aim to decide whether or not the witnesses revealed the truth, but to explore the moral values and norms of early modern Venetian communities which underlay interventions, expressions of resentment, and attempts at reconciliation.

[75]King, "Personal, Domestic, and Republican Values," 557.

[76]See the analysis of Caldiera's *De oeconomica veneta* by Dennis Romano, *Housecraft and Statecraft: Domestic Service in Renaissance Venice, 1400–1600* (Baltimore: Johns Hopkins University Press, 1996), 14-15.

[77]See the fundamental work of Frigo, *Il padre di famiglia*, esp. 84, 155–56.

[78]Romano, *Housecraft and Statecraft*, 4.

[79]Referred to in Finley, *La vita politica*, 52.

[80]According to Gilmore, Contarini's ideas existed "in a somewhat unformulated way in the consciousness of the Venetian patricians and they found occasional expression in the ambassadors' reports." Gilmore, "Myth and Reality," 439.

[81]Female Venetian writers utilized the myth of Venice both to criticize the "condizione femminile" and to claim a "libertà donnesca." See Ginevra Conti Odorisio, *Donna e società nel Seicento: Lucrezia Marinelli e Arcangela Tarabotti* (Rome: Bulzoni, 1979), 49.

THE PERCEPTION OF DOMESTIC VIOLENCE

Since they were noticed and commented on outside the physical walls of the house by neighbors, friends, and relatives, domestic disputes were not private conflicts. The household was not yet a private and intimate sphere; domestic disputes were subject to public evaluation. Balconies and windows offered direct views into neighboring homes, and gossip about crying daughters and parents who inflicted severe punishments spread quickly within the neighborhood long before the details of the domestic dispute were presented in court. Sometimes the litigating family members themselves directly informed neighbors about the particulars of family disagreement. Both parents and offspring turned to their neighbors in order to present their version of events. Neighbors became involved especially when they supported the distressed offspring. After she had left her husband, whom she had been forced to marry, Paulina, daughter of the tailor Giovanni Perron, for instance, was offered a place in a painter's household by his wife.[82] Negotiations and attempts at reconciliation—concealed in the accusations but revealed by witnesses—were carried out before a suit was initiated in court. Witnesses testified that they had been asked by parents and offspring to intervene in order to convince the other party of the righteousness of their point of view.[83] Such interventions aimed at reconciliation in order to prevent a violent escalation of the disputes. The shoemaker Gugliemo, for example, testified in court that he was present when a certain Leonardo told his daughter while eating that she was to marry the journeyman of his *bottega*. Gugliemo advised the stubborn daughter to consent to this match, since only in this case would her father leave her an inheritance.[84]

Such advice to respect the parents' will, given to unwilling daughters in other cases as well, shows the important roles that authority and obedience played within hierarchic households in early modern Venetian communities and reveals how these attributes were utilized during negotiations. By highlighting the daughter's duty to be modest and to respect her parents' authority,[85] since it was not her business to choose her own husband,[86] neighbors powerfully reminded a young woman of the limits of her freedom of choice. Both men and women gave such advice. That a woman might have had a similar experience at the time of her own marriage did not inevitably produce loyalty to her sex. The principle of obedience was not always opposed to the Tridentine decree concerning consent. Parents and children could be

[82]ASPV, C.M., Reg. 90: 20 April 1629, Pauline filie Joannis Sutoris cum Laurentio Comelli, fols. 7v and 13r–v.

[83]ASPV, C.M., Reg. 90: 1 July 1628, Victorie Cesana cum Joe Baptista Barbaro, fols. 11r–v and 16v–17r.

[84]ASPV, C.M., Reg. 74: 10 January 1579, Morosine filie Leonardi Pectinary cum Joanne Maria Pectinario, fol. 4r.

[85]ASPV, C.M., Reg. 86: 13 August 1618, Magdalene Filosi cum Angelo Faniente, fols. 37v–38r.

[86]ASPV, C.M., Reg. 82: 21 April 1593, Hersilie Pegorini cum Bernardio Struppiolo, not foliated, 16 June 1593.

in perfect harmony about the future spouse, as shown in the case of Zanetta, whose father agreed to her choice of groom without any hesitation.[87] But according to secular notions, in contrast to the Catholic theory of consent, marriage formation was not to take place without the explicit agreement, and certainly not against the will, of the parents.

Attempts at reconciliation also reveal the popular notion that parents and legal guardians should not violently force their offspring's obedience but use their power with moderation in attempting to convince them. Such expectations are distinctly audible in the testimony of Marietta Tacca. She criticized the cruel means by which a mother called Isabella had tried to enforce her will on her daughter by threatening and battering her severely, without attempting to persuade her with kindness ("con le buone").[88] In another dispute, Laura Contarini intervened precisely at the moment when the domestic conflict between a widowed mother, Chiara, and her daughter Orsetta was about to escalate. With words that strongly recall the theory of consent, she reproached the mother by stressing that one was not allowed to force children into marriages to which they did not consent.[89] As in other cases, the necessity of consent was brought forward to make the limits of parental authority explicit.[90]

In marriage formation, the right balance between authority and obedience on the one hand and the acceptance of filial free will on the other was hard to achieve. Even the Council of Trent did not resolve this problem, since it did not define the extent of control to which parents were entitled notwithstanding the theory of consent.[91] In everyday life, as the negotiations reveal, emphasis was laid on a prudent and moderate use of power. The fact that responsible parents had to correct disobedient offspring was never in question. "Moderate corrections," aimed at the maintenance of social order, were an accepted practice in early modern Venice.[92] Because corporal punishment was an expression of parental authority, it was not denied in court. Cruel and severe punishments, however, were quite differently perceived, as were domestic conflicts which were about to escalate. In these cases, neighbors tried to reconcile the opposed parties, advising parents to behave moderately and patiently.[93] More dramatic were the events that occurred in the household of the previously mentioned Vancastra family. As the widowed washerwoman Giacoba tes-

[87]ASPV, C.M., Reg. 90: 4 May 1628, Joanette q.m Valentini Hortulani cum Francisco Fabrilignario Arsenatus, fols. 32r–34r.

[88]ASPV, C.M., Reg. 93: 30 March 1661, Benedicta Gregory Marinary cum Jacobi Mucchietti, fols. 9v–10r.

[89]ASPV, C.M., Reg. 74: 4 November 1579, Francisci de Vulgaris cum Ursetta de Coltis, not foliated, 27 November 1579.

[90]Cf. ASPV, C.M., Reg. 81: 5 August 1588, Isabelle Floriani cum Ambrosio Mazzoni, not foliated, point 17.

[91]Seed, *To Love, Honor, and Obey,* 35.

[92]ASPV, C.M., Reg. 90: 20 April 1629, Pauline filie Joannis Sutoris cum Laurentio Comelli, fol. 4r.

[93]ASPV, C.M., Reg. 93: 30 March 1661, Benedicta Gregory Marinary cum Jacobi Mucchietti, fol. 6v.

tified in 1618, she and Zavonetto Becher arrived just in time to prevent the mother's murdering her daughter. Although Giacoba supported the mother's view that a daughter should pay respect and obedience to her superiors, she strongly disapproved of the violent and life-threatening means which the mother had employed.[94] That corporal punishment and daughters' resistance were judged differently according to the circumstances is revealed in several cases. The choice of groom, quite important in this respect, could motivate sympathy for or disapproval of the daughter's resistance. Planned marriages involving a large age gap between the prospective husband and wife, a different social station, or a future groom reputed to be a womanizer and/or a drunkard, called parental decisions into question and elicited a lack of understanding and amazement on the part of the neighbors.[95]

CONCLUSION

Especially as annulment suits because of fear and force give us many insights into the conflicted parent-child relationship, these sources allow us to draw a more complex and vivid picture of Venetian household life, marriage formation, and the role of women within. Rather than highlight paternal authority and the submissiveness of daughters (as normative texts tend to do), trial records demonstrate forcefully the different ways in which young women could undermine paternal authority, before it was reinforced and implemented. They point to the limits of and the challenge to paternal authority and thus to the cultural expectations that were linked with the roles of fatherhood and motherhood. Households were places of "cultural meaning and interaction"[96] and the interventions and attempts at reconciliation carried out by neighbors and friends elucidate the contemporary social values and norms that underlay (or structured) their behavior. They reveal that although parents should strictly and righteously govern their children, they should nevertheless use their authority responsibly and wisely; only then was their rule perceived as just and appropriate. This cultural notion of a rule oriented toward a well-balanced, righteous, and prudent use of authority, which emerges from the written statements and witnesses' testimonies, strongly reflects the discussion of a "good government" as expressed in political theory. Here and there, the problem posed by tyranny and "bad government" could only be prevented by a moderate use of authority. In this way, the metaphor of the family as a microcosm of the city, with the father ruling over his household members just as magistrates rule over their citizens, could be brought forward in court as an argument against tyrannical rule.

---

[94]ASPV, C.M., Reg. 86: 13 August 1618, Magdalene Filosi cum Angelo Faniente, fol. 37r–v.

[95]In this order: Archivio di Stato di Venezia, Avogaria di Comun, *Miscellanea penale* 366.5: Veglia, da Gregorio, adulterio, 1587, foliation not readable because of damage, testimony from 20 September 1587; ASPV, C.M., Reg. 74: 10 January 1579, Morosine filie Leonardi Pectinary cum Joanne Maria Pectinario, fol. 14r; ASPV, C.M., Reg. 90: 1 July 1628, Victorie Cesana cum Joe Baptista Barbaro, fol. 12r.

[96]Kuehn, *Law, Family, and Women*, 4.

Becoming a Mother in the Seventeenth Century
The Experience of a Roman Noblewoman

Marina d'Amelia

There are many different approaches to the study of motherhood in the modern era. One of the most significant, and least common, is an analysis of female perception and experience. Historians have increasingly recognized the influential role of female networking in building family fortunes, as well as the importance of the female lineage in the family policies of the early modern aristocracy.[1] But much less attention has been given, at least in Italian historical studies, to understanding what women had to say about this importance and how they perceived and fulfilled their role in society. The period stretching roughly from the beginning of the Reformation to the advent of Romanticism witnessed an extraordinary blooming of the autobiographical genre. Yet there are relatively few writings by women concerning the role of mothers in the family life cycle or evoking a woman's experience of motherhood. This dearth is especially striking when compared to the abundance of female accounts of spiritual or mystical experiences.

---

[1]Ample literature has put the patrilinear image of families in early modern Italy into better focus and offered a more balanced view of male and female roles in the life cycle of families and their strategies for power and social ascent. Only a few references are given: Anthony Molho et al., "Genealogia e parentado: Memorie del potere nella Firenze tardo medievale; Il caso di Giovanni Ruccellai," *Quaderni Storici* 86 (1994): 365–403; Christiane Klapisch-Zuber, "Albero genealogico e costruzione della parentela nel Rinascimento," *Quaderni Storici* 86 (1994): 405–420; Giulia Calvi, *Il contratto morale: Madri e figli nella Toscana moderna* (Rome: Laterza, 1994); Renata Ago, *Carriere e clientele nella Roma barocca* (Rome: Laterza, 1990); idem, "Giochi di squadra: Uomini e donne nelle famiglie nobili del XVII secolo," in *Signori patrizi e cavalieri nell'età moderna*, ed. Maria Antonietta Visceglia (Rome: Laterza, 1992), 256–64; idem, "Giovani nobili nell'età dell'assolutismo: Autoritarismo paterno e libertà," in *Storia dei giovani: Dall'antichità all'età moderna*, ed. Giovanni Levi and Jean-Claude Schmitt, vol. 1 (Rome: Laterza, 1994), 375–426; Irene Fosi and Maria Antonietta Visceglia, "Marriage and Politics at the Papal Court in the Sixteenth and Seventeenth Centuries," in *Marriage in Italy, 1300–1650*, ed. Trevor Dean and Kate J. P. Lowe (Cambridge: Cambridge University Press, 1998), 197–224.

The relative preponderance of religious writings in the sixteenth and seventeenth centuries may have several causes; the greater proportion (compared to the past) of women who were sent to convents compared to those who married and had children, the difference in literacy rates among these two groups, and the Church's encouragement of religious women to give voice to their faith, albeit within well-defined limits. But religious writings do not tell the whole story. Italian historical archives hold numerous archives of noble families which, besides containing documentation on the public and economic history of the family, also include collections of letters and writings by the female members of the family. These materials shed an interesting light on both women's role in family relations and their involvement in their families' public life and patrimony. One of these archives, the large collection of letters belonging to the Spada Veralli family, is the source for this study.

A brief introduction to the family and to the letters will provide necessary background to the experiences of motherhood to be explored in this paper. The Veralli and Spada families were typical examples of those family groups that owed their social ascent to their ties with the Roman Curia and court.[2] The female members of these families entered into a sort of tacit pact with the ecclesiastics of their family, based on a sense of alliance and complicity. The overarching objective of this alliance was the social rise of their family, in the wake of the curial career of its members, but the pact also appeared to have a profound impact on family models. The women were allowed considerable leeway, and relations between parents and children seemed to be patterned more on persuasion than on coercion.[3] The origins of the Spada family were in the region of Romagna, whence they moved to Rome in the early seventeenth century to follow the ecclesiastical career of Cardinal Bernardino and his brother Virgilio, a member of the Congregation of the Oratory. The nephew of Cardinal Bernardino, Orazio, initiated his social rise and that of his children at the Roman court under the wing of his uncle, and thanks also to his marriage to Maria Veralli.

The Veralli Spada archives include the official, personal, and business correspondence of many members of the Veralli and Spada families from the first half of the sixteenth to the end of the eighteenth century. Though only a small share of the total collection, the letters by the women of the family are quite remarkable. For instance, the archives contain the correspondence between Maria Veralli Spada and

---

[2]For a general history of the Veralli family, see Marina D'Amelia, *Orgoglio baronale e giustizia: Castel Viscardo alla fine del Cinquecento* (Rome: Gangemi, 1993), esp. 21–25. On the origins of the Spada family and the settlement of a branch of that family in Rome following the marriage of Orazio and Maria Veralli, see Cesarina Casanova, "Le donne come risorsa: Le politiche matrimoniali della famiglia Spada (XVII–XIX secoli)," *Memoria: Rivista di storia delle donne* 21 (1987): 56–78; Ago, *Carriere e clientele*; idem, "Maria Spada Veralli, la buona moglie," in *Barocco al femminile*, ed. Giulia Calvi (Rome: Laterza, 1992), 51–70. For the career of Bernardino Spada in the Roman Curia, the primary reference is Ludwig von Pastor, *Storia dei papi dalla fine del medioevo*, vol. 13 (Rome: Desclée, 1931), ad indicem.

[3]See Ago, "Giovani nobili nell'età dell'assolutismo," 406, 420–21.

her daughter Eugenia in the second half of the seventeenth century. Almost all the letters written by Eugenia to her mother between 1656 and 1685 have been preserved, along with a large number of those written to her father. Moreover, the archives contain the correspondence (1671–79) between Eugenia and Ippolito Pieri, the man who administered her family's estate during the years in which Eugenia lost the guardianship of her children to her mother-in-law following her second marriage.[4] This correspondence is precious evidence of the ways in which a mother could continue to take care of her children from her first marriage, even after having lost formal guardianship of them. This form of "dual management," to use the term coined by Yan Thomas, was relatively widespread in the seventeenth century.[5]

During the period documented by these letters, Eugenia married Marquis Domenico Maidalchini and went to live in Viterbo, where she gave birth to four children before being widowed in 1662. After having assumed the guardianship of her three surviving children, she turned down two marriage proposals before finally agreeing, upon her father's strong insistence, to marry Duke Girolamo Mattei in 1666. The marriage to Mattei meant that she had to give up the guardianship of her children to her former mother-in-law. In later years, she gave birth to another son and was once again widowed before finally regaining the guardianship of her surviving children from her first marriage. Eugenia, who was born in 1639, lived long enough to see her children reach adulthood. She became a grandmother and played in her turn the role of advisor to the new generation that had been her mother's before her. She died in 1715.

The correspondence between Maria Spada and Eugenia Maidalchini is used here to explore three basic themes: first, the way in which pregnancy and motherhood were experienced in the mid-seventeenth century by members of the female elite and the place that pregnancy had in the life cycle of women; second, the model of communication between mother and daughter that is suggested by this correspondence; and third, the ways in which the different generations of women modified their heritage and the female models handed down to them by their families of origin.

A RITE OF PASSAGE

The marriage between Eugenia Spada and Domenico Maidalchini was worked out in every detail by Cardinal Bernardino, confirming the observation by Renata Ago

---

[4]For the correspondence between Eugenia Maidalchini and Ippolito Pieri, see Archivio di Stato di Roma (henceforth ASR), Archivio Spada Veralli, b. 442, 443.

[5]Yan Thomas uses the term "dual management" to describe a well-known phenomenon consisting of the split between the appointment of a formal guardian and the de facto responsibility held by Roman widows for the administration of their children's inheritance. See Yan Thomas, "The Division of the Sexes in Roman Law," vol. 1, *From Ancient Goddesses to Christian Saints, A History of Women in the West*, ed. Pauline Schmitt Pantel (Cambridge: Belknap Press of Harvard University Press, 1992), 83–137, esp. 130–31.

that "the ecclesiastic, especially if he had reached an authoritative position, was the real head of the family."[6] This marriage also highlighted the importance that women had assumed in their families of origin. The real counterparts of the cardinal in the marriage negotiations were Olimpia Pamphili Maidalchini, who was the bridegroom's aunt and also the highly influential sister-in-law of the late Pope Innocent X,[7] and Maria Veralli Spada, the bride's mother. The kinship that the bridegroom brought to the marriage through Olimpia Pamphili was very valuable to the Spada family, who had only recently settled in Rome to build their network of court relations. As Maria Spada wrote, Domenico Maidalchini was not only "a handsome young man, who also seems to be good"; more important, he was "a first cousin of the Princess Pamphili, and of the Princesses Giustiniani and Ludovisi, as well as being a blood uncle of the Princess of Palestrina."[8] On their side, the Spada family could offer the influence of Cardinal Bernardino and his brother Virgilio in the Curia, as well as the backing of the Barberini family. This was essential to bolster the career of Cardinal Francesco Maidalchini, a brother of Eugenia's future spouse, who, after having enjoyed the favor of Innocent X, largely thanks to Olimpia's influence,[9] had quickly fallen into disgrace. The powerful position of the two ecclesiastics enabled the Spada family to keep Eugenia's dowry to 10,000 scudi—the average dowry for the young Spada women in the first half of the seventeenth century. The role of Orazio Spada, the father of Eugenia, in brokering this marriage was marginal, to say the least. As Maria Spada aptly put it, her husband found himself in the happy position of a man who "had married off his daughter without any trouble whatsoever."[10]

After their wedding in Rome, Eugenia and Domenico began their married life in Viterbo in the house of his mother, Pacifica Maidalchini. This cohabitation soon became a problem because of the sharp conflict between mother and son on economic matters and also because of Pacifica's bad temper. She saw her role as mistress of the house being threatened by the presence of a daughter-in-law. The clashes between mother and son seemed to have cemented the union of the two young

[6]See Ago, "Giovani nobili nell'età dell'assolutismo," 413. For a detailed background of the various phases of the marriage negotiations conducted by Cardinal Spada, see ASR, Archivio Spada Veralli, b. 459. Concerning the role of the cardinal between 1630 and 1640, when he was legate in Bologna, in arranging the marriages of his nieces as a means of introducing the Spada family into the senatorial aristocracy of Bologna, see Casanova, "Le donne come risorsa," 61–67.

[7]As there is no recent biography of Olimpia Pamphili Maidalchini, see von Pastor, *Storia dei papi*, vol. 17.1, 27–37; Ignazio Ciampi, *Innocenzo X Pamfili e la sua corte* (Rome: Galeati, 1878). Concerning the lengthy marriage negotiations, the role of the cardinal, and the parts played by Olimpia Pamphili and Maria Spada, see ASR, Archivio Spada Veralli, b. 459.

[8]ASR, Archivio Spada Veralli, b. 459, f. 227.

[9]The support of Bernardino and Virgilio Spada for the future career of the young cardinal—at the time of his appointment in 1647, the nephew of the powerful Olimpia was only seventeen years old—was one of the unspoken components of this marriage settlement.

[10]ASR, Archivio Spada Veralli, b. 459.

spouses, and Eugenia became her husband's confidante. Maria Spada, too, assumed the role of a cautious advisor to her son-in-law, as may be surmised from their correspondence.[11] In this tense climate, which fostered complicity between husband and wife, Eugenia soon became pregnant. Her doubts about her possible pregnancy were promptly relayed to her mother following the first delay in her menstrual cycle. On 1 October 1656, the young spouse wrote, "the person who was supposed to come on the 25th has not appeared. I do not know what it means because I feel well, only sometimes my stomach bothers me a little. I do not know what to say, because I know no one who can tell me anything."[12]

This news kindled an intense dialogue with her mother that accompanied Eugenia throughout the nine months of her pregnancy and helped her to cope with the many changes to her life, thanks to the support of her mother's remarkable advice and experience. Every detail was carefully thought out, from what to do in the case of the many unexpected events that may occur in a pregnant body to the practical preparations for the birth of a baby, ranging from the sort of cradle—which Eugenia wanted to be like the wicker cradle used by her mother, and not one of those wooden cradles which "rock from head to foot" that were common in Viterbo—to the frocks and swaddling clothes which were part of a baby's layette.[13]

Everything the young girl did to cope with the daily events and emergencies seems to have been suggested to her in her mother's letters, starting from the care for her body before and after delivery and the important measures used to block lactation to the weaning of the baby and what to do in the case of dreaded childhood diseases. Maria seemed to have an answer to everything, and she was attentive to the most trivial of details in her daughter's life. If ever she had even the slightest suspicion that she was not being told the whole truth, she had no qualms whatsoever about using her son-in-law, and especially Eugenia's personal maid, as informers about her daughter's health, humor, and habits.[14]

The course of Eugenia's morning sickness can be followed in the letters, from the early days when her frequent bouts of nausea almost prevented her from moving about (with bland remedies suggested by her mother such as "lime juice" and the admonition "do not bother to tell the doctor")[15] until Eugenia's relieved announcement to her mother that her stomach bothered her "so little that I do not pay any attention to it, and if it continues this way, I will be very happy."[16] The young girl had a hard time coping with her homesickness and loneliness. Eugenia and Pacifica

[11] ASR, Archivio Spada Veralli, b. 623.

[12] ASR, Archivio Spada Veralli, b. 410/3, letter of 1 October 1656.

[13] See Marina D'Amelia, "La presenza delle madri nell'Italia medievale e moderna," in *Storia della maternità*, ed. Marina D'Amelia (Rome: Laterza, 1998), 26.

[14] An example of this parallel source of information is the letter sent by Camilla, Eugenia Maidalchini's handmaid, to Maria Spada on 15 October 1656. ASR, Archivio Spada Veralli, b. 410/3.

[15] ASR, Archivio Spada Veralli, b. 410/3, letter of 18 October 1656.

[16] ASR, Archivio Spada Veralli, b. 410/3, letter of 25 October 1656.

Maidalchini never did develop a close relationship. Despite Maria's advice to her daughter to rely on her mother-in-law, the tension and antagonism between the two women were to continue into the future. The young girl received a steady stream of often contradictory messages: for example, while it was wise for her not to go outdoors too often and to avoid the bumpy roads, it was also necessary to get some exercise, especially just before childbirth, to ease the delivery.

Two different aspects of the aristocratic culture of that time can be seen at work in relation to Eugenia's pregnancy. Maria Spada was urbane and very conscious of the ceremonial implications of the event. The young mother's attire when she was to receive the visits of relatives and friends in the days immediately following delivery was the subject of many recommendations. Maria was also unexpectedly "modern," for instance, when she advised her daughter to wash her hair because this would in no way jeopardize her pregnancy. The mother-in-law's culture was very different. Pacifica Maidalchini was not only closer to the sort of bodily taboos which were part of a woman's life, but she also had a much more basic approach to the customs surrounding childbirth. For her, a woman's job consisted mainly of preparing the baby's layette.

In those years, the traditional visit to the new mother shortly after childbirth changed in nature. From being a ceremony involving the mother's family of origin and her acquired family alone, it became a wearisome social event, with all the other noble families, in large groups including male visitors, coming to pay their respects. The comments contained in the letters sent by Maria Spada at the time of her grandchildren's births show her to be a careful observer of the evolution in custom. The new habits included minor innovations which Maria Spada at times saw unfavorably, such as the husband's offering a gift in money to his wife immediately after she gave birth.

On the occasion of the birth of her first grandchild, the son of Bernardino and Vittoria Patrizi, Maria Spada wrote to her husband, "I have heard that her husband gave her fifty scudi, and they say that this is now the custom."[17] This habit, which first appeared around 1670, soon became a tradition for the whole of the Roman nobility. In contrast to fifteenth-century Florence, where the gifts to the mother after the birth of a child consisted of traditional objects linked to ancient customs,[18] in Rome there was greater freedom of choice. Indeed, gifts were at times recycled, with little enthusiasm, simply to keep up appearances. "As soon as she had her baby," wrote Maria Spada in 1679 (referring to Vittoria Patrizi, the wife of her elder son, Bernardino, on the occasion of the birth of their first son), "because I thought of this custom, and to get it over and done with, I gave her a gold reliquary with a matching

---

[17]ASR, Archivio Spada Veralli, b. 618, letter of 18 April 1679.

[18]The reference is obviously to the *deschi da parto*, which were studied by Anne Jacobson Schutte in "'Trionfo delle donne': Tematiche di rovesciamento dei ruoli nella Firenze rinascimentale," *Quaderni storici* 44 (1980): 474–88.

chain, which had been a present to me from Cardinal Rocci when he baptized my poor baby Lucrezia."[19]

While Maria Spada was thinking about the ceremonial setting to be respected when she urged her daughter to prepare herself for the birth, for Eugenia preparing for her imminent motherhood meant having to cope with a difficult shift in identity and finding her own way to make ready for the birth of a baby. Despite her many promises to obey her mother's advice to the letter, Eugenia decided to adapt these recommendations to her personal situation. While she did defy her mother-in-law's disapproval by washing her hair, after the birth she did not wear the richly embroidered velvet jackets suggested to her by her mother.[20]

Another difference of opinion between mother and daughter regarded what was truly important and what instead could be overlooked during the period of pregnancy and the rituals preceding and following the birth. One of the disagreements concerned the role that devotional practice should have in the daily life of a future mother. As the time of delivery drew near, Maria Spada appealed to her daughter to turn to God more assiduously. Her letters repeatedly recommended that Eugenia make greater efforts in her devotional practices and in reciting the novena, and that masses with special intentions be celebrated close to the time of the birth. Eugenia promptly followed all of her mother's suggestions concerning her bodily care and the preparation of the baby's trousseau, but she seemed to be much less diligent in accomplishing her religious duties. Not only did she fail to follow the Lenten preaching, but she also avoided reciting the novena that her mother had so strongly suggested. When questioned once again about the matter, she brusquely informed her mother that "if I do not recite the novena, I will have someone else do it for me."[21] The reasons for her nonchalance appeared to be linked to Eugenia's decision at the beginning of her pregnancy to drastically simplify the clothes which she was to wear in public. She also decided on a more lukewarm devotion than the Spada family was used to in Rome. Eugenia clearly revealed the low level of religious literacy that was typical of the new generations of the aristocracy who were close to the Curia in the mid-seventeenth century. Though she did go to mass at the monastery of the Madonna della Quercia forty days after the birth of her first son, when it was customary for all young mothers of Viterbo to do so, she was forced to admit to her mother that she had not taken communion, the taking of which was prescribed by tradition.[22]

The outbreak of the plague in Viterbo resulted in all sorts of precautions and led to a quarantine in September 1657. The situation was exasperated to the point

---

[19]ASR, Archivio Spada Veralli, b. 618, letter of 12 April 1679. Lucrezia, a daughter of Maria and Orazio Spada, died in 1666.

[20]ASR, Archivio Spada Veralli, b. 410/3, letter of 28 March 1657.

[21]ASR, Archivio Spada Veralli, b. 410/3, letter of 28 March 1657.

[22]ASR, Archivio Spada Veralli, b. 410/3, letter of 22 July 1657.

that Eugenia, having reached Capranica in December 1657 on her way to Rome to spend Christmas with her parents, wrote to her mother that "We go to mass on all the holy days, so much so that we have begun to feel as if we are Christians again."[23] In later years, the situation gradually changed. Fear of her children's diseases induced Eugenia, like so many other mothers, to use oil and waters somehow connected to saints. She also used the real relics of saints, such as those associated with Saint Filippo Neri, which had entered the possession of many Roman noble families following the death of the saint, as well as more recent relics that were typical of Viterbo, like the water in which the body of St. Rosa had been washed.[24]

FEAR, EMOTIONS, AND EXPECTATIONS

Eugenia's accounts of her experience of pregnancy seem to revolve around such physiological aspects as the need for proper eating habits and the right balance of rest and exercise. No traces are to be found in her letters of any of the more common fears that were the subject of much theoretical controversy between physicians and theologians, ranging from the birth of deformed babies to the possible negative effects on the fetus of bad impressions produced by the surrounding environment.[25] Eugenia never referred to a craving for special foods, nor did the other daughters, daughters-in-law, or acquaintances whose pregnancies Maria Spada followed closely; it was not considered to be a typical behavior of pregnant women.

There were, however, many commonalities between Eugenia's attitudes and some of the more widespread practices in both traditional medicine and the daily habits of that time. The uncertain system for calculating the nine months of pregnancy, which was based both on lunar cycles and a haphazard recording of the last menstrual cycle, meant that women usually anticipated the time of delivery for each pregnancy. This uncertainty in estimation was common in women of the aristocracy well into the eighteenth century.[26] Another very common habit in popular culture was to bet on the sex of the unborn child. This custom had been forbidden since the sixteenth century but obviously to little effect, as the decrees banning the practice

[23]ASR, Archivio Spada Veralli, b. 410/3, letter of 22 December 1657.

[24]For examples of the special oils and relics used, see ASR, Archivio Spada Veralli, b. 1115, letters of 1 September 1658; 12 and 21 June 1661.

[25]On the fears of pregnant women in this period, the following are some surveys. For Holland, see Herman Roodenburg, "The Maternal Imagination: The Fears of Pregnant Women in Seventeenth-Century Holland," *Journal of Social History* 21 (summer 1988): 701–16. Concerning the literature on monstrous births, see Ottavia Niccoli, "Menstruum quasi monstrum: Parti mostruosi e tabù mestruali nel'500," *Quaderni storici* 44 (1980): 402–28; Katharine Park and Lorraine Daston, "Unnatural Conceptions: The Study of Monsters in Sixteenth- and Seventeenth-Century France and England," *Past and Present* 92 (1981): 20–54. *Il primo processo per S.Filippo Neri*, ed. Giovanni Incisa della Rocchetta and Nello Vian, 2 vols. (Vatican City: Biblioteca Apostolica Vaticana, 1957–58), 2, offers much evidence on how the Roman aristocracy entered into possession of relics of the saint.

[26]See Randolph Trumbach, *The Rise of the Egalitarian Family: Aristocratic Kinship and Domestic Relations in Eighteenth-Century England* (New York: Academic, 1978), 183–84.

were reiterated over the years,[27] and it was a common occurrence in the streets and squares of Rome. Eugenia also referred repeatedly to the negative influence that leap years could have on births.[28]

The lack of any mention in her letters of the sort of fears and anxiety which are to be found so abundantly in other women's writings, such as the fear of dying or other worries linked to the health of the baby to be born,[29] does not seem to be due so much to a form of self-censorship as to the relatively calm and serene environment in which Eugenia was preparing to give birth. It should also not be forgotten that her mother had fourteen healthy children, and that all her sisters-in-law had been pregnant several times and were in very good health.

The letters do reveal how difficult it was for this young woman to put her emotions into words, as shown by a description of her moodiness around her fourth month of pregnancy: "I do not know how many days have gone by that I cannot say if I am feeling better or worse, because before my stomach hurt and now I never want to get dressed because I feel as if everything bothers me and I am so faint that I cannot sit up—that is, I do not know how I feel and I cannot say it."[30] Her interest in the movements of the baby in her womb appeared at first to have been induced by others, and by the sort of questions they asked her: "I think I felt the baby because of what they said, but I am not sure because I do not know if I can recognize it." On the contrary, she wrote spontaneously about the physical changes to her body: "My breasts are beginning to grow," she wrote, "and they continue to swell, but if I squeeze them, they do not hurt."[31] The way in which Eugenia faced the changes in her body over the months, starting with her gain in weight, swung between pride in her visible pregnancy and the need for reassurance that her girlish body was not completely lost. Her ambiguity in admitting the changes to her body was exasperated by the different reactions of her entourage, who observed and pondered their meaning. The pregnant body did not appear to be subjected to any form of censorship whatever, at least judging by how frequently the comments and remarks that relatives and visitors made on the progress of her pregnancy were recorded in her letters.[32]

What were the expectations of young Eugenia concerning the baby's sex? It is hard to say, even though she touched upon the subject several times and made precise

[27]ASR, Bandi, b. 35.

[28]ASR, Archivio Spada Veralli, b. 1115, letter of 23 October 1660.

[29]See Sarah Heller Mendelson, "Stuart Women's Diaries and Occasional Memoirs," in *Women in English Society 1500–1800*, ed. Mary Prior (London: Methuen, 1995), 196–97; Patricia Crawford, "The Construction and Experience of Maternity in Seventeenth-Century England," in *Women as Mothers in Pre-Industrial England: Essays in Memory of Dorothy McLaren*, ed. Valerie Fildes (London: Routledge, 1990), 22–23; Trumbach, *Rise of the Egalitarian Family*, 183.

[30]ASR, Archivio Spada Veralli, b. 410/3, letter of 7 February 1657.

[31]ASR, Archivio Spada Veralli, b. 410/3, letter of 26 November 1656.

[32]ASR, Archivio Spada Veralli, b. 410/3, letters of 31 March, 11 and 15 April 1657; b. 1115, letter of 14 July 1660.

remarks on the occasion of the birth of other babies or statements that can be interpreted in more than one way. For instance, in April, Eugenia commented on the birth of a baby girl to the princess of Palestrina as follows: "And I will surely follow her. But I will love him if he is a boy just as I would a girl."[33] A few days later, the young woman added a qualification which muted the innovative thrust of the previous statement: "I do not mind whether the baby is a boy or a girl, because I do not think it will be the latter."[34] If one considers the expressions of joy or, on the contrary, of disappointment with which Eugenia and the other relatives and acquaintances of the Spada family reacted to the birth of a baby, then clearly the expectations concerning the gender of children were guided by a twofold consideration: the number of children and the balance between males and females. This dual awareness oriented female reactions, and Eugenia's letters over the years showed her deep assimilation of these principles.[35]

THE SEARCH FOR A WET NURSE

The dialogue between mother and daughter and the concerns surrounding the pregnancy show that the search for a wet nurse was by far the most important of all of the preparations for the birth. Wet-nursing was still the norm for child rearing in the aristocracy of the seventeenth century, even though the strong pact between the father of the baby and the husband of the wet nurse, which had been the basis for sending out the baby to an external wet nurse in Renaissance Florence,[36] was not one of the essential aspects of the system in Rome. By the mid-seventeenth century, the choice of the wet nurse, who would live in the home of the baby's parents, lay firmly within the hands of the women of Roman aristocratic families. As revealed by Eugenia's letters to her mother and by the letters of Maria Spada—whose sphere of interest extended to the homes of many other families with whom the Spada family had relations—the choice of the wet nurse was entrusted to a female circle, whose members consulted one another, closely supervised the different "rearings," and were well acquainted with the qualities and defects of the various wet nurses. This female network developed into a sort of hidden but very efficient agency for the recruitment

[33]ASR, Archivio Spada Veralli, b. 410/3, letter of 18 April 1657.
[34]ASR, Archivio Spada Veralli, b. 410/3, letter of 21 March 1657.
[35]In 1660, on the occasion of the imminent birth of a baby to a sister-in-law, Eugenia emphasized the necessary balance between males and females as follows: "The Marchioness Astalli has sent for a midwife and by now she will have given birth, and it really should be a male because she has had so few, and when she has baby girls I know that she is very upset." In 1661, she expressed the belief that it was better for the firstborn baby to be a boy. ASR, Archivio Spada Veralli, b. 1115, letters of 13 October 1660 and 7 September 1661.
[36]In Florence, it was the father who chose the wet nurse and who reached an agreement with the husband of the woman. See Christiane Klapisch-Zuber, *Women, Family, and Ritual in Renaissance Italy,* trans. Lydia Cochrane (Chicago: University of Chicago Press, 1985), 143–44. A different opinion is held by Louis Haas, "Women and Childbearing in Medieval Florence," in *Medieval Family Roles: A Book of Essays,* ed. Cathy Jorgensen Itnyre (New York: Garland Publishing, 1996), 96.

of wet nurses. Husbands or fathers played only a marginal and supporting role. For instance, they might check the time at which a wet nurse had given birth if she lived in a family feudal possession in the countryside, or they might take care of sending the wages to the wet nurse's husband. More than a recognition of male authority, the functions performed by the men were in keeping with the greater mobility of men's lives in that period.

A chorus of voices took part in the search for a wet nurse, and most of the female relations, including those who had taken the veil, seemed to have something to say in a choice that was very meaningful from the point of view of family relations and sensibilities. There was a sort of hidden competition between the family of the husband and that of the wife as to who would have the final say on this matter. The choice of the wet nurse was not only, or at least not exclusively, an expression of the mother's wish, though she did make her personal inclinations known. Rather, it seemed to be the result of a complex system that took several elements into account, including a careful harmonization of family influence, a respect for generational hierarchies, and the approval of husbands, as well as the acceptance of both the future mother and the wet nurse. At the end of the negotiation process, the wet nurse's husband could also exercise a right of veto. The shift of wet-nursing from "men's business" to "women's business" did not translate automatically into a possibility for a mother to impose her will. On the occasion of the birth of her first child, the mother was usually given greater autonomy than in the balance of relations and generational hierarchies that would be sought at the time of subsequent births.

The mother's will did have an impact in this age. Eugenia's position was very clear: child rearing was to remain narrowly within her competence, and she was to be independent and free from the influence and interference of her mother-in-law, which would have been inevitable if the wet nurse had been chosen in Viterbo. In this latter case, Pacifica would have been able to meddle in everything that happened in the house of her son and daughter-in-law "as she does now when she wants to know how many steps we take."[37] Eugenia, therefore, opted for a wet nurse from Castel Viscardo, from one of those families that customarily sent their women to Rome to nurse the Spada offspring.[38] However, at the time of later births, the mother had to comply with the delicate balance of relationships. In 1657, following lengthy consultations which had started in the third month of pregnancy, the final choice fell on Caterina, who in the past had brought up two of Eugenia's brothers, and who agreed to leave Castel Viscardo and to raise Eugenia's firstborn son. The situation at the time of the birth of the couple's second child,

---

[37]ASR, Archivio Spada Veralli, b. 410/3, letter of 10 January 1657. A similar position seeking independence from her mother-in-law's control was expressed by Eugenia during the search for the wet nurse of her third baby. ASR, Archivio Spada Veralli, b. 1115, letter of 25 August 1660.

[38]All the wet nurses of Maria Spada's fourteen children for whom we have records came from Castel Viscardo, a feudal possession of the Spada family.

Olimpia, was very different. Pacifica Maidalchini not only imposed a wet nurse chosen by herself but personally took care of her granddaughter for a certain period of time, much to Eugenia's anger and displeasure. In the autumn of 1660, when Eugenia was expecting her third child, she wrote that she would do anything rather than go through such an experience again.[39]

The real novelty in the female management of wet-nursing in the seventeenth-century aristocracy was that no wet nurses were chosen without the mother-to-be and the woman who was to nurse her baby having met face to face. There are many traces in the Spada correspondence of the "investigations" of wet nurses (this is, significantly, the term used by women in that time to describe their interviews with the would-be wet nurses), and there are many accounts of the outcomes of these encounters. In this setting, where female networks played a much more active role than in Renaissance Florence, the guidelines that led to the preference of one wet nurse over another appear to have been less complex than in the past. For instance, the time-honored principle of "fresh milk" could be ignored if the circumstances so required, and a wet nurse who had already breast-fed one baby could be used for the next baby after the weaning of the first. Also, the wet nurse's age was not as important as it once had been.

With the passage of the selection of the wet nurse into female hands, another remarkable development occurred: the wet nurses themselves negotiated their wages and the conditions of their employment with the families. They showed a clear understanding of the value of the service they offered and also had an acute perception of the special favor that rearing the children of the noble families would have afforded their family as a whole. This explains the devices adopted at times by the wet nurse's family to win or to be reconfirmed in a service that was likely to bring many advantages over the years. The first precaution was to hide from sight any children who did not turn out "well," as the health and robustness of the wet nurse's children had become one of the most important criteria for recruitment into the select group of well-reputed wet nurses.[40] Rather oddly, if compared to the elaborate process of choosing a wet nurse, the selection of the midwife and the evaluation of the skill of a woman who was to play such an important role in the birth of the baby appeared to be a low-key, undramatic choice, at least judging by the scarcity of comments on this subject in the correspondence.[41]

Uncertainty concerning the timing of delivery made the last months of pregnancy the most tiring, marked as they were by an indefinable restlessness: "I have not

---

[39] ASR, Archivio Spada Veralli, b. 1115, letter of 26 September 1660.

[40] This is what happened in 1669, when the first child of Eugenia and Girolamo Mattei was born. Eugenia had a negative impression of a woman called Rosaria, who was appreciated by her mother and sister, because she said that the woman had hidden her last son, "who they say is very ugly," from her sight. ASR, Archivio Spada Veralli, b.1115, letter of 25 September 1669.

[41] ASR, Archivio Spada Veralli, b. 410/3, letter of 1 April 1657.

been able to sleep for four or five days, and I keep twisting and turning in my bed," wrote Eugenia to her mother on 25 April. The movements of the baby were carefully monitored by Eugenia who by then could perceive them clearly and so described them to her mother: "I feel the baby down below, I can feel the whole baby, but usually I feel the baby to the right, close to the mouth of my stomach."[42] The purpose of these descriptions was obviously twofold: Eugenia wanted to reassure her mother that all was well and that the baby was alive, and she also wished to draw auspices from the position it took concerning the sex of the baby to be born.[43] As Eugenia clearly stated in 1660, after having given birth to her third child, "when you are at the end, every day seems like a month."[44]

In May 1657, when the alarm about the plague epidemic had subsided, the quarantine was lifted in Rome and Maria Spada, even though she had delivered her last baby only five months earlier, left to join her daughter in Viterbo so as to be with her at the time of delivery. The grandmother's presence at childbirth, which was the true rite of passage for women,[45] meant that we have no accounts on the birth of Innocenzo, Eugenia's firstborn son.

MOTHER AND SON

In the months following childbirth, when Eugenia resumed her correspondence with her mother,[46] what emerged were her concerns about the forced blocking of lactation and the consequences that this could have, as well as a report on the daily life of the baby. It is hard to overemphasize the problems and worries that the blocking of lactation represented for these young mothers, who were obliged by their family's priorities to privilege fecundity over their relationship with their babies. While there are few clues to the medical approach at that time, thanks to Eugenia's comments we can at least understand the dramatic nature of those moments and roughly outline the inventory of therapeutic remedies. The threat of mastitis was dealt with by using blocking agents, injected with a syringe, and by surgical incisions for the expulsion of pus if other treatments were unsuccessful. Eugenia underwent both procedures and anticipated with terror the time when she would have to squeeze her breast back into her bodice once again. The operation had to be completed within forty days so that the woman could go to church. Eugenia repeatedly tried to reassure her mother that all was fine: "Believe me, I am well: my breasts have almost healed and they are back to the size they used to be, both the one that was cut when

---

[42]ASR, Archivio Spada Veralli, letter of 14 March 1657.

[43]For examples of the beliefs concerning the prediction of the baby's sex based on the position taken by the baby in the womb and the shape of the mother's belly in non-Italian contexts, see Mireille Laget, *Naissances: L'accouchement avant l'âge de la clinique* (Paris: Editions du Seuil, 1982), 84–93.

[44]ASR, Archivio Spada Veralli, b. 1115, letter of 29 December 1660.

[45]See Crawford, "The Construction and Experience," 21.

[46]Eugenia's letters to her mother ceased in early June 1657, just before her delivery and the arrival of Maria Spada in Viterbo, and resumed on July 15 of that same year.

your honored ladyship was here and the other one too, although I have not squeezed either of them because they are oozing a little."[47] The mother insistently asked about how the breasts were healing and offered her advice. The blocking of lactation resulted in different forms of pathology in the lives of the aristocratic women. In some cases, it meant that the months between one pregnancy and the next were an extremely difficult period, not at all like the period of rest that many imagine would be enjoyed by women who entrusted their children to a wet nurse.

The second theme of the letters was the daily life of the baby. The letters reflected many of the attitudes that were typical of families of this social class and their approach to child rearing and health. They also reveal some previously unknown facts and deviations from what used to be considered the current practice of the period. Prompt suckling was generally considered to be a sign of the baby's vitality, and this explains the proud publicity given by Eugenia to the feeding feats of little Innocenzo: "The wet nurse says," wrote the young mother, "that Innocentio sucks much more than Liberata and Guido did and that one breast was enough for them, but Innocentio wants both."[48] A less well known habit of that period was the integration of a milk diet with bread and water mush from the third month onwards.[49]

Choosing the right time for weaning was a crucial concern, in which all sorts of precautions were required. To judge from Eugenia's letters, weaning was a cause of great anxiety for the mother, who in most cases took responsibility for this decision. In the Spada family, child weaning was followed very closely, with a degree of flexibility, and it offered abundant subject matter for a steady stream of comments and suggestions between mother and daughter, especially when the baby refused to give up the breast. In 1662, the letters offered a lively portrait of the difficulties that Andrea, Eugenia's third son, experienced in this delicate transition and the mother's relief when the situation returned to normal.[50] Eugenia's description aptly portrays what was to become a common habit in the lives of many mothers in the centuries to come. "Weaning," wrote Eugenia to her mother on 16 April 1662, "was not as easy as I had thought because after the first day Andrea did not want to eat anything but broth with egg yolk, bread crumbs, and liquid to drink; and I tried many types of soups, and he did not want any. And he does not eat bread in the soup, but he sucks it well and then spits it out; and because I put some bread crumbs in the broth this morning, he did not want it and we were not able to force him to drink it. He was a little queer, but today he seems more cheerful; in the evening he falls asleep

---

[47]ASR, Archivo Spada Veralli, b. 1115, letter of 29 December 1660.

[48]ASR, Archivio Spada Veralli, b. 410/3, letter of 15 July 1657.

[49]ASR, Archivio Spada Veralli, letters of 23 September and 17 October 1657. For the medical literature on child rearing and weaning, see Peter Garnsey, "Child Rearing in Ancient Italy," in *The Family in Italy from Antiquity to the Present*, ed. David I. Kertzer and Richard P. Saller (New Haven: Yale University Press, 1991), 48–65.

[50]ASR, Archivio Spada Veralli, b.1115, letter of 16 April 1662.

immediately, and during the night he is good sometimes and sometimes not." At the end of her letter, Eugenia noted a reassuring detail for the future: "Andrea today was better and he ate two slices of dry bread."

In the Spada family, the attention given to the baby's reactions when breast-feeding was ended was only the beginning of the close relationship between mother and children, which was tested most severely during the various childhood diseases. Eugenia provided a rough description of her children's diseases, which became much more careful and detailed when the fevers lasted a long time and were a true cause for alarm. Accounts of the childhood diseases, just like those of adults, were a common subject in family correspondence in the sixteenth and seventeenth centuries, and there are plentiful examples. These records did not always, however, contain such a wealth of detail on the remedies adopted as may be found in this dialogue between mother and daughter. It is also rare to find such a sensitivity to the subjective reactions of the little patients as Eugenia showed toward her children. Her descriptions were enlivened by comments on the children's moods and humor, which were often the focal point of the story. This sensitivity was not unimportant, as her attentiveness to her children's reactions guided Eugenia's dialogue with the physicians, which led at times to clashes and to her decision to disobey the doctor's orders. A typical example of this was Eugenia's behavior in August 1658, when her elder son, Innocenzo, developed a hernia. After trying to treat it with an oil to no avail and prescribing total immobility, which was very hard to achieve in a one-year-old baby, the physician suggested using an iron belt. The mother rejected this solution because of "his great crying, so much that I had to take it off, and I never want to try to put it back on him again."[51] The therapeutic approach to the main childhood diseases was equally rich and diverse. This latter aspect deserves greater study in order to understand the different types of medical remedies and the various forms of female knowledge.

Eugenia gave birth to four children in five years, which meant an average spacing of little over fourteen months between one child and the next. If her husband had not died, the young woman would most probably have followed in her mother's footsteps. It is hard to gain insight into Eugenia's feelings about the succession of pregnancies, which occurred at a more rapid pace than that to which the Florentine wives studied by Christiane Klapisch-Zuber were accustomed. Certainly, that feeling of intimate pride with which she welcomed her first pregnancy was not voiced at later times. One aspect that Eugenia's letters described very effectively was the atmosphere of control exercised by the older generations over the bodies of the young wives, the sites of reproduction. The expropriation of the woman's corporeal and sexual intimacy, and the collective and familial appropriation of the female body were the counterpoint to the familial protection which the young aristocratic brides enjoyed. And while the control exercised by Eugenia's own mother was compensated

---

[51]ASR, Archivio Spada Veralli, b.1115, letter of 8 September 1658.

for by her practical help and caring attitudes, her mother-in-law's control was at times exasperating and intolerable.

An episode suggestive of the sort of oversight that the family had on the woman's body took place in July 1658. In that period, Eugenia had already had a one-year-old child, and she had a hard time dispelling rumors concerning a new pregnancy. Despite the young woman's denial, her mother-in-law was convinced that she was pregnant and talked about it with Maria Spada in Rome, who immediately wrote a letter to her daughter asking her to confirm it. Upset about the rumors circulating behind her back, Eugenia wrote to her mother revealing both the forms of interference of the families and the weak sort of rebellion that young women could afford: "I hear that the Marchioness has told you that the time passed by ten or twelve days but it is not true; the period came to me on the very right day, but I did not want to tell her so. I told her that it was not the right time because I did not want her to know when my period was due, and in fact this time it came six days early."[52]

Certainly, Eugenia's acceptance of her second, third, and fourth children was not the same as it had been in the case of her firstborn. Caring for her children, whether it was the weaning of one or the sickness of another, fully absorbed her energy and detracted not only from the sort of attention that she could dedicate to her emotional life and fears, but also from the involvement she could have with the last-born child. As the family grew in size, a baby no longer seemed to attract the mother's attention to a great extent unless a wet nurse's sickness raised the fear of having to look for a sudden and difficult replacement, which brought the newborn baby back to the center of the mother's concern.[53] There are many hints of this lessening in attention, such as earlier weaning, along with the fact that the timing of this may have been left by Eugenia to her mother-in-law (as in the case of her second-born daughter, Olimpia, who died in August 1661, only a few months after having been weaned[54]) or to the wet nurse (in the case of her fourth child, Cecilia). It is also true that Eugenia's distance from the weaning of her daughters was due to such inescapable difficulties as giving birth to a new baby in the autumn of 1660, and the problems arising from the death of her husband in the summer of 1662.

Domenico Maidalchini died only a few months after the birth of their last child. Eugenia's long stay with her elder son in Rome to organize her return to her parents' house kept her away from the baby girl for many months. She was to describe Cecilia's gifts and the reactions of the baby to weaning one year later, in October 1663, as if she were recounting a happy discovery.[55]

---

[52]ASR, Archivio Spada Veralli, b.1115, letter of 9 July 1658.

[53]ASR, Archivio Spada Veralli, b.1115, letter of 6 August 1662.

[54]Eugenia commented on the death of her daughter in these words: "Well, the loss of a child is a great sorrow, and I felt it early, and I felt it so much that it seems to me as if she has been robbed from me, and I always think about her" (ASR, Archivio Spada Veralli, b.1115, letter of 14 August 1661).

[55]ASR, Archivio Spada Veralli, b.1115, letter of 17 October 1663.

The central role enjoyed by the firstborn son was not accorded, therefore, to the other children. The novelty of having a child and her curiosity about a first-time experience seemed to have led Eugenia to follow Innocenzo's development more closely. Eugenia was later to summarize the situation in a formula: "Now that I have three children, so as not to recite the litanies, I will simply say that in general they are all well."[56]

WIDOWHOOD

In the summer of 1662, at only twenty-four years of age, Eugenia was widowed. She resigned herself to this condition and was once again sheltered by her family. Her brother Bernardino, then twenty-three years old, rushed to Viterbo at the first signs of Domenico Maidalchini's serious illness, and took care of his sister after the death of her husband, helping her in her first duties as a widow. The letters sent by Bernardino to his father in this circumstance show how the family guaranteed the estate of one of its members in a decisive moment, while Eugenia's letters reveal the sort of supervision that her mother, Maria Spada, had over the clothes and behavior suitable for a newly widowed woman.[57] As a widow, Eugenia was able to fulfill her dearest wish, which was to return to Rome and live with her mother. Her husband's will appointed her guardian and administrator of their children and expressly allowed her to move to Rome and live with her children there for six months of the year.

It took all her father's ability to convince Eugenia to accept a second marriage, to Duke Girolamo Mattei, which was of use to the Spada family strategy. A long letter from Orazio bears witness to his persuasion. While understanding Eugenia's wish not to leave her children, he carefully pointed out the advantages that would accrue to both Eugenia and her children from the more prestigious social position of the mother.[58] However, the loss of guardianship and separation from her children was a trial for Eugenia. The only comfort in this harsh separation was the permission that Eugenia obtained from her second husband to keep her youngest child, Cecilia, by her side. In the autumn of 1666, the two male children were handed over by Maria Spada to Pacifica Maidalchini, who took them to live with her in Viterbo, as the laws on guardianship provided. This transfer was very painful for Eugenia "because as long as they were in your hands [those of her mother, Maria Spada] I felt as if I could see them again soon."[59]

---

[56]ASR, Archivio Spada Veralli, b.1115, letter of 29 December 1660.

[57]For the letters of Bernardino Spada, see ASR, Archivio Spada Veralli, b. 627, esp. ff. 251–72. For the correspondence between mother and daughter, see b. 1115, letters of 20 and 27 August 1662, as well as the letters of 2 and 10 September.

[58]The letter is a masterpiece in the rhetoric of persuasion, and the most important passages have already been published by Casanova, "Le donne come risorsa," 73–74. A brief account of Eugenia's long refusal to accept a second marriage and of the negotiations and the marriage by proxy with Mattei is contained in *Memorie domestiche...di Orazio Spada* in ASR, Archivio Spada Veralli, b. 285. For the marriage contract, see ASR, Archivio Spada Veralli, b. 359, no. 508.

[59]ASR, Archivio Spada Veralli, b. 1115, letter of 23 October 1666.

In the meantime, Eugenia tried her best to induce Mattei to accept her young-est daughter, Cecilia. She had to strike a difficult balance between her duties as a wife and those of a mother. There are many traces of this in her letters to her own mother: the painstaking care with which Cecilia's arrival was prepared, the anxiety with which Eugenia observed the first signs of a possible bond developing between her daughter and her second husband, and the interest with which she followed her husband's trips, hoping that they would take her to Viterbo, where she could see her children again.[60] These visits, however, risked reopening wounds and creating a con-flict between the siblings. Eugenia showed that she was painfully aware of this possi-bility: "The Duke is thinking about going to San Martino this week and I like the idea of being able to see my children again, but I know it will be all the more painful when I have to leave them, and I do not know whether I would do the right thing to bring Cecilia along."[61]

For the time being, all Eugenia could do was to wait for more favorable circum-stances and use her influence and the mediation of her father whenever she disagreed with her mother-in-law's decisions. This was the case, for instance, regarding the choice of the future education of the elder son, Innocenzo. Eugenia would have liked to see him study in a college in Rome, while the mother-in-law wanted him to live in Viterbo so that he "will learn to love the possessions."[62] Besides these negotiations, additional direct evidence of Eugenia's involvement in the guardianship of her mother-in-law was the frequent correspondence between Eugenia and Ippolito Pieri, the man who in practice administered the orphans' estate. The young woman, who knew virtually nothing and had needed the practical advice of Bernardino in 1662 after her husband's death, was later to become strongly aware of her role as a guard-ian and administrator of her children's estate.

In 1660, Eugenia gave birth to her second husband's first and only child, Alessandro. The fact that she had given a long awaited heir to a family nearing extinction made it possible for her, as her father had hoped, to take on a role of great prestige in the life of the Mattei family. It also imposed strict self-discipline and a limitation on her contacts with her children from her first marriage, at least in the beginning, to avoid any risk of infection to the newborn. Clearly, the way she kept away from her daughter, Cecilia, who had had a "mild case of smallpox" in the sum-mer of 1673, was due to her fear of infecting Alessandro. Describing the virulence of the disease in her usual style, which was so attentive to her children's feelings, Euge-nia wrote, "I have never heard anyone moan as much as she did." She also observed that "what bothers Cecilia most is that she has come to Giove to stay in bed and receives little attention, because for the love of Alessandro no one goes near her, and I only so very little, but I am sorry about it, even though I know that she is wanting

[60]ASR, Archivio Spada Veralli, b. 1115, letter of 30 October 1666.
[61]ASR, Archivio Spada Veralli, b. 1115, letter of 30 October 1666.
[62]ASR, Archivio Spada Veralli, b. 1115, letter of 9 November 1666.

for nothing."[63] Eugenia's project in the long run was to foster the emotional bonding of all her children from her first and second marriages, just as the Florentine noblewoman Maddalena Nerli Tornabuoni had done around 1630, as described by Giulia Calvi.[64]

The case of Eugenia Maidalchini reveals the precise limitations imposed upon mother guardians by the law. But it shows equally well how the emotional and social bonds between mothers and children from a first marriage could be maintained even after a second marriage and the loss of guardianship. Eugenia's experience may be viewed either as an interesting exception in aristocratic circles, or as an expression of a way of conducting family affairs where there was a nominal guardian, who could in practice be limited or contained, and on the other hand there was a mother who, although deprived of all formal powers, still tried in all ways to influence the guardian and to take over his role in the care and education of minor children.[65] In this case, this form of dual administration was made much easier by the solid family culture of the Spadas, who had an outstanding family ethos,[66] and by the fact that the guardianship was basically the business of two women. The first, the guardian, was the grandmother, old and not looking to make life more difficult for herself, and therefore ready to accept forms of lessened responsibility. The other woman was the young mother, who could rely on the support of a network of relations who mediated her desire to maintain her bond with her children from her first marriage.

CONCLUSION

The life of Eugenia Maidalchini depicts the experience of motherhood with a sense of immediacy and a depth of understanding that are far removed from the moral maxims of that time and the dry pronouncements of medical thinkers. It is an extraordinary compendium of the main problems in the experience of maternity for the elite of the *ancien régime*. It offers a glimpse into the interweaving of maternities in the different generations of aristocratic families at different stages of their life cycle which was so typical of this period. It also reveals the host of therapeutic remedies to which the bodies of mother and children were subjected. When Eugenia was giving birth to her children and taking her first steps along the path traced by her mother before her, her mother was weaning her last child, her sister had married and become a mother in her turn, and her younger brothers were just beginning to go outdoors to play.

For the young woman, her dialogue with her mother was the basic feature of her apprenticeship in motherhood and the many duties that motherhood entailed in

---

[63]ASR, Archivio Spada Veralli, b. 1115, letter of 14 October 1673.

[64]See Calvi, *Il contratto morale*, 60–61.

[65]Even though the guardian was in all cases responsible before the law for the administration; see Thomas, "The Division of the Sexes in Roman Law," 130-31.

[66]There are steady signs of relations between Orazio and Maria Spada and their Maidalchini grandchildren during the years of Eugenia's second marriage, from summer holidays spent at Castel Viscardo to educational journeys. On this, see ASR, Archivio Spada Veralli, b. 1113, letter of 29 May 1677.

the public sphere, just as much as in private life. Especially at the beginning, her correspondence was full of the tiny daily problems that a timid young woman had to face for the first time when she was confronted with this experience. The dialogue between mother and daughter was not without some dissimulation, but it was essential for channelling Eugenia's emotions and anxiety, and enabling her to voice her many needs: from that of having a wet nurse who would allow the young mother to feel independent of her mother-in-law's control, to the way to cope with her children's diseases, and finally, for the parenting role of the Spada family for Eugenia's children from her first marriage.

A marriage arranged by parents was not solely a form of compliance with the family's interest, which required building a web of alliances. At least in the Spada family, it also meant that the daughter could count on an active and caring attitude towards her future life and a possibility of negotiating over time between the imperatives of the older generation and the problems faced by the younger generation. Eugenia's experience of maternity perfectly matched the cultural models of her social class and the instructions of her own mother. Not only was the wet-nursing system fully assimilated, but the model of domestic intimacy described in Eugenia's letters was not at all unlike that of the Spada family in the 1640s and 1650s. Eugenia's interest in her children, the feeding patterns she adopted, her concern about weaning, her attention to the children's physical well-being, her sensitivity to their emotional reactions, her way of coping with diseases, and her relations with the various physicians she consulted were all very much the same as those seen in her mother, Maria Spada. Regarding child care, the aristocratic culture of the second half of the seventeenth century showed a great continuity between the mothers' generation and that of their daughters. The minor differences between the advice offered by Maria Spada and the solutions adopted by her daughter were linked to adjustments the Maidalchini family made to the rural context in which they lived, where social obligations were fewer than those of the Spada family in Rome. There were no real breaks with a tradition that included the experience of maternity among the social obligations that an aristocratic woman had to fulfill.

Other new developments that characterized motherhood in these social classes, from the direct link between mother and wet nurse, to the more spectacular versions of the visits paid to the new mother, suggest both the cares and worries of child rearing and an aristocratic socialization which was ever more conditioned by class awareness and relations. The cultural universe suggested by the letters concerning the diseased body and therapeutic measures shows a great continuity between the generation of the mothers and the daughters. The influence of medical thinking on the treatment of children had already become clear by this period, and not only among the wealthier families of the upper classes.[67] But it was equally obvious that a trove mother's sensitivity in perceiving her child's reactions, and her access to a treasure of

---

[67]On the socially diverse clientele of physicians in the Italian cities of the *ancien régime*, see Gianna Pomata, *La promessa di guarigione: Malati e curatori in Antico Regime* (Rome: Laterza, 1994).

female knowledge and experience in coping with the most common problems, were powerful filters against an all-pervasive medicalization.

Eugenia's approach to her children was certainly not that professional approach that the physician Heroard had towards his small but exceptional patient, Louis XIII, as handed down to us in his memoirs, to which we owe much of our knowledge about infancy and the relations between adults and children in the seventeenth century.[68] Eugenia's descriptions focused on some aspects, such as prompt suckling, good appetite, physical strength, and other signs which her culture considered to be evidence of vitality, but she ignored many others. We know little about many of the stages of growth of the noble Maidalchini youngsters after their first years of life. But we do know something about the sort of sudden panic that can seize a two-year-old child facing the prospect of travelling in a carriage, and the gentle understanding with which a mother was able to cope with this sort of crisis.[69] We are the spectators of the pleasure of a walk in the countryside for mother and son.[70] We can imagine the children as they show off their little achievements, and the pleasure and pride of the mother and father looking on. A mother's eye caught from a few traits the emergence of extroverted personalities or of more bashful characters, and she patiently accepted sudden regressions, such as that of her third child, Andrea, who after a few weeks of sickness, during which he lay between life and death, refused to start walking again and wanted to be held in her arms.[71]

The outlook on children that Maria Spada and her daughter Eugenia set forth would seem different from that of women of the late sixteenth century, at least within the Veralli Spada family itself. In fact, if we make a comparison between the epistolary space given to maternal identity by Maria and Eugenia Spada, and that given to it in the 1590s by Geronima Veralli, Maria Spada's aunt, we see how Geronima Veralli appears less inclined to fill her letters to her brother Giovan Battista with the day-to-day realities of motherhood.[72] This lack of detail, however, is not directly equivalent, so far as we know, to a lesser involvement in the daily well-being of the children. The fact that Geronima Veralli addressed a male interlocutor, linked with the pressing economic difficulties besetting her and which constituted the principal subject matter of her communication with the head of the family, can justify in part the differences in style and the preference given to certain topics.

The experience of maternity for Maria Spada and her daughter, Eugenia Maidalchini, was certainly different from that of the female generations of the late sixteenth

---

[68]On the atypical features of this childhood, see Sara Micotti, "Un'infanzia ambigua: Luigi XIII bambino nel Journal di Heroard," *Quaderni storici* 57 (1984): 793–818.

[69]ASR, Archivio Spada Veralli, b. 1115, letter of 2 April 1662.

[70]ASR, Archivio Spada Veralli, b. 624, letter of 17 October 1673.

[71]ASR, Archivio Spada Veralli, b. 624, letter of 23 July 1662.

[72]ASR, Archivio Spada Veralli, b. 465. For a preliminary reading of Geronima Veralli's letters, see Marina d'Amelia, "'Una lettera a settimana': Geronima Veralli Malatesta al Signor Fratello, 1575–1622," *Quaderni storici* 83 (1993): 381–413.

century, who were not only less inclined to fill their letters with the daily reality of motherhood, but were also less emotionally involved in their relations with and the destinies of their children. In these seventeenth-century families, as far as maternal care was concerned, the order in which the children were born mattered more than the male or female gender of the children; but this disparity, which was quite common in the early years of life of the children, became less important later on, when the mother's role was to help her adolescent sons make choices befitting their rank and help her daughters in their life as mothers. The letters of Eugenia to her mother, which showed her craving for reassurance and intimacy, offer many examples of the heavy responsibility borne by mothers in their life cycle. Maria Spada's responsibilities extended well beyond the need to bring up her own numerous children, to supporting her daughters and daughters-in-law. The main contradiction between being a wife and a mother, which was characteristic of the medieval world, was compounded by a new contradiction in the maternal role that developed in the seventeenth century. The pace of childbearing obliged them to a reproductive tour de force, which meant that the mother's presence for her various children could at best be discontinuous and uneven. However, women experienced their maternity in a family climate that induced them to develop an intense involvement in the physical and psychological well-being of their offspring, both as young children and as adults.[73]

---

[73]I am grateful to Valerie Conklin for translating this chapter into English.

Space, Time, and the Power of Aristocratic Wives in Yorkist and Early Tudor England, 1450–1550

Barbara J. Harris

One night in March 1534, Thomas Howard, the third duke of Norfolk, arrived at Kenninghall, his main residence, in a furious rage. He grabbed his wife, locked her up, and seized all her clothes and jewelry. Shortly thereafter he moved her to a house in Hertfordshire, where she remained a virtual prisoner until 1547. The effective end of the Norfolks' marriage was the final act in a drama that had begun eight years earlier, when the duke took a woman named Bess Holland as his mistress and installed her at Kenninghall over his wife's protests. In the years that followed, the Norfolks' quarrels became more and more public, creating an open scandal at court and goading the duke into physically abusing his wife in a futile effort to silence her. He finally resolved the situation by expelling her, not his mistress, from their home.[1]

In the same decades, Sir William Paget, one of Norfolk's colleagues on Henry VIII's Privy Council, enjoyed an entirely different kind of marriage. Paget praised his wife as "obedient, wise, gentle and chaste." In 1545 he collapsed in despair when he heard, falsely as it turned out, that his wife had died. "If she be dead, I am the most unhappy man in the world," he wrote, "and desire no longer to live, for it is the plague of god that is fallen upon me...."[2] Three days later, he declared that his heart was about "to burst for pain and anguish. The world is but a vanity, which, as I have always thought in opinion, so now the experience of my great grief and regret does confirm it in me."[3]

The Norfolks and Pagets provide opposite examples of the emotional relationships that developed among Yorkist and early Tudor aristocratic couples. Between

---

[1]For a full account of this dramatic story, see Barbara J. Harris, "Marriage Sixteenth-Century Style: Elizabeth Stafford and the Third Duke of Norfolk," *Journal of Social History* 15, no. 3 (spring 1982): 371–82.

[2]Public Record Office (henceforth PRO), SP1/199, f. 176 (1545).

[3]PRO, SP1/199, f. 209.

these extremes lay a wide variety of marriages characterized by different degrees of emotional intensity and of couples who cooperated more or less successfully in promoting their families' political and economic interests. In recent years, recognition of this variety has led historians to discard the previously hegemonic, oversimplified model which assumed that arranged marriages necessarily produced cool, deeply hierarchical marital relationships.[4] They have replaced it with recognition that arranged matches had many different emotional outcomes and that the degree and intensity of women's subordination to their husbands varied from couple to couple within the limits set by law and custom.[5] In practice, women's contributions to the fortunes of their marital families had a major influence on the degree of power and autonomy they exercised as wives. A more nuanced picture of the emotional relationships between aristocratic couples in the period has therefore been created.

Despite this revision, however, historians have continued to treat wifehood itself as a relatively static role, both temporally and spatially. From a spatial point of view, they have taken the exclusion of aristocratic women from public or political affairs too literally, and inaccurately conflated private concerns with interior, domestic spaces. As a result, they have exaggerated wives' confinement to and isolation in their great country houses. From a temporal point of view, the strategy of organizing studies of the family around the life cycle has encouraged historians to conceptualize women's lives in terms of their sequential roles as daughters, wives, and widows. In England, the common-law doctrine of coverture, which literally meant that husbands effaced their wives' legal personhood, has reinforced this tendency to treat wifehood as a unified role, since it created a unique legal category that distinguished wives from all other adult women and from all men.

I shall argue in contrast that wifehood was a temporally and spatially complex stage of life that changed markedly as women moved through the uxorial cycle.[6] Wives were sequentially dependent young brides and mothers, inexperienced managers of their own households, and mature women whose responsibilities were crucial to their families' prosperity. In the case of some wives—those who died in

---

[4]Lawrence Stone, *The Family, Sex, and Marriage in England 1500–1800* (London: Weidenfeld and Nicolson, 1977), esp. 85–91, 102–5.

[5]For revisionist work, see for example, Keith Dockray, "Why Did Fifteenth-Century English Gentry Marry? The Pastons, Plumptons, and Stonors Reconsidered," in *Gentry and Lesser Nobility in Late Medieval England*, ed. Michael Jones (New York: St. Martin's, 1986), 61–80; Amy Louise Erickson, *Women and Property in Early Modern England* (London: Routledge, 1993); Ann S. Haskell, "The Paston Women on Marriage in Fifteenth-Century England," *Viator* 4 (1973): 459–71; Ralph Houlbrooke, *The English Family 1450–1700* (London: Longman, 1984); Ann J. Kettle, "'My Wife Shall Have It': Marriage and Property in the Wills and Testaments of Later Medieval England," in *Marriage and Property*, ed. Elizabeth M. Craik (Aberdeen: Aberdeen University Press, 1984), 89–103; Colin Richmond, "The Pastons Revisited," *Bulletin of the Institute of Historical Research* 58 (1985): 25–36; Keith Wrightson, *English Society 1580–1680* (New Brunswick, N.J.: Rutgers University Press, 1982), 89–104.

[6]Stanley Chojnacki, "The Power of Love," in *Women and Power in the Middle Ages*, ed. Mary Erler and Maryanne Kowaleski (Athens, Ga.: University of Georgia Press, 1988), 128.

childbirth or whose marriages collapsed, for example—the whole cycle might well be attenuated. Furthermore, as they moved through the uxorial cycle, the places in which women lived and the spaces through which they moved expanded along with their responsibilities. Even when they remained in the country, aristocratic women regularly visited relatives and friends living in their neighborhoods and occasionally made longer journeys to visit their kin in other counties. They also went to London, often without their husbands, to conduct legal and family business of all kinds. Pilgrimages to local shrines, a customary part of contemporary religious life, provided another reason for wives to leave home. In addition, wives from families who held offices in the king's and queen's household moved continually between their great country houses, London residences, and the court, while a far wider group attended the court much more episodically to participate in major diplomatic events and royal family celebrations.

Even among mature wives, important differences existed among those in first and second marriages. Remarriage was a common if not typical experience among the aristocracy; in a sample of 2,557 women, 23.8 percent married two or more times. If one looks at the widows of peers, a much smaller group at the top of the aristocracy, remarriage was even more common—in a sample of 193 widowed noblewomen, 58.5 percent married more than once. In addition to their normal responsibilities, most remarried women managed their jointures or dowers, and acted as executors of their deceased spouses' wills and guardians of their children. Despite the disabilities of coverture, the common law held that a married woman could deal as fully as anyone else with property she administered as executor of a will, because wives were not personally incompetent, but suffered from specific proprietary incapacities.[7] The reality was that husbands trusted their widows more than anyone else to administer their estates: 77 percent (403) of a sample of 523 knights and noblemen with surviving wives appointed them executors or supervisors of their wills. Over a third of the 403 (139 or 34.5 percent) made them their sole executors.[8] Their choice is particularly striking because a large minority of the widows would remarry, which gave their new spouses the opportunity to meddle with their predecessors' property whatever the formal legal situation. Even so, only a tiny number of husbands—eight in our sample of 523—made their widows' appointments conditional on their remaining single. Men also gave their widows custody of their noninheriting minor and unmarried children:

---

[7] William Searle Holdsworth, *A History of English Law* (London: Methuen, 1923), 3:528.

[8] Ann J. Kettle found even higher percentages of men appointing their widows as their sole or coexecutors in the early fifteenth century, but because she drew it from a broader socioeconomic group, her sample was not precisely equivalent to mine. In a sample of 116 male testators with living wives between 1414 and 1443, 77.5 percent left wives as their executors; between 1280 and 1500, 80 percent of men with living wives in the Lincoln episcopal registers appointed them as their executors; in Bristol between 1381 and 1500, 82 percent of those whose names were entered in the Great Orphan Book did so; Kettle, "'My Wife Shall Have It,'" 100–1.

86 percent (ninety-eight) in a sample of 114.[9] Here too, they evidently felt that the advantages of leaving their offspring in the care of their mothers far outweighed the disadvantages of their widows' remarrying.

At the outset of their first marriages, aristocratic women usually remained under the tutelage of their parents and in-laws because they married young—almost always in their teens or very early twenties—and their husbands were usually of a similar age.[10] In a sample of forty-nine first-time brides, for example, thirty were under sixteen and eleven of the thirty were under twelve.[11] On the other hand, only one was over twenty-one. The length of the period when young couples lived in one of their parents' homes and continued to be treated much as they had been before their marriages depended, of course, on their ages. In the late fifteenth century, three of Sir John Howard's daughters married before they were sixteen and remained in their

[9]Wardship was the right of a feudal lord to custody of minor heirs (girls under fourteen; boys under twenty-one). The lord also had the right to arrange his wards' marriages and to collect the profits of their lands during their minorities. In the case of boys, only the inheriting son became a ward; in the case of girls, since they inherited as coheirs, they all became wards at the same time. In practice, since virtually all the members of the upper gentry and nobility held at least some lands as tenants-in-chief of the crown, almost all aristocratic minor heirs became the king's wards. The king's right of prerogative wardship meant that holding even one acre of land from the crown made an entire estate liable to wardship. The crown often sold its rights for profit.

[10]J. Hajnal, "European Marriage Patterns in Perspective," in *Population in History: Essays in Historical Demography*, ed. D. V. Glass and D. E. C. Eversley (Chicago: Aldine, 1965), 101, defines the Northern European marriage pattern, whose salient characteristics were high rates of celibacy and a relatively late age at first marriage. Hajnal does not think, however, that this pattern prevailed as early as the late fifteenth and early sixteenth century. He especially notes statistics about the aristocracy in arguing this point (113–20, 134). Alan Macfarlane argues forcefully that the northern European marriage pattern prevailed in England by the late medieval period, but even he explicitly notes that it did not apply to the landed aristocracy. Alan Macfarlane, *Marriage and Love in England: Modes of Reproduction 1300–1840* (Oxford: Basil Blackwell, 1986), 46–48.

[11]Marriage contracts from the period strongly suggest that however young the bride and groom were at the time of their betrothal, they postponed consummating, and sometimes also solemnizing, their marriages until they were both sixteen. See Essex Record Office (henceforth ERO), D/DP F143, marriage between John Tyrrell, son and heir of Sir Thomas of Heron, and Anne Brown, daughter of William, a citizen and alderman of London (1513); SP1/137, f. 43, marriage between Robert Constable, son and heir of Marmaduke, and Dorothy, daughter of Sir William Gascoigne (1532); Keith Docray, introduction to *The Plumpton Correspondence*, ed. Thomas Stapleton (Gloucester: Alan Sutton, 1990), 9, marriage between Robert Plumpton, son of Sir William, and Elizabeth, daughter of Lord Thomas Clifford (1446). Sometimes solemnization of the marriage took place before the bride and/or groom attained the age of sixteen; it is not clear, however, whether consummation also took place at this time. See *Calendar of Patent Rolls* (henceforth CPR), Edward VI, 1, 165, marriage of a daughter of Sir William Paget and Michael Pulteney, son and heir of Francis, esq. (1547); Warwickshire Record Office (WRO), Throckmorton Papers, CR 1998, Box 72, 3, marriage of John Conway, grandson of Edward, esq., to Mary Throckmorton, daughter of Robert, son and heir of Sir George (1544). Occasionally the marriage was (or was intended to be) consummated before the bride was sixteen. See British Library (BL), Additional Charters 73,901, marriage between Elizabeth, daughter of John Nevill, earl of Northumberland, and Thomas, Fifth Lord Scrope of Masham (1468).

father's household. In two of the cases, their husbands were his wards and were also therefore in residence. In the third, the fourteen-year-old groom resided with his mother and stepfather. The family accounts indicate that as long as the young women lived at home, the Howards treated them as dependent daughters.[12]

Arrangements of this sort continued well into the sixteenth century. Jane Paget and Thomas Kitson, who married in their mid-to-late teens in 1557 or 1558, lived with his mother, the countess of Bath.[13] In June of the latter year, Jane visited her parents while one of her sisters was lying-in at their London residence. Her father wrote to the countess asking for permission to extend Jane's stay with them because she was suffering from a condition he called green sickness. He hoped doctors in the city would be able to cure her.[14] A year and a half later, Jane visited her parents once again. This time Lady Paget thought her daughter was ill with consumption. She not only wanted her to remain at home indefinitely but hoped the countess would allow Jane's husband to join her. The countess's servant doubted Lady Paget's diagnosis— he remarked that her father thought Jane had never looked better—and suggested that her mother was inventing an excuse to keep her in London.[15]

---

[12]The three girls were Anne, Margaret, and Catherine. There is no record of Anne's age, but her mother had six children between 1443 and 1455. Anne was the fourth of the Howards' offspring and the second of their daughters. It is likely therefore that she was born by 1451. Anne appeared as Mistress Anne in the household accounts for 1467; if she were married, she would probably have been referred to as Mistress Gorges, as she was in an entry for 1482. Anne was almost certainly married at least a year before the child mentioned in the accounts for November 1481 was born. We have no way of knowing if this was her first child or if it was newborn at the time. Anne married her father's ward Edmund Gorges between 1468 and 1480. Margaret, the fifth of his children, married another of his wards, John Wyndham, in 1467. Catherine, his youngest child, was the daughter of Howard's second wife, whom he married c. January 1467. Catherine married Lord John Berners, whose mother married Sir John Howard's son Thomas as her second husband. Anne Crawford, *The Career of John Howard, Duke of Norfolk, 1420–1485* (Ph.D. diss., University of London, 1975), 103; *The Household Books of John Howard, Duke of Norfolk, 1462–71, 1481–83*, ed. Anne Crawford (Wolfeboro Falls, N.H.: Alan Sutton Publishing, 1992), xiii, xv–xvi, xxxviii; 1: 582; 2: 104, 152, 154, passim.

[13]Jane was the daughter of Sir William Paget, whose relationship with her mother we discussed above. He was created Lord Paget in 1549. Thomas was the countess's son by her first husband, Sir Thomas Kitson (d. 1540). The Kitson-Paget marriage took place between June 1557, when Lord Paget still referred to Thomas formally as Master Kitson and mentioned the possibility of the marriage obliquely, and the following year, when he spoke of "my daughter Kitson." Cambridge University Library (henceforth CUL), Hengrave Hall MS 88, 1: f. 91; f. 115.

[14]CUL, Hengrave Hall MS 88, 1: f. 115 (1558); Jane was married to Thomas Kitson II, the son of Margaret, countess of Bath by Sir Thomas Kitson, her first husband.

[15]CUL, Hengrave Hall MS 88, 1: f. 83 (1559); Jane's mother may well have been correct since she died by Nov. 1560; CUL, Hengrave Hall MS 88, 1: f. 88, f. 57. For another sixteenth-century example, see the first earl of Rutland's household, Historical Manuscript Commission (HMC), *Report on the Manuscripts of the Duke of Rutland, Belvoir*, 4 (London: HM Stationery Office, 1905): 295, 302–3, 306; the Rutlands' daughter, Gertrude, and her husband appear in the accounts as Lord and Lady Talbot; their eldest son and heir, styled Lord Roos, married to the earl of Westmorland's daughter Margaret, and their daughter Anne, styled Lady Nevill, married to Westmorland's son and heir, Henry, were also living at home. Although Anne's husband does not seem to be a member of the household, they must have cohabited at

As this discussion indicates, parents, not the young couple, decided where they would live. The decision often depended upon who had agreed to support them until the groom was old enough to receive the income assigned to them in their marriage contract or, if the groom's father was dead, until he came of age and gained possession of his inheritance. Thus, in 1458, the first duke of Buckingham assumed custody of Constance Green, the heiress marrying his younger son, and promised to support the young couple.[16] When Sir Thomas Lestrange's seventeen-year-old heir, Nicholas, married Ellen Fitzwilliam in 1528, he agreed to "govern" and support them and any children they had until Nicholas was twenty-one.[17]

The pattern of young marriage and residence with the brides' parents or in-laws meant that many women gave birth to some or all of their children before they had households of their own. Thus, Ursula Pole Stafford gave birth to her first child in the household of her father-in-law, the third duke of Buckingham, in 1519.[18] Three decades later, the earl of Rutland's daughter, Lady Anne Nevill, was living with her parents when her first child was born. Her contemporary Ellen Fitzwilliam Lestrange gave birth to all five of her children in her in-laws' household.[19] The presence of their mothers or mothers-in-law, who could give them practical assistance and emotional support during their confinements and deliveries, was one of the obvious ways young wives benefited from these living arrangements.

Residing with their in-laws did not mean that young wives ceased to be members of their natal families. Their parents and older siblings often contributed to

---

least occasionally, since she had at least one child during the period she resided at Belvoir after her marriage.

[16]Robert Halstead, *Succinct Genealogical Proofs of the House of Green* (London, 1685), 197.

[17]Norfolk Record Office (henceforth NRO), Lestrange of Hunstanton, A42; Cord Oestmann, *Lordship and Community: The Lestrange Family and the Village of Hunstanton, Norfolk, in the First Half of the Sixteenth Century* (Woodbridge, Suffolk: Boydell, 1994). Ellen was the daughter of Sir William Fitzwilliam, later created earl of Southampton.

[18]Barbara J. Harris, *Edward Stafford, Third Duke of Buckingham, 1478–1521* (Stanford: Stanford University Press, 1986), 56.

[19]Stanley T. Bindoff, *The House of Commons 1509–58* (London: Secker & Warburg, 1982), 2: 522; NRO, Lestrange of Hunstanton, A42. Ellen died less than three years after her father-in-law. Isabel Babthorpe Plumpton, wife of William, esq., who was married in 1496 and spent her entire married life at Plumpton, undoubtedly gave birth to her two sons there. Her father-in-law headed the household until 1515 and died in 1523; her mother-in-law survived him and continued to live at Plumpton. *The Plumpton Correspondence, cxxv; Plumpton Letters and Papers*, ed. Joan Kirby, Camden Society, 5th ser., 8 (1996): 192, 221, 229–31, 252; and appendix 2, 78. For other examples, see Calender of Close Rolls (henceforth CCR), Henry VII, vol. 2: 694 (Anne Grey, sister of Richard, earl of Kent, and Henry, son of Charles Somerset, Lord Herbert, 1506); Huntington Library, Hastings Collection, HAP Box 2, folder 28 (Anne, daughter of Sir Leonard Hastings and wife of Thomas, son of Thomas Ferrers, esq., 1448); *Willoughby Letters of the First Half of the Sixteenth Century*, ed. Mary A. Welch, Nottinghamshire Miscellany, no. 4, Thoroton Society, Record Series 24 (1967): 31, Anne, daughter of Thomas, 2nd marquess of Dorset, and Henry, son of Sir Edward Willoughby.

---

their support and intervened on their behalf in a wide variety of matters. Sir William Stonor, for example, apparently paid for his sister Mary's clothing after she married John Barentine. In a letter written in October 1476, his wife reported that the duchess of Suffolk was displeased because Mary, then living in her household, was "no better arrayed" and threatened to send her away if the situation were not corrected. Lady Stonor also warned that John's stepfather wanted the young couple to live with him and John's mother, and speculated that his motive was to get his hands on young Barentine's property. Five years later, Mary wrote to her brother herself because she suspected, rightly as it turned out, that her mother-in-law had convinced her son to sell some of his land. Mary, who was pregnant, was anxious to protect her jointure and her child's inheritance.[20]

Fifty years later, Charles Brandon, duke of Suffolk, kept a paternal eye on his daughter Eleanor following her marriage to the earl of Cumberland's heir.[21] During the Pilgrimage of Grace, he worried that his daughter was in danger "by reason of the rebels in your parts" and asked the earl to send her home if he could do so safely.[22] On another occasion, he expressed concern that Roche Abbey, where Eleanor and her husband were living, was unhealthy and asked Cumberland to give them his castle at Brougham instead."[23] Suffolk also took charge when the young couple went to London to participate in the celebrations surrounding Anne of Cleves's arrival in England to marry Henry VIII. On this occasion, both fathers contributed to the heavy expenses involved in clothing and otherwise equipping them in a style suiting their high rank.[24]

Wives entered the next phase of the uxorial cycle when they and their husbands became heads of their own households. If their fathers-in-law were dead, this stage of their lives began when their husbands turned twenty-one. Thus, Sir Robert Plumpton's daughter Anne and her husband, Germain Pole, lived with him during Pole's minority, but moved to Pole's estate in Derbyshire soon after he came of age in 1504.[25] Three decades later, Henry Grey, marquess of Dorset, and his wife took control of the Greys' family seat shortly after his twenty-first birthday.[26]

---

[20]Christine Carpenter, *Kingsford's Stonor Letters and Papers, 1290–1483* (Cambridge: Cambridge University Press, 1996), 172, 255, 294.

[21]*Clifford Letters of the Sixteenth Century*, ed. A. G. Dickens, Surtees Society, 172 (1957): 141, 144; they married c. 1535.

[22]"Letters of the Cliffords, Lords Clifford and Earls of Cumberland, c. 1500–c. 1565," ed. R. W. Hoyle, *Camden Miscellany* 31 (1992): 55.

[23]Hoyle, "Letters of the Cliffords," 60.

[24]Hoyle, "Letters of the Cliffords," 61.

[25]Kirby, *Plumpton Letters and Papers*, 159, 193, 195.

[26]BL, Vespasian, f. xiii, article 136, f. 187; on his age, GEC, 4: 420; on his quarrel with his mother, see Barbara J. Harris, "Property, Power, and Personal Relations: Elite Mothers and Sons in Yorkist and Early Tudor England," *Signs* 15, no. 31 (1990): 626–27. Grey was married to Frances, daughter of Charles Brandon, duke of Suffolk, and Henry VIII's sister Mary. They were the parents of Lady Jane Grey.

This transition was delayed, often for years, if women's fathers-in-law were still alive when their husbands came of age, since only the wealthiest families could establish their heirs in independent households. The future second earl of Cumberland and his wife were unusual, even in a privileged class, in having their own establishment at Brougham Castle while his parents resided at Skipton.[27] Ellen Lestrange had a more typical experience. She was married for seventeen years before her father-in-law died in 1545 and she became mistress of her own household. Even then, she may have felt some doubt about her authority because her mother-in-law remained in residence.[28] Isabel Plumpton waited even longer to assume the full duties of aristocratic wifehood. She lived with the parents of her husband, William, from 1496 until 1515, when his father, who was then seventy, surrendered control of his property and finances to his son. Since the elderly Plumptons continued to live with them, Isabel may still have had difficulty taking charge of the establishment in which she had resided for so long.[29]

During the period when wives were first assuming control of their households, their letters often conveyed insecurity about their position and recounted their efforts to prove their value as partners in managing the family enterprise. The first countess of Rutland asked her father, one of the executors of Sir Thomas Lovell's will, to use his position to do as much as he could for her husband, who was one of Lovell's beneficiaries. "I beseech you," she wrote, "as ever you loved me, that there may be no fault found in you."[30] Another noblewoman, Elizabeth, countess of Kildare, wife of the ninth earl, petitioned Cardinal Wolsey, Henry VIII's chief minister, "to be good and gracious…unto my lord my husband.…That it may appear unto [his servants]…that your grace is so much all the better unto them at this my humble petition." She explained that she was especially anxious to assist him because her mother had not yet paid her dowry.[31]

Young wives did not always find growing into their role as household and estate managers easy. Even Margaret Paston, who is legendary among historians for her

---

[27]Kirby, "Letters of the Cliffords," 42, 60; GEC, 3: 567–68.

[28]Bindoff, *The Commons*, 2: 522; NRO, Lestrange of Hunstanton, A42; Oestmann, *Lestrange Family,* 13.

[29]*The Plumpton Correspondence*, ed. Stapleton, cxxv; *Plumpton Letters and Papers*, ed. Kirby, 192, 221, 229–31, 252; appendix 2, 78. Sir Robert died in 1523; his wife survived him and continued to live at Plumpton.

[30]BL, Additional MS 27,447, f. 74 (1529). The countess's father was Sir William Paston (d. 1554). Her husband was born in 1492; his first wife died in 1513. He married Eleanor sometime before 1523; their first child, a son, was born in 1526. Although there is no record of the countess's age, she could not have been more than twenty when they married, since she did not give birth to her tenth and last child until 1539 (GEC, vol. 11, 253–55; *Rutland MS*, vol. 4: 290–92). Lovell, who had no children, divided his real property between Rutland and his nephew Francis Lovell. Lovell's first wife was Rutland's great-aunt and Rutland's first wife was Lovell's niece. PRO, Prob11/23/27; GEC, 11: 105–8; Bindoff, *The Commons*, 2: 548.

[31]BL, Titus B1, XI, f. 362 (1523).

effectiveness, had difficulty asserting herself as long as her mother-in-law, Agnes, remained involved in Paston affairs. In 1448, four years after her husband inherited his estates, Margaret's account of her efforts to persuade Lady Morley not to sue him reflects her anxiety about convincing him that she had done everything possible to press his case. She was clearly humiliated that Lady Morley had refused her request and then yielded to Agnes.[32] Another young wife, Anne, countess of Oxford, was unable to influence her spendthrift husband, the fourteenth earl, or cooperate with him in managing their affairs. In desperation she appealed to Cardinal Wolsey to pressure him into reforming. In 1523, Wolsey ordered the recalcitrant young noble-man to give up his independent establishment altogether and live instead with the countess's father.[33]

As they gained experience, many wives—probably the majority—emerged as their husbands' de facto, if junior, partners in supervising their families and managing their assets. Once their wives proved their competence, it was hard for men to resist allowing them considerable power and control over their resources, whatever they thought in the abstract about women's abilities and male authority. The large numbers of their children,[34] huge households,[35] far-flung estates, and numerous servants demanded an enormous amount of supervision. In addition, as their children reached or approached adolescence, planning and advancing their careers[36] and negotiating their marriages[37] became a major preoccupation. Although aristocratic men employed professional and semiprofessional household and estate officials to assist them in managing their affairs, no substitute existed for a competent wife who

[32]*Paston Letters and Papers*, pt.1, 128 (Ap. 1448; John's father died in Aug. 1444).

[33]GEC, 10: 245; PRO, SP1/27, 147, 148, 150, 151, 152d; BL, Hargrave MS 249, f. 223 (orig. 226). She was a daughter of the second duke of Norfolk.

[34]In a sample of 2,557 women, 91 percent had at least one child. The average number of recorded children born to the 2,333 fertile women was 4.42. This figure is undoubtedly an underenumeration, since it almost certainly misses some infants who were stillborn or died within a few days of birth as well as some children who survived birth but died before reaching adulthood. A substantial minority of aristocratic women had large numbers of recorded offspring: just under 40 percent gave birth to five or more children; just under 30 percent to six or more. This figure refers to all of an individual woman's marriages. Since some women had children with only one of their husbands, the percentage of infertile couples is somewhat higher. Of 2,654 couples, 87 percent had children. T. H. Hollingsworth gives a similar figure, 86 percent, for couples in which the wives were peers' daughters born 1550–74: "Demography of the British Peerage," *Supplement to Population Studies* 18 (1964): tables 36, 46.

[35]The households of the nobility ranged in size from 75 to 140; of knights, from 25 to 50. In addition to the nuclear family, residents of the aristocratic household included widowed parents, unmarried siblings, young married children and their spouses, adolescent offspring of their friends and kin who were "in service" with them, and household servants and estate officials of every description and status. Harris, "Property, Power, and Personal Relations," 611.

[36]Crawford, *Career of John Howard*, 95–96; *Lisle Letters*, 5: 432, 1379; Dickens, *Clifford Letters of the Sixteenth Century*, 25; PRO, SP1/114, f. 155 (1537).

[37]Davis, *Paston Letters*, 1: 226, 378, 605, 606; *The Paston Letters, A.D. 1422–1509*, ed. James Gairdner (1904 ed.; New York, 1973), nos. 894–96.

paid continual attention to her family's business. Wives' participation was particularly important because their husbands were frequently away from home visiting their scattered estates, pursuing legal business in London during term time, and attending the king or otherwise serving the crown. In their absence, they needed someone who shared, even identified with, their interests to take charge of their affairs and to keep them informed of any local news that they ought to pass on to the crown. In times of crisis, they depended on their wives to protect their families and estates until they could return or the central government could act.[38]

As a result, virtually all the substantial Yorkist and early Tudor family archives document aristocratic wives actively involved in managing their households and families. The women who cut such large figures in the published Paston, Plumpton, Stonor, and Lisle letters are well known in this respect; but material about scores of other wives demonstrates that they were not exceptional in the initiative, energy, and competence with which they fulfilled their roles.[39]

To substantiate these generalizations, we will look more closely at two less well known women—Lady Anne Lestrange and Eleanor, countess of Rutland—to create a composite picture of the activities, skills, and concerns of mature wives. Lady Anne Lestrange was the daughter of Nicholas, Lord Vaux, a successful courtier under Henry VII and Henry VIII, and the wife of Sir Thomas Lestrange, a landowner in Norfolk.[40] The Lestranges married in 1501, when Anne was seven and Thomas ten. Anne gave birth to Nicholas, her oldest son, between 1511 and 1513. He was probably the first of her thirteen or more children, since aristocratic parents rarely allowed their offspring to consummate their unions before they were sixteen.[41]

Lady Anne's activities are documented in household accounts, which list all the Lestranges' cash outlays, no matter how small, and name all the visitors who dined at their great house at Hunstanton. For historians interested in the uxorial cycle, the Lestrange accounts track the experience of a woman who married as a child and gradually grew into her role as a wife. Since they note the purpose and place of each disbursement, they provide information on the spatial dimension of Anne's life as well as on her activities.

The earliest annual accounts used here began in September 1519. Anne, then twenty-five and pregnant, was playing a relatively marginal role in her household.

---

[38]Barbara J. Harris, "Women and Politics in Early Tudor England," *The Historical Journal* 33, no. 2 (1990): 259–81. For the fifteenth century, see *Paston Letters and Papers*, pts.1 and 2, passim; and Kirby, *Plumpton Letters and Papers*, passim.

[39]For a detailed discussion of this aspect of Margaret Paston's life, see Haskell, "The Paston Women on Marriage," 460–66.

[40]Oestmann, *Lestrange Family*, 16. Sir Thomas was knighted in 1529.

[41]NRO, Lestrange of Hunstanton, A38; Blomfield, 10: 114–115; at least nine survived long enough to marry. Oestmann, *Lestrange Family*, 15. In light of contemporary mortality rates and the documented experience of other families, I doubt that Oestmann is correct that their only children were the thirteen that clearly survived infancy and childhood.

She occasionally ordered clothes for her children and once received a small lump sum for their expenses and hers.[42] The accounts for the early and mid-1520s create a similar impression.[43] By 1530, however, Lady Anne was supervising the Lestrange household and estates and keeping detailed accounts of her cash transactions.[44] This striking change coincided with two major developments in the Lestranges' lives: Lady Anne had stopped having children and her husband had become more prominent at court. His increased visibility there was almost certainly related to his marital connection and friendship with the Boleyns and his support for the king's divorce from Katherine of Aragon. In 1532, Sir Thomas was among the royal servants who accompanied Henry VIII when he took Anne to Calais to meet the king of France. In 1533, he attended their wedding and the new queen's coronation.[45] In his absence, Lady Lestrange managed their affairs in Norfolk.

The accounts for 1533–34 provide a fair representation of Lady Anne's activities during this period. She received rent and tithes from the Lestranges' tenants, profits from the sale of wood and malt, her husband's fee from the abbot of Ramsey, and money Sir Thomas himself collected. She used this money to pay the rent they owed, to buy supplies for the household, to pay their servants, to purchase clothes and other necessities for the children, to make repairs, and to reward or reimburse the scores of people who ran their errands and delivered goods and letters to them. She also sent her husband cash when he needed it.[46] In addition to such routine expenses, Lady Lestrange paid her mother-in-law's annuity, installments on her daughter Alice's dowry, and Sir Roger Lestrange's bequest to Gonville Hall, Cambridge.[47] She also supplied funds for a number of land transactions, including the lease of a manor that cost the substantial sum of £116 13s 4d.[48]

The accounts also contain evidence about the spatial dimensions of Lady Lestrange's life. The only recorded time she left Norfolk was in 1520 when she

[42]Daniel Gurney, "Extracts from the Household and Privy Purse Accounts of the Lestranges of Hunstanton," *Archaeologia* 25 (1834): 416–30; 428–29 for her lying-in.

[43]There are accounts for 1520, 1522, 1525, and 1526; see Gurney, "Accounts of the Lestranges of Hunstanton," 428–89; 449 and 489 for births.

[44]Gurney, "Accounts of the Lestranges," 480–510, 544–45, passim. I assume that Lady Lestrange kept the accounts which refer to "my husband" (for example, 502, 506, 510–53). She seems to have kept the entire accounts for 1530, 1532, and 1533.

[45]Oestmann, *Lestrange Family*, 16; Gurney, "Accounts of the Lestranges of Hunstanton," 522.

[46]Gurney, "Accounts of the Lestranges of Hunstanton," 432–33, 532–42, 545–46, 548–49.

[47]Gurney, "Accounts of the Lestranges," 500, 544–45. Alice married Thomas Calthorp in February 1545; the payments were made to her mother-in-law. Sir Thomas's mother married Sir Edward Knyvett the year after his father died, and appears in the accounts as Lady Knyvett. Sir Roger Lestrange (d. 1505) was the older brother of Sir Thomas' father (Robert, d. 1511). When Sir Roger's only child, John, died without heirs in 1515, Sir Thomas inherited Hunstanton and the other family estates. Neither Sir Thomas nor his father was named executor in Sir Roger's will, but Sir Thomas apparently had acquired the responsibility by 1534. Oestmann, *Lordship and Community*, 13–15, 20; Sir Roger's will is in PRO 11/15/2 (1505).

[48]Gurney, "Accounts of the Lestranges of Hunstanton," 543–44.

journeyed to Northamptonshire, perhaps to visit her father, whose main residence was in that county. Two years later, she made a much shorter journey to Walsingham, the most important English pilgrimage site after Canterbury, which was about fifteen miles away from Hunstanton.[49] Otherwise Lady Anne apparently remained very close to home. With a single exception, when she and her husband traveled to the home of his distant kinsman, Sir Roger Woodhouse, she does not even seem to have engaged in the constant visiting reflected in the guest lists at Hunstanton.[50] Since the lists show that other wives frequently visited the Lestranges, she appears to have been unusual in this respect. The large number of her pregnancies and health problems they caused may explain her immobility.

In any case, Lady Anne was not isolated at Hunstanton, which received a steady flow of aristocratic female visitors. In 1519–20, for example, Lady Elizabeth Woodhouse, Sir Roger's wife, assisted Anne during her month of confinement. Another aunt, Margaret Lestrange, Lady Elizabeth Robsart, and Anne Boleyn's first cousin Anne Shelton also visited during that year.[51] The guests in 1526 once again included Lady Robsart and Anne Shelton (now identified as Mistress Knyvett on account of her marriage), suggesting their ongoing friendship with the Lestranges. In fact, the Knyvetts visited Hunstanton more than once in 1526. The first time, Elizabeth Boleyn, the future queen's mother, accompanied them. On another occasion, they stayed for a week and a half.[52] The most frequent guests were Sir Thomas's sister Catherine Hastings and her husband. Sometimes they came together, sometimes Catherine came alone.[53] The Lestranges recorded entertaining four other aristocratic wives that year.[54]

---

[49]Gurney, "Accounts of the Lestranges," 449. Anne gave birth to a daughter about ten weeks later.

[50]Gurney, "Accounts of the Lestranges," 523. As so often happened, the simple kin term "uncle" used in the accounts actually referred to a far more distant affinal tie. Sir Roger Woodhouse's wife, Elizabeth, was the daughter of Sir Robert Radcliffe and Katherine Drury, widow of Henry Lestrange, Sir Thomas' grandfather; therefore, at the time he was an uncle by virtue of two marriages, his mother-in-law's and his own. Both Sir Roger and Lady Woodhouse visited Hunstanton frequently, suggesting a cordial relationship between the two families.

[51]Gurney, "Accounts of the Lestranges," 427–30; see 425 for another of Lady Woodhouse's visits that year; three other nonaristocratic women also attended her during her lying-in. Elizabeth Robsart was the daughter of Sir Thomas Kerdeston and wife of Sir Theodore. Lady Shelton, the daughter of Sir John and Anne Shelton, was a sister of the future queen's father.

[52]Gurney, "Accounts of the Lestranges," 483, 485.

[53]Gurney, "Accounts of the Lestranges," 484–85, 488. Catherine was married to Sir Hugh Hastings.

[54]Gurney, "Accounts of the Lestranges," 482–83. The women were Lady Catherine Lovell, Anne Lovell, Lady Bedingfield, and Mary Mordaunt. Catherine Lovell was married to Sir Thomas, son of Sir Gregory; Anne Lovell was the wife of Sir Thomas's younger brother Francis; Francis was the heir of their uncle, Sir Thomas (d. 1524), and a future knight. The identity of Lady Bedingfield is unclear; she could have been Alice, the wife of Sir Thomas (d. 1539), or Grace, the wife of his son and heir, Sir Edmund (d. c.1553). Mary Mordaunt was the daughter of John Lestrange, the younger brother of Robert (d. 1511), and therefore Thomas's first cousin; her husband, Robert Mordaunt, was from a junior branch of the family. Oestmann, *Lordship and Community*, 14 n.5.

All of the women mentioned here lived within forty miles of Hunstanton, suggesting a pattern of sociability concentrated on relatively small local areas. With two exceptions, available evidence does not indicate whether these women journeyed outside their neighborhoods regularly. The exceptions, Elizabeth Boleyn and Anne Shelton Knyvett, belonged to important court families and travelled regularly between Norfolk, London, and the royal palaces along the Thames where Henry VIII usually resided.[55]

Because attendance at court was the major reason aristocratic women left their homes for extended periods, the second mature wife we have chosen to look at is Eleanor, countess of Rutland, who married the first earl by 1523.[56] She gave birth to the first of her eleven or more children, a daughter named Anne, that year or soon thereafter. Her last child, Katherine, was born in 1539.[57] The countess's career at court began during the same years she was bearing children. Her first recorded appearance took place when she attended Anne Boleyn at the ceremony creating her marchioness of Pembroke in 1532.[58] Lady Rutland probably served as one of Anne's ladies-in-waiting after she became queen and certainly held this position under Jane Seymour, Anne of Cleves, and Catherine Howard.[59] During this period,

---

[55]Lady Boleyn was the daughter of the second Howard, duke of Norfolk, the wife of Thomas Boleyn, one of Henry VIII's most successful courtiers, and mother of Queen Anne. She belonged to Katherine of Aragon's household from 1509 until at least the mid-1520s. As a member of the inner court circle, she attended royal celebrations and diplomatic events throughout this period. In 1520 she made what was probably her longest journey, when she served Queen Katherine in France at the Field of the Cloth of Gold. *Letters and Papers, Foreign and Domestic, of the Reign of Henry VIII* (L&P), ed. J. S. Brewer, James Gairdner, and R. H. Brodie (London: HM Stationery Office, 1867–1910), 1: 82, 41; 2 (2): 3446; 3 (1): 491, 704, 245; *Rutland MS*, 4, 22. Anne Shelton's mother was a Boleyn (Thomas Boleyn's sister and Queen Anne's aunt) and her husband, Sir Edmund Knyvett, a Howard (his mother was a daughter of the second duke of Norfolk and Lady Boleyn's sister). Equally important, Sir Edmund's father, Sir Thomas, was one of Henry VIII's favorite companions in the opening years of the reign and died heroically at sea during the war against France in 1512. Anne was a member of Princess Mary's household in the mid-1520s, when she appears as Mistress Knyvett since her husband was not knighted until 1538. In the 1540s, she lodged at court with her husband, by then a member of Henry VIII's privy chamber. Bindoff, *The Commons*, 2: 482; L&P, 4 (1): 1577 (13); 21 (1): 969 (iii).

[56]HMC, *Rutland Manuscripts*, 4: 260.

[57]Anne gave birth to her first child in 1540. Since aristocratic couples of this period rarely cohabited before they were sixteen, she was probably at least seventeen at this time and therefore born in 1523. She appears in the Rutland accounts as Lady Nevill. The Rutlands' first son, Henry, was born in 1526. Ten of the countess's children survived; a daughter named Katherine died in 1533. *Rutland Manuscripts*, vol. 4: 275, 295; GEC, 11: 255, 291.

[58]E. W. Ives, *Anne Boleyn* (Oxford: Basil Blackwell, 1986), 198. Later in 1532, she and her husband accompanied the king to France when he took Anne to meet Francis I. They almost certainly attended Anne's coronation eight months later. HMC, *Rutland Manuscripts*, vol. 4: 271, 274; *Lisle Letters*, 1: 350; GEC, 11: 254.

[59]The countess's role in events leading up to Anne Boleyn's marriage to Henry include a letter, dated Shrove Thursday, to her father indicating that the queen was going to visit her at Endfield and that the marriages between her children and those of the earl of Westmorland were not yet settled (the

---

she travelled regularly between the court, the Rutlands' main residence at Belvoir Castle, Lincolnshire, their London mansion at Holywell, and their manor at Endfield, Middlesex, just outside the city.[60] Her mobile lifestyle was at the opposite end of the spectrum from Lady Lestrange's.

Residence at court and in London or its vicinity opened the possibility of a rich social life to Lady Rutland. She developed friendships with a number of the other members of the queen's privy chamber, notably Lady Coffin, the countess of Sussex, Lady Beauchamp, and the duchess of Suffolk. In fact, in 1539, she named her last daughter, Katherine, for the duchess, who visited Belvoir Castle at least once.[61] Lady Coffin sent a gift after the child's birth. Some years later, she married the countess's brother-in-law, Sir Richard Manners, as her third husband.[62] Lady Rutland also became friends with women like Honor Lady Lisle, who came to court occasionally but did not hold offices there.[63]

Since members of their circle at court were unlikely to travel as far north as Belvoir Castle, the Rutlands entertained them at Holywell, their London mansion. In July 1536, they used Holywell for the triple wedding of their eldest son and the heirs of the earls of Westmorland and Oxford, which was undoubtedly the major social event of the year outside the court itself.[64] All the highest-ranking members of the peerage attended, while the king himself appeared after dinner to dance and feast at a late-night banquet.[65] Three years later, the Rutlands used Holywell to celebrate their daughter Gertrude's marriage to the earl of Shrewsbury's heir.[66]

The countess's peripatetic existence prevented her from supervising the Rutlands' numerous households or recording their daily expenses as closely as Lady Lestrange did at Hunstanton. Instead, the earl employed a treasurer who kept records of their expenditures. The officials sometimes noted that they were making payments "by my Lady's commandment."[67] In addition, Lady Rutland occasionally

---

weddings took place on 3 July 1536). References to the countess's being at court before Anne Boleyn's execution (19 May 1537) and Henry's marriage to Jane Seymour (30 May 1536) strongly suggest that she belonged to Anne Boleyn's household. Unfortunately, no complete list of Anne Boleyn's household survives. Ives, *Anne Boleyn*, 198; *Lisle Letters*, 4: 855, 855a, 874, passim; M. A. E. Wood Green, *Letters of Royal and Illustrious Ladies of Great Britain* (London: Colburn, 1846), 3: 168.

[60]For Lady Rutland's movements see HMC, *Rutland MS*, vol. 4, passim; *Lisle Letters*, 4 and 5, passim.

[61]HMC, *Rutland MS*, 4: 294; *Lisle Letters*, 4: 880, 887; A. G. W. Murray and Eustace F. Bosanquet, *The Manuscripts of William Dunche* (Exeter, 1914), 15.

[62]Bindoff, *The Commons*, 1: 667.

[63]Bindoff, *The Commons*, 1: 350; 4: 883; 5: 1091, 1223, 1404.

[64]Rutland's heir married one of Westmorland's daughters and Oxford's heir married another; Westmorland's heir married one of Rutland's daughters.

[65]BL, Additional MS 6113, f. 199d; Charles Wriothesley, *A Chronicle of England during the Reign of the Tudors, AD 1485–1559*, Camden Society, n.s., 11 (1875): 50.

[66]*Lisle Letters*, 5: 1396.

[67]HMC, *Rutland MS*, vol. 4: 314–15, 318.

paid for extraordinary or nonrecurring items on her own, keeping separate accounts of her expenditures. During the year beginning December 1530, for example, she purchased satin for a nightgown for her husband; paid a glazier to make a window for the parish church at Endfield, Middlesex; rewarded servants who delivered gifts and other goods to her; paid for her and her husband's New Year's gifts to the king; and rewarded itinerant entertainers such as minstrels. Expenditures of this sort recur year after year in her accounts.[68] She also paid some of her children's expenses, although, once again, she was far less likely to make routine purchases for them than Lady Lestrange. Her disbursements included such unusual items as her eldest son's dancing lessons, a "physic" to cure the children's worms, and a bow and arrows for Anne.[69] In addition, she assumed responsibility for payments to her husband's brothers and married sisters. Although these occasionally involved large sums, such as the final installments on the dowries of two of her sisters-in-law, these payments were more likely to be one-time gifts or the modest allowances the earl gave his sisters.[70] The countess explicitly noted when she spent money "by my lord's commandment," which suggests that she usually acted independently.[71]

Lady Rutland's duties at court, high rank, and multiple households thus created a variation on the pattern of mature wifehood we saw in the case of Anne Lestrange. Because of her frequent absences from home and itinerant lifestyle, she could not assume day-to-day responsibilities for her children or domestic arrangements. Nonetheless, like her husband, who was also often away from Belvoir, she played an essential part in managing their joint affairs. When it came to crucial issues such as finding husbands for her daughters and negotiating the terms of their matches, she was very much involved. In a letter to her father written from Holywell, for example, she reported the apparent failure of her discussions with an unnamed gentleman. "Howsoever it goeth," she wrote," I trust by your good help, and with the help of my lord, to provide her of another as good as he...." The countess's wording and use of the first person singular indicate that she had taken, and expected to continue to take, initiative in this area.[72] Likewise, in 1539, she, not the earl, paid the first installment of their daughter Gertrude's dowry.[73] Her husband's confidence in her was evident in the will he wrote in 1542 before he departed to fight for the king in Scotland.[74] In addition to naming her as one of his executors and leaving her all his jewels, plate, and household goods, he assigned her land worth almost £700 a year

---

[68]HMC, *Rutland MS*, vol. 4: 267, 269–70, 276–77.

[69]HMC, *Rutland MS*, vol. 4: 271, 275, 281, 288.

[70]HMC, *Rutland MS*, vol. 4: 268; 273–74, 276.

[71]HMC, *Rutland MS*, vol. 4: 269–70. The countess Eleanor, daughter of Sir William Paston, was the earl's second wife.

[72]Green, *Letters of Illustrious Ladies*, 3: 168.

[73]HMC, *Rutland MS*, vol. 4: 288.

[74]HMC, *Rutland MS*, vol. 4: 337.

for her jointure and dower—far more than the traditional third—because he trusted her "to be loving, benevolent, and favorable to our children."[75]

The two mature wives we have looked at were in first marriages. Women who married more than once almost always had heavy additional obligations and more complex households. As we saw at the beginning of this paper, the great majority served as executors of their deceased husbands' wills and retained custody of their noninheriting children. In addition to managing their dowers and jointures, many of them also disposed of considerable wealth in the form of plate, jewelry, luxury clothing, and household goods which they had inherited from their deceased husbands and protected from their new spouses with prenuptial contracts.[76] Remarried women often acquired stepchildren, who complicated their role in their new households and caused difficulties if they once again outlived their spouses and were named executors of *their* estates. These aspects of their lives are well documented because they frequently had to resort to the courts to protect their rights as widows, executors, and guardians. Thus, of 551 lawsuits involving aristocratic women in the courts of Chancery, Requests, and Star Chamber, 43.5 percent (240) were about their dowers or jointures or their duties as executors and guardians. In 5.4 percent (thirty) of the cases, their stepchildren were their opponents in these suits.

Margaret, countess of Bath (d. 1561), who outlived three husbands, is a well-documented example of how successive marriages affected the model of wifehood we have been discussing.[77] The countess, daughter and heir of an ordinary Middlesex gentleman, first married a successful London merchant, Thomas Kitson. They had five children, including one son. Before Kitson died in 1540, he had acquired a knighthood and great country house at Hengrave, Suffolk. In accordance with his deathbed wishes, his widow received use of the Suffolk estate for life and was appointed administrator of his movable goods.[78] She purchased their son's wardship from the king and continued to live at Hengrave.[79]

---

[75]*North Country Wills, 1338–1558*, ed. J. W. Clay, Surtees Society, 116 (1908): 188–89. The earl was able to dispose of land worth £1,862 20d in his will. Because his heir was a minor, land worth £552 16s 5³/₄d. was reserved for the king.

[76]Forty-eight (9 percent) of 523 husbands who wrote testaments and predeceased their wives left them personal property the women had brought into their marriages. All but five of these women had been married before and had probably inherited these goods from their first husbands. Some of these wills state or strongly suggest that the testators were honoring prenuptial agreements giving their wives sole control of their property *during* their marriages.

[77]On Margaret Donington Kitson Long Bourchier, countess of Bath, see Bindoff, *The Commons*, 2: 545–46; GEC, 2: 17; the earl died in 1561. To avoid confusion, I will refer to her as the countess of Bath throughout this discussion although she would have been known as Lady Kitson and then as Lady Long during her first two marriages.

[78]PRO, Prob11/29/30; CUL, Hengrave Hall MS 89 (3), f. 229 and MS 91; West Suffolk Record Office, 449/5/2.

[79]For definition of wardship, see n. 9 above; CUL, Hengrave Hall MS 90, doc, no. 40.

Lady Kitson, now a wealthy widow as well as an heiress, remarried within the year, making a brilliant match that carried her into the inner circle of the early Tudor political and social elite. Her new husband, Sir Richard Long, belonged to Henry VIII's privy chamber. Their marriage gave her the right to lodge at court and opened its social and ceremonial activities to her.[80] During this marriage, Margaret gave birth to another son and three more daughters. When Sir Richard died in 1546, he left her two-thirds of his land for her jointure and named her sole executrix of his estate.[81]

Two years later, Margaret used her still greater wealth and enhanced status to secure a title by marrying John Bourchier, second earl of Bath, as her third husband. Her social ambition was evident in the provision in the Baths' marriage contract that arranged a match between the countess's daughter Frances Kitson and the earl's son and heir.[82] During this, the longest lasting of her three marriages, Margaret had two more daughters. Her husband also had nine children by his two former wives. Lady Bath continued to live at Hengrave, which served as the couple's main residence, although she wanted her husband's daughters to live elsewhere.[83]

Lady Bath's previous marriages had taught her enough about coverture to lead her to insist on limiting her husband's rights over the movable property she brought into their marriage. Before their wedding, he signed a prenuptial contract which contained an inventory of all her possessions and gave her the right to dispose of them as freely as if she were single. The earl promised to compensate her from his estate if he diminished her goods in any way or if they were lost or stolen. Bath also agreed to leave her all the movable property she brought into the marriage when he died, and to permit her to bequeath it by will if she predeceased him.[84] Since the countess could not enforce the agreement herself while she was under coverture, the husbands of two of her Kitson daughters signed the document for her, a precaution giving them standing to sue on her behalf should the necessity arise. In the event, the countess's foresight proved to be wise, since her husband did sell some of her goods to pay his creditors. In compensation, he signed a bond promising to repay her after he died by leaving her all his household goods and a large proportion of his horses, livestock, corn, and farm equipment.[85] What is not clear is whether the couple had

---

[80]L&P, 21 (1): 969 (iii); 1384, 696–97.

[81]PRO, Prob11/31/18.

[82]CUL, Hengrave Hall MS 90, document marked 72 (1548). Frances's husband predeceased his father. GEC, 2: 17.

[83]CUL, Hengrave Hall MS 88, 3: 35, 48, 75. Three of her Kitson daughters were already married: Catherine to Sir John Spencer; Dorothy to Sir Thomas Packington; and Anne to Sir William Spring. SRO, Kitson of Hengrave, 449/4/1 is Catherine's marriage contract; her mother gave her a dowry of 1,000 marks and a yearly rent of £8 during her (that is, her mother's) lifetime.

[84]CUL, Hengrave Hall MS 90, document marked 72 (1548).

[85]West Suffolk Record Office, Kitson of Hengrave, 449/5/5.

agreed on the new arrangement before the sales or the earl had acted unilaterally. In either case, Bath abided by the second agreement in his will.[86]

The letters between Lady Bath, her husband, and their servants show that she was actively involved in managing their property and finances. Both the earl and his servants regularly reported to her about his estates. In her responses, she had no reservations about expressing her opinions about what should be done.[87] Lady Bath was especially concerned about curtailing the earl's expenses, and habitually reminded him of his imprudence.[88] She reported angrily when she thought his heir was trying to prevent him from raising cash to pay his debts by selling some of his land and woods.[89] She also pressured him to save money by spending as little time as possible attending the queen or performing other services for the crown.[90]

Bath displayed the greatest confidence in his wife's ability and judgment. In 1552, for example, he asked her to conduct legal and other business for him in London. Five years later, he wanted her to petition the privy council on his behalf.[91] That same year Bath sent her a memorandum that gives an idea of the wide variety of matters she handled for him: he directed her to speak to his lawyer about leasing a house to his daughter-in-law; to consider the possibility of raising money by selling one of his wards, leasing some pasture, increasing the income from his fishing rights, and selling wood; and to generally advise him on how he might increase his income.[92] Two days before his death in 1561, he wrote an indignant letter to a nephew who had seized the deeds and other evidence about Bath's estates when he heard incorrectly that his uncle had died. Bath told him angrily that he had no intention of trusting him with any business related to his heir or inheritance; rather, for their "greater trust and surety," all matters "were to be committed to my said wife…."[93] He appointed her sole executor of his estate.[94]

As we might expect, the countess took charge of her own and her husbands' children with as much energy and determination as she displayed managing their estates and finances. On one occasion, when she was in London and the earl reported that "a sickness" had broken out at Hengrave, she responded with prompt instructions about where to move their offspring. Her expectation that he would do

[86]PRO, Prob11/44/12 (Jan. 1561).
[87]See for example CUL, Hengrave Hall MS 88, 1: 21, 23, 31, 46, 48, 54, 84, 87.
[88]CUL, Hengrave Hall MS 88, 1: 23, 37.
[89]CUL, Hengrave Hall MS 91, 12 May. One of the countess's daughters by Sir Thomas Kitson married the earl's son and heir. He died before his father in 1556 at the age of twenty-seven. GEC, 2: 17.
[90]The earl participated in suppressing the rebellions against Mary and was lord lieutenant of Dorset, Devon, and Cornwall from 1556. See, for example, CUL, Hengrave Hall MS. 88, 1: 22, 24, 54.
[91]GEC, 2: 40, 88.
[92]CUL, Hengrave Hall MS 91 (in wrapper marked "18 memoranda, acquittances," etc.).
[93]CUL, Hengrave Hall MS 88, 86. Bath's heir, who had married Frances Kitson, predeceased his father in 1556, but they had a son who became his and his father's heir. GEC, 2: 17.
[94]PRO, Prob 11/44/12.

as she instructed was clear in her concluding remarks: "If you will follow these orders which I have appointed ye in, I will tarry....If not, I will make speed to come home...."[95] Another time, it was she, not the earl, who took responsibility for placing her stepson George in Furnivall's Inn to prepare him to enter one of the major Inns of Court. Only after explaining all she had done, did she add—perhaps sincerely, but perhaps only for form's sake—"I will do nothing without your advice, and therefore I pray you send me word." As she probably expected, the earl was "well pleased" with the arrangements.[96] Another stepson, Henry, wrote to her, not his father, when he needed money, clothes, and a horse.[97]

Understandably, the countess was most involved with her husband's heir, Lord Fitzwarren, who married her daughter Frances in 1548. She was very worried about his extravagance and on one occasion advised her husband to arrange for him to live more cheaply.[98] On another, one of her lawyers reported that Fitzwarren had mortgaged a farm and almost lost it because he did not have the funds to redeem it. Fortunately, the lawyer heard about the impending default two days before the deadline and paid off the mortgage himself. The countess had obviously already discussed her concern about Fitzwarren with him; he now advised her to avoid further danger by insisting that her son-in-law place his inheritance in feoffment (that is, trust) for the benefit of his heirs by the countess's daughter.[99]

During these years, Lady Bath looked actively for suitable matches for her unmarried children by her first two husbands. She arranged a marriage between her elder son, Thomas Kitson, and William Paget's daughter Jane. When Jane died a few years later, the countess negotiated a second match for him with Elizabeth Cornwallis, daughter of Sir Thomas, head of a distinguished Norfolk family.[100] She was less successful with her five single daughters, although her correspondence shows she had been trying to find mates for them before her death in 1561.[101] In her will, the countess added 600 marks each to the marriage portions Sir Richard Long had left their three daughters and 900 marks each to the dowries of her two daughters by the earl.[102]

---

[95]CUL, Hengrave Hall MS 88, 1: 35.
[96]CUL, Hengrave Hall MS 88, 1: 63, 65.
[97]CUL, Hengrave Hall MS 88, 1: 118.
[98]CUL, Hengrave Hall MS 88, 1: 37.
[99]CUL, Hengrave Hall MS 88, 1: 120.
[100]Kitson married Jane Paulet c. 1556; she died, apparently of consumption, before 1560, when he married Elizabeth Cornwallis. Norfolk actually offered to host the Kitson-Cornwallis wedding at Kenninghall. CUL, Hengrave Hall MS 88, 1: 57, 89, 91, 159. Sir William Paget was created Baron Paget in 1549; GEC, 10: 278.
[101]CUL, Hengrave MS 88, 1: 140, 149, 150.
[102]CUL, Hengrave MS 90, 42 (1561). Catherine Long married Edward Fisher of Warwickshire after her mother died; Bridget Bourchier, one of her two daughters by her third husband, the earl of Bath, married Sir Arthur Price. I have no indication of what happened to her other daughters by Bath or Long.

The life of Margaret, countess of Bath, exemplifies the most expansive version of the role open to Yorkist and early Tudor aristocratic wives. The scope of her responsibilities, her obvious competence, and the authority she exercised within her family put her at the opposite end of the spectrum from her daughter-in-law, Jane Paget Kitson, whom we discussed above as an example of a young and dependent wife, and Elizabeth, duchess of Norfolk, with whom this paper began. While the countess moved regularly between Hengrave and London and, in some periods of her life, the court, her daughter-in-law travelled only between her in-laws' and parents' home in accordance with their wishes, while the duchess of Norfolk was deprived entirely of her role as a wife. On the spectrum that ran between these extremes, the extant evidence strongly suggests that the lives of the majority of aristocratic women were more like the countess of Bath's than the duchess of Norfolk's.

This conclusion is not meant to deny the significance of patriarchal institutions in constructing the boundaries within which aristocratic women could shape their relationships and activities and respond to their circumstances. As we have seen, coverture affected all women—including those like the countess of Bath who stretched their roles and power to the fullest possible extent. Experiences like the duchess of Norfolk's warned even the highest-ranking wives about the limits of their power to protect themselves, their children, or their property, and surely influenced the way they interacted with their husbands when they disagreed. Nonetheless, to construct a narrative that overemphasizes the oppressive and restrictive aspects of wifehood among the late medieval and early modern English aristocracy is to underestimate both men's dependence on their wives to manage their families and estates *and* women's ability to exploit this need and take advantage of their personal relationships with their husbands. From a feminist point of view, it is as unacceptable to ignore women's agency as to ignore their institutional oppression. The challenge to historians of women is to create a narrative that encompasses both these dimensions of the past.

Eighteenth-Century Marriage Contracts
Linking Legal and Gender History

Gunda Barth-Scalmani

In October 1777, on his way to Paris, Wolfgang Amadeus Mozart received a letter from his father in which Leopold Mozart announced plans for the marriage of his son's friend Johann Baptist von Schidenhofen. The bridegroom was a lower-ranking aristocratic civil servant ("*Beamter*") in Salzburg; the bride was the daughter of a nobleman of rank and profession equal to Schiedenhofen's. Leopold Mozart reported that "how they have agreed on their property interests we do not know yet."[1] When the wedding had been arranged for early February 1778, the twenty-two-year-old Mozart wrote home:

> I wish him joy with my whole heart; but his, I daresay, is again one of those money matches and nothing else. I should not like to marry in this way; I want to make my wife happy, but not to become rich by her means. So I shall let things be and enjoy my golden freedom until I am so well off that I can support a wife and children. Herr von Schiedenhofen was obliged to choose a rich wife; his title demanded it. People of noble birth must never marry from inclination or love, but only from interest and all kinds of secondary considerations.[2]

Mozart's comment points out the new ideal of a love match, in contrast to the traditional marriage of fortune and rank, which was really little more than a contract regulating marital property rights during the marriage.

The subject of marriage contracts concerns legal as well as historical science. The two disciplines have dealt with this subject differently. In the German-language

---

[1] Leopold Mozart, *Briefe und Aufzeichnungen*, ed. Wilhelm Bauer and Otto Deutsch, vol. 2 (Kassel: Barenreiter, 1962), 50, letter from 13 October 1777. (The German text says "Hayratgut," which is not equivalent to dowry.)

[2] *The Letters of Mozart and His Family*, ed. and trans. Emily Anderson, 2nd ed. (London: Macmillan, 1985), 467, letter 283a, Mozart to his father, 7 February 1778.

literature about the history of law, almost no special attention has been given to the history of private law and the community of property between spouses. Helmut Coing's works on European private law are an exception.[3] For Austria, Wilhelm Brauneder's studies of the matrimonial property regime are worth mentioning.[4] The specialized juridical literature about the history of law, however, often presents difficulties to historians. In Austrian and German law schools, academic scholarship traditionally focuses on the history of doctrines and the development of legal instruments. Attempts to link legal questions of the past with the sociohistorical surroundings rarely go deep enough into the relevant subject, and do not meet the standards required by historians.[5] New interdisciplinary approaches in legal history concentrate, therefore, on the social practice of law rather than on the history of legal rules and rights.[6] In studies of subjects such as marriage, it is thus necessary to consider categories of social difference as well as gender-specific questions.

STARTING POINT AND FORMULATION OF THE PROBLEM

Research in marriage contracts offers the chance to include both categories in the analysis. Until recently, except for some dynastic settlements, historians have shown little interest in marriage contracts, seen merely as connected with certain legal acts characterizing a wedding as a "rite de passage," which is a general term for the transition from one period of life to the next, including marriage.[7] Alternatively, they make the general statement that contrary to French custom, written marriage contracts in Germany were customary only in some areas.[8] Such statements may be applicable to the Middle Ages, but definitely not to the early modern era, because the question of which social strata made which kinds of marriage contracts in these centuries has been completely ignored. I have the impression that in regard to matrimonial cases, an exact analysis of the numerous particular rights applicable only to certain territo-

[3]Helmut Coing, *Europäisches Privatrecht,* vol. 1 (Munich: Beck, 1985); *Handbuch der Quellen und Literatur der Neueren Europäischen Privatrechtsgeschichte,* ed. Helmut Coing (Munich: Beck, 1976; reprint, 1982, 1985).

[4]Wilhelm Brauneder, *Die Entwicklung des Ehegüterrechts in Österreich: Ein Beitrag zur Dogmengeschichte und Rechtstatsachenforschung des Spätmittelalters und der Neuzeit* (Salzburg: W. Fink, 1973), 25; idem, *Studien II: Entwicklung des Privatrechts,* 2 vols. (Frankfurt a/M: P. Lang, 1994).

[5] This is obvious in law dissertations such as Eva Tressel-Schuh, *Frauen in Frankfurt: Das gesellschaftliche Verhältnis der Frau und ihre privatrechtliche Stellung im Normensystem des Frankfurter Partikularrechts von der Spätaufklärung bis zum Bürgerlichen Gesetzbuch,* Europäische Hochschulschriften, ser. 2, Law, vol. 2045 (Frankfurt a/M: P. Lang, 1997). This study is based solely on norms.

[6]Cf. *Frauen in der Geschichte des Rechts: Von der Frühen Neuzeit bis zur Gegenwart,* ed. Ute Gerhard (Munich: Beck, 1997), 15.

[7]For example, Richard van Dülmen, *Kultur und Alltag in der Frühen Neuzeit,* vol. 1: *Das Haus und seine Menschen* (Munich: Beck, 1990), 140.

[8]Heide Wunder, *"Er ist die Sonn', sie ist der Mond": Frauen in der Frühen Neuzeit* (Munich: Beck, 1992), 83; Coing, *Privatrecht I,* 241, n. 16, refers to Stryk, *Usus Modernus,* who claims that marriage contracts were very common in the early modern period.

ries is still lacking. In other words, neither within its normative framework nor in its practical consequences for marriage settlements, has matrimonial law so far been historically researched. The main reason may be that neither legal experts nor historians have been interested in the legal regulations of marriage in the time before the great codifications of private law in Europe (that is the Prussian *Allgemeines Landrecht* in 1794, the *Code Napoleon* in France in 1803, or in 1811 the *ABGB* or *Allgemeines Bürgerliches Gesetzbuch*—the General Civic Law—in the Habsburg territories).

The hasty assumption that marriage contracts were not common is probably due to the fact that these contracts are not easily available to historians.[9] Only in the private archives of noble families are they more or less accessible.[10] In regard to the bourgeois/middle and lower classes in towns, the quest for marriage contracts is more difficult because the source material has been organized differently in the public archives. One needs to look for documents that settled a deceased's estate (*Verlassenschaftsabhandlungen*)—which may include such important documents about his or her life as marriage contracts—and for town council documents, in which private contracts like marriage contracts were often enclosed. Relevant information or hints as to marriage agreements among farmer families can be found in land registers (*Notlbücher*) and tax records, as marriages often led to a transmission of possessions. These specific locations of the source material give a first hint that marriage contracts cannot be studied and analyzed in isolation but have to be seen within the context of legal strategies covering several generations.

This essay is based on sources from Salzburg, a small residential town and capital of an ecclesiastical principality of the same name. In the late eighteenth century, the town numbered approximately 16,000 inhabitants.[11] Salzburg belonged to the group of those small states which lost their sovereignty as a result of the new territorial organization of the Holy Roman Empire according to the *Reichsdeputationshauptschluß* in 1803. For legal historians, Salzburg around 1800 is certainly an interesting case; although it was part of the empire, it was a sovereign state and thus did not automatically adopt those reforms and changes in law which were introduced in larger political entities like in the neighboring Habsburg monarchy at the end of the eighteenth century. This applies, for example, to Emperor Joseph II's marriage law (*Ehepatent*) of 1783, which established a coherent system of state matrimonial law; in Salzburg, however, the matrimonial provisions of canon law remained in

---

[9]For the question of source material, see Helmuth Feigl, "Heiratsbriefe und Verlassenschaftsabhandlungen als Quellen zur Alltagsgeschichte," in *Methoden und Probleme der Alltagsforschung im Zeitalter des Barock*, ed. Othmar Pickl and Helmuth Feigl, Veröffentlichungen der Kommission für Wirtschafts-, Sozial- und Stadtgeschichte der Österreichischen Akademie der Wissenschaften (Vienna: Österreichische Akademie der Wissenschaften, 1992), 83–99.

[10]See the studies of Beatrix Bastl and Markus Hillenbrand, *Fürstliche Eheverträge: Gottorfer Hausrecht 1544–1773*, Rechtshistorische Reihe, vol. 141 (Frankfurt: P. Lang, 1996).

[11]Kurt Klein, "Bevölkerung und Siedlung," in *Geschichte Salzburgs: Stadt und Land*, ed. Heinz Dopsch and Hans Spatzenegger, vol. 2 (Salzburg: Universitätsverlag Pustet, 1988), 1341.

force until the end of the archbishopric in 1803.[12]

Assuming that marriage contracts are a suitable source material for gender relations in early modern history, I intend to address several questions. First, I will examine which social classes marriage contracts were customary for in the eighteenth century. Second, I will describe the characteristics of such contracts. Finally, I will analyze the function of marriage contracts in regulating the lives of the old and young. The sources for this article are numerous marriage contracts of urban populations of all social strata. This might be seen as a limitation to my argument, yet we can safely assume that marriage contracts were also common among farmers who owned land and property.[13] Salzburg in the eighteenth century was a so-called *Anerbengebiet,* which means that due to traditions for inheriting farms and forestland, the most suitable son always took over the farm, while the other offspring were paid a lump sum.[14] My basic approach is to show what contracts under private law reveal about gender relations in the everyday practice of matrimonial law. My contribution focuses deliberately on the time before the introduction of the *ABGB,* which in 1811 codified private law in the Habsburg territories for the first time. The moment facts and cases were integrated with legally binding norms, subsequent discussions of this fact or that case tended to refer exclusively to the norms and take them for reality, while ignoring the question of how influential legal norms and rules were actuated in contemporary everyday life.[15] Therefore I see this article on eighteenth-century variations of the matrimonial property regime also as a contribution to what in German is called *historische Rechtstatsachenforschung,* historical research that is primarily interested in the social practice of laws, not in the development of their normative framework.[16]

SOCIAL CLASSES IN WHICH MARRIAGE CONTRACTS WERE COMMON IN THE EIGHTEENTH CENTURY

Disregarding the aristocracy and the farmers, we may establish that marriage contracts were a common practice among *Buerger* (burghers). Among *Buerger,* we include those town dwellers who were engaged in bourgeois/middle class professions (that is merchants and craftsmen) which were connected with certain titles

---

[12]*Die andere Geschichte: Eine Salzburger Frauengeschichte von der ersten Mädchenschule (1695) bis zum Frauenwahlrecht (1918),* ed. Brigitte Mazohl-Wallnig (Salzburg: Pustet, 1995), 50. For divorces, see Barbara Egger, "Bis daß der Tod euch scheidet...': Die katholische Ehescheidungsvariante der Trennung von Tisch und Bett im Spiegel von Salzburger Ehegerichtsakten 1770–1817" (Ph.D. diss., University of Salzburg, 1994).

[13]This assumption is based on random samples I took, and on information from archivists.

[14]Brauneder, "Entwicklung des bäuerlichen Erbrechts," in *Studien II,* xx–xxx

[15]For example, Jürgen Schlumbohm, "Gesetze, die nicht durchgesetzt wurden—ein Strukturmerkmal des frühneuzeitlichen Staates?" in *Geschichte und Gesellschaft,* vol. 23 (1997): 647–63.

[16]Brauneder, "Rechtstatsachen," in *Studien II,* 142.

and obligations. Marriage contracts were entered into when property existed or when important rights and claims were attached to it. In towns of the late eighteenth century, however, *buergerlich* did not mean any longer only a corporative feature, but already implied a certain conduct of life. According to a contemporary description,[17] a *Buerger* was an inhabitant of a small or large town who differed in profession, dress, customs, and manners from the local country folk. Thus the definition of *Buerger* lost its original economic-corporative meaning. In this new, emerging social class, marriage contracts were not common, as marriages did not necessitate alterations in possessive rights. Mozart's father can be mentioned here as a perfect example: then a court musician, he married the daughter of a deceased civil servant without any prenuptial contract. According to legal historians, if no legal acts preceded the marriage, the pecuniary circumstance of either spouse was not altered because of the separation of goods.[18] In the case of Mozart's parents and other similar examples, social historians will add that apart from the household effects, there were no objects of considerable material value to share. But for *Stadt-Buerger*, in the pre-1800s sense of the word, *altstaendisch* marriage contracts can still be found. In Salzburg, *Stadt-Buerger* comprised the merchants at the top of the local economic structure,[19] brewers, innkeepers, and other persons carrying on business trades and crafts. In this social class, marriage contracts are no great surprise, of course. All contracts were put down in writing, mostly out of court; only a few contracts were deposited in the municipal court or recorded in the minute books of the town council (*Ratsprotokolle*). With the economic activity and the educational level of the members of these urban groups, such literate recording does not seem unusual.

In this context it is quite appropriate to point out that many women could obviously write, given the ease with which they put their signature to the documents. This is surprising only to those not familiar with research results in gender studies and early modern history. Calculation, writing, and reading were essential to managing a household. It has even been proved that the wives of some small traders

---

[17]Lorenz Hübner, *Beschreibung des Erzstiftes und Reichsfürstentumes Salzburg in Hinsicht auf Topographie und Statistik*, vol. 3 (Salzburg: Verlage des Verfassers, 1796), 896.

[18]Brauneder, "Frau und Vermögen im spätmittelalterlichen Österreich," in *Studien II*, 217–28, at 218; Werner Ogris, "Mozart's 'Heuraths=Contract' vom 3. August 1782," in *Festschrift zum 80. Geburtstag von Hermann Baltl*, ed. Kurt Ebert (Vienna: Verlag Österreich, 1998), 225–36. Ogris's interesting article was published after this contribution was finished.

[19]Gunda Barth-Scalmani, "Der Handelsstand in der Stadt Salzburg am Ende des 18. Jahrhunderts: Altständisches Bürgertum in Politik, Wirtschaft und Kultur" (Ph.D. diss., University of Salzburg, 1992); idem, "Die Lebenswelt des altständischen Bürgertums am Beispiel des Handelsstandes in Salzburg," in *Bürger zwischen Tradition und Moderne*, ed. Robert Hoffmann, vol. 6, Bürgertum in der Habsburgermonarchie (Vienna: Bohlau, 1997), 29–52.

were in charge of keeping the books.[20] Basic literacy was spread among women of other social strata as well. When, for instance, the sacristan of the Muelln monastery and his wife leased a small farm belonging to the monastery and signed a marriage contract stipulating the community of property, the wife, Monika Reischlin, employed a much more fluent hand than her husband.[21]

The concept of contracts implies today a written document. Yet, in this period, verbal agreements were also used to regulate property rights during marriage, as two examples will show. Maria Anna Fentschin, a small umbrella manufacturer, died in early May 1789. When the municipal court was taking an inventory of her few belongings, her husband made a statement that no marriage settlement had ever been put down and no property had been brought into the marriage by his wife. He added that he and his deceased spouse had agreed that all they owned would belong to both of them.[22]

The second example comes from the same social background. When Gertrud Seidl, a dealer of secondhand articles and old garments, died after thirty-four years of independent work in 1792, her husband declared that he and his wife had agreed on community property; thus he claimed to own half of her secondhand business. After the authorities made inquiries among their adult children and investigated an old borrower's note (*Schuldverschreibung*), which was in the name of both spouses, they permitted the liquidation of the small inheritance.[23]

No written agreement was made when small-scale traders like these couples got married. Most sources considered by historians to be relevant for early modern history are in writing and today's science of law is based primarily upon documents in writing. As regards verbal marriage settlements, research work should therefore direct its attention to references connected with *Verlassenschaftsabhandlungen*. They provide valuable information about how legal acts—verbal or written—were put into effect in everyday life. Written marriage contracts were customary among members of the urban bourgeois/middle classes, but men and women from lower social strata were also well aware of the legal nature of marriage and the consequences for property rights. Agreements may have remained unwritten for many reasons, such as illiteracy of the spouses or high fees for scribes, notaries, or lawyers. In any case, verbal marriage agreements were accepted by the authorities in the eighteenth century.

[20]Salzburger Landarchiv (henceforth SLA), M 81: "*Zinsbüchlein*" of Elisabeth Haffner, a merchant's wife; Konsistorialarchiv Salzburg (henceforth KAS), Ehescheidungen 1792–1805, 22/4. The town curate about the bookkeeping of the wife of the master glazier Hörmann; SLA, Verlassenschaftsabhandlungen: references to the books that belonged to female cooks.

[21]SLA, Verlaß Stadtgericht, 925, marriage contract made out of court, 28 May 1808.

[22]"Keine Heurathspakten vorhanden und seine Ehewirthin (habe) ihm kein Vermögen zugebracht, doch hätten sie ihr vorhandenes Vermögen als ein gemeinschaftliches bisher angesehen, sohin die Helfte seiner abgeschiedenen gattin angehöre." SLA, Verlaß Stadtsyndikat, 203, 9 May 1789.

[23]SLA, Verlaß Stadtsyndikat, 1002 through 998. For details, see Gunda Barth-Scalmani, *Salzburger Handelsfrauen*, 35–37.

FORM AND CONTENT OF MARRIAGE CONTRACTS

All marriage contracts begin with a stereotyped introduction. After the invocation of the Holy Trinity, they name the bridegroom, his rank and/or profession, the bride, and usually both the parents of both man and woman. The phrasing of these contracts remained unaltered in the course of the eighteenth century; it was only the spelling that changed toward up-to-date orthography.[24] The little piece of gossip in Leopold Mozart's letter quoted at the beginning illustrates that negotiations over such marriage contracts lasted a relatively long period before the wedding ceremony. Thus the first paragraph in a contract always stipulates that the wedding should be celebrated before long.[25]

Specific regulations concerning the *Heiratsgaben* (wedding gifts) followed and marital property rights were settled. The contract concluded with detailed statements concerning dispositions after the deaths of the spouses. In connection with the *Heiratsgaben*, terms such as *Heiratsgut, Morgengabe* (morning gift), *Wi(e)derlage* (return gift), and *Paraphernalgut* (paraphernalia) are instrumental. They are part of an old and thoroughly constructed system of mutual gifts between spouses.[26] In early modern history, the term *Heiratsgut* meant what can in some degree be paraphrased as "marriage portion" or "dowry" of the wife in the sense of material assets. But it could also be used to mean gifts to the bride, or money given by the wife to back the marital property.

In a contract from 1781, the second paragraph stipulated that the father of the bride had to give his daughter 2,000 gulden as a *Heiratsgut* plus a trousseau befitting her social position.[27] As indicated by the high amounts given in this contract and the transfer of money, both parents of the bridal pair were prominent members of the trading class. Here, the daughter of the richest merchant in an important market town, which was also a stop for mail-coaches on the main route to Vienna, married the heir of one of the richest hardware dealers in the capital.[28] In another case dating

---

[24]"In dem Nammen der Allerheiligst: Unzerthailten Dreyfaltigkait Gottes Vatters, Sohn und Heiligen Geists ist zwischen Titul. Herrn Andreen Mayr, angehender Bürger und Handls-Factor alhier in Saltzburg als Herrn Hochzeitern an ainem dan der edl vill ehrn tugendreichen Jungfrauen Anna Margaretha Mohrin, des edl und vesten Herrn Mathias Mohrs auch Handls-Factores alda bey dessen Ehefrauen Maria Ursula geborenen Rottin conlich erworbene Tochter als Jungfrau Hochzeiterin andern Thails volgender Heuraths-Contract zu beyderseits contento abgeredt: und beschlossen worden, inmassen wir hernach zu vernemmen...." SLA, Verlaß Stadtsyndikat. 4039 through 708, from 17 June 1713.

[25]"ERSTLICH sollen beede Brautpersonen von nun an ehelich versprochen seyn, sohin schuldig und gehalten seyn, dieses ihr Eheversprechen christ-katholischen Gebrauch noch durch priesterliche Einsegnung an einen von ihnen nächst zu wählenden Tage bestättigen zu lassen." SLA, Stadtgericht (town court), 192, contract made between Franz Egg, a baker, and Maria Josepha Eschenbacherin, a brewer's daughter, on 30 November 1783.

[26]Brauneder, *Frau und Vermögen*, 225.

[27]The German text says: "der Jgfer Braut Herr Vatter (verspricht) dem Herrn Hochzeiter zu einem ordentlichen und rechtmässigen HeurathsGut 2000fl sage zweitausend Gulden in baarem Gelde nebst einer standmässigen Ausfertigung zu überanworten." SLA, Stadtsyndikat, 2235 through 279.

[28]Barth-Scalmani, *Handelsstand*, 131.

from 1731, Maria Catharina Prötzin, a widow and heiress to a cloth and silk business, brought a *Heiratsgut* of six hundred gulden to her marriage with Franz Anton Spängler. She insisted, however, that her husband should have only two hundred gulden—a third of the sum—at his own disposal.[29]

The husband's return for the *Heiratsgut* was the so-called *Widerlage*. With scientific and academic definitions of rights and obligations gaining increasing influence in the eighteenth century, the term *Widerlage* was equated with *donatio propter nuptias*, a term from Roman law.[30] In the above-mentioned contract from 1781, the bridegroom promised to add 2,000 gulden to the 2,000 his future wife was to bring into the marriage, and to have these 4,000 gulden entered in the land register. Moreover, he would give one hundred ducats as a *Morgengabe* and would delight in presenting his bride with beautiful jewels and dresses on their wedding day.[31] *Morgengabe* in the eighteenth century was a gift to the wife from the husband. It became her property[32] and was part of what was sometimes called *Schazgeld*.[33]

The extensive marriage contract from 1781, which covers twelve detailed paragraphs, can serve as an example of how contracts were created between spouses of equal rank and of an economically leading class. The financial security of the wife was not only ensured by the *Heiratsgaben*, but also by additional comprehensive provisions that protected the wife's property and her right to use her assets as capital for business. The basis of all these regulations was the system of the community of property.[34] There were two forms, partial or joint community. Which form was chosen depended on the socioeconomic and sociocultural context of the spouses. If the man and woman to be married both owned or expected to inherit property, in most cases a partial community of property was agreed upon. In a marriage contract from 1747, entered into by spouses of the same rank and from the trading class, the fifth paragraph points out that each spouse was entitled to get half of the property they had worked for during their marriage.[35] This *Errungensgemeinschaft*[36] (community of property acquired during marriage), legal experts assume, was the oldest form of lim-

---

[29]SLA, Verlaß Stadtsyndikat, 807, marriage contract from 16 July 1731.

[30]Brauneder, "Widerlegung," HRG, vol. 5 (Berlin, 1998), cols. 1346–49; idem, *Ehegüterrecht*, 56.

[31]"Drittens wiederlegt Herr Hochzeiter das HeurathsGut mit gleichen 2000fl...und verhypotecirt sowohl diese Summe als auch das HeurathsGut selbst, also in allem 4000 fl...mit seinem ganzen Vermögen. Ausserdem gibt er seiner Jgfr Braut für eine Morgengabe einhundert Stück Species Dukaten als ein stätes und unwiederrufliches Eigenthum und behält sich noch das Vergnügen vor, sie am Hochzeitstage mit anständigem Schmuck und Kleidung aus seinen eigenen Mitteln zu versehen." SLA, Verlaß Stadtsyndikat, 2235 through 279.

[32]Like so many other historians, van Dülmen mentions only the "Morgengabe" as a means to provide financial security for widows, but ignores completely the well-devised system of wedding gifts and provisions regulating property rights.

[33]Brauneder, *Ehegüterrecht*, 50; Th. Mayer-Maly, "Morgengabe," HRG, vol. 3, (Berlin, 1984), col. 678–83. Thus it says in the 1781 marriage contract: "Die Morgengabe /: welche ohnehin als ein Theil ihres Schazgeldes jederzeit anzusehen ist." SLA, Verlaß Stadtsyndikat, 2235 through 279.

[34]Werner Ogris, "Gütergemeinschaft," HRG, vol. 1 (Berlin, 1971), cols. 1871–74.

ited community of property between spouses. It was widespread in Southern Germany and can be traced back in Salzburg to a written *Landesordnung* (Constitution) from 1526. In the case of Gschwendtner and Socher (1781), the wife was entitled to half of the capital as well as the profits of the business during her lifetime. The property she inherited or got as donations during her marriage was destined for her and her husband's joint benefit, but with the reservation that she could use her property as she wished at any time.

This clause in particular was modified individually according to economic and social circumstances. In the 1747 contract between Ranftl and Lechnerin—again a marriage between equal-ranking members of Salzburg's trading class—joint holding of the paraphernalia was agreed upon as usual. But the condition was added that the husband had to give 25 percent of the returns of this investment to his wife, who was entitled to use the money freely—not just for meeting the household expenses. Of course, many things can be stipulated in contracts without ever becoming reality. In my view, however, variations of a common pattern show how much margin could be left to women. If we look at the custom of specifying the joint benefit of separate assets in a positive light, we may assume that the wife could decide freely how to assess the interests of her capital, just like her husband. In yet another marriage contract, the detailed instruction is included that at least 25 percent of the income from a wife's capital could be used at her own discretion. From this follows that normally the husband, who owned and ran the business, could decide about the usufruct of his wife's capital.[37] Thus was made the above-mentioned provision in the contract between Ranftl and Lechnerin, which limited the husband's usufructuary right. Such an analysis of contracts under private law shows the epistemological limits of the history of law. A husband's decision about joint or separate capital was never a mere legal question. His decision was determined by the distribution of power within the families that owned the business, and his bourgeois background.

But even in the *altstaendisch* society, spouses of the same social rank did not always have equal wealth. On 4 February 1748, Martin Adam Prötz, son of a merchant, entered into a marriage contract with Anna Theresia Frankenbergerin, whose father owned a shop for fashionable articles. Since he had brothers, Martin Prötz had never been eligible to take over his father's business, but had learned the profession and was conducting the Frankenberger business at the time of the wedding. As regards the paraphernalia of the spouses, both owned their respective assets but had

---

[35]"Was künfftige Eheconsorten während ihrer Ehe mit ihrem Fleiß und guten Hauswürtschafft durch reichen Seegen Gottes gewünnen und erhausen werden, hervon solle iedem Theile durchgehendts die ungefortlete Helfte eigentümlich gebühren." SLA, Verlaß Stadtgericht, fas. 6, 1266 ex 1820, § 5: marriage contract between the merchant Joseph Ranftl and Maria Anna Lechnerin, a merchant's daughter, 15 October 1747.

[36]Ogris, "Errungensgemeinschaft," HRG, vol. 1 (Berlin, 1971), cols. 1004–6; Brauneder, *Ehegüterrecht*, 233, 235, 256.

[37]Anna Maria Lechner's inventory shows that she reinvested her capital assets plus interests in her business.

to invest them as capital for the business.[38] As the bridegroom had more property than Anna Theresia Frankenbergerin, it was agreed that if his wife should die before him, he would get the *Gerechtsame*, the privilege or license to take over the fancy goods business completely. In an urban economy in which a constant number of licenses or privileges limited the only possible entry to the market, a *Gerechtsame* was of great value. The "intangible" property of his wife was equal to his capital assets.

Women's freedom of decision is obvious in those cases in which they brought more assets and property to the marriage than their future husband. In 1789 the young widow of a *Gürtlermeister* (a manufacturer of miscellaneous items made of brass or metal) married Nikolaus Ort, the poor son of another manufacturer in the same professional group, and assigned her *Gerechtsame* to him. They established a partial community of property or, to be precise, a community of property acquired during their marriage. Their other assets and property holdings were not affected. This was of course relevant only to the wife, as her husband did not have any property to speak of. Logically, it was the wife who bought a second salesroom in the so-called *Gusettihaus*.[39]

In summation, we can observe that a partial community of property during marriage was established by those *Buerger* who owned titles or privileges such as licenses, capital, estates, and cash assets. Wives kept their legitimate claim to their parents' fortune. If they brought cash assets into the marriage, the money was put into the business and the women became more or less dormant partners.

A joint community of property—the other form of property sharing—was above all characteristic for farmers in the alpine regions.[40] It had to be agreed upon explicitly, but contrary to the partial community of property, it could be established sometime after the wedding. This variation applies, for example, to the above-mentioned tenants of a farm belonging to the Muelln monastery. The contract of lease was signed by both husband and wife on 28 May 1808; the marriage contract was made four months later.[41] Among the urban social strata, joint community of property was more prevalent among those whose professions did not require enormous capital investments. For the guild of bakers, there are two contracts from 1764 and 1783, each with different provisions for the marital property. The settlement dating from 1764 creates a joint community of property,[42] while a partial community of property is stipulated in the contract from 1783. Here, however, the bride was a brewer's daughter and expected a substantial inheritance.[43] According to the third

---

[38]SLA, Verlaß Stadtsyndikat, 807, 4 February 1748.

[39]SLA, Verlaß Stadtsyndikat, 183, inventory taken after her death, 21 January 1800.

[40]Brauneder, *Ehegüterrecht*, 323–24.

[41]SLA, Verlaß Stadtsyndikat, 964.

[42]SLA, Verlaß Stadtsyndikat, 2124 through 2202: contract between Joseph Fux and Anna Kallin.

[43]SLA, Verlaß Stadtsyndikat, 192, contract between Franz Egg and Maria Josepha Eschenbacher, daughter of Engelwerth Eschenbacher, brewer and innkeeper.

paragraph, the master baker Franz Egg promised to observe the obligations cussedly the partial community of property and to record the joint ownership of house and *Gerechtsame* at the town court.[44]

Josepha Gerlich, the daughter of a Salzburg *Kaffeesieder* (coffee roaster) and confectioner who, in spite of the compulsory guild membership, was not a member of the guild (*hofbefreit*), was married to Michl Pachmayr in 1769. Pachmayr, too, was a coffee roaster but was a guild member. Since the Pachmayrs had no children and had agreed on a joint community of property in their marriage contract, Josepha Pachmayrin was the sole heiress to her husband's 50 percent of the marital property. In her second marriage with a civil servant, again a joint community of property was established. In my view, this was just a clever legal structure enabling the civil servant to participate in Josepha's business profits. On their wedding day, he presented one thousand gulden, partly in borrower's note bonds (*Schuldverschreibungen*), partly in cash. This amount was equivalent to the sixfold value of her *Gerechtsame*. As her husband thus possessed half of their joint property,[45] real estate bought on 1 December 1790 belonged consequently to both spouses.

Let us now take a brief look at the lower ranks in the social spectrum. A marriage contract from 1808 made between the silver worker Georg Sedlymayr and Anna Pendle, the daughter of a clockmaker, illustrates how property was divided up by small businessmen. Together with the *Gerechtsame* her husband had bought for 450 gulden, the wife's *Heiratsgut* (300 gulden) and her trousseau became the foundation of a joint property.[46] In 1768, Joseph Schintlauer bought the *Gerechtsame* for a *Fragnerei*, a little grocery outside the town walls of Salzburg. Shortly afterwards he married Theresia Eschlberger, the daughter of a *Wegmacher* (someone in charge of road repairs). In the written marriage contract, he assigned 50 percent of the worth of his *Gerechtsame* to his future wife and expected *fleissige Hauswirtschaft* (proper housekeeping) from her in return. She brought the basic parts of their household effects into the marriage.[47]

By way of summarizing both legal forms of marriage contracts, one point has to be stressed. It is condensed in the formula, "what both spouses acquire and obtain

---

[44]"Sein gegenwerthig und zurkonfftiges Vermögen nicht hiervon besonders noch auß genommen seiner Jungfrau Hochzeiterin Maria Anna Kallin auch getreulich zurbringen und zu ihren Vermögen beylegen solle, als ihr der beeden PrautPersonen ganz völlige Vermögenschafft iezig und konfftig auf solche Weise zusammen geworfen seye, daß sie hiemit *societatem omnium tam presentium quam futurorum bonorum* wollen controllirt haben und hiervon ainen Thaill so vill als dem anderen /weillen sye nun würklich hierinnen reciproce in der Hellfte stehen:/ gebühren...." SLA, Verlaß Stadtsyndikat, 192, contract between Franz Egg and Maria Josepha Eschenbacher, third paragraph.

[45]SLA, Verlaß Stadtsyndikat, 191, contract between Leopold von Ehrich, civil servant at the chapter administration in Salzburg, and Maria Josepha Pachmayrin, 13 June 1787, and inventory taken after her death, 11 March 1803.

[46]SLA, Verlaß Stadtsyndikat, 859, 28 August 1808, § 1–3.

[47]SLA, Verlaß Stadtsyndikat, 1054, 18 July 1799.

during their marriage with their diligence and good housekeeping due to God's blessing."[48] This clearly shows that, first of all, marriage was an economic community of a wife and a husband. Certainly marriage was then the only way to a legitimate partnership in which man and woman could enjoy their sexuality and have legitimate descendants. Marriage contracts, however, let us perceive a community of life whose priority was to cope with the struggle of everyday life. This fact was vital for both forms of financial conditions in marriage contracts in the eighteenth century. The husband as the master of the house, representing the family members as well as the servants and employees of his business, was in a relatively high-ranking position, compared to his wife's status as housewife. When it came down to the protection and growth of property for the benefit of the next generation(s), however, it did not matter at all whether the household in question was headed by a prominent businessman or a small grocer. To accomplish this task, both wife and husband worked equally hard and prudently.[49] Before the nineteenth century, marriage was a legal community that did not distinguish between the rights of the individual and the property rights; even if the wife required a male advisor to enter into a business transaction,[50] she was always a fully accepted legal personality like her husband. When assets and titles of the spouses are counterbalanced, it appears that the different economic contributions by a wife and a husband were seen as equal.

A major change, however, came with the codification of private law, for the authors of the *ABGB* of 1811 proceeded on a different assumption about the wife's role. In the preliminary stages of the *ABGB* (that is, the *Codex Theresianus* of 1766, the *Josephinisches Gesetzbuch* of 1786, and the *Westgalizisches Gesetzbuch* of 1797), the marital community of property was still described as *societas* under the influence of *Gemeinrecht*.[51] Around 1800, however, a strong influence of natural law was beginning to alter the concept of marriage. Karl Anton von Martini and Franz von Zeiller, the founding fathers of the *ABGB*, emphasized the rights and obligations in a marriage, pointing out the husband's obligation to nourish and provide support. Neither Martini nor Zeiller saw the marriage as a partnership primarily for the purpose of securing and increasing the family fortune *(Erwerbsgemeinschaft)*, as had the

[48]"Was...beede künfftige Eheconsorten während ihrer Ehe mit ihrem Fleiß und guten Hauswürtschaft durch reichen Seegen Gottes gewünnen und erhausen werden...." SLA, Verlaß Stadtgericht, 1266 ex 1820, Ranftl vs. Lechner ex 1747, §5.
[49]Gunda Barth-Scalmani, "Salzburger Handelsfrauen, Frätschlerinnen, Fragnerinnen: Frauen in der Welt des Handels am Ende des 18. Jahrhunderts," in *L'Homme: Zeitschrift für feministische Geschichtswissenschaft*, vol. 6 (1995), 23–45; Barth-Scalmani, Ingrid Bauer, Sabine Fuchs, "Frauen und Arbeit," in Mazohl-Wallnig, *Die andere Geschichte*, 153–212, at 171 and 209.
[50]The need for male advisors for contract negotiations did not necessarily mean that women were worse off by law compared to men; see Ernst Holthöfer, "Die Geschlechtsvormundschaft: Ein Überblick von der Antike bis ins 19. Jahrhundert," in *Frauen in der Geschichte des Rechts*, 390–451, at 399, 424, 436–37.
[51]Brauneder, *Ehegüterrecht*, 270–71, 256–57; Brauneder, "Gesellschaft-Gemeinschaft-Gütergemeinschaft," in Brauneder, *Studien II*, 229–65; Brauneder, *Zu...den Ehepakten*, esp. I.A–D.

drafters of marriage contracts of the eighteenth century.[52] With the *ABGB,* a new concept of marriage became the model. According to paragraph 91 in the *ABGB,* the husband was destined to be the head of the family and had to do his best to nourish and support his wife. Paragraph 1237 established that in case of doubt, if no prior agreements concerning the marital property had been made, all earnings and profits would stem from the husband's work.[53] That clause simply ignored women's contribution to the household in general. It is no coincidence that in his commentary on the new marriage law, Zeiller failed to consider the assistance and work of women that was not confined to the house.

In the early nineteenth century, the working cooperation of spouses that had so long been taken for granted in agriculture, crafts, and trade was increasingly overlooked. According to a contemporary lawyer, the new marital property regime as defined by the *ABGB* was initially opposed by parts of the population.[54] In time, however, the bourgeois/middle class family model as set up in the *ABGB* gained ground as a norm for all, and women's work was no longer considered equal to that of a man. Instead, it was interpreted as the result of a woman's biologically determined yet voluntary and self-sacrificing kindness.[55]

MARRIAGE CONTRACTS AND THE SUCCESSION OF GENERATIONS

Within the life cycle of a *Buerger* marriage, there was often a moment in which responsibility for the family's business, trade, or craft was transferred. The transfer of the *Gerechtsame* from the parents to a son or daughter was often agreed upon in an *Übergabevertrag.* Such contracts made detailed arrangements for the transfer of the business[56] as well as the parents' dwelling rights, or how much money and property they would keep for their old age.[57] Such transfers and marriage contracts bound generations together. Marriage contracts very often included extensive provisions for

---

[52]U. Flossmann, "Franz von Zeiller," in *HRG,* vol. 5 (Berlin: 1998), cols. 1637–42; see also *Forschungsband Franz von Zeiller: Beiträge zur Gesetzgebungs- und Wissenschaftsgeschichte,* ed. W. Selb and H. Hofmeister, vol. 13, Wiener Rechtsgeschichtliche Arbeiten (Vienna, 1980).

For Martini's and Zeiller's difference of opinion, see Flossmann, "Die beschränkte Grundrechtssubjektivität der Frau: Ein Beitrag zum österreichischen Gleichheitsdiskurs," in *Frauen in der Geschichte des Rechts,* 293–324, esp. 295–305. For Martini, both spouses are equal by nature; in his view, they should both represent the head of the family (296); contrary to him, Zeiller saw the man as the head according to "natural" reasons (302).

[53]See *Das Allgemeine bürgerliche Gesetzbuch für die gesammten Deutschen Erbstaaten der Oesterreichischen Monarchie* (Vienna: 1811), § 1237.

[54]Oskar Lehner, *Familie-Recht-Politik: Die Entwicklung des österreichischen Familienrechts im 19. und 20. Jahrhundert,* vol. 13, Linzer Universitätsschriften (Vienna: Springer Verlag, 1987), 24 n. 49. Until now, the important question of how the population reacted has not been researched in detail.

[55]For the role of women's work as political economists saw it, see Gunda Barth-Scalmani, "Die Thematisierung der Haus/Frauenarbeit bei Lorenz von Stein," in *Bürgerliche Frauenkultur im 19. Jahrhundert,* ed. Brigitte Mazohl-Wallnig, vol. 2, L'Homme Schriften: Reihe zur feministischen Geschichtswissenschaft (Vienna: Bohlau, 1995), 81–124.

[56]For example, SLA, Verlaß Stadtsyndikat, 683, *Übergabevertrag* between Johann Peter Metzger and Kajetan Metzger, 23 November 1794.

the death of a spouse. Depending on whether a partial or joint community of property had been agreed upon, the surviving party was the sole heir(ess) to one half of the property; the paraphernalia were returned to the family from which they had originally come. Precise provisions were added concerning succession in case of childlessness, or if there were offspring to remember. If decedents had no children, usually the parents and siblings of both spouses were provided with endowments. The amounts were dependent on how much wealth the spouses brought into the marriage. Bride and groom had to provide for the relatives of each side. An upper limit to these endowments was fixed in order to ensure the interests and needs of the surviving spouse, thereby first of all securing the survival of the business or trade.[58]

Sometimes it was painstakingly specified how much money had to be considered for the various degrees of relationship.[59] The *Ort*-contract, for example, provided that if the (poor) husband died before his wife, his parents were entitled to his 50 percent of what had been acquired during the marriage.[60] If there were children, they inherited the deceased parent's 50 percent. Thus the surviving spouse, if he or she married again, and the children from the first marriage made a contract that settled claims to the inheritance and the transfer of the business.

When, for example, the father of the above-mentioned baker Franz Egg died in April 1775, Egg's widowed mother, Barbara Ratzinger, and her four children entered into a contract that specified how the bakery should be transferred. Her husband had stated in his will that his wife and children should own the bakery together, and that Barbara Ratzinger should run it for ten years until the most suitable offspring took over and became the new owner. To avoid difficulties that could be raised by the children's guardians while she was running the bakery, Barbara Ratzinger alone should dispose of the entire fortune during these ten years. The property which the children inherited from their father remained invested in the business and yielded 4

[57]SLA, Verlaß Stadtgericht, 204, *Übergabevertrag* between Joseph Kaspar Freysauff and his son Benedikt, 10 June 1787; see also Verlaß Stadtsyndikat, 346, *Übergabevertrag* between Georg Christoph Hagenauer and his son-in-law Christian Reiffenstuhl on provisions made in the marriage contract, 7 October 1741.

[58]"Drittens ist auf die Todfälle...beschlossen worden, daß im Fall Herr Hochzeiter vor seiner Jungfrau Hochzeiterin ohne Kinder aus dieser Ehe verstürbe, sodann die überlebende Witwe von dem gemeinsamen Vermögen, nemlich was dermalen zusammen geleget und bis dahin erhauset wird, seinen nächsten Anverwandten oder nach seiner Disposition nur 1200 fl. ... und was sich an Paraphernal Gut zeiget, hinauszugeben, all übriges aber ihr getreulich zu Händen verbleibe habe. Soll aber Viertens Jungfrau Hochzeiterin eben ohne Hinterlassung eines Kindes vor ihren H: Hochzeiter das Zeitliche segnen, so giebt selber ihren nächsten Anverwandten oder nach ihrer Disposition vom gemeinsamen Vermögen 1500 fl. ... nebst dem eingebrachten Paraphernal und ihrer Einrichtung hinaus, alles übrige aber bleibe ihm in unangefochtenen Eigenthum." SLA, Verlaß Stadtsyndikat, 192: marriage contract between Franz Egg/baker and Maria J. Eschenbacher/brewer's daughter, 30 December 1783.

[59]SLA, Verlaß Stadtsyndikat, 191: contract between Maria Josepha Pachmayrin and Leopold von Ehrich.

[60]SLA, Verlaß Stadtsyndikat, 183.

percent interest until the children's eighteenth birthdays. Only then was their mother permitted to pay out their share of the inheritance. She also had to pay for educational and training costs. The children in turn had certain obligations toward their mother; for example, if the only daughter still lived at home after her eighteenth birthday, she was expected to pay up to thirty-five gulden each year for board. This was twice what female servants in urban households were paid yearly. The cook and the maidservant employed in the household of a young merchant's wife, Elisabeth Haffner, were paid eighteen gulden in 1781, plus five gulden in *Biergeld*, a sort of allowance; board and lodging were free.[61] If one of the children was out of work or fell ill, he or she could expect meals to be cooked and someone to look after him or her at the mother's home.[62]

When a wife survived her husband, she was usually given a free hand concerning the *Gerechtsame*. Such a license was no mere legal title, but of great value in an eighteenth-century corporative urban economy. Therefore the private-law provisions in marriage contracts have to be considered together with the rules of the guilds or trade associations. Widows, for example, had the right to carry on the business if they were competent, but in most cases only for a limited period of time, after which they were expected to get remarried to a member of the guild. They could not decide according to their own personal judgment, but had to act in consideration of the duties implied by their rank and class. Only when widows married for the second or even third time, could they leave the confines imposed by the maxims and principles of their own rank.

To conclude, precautions taken in marriage contracts included provisions for the death of a partner. In most cases, marriage contracts were accompanied by settlements arranging for the passing on of fortune between parents and children. Not only did they serve to ensure the passing on of material goods over several generations; they also wove a net of mutual responsibility which secured the succession of generations in a household and created the notion of continuity in those social groups that in early modern history were beginning to form the middle classes.[63] The generations accepted mutual responsibility for each other. The basic function of marriage and transfer contracts was to keep the family's business, trade, or craft profitable. Therefore the role of women was vital. As daughters, wives, mothers, and widows, they kept the substance of a family fortune and a business intact.

---

[61]SLA, HS M 81; for details, see Gunda Barth-Scalmani, "Weibliche Dienstboten in der Stadt des ausgehenden 18. Jahrhunderts: Leopold Mozart's 'Seccaturen mit den Menschen,'" in *Mitteilungen der Gesellschaft für Salzburger Landeskunde*, vol. 137 (1997), 199–218, at 209.

[62]SLA, Verlaß Stadtsyndikat, 192, *Übergabevertrag*, 3 November 1775.

[63]Wunder, *Er ist die Sonn'*, 95; see also Josef Ehmer, *Sozialgeschichte des Alters* (Frankfurt: Suhrkamp, 1990).

SUMMARY

To take up the opening question of whether marriage contracts can give insight into gender relations in early modern history, it can be said that it is difficult to analyze these relations, as they are embedded in a typical legal discourse which acts as a barrier to an immediate historical understanding. A clear legal position of women before 1800 cannot be defined because there was then no uniformly settled and binding law. The position of women bound by contract was dependent on their status within the family, rather than solely on their gender. Additional influential factors to consider were the financial circumstances of the families from which the spouses came, and the social rank of both families within the professional group they belonged to. Moreover, the kind of trade families were involved in also played a role: for example, the wife of a merchant could understand the development of the family fortune only with the help of experts in order to gain insight into the intricacies of bookkeeping. Wives of brewers or bakers, however, could judge business prospects by keeping an eye on the goings on in their immediate sphere of work. Marriage contracts therefore reflect primarily the economic everyday life of members in a corporative society. These contracts should not be analyzed in isolation, but within the context of the succession of generations. Like men, women could keep property and assets intact and pass them on, thereby mobilizing capital for a corporative urban economy.

It must be emphasized, though, that "marriage" in the analyzed contracts of the eighteenth century means a concept that from the nineteenth century was labelled "premodern" or "traditional" under the influence of the then so-called "modern" European codifications of private law. In the eighteenth century contracts, "marriage" still stood for a legal partnership in which the idea of additional wealth jointly created during the marriage was well in the forefront.

The role of women as depicted in the *ABGB* is unthinkable without these philosophical and anthropological concepts, which were defined in the last decades of the eighteenth century, to prove that it was in woman's "nature" to be weak not only in body, but also in mind.[64] Although in the *ABGB* marriage was interpreted as a contract based on natural law, this concept depended on the precondition that the wife subordinated herself voluntarily to the physically and intellectually stronger man.[65] The authors of the *ABGB* took the marriage and family model which was familiar to them as high-ranking civil servants[66] as a norm for all: the husband

---

[64]Claudia Honegger, *Die Ordnung der Geschlechter: Die Wissenschaften vom Menschen und das Weib 1750–1850* (Frankfurt: Campus, 1991); Ute Frevert, "Bürgerliche Meisterdenker und das Geschlechterverhältnis: Konzepte, Erfahrungen und Visionen an der Wende vom 18. zum 19. Jahrhundert," in *Bürgerinnen und Bürger: Geschlechterverhältnisse im 19. Jahrhundert,* ed. Ute Frevert (Göttingen: Vandenhoeck & Ruprecht, 1988), 17–48.

[65]Zeiller, *Natürliches Privatrecht,* § 161.

[66]For biographical hints of some of the *ABGB* collaborators, see Lehner, *Familie-Recht-Politik,* 50–51, nn. 20, 21.

attended to his business outside the house, while the wife ran the household. This family model—in 1811 confined to a small urban group—was adopted widely in the course of the nineteenth century when more and more social groups modelled their life upon the principles and practices of the bourgeois/middle class. The idea of marriage as an economic community of two equal partners got gradually lost. Consequently housework was no more regarded as an adequate contribution for the maintenance of a family. It was not until 1975 that this relevant point in the *ABGB* was reformed in Austria.

PART 5

En-Gendering Selfhood
Defining Differences and Forging Identities
in Early Modern Europe

Kristin Eldyss Sorensen Zapalac

*Once upon a time a man lost his wife, who left behind her a suckling baby. The man
was so poor that he could not afford to hire a nurse for the child. But a miracle happened
to him, and his breasts grew so large that he was able to feed his child like a nurse.*

Not surprisingly, the miracle attracted comment, in this case from three teachers
who, naturally, had to make a lesson of it. One insisted that the man must have been
very virtuous, since God had "performed such a miracle for him." Another insisted
instead that the man must have been quite bad, since "for his sake the order of creation had to be changed." Finally, the third spoke: "Come," he said,

> and see how many difficult tasks God must perform for man before He
> provides his food for him, seeing that God changed the order of creation
> for his sake and made it possible for him to suckle the child. For the Lord
> could have created food for the baby, and yet He performed a miracle so
> that the man himself could feed the child.

That story was printed in 1602; another, printed in English in the same period,
involved not a man who developed breasts, but rather a man who was told by the
local doctor that he was pregnant. On hearing the diagnosis,

> in despairing manner he beganne to rage, and cry aloud, saying to his wife.
> Ah thou wicked woman. ...thou hast done me this mischeefe: for alwayes
> thou wilt be upon me, ever railing at mee, and fighting, untill thou hast
> gotten me under thee....

According to the narrator of the tale, however, "The Woman, being of verie
honest and civill conversation, hearing her husband speake so foolishly, blushing
with shame, and hanging downe her head in bashfull manner, without returning
any answer, went forth of her chamber." Neither her silence nor her departure

assuaged his rage:

> How shal I be delivered of this child? Which way can it come from me into the world? I plainly perceyve that I am none other than a dead man, and all through the wickednesse of my Wife....Were I now in as good health, as heeretofore I have beene, I would rise out of my bed and never cease beating her....Hang me, if ever she get me under her againe, or make me such an Asse, in having the mastery over mee.

The reader knows, of course, that the husband is not pregnant. Not because the narrator says that a man could not become pregnant if he were to allow his wife to assume his rightful position of dominance: he doesn't. And not even because the reader has been in on the joke from the beginning. The reader knows that the husband is not pregnant because the narrator has assured us that in this case the wife was "verie honest and of civill conversation"—in other words, not that sort of woman.

This second story is familiar to most scholars of early modern Europe and to many others as well. It is the famous tale told by Philostratus on the ninth day of the *Decameron*, reproduced here in an anonymous English translation first published in 1620.[1] My first story, taken from a collection published in Basel by Konrad Waldkirch in 1602, is considerably less familiar. The collection was assembled not by Giovanni Boccaccio, but by an unknown collector, and published on behalf of Jacob ben Abraham of Mezeritch, whose relation to the text is unclear. He may have translated a portion of it or even edited the whole between 1581 and the end of the century.[2]

Despite the fact that one lived in the era of manuscripts and the other in the era of printed books, both Boccaccio and Jacob ben Abraham (whom for convenience I shall treat as editor of the *Ma'aseh Book*) intended their collections for the popular audience. Each published his collection in his community's vernacular: Boccaccio in Italian, ben Abraham in Judeo-German, that is, in Hebrew characters representing the Judeo-German (Yiddish) dialect spoken in Switzerland and along the Rhine. Each took his tales from a variety of sources. According to the title page of the 1602 *Ma'aseh Book*, its "three hundred" tales had been drawn from the Gemara, the *Midrash Rabbah*, the writings of Bechai ibn Pakuda, an eleventh-century philosopher, and the life of Judah the Pious, the head of the Jewish community in Regensburg in the twelfth century.[3] In fact, 157 of the 254 stories in the 1602 edition were taken from the Babylonian and Palestinian Talmuds, and from learned commentar-

---

[1]Giovanni Boccaccio, *Decameron*, trans. Edward Hutton, vol. 4 (1620; reprint, London: AMS Press, 1909), 144.

[2]*Ma'aseh Book: Book of Jewish Tales and Legends*, trans. Moses Gaster, vol. 1 (Philadelphia: Jewish Publication Society of America, 1934), 1: xxix, xxxv–vi; the story appears on 16–17. For a discussion of the identity of the compiler, see Jakob Meitlis, *Das Ma'assebuch, seine Entstehung und Quellengeschichte zugleich ein Beitrag zur Einführung in die altjiddische Agada* (Berlin: R. Mass, 1933), 21–22, 127–48.

[3]The title page is given by Meitlis, *Das Ma'assebuch*, 23–24.

ies on the Mishnah, the oral law held to have been given by Moses contemporaneously with the written law (the familiar commandments of the Hebrew Bible) and fixed early in the third century CE by Judah ha-Nasi on the basis of an oral tradition dating back to the time of Ezra the scribe (ca. 450 BCE).[4]

As the discussion engendered by the widower's story makes clear, the compilers of the Talmuds approached the task of interpreting divinely inspired texts differently than did their Christian contemporaries Jerome, Augustine, and Gregory the Great. To those accustomed to the church fathers' insistence on a single (revealed) truth and their efforts to resolve all apparent dissonance, the Talmud may seem cacophonous—a collection of exempla and conflicting interpretations couched as a seemingly endless series of debates without resolution. By the same token, a closer comparison of Jewish and Christian versions of some key stories reveals that the Judeo-Christian fear of "the indeterminacy of the body"[5] and the anxiety often associated with "the oxymoronic one-sex body" of medical literature[6] is a peculiarly Christian phenomenon. References to manly women (IV Maccabees) and effeminate men (Philo's "On the Contemplative Life") disappear from Jewish texts with the rise of rabbinic Judaism after the destruction of the temple in 70 CE.

It is among *Christian* Europeans that we encounter "gender dissonance," that is, a psyche described as masculine or effeminate attached to a body of the "wrong" sex. The anxiety about gender dissonance so characteristic of Christian writings in the early modern period requires a notion of a selfhood (psyche or soul in the parlance of the period) engendered not so much by bodily sex, as by the soul's ability to dominate or control that sexed body. That is, it requires a Hellenistic view of the engendering of selfhood, a view that was effectively banished from mainstream Judaism with the fall of the temple. It is a paradox peculiar to Christian writers that the woman or man whose successful disciplining of the body proves the "manliness" of the soul (that is, its dominance of the body), may discover the "truer selfhood," that is, abandonment of the individualized self in (feminized) absorption into the divine. Within Judaism, such genderings of self and god are reserved for rarified discussions among the cognoscenti of esoteric mystical writings such as the *Zohar*, the classic thirteenth-century kabbalistic text.

The *Zohar* was unknown to readers of the *Ma'aseh Book*. Like most of the tales in that popular book, the story of the widower and the three rabbis was taken from what is chronologically the second (and therefore more comprehensive) Talmud, whose compilation by the Jewish scholars of Babylon was largely complete by the

---

[4]The source for each story is given in Gassner's notes to his translation of the *Ma'aseh Book*, 2: 665–94, and, with some errors, in the heading that appears above each of the earlier tales in the Basel edition. Cf. Meitlis, *Das Ma'assebuch*, 111 n.5.

[5]Peter Brown, *The Body and Society: Men, Women, and Sexual Renunciation in Early Christianity* (New York: Columbia University Press, 1988), 438.

[6]Thomas Laqueur, *Making Sex: Body and Gender from the Greeks to Freud* (Cambridge, Mass.: Harvard University Press, 1992), 19.

early decades of the sixth century CE. The three rabbis of the tale are Judah bar Ezekiel (220–99), the head of the academy at Pumbedita, Joseph, and Abbaye (d. 339 CE), a student of Judah's successor who himself came to direct the same school.[7]

In both the Talmud and the *Ma'aseh Book,* Rabbi Joseph is the first to interpret the meaning of the event the narrator has already defined as a miracle. Although the context of the story in the Talmud is surprising—it appears in the tractate of the Sabbath in the midst of a discussion of whether or not goats may be sent out on the sabbath carrying a pouch attached to their udders—Joseph's conclusion is the same in each version. "Come," he says, "and see what a good man he must have been that the Lord, blessed be He, should have performed such a miracle for him." To Abbaye, who was involved in the final editing of the Babylonian Talmud, the *Ma'aseh Book* (in Gassner's translation of the 1602 edition), attributes the conclusion that the widower was "bad," a moral judgment considerably less subtle than Abbaye's conclusion in the Talmud. In the Talmud he had insisted instead that God's action was the result of the widower's lowly status. This is, as Epstein points out, a reversal of the position he had taken in an earlier tractate, one which Rashi in his turn explains as a reference to the widower's poverty and inability to earn money for a wet nurse.[8]

Rab Judah, the third speaker in both accounts, broadens the discussion from the status of the widower to the relationship between God and humankind. In contrast to the Rab Judah of the *Ma'aseh Book*, who celebrates God's efforts on behalf of humankind, the Rab Judah of the Sabbath tractate is a Moses wearied by his people's complaints: "Come and see how difficult are man's wants [of being satisfied], that the order of creation had to be altered for him!" Both versions conclude with what we might call a moral: the observation that God, who performs many miracles for the protection of the human race, nevertheless does not create its food for it. Neither the narrator of the *Ma'aseh Book* nor Rabbi Nahman, who voices this truth in the Talmudic *exemplum*, makes the obvious link back to the curse laid on Adam after the Fall. Perhaps the connection can be considered literally to have gone without saying. More to the point, no one in either version of the tale of the widower and the rabbis' conclusions displays any of the anxiety about the relation between the widower's growth of breasts and the widower's masculinity we have come to expect from other (Christian) sources.

Clearly, the Jewish tale depends on an understanding of the relation between body and gender as foreign to the stories of Boccaccio as it is to recent scholarship on the meaning of gender in early modern Europe. In the *Decameron,* the possibility is left open that behaving "like a woman"—allowing her to assume the dominant role (Natalie Davis's famous "woman on top"[9])—can lead to biological transformation,

[7]Shulamis Frieman, *Who's Who in the Talmud* (Northvale: Jason Aronson, 1995); *A Rabbinic Anthology*, ed. C. G. Montefiore and H. Loewe (London: Jewish University Press, 1938), 492, 704, 706.
[8]Shabbath 53b = *Babylonian Talmud: Seder Mo'ed I*, trans. and ed. Isidore Epstein (London: Soncino, 1938), 245–46.
[9]Natalie Zemon Davis, "Women on Top," in *Society and Culture in Early Modern France* (Stanford:

to literal degen(d)eration. In contrast, the arrangement of the rabbis' comments in both the Talmud and the *Ma'aseh Book* effectively excludes the suggestion that the widower's biological transformation is a marker of anything other than his god's miraculous intervention. Although a leading commentator on biblical and Talmudic medicine describes the Talmudic case as "expressly denoted to represent a 'change in nature,'" it is nowhere interpreted as a change in the nature or the selfhood of the widower himself.[10]

According to a midrashic source, another contemporary rabbi, Abbahu (ca. 279–320 CE), the leading scholar at the yeshiva in Caeserea (the school responsible for the tractate on civil law in the earlier Palestinian Talmud), once suggested that Mordecai, who elsewhere was said to have "illumined the eyes of Israel," and to have been "heard by God when he offered up prayer," had himself nursed his ward Esther, the Jewish heroine celebrated in the feast of Purim, with milk miraculously produced from his own breasts.[11] Although the congregation to whom Abbahu spoke is recorded as having laughed at their learned rabbi, the twentieth-century compiler of *The Legends of the Jews* writes approvingly that Mordecai "himself did not hesitate to do services for the child that are usually performed only by women." This line is oddly reminiscent of Martin Luther's recommendation that fathers should not be ashamed to change their children's diapers—and the Mishnah itself refers to the "milk of a male" in another context.[12] Despite his congregation's response, there is no hint that Abbahu's interpretation was denigrating a Jewish hero; instead, it was seen by the rabbi and his successors as indicative of the providential nature of Mordecai's collaboration with Esther.

I dwell on the story of the Jewish widower not only because it reveals a striking lack of the anxiety about masculine identity that most historians of early modern Europe and their readers have come to expect, but also because it is a tale with a history. Boccaccio's tale of Calandrino's "pregnancy" also has a history, one that provides even more striking evidence of the differences between the Jewish and Christian conceptions of the engendering of selfhood and the relation between body and behavior.

The earliest extant versions of the story of a man diagnosed as pregnant by his doctor date from the end of the twelfth century, where they form part of the lively interchange of fables between Christian and Jewish (and, through intermediaries,

---

Stanford University Press, 1973), 124–51

[10]Julius Preuss, *Biblical and Talmudic Medicine*, trans. and ed. Fred Rosner (New York: Sanhedrin, 1978), 410.

[11]Reported in Preuss, *Biblical and Talmudic Medicine*, 410.

[12]Louis Ginzberg, *The Legends of the Jews* (Philadelphia: Jewish Publication Society of America, 1939), 4: 383, 6: 459 n. 66. My thanks to David Hadas for this reference. Preuss, *Biblical and Talmudic Medicine*, 410, cites Machshirin 6:7 for the "milk of a male"; Genesis Rabbah 30:8 for the congregation's laughter.

Arabic and Persian) writers in England and France before the expulsion of the Jews from those countries.[13] As one scholar of such folktales puts it, "There is in the domain of fable...a continuous, rather complex interaction between literary and oral tradition, each trend and stream nurturing and reinforcing the other."[14] As we shall see, the fable at the root of Boccaccio's tale is not only a part of a genre that blurs the boundaries between high and low; the first recorded versions of that fable reveal the extent to which other boundaries could also be breached.

Although scholars have discovered no trace of the tale before 1150,[15]after that date it appeared almost simultaneously in three fable collections. The best-known of these (and quite possibly the first) is the *Ysopet* or *Esope* (to use the title common in the manuscripts) composed in Old French by a Christian whose name scholars take

---

[13]In 1198, Philip Augustus readmitted the Jews he had expelled from his territories in 1182, and thereby enriched his treasury through the taxes and duties he assessed on the banking industry. The Jews were not expelled from England until 1290.

[14]Haim Schwarzbaum, *The Mishlé Shu'lim (Fox Fables) of Rabbi Berechiah ha-Nakdan* (Kiron, Israel: Institute for Jewish and Arab Folklore Research, 1979), xxi.

[15]I can give no explanation for Roberto Zapperi's assertion that this and another story appear only in two German manuscripts of the [Romulus] collection, which show signs of subsequent and much later editing. They are certainly earlier than [Marie's?] translation into old French, which dates from the second half of the twelfth century. The collection is undoubtedly monastic in origin, and enjoyed great success in northwestern Europe, from where it originally spread abroad.

The Pregnant Man, trans. Brian Williams (Chur, Switzerland: Harwood, 1991), 63, 233. I used the English edition of *L'uomo incinto* (Cosenza: Lerici, 1979) since it is described as the "fourth edition, revised and updated for English translation."

Zapperi referenced only Ben Edwin Perry's *Aesopica: A Series of Texts Relating to Aesop or Ascribed to Him or Closely Connected with the Literary Tradition That Bears His Name* (Urbana: University of Illinois Press, 1952), 671, 682, no. 684, where the story appears in the Latin of the codex Bruxellensis 536, a fable collection to which Perry did not assign a date, but identified only as "related to [*cognatae*] Robert's Romulus," an identification he omitted in 1965 when he published an English translation of the fables in the collection in the appendix to his Loeb edition of *Babrius and Phaedrus* (Cambridge, Mass.: Harvard University Press, 1965), 572, 583–84, no. 684. Perry's own source appears to have been Léopold Hervieux, *Les fabulistes latins depuis le siècle d'Auguste jusqu'à la fin du moyen âge* (Paris: Firmin-Didot, 1884–99), to which he refers frequently albeit never with complete citation. Much of Perry's preface is devoted to a critique of Hervieux's organization of the fables, and Perry cites the work frequently in the Latin section of his *Aesopica*; despite this, I can find no indication of the edition he has used except the following midsentence reference on 553: "Leopoldus Hervieux: *Les Fabulistes Latins*, Parisiis 1894." Based on this date and the pagination differences between Perry's citations to Hervieux and my own, I assume that he had access to the corrected and apparently expanded edition (1893–94) of vols. 1 and 2 of Hervieux's work. I had access only to the 1884 edition of those volumes, a fact reflected by my own pagination in what follows.

Although both Perry's *Aesopica* and the *Babrius* are frequently referenced in the most recent catalogue of German fables in the medieval and early modern period, the tale of the pregnant man does not appear in the German collections known to Gerd Dicke and Klaus Grubmüller, *Die Fabeln des Mittelalters und der frühen Neuzeit: Ein Katalog der deutschen Versionen und ihrer lateinischen Entsprechungen*, Münstersche Mittelalter-Schriften 60 (Munich: Wilhelm Fink, 1987). It appears therefore to have been unknown to German collectors of fables before the Boccaccio (that is, Hans Sachs) version.

---

from a line in the epilogue to her collection: "*Marie ai nun, si sui de France*" ("Marie is my name, I am from France").[16] No name is attached to another closely related Latin (and therefore obviously Christian) collection now in the Royal Library in Brussels. Finally, in addition to the collections in Old French and Latin, there is a Hebrew collection called the *Mishle Shu'alim* or *Fox Fables*, compiled by Berechiah ben Natronai he-Nakdan, a French or English Jew employed as a copyist punctuating Hebrew texts and translating from Latin and French into Hebrew.[17]

Sadly, little more is known about the compilers for whom we have names than about the one who remains anonymous. The provenance and orthography of the earliest of the twenty-three surviving manuscripts of Marie de France's collection seems to place her residence in Norman England. Like the learned Berechiah, she mediated between linguistic cultures; she was knowledgeable in Latin, French, and probably English.[18] Self-consciously locating herself in the tradition of Aesop, whom she held (incorrectly but typically for her day) to have translated fables from Greek into Latin, Marie concluded her collection with an epilogue in which she declared:

> For love of Count William,
> most valiant in the realm,
> I was driven to make this book
> and to translate from English into [Old French].
> This book is called "Esope,"
> after the one who translated and wrote it,
> turning the Greek into Latin.
> King Ælfred, who loved it greatly,
> then translated it into English,
> from which I have rhymed it in French.[19]

Although, as we shall see, Marie's is not the only reference to an "Ælfredic" collection, no trace of it survives. It is nevertheless clear that either Ælfred or Marie knew the Aesopian fables of the Phaedrus tradition from the medieval *Romulus nilantii*—it is the source for the first forty fables in Marie's collection.[20] Below is my

---

[16]*Die Fabeln der Marie de France*, ed. Karl Warnke on basis of materials by Eduard Mall, Bibliotheca Normannica 6 (Halle: M. Niemeyer, 1898), 369, Ep. 13.

[17]Although he is generally referred to by recent scholars as "Rabbi," Berechiah did not describe himself so in his own work. Nor is there any evidence that he led a yeshiva. I therefore omitted the title.

[18]For what we know of the life of Marie de France and her composition of the fables, see Marie de France, *Fables*, ed. and trans. Harriet Spiegel (Toronto: University of Toronto Press, 1987), 3–6; Warnke, *Fabeln*, cxii–cxviii.

[19]My translation of Marie de France, fable 42, from the Old French text given in Warnke, *Fabeln*, 328. Hervieux also gives a Latin translation of Marie's text from codices MS 347b and c in the Bibliothèque nationale, Paris: *Fabulistes*, 2 (1884), 486 no. 8.

[20]Numbers 49 and 66 are also to be found in the *Romulus nilantii*, a collection that was itself already several generations removed from the Aesopic originals. Numbers 60, 66–67, 72, 75, 85–86, 88–89, and 102 are to be found in other manuscripts from the *Romulus* tradition. Schwarzbaum, *Mishlé Shu'lim*, xxxii–xxxiv.

translation from the Old French of Marie de France's forty-second tale, the second in her collection that comes not from the *Romulus* but was apparently added by Ælfred:

> Concerning a physician who served
> a rich man, caring for him
> during a grave illness.
> After he had drawn blood, he gave orders
> to his daughter, that she
> preserve it from harm.
> From that blood, he said, he would identify
> her father's illness.
> The maiden carried the blood
> into her chamber to a bench.
> But things went badly for her—
> she spilt all the blood.
> This she dared not tell or show...
> She could hit on no other plan
> but to replace it with her own.
> So she let the blood cool down
> before the doctor examined it;
> He, when he saw it, knew that
> the one from whom it had come was pregnant.
> The rich man was dumbfounded—
> he really thought he was with child!
> He called for his daughter.
> Partly from anxiety, partly from love,
> she revealed the truth:
> she had spilled the blood drawn from him,
> and the other was from her.

Marie's fable ends with the daughter's confession: we know nothing of her father's reactions to her admission. Instead, the narrator admonishes her reader that

> So it goes with tricksters,
> with thieves and drunkards:
> those who deal in treachery,
> will be snared by it as well.
> However they take care to escape the fine,
> they will be burdened with death.[21]

[21]My translation based on the text given in Warnke, *Fabeln*, 138–39.

Without the benefit of the father's reaction, and told of the daughter only that (1) she spilt the blood, (2) she tried to hide her mistake, (3) she was pregnant, and (4) she both loved and feared her father, we are surely entitled to wonder why Marie has classed her with tricksters, thieves, and drunkards. There is, however, still more reason to wonder at the rich man. Why does he accept his physician's diagnosis? Like Calandrino, the rich man does not question his "pregnancy." Unlike Calandrino, however, he is not the butt of joke; he is not depicted as a fool at whom we are to laugh when he is tricked by a false physician. Again, unlike Calandrino, the rich man appears to have no wife to blame for his predicament. Marie, in fact, does not tell us to what behavior or cause the rich man ascribes his predicament. We are told only that the rich man does not question the doctor's diagnosis. As far as he and his doctor are concerned, men can become pregnant without warning!

Marie's is not the only Christian version of the fable of the pregnant man to have come down to us from the high Middle Ages. A somewhat more expansive prose version appears in an anonymous Latin codex in the Bibliothèque Royale in Brussels shortly after the line "*Hactenus Aesopus; quod sequitur addidit rex Affrus*" ("Thus far, Aesop; King Affrus added what follows").[22] As Karl Warnke pointed out in his edition of the fables of Marie de France, the transformation of "King Ælfred" into "King Affrus" by an author believed to have been English appears extremely unlikely, unless the author was working from an Old French manuscript such as Marie's, in which it would have been possible to misread the "l" in "Alfrez" or "Alfres" as an "f," and thus to latinize the unfamiliar name as "Affrus."[23] Regardless of the relation between the *Esope* of Marie de France and the anonymous Latin codex, the author of the latter appears to have been rather more interested in accounting for the moral's harshness than was Marie. According to the Latin prose version,

> A certain rich man let some blood which he gave into his daughter's care, in order that the physician might later inspect it and discover in it reliable markers of his illness. But in fact the negligent daughter guarded the blood badly. Indeed, overturned by a dog, it spilled out partially and was partially lapped up. When she discovered this, the girl, fearing her father's anger, was so disturbed she told a friend. In consolation this girl said: "I know what you should do—let your own blood into the same container. Give that to the physician when your father orders it!" The advice pleased her and she hastened to follow it. As soon as he saw the blood, the physician, an observer incapable of being deceived in his art, read in it the absolutely certain markers of pregnancy. He said to the lord: "I'm certain, according

[22]According to Hervieux, *Fabulistes* 2, 569, the line appears immediately before the fable that precedes "Of the rich man from whom blood was drawn" in the codex Bruxellensis 356 in the Bibliothèque Royale Albert 1er, Brussels.
[23]Warnke, *Fabeln*, li.

to the rules of my art, that this blood reveals that the one from whom it was drawn is pregnant!" The lord was shocked. It wasn't enough that he couldn't conceive how this unheard of thing was happening in him; he also conceived great fear concerning his future parturition. His whole household was shocked and dumbfounded, and distressed about their pregnant master. Not knowing what to do, they called the physician a liar and a cheat. While the household was so stirred up and terrified of the coming dangers, they began urgently asking how this had happened, and—the blood stain having been discovered—as soon as they surmised the truth, they surrounded the girl and interrogated her. Seeing that it was impossible to deceive the physician, the girl told them what had happened, and revealed her disgrace to her father.

The narrator concludes the substantially wordier fable with a moral paradoxically brief: "Thus that which through infidelity and negligence is less than honorable shall be made known."[24]

It is not, however, only in the brevity and comparative mildness of its moral that this fable differs from Marie's. Where Marie was content to cap a bare outline of an event with its moral, this author likes the liveliness of direct discourse. Together with details designed to cast the daughter in a bad light, this preference prepares us for the moral that is ironically less harsh. As was not the case in Marie's version, the reader is informed that (1) "the negligent daughter guarded the blood badly"; (2) she confessed her misdeed to a friend and allowed herself to be led into further error; and most damningly, (3) far from confessing to relieve her father's anxiety about his condition, she spoke only after members of the household had been led by their discovery of the bloodstain to discern the truth and force the confession from her, and even then only because it was clear that she could not bluff the physician.

Nevertheless, the differences between the two Christian versions of the fable can be said to be more apparent than real. They agree in the essentials. Thus, although the servants are prepared to call the physician a liar and a cheat, the rich man himself does not question the diagnosis or its application to himself. Although he himself is no fool, the rich man is like Calandrino in that he worries about the biological practicalities of his parturition. Although only Boccaccio's fool seeks and assigns a cause for his pregnancy, not one of the pregnant males in the three Christian versions of the tale doubts his pregnancy. As we shall see, this is not the case in the contemporaneous Jewish version of the same story.

[24]My translation of the text given in Hervieux, *Fabulistes* 2, 569–70, no. 114. Perry's English version in *Babrius and Phaedrus*, 583-84, no. 684, is actually a paraphrase that substitutes indirect discourse for the much more active Latin account. Cf. the Latin in his *Aesopica*, 682, no. 684. Although Hervieux himself dates the Brussels codex to the fifteenth century in the 1884 edition of vol. 1 (600) of the *Fabulistes*, its dating and thus its relation to Marie's collection is disputed by scholars: cf. Warnke, *Fabeln*, xlviii–lx.

Our final early version of the tale of the man told he was pregnant comes from the Hebrew collection by Marie de France's Jewish contemporary Berechiah. Although Marie de France's work is generally ascribed to the 1170s, the date for Berechiah's *Mishle Shu'alim* or *Fox Fables* is less certain. According to an Oxford document, a certain "Benedictus le Puncteur" was resident there in the late twelfth century. "Benedictus" is, of course, the Latin for "blessed," a translation of the Hebrew "berechiah." Similarly, "le punctuator" seems intended to be read as "pointer," and thus a rough Latin equivalent of the Hebrew "ha-nakdan."[25] If indeed he was at Oxford at the end of the century, Berechiah could well have known Marie de France's work or even the "Ælfred" collection to which she attributed her fables. Moses Hadas sums up the scholarly consensus: "The uncertainties about the exact dates of both Marie de France and Berechiah preclude any final decision about which of them was the source for the other, but all the evidence we have indicates that Berechiah drew on the collection of Marie de France."[26] Whether her collection was indeed the source of both the fable in the anonymous Latin collection and Berechiah's eighty-first tale, or whether each of the three found the tale in a third (Ælfred's?) collection no longer extant, the similarities and differences among the three are instructive.

Berechiah's version is—as usual—much more detailed than that of Marie de France, more detailed even than that of the anonymous Latin author. One scholar has described Berechiah as "breit" (broad) and "weitschweifig" (detailed, circumstantial, or tedious) in contrast to Marie, who is "kurz" (brief) and "knapp" (terse). Since it is the details that interest me, I again give the whole of the fable, this time in the translation made by Hadas shortly before his death:

> A physician let blood for a patient and said to him: "This blood thou shalt watch over strictly until the third day, and upon the third day I shall see whether thou wilt go free of the disease that troubles thee and how thou mayest be relieved of it. By the blood I shall recognize every stumbling block, every plague and source of ill. All that plagues a patient is made manifest by the blood, whether it be green, black, white, or ruddy, for blood is the soul of all flesh.

Clearly Berechiah's style is as advertised, his account enriched with details of medical practice and with a quotation from the Torah. The line "for blood is the soul of all flesh" is an almost direct quotation from the Torah: "For the life of the flesh [is]

[25] *Fables of a Jewish Aesop Translated from the Fox Fables of Berechiah ha-Nakdan*, trans. Moses Hadas (New York: Columbia University Press, 1967), ix; Schwarzbaum, *Mishlê Shu'lim*, xxxii–xxxv, liv–lv, ns. 143–46; and more extensively Albert C. Friend, "The Tale of the Captive Bird and the Traveler: Nequam, Berechiah, and Chaucer's *Squire's Tale*," *In Honor of S. Harrison Thompson*, ed. P. M. Clogan, *Medievalia et Humanistica*, n.s., 1 (1970): 57–65, at 64–65 n. 9.

[26] *Fables of a Jewish Aesop*, viii.

in the blood: and I have given it to you upon the altar to make an atonement for your souls: for it [is] the blood [that] maketh an atonement for the soul." Nevertheless, the passage in Leviticus 17:11, 14 serves a very different purpose than the physician's words in Berechiah's fable. In Leviticus, it is God who tells Moses that "the life of the flesh [is] in the blood" in order to explain the prohibition against consuming the blood of an animal, and thus the restrictions on the manner in which animals were slaughtered. "For [it is] the life of all flesh; the blood of it [is] for the life thereof: therefore I said unto the children of Israel, Ye shall eat the blood of no manner of flesh: for the life of all flesh [is] the blood thereof: whosoever eateth it shall be cut off." Spoken by Berechiah's doctor, the passage becomes evidence of his knowledge not only of Torah but also of medicine; not only Moses, but also the Greek philosophers Empedocles, Critias, and Aristotle had located the rational soul or animating principle (Greek ψυχή, Latin *anima*) in the heart or blood.[27] As Berechiah composed his text in Hebrew, Jews and Christians such as Gerard of Cremona (1115–85) were laboring in the libraries of Toledo, translating the works of Aristotle, Hippocrates, Galen, and other natural philosophers from the Arabic in which they had been preserved after the destruction of the library at Alexandria into Latin— often via an intermediate Hebrew translation.

> The patient bade his daughter to take the blood from him and guard it as the apple of her eye from being spilt hither or yon; for any that overturned the vessel, by man would his blood be shed. She took the blood and carried it away and put it underneath her chest. A cat walking by in innocence spilt the blood, whereupon her hands waxed weak and her spirit was darkened, and she said: "Alas, hope is perished! How can I say to my father, 'It is no more'? If he demands it, what answer can I give? May a lion rend him that spilt it; whether beast or man he shall not live." As her thoughts oppressed her, her reins counseled her to empty into the vessel so much of her own blood as the measure of what had been there. She bethought her of a leech and summoned him to her chamber and bade him drain her blood into the vessel. The physician came in his season to ascertain the source of the ailment, and the patient described his state. The physician asked for the blood which he had bidden him keep, and the patient replied that it had not been moved. The blood was sought, and the daughter brought it. When the physician saw the ruddiness of the blood and its aspect, it was accounted unto that man as an offense of blood. [The physician's] rath was kindled and he said in passion: "Thou art pregnant! Never has there been such a thing and never shall be, that an embryo be found in

---

[27]On the blood as the soul in Greek thought and Plato's rejection of that thesis, see James Longrigg, *Greek Rational Medicine: Philosophy and Medicine from Alcmaeon to the Alexandrians* (London: Routledge, 1993), 75–76, 134, 165, 173.

the body of a male. I do not wonder thou art sick; thy sins have caused these things. Thy guilt becometh such a man as thou; thou shalt put a knife to thy throat."

Alone among the early tellers of the fable, Berechiah clearly divides practitioners of medicine into the mere blood-letters (leeches or barbers) and those who diagnose learnedly (physicians). And alone of the physicians we have seen in the early fables, Berechiah's displays emotion. More importantly, he alone diagnoses not only his patient's illness, but also its cause! In sharp contrast to Boccaccio's fool, who would attribute his own pregnancy to having allowed his wife to dominate him sexually, Berechiah's physician—like Abbaye in the tale from the *Ma'aseh Book*—diagnoses the cause of the unlikely event as sin. As in the Talmud and the *Ma'aseh Book*, the transformation of the body requires divine intervention. Impossible in nature (biology), it cannot be the result of human behavior unless that behavior inspires God to disrupt the order of creation.

> The physician returned upon his way, and the patient sorrowed in his heart, for his heart misgave him.

For the learned physician the blood was the soul or animating principle of the flesh. For the patient himself the older formula suffices: the heart is the seat of the passions and the intellect. Precisely because the formula is so familiar, it strikes the twentieth-century reader as less curious than the fact that here, as in the other versions of the fable, the patient accepts his physician's reading of the evidence in the blood. Not one of the men challenges the physician's diagnosis of pregnancy. Nor, in the case of this Jewish version, does the patient challenge his physician's diagnosis of the cause of pregnancy in a male; male parturition would indeed require divine intervention and thus prove that its subject had displeased God. Since this is the case, Berechiah's patient searches his own heart to ascertain if he is indeed guilty. On the basis of the evidence of his heart, he doubts not the physician's diagnosis—the assumption of its accuracy is the basis for the conclusion he reaches—but that the blood was his own:

> He summoned his daughter and again and again adjured her to know whether it was his blood she had brought without diminution just as she had received it, or whether she had spilt it on the ground and substituted other blood in its place; for that cause was his reason unsteady.

Unlike the daughter of the rich man in Marie's fable, who confessed in order to relieve her father's anxiety, or the daughter of the rich man in the Latin manuscript, who confessed only after other members of the household had found the spilled blood, the daughter in Berechiah's fable confesses because her father, convinced that the blood is not his own, suspects what has really happened.

The girl answered: "I did not spill the blood, nor do I know who spilt it. I found the vessel overturned and all the blood spilt out of it; and lest thou fall angry with me, I substituted my blood for thine."

Now, at last, we encounter a response that can be seen as foreshadowing both the moral of this fable and the anger displayed by Calandrino in Boccaccio's story. Once his persistent questioning has forced the confession from his daughter, he cries, "I thought thee a wall but thou art a door," an apparent echo of the use of terms from domestic architecture to describe the female genitalia in the Niddah, the Mishnaic tractate on the ritual uncleanliness of the menstruating women.[28] The sweeping range of the metaphors that follow suggests extreme, almost incoherent, agitation:

From bran I hoped for fine flour. I thought thee shut in, but thou art pregnant of a man, and of men hast thou sown seed. I had hoped for good and there came evil. Repeatedly I adjured thee in thy chambers not to go after young men. By the cords of thy guile hast thou stumbled; thou hast not clothed thee with beauty and majesty.

Berechiah's moral follows naturally from this tirade:

The parable is for those who think to trip others by their wiles so that they might suddenly smite them, but in the ambush in which they lurk they are caught by the guile they themselves contrived. Their evil and deception is revealed when their foot is caught in the snare they have hidden. He who plots to capture his fellow with false lines, false will be his return. So it befell the girl in her deception; her father thought her a virgin but learned that a man had uncovered her source, and he despised the soul that had been precious in his sight.[29]

It is not, then, only in length that Berechiah's fable differs from the two contemporary Christian versions. Like the Yiddish *Ku-Bukh*,[30] Berechiah's *Mishlé Shu'lim* "already exhibits [some of the] features that would come to be seen as characteristic of Yiddish popular literature: loquacity, earthiness, humor, and interest in the quotidian life of the Jews."[31] In his preface Berechiah boasted: "Verily these parables are current upon the lips of all earth's progeny, and men of diverse tongues have set them forth in a book. But my practices are different from their practices, for I have enlarged and augmented them with like and similar matter, in verses and poems."[32]

---

[28]For the Mishnaic terms, see Preuss, *Biblical and Talmudic Medicine*, 115–17.

[29]Berechiah, fable 82, as translated by Moses Hadas, *Fables of a Jewish Aesop*, 149–50.

[30]Introduction to Moshe Wallich, *Book of Fables: The Yiddish Fable Collection of Reb Moshe Wallich, Frankfurt am Main, 1697*, ed. and trans. Eli Katz (Detroit: Wayne State University Press, 1994), 17.

[31]Katz, *Book of Fables*, 17.

[32]Hadas, *Fables of a Jewish Aesop*, 1.

As we have seen, Berechiah himself had expressed pride in his augmentation of fables collected by gentiles, "men of diverse tongues." According to Schwarzbaum, "even when there is a Jewish version of a certain fable [Berechiah] nevertheless clings to the non-Jewish one, 'cleansing' it from its 'objectionable' features"; he delighted in his ability to transform even the most pagan story into a Jewish one.[33]

Not surprisingly, much of the material added by Berechiah was scriptural. Like the doctor's insistence that the blood is "the soul of the flesh," the narrator's reference to the daughter's sexual activity ("a man had uncovered her source") is an explicit reference to Leviticus, in this case to the prohibition of sexual intercourse during a woman's menses: "If a man shall lie with a woman having her menses, and shall uncover her nakedness, he hath discovered her fountain, and she hath uncovered the fountain of her blood: and both of them shall be cut off from among their people" (Leviticus 19:18). The same language occurs in the Niddah, the Mishnaic tractate on menstruation and ritual (un)cleanliness whose language had already been echoed in the father's tirade, a text whose discussion of blood and intercourse would have made it an obvious source for material appropriate to this particular fable.[34] Despite this, in this fable it is not so much that Berechiah's (and his community's) "practices are different from their practices," but rather that his (and his audience's) understanding of the relation between body and soul, biology and behavior differs from that of their Christian contemporaries.

For Berechiah's doctor, wise in his art, as for his apparently virtuous patient, male pregnancy was obviously the result of sin. For the rabbis in the Talmud and *Ma'aseh Book,* male lactation could be the result of virtue or sin or simple necessity. The rabbis, the physician, and his patient all agreed that such events were miracles, the result of divine intervention. Perhaps, then, we should read the physician's insistence that "blood is the soul of all flesh" as something more than evidence that Berechiah was up to date on the philosophers whose works were being translated in Toledo, or that he wanted to display his physician in such a light. There is, as Alon Goshen-Gottstein has put it, "much talk of soul and body in the rabbinic sources." Nevertheless,

> There is not a fundamental metaphysical opposition between these two aspects. There may be an existential confrontation, but metaphysically soul and body form a whole, rather than a polarity. Crudely put—the soul is like a battery that operates an electronic gadget. It may be different and originally external to the gadget. However, the difference is not one of essence. Nowhere in rabbinic literature is the soul regarded as Divine. It

---

[33]Schwarzbaum, *Mishle Shu'alim*, xxv.

[34]Preuss, *Biblical and Talmudic Medicine*, 115–16, 125. The Mishnaic passages are found at Niddah 2:5 and 16a. Berechiah's famous Spanish contemporary Maimonides made a notable attempt to clarify the Mishnaic terms in his own commentary on Niddah 2:5; see Preuss, *Biblical and Talmudic Medicine*, 117.

may be of heavenly origin, but it is not Divine. More significantly, the gadget and its power source ultimately belong together, rather than separately. Thus the soul is the vitalizing agent, whose proper place is in the body, not out of it.[35]

It is therefore not in Rabbinic Judaism and its nonmystical successors in Northern Europe that actions of the body can jeopardize gender identity, but in its Hellenized offshoot, Christianity. In Rabbinic Judaism, neither lactation nor pregnancy is a marker that a male has behaved in an unmanly fashion; neither prompts the fear that masculine identity may be lost. So stably is the Jewish male's selfhood engendered that neither the growth of breasts nor their production of milk can disrupt it. Such biological transformation is neither symptom nor cause of psychological transformation; it is instead proof that God intervenes in cases of necessity. In fact, even to label the growth of breasts "transformation" is to cast the story in terms appropriate to the tangled spirit-body dichotomy that permeated medieval Christian thought in the West, but had little impact on Jewish thought in medieval and early modern Europe outside the rarified writings of the Kabbalists.

Neither do the actions of a Deborah, a Jael, or a Judith elicit from Jewish commentators the references to the heroine's possession of a "manly" spirit, as in the comments commonly elicited from their Christian contemporaries. For the Jews of medieval and early modern Europe, biological transformation was not rooted in behavior. It was neither symptom nor cause of psychological transformation; it was instead proof that God might intervene in the natural world. In contrast to Christian ethical codes, Halachah itself was generally justified, not in terms of nature or even of God's supposed ability to judge behaviors appropriate to women and men, but in terms of its role in the covenant between the Jews and their god; the very difficulties, even apparent absurdities, of its observance served to confirm the covenant.

Similarly, a woman's activity in what we might call "public space"—even a display of judicial wisdom or lethal swordplay—did not require explanation so long as it did not violate the code of Halachah. Glückel of Hameln was not alone. Since her financial dealings did not violate Halachah, the good wife in the book of Proverbs earned praise for them, as well as for her charity.[36] In contrast to the few women who were depicted reading prayer books, always alone, in Christian illuminations and paintings, Jewish manuscripts depicted women as well as men reading

[35]Quoted from "The Body as Image of God in Rabbinic Literature," a paper presented by Alan Goshen-Gottstein at the conference "People of the Body/People of the Book" (Berkeley 1991), by Daniel Boyarin, *Carnal Israel: Reading Sex in Talmudic Culture* (Berkeley: University of California Press, 1993), 33–34, to whose own work the words "brilliantly articulated," applied by him to Goshen-Gottstein's exposition, can be applied with no diminution of the praise he intends to bestow.
[36]See Natalie Zemon Davis, "Arguing with God," *Women on the Margins: Three Seventeenth-Century Lives* (Cambridge, Mass.: Harvard University Press, 1995), 5–62.

the Haggadah at the family table during the Passover seder—even depicted women reading while men listened.

The term "transformation"—misplaced when we attach it to the lactating widower in the Talmud—appropriately describes the story of the pregnant man told in the fourteenth century by Boccaccio's Philostratus, the first Christian version in which an explanation is given for male pregnancy. The explanation is, of course, offered by Calandrino, not by a learned physician nor by a wealthy man who is surrounded by servants bearing witness to a social standing the events do not undermine. Calandrino, we are told from the beginning, is a fool whose bit of money is a sudden inheritance; he is surrounded not by servants and learned physicians, but by knaves. Nevertheless, our knowledge that his causal diagnosis is false depends less on these facts than on Philostratus' description of the honest modesty of Calandrino's wife. A dominant woman might in fact make her husband pregnant, but Calandrino's wife is simply not that sort of woman.

The explanation—the punchline after which Philostratus' tale loses its steam—is directly opposed to Berechiah's. It is not divine intervention but the natural relation between human behavior and biology, that is, biology determined by rather than determinative of behavior. The cause is not relation to God, but relation to spouse. Yet here again we see the impact of the ancient natural philosopher so respected that Albertus Magnus and others referred to him simply as "the Philosopher."[37] The efforts of Gerard of Cremona and the others who had translated the works of Aristotle and other ancient writers resurrected among Christian theologians the ancient debates about the location of the human soul. The *Canon* or systematization of Greek and Muslim medical knowledge by the Persian philosopher ibn Sina (Avicenna, 980–1037), who tended to side with Aristotle in the debate over the seat of the psyche, was soon translated into Latin and circulated widely in manuscript and (later) printed versions. Christian readers of ibn Sina's *Canon* struggled to integrate the essentially Neoplatonic view of the relation between the body and the immortal (and therefore fundamentally separate) soul that was their inheritance from Paul and Augustine—and, more radically, Pseudo-Dionysius—with the functionalist view of Aristotle, for whom the soul was the "life principle" in something material (whether vegetable, animal, or human) and therefore connected in the latter two cases with the heart and blood without which they could not live.

The debate begun among the Greeks and resurrected in the West by the rediscovery of ancient treatises in medicine and natural philosophy was continued in the sixteenth century in works such as Philipp Melanchthon's *Liber* or *Commentarius de anima*, first published at Wittenberg, Augsburg, and Paris in 1540, and reissued

---

[37]On Aristotle's view of the heart, see Longrigg, *Greek Rational Medicine*, 170; for Ibn Sina, see Preuss, *Biblical and Talmudic Medicine*, 105; Albertus Magnus, 2, Sent. Dist. 13, C art. 2.

throughout the century.[38] Even after the publication of William Harvey's *Exercitatio anatomica de motu cordis et sanguinis in animalibus* (*Anatomical Exercise on the Motion of the Heart and Blood in Animals*) (1628), the debate was carried on by Johannes Antonides van de(r) Linden, a leading Dutch physician and professor of medicine, who in 1653 published a tirade complete with scriptural citations against Galen's cerebral siting of the soul.[39] If the soul whose location was being debated was less clearly the immortal soul of Paul and Augustine than the animating soul of Aristotle, the debate itself reveals the difficulties faced by Christians (including Augustine) who attempted to explain the obvious connection between body and soul, individuating matter and selfhood.

Hans Sachs's willing embrace of Boccaccio's tale suggests that the psychologies of the dominant strands of Protestantism did not so much challenge the soul-body dichotomy as turn it inside out. Protestants all over Europe had rejected the possibility that disciplining the body might enable the soul to achieve true virtue in this life. This was not a rejection of the dualistic metaphysics per se, but a rejection of the optimistic possibilities such a metaphysics had implied for Augustine and his successors. Mastery and virtue formerly demonstrated by both women and men in their ability to detach their truer selves from the things of this world, however much their bodies might appear to later historians to be controlled by others, could now be demonstrated only in the world and in relationships of the flesh.

The dichotomy, however, did not vanish. Although thinkers as diverse as Martin Luther and John Locke declined to believe the human being capable of discerning or correctly assessing an invisible truer self, they did not deny its existence. Luther insisted that his belief in Christ's "real presence" in the bread consecrated in the mass was based not on medieval science or on mystical experience, but solely on God's word, the scriptural assurance "hoc est corpus meum." Concerned with different issues, Locke conceded that material objects might have a "real essence"; he also insisted that the "different names...of man's making [were] seldom adequate to

---

[38]The BVB or on-line catalogue of the Bibliotheksverbund Bayern lists at least twenty-seven different editions from the sixteenth century in the collections of its member libraries: <http://bvbx3.bib-bvb.de/bvb-bin/isuche.cgi?uid=BIBBVB–30101996–15222200&opacdb=BVBpercent 2BVerbundkatalog&lang=deutsch&field1=TI&name1=anima&opt1=OR&field2=TI&name2=seele&op t2=OR&field3=TI&name3=geist&opt3=AND&field4=AU&name4=melanchthon&select=X0&selval= Bitte+Selektionskriterium+waehlen&experte=&Aktion=Suchen> (search conducted 30 Oct. 1996). Before turning to questions of the freedom or bondage of the will and the immortality of the soul, Melanchthon investigated human physiology. His discussion of the "sympathy" (μ) or "consensus" that must exist between heart and mind if the heart is to be moved by "affections" as well as by the dilations and contractions that take place without the intervention of mind or nerves concludes with the curious statement that "explication is easier for those who say that the heart is the domicile of the *substantive* soul." Philipp Melanchthon, "De motibus cordis," in *Liber de anima = Opera quae supersunt omnia*, ed. Karl Bretschneider, Corpus Reformatorum, 13 (Halle: C.A. Schwetschke et filium, 1846), cols. 57–59.

[39]Preuss, *Biblical and Talmudic Medicine*, 104 n.1016.

the internal nature of the things they were taken from."[40]

Since exploring the tensions between engendered selfhood and sexed body from Luther to the present goes far beyond the scope of this paper, I will instead o'erleap the intervening centuries (and the unsexed bodies of female Christendom from Shakespeare's Lady Macbeth to Conan Doyle's Dr. Verrinder Smith) to conclude on a more modern note. Although I have retold stories, they are stories with implications for the ways in which lives were and are shaped and lived. The dualistic metaphysics embraced by churchmen from Paul on remain curiously implicit in the constructs of modern liberal individualism. These are constructs in which the individual's willingness to ignore the individuating factors of visible difference and bodily experience—what Augustine had called "connections contingent upon birth and death"—seem to call for an act of self-abnegation worthy of a medieval mystic.[41] In contrast, psychologists such as Erik Erikson have written of identity as an amalgam "of past and future both in the individual and in society."[42] For Erikson, our very sense of self, of identity, is rooted in our experience of ourselves in relations in which our sexes, ages, races, generations, religions, classes, and abilities are experienced. This is not to assert the validity of any of these categories, but rather to assert the reality of our experience of ourselves in terms of them. While a close reading of historical sources demonstrates that, as Locke insisted, it is not any essential difference "that distinguishes them into species; it is men, who…range them into sorts…under which individuals…come to be ranked," our experience of these sorts and their ranking requires that we integrate them into our sense of ourselves and the selves of others.

As history makes clear, the differentiation between self and other may serve not only to define the individual, and not merely for what Locke termed "the convenience of comprehensive signs." Some differentiations constitute what Joan Scott has called "recurrent references by which political power has been conceived, legitimated, and criticized." To shift the ground for the moment from sex to a generally less controversial means of "sorting": all the evidence collected by biologists, geneticists, and anthropologists may prove that race does not exist; it cannot disprove a single individual's experience of racism.

[40]John Locke, *Essay concerning Human Understanding* (1690), 3.6.37 (1: 500 of 21st ed.) (London: J. Johnson, 1805).

[41]John Rawls, "The Original Position," *A Theory of Justice* (Cambridge, Mass.: Belknap Press of Harvard University Press, 1971), 24; John Rawls, "The Veil of Ignorance," *A Theory of Justice,* 137. Although Rawls in this work uses the masculine language of the French Revolutionaries, Schneewind has insisted on Rawls's behalf that Rawls's "self as morality requires us to think of it" must "consider irrelevant any individuating information about myself, such as my sex, age, race, generation, religion, class, or abilities." J. B. Schneewind, "The Use of Autonomy in Ethical Theory," in *Reconstructing Individualism and the Self in Western Thought,* ed. Thomas C. Heller and Chistine Brook-Rose (Stanford: Stanford University Press, 1986), 64–75, at 71.

[42]Erik Erikson, *Identity: Youth and Crisis* (New York: W.W. Norton, 1968), 310.

For the historian, as Scott has written, these experiences must be "not the origin of our explanation, but that which we want to explain." I have tried to talk "about identity without essentializing it," "not denying the existence of subjects, [but] instead interrogat[ing] the processes of their creation."[43] To return once more to the early modern period and paraphrase Marsilio Ficino: "it is by means of our sense of identity and for its sake that one wants to understand history."[44]

[43]Joan W. Scott, "Experience," in *Feminists Theorize the Political*, ed. Judith Butler and Joan W. Scott (New York: Routledge, 1992), 22–40, at 33.

[44]According to a letter written by Ficino to Jacopo Poggio, the study of history "est ad vitam, non modo oblectandam, verumetiam moribus instituendam summopere necessaria." "Animae natura & officium, laus historiae: Marsilius Ficinus Jacobo Pogi; oratoris filio, paternae artis haeredi," in *Marsilii Ficini...Opera* (Basel: Henricpetri, 1596), 657–58.

Construction of Masculinity and Male Identity in Personal Testimonies
Hans Von Schweinichen (1552–1616) in His *Memorial*

Heide Wunder

In *The Courtier,* Baldasar Castiglione unravels with masterful skill the whole spectrum of the discursive construction of masculinity and male identity.[1] He uses self-reference (that is, a man's relationship to other men) and defines women as an opposing image, but also justifies the differences between and the equality of Man and Woman within divine creation. In particular, in the third book Castiglione reflects (not without irony) on the way male and female courtiers are "developed" and "shaped"—constructed as ideal beings and then allowed to take the stage. As his backdrop, taking real conditions of the day very much into consideration, he chooses the court of Urbino, where court society met every evening to amuse itself.[2] Direct contact between the sexes when dancing together or in conversation forms the background for the discursive development of masculinity and femininity through the figures of male and female courtiers.

This is only part of the story, however, since in the dialogues, where views are exchanged concerning the most perfect male or female courtier, the ladies cannot be allowed to speak for themselves, but are obliged to select a "champion" for their interests. This may follow in the tradition of chivalric jousting, but it can also be seen as a means for the author to distance himself from and thus criticize the behavior of the Italian ladies with their humanistic education, women who were very much in evidence in the *querelle des femmes.*[3] Nonetheless, by their questions and their interjections, a number of the ladies guide the conversation. The princess is

---

[1] I am grateful to Jeremy Gaines and Merry Wiesner-Hanks for translating this chapter into English.

[2] See Baldesar Castiglione, introduction to *Das Buch vom Hofmann,* ed. Fritz Baumgart (Bremen: C. Schünemann, 1960), esp. xiv–xxi.

[3] *Beyond Their Sex: Learned Women of the European Past,* ed. Patricia A. Labalme (New York: New York University Press, 1980).

allowed a role in the soirée, apparently because the prince has already retired on account of his weak health, and she represents him in his absence. We might also understand this constellation of persons to mean that the prince's authority is not necessary to "shape" the man, the male courtier who serves him, whereas the personal presence of the princess and her ladies *is* required to project an image of the perfect female courtier.

Perhaps it is even possible to go one step further in this interpretation, and to presume that the presence in the conversation of the highly cultivated princess is meant to create a situation in which the respect due to the princess sets limits to male strategies for misogynous argumentation. Nonetheless, it is quite obvious that although the male and female courtiers are constructed analogously, symmetry between the sexes does not exist, for the speaking parts are not equally distributed. It is only because of the presence of the princess and her ladies that a balance of some kind, albeit a precarious one, is achieved. Admittedly, according to their roles, the male and female courtiers are assigned to the prince or the princess, but at the same time they reflect the royal couple, which represents joint dominion by appearing together in court ceremonies.[4] It would therefore be a fundamental mistake to take account merely of the discourse on equality/inequality in Castiglione's artistic and complex presentation of the question of gender. On the contrary, he was well aware of the view that in many ways gender represents a "relational category," as Joan Scott calls it,[5] but obviously only within the scope of knowledge and the modes of thinking of Castiglione's day.

The Courtier was read throughout Europe, as can be seen from the various editions and translations, as well as its inclusion in library catalogues and reading lists.[6] It formed part of the educational canon not only in the courtly world but also—because of its humanist view of mankind—among all educated groups.[7] Gender constructions, however, are not only to be found in scholarly and theological treatises and other pragmatic forms of literature with a similar orientation, which have to date been the preferred subject of analysis. They are also encountered in various autobiographical testimonies, mainly by male authors, from the fifteenth century on.[8] It would thus seem reasonable to investigate these "men's lives," which have

[4]Dirk Schümer, "Der Höfling: Eine semiotische Existenz," *Journal für Geschichte* (1990): 15–23; Beatrix Bastl and Gernot Heiss, "Hofdamen und Höflinge zur Zeit Kaiser Leopolds I: Zur Geschichte eines vergessenen Berufsstandes," *Opera Historica* 5 (1996): 187–265.

[5]Joan Wallach Scott, "Gender: A Useful Category of Historical Analysis" in her *Gender and the Politics of History* (New York: Columbia University Press, 1988), 28–50.

[6]Peter Burke, *The Fortunes of the Courtier: The European Reception of Castiglione's "Cortegiano"* (Cambridge: Cambridge University Press, 1995).

[7]Klaus Ley, "Castiglione und die Höflichkeit: Zur Rezeption des *Cortegiano* im deutschen Sprachraum vom 16. bis zum 17. Jahrhundert," *Chloe* 9 (1990): 3–108.

[8]Hans-Rudolf Velten, *Das selbstgeschriebene Leben: Eine Studie zur deutschen Autobiographie im 16. Jahrhundert* (Heidelberg: Carl Winter, 1995); Günter Niggl, *Die Autobiographie: Zu Form und Geschichte*

their roots in different social groups and were produced at different times, and to look more closely at the image of masculinity and male identity they constructed. I shall purposely not rely on any fixed definition of masculinity, but will instead look at the way these men portray themselves in the "lives they have written themselves," to use Hans-Rudolph Velten's phrase, in order to determine which elements of their self-perception appear fundamental, what significance should be accorded to the construction of gender (anatomical/social gender), what role the normative precepts of Christian/humanist anthropology played in this process, what age or class-specific characteristics and what agencies of social authority and significant personal constellations (social stratum, parents, school, training, age group) emerge as being of importance. My concern is not with the question of historical truth, of history "as it actually happened," but with how the author gives his life meaning; that is, how he deals with the contradictions between his actions and his conduct, how he constructs his own biography so that it culminates in him and he can recognize and explain himself in it.

For this purpose I have chosen one specific example: the *Memorial* by Hans von Schweinichen (1552–1616), a member of the Silesian lesser nobility who spent most of his life in the service of the dukes of Liegnitz. His *Memorial* appears suitable because what remains of it has been published in its entirety. Though the language has been modernized,[9] the modern editor did not, as is frequently the case, omit

---

einer literarischen Gattung (Darmstadt: Wissenschaftliche Buchgesellschaft, 1989); Helmut Winter, *Der Aussagewert von Selbstbiographien: Zum Status autobiographischer Urteile* (Heidelberg: Carl Winter, 1985); Heide Stratenwerth, "Selbstzeugnisse als Quelle zur Sozialgeschichte des 16. Jahrhunderts," in *Festgabe für Ernst Walter Zeeden*, ed. Horst Rabe et al. (Münster: Aschendorff, 1976), 21–35; *Ego-Dokumente: Annäherung an den Menschen in der Geschichte*, ed. Winfried Schulze (Berlin: Akademie Verlag, 1996); *Biographie als Geschichte*, ed. Hedwig Röckelein (Tübingen: Edition Diskord, 1993); Benigna von Krusenstjern, "Was sind Selbstzeugnisse? Begriffskritische und quellenkundliche Überlegungen anhand von Beispielen aus dem 17. Jahrhundert," *Historische Anthropologie* 2 (1994): 462–71.

[9]Hans von Schweinichen, *Denkwuerdigkeiten*, ed. Hermann Oesterley (Breslau: W. Koebner, 1878). References to quoted passages of the text are provided in parentheses in the body of the text. On Schweinichen, see Conrad Wutke, s.v. "Schweinichen," *Allgemeine deutsche Biographie* 33 (Leipzig: Duncker & Humblot, 1891), 360f.; *Zur Geschichte des Geschlechts der von Schweinichen,* ed. Constantin von Schweinichen, K. Wutke, and O. Schwarzer (Breslau: W. Gikorn, 1904–8). On textual criticism and critical discussion by literary scholars, see Stephan Pastenaci, *Erzählform und Persönlichkeitsdarstellung in deutschsprachigen Autobiographien des 16. Jahrhunderts: Ein Beitrag zur historischen Psychologie* (Trier: Wissenschaftlicher Verlag, 1993), 151–85. Publications offering selected perspectives on Schweinichen include Hans-Jürgen Bachorski, "Der selektive Blick: Zur Reflexion von Liebe und Ehe in Autobiographien des Spätmittelalters," in *Eheglück und Liebesjoch: Bilder von Liebe, Ehe und Familie in der Literatur des 15. und 16. Jahrhunderts*, ed. Maria E. Müller (Weinheim: Beltz, 1988), 23–46; Michael Schröter, "Zur Intimisierung der Hochzeitsnacht im 16. Jahrhundert: Eine zivilisationstheoretische Studie," in *Ordnung und Lust: Bilder von Liebe, Ehe und Sexualität im Spätmittelalter und Früher Neuzeit*, ed. Hans-Jürgen Bachorski (Trier: Wissenschaftlicher Verlag, 1991), 359–414; and Christoph Lumme, *Höllenfleisch und Heiligtum: Der menschliche Körper im Spiegel autobiographischer Texte des 16. Jahrhunderts* (Frankfurt a/M.: Lang, 1996).

passages which he considered offensive or boring.[10] It is also suitable because it is not constructed as a single retrospective passage like, for example, Götz von Berlichingen's "Vhedt vnd Handlungen"[11] but takes the form of continuously recorded notes. Even if many of these daily notes, which Schweinichen started committing to paper when he was about twelve years old[12] (perhaps in diary form), may have been deleted when he edited them at the end of each year, the *Memorial* still contains a considerable variety of individual pieces of information which are relevant to my investigation. Schweinichen's goal in writing his notes is a good indication of their relative reliability ("truth"):

> Having reached a certain age and sense of reason, I have taken it upon myself, inspired, no doubt, in some special way by the Holy Ghost, to note down as much as possible of what God allows to occur in my life as long as he grants me life on this earth: all the good things he gives me and the evil things he allows to happen to me, also what I have done and what I have omitted to do, how and where I have spent my life…in order that I might therefore reflect upon God's wonders and deduce from this with certainty that a God does exist.…

The *Memorial*, then, also amounts to a type of bookkeeping. Schweinichen provides both God and himself with an account of his conduct throughout his life. This goal does not allow the author to keep silent on important matters. What is more, such reticence would not have served his second purpose, the didactic goal of leaving a testament for his heirs. Schweinichen's strict instructions to his heirs not to grant others access to the *Memorial* enhances the credibility of these self-revelations. Schweinichen also makes some very critical comments on life at the court of Liegnitz, particularly on the behavior of the dukes. Such comments should under no circumstances be seen as the usual type of "court criticism." On the contrary, it would be correct to consider them as "personal" criticism.

The three parts of the *Book* or *Memorial* which have come down to us cover the period 1552–1602. The third book ends in the year of Schweinichen's second marriage and the death of his fifth lord, Duke Joachim Friedrich of Liegnitz. The first fifty years of Schweinichen's life were a turbulent period in Silesian history, not only for the duchy and the empire, but also for the countries bordering it to the west. At this time, confessionalism, the Counter-Reformation, and religious wars shaped the lives and activities of the princes and their advisors. Schweinichen's *Memorial* was

---

[10]See Heide Wunder, "Wie wird man ein Mann am Beginn der Neuzeit?" in *Was sind Frauen? Was sind Männer? Geschlechterkonstruktionen im historischen Wandel*, ed. Christiane Eiffert et al. (Frankfurt a/ M.: Suhrkamp, 1996), 122–55, esp. 144 n. 20.

[11]Helgard Ulmschneider, *Götz von Berlichingen: Mein Fehd und Handlungen* (Sigmaringen: Thorbecke, 1981).

[12]On the genesis of the text, see also Pastenaci, 160f. n. 8.

not his only work to take issue with the events and developments of this period; he also addressed them in a history of Duke Heinrich XI.[13] For a comprehensive analysis of the *Memorial*, it would be necessary to take into consideration both this history and the documents relating to Schweinichen's administrative duties.[14] For example, Schweinichen describes how, during the period of his employment at the Liegnitz court, he was involved in 1580 in setting up "court regulations," and in 1602, in drawing up an inventory.[15] For my specific investigations, however, I limited myself to the *Memorial*.

In analyzing the *Memorial* with regard to the fundamental elements of Schweinichen's portrayal of himself, I wish to develop the following main theses. First, the introductory passages to the first book on creed and social standing are of special importance for the way in which Schweinichen sees himself. He summarizes the contents of these passages at the beginning of the two following books in order to impress them upon his heirs. Second, Schweinichen's retrospective portrayal of his childhood and youth offers important insights into the way he constructs his own personal development. This phase of his life concludes with his marriage and his release from the services of Duke Heinrich XI in the year 1581. The fact that this marks a turning point is supported by Schweinichen's annual review of 1581, in which he critically sums up his service with the dukes of Liegnitz as having taken place "from my youth onwards." An analysis of the subsequent phase of his life, including the question of how masculinity and male identity developed as he grew older would be equally worthwhile. It would, however, require a separate discussion.

A NOBLE AND CHRISTIAN GENEALOGY

At the beginning of the first book stands a "confession of my belief and creed," which is followed by a "preface to and explanation of my subsequent book or memorial" and by "my eight ancestors and coats of arms," "the origins of my advent," and the "four escutcheons of my lady mother." Schweinichen doubtless chose this sequence carefully, as these five sections are especially significant in giving meaning to the themes he addresses in his self-portrayal. Whereas the discussions of origin and advent fit the normal pattern of biographical texts and a justification of portraying one's own life was in no way unusual, the confession most certainly does not fit into such a frame. In his normative definition of the reasons for setting forth his life, Schweinichen gives first priority to his Protestant creed. Thus he not only accords God the honor due to Him and defines himself as a Lutheran with a strong inclination towards a belief in divine providence, but also, when revising his diary, he

---

[13]Hans von Schweinichen, *Leben Herzog Heinrichs XI. von Liegnitz*, in *Scriptores rerum Silesiacarum*, ed. Gustav Adolf Stenzel (Breslau: Josef Max, 1850), 21–162; Pastenaci, *Erzahlform*, 184f.

[14]Schweinichen, *Denkwuerdigkeiten*, XVIf.

[15]Schweinichen, *Erzählform*, 243, 554.

explicitly establishes a close link between religious confession and one's personal self-understanding.

Schweinichen justifies the account he keeps of his life by asserting that he was divinely inspired to write it. This appears all the more important to him since, in contrast to other authors, he does not portray his life principally as an example for posterity.[16] Even though he sometimes offers stern advice to others, his main avowed intent is to write for his own pleasure. His proof of his own membership in the nobility is something which Schweinichen also associates with his personal creed. He introduces the story of his origins, which is inserted between an examination of his maternal and paternal lineage, by talking about how the human race was created by God in His own image and how all men are descended from Adam and Eve, the first human couple. This association of Christian anthropology (based on Genesis 1:1) with aristocratic genealogy is surprising and unusual. In Protestant communities, Genesis 1 was one of the texts read out to couples and the congregation as a whole before the actual marriage ceremony, after Genesis 2 and 3, as a form of "consolation"—that is, Genesis 1 was not intended to be applied to life in this world, but to hold out the prospect of eternal life.[17] Hence Schweinichen's quoting only Genesis 1, and his placing of this biblical reference between an examination of his maternal and paternal lineage, warrant further discussion. Whereas other nobles drew attention to the quality of their nobility by tracing their ancestors back to outstanding Roman or Greek persons or families, Schweinichen reduces the number of his references to noble ancestors to an absolute minimum, considering anything which went beyond this as mere invention.[18] Instead, he draws up another much longer and more honorable genealogy, establishing a relationship between the origins of man and his own origins as a nobleman. The connection could lie in the way that lineage needed to be proven at the time. For both his mother and his father, this proof was conducted via the respective mother's line. In other words, the prevalent interpretation of the Creation, whereby woman was considered inferior, could not be reconciled with the system used to prove one's noble lineage. The idea that the first couple was created in God's image, however, could. By associating man's origins with his own origins as a nobleman to produce a "noble and Christian" (*christ-adelig*) genealogy, Schweinichen unites an expressly Christian viewpoint with a nobleman's awareness of his social status, thus modifying standard gender constructions to suit his status as a member of the aristocracy.

---

[16]Hannah S. M. Amburger, "Die Familiengeschichte der Koeler: Ein Beitrag zur Autobiographie des 16. Jahrhunderts," offprint from *Mitteilungen des Vereins für Geschichte der Stadt Nürnberg* 30 (1930).

[17]Martin Luther, *Ein Traubüchlein für die einfältigen Pfarrherr*, in *D. Martin Luthers Werke: Kritische Gesamtausgabe [Weimarer Ausgabe]*, vol. 30, 3. *Abteilung* (Weimar: Hermann Böhlaus Nachfolger, Akademische Druck-und-Verlagsanstalt, 1964), 43–80.

[18]Schweinichen, *Memorial*, 13.

One would be fully justified in stating that Schweinichen's nobility and his (Lutheran) confession represent constructive principles in his presentation of himself. In this respect, not only did he differ from many of his peers, but in his *Memorial* it is also possible to see just what consequences this system of references had in structuring his life. As this portrayal of his life reveals, the values and standards of his creed and his class (Christian virtues/aristocratic virtues) are by no means identical. The story of Schweinichen's life, therefore, should be read and interpreted with a view to the tension implicit between this "confession of my belief and my creed" and his life as a nobleman.

"ON THE PROGRESS OF MY LIFE AND THE GENERAL COURSE OF THE SAME"

Hans von Schweinichen was the first son to be born of his father's second marriage to Salome Gladis von Gorpe in 1551. His father, Georg von Schweinichen, was the squire of Mertschütz and at the same time a high court official, primarily in the service of the dukes of Liegnitz. He already had one son, Georg, and three daughters, Anna, Barbara, and Katharina, by his first marriage; after Hans was born, three more daughters (Salome, Elena, and Eva) and two more sons followed.[19] The first of the latter sons died in infancy, and the following son was given his name, Heinrich. Hans's position in the sequence of children indicates that, as far as inheriting his father's estate was concerned, he was only second in line.

Schweinichen was raised by his parents "in the fear of God." When he was nine years old, they sent him to the village scribe to learn to read and write. In 1562, after he had made some progress and before he had even reached the age of ten, a particular educational opportunity presented itself: the chance to be taught and brought up by a tutor at the Liegnitz court together with the future Duke Friedrich IV—the same age as he, who was in the custody of his elder brother, Duke Heinrich XI—and another noble boy.[20] Hans thus moved out of his parents' home into a male-dominated world. The tutor made his pupils learn their catechism, litany, and rosary by heart and taught them to read Latin. He was also responsible for supervising the boys and for their general upbringing. Corporal punishment played a role in this upbringing; the prince was known to beat his son personally, and even the page Hans had his ears boxed on several occasions. Schweinichen's education in all the noble virtues[21] started at the same time. He was granted an office by Duke Friedrich III, the father of the young lord. It is indicative of Duke Friedrich's situation that Hans became his "keeper of the wine cellar" and was also charged with looking after rapiers and shot.

---

[19]Eva is not mentioned the first time he lists his siblings. Born in 1564, she was still "mistress Eva" in 1601.

[20]Schweinichen, *Memorial*, 15.

[21]See Ernst Reimann, *Prinzenerziehung in Sachsen am Ausgang des 16. und im Anfange des 17. Jahrhunderts* (Dresden: Wilhelm Baensch, 1904).

On the one hand, Schweinichen describes himself during this initial period at Liegnitz as "a little boy" and a "small child." On the other hand, he was serving the duke as a page (*Junge*) in the lowliest position which a nobleman's son could occupy at the beginning of a career. He observed male behavior from this perspective: his lord's drinking bouts, his treatment of his wife in the bedchamber, the coexistence of debauchery and piety. These experiences made an impression on Schweinichen, as did short visits to court he made at a later date, for example in 1563 for the marriage of Princess Catharina of Liegnitz to Duke Casimir of Teschen:

> On this occasion I remember that in the morning Princess Catharina was carried away from the table in a chair. On the way, she met Balthasar Axleben's wife, née Spiegel, who had married fourteen days previously. The latter asked what was wrong with the princess and gave her to understand that she felt the way that brides normally feel, saying, so that I could hear: "Oh, madam, I felt the same way the first time. It will not harm your marriage and when you are used to it you will not need to ask about it." Thus it was that the young woman comforted the princess.[22]

And five years later, when he was doing more than just remembering, but had already started organizing his notes into reviews of the various years, he again highlights this subject. In 1568 he served as a page at the marriage of Duchess Elena of Liegnitz to Sir Siegmund Kurzbach at Liegnitz castle:

> One thing comes to my mind, and it occurred when I was present. On the first evening when the bride and groom first lay together and the princely personages were also on the point of retiring, the bride suddenly cried out loudly from the high chamber which overlooked Castle Raunstein, "O my dear Sir Siegmund!" and kept repeating this over and over again. Young gentleman-in-waiting that I was, I then appeared in her ladyship's room, and when the duchess heard the noise, she told me to light the lights, ran down the narrow corridor, knocked on the door at the end of it, and cried out, "Sir Siegmund, are you mad? Spare the poor girl! Do you think she's a dairymaid?" Lord Siegmund paid no attention, until finally everything went silent (and you can imagine why everything went silent). And when everything had gone silent the Duchess went away again. The next morning the Duchess reproached Sir Kurzbach and asked him why he had not opened the door. Sir Kurzbach replied that he had not heard anything because he had been courting like a capercaillie, laughed, and went on his way. After this no one made any more fuss, and the wedding was celebrated with great joy.[23]

[22]Schweinichen, *Memorial*, 19.
[23]Schweinichen, *Memorial*, 26–27.

Schweinichen also reports on a number of experiences with women which "as a child" he is unable to understand, as for example, a maid showing herself to him naked.[24]

Schweinichen's life at court lasted only a year and a half. He became caught up in a court intrigue and to his great chagrin, his father had him sent back to Mertschütz. He was even more annoyed, in retrospect, when his parents turned down an offer made by the Prussian duke Albrecht to let him be educated with his own son at the Königsberg court. For want of a better alternative, he initially continued his education with the village scribe and then began to take an interest in the management of the estate. He was called to duties at court in Liegnitz on special occasions, as was his father, and was part of the entourage on any major journeys the duke embarked upon. His position was now no longer that of a small child but that of a page (*Junge*) and his main role was to wait upon his father, to accompany him on any journeys he undertook, and to learn about various fields of activity from him.

However, since as a second son Hans could not inherit, his father wished to open up other career possibilities to him. Thus, after he had received two years' induction from the Mertschütz pastor Balthasar Thieme, he was sent at age fourteen to the renowned school in Goldberg. However, Hans had no great desire to study, even if he did make a certain amount of progress and learned to speak Latin and debate. But ever since his time at Liegnitz, his head had been spinning with life at court and horsemanship.[25] He used tricks to ensure that he was quickly sent back, something which he later deeply regretted.[26] Although his sojourn in Goldberg was only a short one, Schweinichen marked it as a decisive turning point between childhood and youth. He was suddenly confronted with a reasonably large group of boys the same age as himself, more than 140 gentlemen and members of the nobility, and more than 300 other students, some of whom made his life hard. Alone and far away from his home, he was forced to come to terms with these hardships and develop an independent sense of responsibility. The social opportunities the town offered, however, appear to have been equally important to him. It was here that he first assumed a man's role, escorting noble maidens who were invited to the weddings of the townspeople.

On his return from Goldberg in 1567, the fifteen-year-old Schweinichen devoted himself to the hunt and estate management, practiced "writing the German language," and copied all his father's correspondence. In this way he not only became familiar with the style of the chancellery but also gained an insight into official business: "Thus I did not idle away my time but was occupied at all times."[27] At the same time, he noted his progress in acquiring the virtues of a noble. And if in

---

[24]Schweinichen, *Memorial*, 16.
[25]Schweinichen, *Memorial*, 21.
[26]Schweinichen, *Memorial*, 23.
[27]Schweinichen, *Memorial*, 24.

1564, as a young halberdier on the journey to Ansbach in Franconia, he did not have the strength to travel all the way on horseback, eventually having to transfer to his father's coach, one year later he was able to accompany his father "on a steed," as he stresses.[28] It was many years before he received a horse of his own, but as early as 1567, his father bought him his first sword, "something which I noted down in order to remember."[29]

One might assume that, having been given a sword and learned to ride and hunt, Schweinichen had achieved his goal of chivalrous manhood. More was required of him, however. He still had to find his place within the society of landed gentry and thus to adopt a stance on the forms of male behavior which had impressed him so much as a child at the Liegnitz court: drinking and violence in relationships with women.

Schweinichen was particularly concerned about his behavior in regard to drinking. Here, Christian virtues were very much at odds with those of a noble. To a Christian mind, drinking was a deadly sin and a vice. In contrast, the ability to hold one's drink was one of the epitomes of aristocratic manliness. In the *Memorial* for the remaining years until he came of age in 1572, Schweinichen records this ongoing dilemma. For 1567, he reports, "At that time I had not started to drink wine, but remained sober at all times."[30] In other words, he did drink beer,[31] but "to my knowledge never got drunk on wine."[32] Although both formulations are a retrospective interpretation, we may assume that he had thought about drinking even while still a youth. It is impossible to know whether he was influenced by the warnings against drinking found in edifying literature and the guides on leading a Christian life which would have been known to him from his time in Goldberg, from his lessons with the Mertschütz pastor, from his own reading, and from sermons. Only in 1570 does he describe in detail being intoxicated for the first time, stating that from that day onward, "I gorged and drank half or all the night long and went along with everything they wanted."[33] By "they," Schweinichen meant the noblemen of his own age, whose ranks he thus joined and to whom he now felt that he belonged. Indeed,

---

[28]Schweinichen, *Memorial*, 21.

[29]Schweinichen, *Memorial*, 25. Schweinichen does not mention ever using the sword. In contrast, Johann V (born 1436), Wild- and Rheingraf, remarks on having participated in the siege of Besançon, in which he "hewed off the heads of four of them." Hans-Walter Herrmann, "Autobiographische Aufzeichnungen des Wild- und Rheingrafen Johann V," in *DEVS QVI MVTAT TEMPORA: Menschen und Institutionen im Wandel des Mittelalters: Festschrift für Alfons Becker zu seinem fünfundsechzigsten Geburtstag,* ed. Ernst-Dieter Hehl, Hubertus Seibert, and Franz Staab (Sigmaringen: Thorbecke, 1987), 335–53. My thanks to Karl-Heinz Spiess (Greifswald) for drawing my attention to this point.

[30]Schweinichen, *Memorial*, 25.

[31]Schweinichen, *Memorial*, 23.

[32]Schweinichen, *Memorial*, 32.

[33]Schweinichen, *Memorial*, 34.

this ability to hold his drink earned him high esteem among both the nobility and the princes whom he served.[34]

Schweinichen describes his approaches to the opposite sex quite differently. It was also in 1570, when he was eighteen years old, that he began to take an interest in maidens and would have liked more than anything to marry.[35] Apparently he noted down all the journeys he made through the neighborhood in order to see maidens.[36] But also at the Liegnitz court he enjoyed the conviviality taking place in the ladies' apartments, bringing together young people of both sexes. Here, for instance, is his report on a banquet at the Liegnitz court on 27 August 1574:

> In the evening his lordship organized a banquet, and after the meal he held a dance, which lasted all night. The music was pleasant, the wine good, the maidens beautiful and the society intimate, and above all his lordship joined in the fun. For this reason no one was sad or troubled; joy and delight abounded. If I had fallen from heaven to earth at the time, I would not have fallen anywhere but to Liegnitz, to the women's quarters (*Frauenzimmer*), where there was daily joy and delight: riding, racing, music, dancing, and other distractions which pleased the young people like myself.[37]

His first great love came in 1573. "That year I discovered what love is, falling so deeply in love with a maid that I could no longer sleep. But I was not so bold as to pester her."[38] Thus Schweinichen distinguished very clearly between desire and love. If he had given way to peer pressure with regard to drink and nurtured a typically male vice, in his relations with women he maintained a certain distance. Admittedly, he attached great importance to portraying himself as a highly desirable man, but in all his amorous dalliances he always stressed his honorable intentions.

It is possible that the memory of the scenes of male violence toward women that he had observed as a child and youth played a role in this. Perhaps this is also the reason for the interest in erotic practices between the sexes he reveals during his journeys: in the Lüneburg region the practice of "sleeping together in good faith," that is, of a young lord and lady lying in bed together fully clothed;[39] or at

---

[34]On drinking, see Pastenaci, *Erzählform*, 178 n. 110; Lumme, *Hoellenfleisch und Heiligtum*, 90; Lyndal Roper, "Blood and Codpieces: Masculinity in Early Modern Germany," in her *Oedipus and the Devil: Witchcraft, Sexuality and Religion in Early Modern Europe* (London: Routledge: 1994), 107–24; and Hasso Spode, *Alkohol und Zivilisation: Berauschung, Ernüchterung und Tischsitten in Deutschland bis zum Beginn des 20. Jahrhunderts* (Berlin: Tara-Verlag Hartmut Hensel, 1991).

[35]Schweinichen, *Memorial*, 32.

[36]Schweinichen, *Memorial*, 46.

[37]Schweinichen, *Memorial*, 46.

[38]Schweinichen, *Memorial*, 37.

[39]Schweinichen, *Memorial*, 38–39.

patrician banquets in Augsburg, where the male and female dancers were allowed to embrace one another.[40]

According to his *Memorial*, by the time he came of age at twenty, Schweinichen was socially integrated into the landed gentry. His coming of age, however, did not represent any fundamental changes in his status. He was admittedly no longer in "his father's power,"[41] but he continued to obey orders and to receive clothes from his father,[42] and his father kept a tally of the relevant expenses.[43] Indeed, it was only two years later, in 1574, that he entered the services of Duke Heinrich XI, and was paid and clothed by the latter. As soon as he was emancipated from his father, then, Schweinichen entered upon a new relationship of subordination to the duke, although this time with a great range of responsibilities and authority of his own.

Entering the duke's services meant that Schweinichen finally received the opportunity to go on the sort of grand tour that young gentlemen customarily undertook. In 1575 he left Silesia with Duke Heinrich XI and, with the exception of a few trips back home, spent almost five years travelling through Poland, Bohemia, the Holy Roman Empire, the Netherlands, and parts of France, until in 1580 Duke Heinrich again took up his responsibilities in Liegnitz. As the duke's steward, Schweinichen was responsible for taking care of the court when in transit and in particular for arranging its financing. In describing this life with its ups and downs, he does not downplay his own role, nor does he see himself as a "knight without fear or reproach." When he speaks of courage, it is a courage born of despair. In contrast, he underscores his own industriousness, resourcefulness, application, steadfastness, and devotion, describing his attitude as "pious" (*fromm*), in other words, upright.[44] Thus he portrays himself in sharp contrast to his princely master. He distances himself from the duke and the latter's lifestyle, even though he participates in it, and not only out of necessity. Despite the fact that he felt himself to be bound to the duke by duty and allegiance,[45] he still enjoys the "topsy-turvy world" at a society wedding in Augsburg which his lord was only able to attend dressed up as Schweinichen's servant.[46]

As the years went by, Schweinichen's desire to be released from the services of the duke increased. He wanted to be able to devote himself to family business, in

---

[40]Schweinichen, *Memorial*, 77.Other interpretations of Schweinichen's relationships with women can be found in Lumme, *Hoellenfleisch und Heiligtum*, 45–47.

[41]Schweinichen, *Memorial*, 229.

[42]On the significance of paying for clothes, see Wunder, "Wie wird man ein Mann"; and Lumme, *Hoellenfleisch und Heiligtum*, 65–69.

[43]Schweinichen, *Memorial*, 23.

[44]Heide Wunder, "Iusticia, Teutonice fromkeyt: Theologische Rechtfertigung und bürgerliche Rechtschaffenheit: Ein Beitrag zur Sozialgeschichte eines theologischen Konzepts," in *Die frühe Reformation in Deutschland als Umbruch*, ed. Bernd Moeller and Stephen E. Buckwalter (Gütersloh: Gütersloher Verlagshaus, 1998), 307–32.

[45]Schweinichen, *Memorial*, 226.

[46]Schweinichen, *Memorial*, 76.

particular to his father's financial problems. The latter had become embroiled in severe difficulties because of a loan which he had been forced to co-sign on the duke's behalf:[47]

> While I enjoyed myself in foreign parts, my dear father was having a terrible time at home, for he was greatly plagued as a warrantor for Duke Heinrich's debts. Also because he had to encumber his estate at Mertschütz to Christoph Schweinitz under seal, whereby he would pay 800 Hungarian florins for his lordship should he default, and if he did not pay by Michaelmas 1576, the other would be entitled to seize the property. This caused my father a great deal of distress in his old age, and was the beginning of my father's ruin and the downfall of my brothers and sisters.[48]

When his lord took up residence in Liegnitz again, Schweinichen initially remained in his service, but he continued to follow his own plans with determination, namely both to marry his beloved, Margarethe Schellendorf, who had remained true to him throughout the years of his absence despite other good offers of marriage, and to lead an independent life as a country gentleman. He explicitly formulated the twofold requirements of "Christian" and "noble": the bride would have to come from a family which was not only good and noble but also pious. In choosing a wife, Schweinichen sought both the advice of his maternal relations and the necessary consent from the duke. His major aim, though, was "to conduct my life in a different way and to be guided by God's word and his commandments." In order to be sure of his undertaking, on the morning of Christmas Day 1581 at church he asked God:

> If it should be for my blessing and His Godly will, that the dear Lord should let me know in my heart whether I should enter upon such a Christian duty and take and bestow upon myself the maiden Margarethe Schellendorf (if it should be His will). And now I can say in truth that during the sermon the following entered into my heart and at the same time was whispered into my ear: "Take the duke with you and ask for the maiden's hand and drive out in the sleigh. If you do not come out in the morning, the maiden will not be yours."

This divine message was repeated the following night, and so the next morning Schweinichen embarked upon his suit, which was successful.[49] Nevertheless, Schweinichen had not been sure of his success; he had trembled at the idea that one of his rivals might win his beloved from him and that such a rival might be able to put him in the shade, something which would have been very injurious to his manly

[47]Schweinichen, *Memorial*, 34.
[48]Schweinichen, *Memorial*, 117.
[49]Schweinichen, *Memorial*, 247–48.

pride. He had been preparing himself for a rejection until the last moment and had taken precautions in case this were to happen. But everything went well; the marriage took place and Schweinichen could not refrain from describing his wedding night. Whatever the case, Schweinichen describes his wedding night with Margarethe Schellendorf in 1581 as follows: "His lordship's rose room had been prepared for us, where I lay with her in honorable delight. Like the bride, I was a pure virgin, which meant that neither of us had to catch up with the other."[50] He continues ironically: "Her Ladyship the Duchess [and] the Lady Kurzbach, along with the maiden's mother, led the bride to my bed and instructed me to spend the night peacefully, which I respected, and my strong state of intoxication will also have helped me to spend the night peacefully."[51] Schweinichen does not hold back further details of his married life. After several days of wedding festivities the guests departed again, but Schweinichen "stayed at Mertschütz for fourteen days and practiced that which newly married couples practice. In this I was diligent and allowed it to be my great concern."[52]

Securing his release from the service of the duke was even more difficult. He finally succeeded, but only because he managed to convince Duke Heinrich, who was by this time being held prisoner in Prague, that the latter did not require a steward under such circumstances. Thus, after again earning high praise for his role as a mediator between the two princely brothers in the Liegnitz war, Schweinichen was finally in a position to commence his life as a member of the landed gentry and proprietor of the Mertschütz manor with his "dear wife." After releasing himself from a state of dependence upon his father, he also succeeded in freeing himself from his obligations to the prince and thereby became his own master, a position in which role models and practical experience came together. Evidently, Schweinichen now saw the fulfillment of the first part of an old monk's prophecy to him. In 1576 in Cologne this monk had cast his horoscope: "After my thirtieth birthday God would raise me up to a position where I would rule over other people and God would truly give me my bread, for I would find great favor with great lords and would achieve and experience advancement."[53]

"A MAN'S LIFE": THE CONSTRUCTION OF MASCULINITY

Without doubt, Schweinichen led the life of a nobleman of his day. In his *Memorial*, the plan for his life clearly emerges from both the variety and selection of experiences recounted. He makes retrospective comments on the selected sequence of events and does not fail to highlight occasions where his youthful perspectives and views differ

---

[50]Schweinichen, *Memorial*, 254.
[51]Schweinichen, *Memorial*, 255.
[52]Schweinichen, *Memorial*, 256.
[53]Schweinichen, *Memorial*, 118.

from later ones. When we investigate the constructive elements of Schweinichen's portrayal of himself in this "life written by himself," several trends become apparent.

As a nobleman, he went through various stages—from "page" to "young gentle-man" to "squire" (*Junker*)— of an education in all the noble virtues and then led an eventful life at the Liegnitz court. He presents his individual circumstances within the standard pattern of a noble life, using the noble ideals of masculinity as his point of orientation. These included physical strength and discipline, which played an important role in riding, wielding weapons, displaying prowess when hunting, and equally important, dancing gracefully. Another structural element in Schweinichen's self-portrayal is provided by his attempt to reconcile his Christian beliefs with the noble way of life. Since both at court and in the society of the landed gentry, drinking and violence formed an integral part of male identity, Schweinichen found himself faced with a conflict between normative forms of behavior which threatened his identity, given that the notions of noble honor, male honor, and honoring God were widely divergent on these points.

As far as male vices were concerned, only drinking remained a lifelong problem for Schweinichen. He was able to date the first time he was intoxicated exactly, which implies that he started to include his drinking behavior (*Räusche*) in the accounts he kept from at least this occasion onwards. His behavior towards the opposite sex, on the other hand, was not typical of his peers. Although he was deeply attracted to women, he could see no reason for surrendering to the demands of his male potency. In this he demonstrated his "male strength" by showing self-restraint.

The theme of violence, on the other hand, appears in a number of different guises. At the Liegnitz court, certainly, Schweinichen often spoiled for a fight, but by the time he went to Goldberg he had started to prefer letting others do the fighting for him. In the years that followed, he took an interest when other young people argued and bragged,[54] but he presents himself as somewhat restrained.[55] In later years, he proved a valiant defender of his "noble honor." In his service to the duke, however, he distinguished himself through his ability to mediate. He was even asked to reconcile the duke and the duchess after the duke had mortally wounded the duchess's honor by boxing her ears in Schweinichen's presence. In dangerous situations he demonstrated "a man's courage" not so much through belligerence, but by thinking before he acted. Through this he acquired the male identity of mediator, not only in his service of the duke but also in aristocratic society in general. Such behavior corresponded to the required Christian notion of peacefulness, but also perhaps to Schweinichen's own disposition.[56] One important factor in an assessment

---

[54]Jacob and Wilhelm Grimm, s. v. "Unfläterei," in *Deutsches Wörterbuch* 24 (1936; reprint, Munich: Deutscher Taschenbuch Verlag, 1984), 556.

[55]Schweinichen, *Memorial*, 34.

[56]Pastenaci, *Erzählform*, 183, n. 128, on the other hand, assumes an "alienation from the profession of arms" and considers this to be a "typically unsoldierly attitude."

of his role as mediator may be that he often had to act with a sharp mind from a weak rather than a strong position in order to achieve his goal, and so he made this into a virtue in his self-image.

It is striking in how many ways Schweinichen shaped existing ideals of masculinity, such as courage and honor, for his own purposes. Identification and delimitation play an important role not only in regard to men and women but also, and in particular, in his attitude to other men, for example, rivals or enemies. An example of this is his relationship with his father. He associates orientation, contrast, and identification with the figure of his father. Schweinichen's education in the noble virtues and his initiation in estate management and practical administration lay very much in his father's hands. The principal characteristic of this relationship was obedience. Initially, what was involved was the obedience of a small, ignorant child toward his father and mother. This then became the son's obedience to his father, and finally the youth's (*Junge*) obedience to his Lord Father (*Herr Vater*). Schweinichen proved an obedient child in every way, and the only wish of his father's which he disregarded was that he complete his education in Goldberg, an instance of disobedience which he later regretted because of the effects it had on his career.

Obedience obviously did not conflict with masculinity. On the contrary, it was essential in order to be able later to command obedience as lord of the manor, aristocratic administrator, and husband. The term obedience, which played such an important part in the normative definition of the relationship between man and woman, must therefore be taken into consideration as regards the balance of power between men. In this respect, the father/son relationship appears highly ambivalent. Admittedly, Schweinichen only reports one major conflict, the disagreement about schooling. However, his father, who spent many years preparing his son for his life as a noble and set a great example for him in this regard, was at the same time a source of provocation to Hans, since he was allowed to participate in his father's work but was not allowed any great degree of independence. Schweinichen's formulation of the father/son relationship using the terms youth (*Junge*) and Lord Father (*Herr Vater*) expresses more than a difference in generation; it also implies a distancing and objectification of what initially appears to be a close family relationship. His distancing from his father created the conditions necessary for Schweinichen later to identify with his father. In many ways, in fact, Schweinichen portrayed himself as his father's successor: he even took on the role of the father for his brothers and sisters. It is thus fitting that his siblings rarely come to the fore in the earlier sections of the *Memorial*. His relationship with them only gains definition once he has made a name for himself at court, when with his knowledge, experience, and connections, he can intervene in order to straighten out his family's financial difficulties in order to "save the honor and the good name of my father."

Schweinichen depicts his long-standing obedience to Duke Heinrich in a completely different manner. As the latter's "loyal and obedient subject and servant,"[57]

---

[57]Schweinichen, *Memorial*, 226.

Schweinichen did everything within his powers to obey—even when this went against his own principles—but received little recognition in return. Duke Heinrich could never serve as an example to Schweinichen. On the contrary, his rule and his lifestyle seemed to be a perversion of good sovereignty, not to mention the male vices he displayed.

Schweinichen's relationships with women were of course different, but no less complex. His mother came first. He was her first child and her "dear little Hans."[58] She died when he was seventeen years old, and he mourned her not only for the sake of appearances but with his whole heart.[59] Nevertheless, in the *Memorial* she appears mainly in situations of delimitation, as in one episode which occurred around 1551. His mother entrusted Hans with looking after the geese. One day he had nothing better to do than to wedge open all the geese's mouths with little sticks, and they would have died of thirst if Hans' mother had not saved them. After duly punishing him, his mother charged him with looking for eggs in return for a small sum of money, which he then spent on marbles. This prank seems to be more than the kind of anecdote that many authors incorporate into their autobiographies.[60] Obviously, the boy could not identify with the work his mother had given him and was unable to accept responsibility for the animals she had entrusted to him, although he must have known how important these animals were to her. Looking after the geese was considered a menial task, if not a job for girls, and it is possible that he could not reconcile this kind of work with his new status as a schoolboy. His mother may have recognized this when she gave him a job for which he received a financial reward.

This distancing from his mother, which takes the guise of an anecdote here, is expressed explicitly at a later point, where he makes the following comment on her refusal to let him move to the distant court of Duke Albrecht of Prussia as an eleven-year-old (1563) in order to study with the young lord there:

> But as is so often the case with beloved children, their mothers are unwilling to let them out of their sight but prefer to keep them at their own side, irrespective of what they learn there: this was what happened to me....She begged my Lord Father not to send me away. He let her convince him and kept me at home, thus tacitly impeding the happiness which God would doubtless have granted and accorded me had I gone there.[61]

It is true that in the final analysis Hans blames both parents—including his father, who cannot resist the pleas of his young wife—for the opportunity he missed, but in reality it was his mother who was unwilling to give up her favorite son, even though the duke was prepared to treat Hans like his own son. Although Schweinichen comforts himself with the thought that this was God's will, he uses

[58]Schweinichen, *Memorial*, 30.
[59]Schweinichen, *Memorial*, 31.
[60]Wunder, "Wie wird man ein Mann," 127–29.
[61]Schweinichen, *Memorial*, 18.

this standard formulation to limit the damage, in order to come to terms with his parents' decision. It was not possible for him to develop a more complex attitude toward his mother because she died so young.

Schweinichen's encounters with young women are recounted not as a means of contrasting himself with them, but in order to achieve recognition as a man. The noble youths and maidens who played a central role in the long and frequent festivities (christenings, weddings, funerals, and fairs) which took place among the landed gentry provided the occasions for Schweinichen's initiation into the rituals of masculinity. Finally, the women's quarters (*Frauenzimmer*) in the duke's residence in Liegnitz seemed to him a heavenly place and the right place for the sexes to meet. These relationships hinged not only on Schweinichen's acceptability as a lover, but also and principally on his acceptability as a potential husband. During his apprenticeship years, however, he felt no desire for marriage and reacted irritably to any attempts by his "romantic attachments" or their mothers to coerce him into marriage—sometimes even by means of trickery. He defended himself against such tactics by making stereotyped judgments about women. When he decided to get married and actually took a wife, however, he describes his trusting relationship with his wife Margarethe, "my little Maurausch."[62]

Conclusion

Hans von Schweinichen's *Memorial* offers a number of insights into the construction of a "man's life." What initially appears to be the very narrow basis of a single life turns out to be so broad in scope that it is not possible to evaluate everything systematically, for this portrayal covers not only Schweinichen's life but his life in relationship to other men's lives. Admittedly, other men only put in cursory appearances and are not described in great detail. Nevertheless, they help to define the world in which the gentry moved in the second half of the sixteenth century. For the first years of his life, when Schweinichen had to rely on information from his parents and not on his own memory, these relationships did not play a particularly large role, but from his early youth, the time when he first resided at Liegnitz court, it appears that they became more important.

The structuring function played by social status and creed in Schweinichen's self-portrayal is clearly evident. While there are numerous extant examples of public avowals of an adherence to the Lutheran confession, for example in town chronicles, the *Memorial* demonstrates one man's efforts as an individual to lead a Christian life. However, Schweinichen was also affected in practical terms by his confessional allegiance: his father turned down a generous offer by the bishop of Wroclaw to have his son educated by him, because the bishop would subsequently have expected Hans to enter his service; that is, to convert to Catholicism—in Schweinichen's book, another missed opportunity for a later career. The exceptional significance of reli-

[62]Schweinichen, *Memorial*, 276.

gious confession is even more apparent in Schweinichen's biography of Duke Heinrich XI, whose steadfast profession of the Lutheran faith in the face of the emperor he cannot stress enough.[63] Schweinichen sees this faith as somewhat compensating for his master's negative qualities.

It is not possible to discover exactly when Schweinichen adopted this attitude of dedicated Lutheranism as his own. The genesis of the text, which to date remains unclear, and the fact that it was revised several times could throw some light on the matter. The increasing importance of his religious beliefs to Schweinichen is manifest principally in the lengthy daily prayer recorded in 1591 at the end of his annual review, which concludes the second book of the *Memorial*. It is possible that illness and personal disappointment were not the only contributing factors here, but that he was also influenced by the political situation in the duchy, where the pressure of the Counter-Reformation exerted by the emperor and the king of Bohemia was increasingly making itself felt—something which would have affected Schweinichen both in his official capacities in the duchy and during his missions within the empire. The *Memorial* is presented as a retrospective autobiography, in which we find personal self-confession, as well as a construction of masculinity and male identity, set fundamentally within the background of confession and Christianity. Schweinichen, however, had no problems in reconciling this strongly Lutheran orientation with other forms of counsel. In 1576, for example, he had his horoscope drawn up by no less a person than a monk. Both the monk's summaries of the past and his predictions for the future Schweinichen found to be correct. Schweinichen naturally regarded his illnesses and the various difficulties he experienced over the years not only as the result of his sins but also as an effect of the climacteric (1514 f.),[64] an explanation prevalent at the time.

Schweinichen considered himself a courtier. He was not, however, a courtier in Castiglione's sense.[65] He was not an uneducated man—indeed, he was familiar with the noble virtues—but he describes himself as "simple," that is, honest, upright, and "pious" (*fromm*), completely committed to the Christian image of man. Whereas Castiglione's intellectual discursive construct of a courtier presents a new humanity, Schweinichen's presentation of himself as a nobleman and a Christian focuses on the question of a Christian way of life. In light of the consequences and renewal of the humanist traditions of education, Castiglione's construct may appear to be the more influential. However, we should not forget that piety like Schweinichen's would eventually extend beyond the boundaries of his social class, culminating in bourgeois society and making social borders obsolete.

---

[63]Schweinichen, *Denkwuerdigkeiten*, 12–13.

[64]See also *Leben im 16. Jahrhundert: Lebenslauf und Lieder des Hauptmanns Georg Niege*, ed. Brage bei der Wieden (Berlin: Akademie Verlag, 1996); Kaspar von Greyerz, *Vorsehungsglaube und Kosmologie: Studien zu englischen Selbstzeugnissen des 17. Jahrhunderts* (Göttingen: Vandenhoeck & Ruprecht, 1990).

[65]Schümer, "Der Hoefling," n. 4.

About the Contributors

Gunda Barth-Scalmani is assistant professor in the Department for Austrian History at the Universität Innsbruck. With Brigitte Mazohl-Wallnig and Ernst Wangerman, she edited the volume *Gienie und Altagbürgerliche Stadtkultur zur Mozartzeit* (1994). She has published articles on the history of gender, medicine, law, and bourgeois society in journals including *L'Homme, Zeitschrift für feministische Geschichtswissenschaft,* and *Mitteilungen der Gesellschaft für Salzburger Landeskunde,* as well as in the collections *Bürger zwischen Tradition und Modernität,* ed. Robert Hoffmann (1997) and *Rituale der Geburt: Eine Kulturgeschichte,* ed. Jürgen Schlumbohm et al. (1998).

Gabriele Beck-Busse was recently appointed Wissenschaftliche Assistentin in the Department of Romance Philology and Linguistics at the Freie Universität Berlin. Her Habilitationschrift is entitled *Grammatik für Damen zur Geschichte der französischen und italienischen Grammatik in Deutschland, England, Frankreich und Italien (1605–1850).*

Stanley Chojnacki, professor of history at the University of North Carolina at Chapel Hill, is the author of essays on the political and social roles of Venetian patricians and gender relations among them. Some of these are gathered in *Women and Men in Renaissance Venice* (2000). Among his recent publications is "La formazione della nobiltà dopo la Serrata," in *Storia di Venezia,* vol. 3, *La formazione dello stato parizio* (1997).

Marina d'Amelia is ricercatore in early modern European history at the Università di Roma la Sapienza. Her book *Orgoglio baronale e giustizia: Castel Viscardo alla fine del Cinquecento* (1996) includes a discussion of the role played by women in establishing feudal family identity and administering estates. Her articles on women and their dowries and female violence have appeared in the journals *Quaderni storici* and *Dimensioni e problemi della ricerca storica,* and she edited the volume *Storia della maternità* (1997). Her recent publication "Lo scambio epistolare tra Cinque e

Seicento: Scene di vita quotidiana e aspirazioni" appeared in *Per Lettera: La scrittura epistolare femminile tra archivio e tipografia,* ed. Gabriella Zarri (1999).

Daniela Hacke is Wissenschaftliche Assistentin in the Lehrstuhl für Frühe Neuzeit of the Historische Seminar der Universität Zürich. She earned her doctorate at the University of Cambridge with her dissertation, directed by Peter Burke, entitled "Marital Litigation and Gender Relations in Early Modern Venice (c. 1570–1700)." She is completing a critical edition and German translation of Moderata Fonte's *Il merito delle donne* (1600).

Barbara J. Harris is professor of history and women's studies at the University of North Carolina at Chapel Hill. Her publications include *Beyond Her Sphere: Women and the Professions in American History* (1978) and *Edward Stafford, Third Duke of Buckingham, 1577–1621* (1986). The essay in this volume is based on material from the book she is currently completing, *Aristocratic English Women 1450–1550: Marriage and Family, Property and Career,* for publication.

Julius Kirshner, a historian of law, is professor of medieval and Renaissance history at the University of Chicago. With Osvaldo Cavallar and Susanne Degenring, he edited *A Grammar of Signs: Bartolo da Sassoferrato's Tract on Insignia and Coats of Arms* (1994). He also edited the English-language version of the proceedings of a conference, "The Origins of the State in Italy," held in Chicago in 1993.

Thomas Kuehn, professor of history at Clemson University, is the author of *Emancipation in Late Medieval Florence* (1982) and *Law, Family, and Women: Toward a Legal Anthropology of Renaissance Italy* (1991). He is currently completing a study of the legal and social position of illegitimate children in fifteenth-century Florence.

Francesca Medioli, lecturer in Italian women's history at Reading University, has worked extensively on forced monachization and enclosure. Her publications include *L'"Inferno monacole" di Arcangela Tarabotti* (1990) and articles in *Rivista di storia e letteratura religiosa, Clio,* and the collection of essays *Il monachesimo femminile in Italia dall'Alto Medioevo al secolo XVII,* ed. Gabriella Zarri (1997).

Anne Jacobson Schutte, professor of history at the University of Virginia, specializes in religion, culture, and gender in early modern Italy. Her publications include *Pier Paolo Vergerio: The Making of an Italian Reformer* (1977), *Printed Italian Vernacular*

Religious Books, 1465–1550: A Finding List (1983), and editions in Italian and English of Cecilia Ferrazzi's inquisitorial autobiography (1991, 1996). She serves as North American coeditor of *Archive for Reformation History/Archiv für Reformationsgeschichte.*

Silvana Seidel Menchi is professor of history at the Università degli Studi di Trento. Among her numerous publications on sixteenth-century religious life, the best-known is *Erasmo in Italia, 1520–1580* (1987), which has appeared in German and French translations. She is now working on the records of matrimonial trials in ecclesiastical courts.

Merry E. Wiesner-Hanks, professor and chair of the Department of History at the University of Wisconsin–Milwaukee, is one of the editors of *The Sixteenth Century Journal.* Among her publications are *Working Women in Renaissance Germany* (1986) and *Women and Gender in Early Modern Europe* (1993). Many of her articles on various aspects of women's lives and gender structures have been collected in the volume *Gender, Church, and State in Early Modern Germany* (1998).

Heide Wunder is professor of early modern social and institutional history at the Universität-Gesamthochschule Kassel. Her research centers on the history of gender and of the rural economy in the early modern era. One of her books has appeared in English translation: *He Is the Sun, She Is the Moon: Women in Early Modern Germany* (1998).

Kristen Eldyss Sorensen Zapalac's first book, *"In His Image and Likeness": Political Iconography and Religious Change in Regensburg, 1500–1600* (1990), was published as she was completing her fellowship in the Harvard Society of Fellows. After several years as a faculty member at Washington University in St. Louis, she is now director of Information Technology at Secora Corporation. She is completing a second book, tentatively entitled *Inside/Out: Judith of Bethulia and the Engendering of Selfhood in the West.*

Gabriella Zarri, professor of modern history at the Università degli Studi di Firenze, has written many articles and books on the history of ecclesiastical institutions and religious life between the fifteenth and seventeenth centuries, with particular emphasis on the relationship between women and religion. She has edited several volumes of essays, including (with Lucetta Scaraffia) *Donne e fede: Santità e vita religiosa in Italia* (1994), in English translation as *Women and Faith: Catholic Religious Life in*

Italy from Late Antiquity to the Present (1999). Among her books are *Le sante vive: Cultura e religiosità femminile tra medioevo e età moderna* (1990) and *Matrimonio tra medioevo e età moderna* (2001).

Margarete Zimmermann, professor of French and Italian literature at the Freie Universität Berlin, has published widely on twentieth-century French literature, Christine de Pisan and medieval literature and culture, the European *querelle des femmes,* and feminist literary history. She now serves as president of the International Christine de Pisan Society. Cofounder and coeditor of the gender studies yearbook *Querelles* and coeditor of the *Ergebnisse der Frauenforschung,* she has recently coedited two books: with Roswitha Böhm, *Französische Frauen der Frühen Neuzeit: Dicterinnen, Malerinnen, Mäzeninnen* (1999); and with Renate Kroll, *Gender Studies in der romanischen Literaturen: Re-Visionen, Sub-Versionen* (1999). She is currently working on a study of Christine de Pisan and a history of French literature by women.

Index

Illustrations are indicated by **bold** locators.